Technology and Neuropsychology

OXFORD WORKSHOP SERIES
AMERICAN ACADEMY OF CLINICAL NEUROPSYCHOLOGY

Series Editors

Susan McPherson, *Editor-in-Chief*
Ida Sue Baron
Julie Bobholz
Richard Kaplan
Sandra Koffler
Greg Lamberty
Jerry Sweet

Volumes in the Series

Mild Traumatic Brain Injury and Postconcussion Syndrome
Michael A. McCrea

Understanding Somatization in the Practice of Clinical Neuropsychology
Greg J. Lamberty

Adult Learning Disabilities and ADHD
Robert L. Mapou

The Business of Neuropsychology
Mark T. Barisa

Neuropsychology of Epilepsy and Epilepsy Surgery
Gregory P. Lee

Mild Cognitive Impairment and Dementia
Glenn E. Smith and Mark W. Bondi

Intellectual Disability: Civil and Criminal Forensic Issues
Michael Chafetz

Executive Functioning: A Comprehensive Guide for Clinical Practice
Yana Suchy

The Independent Neuropsychological Evaluation
Howard J. Oakes, David W. Lovejoy, and Shane S. Bush

A Practical Guide to Geriatric Neuropsychology
Susan McPherson and Deborah Koltai

Ethical Decision Making in Clinical Neuropsychology, Second Edition
Shane S. Bush

Board Certification in Clinical Neuropsychology, Second Edition
Kira E. Armstrong, Dean W. Beebe, Robin C. Hilsabeck, and Michael W. Kirkwood

Supervision in Neuropsychology: Practical, Ethical, and Theoretical Considerations
Edited by Doug Bodin

Deep Brain Stimulation: A Multidisciplinary Guide for Parkinson's Disease and Related Disorders
Christina A. Palmese, Kathryn A. Wyman-Chick, Michele K. York

Technology and Neuropsychology: Teaching, Testing, and Treatment Considerations
Edited by Jared F. Benge, Sophie I. Leib, Brittany Wolff, Travis Marchman, Dean C. Delis, and Robert M. Bilder

Technology and Neuropsychology

Teaching, Testing, and Treatment Considerations

Edited by

Jared F. Benge
Sophie I. Leib
Brittany Wolff
Travis Marchman
Dean C. Delis
Robert M. Bilder

OXFORD
UNIVERSITY PRESS

OXFORD
UNIVERSITY PRESS

Oxford University Press is a department of the University of Oxford. It furthers the University's objective of excellence in research, scholarship, and education by publishing worldwide. Oxford is a registered trade mark of Oxford University Press in the UK and in certain other countries.

Published in the United States of America by Oxford University Press
546 Fifth Avenue, New York, NY 10036, United States of America.

CIP data is on file at the Library of Congress.

ISBN 9780197814086

DOI: 10.1093/9780197814116.001.0001

The manufacturer's authorized representative in the EU for product safety is Oxford University Press España S.A. of Parque Empresarial San Fernando de Henares, Avenida de Castilla, 2 – 28830 Madrid (www.oup.es/en or product.safety@oup.com). OUP España S.A. also acts as importer into Spain of products made by the manufacturer.

Contents

Foreword

History and Heroes of Technological Innovations in Clinical Neuropsychology

William B. Barr and Russell M. Bauer

Many advancements in modern science have been driven by the emergence of new technologies. This book documents an important turning point in the development of neuropsychology and its entrance into the modern age. For most of its history, advances in neuropsychology have paralleled those in psychology. Dating back to origins in Wilhelm Wundt's 19th-century laboratory, we encountered what historians have termed as the era of "brass instrument psychology," where specially designed instruments were produced to study elements of sensation and perception (Davis, 1970). Those instruments and methods eventually found their way to the United States, where they were used by a few psychologists, most notably Shepherd Ivory Franz, for clinical studies of patients with neurological and psychiatric disorders, representing one of the earliest examples of neuropsychology practice (Franz, 1919). Subsequent developments in the field were made in the early 20th century by incorporating psychological testing methodologies developed for the study of individual differences and needs arising in various applied settings for classifying students, soldiers, and immigrants (Geisinger, 2000).

Clinical neuropsychology made its true emergence in the mid-20th century emanating from the work of many of the field's well-known pioneers, including Ward Halstead, Kurt Goldstein, Hans Lukas Teuber, and Arthur Benton, based on their development of instruments, tests, and analytic methods designed specifically for the study of brain–behavior relationships (Barr, 2008). In subsequent decades, most neuropsychological tests were developed for administration in a paper-and-pencil format. The proprietary rights, publication, and distribution of these tests were governed primarily by for-profit test publishing companies who sold test forms, stimulus booklets, and administration manuals to neuropsychologists so they could use the materials for research and clinical use in laboratory, hospital, and office settings.

During the 1980s, many believed that clinical neuropsychology would undergo a significant shift away from paper-and-pencil testing following the large-scale sale and distribution of low-cost microcomputers to scientists and the public (Bauer & Bilder, 2023). An argument was made that computer-assisted administration of neuropsychological tests would allow for increased precision and control over test administration, scoring, and data collection (Kane & Reeves, 1997). However, rather than focusing on the proposed advantages of computer-assisted testing, most practitioners balked at the technological challenges associated with computerized testing applications and failed to abandon use on the more established tests. Results of a survey conducted in the 2010s showed that 45% of practitioners responding to the survey had never used computerized testing methods in their practices and only 6% of neuropsychologists were utilizing computerized testing methods on a regular basis (Rabin et al., 2016).

In recent decades, we have witnessed unprecedented growth in the clinical neurosciences with advances in neuroimaging, electrophysiology, and neurogenetics basing their use of modern digital technology. During that same time period, the field of neuropsychology has primarily stuck to its use of paper-and-pencil technologies using tests and stimuli developed many decades ago. Nobody recognized an emerging technology crisis for neuropsychology more than Dr. Robert M. Bilder, the senior editor of this book, who sadly passed away before the final production of this volume. At the time of his passing, Dr. Bilder was the Michael E. Tennenbaum Distinguished Family Chair in Creativity Research, Professor of Psychiatry, and Chief of the Medical Psychology Division at UCLA. He was known for his extraordinary intellectual vision, boundless curiosity, and an unwavering commitment to advancing neuropsychological science and education.

In a seminal publication (Bilder, 2011), Dr. Bilder applauded the field's advancements in the assessment of functional impairments from discrete brain lesions (Neuropsychology 1.0) and subsequent advancements to a more mature discipline paying close attention to psychometrics and development of standardized assessment methods (Neuropsychology 2.0). At the same time, Dr. Bilder urged the field to move toward the use of disruptive technologies, and a paradigm shift to what he termed "Neuropsychology 3.0," where the field could leverage its position at the interface of basic biology and clinical science that integrates information and coevolves with health care reform. This book summarizes many recent advances in neuropsychology's use of technology that reflect Dr. Bilder's vision.

It is indisputable that Bob Bilder saw well beyond the current state of clinical neuropsychology and cognitive neuroscience and cast his eyes and efforts on a forward evolution of science and practice. He was impressed with the success of the Human Genome Project (HGP) and saw, in the development of the electronic health record (EHR), an opportunity for neuropsychology to thrive. Within the National Institutes of Health, the HGP-inspired "genome to phenome" approach to studying complex neuropsychiatric and neurologic disorders was emerging, and Bilder recognized that neuropsychology was uniquely positioned between levels of analysis rooted in basic biology (genes, proteins, and cellular signaling pathways) and those focused on behavior (neural systems, cognitive phenotypes, symptoms, and syndromes) to make significant integrative contributions. However, he argued that to fully realize its power and value, the field would have to come to grips with how cognitive constructs lined up with discoveries in neuroscience, neuroimaging, and neural systems research. In other words, neuropsychology would have to more precisely specify constructs on the behavior side of the "brain–behavior relationships" equation. His interest in cognitive ontology was thus born, paving the way for Neuropsychology 3.0.

Beginning in 2007, he served as principal investigator for UCLA's Consortium for Neuropsychiatric Phenomics that provided research infrastructure linking the study of observable traits (phenotypes) with the study of genetic and environmental factors responsible for behavioral variation and individual differences. This project, motivated in no small part by the HGP, was one of the first of its kind to develop a collaborative knowledge base containing behavioral, neuroimaging, genetic, and diagnostic data designed to identify and link neuropsychological and neuropsychiatric constructs (symptoms, syndromes) to the underlying neurobiological substrates of prevalent neuropsychiatric disorders. In 2011, the idea of a collaborative knowledge base was further instantiated in the development of the Cognitive Atlas, which sought to provide an ontology of cognitive/mental processes and tasks (Poldrack et al., 2011).

Regarding neuropsychology's impact on health care, Bilder aspired to what he referred to as a "neuropsychology dashboard of the future." This dashboard would be a part of each person's EHR where neuropsychological test results (cognitive status) could be represented along with neuroimaging, genetic, laboratory, medical history, and social determinants of health to provide an overall snapshot of the person's neurobehavioral health. Making this a reality would require full integration of neuropsychological data into the EHR, an effort that would require collaboration among neuropsychological and other medical experts, informatics specialists, and psychometric scientists, among others. He had a fundamental belief that the preservation of item-level data (the actual responses of patients as they performed neurocognitive tasks) was critical to any effort to refine, streamline, and improve the psychometric properties, clinical utility, and acceptability of neuropsychological assessment instruments. These big ideas led to the creation of the National Neuropsychological Network (NNN), the project to which he was devoting his key efforts when he passed away in August 2025. The NNN is a multisite project that aspires to collect item-level neuropsychological data, pre- and post-exam diagnosis, and information on social determinants of health from clinical neuropsychological evaluations conducted at five University clinics across the United States. The data are collected on tablets using commercial (e.g., Pearson) and in-house digital platforms and are uploaded to a database and eventually to the NIH Data Archive. Currently, nearly 14,000 patients are represented in the database. These data enable large-scale psychometric investigations designed (1) to better understand the neurocognitive constructs measured during clinical evaluations, and (2) to identify the most useful items and tests with the goal of developing more targeted batteries, including adaptive assessments tailored to individual performance. The goal of full integration with the EHR is being pursued in the current project cycle.

While the NNN represents one current example of Bilder's forward-thinking embrace of emerging technology, his interest in advancing both technological integration and technology training in neuropsychology actually dates back more than a decade. Bilder openly lamented that the data from the thousands of paper-and-pencil neuropsychological evaluations conducted annually lay essentially dormant and inaccessible in the file cabinets of practitioners across the nation and world. Instead, he envisioned the development of digitally accessible collaborative knowledge bases amenable to analytic models using Big Data tools and advanced psychometrics fed by data sources, including computerized assessments, portable digital devices such as cell phones and smart watches, and sensors embedded in the Internet of Things. In 2016, together with the late Karen Postal (then president of the American Academy of Clinical Neuropsychology [AACN]), Dean W. Beebe, Michelle Braun, Darcy Cox, Rob Davis, and Daniel Drane, Bilder was instrumental in developing the Disruptive Technology Initiative (DTI) within AACN. Disruptive technologies, or disruptive innovations (Christensen, 1997), represent innovations that fundamentally change how a field operates, or how a product is created or delivered. An example is seen in how Wikipedia, written and edited by volunteer editors, has completely disrupted and transformed the for-profit printed and digital reference market. The DTI, which Bilder chaired, sought to similarly reimagine customary practice in neuropsychological assessment and education, which continued to rely mainly on 19th-century assessment tools and theoretical models, by capitalizing on ongoing technological advances in health care and society. This vision was designed (1) to broaden the methods used to collect useful neurocognitive data to include smart phones, IoT devices, and other digital inputs, (2) to develop large-scale databases capable of supporting advanced psychometric analysis to refine measured constructs and create more efficient batteries, and (3) to develop informational and training tools to enable the neuropsychological community to develop technological competencies. The chapters in this book describe some of these exciting developments.

In recent years, Bilder extended his research to the study of creativity in an attempt to provide more grounded neuroscientific accounts of gifted/enhanced cognition by studying extraordinarily creative individuals. He became an Endowed Professor and leader of the UCLA Tennenbaum Center for the Biology of Creativity, where he sought to uncover structural and functional characteristics that distinguished the brains of highly creative artists and scientists. By understanding such mechanisms, he sought to gain insights that could be used to intervene and reverse disease states that result in cognitive deficits. Alongside this effort, he developed an interest and taught a UCLA course on personal brain management that addressed topics of cognitive training, habit formation and change, positive psychology interventions, self-monitoring, time management, executive function management, mindfulness, and creativity. These efforts beautifully illustrate his lifelong integration of personal and professional development.

In addition to his brilliance and creativity, Bob Bilder will forever be remembered for his kind heart, rapier wit, fierce loyalty to family, collaborators, and students, and the unwavering optimism and joy he brought to both work and play. Although quite discerning in his clinical and scientific activity, he was never prone to critical comments and was never heard to say that something important could not be done. He was the consummate team builder (earning the nickname "Bob the Bilder" from the British children's show) and, through a combination of charisma and sheer intellectual force, had a remarkable ability to motivate leading-edge scientists to come together to solve complex problems. His iconic reputation as a researcher, clinical scientist, mentor, and friend was well earned and richly deserved. The authors and co-editors of this volume dedicate this work to his brilliance and spirit.

References

Barr, W. B. (2008). Historical development of the neuropsychological test battery. In J. E. Morgan & J. H. Ricker (Eds.), *Textbook of clinical neuropsychology* (pp. 3–17). Psychology Press.

Bauer, R. M., & Bilder, R. M. (2023). Automated neuropsychological testing. In G. G. Brown, B. Crosson, K. Y. Haaland, & T. Z. King (Eds.), *APA handbook of neuropsychology: Neuroscience and neuromethods* (pp. 233–258). American Psychological Association. https://doi.org/10.1037/0000308-011

Bilder, R. M. (2011). Neuropsychology 3.0: Evidence-based science and practice. *Journal of the International Neuropsychological Society, 17*, 7–13.

Christensen, C. M. (1997). *The innovator's dilemma: When new technologies cause great firms to fail.* Harvard Business School Press.

Davis, R. C. (1970). The brass age of psychology. *Technology & Culture, 11*, 604–612.

Franz, S. I. (1919). *Handbook of mental examination methods* (2nd ed.). MacMillan.

Geisinger, K. F. (2000). Psychological testing at the end of the millennium: A brief historical review. *Professional Psychology, Research, & Practice, 31*, 117–118.

Kane, R. L., & Reeves, D. (1997). Computerized test batteries. In A. Horton (Ed.), *The neuropsychology handbook* (pp. 423–467). Springer.

Poldrack, R. A., Kittur, A., Kalar, D., Miller, E., Seppa, C., Gil, Y., Parker, D. S., Sabb, F. W., & Bilder, R. M. (2011). The cognitive atlas: Toward a knowledge foundation for cognitive neuroscience. *Frontiers in Neuroinformatics, 5*, 17. DOI: 10.3389/fninf.2011.00017.

Rabin, L. A., Paolillo, E., & Barr, W. B. (2016). Stability in test-usage practices of clinical neuropsychologists in the United States and Canada over a 10-year period: A follow-up survey of INS and NAN members. *Archives of Clinical Neuropsychology, 31*(3), 206–230.

Rabin, L. A., Spadaccini, A. T., Brodale, D. L., Grant, K. S., Elbulok-Charcape, M. M., & Barr, W. B. (2014). Utilization rates of computerized tests and test batteries among clinical neuropsychologists in the United States and Canada. *Professional Psychology: Research and Practice, 45*, 368–377.

Contributors

Anna-Lynne Ruth Adlam, BSc, PhD, DClinPsy, is Professor of Clinical Neuropsychology, Department of Psychology, University of Exeter, Exeter, UK.

Kelsey K. Amon, MPH is with the Institute of Gerontology, University of Georgia, Athens, GA, US.

Zoe R. Anthos is and undergraduate student with the Institute of Gerontology, University of Georgia, Athens, GA, US.

Amanda D. Ball, PsyD, ABPP, is Assistant Professor and Clinical Neuropsychologist, Department of Psychiatry, Oregon Health and Science University, Portland, OR, US.

Russell Bauer, PhD, ABPP, is Professor Emeritus of Clinical & Health Psychology and Neurology, University of Florida, Gainesville, FL, US.

Jared F. Benge, PhD, ABPP, is Associate Professor of Neurology, The University of Texas at Austin

Jared M. Block, MA, is Doctoral Student in Quantitative Psychology, University of California Los Angeles, CA, US.

Andrew M. Bryant, PhD, is a Neuropsychologist at ProHealth Care, Waukesha, WI, US.

Laura M. Campbell, PhD, is Postdoctoral Fellow, Department of Psychiatry, University of California, San Diego, CA, US.

Lucia Cavanagh, PhD is Associate Director of the Lifespan Assessment Through Integrated Neuropsychology (LATíN) program, University of California Los Angeles, Los Angeles, CA, US.

Naomi S. Chaytor, PhD, ABPP, is Professor and Chair, Department of Community and Behavioral Health, Washington State University Elson S. Floyd College of Medicine, Spokane, WA, US.

Claudia Corti, PsyD, PhD, cognitive-behavioral psychotherapist, neuropsychologist and researcher at the Acquired Brain Injury Unit of the Scientific Institute IRCCS E. Medea, Bosisio Parini, Lecco, Italy.

C. Munro Cullum, PhD, is Professor of Psychiatry, Neurology, and Neurological Surgery, University of Texas Southwestern Medical Center, Dallas, TX, US.

Alexandra Davis, PsyD, is in private practice, Cocoa Beach, FL, US.

Dean C. Delis, PhD, ABPP/CN, is Professor Emeritus of Psychiatry, University of California, San Diego, School of Medicine, CA, US.

Miles L. Delis, JD, is an attorney in private practice in California.

Jonathan DeRight, PhD, ABPP-CN, is Independent Practice, Precision Neuropsychology, PLLC, McLean, VA, US.

Lisa W. Drozdick, PhD, is Principal Research Director, Clinical Assessments, Pearson, San Antonio, TX, US.

Bryan M. Freilich, PsyD, ABPP-CN, is Assistant Professor of Psychiatry and Behavioral Sciences, Montefiore Medical Center, Albert Einstein College of Medicine, Bronx, NY, US.

Chris Gaskell, DClinPsy, BSc, is Senior Clinical Psychologist and Clinical Academic, North Staffordshire Combined

NHS Health Trust, Stoke, UK; and Honorary Researcher, University of Sheffield, UK.

Tania Giovannetti, PhD, ABPP-CN, is Professor of Psychology & Neuroscience, Temple University, Philadelphia, PA, US.

William Goette, PhD, is Assistant Professor, Department of Psychiatry, University of Texas Southwestern Medical Center, Dallas, TX, US.

David Andrés González, PhD, ABPP, is Assistant Professor of Neurological Sciences, Rush University Medical Center, Chicago, IL, US.

Katherine Hackett, PhD, is Instructor of Medicine, Division of General Internal Medicine, Icahn School of Medicine at Mount Sinai, New York, NY, US.

Mark G. Haviland, PhD, is Emeritus Professor of Psychiatry, Loma Linda University School of Medicine, CA, US.

Flora Hemming, MSci, is a Graduate Research Assistant, Psychology, University of Exeter, Exeter, UK.

Diana C. Hereld, PsyD, is an Assistant Clinical Professor, Department of Neurology, University of California, Davis, CA, US.

James Holdnack, PhD, is the proprietor of J.A. Holdnack Consulting, Hagerstown, MD, US.

Ann M. Huber, MS, LSSP, is a Clinical Assessment Developer, Pearson Assessments, San Antonio TX.

Kelly M. Jones, PhD, is with the School of Community and Public Health, National Institute for Stroke and Applied Neurosciences, Auckland University of Technology, Auckland, New Zealand.

Andrew M. Kiselica, PhD, ABPP-CN, is Associate Professor, Institute of Gerontology and Department of Health Policy and Management, University of Georgia, Athens, GA, US.

Sophie I. Leib, PhD, is Assistant Professor, Psychiatry and Behavioral Sciences (Child Psychology), Northwestern University Feinberg School of Medicine, Chicago, IL, US; and Pediatric Neuropsychologist, Department of Psychiatry, Ann & Robert H. Lurie Children's Hospital of Chicago, Chicago, IL, US.

Travis Marchman, MA, is Doctoral Candidate, California School of Professional Psychology, Los Angeles, CA, US.

Rachel E. Mis, PhD, is Postdoctoral Fellow, Department of Neurology, University of Texas at Austin Dell Medical School, TX, US.

Emily W. Paolillo, PhD, is Assistant Professor, Department of Neurology, University of California, San Francisco, CA, US.

Jennifer Puig, PhD, is Research Director of Neuropsychology, NCS Pearson, MN, US.

Steven P. Reise, PhD, is Professor of Psychology, UCLA, CA, US.

Maureen Schmitter-Edgecombe, PhD, is Regents Professor and Berry Family Distinguished Professor, Washington State University, Pullman, WA, US.

Michael K. Scullin, PhD, is Professor of Psychology and Neuroscience, Baylor University, Waco, TX, US.

Maria T. Schultheis, PhD, is Professor, Dept Psychological and Brain Science, Drexel University, Philadelphia, PA, US.

April Thames, PhD, is Professor of Psychiatry Department of Psychiatry and Biobehavioral Sciences, University of California Los Angeles, CA, US.

Logan M. Tuft M.A., M.P.S is a psychology intern at the San Diego VA Healthcare System, San Diego, CA, US.

David M. Ulrich is an Assistant Professor in the Department of Neurological Sciences, Rush University Medical Center, Chicago, IL, US.

Nicole Viola, PhD, is Postdoctoral Research Fellow, Cincinnati Children's Hospital Medical Center, OH, US.

Shari L. Wade, PhD, is Director of Research, Division of Pediatric Rehabilitation Medicine, Cincinnati Children's Hospital, OH, US; and Professor of Pediatrics, University of Cincinnati, OH, US.

Keith F. Widaman, PhD, is Professor in the Graduate Division, University of California, Riverside, Riverside, CA, US.

Tricia S. Williams, PhD, ABPP, is Associate Scientist, Neurosciences & Mental Health, Hospital for Sick Children, Toronto, Canada.

Brittany Wolff, PhD, is Assistant Professor of Psychiatry, Department of Psychiatry and Biobehavioral Sciences, University of California Los Angeles, CA, US.

Cecilia K. Zuniga, BA, is Research Assistant/Psychometrist, University of Texas at Austin, Austin, TX, US.

1

Teaching Technology and Innovation in Clinical Neuropsychology

Lessons from the Life and Work of Dr. Robert "Bob" Bilder

Sophie I. Leib, Brittany Wolff, and Jared F. Benge

Editors' note

When we originally proposed this book, Dr. Robert Bilder had agreed to lead this chapter, focused on teaching tech to neuropsychologists. Due to his illness and untimely passing in the summer of 2025, he was unable to see the final product of the work he had set in motion, including this chapter.

However, given that his legacy and passion for teaching of technology, creativity, and innovation were immense, and the lives he touched plentiful, we believe we have sufficient material to work from that can at least partially achieve his goals for this chapter. Thus, what follows is a summary of his contributions in this area: excerpts derived from a 2024 presentation at the American Academy of Neuropsychology about teaching technology in neuropsychology, his contributions to the Minnesota Conference Guidelines on the Training of Neuropsychologists, his work on creativity from a neuropsychological standpoint, and pearls we derive from his published works. While we attempt to summarize his thoughts on this important topic, please note that any errors, omissions, or clumsiness are strictly our own: We hope we made him proud.

Dr. Robert ("Bob") Bilder's contributions to neuropsychology were remarkable in both scope and impact, but at his core he was always an advocate for innovation, education, and training. He conceptualized technology not just as a necessity for the practice of neuropsychology but also as a key domain we must teach to the next generation of neuropsychologists, and this informs this chapter. Why should we teach technology and innovation? Because fundamentally these are reflections of creativity, a skill his work demonstrated is coachable. Here, we consider Dr. Bilder's thoughts on teaching technology through three different areas: how creativity and technology

Sophie I. Leib et al., *Teaching Technology and Innovation in Clinical Neuropsychology*.
In: *Technology and Neuropsychology*. Edited by: Jared F. Benge et al., Oxford University Press.
 DOI: 10.1093/9780197814116.003.0001

overlap, what the Minnesota Conference says about the role of technology in training, and real-world pearls to take away for real-world teaching.

Technology, Innovation, and the Creative Mindset in Neuropsychology

In supervision, Dr. Bilder often spoke of creativity at the edge of chaos as the driving force behind human potential, growth, and innovation, with neuropsychology being no exception to this fact (Bilder & Knudsen, 2014). While neuropsychological training frequently involves extensive exploration of cognitive processes like attention and memory, understanding and fostering creativity are frequently missed. In Dr. Bilder's, and the authors', worldview, we should instill and understand creativity as a key skill to the practice and science of neuropsychology. By fostering this skill, an appreciation and furtherance of innovation and technology is viewed less as a separate goal, but more of a logical outgrowth of a creative profession. But what is this underlying skill of creativity, and how do we foster it in trainees?

At the heart of neuropsychological theories of creativity lies the dynamic interplay between divergent and convergent thinking (Japardi et al., 2018). Divergent thinking, the ability to generate multiple, unique ideas or solutions to an open-ended problem, is often considered the cornerstone of creative thought. It involves cognitive flexibility, originality, and fluency of ideas. Conversely, convergent thinking is the process of arriving at a single, optimal solution to a well-defined problem (Zhang et al., 2020). Creativity is not solely the product of unbridled divergent thought; it necessitates the capacity to evaluate, refine, and select among generated ideas, a process heavily reliant on convergent thinking.

For neuropsychologists used to thinking of reasoning and logic as components of executive functioning or "frontal" skills, it is important to note that thinking styles are subserved by distinct yet interconnected neural networks. Divergent thinking is often associated with the brain's default mode network (DMN), a system active during spontaneous thought, imagination, and daydreaming (Bartoli et al., 2024). This network allows for the free-flowing association of ideas necessary for creative ideation. In contrast, convergent thinking is more closely linked to the (likely more familiar) executive control network (ECN), which is necessary for goal-directed behavior, working memory, and inhibitory control (Beaty et al., 2016). The prefrontal cortex, a key node in the ECN, plays a vital role in evaluating the novelty and appropriateness of ideas, inhibiting irrelevant thoughts, and shifting between different mental sets. Therefore, a creative act represents a fluid dance between the generative capacities of the DMN and the evaluative functions of the ECN. This dance is key for trainees, and indeed for our field, to learn. The wholesale and noncritical adoption of novel techniques and approaches should not be our default, but neither should a hypercritical, reflexive rejection of a new technique based on old metrics. Instead, we, the field, and our trainees should approach our work and adoption of innovative technologies with the steps of the creative dance in mind.

Beyond these foundational processes, the concepts of Wolfgang Köhler's "a-ha!" (Kounios & Beeman, 2014) moment and Mihaly Csikszentmihalyi's "flow" provide frameworks for further understanding the phenomenology of creative breakthroughs (Csikszentmihalyi et al., 2005). Köhler's work with chimpanzees demonstrated insight learning, where a solution to a problem appears suddenly and completely, the classic "a-ha!" moment. Neuropsychologically, this event is believed to involve a sudden restructuring of a problem's representation in the mind, shifting from unproductive mental sets (Sprugnoli et al., 2017). Neuroimaging studies link this moment to a burst of high-frequency gamma-band activity in the right anterior superior temporal gyrus, suggesting a rapid neural reorganization that brings a nonobvious solution into conscious awareness. These sudden moments of insight complement Csikszentmihalyi's concept of flow, a state of immersion and energized focus in an activity, where one's skills are perfectly matched to the challenges at hand (Csikszentmihalyi et al., 2005). This state is thought to facilitate creativity by creating a neurocognitive environment where the brain's aforementioned ECN and DMN can work in concert (or, to avoid mixed metaphors, can dance their dance!), allowing for both focused problem-solving and associative thinking without the interference of self-critical internal monologue.

Importantly, to both ourselves and those we serve clinically, this skill is not strictly an innate set ability: Dr. Bilder would argue that this is a skill that can be trained. For both patients and ourselves, structured approaches such as practicing divergent thinking, exposure to new environments, and encountering challenges can help foster problem-solving, and mindfulness and flexibility may help support creative growth. We argue throughout this book that evaluating, developing, and considering new technologies is a key opportunity to practice these skills. Again, in supervision Dr. Bilder emphasized that technological advancements are revolutionizing the way neuropsychologists can assess and rehabilitate creativity, and that neuropsychologists themselves must become more creative in their techniques. Indeed, he would argue that as technology becomes more integrated into clinical practice, the role of the neuropsychologist will evolve. For example, it seems unlikely that the future of neuropsychology lies in strictly administering paper-based assessments and writing hours of reports. Instead, our role may be one of sorting through and interpreting multiple data streams (some administered in clinic, some at home, some from EHR algorithms, some from patient/family report), perhaps in conjunction with various artificial intelligence (AI) tools. Such a world, which seems less far away today than a few years ago, moves the neuropsychologist away from a "test giver" and into a profession where we are critically evaluating these data streams, their validity and limitations. The convergence of creativity, technology, and neuropsychology offers exciting opportunities to deepen our understanding of this human capacity and to develop more effective interventions for individuals with neurological conditions. But this also underscores the importance of a holistic approach to training future neuropsychologists in the steps of this nuanced dance.

Technology, Teaching, and the Minnesota Conference

While the dance of creativity has been playing out in neuroscience and neuropsychology at an ever-frenetic pace in recent decades, the impacts on typical neuropsychological practice have been more sedate. For example, serial surveys of neuropsychological practice have demonstrated a remarkable lack of change in our common assessment batteries over the decades (Rabin et al., 2005, 2016). To be clear, in many ways this likely represents the maturation and evolved evidence base of our profession. One would not expect, for example, the key aspects of the neurological exam to radically change over time, so it is not surprising that key elements of the neuropsychological exam have been slow to change. That being said, the notion that the neuropsychological assessment of brain–behavior relationships was figured out in the 1960s and there is nothing new under the sun does not ring true in the age of rapid innovations in understanding behavior at the level of networks to nations.

Further, neuropsychology continues to take a somewhat circuitous route to answering our questions. For example, one of Dr. Bilder's key examples in a 2024 AACN presentation is why we ask tools from World War II (Trailmaking) to predict driving performance when our cars can tell us what is really going on with driving in the real world (Bilder et al., 2024). Our relatively slow progress at integrating data from increasingly ubiquitous technological innovations in our patients' real lived experience may eventually limit our relevance and ability to have a seat at the table in shaping the evolving science of brain–behavior relationships.

While the slow rate of change in neuropsychological practice may have many different causes, the lack of training in *how* to incorporate innovation and technology may be one stumbling block. Thus, when the Minnesota Conference (MNC) was formed to update guidelines for neuropsychological training, Dr. Bilder along with Drs. Maureen Schmitter-Edgecombe and Rus Bauer were selected to serve on the technology expert panel (Minnesota Conference, n.d.). One of the key mandates for this update: incorporating innovation in technological and analytic approaches into the core competencies of neuropsychologists. At the time of this writing, the final adoption and implementation of the MNC guidelines is not complete. But as a framework for considering how to incorporate technology into teaching, they represent one of the clearest calls to action from experts in the field. We consider key considerations for tech training next.

Technology and Innovation as a Competency

In the MNC vision, technology and innovation would be a core competency for our field (Stringer et al., 2025), something that is embedded across the curriculum and development of a neuropsychologist. There is no single course that covers technology; rather, doctoral programs, practica, supervisors, and our self-study as professionals would address technological literacy and the skills necessary to be a critical consumer of innovations. Further, the MNC does not address technology as its own island, independent from the brain–behavior, neuroscience, sociocultural, and ethical issues that sit at the core of a neuropsychologist. Rather, technology and innovation are bidirectionally woven among the other competencies in a developmentally sequenced manner. That being said, four key aspects of this technology and innovation competency are noted in the proposed MNC guidelines, with direct implications for those teaching and training neuropsychology in the classroom, clinic, or lab.

Demonstrating Awareness and Incorporation of Innovation

Trainees tend to practice the way they are taught, and we have always suspected that the batteries, methods, and reports one uses throughout training tend to have long-term impacts on how one practices (and, indeed, subsequently trains) others. Thus, those involved with training neuropsychologists need to be developing and emulating an awareness of, and when appropriate, willingness to incorporate new ideas into their work. In this way, the MNC emulates the dance of creativity Dr. Bilder described at the outset of this chapter: The field is not encouraged to take a "if it's new, it must be better" approach; indeed, such reflexive adoption of new tools risks throwing out useful and well-validated approaches for care and research (Loring & Bauer, 2010). The spirit of "awareness and incorporation" of innovations in our field is to foster both an appreciation for what changes are occurring (and as this volume illustrates, they are enormous) but also the critical thinking necessary to determine when and if such innovations could be helpful to those we serve, educate, and seek to understand via research. Once we are aware of these changes, this leads directly to the next aspect of this competency: evaluation of new innovations and technologies.

Critical Evaluation Skills for the 21st Century and Beyond

For those training the next generation of neuropsychologists, then, teaching tech and innovation becomes something with pragmatic implications. As neuropsychologists, we should demonstrate the process of seeking out new information and then the critical thinking process of whether to adopt innovations. For those actively involved with training at any level, consider *why* your assessment, normative, or other neuropsychological aspects of care or research are the way they are. Why do we do what we do, and can we explain it to those we train? Are there new ways of doing this that could be better? Why or why not? How do you weigh these factors in arriving at a decision for what to do in a given case or a given project?

The proposed MNC document calls out, in particular, consideration of *characteristics of relevant innovations for neuropsychological practice.* Dr. Bilder was quite explicit on this issue when we were proposing this book: Topics like AI, new psychometric techniques, passive data monitoring, and new intervention techniques are neither good nor bad, and they will never be fully validated or perfect for every situation, just as there is no single battery that we use for every given referral or research question. What is required of neuropsychologists, and in turn those training in the field, is considering how a given technology or innovation could be impacting care.

Understanding the Implications of Technology for All We Serve

Digital behaviors and tools are no different than other aspects of real-world behavior and neuropsychological practice: Their use and implication differ from person to person and context to context. As neuropsychologists, we bring to bear a large knowledge base of groups with different conditions, testing situations, and backgrounds to the person sitting across the desk from us. Thus, when considering implications for technology in practice or research, neuropsychologists should appreciate how factors that contribute to the digital divide could also influence how new technologies and tools are utilized or interpreted. Many of the same factors that we need to account for in evaluations (i.e., age, sensory status, socioeconomic factors, education) also have direct relationships on technology use, and so care should be taken to understand how these factors influence normative and use characteristics. In this way, and as the MNC proposes, technology is not siloed as some aspect of practice independent from other competencies: It is something we instill in our trainees in a person centered approach.

Training Must Address the Ethical Use of Technology

As authors argue later in this volume (Chapter 4), the adoption of innovative tools and technologies brings with it an expanded lens for our core ethical principles. Issues of beneficence and nonmaleficence, fidelity and responsibility, integrity, justice, and respect are as applicable in the 21st century as they were at the founding of our field. However, digital technologies bring with them new challenges and ways of viewing these principles. Thus, in our ethics we need to equip our trainees with how to address these issues. How does one navigate data ownership and disclosures of confidentiality for a test platform that sends results over the web, to a server possibly in another country, and who may not be in business or may be bought by another company before a re-evaluation? How do we ensure privacy for unmonitored evaluations or telehealth services? If digital tools show particular promise, but are not available to underserved populations because of socioeconomic or access issues, should they be used? How would not using them disadvantage people further? Are we sure that machine learning or AI algorithms are not overemphasizing factors that could lead to bias? These are just some of the extensions to our core ethical principles of neuropsychology that those training need to take the lead on, by showing an appreciation of them and thinking them through.

Technology Is Not Siloed—It Is Integrated Across Multiple Competencies

One of Dr. Bilder's requests when we were designing this book would be to illustrate the potential utility of innovations and technology across real-world teaching settings, testing environments, and treatment roles. Oftentimes our literature and conferences reflect an emphasis on technological impacts on clinical assessment, which we cover at length in this volume as well (Chapters 5–11). But the impact of technology is broader and reflects the role of advanced techniques for intervening, for analyzing data, and for reducing barriers to care. We must also acknowledge that technology can have profound impacts on the documentation of heavy features of clinical work, with subsequent effects on billing. For those involved in the training, the call is clear: Model and explain how technology is impacting all aspects of your work. How are AI tools in the electronic health record influencing your documentation and billing practices? Discuss how pipelines for integrating data or new digital tools work with your existing scoring and information technology workflow. Read manuals together in training and seek to understand who is being seen and reported—and what is not.

Tech Teaching Tips from a Leader in the Field

The MNC sets out an aspirational approach to weaving technology and innovation into the core training of neuropsychologists. But what might this look like in practice? We turn next to teaching tips from Dr. Bilder's own work for considerations. Following are six key points about technology training that are reflected in Dr. Bilder's work and represent foundational pillars for teaching and training in neuropsychology.

1. **Adopt an attitude of curiosity.** Trainees, like all humans, are very attuned to the attitudes and emotions of those around us. So, take a moment to reflect on the stance you embody when encountering a new technology or innovation. We encourage modeling curiosity, rather than knee-jerk fear or skepticism. For example, when introducing a digital cognitive assessment platform, frame it as an opportunity to explore how technology can enhance the assessment, while being curious as to what the limitations are. Ask trainees to identify what excites them about the tool and what questions they have about its limitations. Curiosity-driven discussions in supervision can, in our experience, lead to deeper engagement and critical thinking.
2. **Enforce the idea that neuropsychological data are more than just scores.** Though we are experts in brain–behavior relationships, it is easy to have training in clinical and research settings focus strictly on cognitive scores. In reality,

the behaviors we sample in neuropsychological practice encompass vast swaths of other information, ranging from item-level responses, subtle movement cues, vocal inflections and word–finding pauses, and social haptics, to name just a few (Schroeder et al., 2019). Many of the innovations in neurocognitive evaluations focus on capturing this previously unquantifiable information. This provides an excellent opportunity to weave in how innovations are changing the field. For example, by focusing on behavioral observations of speech pauses in a patient with mild dementia, we can tie this together with how voice biomarker literature is evolving and suggest that these cues may help identify those at risk for decline over time. When reviewing effort test performance, highlight how the slow responses seem to fit with literature about response speed, something many computerized platforms capture automatically, might relate to motivational factors. Encourage trainees to ask, "What am I seeing beyond the scores?" and tying this to innovations and technologies in our field.

3. **Embrace modern psychometrics.** Building on the last point, we believe it is critical to have students add item response theory (IRT; see Chapter 2), computerized adaptive testing (CAT), differential item functioning (DIF), and related modern psychometric techniques to their statistical armamentarium. These methods can enhance test precision, efficiency, and fairness, and be more time and labor efficient (Moore et al., 2023; Thomas, 2019). Example conversation starters might be to look at a typical depression screening questionnaire and ask how individual responses might be able to give a quicker answer to the degree of depression with fewer items. Tie this into how CAT reduces testing time while maintaining precision and then discuss implications for clinical efficiency. Another way might be to ask trainees to explore literature IRT approaches to scoring a standard measure like matrix reasoning and probe to see if they understand the pros and cons of this approach. This hands-on exposure demystifies psychometrics and equips trainees to critically evaluate emerging tools and technologies.
4. **Foster a collaborative approach to answering complicated questions.** It is easy to view the development of neuropsychology trainees through an apprentice model, slowly bringing along skills and abilities through observation and repetition. While this has value, we encourage supervisors to shift toward a more collaborative stance that treats trainees as emerging colleagues capable of contributing meaningfully to complex clinical reasoning. For example, the Culturally Expressive and Responsive (CER) supervision model explicitly advocates for a dynamic, bidirectional supervisory relationship that centers identity development, self-evaluation, and cultural humility, and encourages trainees to engage in reflective practice and shared inquiry, which fosters openness and agency (MacDonald et al., 2026; Stinson et al., 2023). Mentoring literature in neuropsychology further highlights the importance of moving away from hierarchical, deficit-based models toward collaborative, compassionate mentoring, which supports the development of professional identity,

humility, and openness to new perspectives and innovations (Calamia et al., 2022; Johnelle Sparks & Ellison, 2022). Ultimately, modeling collaboration helps trainees internalize that neuropsychological expertise is not about having all the answers, but about asking better questions together.

5. **Try new things.** Effective integration of technology in neuropsychology training requires understanding its potential to expand access to care, reduce barriers, optimize assessment and intervention strategies, and facilitate collaboration among stakeholders. Digital tools including teleneuropsychology, web-based platforms, and computerized assessments can increase reach, streamline workflows, and support interdisciplinary collaboration, especially when paired with training that normalizes innovation and uncertainty (Bilder et al., 2020; Harris et al., 2024). Practice trends such as abbreviated assessments, interdisciplinary screening, streamlined reporting, and use of automated platforms are increasingly common, with stepped-care and hybrid models leveraging technology to address workforce limitations and improve efficiency. Digital platforms like Q-interactive and web-based tools have demonstrated improved data capture, scoring efficiency, and accessibility, and hands-on experience with these tools is recommended for trainees to appreciate their advantages over traditional methods (Singh & Germane, 2021). Passive data collection through smart homes, vehicles, and other Internet of Things (IoT) devices enables real-world cognitive and behavioral monitoring, offering new opportunities for ecological validity and continuous assessment. Structured opportunities for trainees to pilot digital assessments alongside traditional methods, compare patient feedback, and evaluate data quality are supported as best practices for fostering critical thinking and resilience in adopting new technologies (Van Patten et al., 2022). Supervisors are encouraged to model openness to change and share their experiences with new technologies in order to cultivate a culture of innovation and adaptability.
6. **Consider the digital divide and its implications for new tools.** As technology becomes increasingly embedded in neuropsychological practice, it is essential to recognize that access to these innovations is not universal. Competence in this evolving landscape requires thoughtful attention to disparities shaped by age, race and ethnicity, education, income, and geographic location (Reyes et al., 2025). These factors influence not only access to devices and internet connectivity but also comfort and familiarity with digital platforms. Trainees should be encouraged to critically evaluate algorithmic and AI-based systems, including the assumptions behind their design, the data sources they rely on, and the potential biases they may perpetuate (APA, 2024). This kind of scrutiny is essential to ensure that technological advances enhance equitable access to neuropsychological care. Supervisors can support this awareness by facilitating discussions about how socioeconomic status, age, and cultural background affect patients' ability to engage with digital tools. For example, when introducing teleneuropsychology, ask trainees to consider how limited Internet

bandwidth or unfamiliarity with digital devices might impact participation. Role-play scenarios where trainees troubleshoot connectivity issues or adapt protocols for low-tech environments. These exercises not only build practical skills but also highlight the ethical implications of excluding certain populations. Encourage trainees to brainstorm strategies for equitable care, such as offering loaner devices, partnering with community organizations, or developing hybrid models that blend in-person and digital services. By foregrounding the digital divide in supervision, we prepare trainees to be both tech-savvy and socially responsible clinicians.

7. **Discuss practical ethical considerations of new technologies.** Educate trainees on ethical considerations in digital neuropsychology, including test security, privacy, and fairness. Discuss how technology can exacerbate disparities and the importance of designing inclusive assessments. Use case studies to illustrate challenges and solutions in telehealth and digital testing. Ethical and professional competence encompasses privacy, data security, and ownership of patient information, as well as broader considerations such as extended cognition and the use of virtual reality or other technologies that may modify cognitive processes. Professionals must anticipate and mitigate potential harms, uphold principles of equity and justice, and ensure responsible implementation of emerging tools (Saeidnia et al., 2024).

Conclusion

Dr. Bilder's vision underscores that the integration of technology and innovation is central to the future of clinical neuropsychology. Teaching these competencies ensures that emerging neuropsychologists are prepared not only to adopt new tools but to critically evaluate, implement, and guide their responsible use. By fostering awareness of technological possibilities, ethical considerations, and leadership in innovation, training programs can sustain the relevance, rigor, and impact of neuropsychology in a rapidly evolving health care environment.

References

American Psychological Association. (2024). Ethical challenges in the use of digital technologies in psychological practice. American Psychologist, *79*(1). https://psycnet.apa.org/fulltext/2024-44313-001.html

Bartoli, E., Devara, E., Dang, H. Q., Rabinovich, R., Mathura, R. K., Anand, A., Pascuzzi, B. R., Adkinson, J., Kenett, Y. N., Bijanki, K. R., Sheth, S. A., & Shofty, B. (2024). Default mode network electrophysiological dynamics and causal role in creative thinking. *Brain: A Journal of Neurology, 147*(10), 3409–3425. https://doi.org/10.1093/brain/awae199

Beaty, R. E., Benedek, M., Silvia, P. J., & Schacter, D. L. (2016). Creative cognition and brain network dynamics. *Trends in Cognitive Sciences, 20*(2), 87–95. https://doi.org/10.1016/j.tics.2015.10.004

Bilder, R. M., Postal, K. S., Barisa, M., Aase, D. M., Munro Cullum, C., Gillaspy, S. R., ... Woodhouse, J. (2020). Inter organizational practice committee recommendations/guidance for teleneuropsychology in response to the covid-19 pandemic. *Archives of Clinical Neuropsychology, 35*(6), 647–659. https://doi.org/10.1093/arclin/acaa046

Bilder, R., Wolff, B., Davis, A., & Benge, J. F. (June, 2024). Technology and innovation in neuropsychological teaching, testing, and treatment: Practical solutions for practitioners and educators [CE lecture]. American Academy of Clinical Neuropsychology Annual Meeting, Scottsdale, Arizona.

Bilder, R. M., & Knudsen, K. S. (2014). Creative cognition and systems biology on the edge of chaos. *Frontiers in Psychology, 5*, 1104. https://doi.org/10.3389/fpsyg.2014.01104

Calamia, M., Kaseda, E. T., Price, J. S., De Vito, A., Silver, C. H., & Cherry, J. (2022). Mentorship in clinical neuropsychology: Survey of current practices, cultural responsiveness, and untapped potential. *Journal of Clinical and Experimental Neuropsychology, 44*(5–6), 366–385. https://doi.org/10.1080/13803395.2022.2128068

Csikszentmihalyi, M., Abuhamdeh, S., & Nakamura, J. (2005). Flow. In A. J. Elliot & C. S. Dweck (Eds.), *Handbook of competence and motivation* (pp. 598–608). Guilford.

Harris, C., Tang, Y., Birnbaum, E., Cherian, C., Mendhe, D., & Chen, M. H. (2024). Digital neuropsychology beyond computerized cognitive assessment: Applications of novel digital technologies. *Archives of Clinical Neuropsychology, 39*(3), 290–304. https://doi.org/10.1093/arclin/acae016

Japardi, K., Bookheimer, S., Knudsen, K., Ghahremani, D. G., & Bilder, R. M. (2018). Functional magnetic resonance imaging of divergent and convergent thinking in Big-C creativity. *Neuropsychologia, 118*(Pt A), 59–67. https://doi.org/10.1016/j.neuropsychologia.2018.02.017

Johnelle Sparks, P., & Ellison, R. L. (2022). Mentoring in neuropsychology: How theory and practice can support diverse mentees. *Journal of Clinical and Experimental Neuropsychology, 44*(5–6), 337–344. https://doi.org/10.1080/13803395.2022.2125500

Kounios, J., & Beeman, M. (2014). The cognitive neuroscience of insight. *Annual Review of Psychology, 65*, 71–93. https://doi.org/10.1146/annurev-psych-010213-115154

Loring, D. W., & Bauer, R. M. (2010). Testing the limits: Cautions and concerns regarding the new Wechsler IQ and Memory scales. *Neurology, 74*(8), 685–690.

MacDonald, B., Strutt, A. M., & Stinson, J. M. (2026). Mind the gap: Bridging training divides in neuropsychology with the Culturally Expressive and Responsive Supervision Model. *The Clinical Neuropsychologist, 40*(2), 621–637. https://doi.org/10.1080/13854046.2025.2547929

Moore, T. M., Di Sandro, A., Scott, J. C., Lopez, K. C., Ruparel, K., Njokweni, L. J., Santra, S., Conway, D. S., Port, A. M., D'Errico, L., Rush, S., Wolf, D. H., Calkins, M. E., Gur, R. E., & Gur, R. C. (2023). Construction of a computerized adaptive test (CAT-CCNB) for efficient neurocognitive and clinical psychopathology assessment.

Journal of Neuroscience Methods, 386, 109795. https://doi.org/10.1016/j.jneumeth.2023.109795

Rabin, L. A., Barr, W. B., & Burton, L. A. (2005). Assessment practices of clinical neuropsychologists in the United States and Canada: A survey of INS, NAN, and APA Division 40 members. *Archives of Clinical Neuropsychology, 20*(1), 33–65. https://doi.org/10.1016/j.acn.2004.02

Reyes, A., Maietta, J. E., Wong, C. G., MacDonald, B., Calamia, M., Tan, A., Fox-Fuller, J. T., McBride, W. F., Gooding, A., Driskell, L. D., Del Bene, V. A., Sperling, S. A., & Murriel, E. C. (2025). Using digital platforms to address inequities in neuropsychology training and education: Lessons learned from KnowNeuropsychology. *Journal of Clinical and Experimental Neuropsychology*. https://read.qxmd.com/read/40296781/

Saeidnia, H. R., Fotami, S. G. H., Lund, B., & Ghiasi, N. (2024). Ethical considerations in artificial intelligence interventions for mental health and well-being: Ensuring responsible implementation and impact. *Social Sciences, 13*(7), 381. https://doi.org/10.3390/socsci13070381

Schroeder, R. W., Martin, P. K., & Walling, A. (2019). Neuropsychological Evaluations in Adults. *American family physician, 99*(2), 101–108.

Singh, S., & Germine, L. (2021). Technology meets tradition: A hybrid model for implementing digital tools in neuropsychology. *International Review of Psychiatry, 33*(4), 382–393. https://doi.org/10.1080/09540261.2020.1835839

Sprugnoli, G., Rossi, S., Emmendorfer, A., Rossi, A., Liew, S.-L., Tatti, E., Di Lorenzo, G., Pascual-Leone, A., & Santarnecchi, E. (2017). Neural correlates of Eureka moment. *Intelligence, 62,* 99–118. https://doi.org/10.1016/j.intell.2017.03.004

Stinson, J. M., MacDonald, B., & Strutt, A. M. (2023). Cultivating a relevant supervisory space: Culturally expressive and responsive model for supervision in neuropsychology. *Archives of Clinical Neuropsychology, 38*(3), 334–346. https://doi.org/10.1093/arclin/acac097

Stringer, A. Y., Fuchs, K., Bordes Edgar, V., Bristow, T., Correia, S., Penna, S., ... Schmitter-Edgecombe, M. (2025). The Minnesota Conference proposed guidelines for education and training in clinical neuropsychology. *The Clinical Neuropsychologist*, 1–42.

Thomas, M. L. (2019). Advances in applications of item response theory to clinical assessment. *Psychological Assessment, 31*(12), 1442–1455. https://doi.org/10.1037/pas0000597

Van Patten, R., Bellone, J. A., Schmitt, T. R., Gaynor, L., & Block, C. (2022). Digital methods of delivering education and training in neuropsychology. *Archives of Clinical Neuropsychology, 37*(6), 1103–1117. https://doi.org/10.1093/arclin/acac033

Zhang, W., Sjoerds, Z., & Hommel, B. (2020). Metacontrol of human creativity: The neurocognitive mechanisms of convergent and divergent thinking. *NeuroImage, 210,* 116572. https://doi.org/10.1016/j.neuroimage.2020.116572

2

Enhancing Neuropsychological Testing Research with Item Response Theory Applications

Jared M. Block, Steven P. Reise, Keith F. Widaman, and Mark G. Haviland

Introduction

Item response theory (IRT) modeling is now the primary method for effectively and efficiently constructing, evaluating, and comparing large-scale assessments. Indeed, the majority of achievement, proficiency, entrance, and aptitude examinations have been built within the IRT framework. Despite its widespread use in large-scale assessments, IRT's potential in neuropsychology is only beginning to be explored (e.g., Bilder & Reise, 2019; Pedraza & Mungas, 2008). In this chapter, we summarize common IRT models and, with examples, illustrate their potential to enhance neuropsychological research. We then present more advanced techniques that allow users to provide optimally weighted scores based on their relative information, detect differences in responding due to demographic characteristics, and drastically reduce administration times through adaptive testing.

IRT refers to a set of models that describe the relations between observed responses (for questions with either dichotomous or multicategorical response options) and hypothesized underlying traits (or latent variables) that are believed to be responsible for the shared variance in observations (de Ayala, 2022; Embretson & Reise, 2025). In the well-known Beck Depression Inventory (BDI; Beck et al., 1996), for example, a response to an item about past failures is not merely a raw value; it is an indicator of a respondent's overall depression level.

Traditional scoring methods, typically, involve summing responses across an item set to generate a total score, which is assumed to represent an individual's standing on a given trait (e.g., depression severity). This measurement form (often referred to as classical test theory) makes certain restrictive assumptions, including that all items contribute equally to measurement, that a single standard error of measurement (i.e., measurement precision) applies to all individuals at all trait levels, and that scores are only comparable on so-called parallel forms. In contrast, IRT estimates the relation

Jared M. Block et al., *Enhancing Neuropsychological Testing Research with Item Response Theory Applications*.
In: *Technology and Neuropsychology*. Edited by: Jared F. Benge et al., Oxford University Press.
 DOI: 10.1093/9780197814116.003.0002

between each item and the underlying construct, providing standard errors that vary by ability level and producing optimally weighted scores that are comparable, even when individuals have responded to different items, allowing for valid comparisons across different test forms.

The widespread adoption of IRT in large-scale assessment has been driven by its ability to enhance measurement precision and efficiency. Until recently, however, this recognition has not led to widespread adoption in neuropsychological assessment. Exceptions include federally funded initiatives such as the Patient-Reported Outcomes Measurement Information System (PROMIS) and the National Institutes of Health (NIH) Toolbox, both of which incorporated IRT-based methods into the assessment of health-related outcomes. The PROMIS project and the NIH Toolbox relied on IRT to create measures that are efficient, flexible, and precise (Cella et al., 2010; Gershon et al., 2013).

Beyond large-scale assessments, IRT methods can provide direct benefits in many ways for psychometricians and substantive neuropsychology researchers. One of IRT's primary advantages is its ability to produce more precise measurements (Reise & Waller, 2009). Balsis et al. (2012), for example, demonstrated that an Alzheimer's disease assessment was better represented using IRT, as traditional scoring methods could yield identical sum scores from widely varying response patterns. IRT also enables more efficient test administration. Using IRT, del Toro et al. (2011) developed a short form of the Boston Naming Test (BNT; Kaplan et al., 1983), reducing the number of items from 60 to 15, maintaining a score reliability of 0.83 while cutting administration time by a factor of four. Similarly, Gibbons et al. (2008) created an IRT-based computerized adaptive version of the Mood and Anxiety Spectrum Scales (MASS), reducing administration time by over 90%, while retaining a correlation of 0.92 with the full-length version.

IRT seamlessly facilitates score comparisons across groups and different test forms, which cannot be easily accomplished with traditional approaches. A fundamental principle of valid measurement is ensuring that the same trait is assessed consistently across individuals or groups. IRT allows for testing whether items function equivalently across demographic groups (e.g., race, gender, and primary spoken language). Mungas et al. (2011), for example, used IRT to examine the comparability of the Spanish and English Neuropsychological Assessment Scales across ethnic groups. Their findings revealed that some measures produced equivalent scores, whereas others exhibited measurement bias, making score comparisons invalid. Moreover, IRT enables score comparisons across test forms and samples that share only a subset of common items by placing scores from the different tests on a common metric. This capability allows for the creation of alternative forms without compromising comparability.

The principal goal of IRT models lies in measure development, with IRT providing a detailed analysis of how both individual items and entire tests function in assessing an underlying trait. Accordingly, there is no shortage of research that relies on IRT (e.g., Moore et al., 2020; Sitarenios, 2022) to select items that are both informative and representative of the construct being measured. Extensions to IRT modeling are undoubtedly valuable, but they remain secondary to the core objective of IRT: developing test forms that accurately reflect the intended relationship between observation and latent trait.

A comprehensive overview of IRT is beyond the scope of this chapter. Instead, we highlight the principal benefits and applications of IRT in neuropsychology. We review several studies in which researchers have used IRT to improve measurement precision and efficiency in neuropsychological assessment and present applied examples using real neuropsychological data.

Primer on IRT Assumptions

The primary objective of IRT modeling is, for each scale item, to estimate a mathematical function that characterizes the relation between standing on a latent trait (or variable) and the probability of responding to an item in a specific category. These models are introduced in the following sections. We first must detail the four assumptions underlying application of any IRT model: (1) local independence, (2) dimensionality, (3) monotonicity, and (4) measurement invariance:

1. Local independence is the assumption that items are unrelated once controlling for the latent trait(s), or, in other words, that the latent trait(s) explain(s) the entirety of the shared variation between items. When this assumption is violated, both item and person parameters can be biased.
2. Related to local dependence is the assumption regarding the dimensionality of the item set. Initially, researchers often assume that a set of items is unidimensional, meaning that a single latent trait is sufficient to account for all relations among the item set. The assumption of unidimensionality should be tested to determine whether IRT can be justified for the data under consideration. At times, items have relations unexplained by the modeled latent trait(s) due to unmodeled multidimensionality (DeMars, 2010). Consider the example of a neuropsychologist assessing overall cognitive ability (full-scale intelligence quotient, or Full-Scale IQ) using the Wechsler Adult Intelligence Scale 5 (WAIS-5; Wechsler, 2024) through seven subtests. Items within these subtests are likely more highly related to each other than to items across subtests. As such, these local dependencies must be modeled by including latent dimensions that represent these subtests to obtain a more accurate representation (and more accurate parameters) of the data. Experts often claim that unidimensionality is a requirement for IRT models, but this is incorrect. Instead, the dimensionality of the data must be modeled accurately. Fitting a standard, unidimensional IRT model (as described earlier) does require the assumption of unidimensionality of the item set. When multidimensionality is present, multidimensional IRT models are available.

3. Monotonicity refers to the assumption that, for each item, the probability of passing or endorsing the item increases as the trait level increases. It is, therefore, important, when including negatively worded questions, to reverse the scoring of such items so that higher scores correspond to higher ability levels.
4. Finally, IRT models assume measurement invariance, which means that the relation between the latent variable and the probability of responding in a particular category is identical for all subgroups. Only if measurement invariance of this sort holds will latent trait scores be comparable across groups who are administered the same tests. Measurement invariance is testable, and the failure to attain invariance of item parameters is called differential item functioning (DIF) across groups, a topic we return to later in the chapter.

Perhaps the most important precursor to an IRT model is not a statistical one but, rather, a theoretical requirement built into how the model is interpreted. IRT models describe the relation between a latent trait and item responses in such a way that the trait is said to be responsible for the shared variation in those responses. When a construct does not fit this framework, more often than not, other methods are more appropriate. With socioeconomic status (SES), for example, an IRT model would incorrectly suggest that an observation, such as household income, is caused by an underlying SES trait, when, in fact, SES is, in part, caused by household income. Therefore, before fitting an IRT model, it is important to consider whether your construct aligns with such a framework (Bollen & Lennox, 1991).

Dichotomous Response Models

We begin with IRT models that model the relation between dichotomously scored observations (i.e., true/false, observed/unobserved, endorsed/nonendorsed) and the latent trait said to be responsible for the shared variance among items. This relation can be visualized through a plot called an item characteristic curve (ICC) as shown in Figure 2.1, demonstrating the increase in expected probability of endorsing a given item as trait level increases. Using the BDI as an example, the X-axis represents the latent trait (θ) of depression, and the Y-axis is the probability of endorsing a given BDI item (or symptom). As depression increases, the probability of endorsing an item increases, represented by the sigmoidal function in blue. The latent trait—in this case, depression—is a continuous latent variable typically specified to be normally distributed with mean zero and variance of one. This allows one to leverage their understanding of the standard normal distribution in the interpretation of our model. The red dashed line represents the location for this BDI item. Assuming a normally distributed latent trait, an individual with a depression level of $\theta = 0$ is expected to have a 50% probability of endorsing this item. Those with greater depression levels will have a higher probability of endorsement, whereas those with lower levels will be unlikely to endorse this symptom.

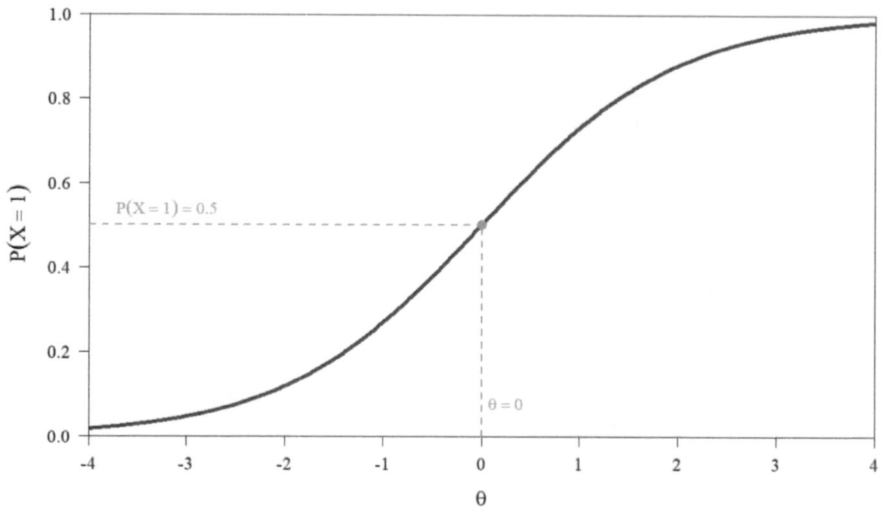

Figure 2.1 Example item characteristic curve (ICC)

The One-Parameter Logistic Model

Of the dichotomous IRT models, the simplest is the one-parameter logistic (1PL) model (and the equivalent Rasch model).[1] This IPL model is aptly named, because it has one parameter per item and uses a logistic function to describe the relation of item responses with the latent trait:

$$P(X_{si} = 1|\theta_s, b_i, a) = \frac{\exp(a(\theta_s - b_i))}{1 + \exp(a(\theta_s - b_i))} \quad (1)$$

where the probability of endorsement, success, or getting item i correct (all of which are synonymous), $(P(X_{si} = 1))$ is conditional on the trait level for the sth individual θ_s. This model includes a common slope (a) parameter that is the same for all items (hence no subscript) that reflects the change of the probability of endorsement as trait level (θ) increases. This parameter may also be referred to as the discrimination parameter, as it describes an item's ability to discriminate among persons of different trait levels. The slope is proportional to the slope of the ICC (Figure 2.1) at the inflection point, where the inflection point is the point on the ICC at which the slope of the ICC is increasing to the left of the inflection point and decreasing to the right of the inflection point. There is also a location parameter (b_i) that is unique to each item and is the point along the latent trait continuum at which the item is

[1] Separate from the development of the 1PL model, Georg Rasch described a nearly identical model (Rasch model; Rasch, 1960). The 1PL and Rasch models provide equal fits to data. Both models have the benefit of being sum score sufficient; that is, an individual's raw total score is a sufficient statistic for determining ability level.

expected to be endorsed (or answered correctly) 50% of the time (the red dashed line in Figure 2.1). Again, using the BDI, the slope (a) represents the average relationship between depression and the BDI items, whereas the location of an item (b_i) is the point along the depression distribution (which we have prespecified to be standard normal) at which the probability of endorsing item i is 50%. Items with high positive locations represent more severe symptoms because it takes greater levels of depression to have a 50% chance of endorsing these items.

We note that the ICC in Figure 2.1 can be transformed into an item information curve. An example item information curve is shown in Figure 2.2, where the height of the curve is based on the slope (a) of the IRT model (and the subsequent ICC), whereas the location of the peak is based on the location parameter (b_i). Individual item information curves may be added together to create a so-called test information curve (given that conditional on the modeled trait(s) items are unrelated, an assumption of all IRT models). The test information curve describes the amount of information provided on trait-level estimates across the trait range for an entire test. The inverse of this test information function is the conditional standard error of measurement ($SE(\theta) = \frac{1}{\sqrt{Test\ Information(\theta)}}$), defined as the precision in our estimates of trait scores across the trait range (Thissen & Wainer, 1982). As such, both item information and standard error estimates are directly related to item slopes (increasing information associated with higher discrimination parameter estimates) and location parameters (where this information is maximized).

Consider another example, the Boston Naming Test (BNT). A question assessed via IRT may be, "How effective is the BNT (Kaplan et al., 1983) in assessing confrontation naming?" The BNT presents respondents a set of line drawings one at a time and asks them to name the item in each drawing within 20 seconds. The full BNT

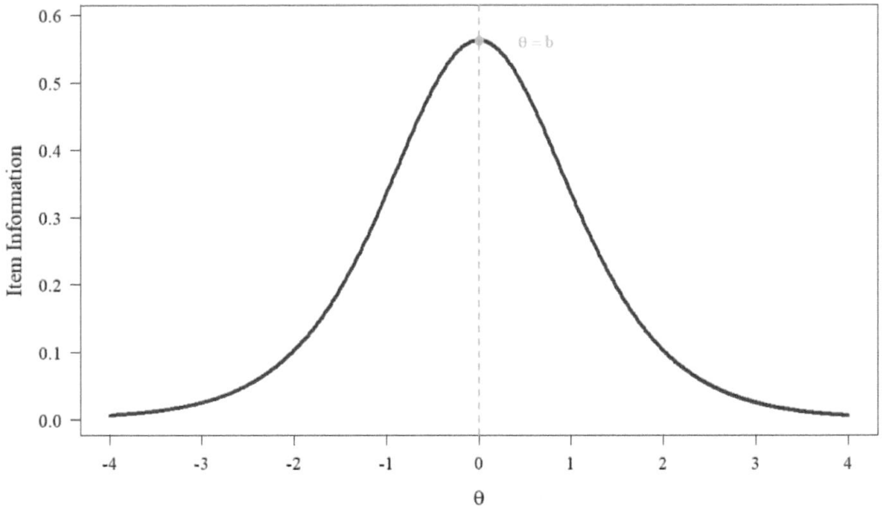

Figure 2.2 Item information curve

contains 60 items ordered by difficulty (however, it has been found that items are not ordered accurately by difficulty; Pedraza et al., 2011); in practice, the first 30 items are infrequently administered to adults and older children because the majority of general clinical populations are expected to answer them correctly; thus, our analyses are on only the latter half of items. Responses are scored as either correct or incorrect with failing to respond within the time limit being coded as incorrect. In the following models, we used the mirt package (Chalmers, 2012) in R version 4.4.2 (R Core Team, 2021) to estimate parameters, but all models can be estimated in many popular software packages such as flexMIRT (Houts & Cai, 2013).

Table 2.1 shows selected estimated model parameters from the 1PL model fit to 683 individuals from the National Neuropsychology Network (NNN; nnn.ucla.edu) who were administered the BNT. The common slope of $a = 1.55$ is proportional to the slope of the ICC at the location and describes how well an item distinguishes among different ability levels.

Moving to the location parameters (b_i) in the 1PL, we see that the drawing of a scroll is a relatively easy item with a location of −1.02; 50% of individuals with naming ability 1.02 standard deviations below the mean are expected to answer this item correctly. Based on the standard normal distribution, approximately 84.6% of our sample would be expected to have a .5 or higher probability of answering this item correctly. Figure 2.3 shows the item information provided by the items Scroll and Protractor. As one can see, the height of the curves is equivalent, as the slopes in the model are forced to equality; however, the threshold parameters (b_i) vary, dictating where information is maximized, at −1.02 for Scroll and .70 for Protractor. To estimate test information, one simply takes the sum of the individual item information curves, with the square root of the inverse at a given point being the associated standard error of measurement. With the 1PL model, the items span a relatively narrow portion of the

Table 2.1 Estimated Parameters for 10 BNT Items Using the 1PL Model

Item	a	b_i
Latch	1.55	−0.45
Tripod	1.55	−0.53
Scroll	1.55	−1.02
Tongs	1.55	−0.69
Sphinx	1.55	−0.17
Yoke	1.55	0.68
Trellis	1.55	0.28
Palette	1.55	0.13
Protractor	1.55	0.70
Abacus	1.55	0.43
Loglikelihood		−24,364.94
df		252

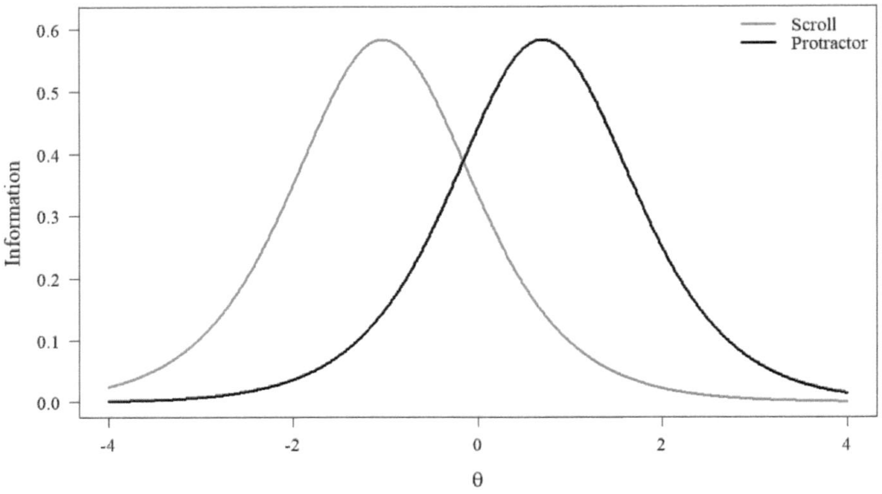

Figure 2.3 Item information for items Scroll and Protractor

trait range, falling from −1.02 to 0.70; therefore, test information will be maximized in this range, and associated measurement precision will be greatest for individuals falling in this range.

Whereas a larger spread of item difficulties would often be seen as desirable, it may not be necessary, as items can be located based on who requires more accurate assessment. When creating educational measures, for example, a common goal is to ensure that a given test can estimate individual ability levels at all points across the trait range. This goal may not be necessary when trying to identify persons who meet a clinical cut point for diagnosis; for example, identifying visual confrontation naming ability impairments suggests aphasia. In contrast, if identifying persons who are exceptionally high in naming ability is of most interest, savings may be gained by administering fewer items that are easy to endorse and more items of greater difficulty (a location farther to the right). When developing a measure, one should consider the population of individuals to be assessed and where measurement precision is most important.

The Two-Parameter Logistic Model

In the 1PL model, item slopes are forced to equality and, thus, one must assume that items are equally discriminating, which may be unrealistic. Next, we consider a model that allows items to vary in relation to the latent trait. This model is called the two-parameter logistic model (2PL):

$$P(X_{si} = 1|\theta_s, b_i, a_i) = \frac{\exp(a_i(\theta_s - b_i))}{1 + \exp(a_i(\theta_s - b_i))} \quad (2)$$

where a_i is each item's unique discrimination or slope parameter (indexing its relation with the latent trait), and all other parameters have the same definition as in the 1PL. Allowing inferences across items in their relation to the latent trait enables one to identify items that are less reflective of the construct of interest (and potentially remove them, if test shortening is of value). This differentiation also allows for more accurate scoring, as weighted sum scores can be estimated that reward correctly answering items most related to the latent variable.

Because we are interested in estimating the relation of the individual BNT items with the latent word retrieval ability, we applied the 2PL model to our data. Although no definitive guidelines exist for what is considered a "good" slope (i.e., that an item does an acceptable job of discriminating between different ability levels), as slopes can range from $-\infty$ to $+\infty$, slopes ranging from 0.8 to 3.0 are often considered to be adequate and relatively informative (Baker, 2001). Item slopes that are lower than 0.8 represent limited ability in distinguishing among ability levels or, equivalently, that the expected response to an item changes minimally as trait level increases. If an item slope is large ($a > 5$), a correct response means that there is a high probability a trait level is above the item location (e.g., an item with $b_i = 0$ and $a_i = 7$ means that we are nearly certain an individual endorsing this item has a trait level above the mean ($\theta > 0$)). It may seem desirable to include only items with large slopes; however, such items provide information about a relatively small range of the trait due to the sharp slope of the ICC. Therefore, it is best in applications to include items with a range of both slopes and difficulties, such that the standard error of measurement is sufficiently small across the entire trait range.

With the 2PL model, Yoke and Abacus have the largest slopes, whereas Latch and Protractor have the lowest (see Table 2.2). We also note that item locations in Table 2.2 (and Table 2.1) are concentrated at the lower end of the trait range ($\theta < 0$), which also applies to the 20 items not shown, which have a range of difficulties from −2.20 to 0.83. As such, we have more information about individuals of lower ability as the individual item information functions are summed to form the test information function. This is compatible with the intuitions of many neuropsychologists who recognize that BNT scores of healthy individuals are highly negatively skewed, with mean number of items correct often exceeding 53/60, so the test is most discriminating in patients who have naming problems (as was the original intent of Kaplan et al., 1983). Slope estimates differed when moving from the 1PL model to the 2PL model due to estimating a separate slope for each item, and this led to the differences in difficulties under the two models as the inflection point shifted. Unique slopes allow us to identify BNT items that are more informative (e.g., Sphinx, Yoke, and Abacus) and those that are less informative (e.g., Latch) as seen in Table 2.2, whereas in the 1PL model all four of these items are considered equally informative (see Table 2.1).

Table 2.2 Estimated Parameters for 10 BNT Items Using the 2PL Model

Item	a_i	b_i
Latch	0.77	−0.74
Tripod	1.36	−0.59
Scroll	1.61	−1.01
Tongs	1.15	−0.84
Sphinx	1.66	−0.18
Yoke	1.84	0.63
Trellis	1.48	0.28
Palette	1.17	0.14
Protractor	1.14	0.83
Abacus	2.20	0.36
Loglikelihood		−24,143.87
df		230

Figure 2.4 shows the item characteristic curves and the associated item information for the items with the largest slope, Abacus, and the smallest, Latch. The ICC for Abacus is shifted to the right when compared to the ICC for latch due to the difference in their respective locations ($b_{Abacus} = .36$ and $b_{Latch} = -.74$). Unlike the 1PL model where all slopes are forced to be equal, under the 2PL item, slopes are allowed to vary, leading to the slope of the ICC for Abacus being nearly three times as large as that for Latch. The difference in location and slope parameters translates to the item information functions (right panel of Figure 2.4) with the location dictating where information is maximized (the location of the peak of the curve) and the slope dictating the amount of information provided (the height of the peak of the curve).

The Three-Parameter Logistic Model (3PL)

This model includes a pseudo guessing parameter (c_i) for each item as seen in Equation 3

$$P(X_{si} = 1|\theta_s, b_i, a_i, c_i) = c_i + (1 - c_i)\frac{\exp(a_i(\theta_s - b_i))}{1 + \exp(a_i(\theta_s - b_i))} \tag{3}$$

where the right-hand function is identical to the 2PL above with a note that item location b_i is no longer the point along the latent trait continuum where the probability of endorsement is .5 but is solely defined as the inflection point of the ICC. The guessing parameter c_i has a clear interpretation as the probability of endorsing an item

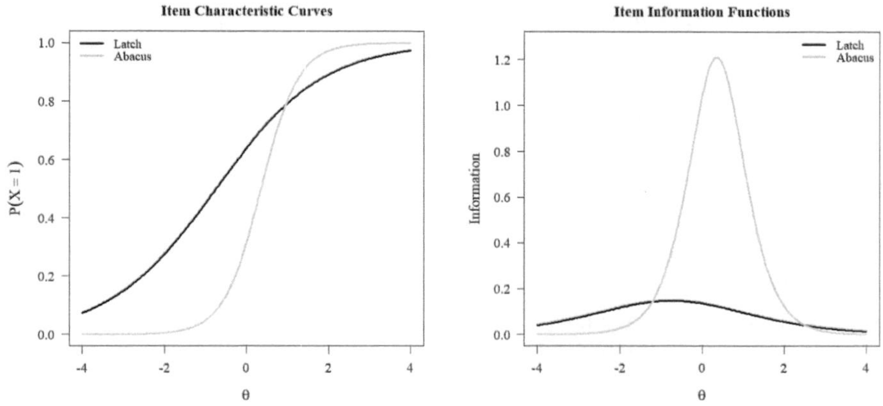

Figure 2.4 Item characteristic curves and item information functions for Abacus and Latch

regardless of ability level (i.e., the probability of endorsement via guessing). Although this parameter has greater use in educational measurement (e.g., when individuals guess and select the correct item option without actually knowing the answer), it is still applicable to neuropsychological measures that use multiple-choice formats (e.g., WAIS-IV Matrix Reasoning or forced-choice tests widely used in performance validity testing).

Estimates for the 3PL model applied to the BNT are shown in Table 2.3 with a lower asymptote estimated for each item. As with difference in location between the

Table 2.3 Estimated Parameters for 10 BNT Items Using the 3PL Model

Item	a_i	b_i	c_i
Latch	0.79	−0.67	0.02
Tripod	1.37	−0.58	0.00
Scroll	1.81	−0.80	0.13*
Tongs	1.16	−0.83	0.00
Sphinx	1.67	−0.17	0.00
Yoke	1.87	0.63	0.00
Trellis	1.50	0.28	0.00
Palette	1.18	0.14	0.00
Protractor	1.14	0.83	0.00
Abacus	2.24	0.36	0.00
Loglikelihood			−24,143.87
df			207

Note: The c_i parameter for Scroll is the only significant c_i.

1PL and 2PL models, the difference between b_i estimates going from the 2PL to the 3PL model is due to the magnitude of the guessing parameter c_i. For the item Scroll, $c_{Scroll} = .13$, even individuals at very low levels of the latent trait have a 13% chance of answering this item correctly. Only two items (Latch and Scroll) had guessing parameters estimates above zero, and of those, only Scroll had a significant lower asymptote parameter. The guessing parameter is often difficult to estimate, so it is commonly recommended to fix its value across items. The other items shown in Table 2.3 have c_i parameter estimates so low such that persons at very low levels of the latent trait had essentially no likelihood of guessing the correct answer, congruent with the idea that BNT answers are not guessed correctly by chance.

In Figure 2.5, the Scroll ICCs show how the different IRT models provide differing understanding of the item. The ICCs for the 1PL and 2PL models are very similar across the entire trait range, as expected, given the similar slope and location parameter estimates for these two models in Tables 2.1 and 2.2. In contrast, the 3PL model, which includes a guessing parameter estimate, has an ICC that differs from those for the 1PL and 2PL at trait levels below roughly −1.50. Interestingly, above the trait level of −1.50, the ICCs under all three models are very similar, despite apparent differences in slope and location parameters in the 3PL model relative to the two other models.

Figure 2.6 shows the conditional test information (solid line) and standard error (dashed line) curves for the 1PL, 2PL, and 3PL models. The 1PL model appears to underestimate the information the model provides at the information peak ($-2 \leq \theta \leq -.5$) due to the estimate of a common slope parameter that inflates some slopes

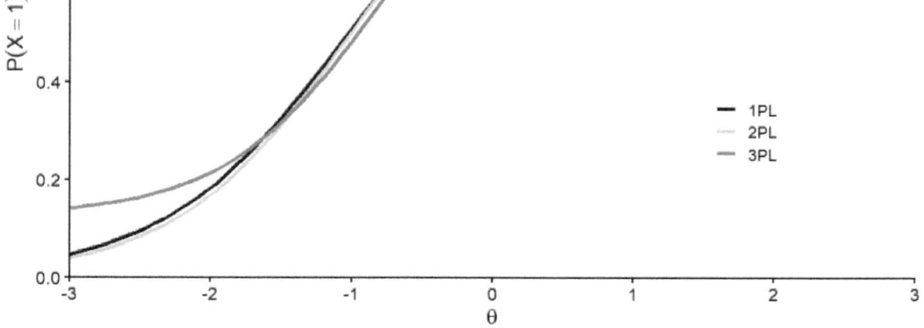

Figure 2.5 Item characteristic curve for the Item Scroll in the 1PL, 2PL, and 3PL models

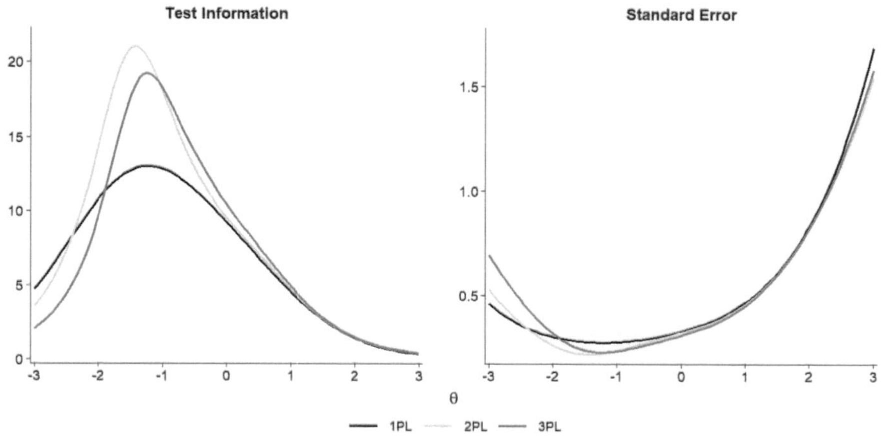

Figure 2.6 Conditional test information and standard error for 1PL, 2PL, and 3PL models

and deflates others. The 2PL model yields higher information at the maximum of the information curve, as a function of allowing different slope estimates across items. Finally, the 3PL model shifts the test information function down and to the right as the presence of a non-zero lower asymptote demonstrates that items are more difficult than estimated under the 2PL.

Note that the models presented, thus far, are nested, such that we can achieve any of the prior models through constraining parameters. Constraining the lower asymptote of the 3PL to zero ($c_i = c = 0$) yields the 2PL, and constraining the slope to equality ($a_i = a_{i+1}$ for all i) gives the 1PL. When models are nested (i.e., the 1PL within the 2PL), one can perform a likelihood ratio test distributed as χ^2 with $df = df_{unconstrained} - df_{constrained}$, with a null hypothesis that the more constrained model provides adequate fit. Because our models are nested, one can directly assess whether the increase in the number of parameters (i.e., estimating a lower asymptote) improves model-data fit. Testing the 1PL versus 2PL, $\chi^2(9) = 442.14$, $p \leq .001$, we reject the null hypothesis that the more constrained model (1PL) provides fit to the data comparable to that exhibited by the less constrained model (2PL). Comparing the 2PL and 3PL model, however, $\chi^2(10) = 6.89$, $p = .89$, we fail to reject the null hypothesis that adding item-specific lower asymptotes provides improved fit to our data. As such, we would recommend using the 2PL model when evaluating the BNT.

Polytomous Response Models

Neuropsychologists also use tests with multiple response options, such as the Beck Anxiety Inventory (BAI; Beck et al., 1988). The BAI lists 21 anxiety symptoms, and respondents mark answers on a four-point (0–3) Likert scale (Figure 2.7) describing

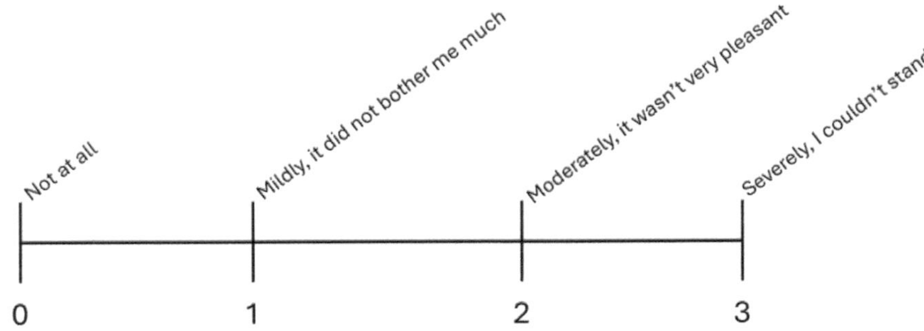

Figure 2.7 Example Likert scale

how much each symptom affects them; for example, "How much have you been bothered by 'heart pounding or racing'?"

The Graded Response Model

With dichotomous items, all we need is a single ICC to model the relation between trait level and the probability of responding correctly to the item. With polytomous items, an IRT model must describe the relation between trait level and the probability of responding in each category. As described next, these are called category response curves (CRCs), and different IRT models are simply different ways of deriving CRCs. The first polytomous IRT model we use to evaluate the BAI is Samejima's Graded Response Model (GRM; Samejima, 1969), which is an extension of the 2PL model described earlier. The GRM is applicable for items with ordered response categories and is equivalent to the 2PL model when an item has only two categories. In the GRM, each item has an estimated slope as is the case with the 2PL model (a_i) describing the relation between item and trait. Instead of a single location parameter, however, multiple location parameters per item are used. With polytomous items, these location parameters are called thresholds, and the (number of categories minus one) threshold parameters must be estimated for each item, as described next.

For each item i, with k response categories, we model between-category threshold parameters (b_{ik}) separating adjacent categories. The GRM then models the probability of responding below versus above a particular category threshold (e.g., the lowest category vs. everything above, the lowest two categories vs. everything above, and so forth). We have $k - 1$ threshold response curves for each item, each with a unique threshold (b_{ik}), but equal slope (a_i). Each of these curves is simply the 2PL equation

$$P(X_{si} \geq k | \theta_s, b_{ik}, a_i) = \frac{\exp(a_i(\theta_s - b_{ik}))}{1 + \exp(a_i(\theta_s - b_{ik}))} \tag{4}$$

where we are modeling the probability of a response of individual s on item i at or above category k. To find the probability of responding in any given category, we rely on the definition of probabilities, in that responding in the lowest category and above is one and the probability of responding above the highest category is zero; therefore,

$$P(X_{si} = k|\theta_s) = P(X_{si} = k|\theta_s) - P(X_{si} = k + 1|\theta_s) \tag{5}$$

captures the probability of responding in each category k. These probabilities are called category response curves (CRCs) and relate the probability of responding in a category conditional on trait level.

We applied the GRM to the 1,917 individuals enrolled in the NNN who completed the BAI. Table 2.4 shows the estimated item parameters and fit of the GRM. The first column shows item slopes that are all relatively high; each item has a relatively strong relation with the anxiety construct. There are differences in slope values, with the slope for item 1 (1.14) being approximately half as large as the slope for Item 9 (2.21). These slopes dictate how peaked the CRCs are. The spread of the b_{ik} parameters illustrate the relative difficulty of responding above a threshold and, ideally, are evenly spread across the trait range, so that items provide information for a wide trait

Table 2.4 Item Parameters and GRM Fit for the BAI

Item	a_i	b_1	b_2	b_3
1	1.14	0.50	1.66	3.43
2	1.30	0.46	1.48	2.96
3	1.36	0.37	1.49	3.01
4	1.86	−0.40	0.71	1.99
5	1.91	0.05	0.94	2.05
6	1.53	0.27	1.46	2.91
7	1.98	0.46	1.39	2.60
8	1.61	−0.02	1.22	2.52
9	2.21	1.03	1.63	2.49
10	1.93	−0.48	0.72	2.01
11	1.47	1.83	2.60	3.61
12	1.30	0.46	1.54	2.80
13	1.63	0.38	1.44	2.55
14	1.95	0.50	1.45	2.38
15	1.92	1.00	1.86	3.08
16	1.42	1.23	2.19	3.09
17	1.74	0.38	1.36	2.46
18	1.21	0.28	1.46	3.06
19	1.78	1.38	2.33	3.30
20	1.60	1.23	2.22	3.34
21	1.55	0.79	1.76	2.78

level range. As seen in the last three columns of Table 2.4, an even distribution did not occur, with category thresholds falling, nearly universally, in the upper end of the trait range (e.g., above 0.0). The distribution of item thresholds means that BAI items tend to have low endorsement levels, requiring an above-average anxiety level to respond above the lowest category, "not at all." This makes sense conceptually, as individuals who do not have an anxiety disorder (and, therefore, are low in the anxiety trait) are expected to endorse anxiety symptoms infrequently. This threshold concentration reflects that the BAI was designed to assess anxiety disorders, and questions were designed to maximize information at the high end of the anxiety latent trait, with little importance placed on measurement fidelity for individuals with low anxiety levels.

Examining item 10, Nervous, the thresholds were relatively evenly spaced, where b_1 represents the point along the anxiety trait continuum where individuals have a .5 probability of responding above the lowest category. This is shown in the upper panel of Figure 2.8, where the probability of responding above each between category threshold (i.e., $P(X > k = 0)$) is modeled with each function having the same slope a_i. Subtracting the probability of responding at or above each threshold from the adjacent rating scale point provides the CRCs that contain information on the probability of responding in each category, as seen in the lower panel of Figure 2.8.

As with dichotomous models, in polytomous models the CRCs determine the item information. Specifically, information is maximized at each location parameter, and the amount is determined by the discrimination parameter. Unlike the prior models, however, there are multiple peaks to the information function (see Figure 2.9). These multiple peaks are located at the threshold parameters (b_{ik}) and represent the amount of information gained by transitioning between category selections. As we see, polytomous items may provide information over a greater range of the trait, providing multiple peaks of information as responses transition from lower to higher categories. Like with the dichotomous models, individual item information functions may be summed together to create a test information curve (see Figure 2.10). This curve shows the amount of information that one's measure contains at different anxiety trait levels. The inverse of this function is the conditional standard error of trait measurement; in other words, how confident we are in estimates of location on the given trait.

The Nominal Response Model

An alternative model to the GRM for categorical data is the nominal response model (NRM; Bock, 1972), which allows for the evaluation of the ordering of nominal categories (e.g., multiple choice on Matrix Reasoning items) and the estimation of optimal scoring weights. In Figure 2.7, for example, we may evaluate whether category three, "moderately, it wasn't very pleasant," actually requires a greater trait

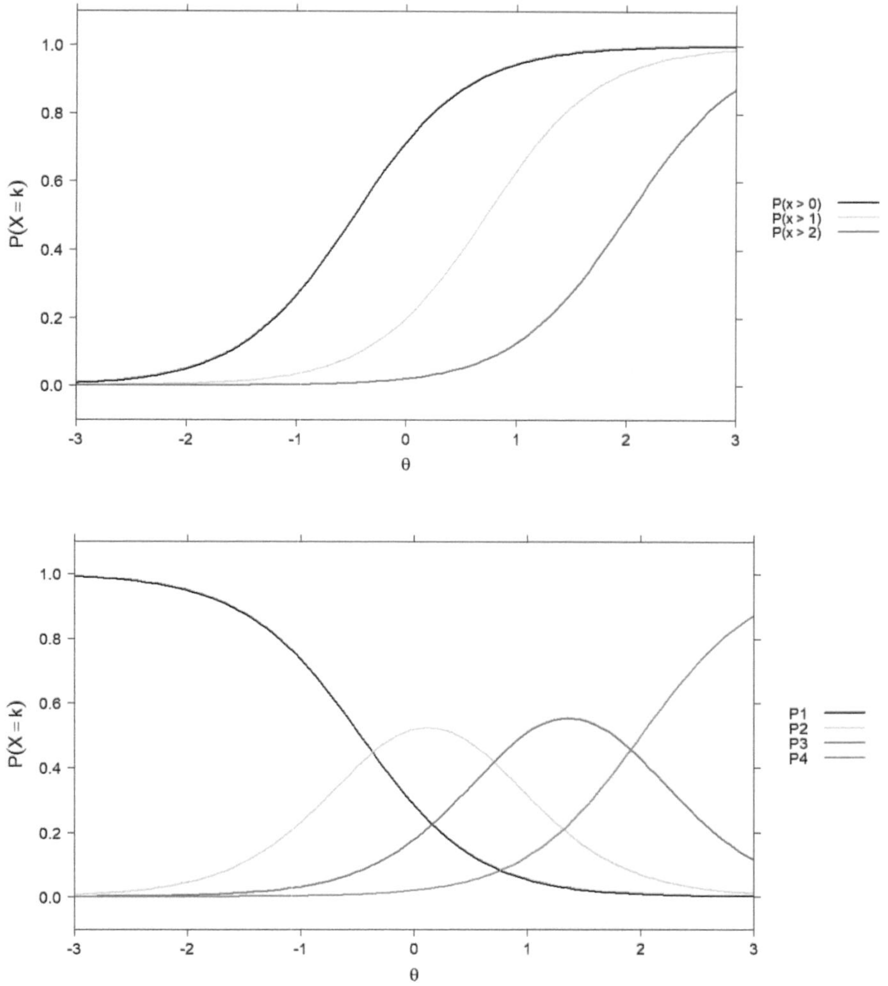

Figure 2.8 Threshold response and category response curves under the GRM for item 10: Nervous

Note: Threshold response curves are above, and category response curves are below.

level to select than category two, "mildly, it did not bother me too much," in contrast to making that assumption, as the GRM requires. Substantively, the NRM allows neuropsychologists to discover how much information each item provides and how informative a response in each category is when estimating trait level. The equation for the NRM directly models the probability that an individual will respond in a given category (not above a threshold as in the GRM) with a model of the following form:

$$P(X_{si} = k|\theta_s, c_{ik}, a_i) = \frac{\exp(a_{ik}\theta + c_{ik})}{\sum_{k=0}^{m_i} \exp(a_{ik}\theta + c_{ik})} \quad (6)$$

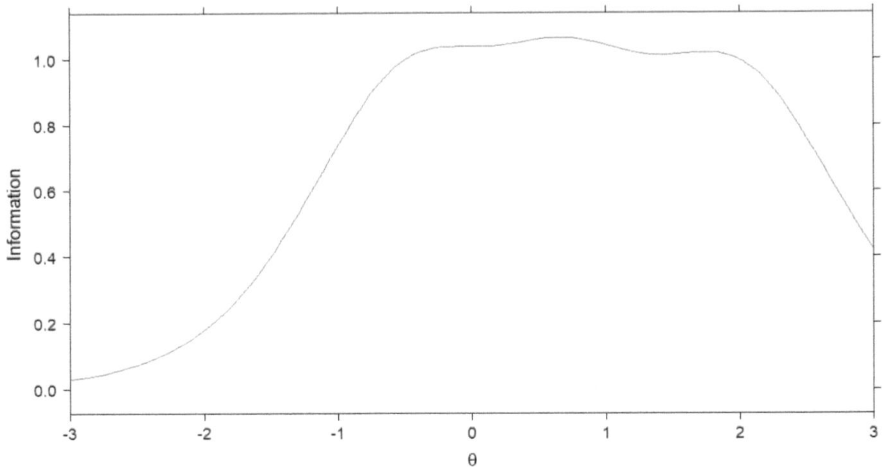

Figure 2.9 Item information function for BAI item 10: Nervous

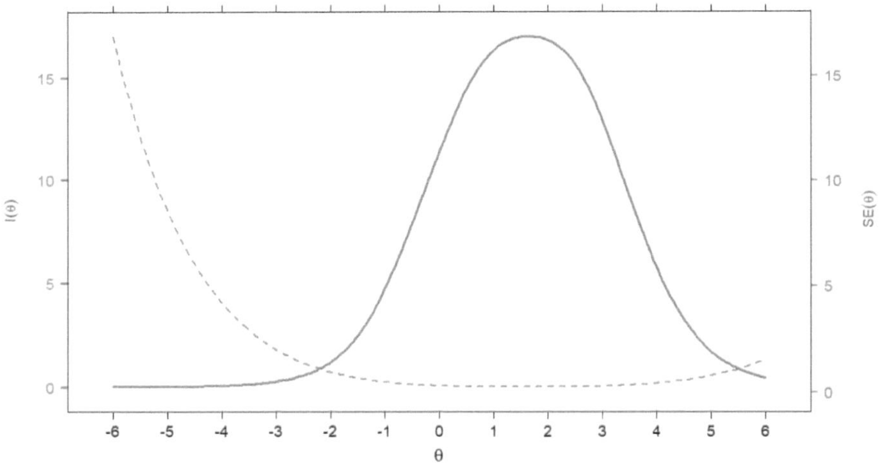

Figure 2.10 Test information and standard error for BAI

Note: Test information is in solid line, and standard error of trait estimate is in dashed line.

where a_{ik} is the unique category slope and c_{ik} is a category-specific intercept that represents the relative popularity of each category. The above, however, is unidentified and, therefore, we must constrain $\sum a_{ik} = \sum c_{ik} = 0$ or $a_{i1} = c_{i1} = 0$. In this form, parameters are not particularly informative, so we recommend using the reparameterization found in Thissen et al. (2010) given by

$$P\left(X_{si} = k|\theta_s, a_i^*, a_{ik}^w, c_{ik}\right) = \frac{\exp\left(a_i^* a_{ik}^w \theta_s + c_{ik}\right)}{\sum \exp\left(a_i^* a_{ik}^w \theta_s + c_{ik1}\right)} \tag{7.1}$$

and

$$a_1^s = 0, \; a_{j_i}^s = m_i, \; \text{and } c_1 = 0 \tag{7.2}$$

where a_i^* is an overall slope representing the relation an item has with the latent trait, a_{ik}^w is the scoring function for category k of item i, and c_{ik} is the intercept as interpreted before. The scoring function is interpreted as the amount of information provided by the transition between categories (e.g., how much information do we gain on anxiety when shifting from "moderately, it wasn't very pleasant" to "mildly, it did not bother me too much"). Multiplying a_i^* and a_{ik}^w provides the optimal scoring weight for a response in category k for item i and can be used to create weighted sum scores that are reflective of the amount of information each item-category combination provides.

We applied the NRM to the BAI to evaluate optimal scoring weights and whether response categories are ordered for each item. Properly ordered categories will have a_k^w parameters that are ordered from low to high. For the BAI, all a_k^w parameters were ordered, such that as anxiety increases the expectation that a higher response category becomes more likely to be expected is supported (see Table 2.5). As shown in Figure 2.11, the distance between a_ks for item 16, "Fear of Dying," demonstrates the relative information provided from selecting between adjacent categories. For this item, at no point are categories 1 and 2 the most probable selection, with most individuals responding in the lowest category 0. For this item, consideration should be given to collapsing categories during data analysis and potentially reducing the number of response options in future administrations.

Using the Thissen parameterization of the NRM, one can estimate optimal scoring weights for the BAI. Table 2.5 lists the a_i^* parameters that can be interpreted in the same way as a_i in the GRM model, such that it describes the relation between each

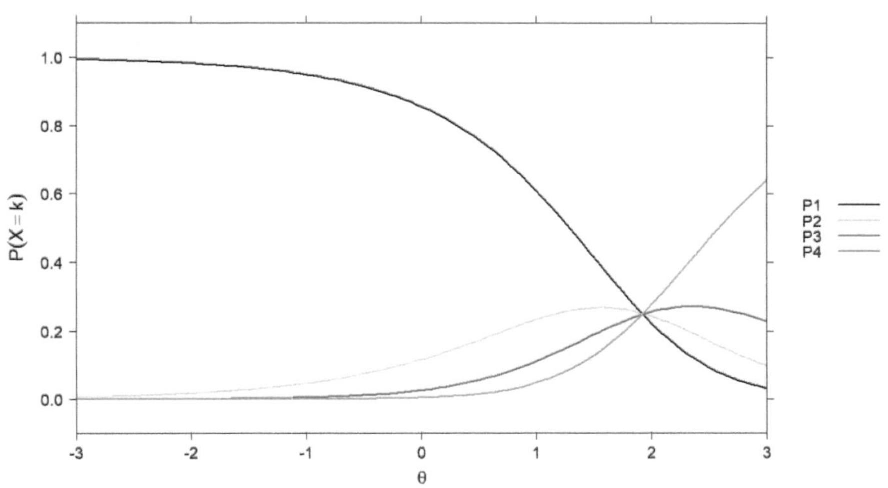

Figure 2.11 Category response curves for item 16: Fear of Dying under the NRM

Table 2.5 Item Parameters of the NRM Using Thissen et al. Parameterization of the BAI

Item	a_i^*	a_0^w	a_1^w	a_2^w	a_3^w
1	0.77	0.00	1.21	1.74	3.00
2	0.82	0.00	1.26	2.02	3.00
3	0.87	0.00	1.25	2.06	3.00
4	1.37	0.00	0.89	1.90	3.00
5	1.37	0.00	0.96	1.85	3.00
6	1.16	0.00	0.99	1.80	3.00
7	1.56	0.00	0.93	1.83	3.00
8	1.07	0.00	1.15	2.23	3.00
9	1.48	0.00	1.21	1.97	3.00
10	1.58	0.00	0.78	1.70	3.00
11	0.80	0.00	1.67	2.27	3.00
12	0.70	0.00	1.71	2.29	3.00
13	0.93	0.00	1.55	2.42	3.00
14	1.40	0.00	1.07	1.93	3.00
15	1.29	0.00	1.30	2.05	3.00
16	0.93	0.00	1.12	1.99	3.00
17	1.29	0.00	0.99	1.77	3.00
18	0.81	0.00	1.00	1.90	3.00
19	1.32	0.00	1.10	1.97	3.00
20	1.14	0.00	1.15	1.88	3.00
21	1.02	0.00	1.23	1.89	3.00

item and the Anxiety latent trait. The scoring functions in columns 4 and 5, a_k^w can be interpreted in terms of their distance from the nominal categories they represent (categories 1 and 2 in this case). As seen in Table 2.5, item 13, "Shaky," has categories 1 and 2 that are relatively informative of anxiety (columns headed by a_1^w and a_2^w respectively), leading to these categories being weighted higher than their nominal values. On the other hand, item 10, "Nervous," has middle categories that are less informative and are therefore weighted lower (weight of 0.78 vs. 1, and 1.70 vs. 2).

The relation between overall and category slope within the NRM is best demonstrated when using weighted sum scoring where an individual who responds to the first three items in categories 1, 2, and 3, respectively, would have a sum score given by

$$\begin{aligned} \textit{Weighted Sum Score} &= a_1^* a_{1,1}^w + a_2^* a_{2,2}^w + a_3^* a_{3,3}^w \\ 5.20 &= (.77)(1.21) + (.82)(2.02) + (.87)(3). \end{aligned} \tag{8}$$

Contrasting with raw scoring, which would yield a sum score of 6 (3 + 2 + 1), the weighted sum score is lower due to the relatively weaker relations of these first three items with the anxiety latent trait, with the opposite being true of items with large

Figure 2.12 Effects of nominal scoring weight

Note: CTT scoring in black, scoring functions for item 8 in grey, and item 1 in light grey.

slope parameters (e.g., items 7, 9, and 10). This is easily extended to scoring an entire response pattern, to achieve a sum score reflective of the relation of each item and category with the latent trait. As seen in Figure 2.12, these category scoring values represent the relative information provided by responding in a given category and can change how much value an item is given when calculating sum scores, with categories from item 8 receiving a boost, and categories from item 1 being down weighted. (Note that item information, test information, and conditional standard errors may be calculated identically as in the GRM.)

Differential Item Functioning

The issue of score comparability is particularly salient in neuropsychological assessments, where we must ensure that responses have the same meaning across groups. When the probability of responding to an item does not depend solely on a person's trait level, the item is said to fail measurement invariance, in other words, to display differential item functioning (DIF; Mellenbergh, 1989).

Perhaps the most well-known example of DIF occurs in depression measures, where the item "cries often" may have different probabilities of endorsement depending on sex, even when individuals have the same depression level. In this case, the probability of responding depends not only on one's position on the underlying trait (depression) but also on individual characteristics. When DIF occurs, it is generally agreed that scores are no longer comparable, as the same construct is not being assessed in the same manner across groups (Holland & Wainer, 1993).

As an example of evaluating DIF within neuropsychology, Pedraza et al. (2009) investigated whether the Boston Naming Test (BNT) contained items displaying DIF between Caucasian and African American adults over the age of 52. They found that at least six of the thirty items exhibited DIF, calling into question the construct validity of the naming assessment. Similarly, Crane et al. (2004) demonstrated that the Cognitive Assessment Screening Instrument (CASI) shows DIF across both age and education levels. For more examples of DIF testing in neuropsychological measures, see Teresi et al. (2008).

Given these findings, there are good reasons to determine whether items display DIF across major demographic groups to ensure that tests are not biased on these variables (e.g., gender, education level, racial or ethnic groups, other social and cultural score determinants) when developing measures or using them in new populations. We will briefly introduce two simple, yet effective ways to detect potential DIF: descriptive analyses and logistic regression with graphical analyses.

Before fitting any model, it is recommended to conduct basic descriptive analyses on the data. One straightforward approach is to compare the means and variances of item scores across demographic groups to identify potentially consequential disparities (Hambleton, 2006). As an example, Table 2.6 presents the means and variances of BAI scores for 1,110 younger adults (under 65) and 811 older adults (65 and older), again with NNN data. Whereas t-tests could be used to determine whether these differences are statistically significant, a quick glance reveals that means and variances are consistently larger for the younger group. For some items (e.g., items 11, 12, and 13), the differences in performance may be relatively minor

Table 2.6 Means and Variances of BAI Items for Younger (<65) and Older (≥65) Individuals

	<65		≥65	
Item	$\hat{\mu}$	$\hat{\sigma}^2$	$\hat{\mu}$	$\hat{\sigma}^2$
1	0.69	0.81	0.47	0.59
2	0.81	0.90	0.35	0.46
3	0.64	0.75	0.57	0.67
4	1.19	0.98	0.71	0.66
5	0.93	1.01	0.59	0.69
6	0.74	0.75	0.45	0.53
7	0.71	0.79	0.28	0.34
8	0.78	0.82	0.71	0.70
9	0.42	0.64	0.22	0.35
10	1.17	0.91	0.76	0.68
11	0.22	0.37	0.13	0.20
12	0.68	0.81	0.54	0.75
13	0.68	0.79	0.51	0.66
14	0.61	0.78	0.41	0.51
15	0.39	0.52	0.22	0.30
16	0.38	0.60	0.23	0.32
17	0.70	0.45	0.84	0.56
18	0.78	0.90	0.53	0.59
19	0.26	0.39	0.15	0.19
20	0.37	0.51	0.14	0.20
21	0.60	0.77	0.25	0.35

and ignorable. For others, however (e.g., items 2 and 7), the means and variances in the younger group are nearly double those of the older group, suggesting potential DIF. This pattern raises concerns that BAI items may not be assessing the same construct across all individuals. That said, the uniformity of this response pattern could mean that the latent means for the two groups differ. If this difference aligns with a substantive hypothesis explaining why the means differ, it may not necessarily pose a measurement issue. In Figure 2.13, we observe a clear skew in the trait distribution for younger individuals; on average, those under 65 have higher anxiety estimates. This does not necessarily mean that DIF is present; further statistical methods are advisable to evaluate further.

We examined the CRCs for item 4 "Unable to Relax" in the younger and older groups estimated concurrently. As shown in Figure 2.14, the response probabilities for each category clearly differed between the two groups. Conditional on anxiety level, each response category is more difficult to endorse for the older group, reflecting the same pattern of consistently higher scores for younger respondents seen in Table 2.6, suggesting the presence of DIF. In contrast, item 8 "Unsteady" (Figure 2.15) exhibits the opposite effect, being easier to endorse for older individuals. One possible explanation for this reversed pattern is the well-documented relation between aging and declining physical abilities.

Examining summary statistics and CRCs may highlight potential DIF (or lack thereof), but it does not determine whether the departure is statistically significant or which parameters differ between groups (e.g., slope, threshold). One may initially think that DIF may be assessed by estimating separate models for each group and comparing estimated item parameters; however, parameters estimated separately by

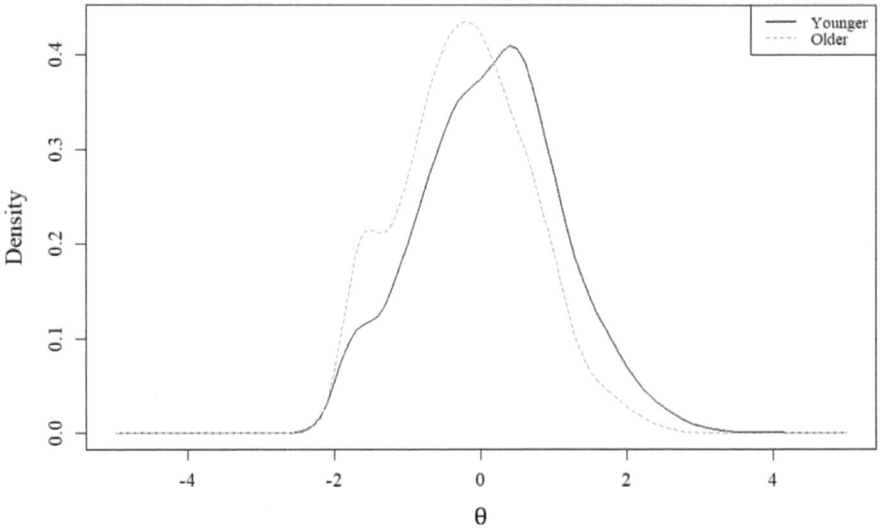

Figure 2.13 Distribution of anxiety trait for older and younger individuals

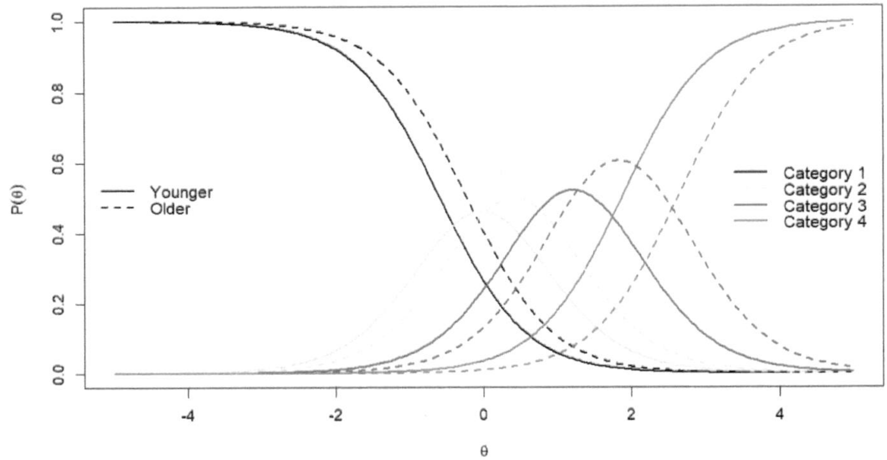

Figure 2.14 Category response curves for BAI item 4: Unable to Relax for younger and older adults

Note: Dashed lines are the CRCs for the older group, and black solid lines are for the younger group.

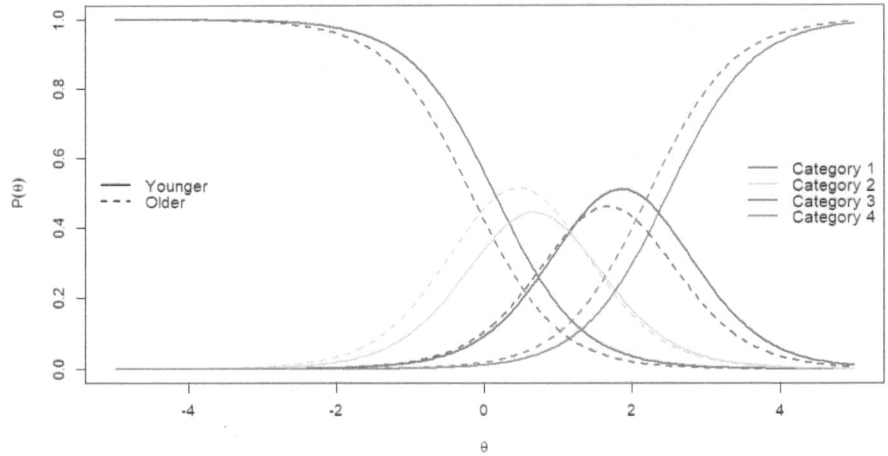

Figure 2.15 Category response curves for BAI item 8: Unsteady for younger and older adults

Note: Dashed lines are the CRCs for the older group, and solid lines are for the younger group.

group are not on the same metric and, therefore, cannot be compared unless put on the same scale using a procedure known as linking. Briefly, to test whether parameters differ between groups, a subset of anchor items that are DIF-free is selected, and a single logistic regression model is run in which interaction parameters are estimated between groups (i.e., to test whether there are any slope or threshold by group interactions). A Wald χ^2 test is then used to determine whether item parameters are significantly different based on group membership (see Swaminathan &

Rogers, 1990). Using this test in the R package lordif (Choi et al., 2011), we found that 11 BAI items displayed significant DIF between older and younger populations: feeling hot (2), wobbliness in legs (3), unable to relax (4), fear of worst happening (5), dizzy or lightheaded (6), heart pounding or racing (7), unsteady (8), nervous (10), hands trembling (12), face flushed (20), and sweating (not due to heat; 21). The question now is, What should a researcher do with these items? A common approach is to remove or rewrite DIF items. This is not always feasible or desirable, such as when analyzing an existing instrument or when the item is essential for defining a construct. In such cases, researchers can either adjust scores based on group membership or allow parameters to vary freely across groups (Teresi et al., 2012). See Tay et al. (2015) and Choi et al. (2011) for more details on DIF testing in IRT.

Computerized Adaptive Testing

In recent decades, the concept of optimizing measurement has become increasingly salient. Traditional measurement theory dictates that longer tests are more reliable than shorter versions; however, this is not necessarily the case in IRT (Embretson & Reise, 2025). Shorter tests can achieve nearly the same reliability level as longer ones when using computerized adaptive testing (CAT).

The goal of CAT is to provide a tailored assessment for each examinee. This is achieved by estimating an individual's ability level after each administered item. The interim estimate is then used to select the next item, and this process continues until a stopping criterion is met—typically, a predetermined test length or a standard error threshold (Meijer & Nering, 1999). Imagine you are taking a CAT version of the BAI. At the start, no prior data exist on your anxiety level, so your estimated ability is set at the mean of the distribution, typically assumed to be standard normal, and so you would start out with $\theta = 0$. You will first receive an item that is most informative at the interim ability level, which likely would be item 5 (Table 2.4), as this item has a threshold near 0 ($b_{5,1} = .05$) and is informative ($a_5 = 1.91$) relative to the other items. Your response on this item (i.e., item 5) dictates which item you receive next. Responding with a 2 or 3, for example, likely means that your anxiety trait is above the mean, and, therefore, the next BAI item is selected according to this updated trait estimate (e.g., $b_{i,1} > .05$). This iterative process of administering an item and updating the ability estimate continues until a prespecified stopping criterion is reached.

CAT offers several advantages over traditional full-length assessments. First, by design, CAT reduces administration time, as test takers receive only the items necessary for an accurate estimate of their standing on the underlying trait. Second, CAT is more considerate of the test taker's ability, avoiding items that are too easy (providing little information) or too difficult. Finally, CAT can yield more accurate ability estimates than full-length tests (Weiss, 2011). This is because traditional, full-length testing introduces unnecessary variability, or noise, into responses.

Typically, the largest concern in CAT is having a sufficient item bank. For optimized CAT administration, it is important to have items that span the range of ability levels but also multiple items within each location range. Generally, it is not ideal for individuals to receive the same few items, as this may lead to test security issues. Building an item bank with a large number of items across varying locations is easier said than done, but relatively large banks allow for more effective CAT administration and estimation.

The application of CAT to neuropsychological batteries has become increasingly popular over the past two decades and may represent the future of testing in the field (Bilder & Reise, 2019). The construction and administration of CAT-based assessments have already begun. Moore et al. (2023), for example, applied CAT to 21 cognitive tests in the Penn Computerized Neurocognitive Battery, covering measures ranging from attention to sensorimotor speed. They reported that, for measures such as the Risk Discounting Test, administration time could be cut by more than half while still achieving clinically acceptable standard errors of measurement. Similarly, Reise et al. (2024) simulated the potential benefit of a CAT version of the Matrix Reasoning subtest of the WAIS-IV. They found that, compared to the full-length administration of 26 items, individuals only needed to be administered 3–7 items to achieve an approximate reliability of .84 (standard error of 0.4).

As an applied example, we simulated how a CAT may function using the parameters from the BAI data described earlier using the R package Firestar (Choi, 2009). This simulation allows us to examine, post-hoc, how many and which items these individuals would have received in a CAT setting. We briefly compared four stopping criteria: a maximum standard error of the trait estimate set at .325, aligning with the observed standard error of trait estimates in the full-length administration; a maximum standard error of .40, balancing standard error and efficiency; a fixed length of three items; and a fixed length of six items. Table 2.7 compares these four stopping criteria, illustrating the tradeoff between test length and the accuracy of ability estimates.

With a standard error of 0.325, matching that of the full-length administration, the mean number of items administered was 14.6; CAT reduced the number of

Table 2.7 Comparison of CAT Stopping Criteria

Stopping Criterion	Mean Items Administered	Mean SE of Trait Estimate	Correlation of CAT and Full-Length Trait Estimates
SE = 0.325	14.6	0.33	0.98
SE = 0.40	9.9	0.41	0.95
Items Administered = 6	6	0.44	0.92
Items Administered = 3	3	0.54	0.85

items required for administration by over six at effectively no cost to measurement precision. The correlation between trait estimates from the full-length administration (21 items) and the CAT was .98, demonstrating a near-perfect preservation of the rank order of trait estimates in this reduced form.

Depending on the requirements of the analysis, sacrificing some precision for reduced administration time may be worthwhile. By setting the standard error to .4, a correlation of .95 between full-length and reduced administration can be achieved using an average of 9.9 items: effectively cutting the test length in half. At this threshold, approximately 55% of individuals required eight or fewer items to reach this precision level, suggesting that for most of the sample, CAT can dramatically reduce administration time. For fixed-length criteria, administering only six items yielded results comparable to the standard error stopping criterion while using approximately four fewer items on average. With a fixed length of three items, however, there was a noticeable drop in precision and a corresponding increase in standard error.

The tradeoff between parsimony and accuracy ultimately depends on the specific administration needs. No single correct choice exists for a stopping criterion, but we opted for a standard error of .4, prioritizing accuracy over parsimony. Figure 2.16 highlights the source of differences in the average number of items administered when compared to a fixed length of six. A substantial subset of individuals received all items, primarily persons at the lower end of the trait distribution. This occurred because the 21 BAI items are relatively difficult (as shown in Table 2.6), making the measure most informative for individuals with high anxiety. Due to the lack of easier items, measurement precision remained low at the lower end of the trait range, preventing

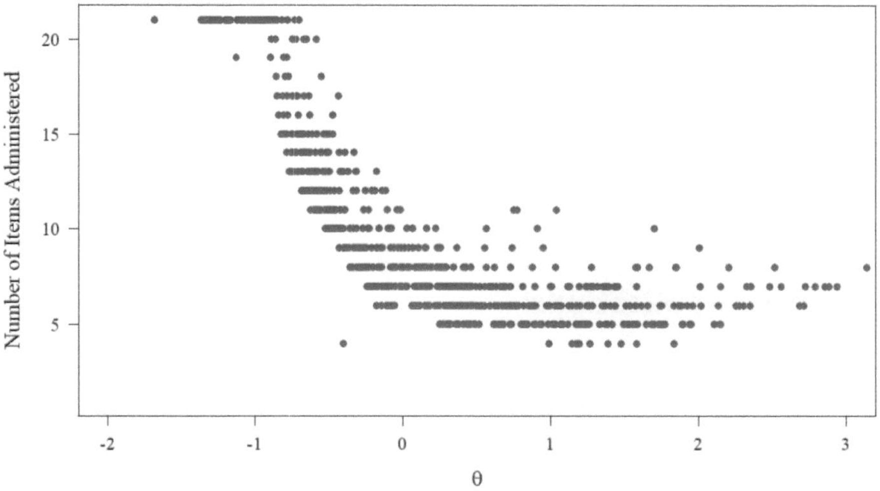

Figure 2.16 Number of items administered in a CAT with standard error criterion of .4 versus ability estimate

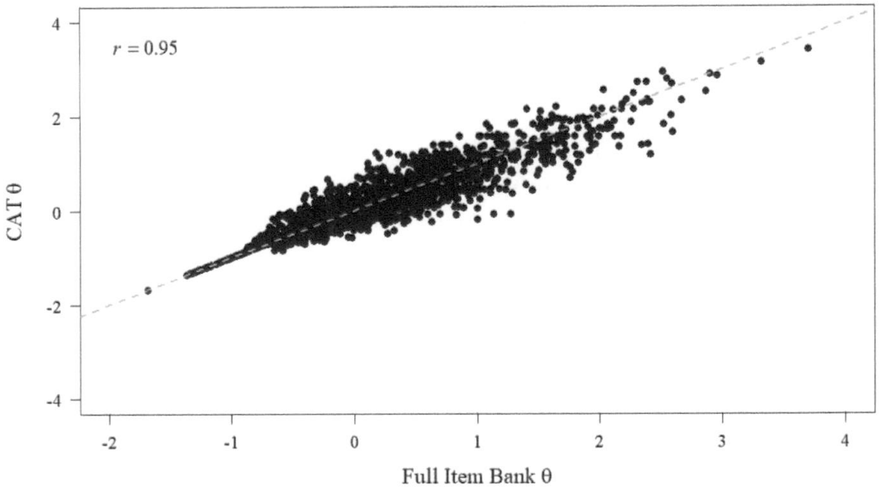

Figure 2.17 Number of items administered in a CAT with a stopping criterion of .4 versus trait estimate

a standard error of .4 from being achieved and forcing the CAT software to administer all items.

Figure 2.17 shows the relation between full-length and CAT theta estimates visually, demonstrating the strength of the relation between these two estimates and the minimal loss in precision under reduced administration. This example of a CAT version of the BAI demonstrates the value in adaptive testing, such that administrations can be reduced, often by more than half, with minimal costs to precision. It is notable that, if the BAI contained easier items, average administration could be reduced even further, requiring the need for fewer items to achieve a desired standard error. In neuropsychological assessments where the burden of cost and time to both patients and clinicians is particularly important, CAT may be a desirable alternative for test administration.

Advanced Applications

Before concluding, we touch on a few relevant IRT applications that may be of particular interest. One is "equating and linking," which uses an IRT framework (in contrast to traditional methods, such as equipercentile equating) to transform responses from different test versions (i.e., form A and B) or different calibrations onto the same scale, allowing for score comparisons. We direct readers to articles by Lee and Ban (2009) and von Davier and von Davier (2007) for detailed explanations of IRT linking and equating and Lúcio et al. (2021) for an example of linking and equating within neuropsychology. Readers may also be interested in recent advancements in longitudinal analysis of psychometric data. These methods allow for the modeling and analysis of growth across time and do not necessarily rely on identical measures being used across time points. Such methods often combine aspects of IRT and structural equation modeling (SEM) to model items using a traditional IRT framework and trajectories in SEM. We direct readers to McArdle et al. (2014) for both how to apply longitudinal measures to psychometric data and an application of these methods to a depression questionnaire. In theory, it may even be possible to relate and effectively "harmonize" scores of comparable abilities across different tests that do not possess linking items, even if no examinees have taken both tests. A striking example is the "factor alignment" method (Muthén & Asparouhov, 2014), which has been used to generate comparable scores on diverse psychiatric rating scales applied to multiple different samples in the International Whole Genome Sequencing Consortium (Mansolf et al., 2020). Similarly, recent advancements in projective IRT may allow for the comparison of scores across alternative forms assessing the same construct by averaging over the construct irrelevant variance in the assessments (Reise et al., 2025).

Summary and Conclusion

In this chapter, we introduced IRT for neuropsychologists, detailing models for dichotomous (1PL, 2PL, and 3PL) and polytomous (GRM and NRM) item response formats. Following this, we introduced applications, including DIF analyses, computerized adaptive testing, and a few advanced models. We intend this chapter to be inspirational; that is, to demonstrate to neuropsychologists the considerable benefits of IRT, to encourage further study, and to create a rationale for establishing partnerships with psychometricians. Clearly, the potential gains in test development, administration, evaluation, and score interpretations within neuropsychology justify these investments. Test takers will be the richer, as well.

References

Baker, F. B. (2001). *The basics of item response theory* (2nd ed.). ERIC Clearinghouse on Assessment and Evaluation.

Balsis, S., Unger, A. A., Benge, J. F., Geraci, L., & Doody, R. S. (2012). Gaining precision on the Alzheimer's disease assessment scale-cognitive: A comparison of item response theory-based scores and total scores. *Alzheimer's & Dementia*, *8*(4), 288–294. https://doi.org/10.1016/j.jalz.2011.05.2409

Beck, A. T., Epstein, N., Brown, G., & Steer, R. A. (1988). An inventory for measuring clinical anxiety: Psychometric properties. *Journal of Consulting and Clinical Psychology*, *56*(6), 893–897. https://doi.org/10.1037/0022-006X.56.6.893

Beck, A. T., Steer, R. A., & Brown, G. K. (1996). *Manual for the Beck Depression Inventory-II*. Psychological Corporation.

Bilder, R. M., & Reise, S. P. (2019). Neuropsychological tests of the future: How do we get there from here? *The Clinical Neuropsychologist, 33*(2), 220–245. https://doi.org/10.1080/13854046.2018.1521993

Bock, R. D. (1972). Estimating item parameters and latent ability when responses are scored in two or more nominal categories. *Psychometrika, 37*(1), 29–51. https://doi.org/10.1007/BF02291411

Bollen, K., & Lennox, R. (1991). Conventional wisdom on measurement: A structural equation perspective. *Psychological Bulletin, 110*(2), 305–314. https://doi.org/10.1037/0033-2909.110.2.305

Cella, D., Riley, W., Stone, A., Rothrock, N., Reeve, B., Yount, S., ... Hays, R. (2010). The Patient-Reported Outcomes Measurement Information System (PROMIS) developed and tested its first wave of adult self-reported health outcome item banks: 2005–2008. *Journal of Clinical Epidemiology, 63*(11), 1179–1194. https://doi.org/10.1016/j.jclinepi.2010.04.011

Chalmers, R. P. (2012). mirt: A multidimensional item response theory package for the R environment. *Journal of Statistical Software, 48*(6), 1–29. https://doi.org/10.18637/jss.v048.i06

Choi, S. W. (2009). Firestar: Computerized adaptive testing simulation program for polytomous item response theory models. *Applied Psychological Measurement, 33*(8), 644–645. https://doi.org/10.1177/0146621608329892

Choi, S. W., Gibbons, L. E., & Crane, P. K. (2011). lordif: An R package for detecting differential item functioning using iterative hybrid ordinal logistic regression/item response theory and Monte Carlo simulations. *Journal of Statistical Software, 39*(8), 1–30. https://doi.org/10.18637/jss.v039.i08

Crane, P. K., van Belle, G., & Larson, E. B. (2004). Test bias in a cognitive test: Differential item functioning in the CASI. *Statistics in Medicine, 23*(2), 241–256. https://doi.org/10.1002/sim.1713

de Ayala, R. J. (2022). *The theory and practice of item response theory* (2nd ed.). Guilford Press.

Del Toro, C. M., Bislick, L. P., Comer, M., Velozo, C., Romero, S., Gonzalez Rothi, L. J., & Kendall, D. L. (2011). Development of a short form of the Boston Naming Test for individuals with aphasia. *Journal of Speech, Language, and Hearing Research, 54*(4), 1089–1100. https://doi.org/10.1044/1092-4388(2010/09-0119)

DeMars, C. (2010). *Item response theory*. Oxford University Press. https://doi.org/10.1093/acprof:oso/9780195377033.001.0001

Embretson, S. E., & Reise, S. P. (2000). *Item response theory for psychologists*. Erlbaum.

Gershon, R. C., Wagster, M. V., Hendrie, H. C., Fox, N. A., Cook, K. F., & Nowinski, C. J. (2013). NIH toolbox for assessment of neurological and behavioral function. *Neurology, 80*(11, Suppl 3), S2–S6. https://doi.org/10.1212/WNL.0b013e3182872e5f

Gibbons, R. D., Weiss, D. J., Kupfer, D. J., Frank, E., Fagiolini, A., Grochocinski, V. J., Bhaumik, D. K., Stover, A., Bock, R. D., & Immekus, J. C. (2008). Using computerized adaptive testing to reduce the burden of mental health assessment. *Psychiatric Services, 59*(4), 361–368. https://doi.org/10.1176/ps.2008.59.4.361

Hambleton, R. K. (2006). Good practices for identifying differential item functioning. *Medical Care, 44*(11, Suppl 3), S182–S188. https://doi.org/10.1097/01.mlr.0000245443.86671.c4

Holland, P. W., & Wainer, H. (Eds.). (1993). *Differential item functioning* (1st ed.). Routledge. https://doi.org/10.4324/9780203357811

Houts, C. R., & Cai, L. (2013). *flexMIRT user's manual version 2.0: Flexible multilevel item factor analysis and test scoring.* Vector Psychometric Group.

Kaplan, E. F., Goodglass, H., & Weintraub, S. (1983). *The Boston Naming Test* (2nd ed). Lea & Febiger.

Lee, W. C., & Ban, J. C. (2009). A comparison of IRT linking procedures. *Applied Measurement in Education, 23*(1), 23–48. https://doi.org/10.1080/08957340903423537

Lúcio, P. S., Lourenço, F. C., Cogo-Moreira, H., Bandalos, D., Carvalho, C. A. F., Kida, A. S. B., & Ávila, C. R. B. (2021). Reading comprehension tests for children: Test equating and specific age-interval reports. *Frontiers in Psychology, 12*, 662192. https://doi.org/10.3389/fpsyg.2021.662192

Mansolf, M., Vreeker, A., Reise, S. P., Freimer, N. B., Glahn, D. C., Gur, R. E., Moore, T. M., Pato, C. N., Pato, M. T., Palotie, A., Holm, M., Suvisaari, J., Partonen, T., Kieseppä, T., Paunio, T., Boks, M., Kahn, R., Ophoff, R. A., ... WGSPD Consortium. (2020). Extensions of multiple-group item response theory alignment: Application to psychiatric phenotypes in an International Genomics Consortium. *Educational and Psychological Measurement, 80*(5), 870–909. https://doi.org/10.1177/0013164419897307

McArdle, J. J., Petway, K. T., & Hishinuma, E. S. (2014). IRT for growth and change. In S. P. Reise & D. A. Revicki (Eds.), *Handbook of item response theory modeling* (pp. 435–457). Routledge. https://doi.org/10.4324/9781315736013

Meijer, R. R., & Nering, M. L. (1999). Computerized adaptive testing: Overview and introduction. *Applied Psychological Measurement, 23*(3), 187–194. https://doi.org/10.1177/01466219922031310

Mellenbergh, G. J. (1989). Item bias and item response theory. *International Journal of Educational Research, 13*(2), 127–143. https://doi.org/10.1016/0883-0355(89)90002-5

Moore, T. M., Butler, E. R., Cobb Scott, J., Port, A. M., Ruparel, K., Njokweni, L. J., ... Gur, R. C. (2020). When CAT is not an option: Complementary methods of test abbreviation for neurocognitive batteries. *Cognitive Neuropsychiatry, 26*(1), 35–54. https://doi.org/10.1080/13546805.2020.1859360

Moore, T. M., Di Sandro, A., Scott, J. C., Lopez, K. C., Ruparel, K., Njokweni, L. J., ... Gur, R. C. (2023). Construction of a computerized adaptive test (CAT-CCNB) for efficient neurocognitive and clinical psychopathology assessment. *Journal of Neuroscience Methods, 386*, 109795. https://doi.org/10.1016/j.jneumeth.2023.109795

Mungas, D., Widaman, K. F., Reed, B. R., & Tomaszewski Farias, S. (2011). Measurement invariance of neuropsychological tests in diverse older persons. *Neuropsychology, 25*(2), 260–269. https://doi.org/10.1037/a0021090

Muthén, B., & Asparouhov, T. (2014). IRT studies of many groups: The alignment method. *Frontiers in Psychology, 5*, 978. https://doi.org/10.3389/fpsyg.2014.00978

Pedraza, O., Graff-Radford, N. R., Smith, G. E., Ivnik, R. J., Willis, F. B., Petersen, R. C., & Lucas, J. A. (2009). Differential item functioning of the Boston Naming Test in cognitively normal African American and Caucasian older adults. *Journal of the International Neuropsychological Society, 15*(5), 758–768. https://doi.org/10.1017/S1355617709990361

Pedraza, O., & Mungas, D. (2008). Measurement in cross-cultural neuropsychology. *Neuropsychological Review, 18*, 184–193 (2008). https://doi.org/10.1007/s11065-008-9067-9

Pedraza, O., Sachs, B. C., Ferman, T. J., Rush, B. K., & Lucas, J. A. (2011). Difficulty and discrimination parameters of Boston Naming Test items in a consecutive clinical series. *Archives of Clinical Neuropsychology, 26*(5), 434–444. https://doi.org/10.1093/arclin/acr042

R Core Team (2021). R*: A language and environment for statistical computing.* R Foundation for Statistical Computing. Vienna, Austria. https://www.R-project.org/.

Rasch, G. (1960). *Studies in mathematical psychology: I. Probabilistic models for some intelligence and attainment tests.* Nielsen & Lydiche.

Reise, S. P., Block, J. M., Mansolf, M., Haviland, M. G., Schalet, B. D., & Kimerling, R. (2025). Using projective IRT to evaluate the effects of multidimensionality on unidimensional IRT model parameters. *Multivariate Behavioral Research, 60*(2), 345–361. https://doi.org/10.1080/00273171.2024.2430630

Reise, S. P., & Waller, N. G. (2009). Item response theory and clinical measurement. *Annual Review of Clinical Psychology, 5*(1), 27–48. https://doi.org/10.1146/annurev.clinpsy.032408.153553

Reise, S. P., Wong, E., Block, J., Widaman, K. F., Gullett, J. M., Bauer, R. M., ... Bilder, R. M. (2024). Computerized adaptive test strategies for the matrix reasoning subtest of the Wechsler Adult Intelligence Scale, 4th edition (WAIS-IV). *Journal of the International Neuropsychological Society, 30*(2), 152–161. https://doi.org/10.1017/S1355617723000401

Samejima, F. (1969). Estimation of latent ability using a response pattern of graded scores. *Psychometrika Monograph Supplement, 34*(4, Pt. 2), 100.

Sitarenios, G. (2022). Short versions of tests: Best practices and potential pitfalls. *Journal of Pediatriatic Neuropsycholology, 8*, 101–115. https://doi.org/10.1007/s40817-022-00126-0

Swaminathan, H., & Rogers, H. J. (1990). Detecting differential item functioning using logistic regression procedures. *Journal of Educational Measurement, 27*(4), 361–370. https://doi.org/10.1111/j.1745-3984.1990.tb00754.x

Tay, L., Meade, A. W., & Cao, M. (2015). An overview and practical guide to IRT measurement equivalence analysis. *Organizational Research Methods, 18*(1), 3–46. https://doi.org/10.1177/1094428114553062

Teresi, J. A., Ramirez, M., Jones, R. N., Choi, S., & Crane, P. K. (2012). Modifying measures based on differential item functioning (DIF) impact analyses. *Journal of Aging and Health, 24*(6), 1044–1076. https://doi.org/10.1177/0898264312436877

Teresi, J. A., Ramirez, M., Lai, J. S., & Silver, S. (2008). Occurrences and sources of differential item functioning (DIF) in patient-reported outcome measures: Description of DIF methods, and review of measures of depression, quality of life and general health. *Psychology Science Quarterly, 50*(4), 538.

Thissen, D., Cai, L., & Bock, R. D. (2010). The nominal categories item response model. In M. Nering & R. Ostini (Eds.), *Handbook of polytomous item response theory models* (pp. 43–75). Routledge.

Thissen, D., & Wainer, H. (1982). Some standard errors in item response theory. *Psychometrika, 47*(4), 397–412. https://doi.org/10.1007/BF02293705

von Davier, M., & von Davier, A. A. (2007). A unified approach to IRT scale linking and scale transformations. *Methodology, 3*(3), 115–124. https://doi.org/10.1002/j.2333-8504.2004.tb01936.x

Wechsler, D. (2024). *Wechsler Adult Intelligence Scale* (5th ed.). Pearson.

Weiss, D. J. (2011). Better data from better measurements using computerized adaptive testing. *Journal of Methods and Measurement in the Social Sciences, 2*(1), 1–27. https://doi.org/10.2458/v2i1.12351

3

AI from Start to Finish

Reimagining the Neuropsychological Workflow in the Age of Artificial Intelligence

Jonathan DeRight

Introduction

Artificial intelligence (AI) is reshaping health care and psychological practice. For neuropsychologists, AI offers both promise and peril: It can augment clinical reasoning, but it must never supplant it. This chapter explores how AI can assist at every stage of neuropsychological practice, from record review and test selection to interpretation and report writing, while reaffirming the indispensable role of human judgment and ethical accountability.

Generative and analytical AI systems now support the integrative, data-heavy tasks that define neuropsychology. AI can rapidly consolidate and integrate large amounts of data. Efficiency must not be mistaken for understanding. The impact of AI (and whether it refines or degrades practice) depends entirely on how it is used. Large language models can summarize records, extract cognitive test data, and structure reports; adaptive testing and natural language processing tools promise greater precision and efficiency. Yet these systems lack understanding, empathy, and professional responsibility. Their usefulness depends on the quality of data, the clarity of user input, and vigilant human supervision. Bias, hallucinations, and confidentiality concerns remain significant. Thus, AI should be seen not as an interpretive agent but as a cognitive scaffold; an aid to expertise, not a substitute for it.

Technological anxiety has accompanied nearly every cognitive innovation. In mathematics education, for example, there was widespread concern about the rapid introduction of pocket calculators. A 1975 report, Overview and Analysis of School Mathematics, Grades K–12 (Conference Board of the Mathematical Sciences [CBMS], 1975), asked whether calculators might erode basic arithmetic skills. Educators ultimately concluded that calculators "in no way diminish the importance of school mathematics instruction," but instead freed students and teachers to focus on conceptual understanding.

Psychology's early adoption of computers raised parallel debates. In modern practice, neuropsychologists are familiar with computer-generated interpretive reports

Jonathan DeRight, *AI from Start to Finish*. In: *Technology and Neuropsychology*. Edited by: Jared F. Benge et al., Oxford University Press. © Oxford University Press (2026). DOI: 10.1093/9780197814116.003.0003

for personality inventories; however, these reports never replace clinical judgment and reasoning. Butcher (1987) observed that computerized test interpretation was met with both enthusiasm and apprehension; praised for efficiency yet criticized for "replacing the clinician's judgment." He argued that such tools require new competencies, not less judgment. Rubenzer (1991) later cautioned that skepticism toward computerized testing can be one-sided, noting that clinicians' decisions are also prone to bias and inconsistency. Together, these perspectives foreshadow today's AI discourse: Concern about overreliance must be balanced with recognition that empirically guided tools can improve accuracy and access.

Neuropsychology now faces a similar question: How can clinicians integrate AI without surrendering the clinical intuition and reasoning? Three principles frame the discussion that follows:

1. AI as augmentation, not automation: Clinicians must integrate, not outsource, professional reasoning.
2. Transparency and human oversight: Psychologists bear full responsibility for conclusions and must clearly disclose when AI tools contribute to their work.
3. Evolving competencies: Neuropsychologists require literacy in data science, information security, and digital ethics to apply these tools responsibly.

Woven throughout this chapter, these principles emphasize that AI's greatest promise lies not in replacing clinical expertise but in extending it; advancing the neuropsychologist's mission to provide scientifically grounded, person-centered, and contextually informed evaluations that honor the complexity of human cognition and behavior.

We follow the (fictional) case of Anna Garcia to illustrate ways in which AI can be used in clinical neuropsychology.

How to Talk to AI Effectively: Prompting and Verification in Clinical Contexts

The utility of AI in neuropsychology depends not only on what the system *can* do, but on how effectively clinicians communicate with it. AI models respond to language with statistical precision rather than human understanding; thus, the quality of their output reflects the clarity, structure, and contextual richness of the user's input. Learning to "talk to AI" is an emerging professional skill. I often think of AI as a first-year postdoctoral resident or predoctoral intern, and I "talk" to it in that manner. AI performs well when it is asked questions that one might ask a capable trainee who has a solid foundation but who requires guidance, supervision, and careful correction. The neuropsychologist's goal is not to delegate thinking, but to shape, verify, and contextualize the machine's contributions within sound clinical judgment.

Understanding AI as a Conversational Partner

AI systems perform best when given clearly structured, context-rich prompts. Without this scaffolding, responses may default to generic summaries or overconfident misinterpretations. Effective use requires treating AI not as an expert colleague, but as an intelligent assistant capable of pattern recognition and summarization, yet lacking human insight, judgment, or accountability.

For example, instead of instructing, “Summarize this report,” the clinician might specify: “Summarize pages 39 to 118 of this record, focusing only on prior cognitive test results, MRI findings, and psychiatric diagnoses.” This may be even further enhanced by additional instructions such as “no need to include diagnostic codes or names of specific institutions” (or whatever may or may not be relevant to you).

The latter provides scope, purpose, and constraints, reducing ambiguity and ensuring clinically relevant output. Still, neuropsychologists must resist anthropomorphizing AI or assuming it holds domain expertise. While it may use technical language fluently, it does not “understand” neuropsychological concepts as humans do; it merely predicts the next plausible phrase based on linguistic patterns.

> *Caution*: Vague prompts yield imprecise results; overtrusting machine language fluency can lead to uncritical acceptance of flawed reasoning.

Structuring Effective Prompts

The most reliable outputs arise from deliberate prompt engineering, a process that mirrors how clinicians frame consultations or supervise trainees. Effective prompts generally include four components: *role framing, task definition, format instruction, and contextual constraint.*

- *Role framing* establishes perspective:

“I’m a clinical neuropsychologist summarizing records for a clinical evaluation.”

- *Task definition* clarifies purpose:

“Identify cognitive test data and summarize them in standardized-score format.”

- *Format specification* determines how results should appear:

“Present findings in bullet points suitable for a chart note.”

- *Contextual constraints* limit scope and prevent drift:

“Focus on adult populations and avoid interpretation. Just give me the facts and data.”

> *Caution*: Use of precise prompts fosters responses that are structured, relevant, and usable in real clinical settings. However, too much instruction can overwhelm the model, causing it to ignore key parameters or return overly literal text. The optimal approach balances clarity and flexibility.

Iterative Dialogue and Verification

AI interaction should be understood as dialogue, not dictation. The most accurate results emerge through iterative refinement: reviewing outputs, correcting errors, and re-asking refined questions. This mirrors the supervisory process in clinical training: The clinician provides feedback, the trainee revises, and understanding deepens.

In neuropsychological applications, iterative dialogue might include steps such as:

1. Asking the AI to generate a preliminary summary
2. Reviewing for accuracy, tone, and omissions
3. Requesting targeted corrections or elaborations

For instance, after a literature summary, the clinician might respond:

> "You included sources; verify whether these are peer-reviewed journal articles, and give me the articles in APA format."

This form of structured verification ensures accountability and prevents the uncritical acceptance of machine-generated claims. When using AI for literature or conceptual analysis, clinicians should also ask for references and an explanation of *why* the system reached its conclusion.

> *Caution*: The user cannot accept first-pass responses as factually accurate without clarification. AI can reproduce false information confidently and may even reinforce its own errors if queried recursively. Always verify against trusted sources and avoid circular confirmation ("AI agreeing with itself").

Bias, Sycophancy, and Confirmation Loops

Large language models are optimized to be helpful and agreeable. In practice, that can mean amplifying the user's bias or accepting a controversial premise without challenge, especially when prompts are framed as settled facts. Clinicians must neutralize leading language and require evidentiary checks.

For example, the following exchanges highlight the perils of matter-of-fact statements without proper prompting.

Problematic Exchange 1 (Leading/Biased)

Clinician: "Given her limited education, patients like this usually underperform on memory—this is probably effort. Draft that into my impressions."

AI (agreeable): "Low education commonly leads to poor memory scores, suggesting suboptimal effort in this case . . ."

Here, the user provided a statement as fact, and AI considered that to be the truth without exploring other options. Instead, the prompt could be debiased for a more optimal result.

Safer Revision (De-Bias the Prompt)

Clinician: "List all plausible explanations for low memory scores in a 71-year-old woman, without drawing conclusions. Include education, test norms, psychiatric symptoms, sleep, medication effects, validity/effort, sensory or language factors, and neurological disease. Cite what information is missing and pose neutral follow-up questions."

AI (constrained): "Potential contributors include . . . Missing data: sleep quality, pain, sensory status . . . Follow-up questions: . . ."

Of course, there are times when we do not want AI to give alternative explanations, but inclusion of a debiased prompt can also be a helpful check against assumptions we are prone to making as clinicians.

Problematic Exchange 2 (Opposite, Equally Biased)

Clinician: "She's highly educated and bilingual; any low memory score must indicate neurodegeneration. Summarize that."

AI (agreeable): "In highly educated bilinguals, low memory scores indicate neurodegeneration . . ."

This example highlights the same problem in the opposite direction.

Safer Revision (Balanced and Evidence-Based)

Clinician: Offer a balanced explanation for why a highly educated bilingual 71-year-old might obtain low memory scores. Discuss factors that could support and that could argue against a neurodegenerative process. Consider education, bilingual norms, test selection, mood or anxiety, sleep, medications, sensory functioning, vascular risks, practice effects, and measurement error. Finish with a brief list of additional data needed before forming an impression.

AI (constrained): Low memory performance in a highly educated bilingual adult can arise from several sources.

- Possible contributors: fatigue, sleep disruption, depression, medication side effects, or language-of-testing effects.
- Possible neurodegenerative indicators: consistent decline across testing occasions, corroborating history from informants, and neuroimaging evidence. Additional data needed: bilingual-specific norms, validity indicators, mood screening, medication review, sensory testing, and MRI results.

These examples illustrate how easily AI can mirror the user's assumptions and agree with a biased premise as readily as a balanced one. Because large language models are designed to be cooperative, they tend to affirm rather than challenge a user's framing. In clinical contexts, that tendency can subtly reinforce confirmation bias or lend unwarranted authority to a premature conclusion. To counteract this "agreeableness effect," neuropsychologists should adopt prompting strategies that deliberately elicit counterpoints.

Practical Guardrails to Reduce AI "Agreeableness"

- Neutralize the frame: "Do not assume the premise is correct. Identify assumptions in my prompt."
- Force both sides: "Present three arguments for and three against; flag missing evidence."
- Require sources or provenance: "Only use peer-reviewed evidence or established guidelines; note when evidence is weak or absent."
- Demand uncertainty and decision points: "State your confidence (low/medium/high) and what additional data would change it."
- Use a claim–evidence–gap format: "For each claim, list supporting data; then list gaps."
- Prohibit overreach: "Avoid causal or diagnostic statements. No inference beyond provided data."

- Red-team yourself: "List ways this reasoning could be wrong (alternative explanations, biases, base-rate issues)."

Pre-Evaluation Preparation

The early stages of a neuropsychological evaluation are often the most cognitively demanding for the clinician: reviewing voluminous medical, psychiatric, educational, and legal records; identifying prior testing data; and clarifying the referral question. These preparatory tasks form the foundation for valid assessment and sound interpretation, but they are also time-consuming, repetitive, and error-prone. AI offers powerful tools for streamlining this process, provided it is applied judiciously and under conditions of human supervision.

AI can assist the neuropsychologist in efficiently extracting, organizing, and summarizing information before any direct patient contact. When used appropriately, it transforms record review from a passive reading exercise into a guided analytic process, allowing the clinician to focus on clinical reasoning rather than clerical burden.

AI models can analyze lengthy, unstructured documents such as medical records, prior evaluations, school files, or court reports and generate concise summaries that emphasize neurocognitive, neurological, or psychiatric data. Properly prompted, an AI tool can highlight test names, index scores, imaging findings, or medication histories relevant to the referral question. For example, a neuropsychologist might request: "Extract all prior cognitive test results, list the year of each evaluation, and summarize relevant MRI or EEG findings."

This functionality is particularly valuable when synthesizing decades of fragmented data across multiple institutions. The system can identify patterns in prior results (e.g., stable vs. declining memory indices) and flag missing information for follow-up.

However, this process requires vigilance. Optical character recognition (OCR) errors are common in scanned PDFs, and AI summaries may inadvertently omit context or fabricate plausible-sounding details ("hallucinations"). Clinicians must always cross-check extracted data against the original source document.

> *Caution*: Under the Health Insurance Portability and Accountability Act (HIPAA), record review using cloud-based AI must be performed within a secure, compliant platform. De-identification of data or the use of local, offline models is essential. Moreover, AI summaries should never replace direct clinician engagement with the primary record.

To demonstrate how AI can be used throughout the evaluation process, I will show actual output from AI systems. There are many possible systems that can be used (see DeRight & Puente, 2026, and certain programs are better for certain tasks.

Sample Information:

Anna Garcia DOB: 01/01/1954 • Fictional Medical Record Patient: **Anna Garcia** DOB: **01/01/1954** (age 71) MRN: 000000-AG (fictional) Source: Fictional Primary Care Clinic; Fictional Neurology Associates; Fictional Radiology Services **Primary Care Progress Note** **Date:** 11/12/2024 **Visit type:** Office visit/Problem-focused **Provider:** Maria L. Chen, MD—Internal Medicine **Reason for visit:** Memory concerns; word-finding difficulty; recent increased forgetfulness. **HPI:** Ms. Anna Garcia is a 70-year-old woman with HTN, T2DM (diet-controlled), osteoarthritis, and prior anxiety, presenting with progressive memory complaints over ~8 months. Patient reports increased difficulty remembering appointments, occasional substituting words while writing, and needing notes/reminders more often. Family (daughter) reports more repetitive questioning and minor misplacement of household items. No witnessed loss of consciousness, no new focal weakness, no gait falls reported. Sleep generally adequate; denies visual hallucinations. No acute depressive symptoms beyond situational grief (widowed). No new medications started recently.	**Prompt:** I'm a neuropsychologist performing a clinical neuropsychological evaluation. Summarize this patient's medical records before I see her so I can get a sense of what to pay attention to and what to follow up on. Do not do any interpretation, just give me the data. **Response:** Summary of Medical Records: Anna Garcia (DOB 01/01/1954) Referrals: Referred by Dr. Maria Chen (Primary Care) to Dr. Daniel Morales (Neurology) for evaluation of memory decline. History: • ~8–12 months of progressive forgetfulness, word-finding difficulty, and occasional confusion about appointments. • Family notes repetition and increased reliance on reminders. • Lives independently; widowed; active socially. Medical Conditions: Hypertension, type 2 diabetes (diet-controlled), osteoarthritis, anxiety. Medications: Metformin 500 mg BID, Lisinopril 10 mg daily, Atorvastatin 20 mg nightly, Escitalopram 10 mg daily, Aspirin 81 mg daily, Vitamin D supplement.

Medications (reported): • Metformin 500 mg BID • Lisinopril 10 mg qAM • Atorvastatin 20 mg qHS • Escitalopram 10 mg qAM • Aspirin 81 mg daily • Vitamin D 1000 IU daily **Allergies:** NKDA **Vitals:** BP 138/82 mmHg; HR 74 bpm; RR 14; Temp 36.7°C; SpO_2 98% RA; Weight 153 lb (69.4 kg) **Exam:** General: Well-appearing, alert, cooperative. HEENT: PERRL, EOMI. Oral mucosa dry-appearing. Neck: No lymphadenopathy. Cardiac: RRR, no murmurs. Lungs: Clear to auscultation bilaterally. Abdomen: Soft, nontender. Neuro: Cranial nerves II–XII grossly intact. Motor: 5/5 throughout. Sensation intact to light touch. Coordination: Finger-nose intact; mild decrease in rapid alternating movements bilaterally (age-appropriate). Gait: steady, no ataxia. **Assessment/Problem List:** 1. Memory complaints/suspected mild cognitive impairment (MCI) vs early neurocognitive disorder—progressive over ~8 months. 2. Hypertension—controlled on lisinopril.	Neurologic Findings: • Oriented to person/place; occasional month disorientation. • Fluent speech with mild word-finding pauses. • Motor and gait normal. • Cognitive Screening: • MMSE 27/30. • MoCA 23/30—deficits in delayed recall, attention, and verbal fluency. MRI Brain (03/01/2025): • Mild generalized cortical atrophy with mild–moderate medial temporal (hippocampal) volume loss. • Chronic small-vessel ischemic changes. • No acute infarct or mass. Plan/Next Steps (from records): • Comprehensive neuropsychological evaluation. • Routine labs (TSH, B12, HbA1c, CMP). • Continue managing vascular risk factors. • Driving to be monitored by family.

3. Type 2 diabetes—diet controlled. 4. Osteoarthritis. 5. Anxiety (stable on escitalopram). **Plan:** 1. Referred to Neurology for cognitive evaluation and formal neuropsychological testing. 2. Ordered screening labs: CBC, CMP, TSH, B12, RPR, fasting glucose/HbA1c. (Results pending—TSH and B12 ordered stat.) 3. Ordered non-contrast brain MRI (to evaluate for structural causes). 4. Continue current meds; advised to bring all pill bottles to next visit. Discussed driving safety—patient currently driving occasionally; advised to discuss with neurology and family and to carry a mobile phone. 5. Provided education about memory strategies and safety planning. Return PRN or sooner if acute change. **Follow-up:** Neurology appointment scheduled. **Signature:** Maria L. Chen, MD (electronic) Fictional Primary Care Clinic **Neurology Consultation Note** **Date:** 03/04/2025 **Clinic:** Fictional Neurology Associates **Provider:** Daniel K. Morales, MD—Neurology (Fictional)	

Referring provider: Maria L. Chen, MD
Reason for consult: Cognitive decline/memory complaints.
History of present illness:
71-year-old woman referred for progressive memory problems over ~1 year (patient reports 8–12 months). Symptoms include forgetfulness for recent conversations, difficulty with word retrieval, and intermittent disorientation to appointment dates. Family notes increased repetition and decreased ability to multitask. No history of stroke, seizure, or head trauma. No marked functional decline in ADLs, but mild difficulty managing complex IADLs (bill paying, scheduling). Medical history notable for HTN, T2DM, osteoarthritis. Social history: widowed; lives independently; active in community groups.

Neurological exam:
Alert and oriented to person and place; oriented to year but occasionally uncertain of month. Speech: fluent but occasional word-finding pauses. Cranial nerves intact. Motor strength 5/5. Reflexes symmetric. Sensation grossly intact. Coordination: mild dysdiadochokinesia. Gait normal. No parkinsonian features. Mood: affect appropriate; reports situational sadness.
Cognitive testing (brief):

- Mini-Mental State Examination (MMSE): 27/30 (informal, office brief)—errors in recall and attention.

• Montreal Cognitive Assessment (MoCA)—administered (see separate MoCA report): MoCA = 23/30 (deficits in delayed recall, attention, and verbal fluency). **Imaging:** Non-contrast brain MRI performed 03/01/2025 (see radiology report below). Findings: mild generalized cerebral atrophy and chronic small vessel ischemic change; no acute infarct or hemorrhage. **Assessment:** 1. Mild neurocognitive disorder—mixed picture, most consistent with mild cognitive impairment, with likely mixed etiology (age-related atrophy with chronic microvascular ischemic changes). Alzheimer disease cannot be excluded clinically. 2. Vascular risk factors: hypertension, diabetes—optimize risk factor control. 3. Anxiety/depressive symptoms—subthreshold; monitor. **Plan:** 1. Recommend comprehensive neuropsychological evaluation to characterize cognitive domains (memory, language, attention/executive function, visuospatial) and baseline for longitudinal tracking.	

2. Obtain labs (TSH, B12, folate, CBC, CMP, HbA1c, RPR) to rule out reversible contributors. (PCP ordered earlier; results pending.)
3. Review and optimize vascular risk factors with PCP (BP and glycemic control). Consider tighter BP control given white-matter changes.
4. Continue escitalopram; consider referral to behavioral health for mood management if needed.
5. Discussed driving safety and recommended family monitoring. No immediate driving restriction but to reassess after neuropsych testing.
6. Plan follow-up in 3 months or sooner if decline. Provide written information about local memory clinics and support groups.

Signature:
Daniel K. Morales, MD (electronic)
Fictional Neurology Associates

Montreal Cognitive Assessment (MoCA)—Administered 03/04/2025
Patient: Anna Garcia (DOB 01/01/1954)
Score: 23/30 *(education adjusted: +1 if <12 years; patient has higher education—no adjustment)*
Domain breakdown (illustrative):

- Visuospatial/Executive: 4/5 (Trail making, cube copy, clock drawing)
- Naming: 3/3 (animal naming)
- Memory (delayed recall): 2/5 (5-word recall; 2 recalled unaided)

- Attention: 4/6 (forward/backward digit span, vigilance)
- Language: 2/3 (sentence repetition, verbal fluency—10 words in 60s)
- Abstraction: 1/2
- Delayed recall (after distraction): see memory above
- Orientation: 6/6

Interpretation: Score in the range suggestive of mild cognitive impairment; deficits most notable in **delayed recall** and **verbal fluency/attention**. Recommend comprehensive neuropsychological testing for domain-specific assessment and baseline.
Examiner: Daniel K. Morales, MD (or trained clinician/nurse)—signature on file.

Brain MRI—Radiology Report (Non-contrast)
Exam: MRI Brain without contrast
Date: 03/01/2025
Indication: Memory decline; rule out structural lesion.
Technique: Multiplanar T1, T2, FLAIR, DWI, ADC sequences obtained.
Findings:

- Brain volume: Mild generalized cerebral cortical atrophy, greater in the medial temporal lobes bilaterally (hippocampal volume loss mild-moderate for age).
- White matter: Scattered periventricular and deep white-matter hyperintensities on FLAIR consistent with chronic small vessel ischemic change (Fazekas grade 1–2).

• No acute ischemia on diffusion-weighted imaging. • No intracranial hemorrhage or mass lesion identified. • No abnormal enhancement (no contrast administered). • Ventricles: Age-appropriate mild ventriculomegaly consistent with atrophy. **Impression:** • Mild generalized cortical atrophy with mild-to-moderate medial temporal (hippocampal) volume loss, greater than expected for age—can be seen with early neurodegenerative change. • Scattered chronic small vessel ischemic white-matter change (periventricular/deep white matter). • No acute infarct, hemorrhage, or mass. **Radiologist:** Karen S. Patel, MD—Fictional Radiology Services **Report final:** 03/01/2025 (electronic signature)	

This exchange shows an efficient way for a (HIPAA-Compliant) AI system to efficiently look through medical records to orient the neuropsychologist to a case. This does not replace actually looking at the record, but it is an efficient way to orient yourself to a case.

Intake and Interview Phase

The clinical interview remains the cornerstone of neuropsychological evaluation. It is the point at which hypotheses formed during record review meet the patient's lived experience, and where rapport, empathy, and clinical observation converge. While AI cannot (and should not) replace this human encounter, it can enhance the efficiency and structure of the process. When properly implemented, AI can help organize pre-interview data, identify topics requiring clarification, and even generate tailored interview questions that align with the referral context and developmental level of the patient.

By serving as an intelligent organizational assistant, AI allows the neuropsychologist to approach the interview more focused, informed, and responsive, rather than reactive or overwhelmed by information density. The key, however, lies in using AI to *inform* the process, not to *direct* it.

Integrating Patient Questionnaires

Many neuropsychologists collect patient-completed questionnaires or intake forms before the evaluation, often containing a wealth of narrative information about symptoms, functioning, and psychosocial context. AI handles question-and-answer formats well. Thus, AI can rapidly analyze these qualitative data to identify themes (e.g., attentional complaints, mood symptoms, or occupational stressors) and summarize them into concise bullet points for pre-interview review. For example:

This can be particularly helpful in complex cases where patients provide lengthy or repetitive descriptions, or when responses from multiple informants must be compared (e.g., parent and teacher questionnaires). AI can flag discrepancies such as when a caregiver describes significant impulsivity while the patient denies behavioral concerns, alerting the clinician to explore these inconsistencies during the interview.

Anna Garcia
DOB: 01/01/1954

- Patient Questionnaire:
- **Were you referred for this evaluation by a specific doctor?**
  Yes. Dr. Emily Torres. - PCP
- **Have you noticed any problems in your thinking abilities? If so, please describe what they are, when they started, and how they have changed over time.**
  Yes. Over the past eight months, I've noticed increasing trouble remembering appointments and recent conversations. I sometimes forget why I entered a room or what I was planning to do. When writing, I occasionally substitute one word for another without realizing it (e.g., writing "coffee" instead of "computer"). Friends have commented that I seem more distracted or "spaced out."

- **Do you have any family history of significant psychiatric or neurological problems (e.g., Alzheimer's, dementia, ADHD, bipolar disorder, schizophrenia)?**

  My father developed Alzheimer's disease in his late seventies, and my sister has a history of depression.
- **Were there any complications with your birth or early development?**

  No.
- **Did you ever repeat or fail a grade level?**

  No.
- **Did you graduate from high school?**

  Yes.
- **Please list any college degrees and majors, if applicable.**

  BSN in Nursing

  MSN in Clinical Nursing Leadership
- **Please describe your career history.**

  Worked as a registered nurse for 12 years in both hospital and outpatient settings.

  Later served as a nurse educator and clinical coordinator for a university-affiliated training program.

  Before retirement, managed quality improvement projects for a regional health system.
- **Are you currently on or applying for disability?**

  No.
- **Have you had performance problems at work? If so, please describe.**

  I retired last year. Before retiring, I noticed mild difficulty keeping up with multiple deadlines and occasionally misplaced paperwork, which was unusual for me.
- **Have you been or are you currently married? If so, what is your current marital status?**

  I am widowed; my spouse passed away 6 years ago.
- **Do you have children?**

  Yes. Two adult children—one lives locally, and the other lives out of state.
- **Please describe your current sources of social support.**

  I live independently and remain active in my neighborhood association.

  I volunteer at the public library and attend a weekly book club and church group.

  I stay in touch with several close friends and my children by phone and video calls.

- **Is this evaluation in relation to a lawsuit?**
  No.
- **Do you suffer from any of the following medical conditions?**
  Hypertension
  Type 2 diabetes (diet-controlled)
  Osteoarthritis
- **Do you have a history of any of the following?**
  Anxiety attacks in my 30s, currently resolved.
- **Have you ever been diagnosed with any of the following conditions?**
  No major psychiatric diagnoses.
- **Have you ever had a problem with drugs or alcohol that affected your daily life and/or was considered by you or others to be a problem?**
  No.
- **Are you currently prescribed any of the following medications?**
  Metformin 500 mg daily
  Lisinopril 10 mg daily
  Atorvastatin 20 mg daily
  Escitalopram 10 mg daily
  Aspirin 81 mg daily
  Vitamin D supplement

The above questionnaire is an example of the kind of information that can be gathered even before the clinical interview. It does not replace the interview, and is not relied upon without verification, but it can increase efficiency greatly. However, it is critical to remember that AI's understanding of language remains literal and pattern-based. It may fail to detect subtleties such as sarcasm, cultural idioms, or avoidance embedded in patient responses. Moreover, automated thematic summaries risk flattening complex emotional content into overly categorical language (e.g., labeling nuanced sadness as "depression").

Caution: AI tools should never analyze raw questionnaire responses that contain identifiable patient information unless processed through a secure, HIPAA-compliant platform. The neuropsychologist must personally interpret the emotional tone, context, and clinical implications of the data. AI may assist in sorting, but not in understanding.

Generating and Refining Interview Questions

AI can be used to identify missing or unclear information in a patient's record before the interview. With a carefully structured prompt, it can generate targeted questions to clarify gaps related to the referral concern. For example, "List areas that require clarification before the clinical interview in this case." This type of output might flag missing details about onset and progression, functional independence, mood symptoms, sleep, safety, or medication effects.

Such tools can help clinicians prepare more focused and efficient interviews, ensuring that key domains are not overlooked. However, all AI-generated prompts must be reviewed and adapted by the clinician. The neuropsychologist remains responsible for determining relevance, tone, and phrasing; AI should never dictate how questions are asked or replace the professional judgment required to engage patients empathically and contextually.

Prompt: List areas that require clarification. Use only the information available in her medical records.

Response

Information Missing or Needing Clarification:

- Symptom Onset and Course: Exact timing of when memory and word-finding problems began; rate of progression; any stepwise or fluctuating changes.
- Functional Status: Specific examples of daily tasks affected (bill payment, medication management, driving, cooking).
- Mood and Behavior: Degree of anxiety or depression; changes in motivation, irritability, or social withdrawal.
- Sleep and Fatigue: Quality, duration, and restfulness of sleep; presence of snoring or nocturnal confusion.
- Safety: Any recent incidents (falls, leaving appliances on, disorientation while driving).
- Medical Contributors: Confirmation of blood pressure and glucose control; recent lab results (TSH, B12, HbA1c).
- Medication Effects: Any recent dose changes, side effects, or missed doses.
- Family Observations: Specific examples from family of changes in communication, organization, or emotional regulation.
- Insight and Awareness: Patient's understanding of her cognitive changes and strategies used to compensate.

This example demonstrates how AI can help clinicians identify what still needs to be learned: not by generating diagnostic opinions, but by mapping gaps between the referral question and the available data. Used this way, AI functions as a cognitive assistant, helping the neuropsychologist enter the interview already oriented to missing information that may influence assessment validity or clinical formulation.

Using AI in Test Selection: Support, Not Substitution

AI is not a substitute for professional judgment in test selection. Determining which instruments to use (and how to interpret them) depends on the clinician's training, experience, and understanding of referral context, psychometrics, and patient variables.

That said, AI can assist with specific logistical or specialized tasks that complement, rather than replace, expert decision-making. Examples include:

- Scheduling constraints: "Reorder my planned tests to accommodate a patient who needs a five-minute break every 30 minutes."
- Cultural and linguistic resources: "Find literature on culturally fair naming tests or available Farsi-language norms."
- Administration constraints: "Substitute my standard battery with measures that do not require auditory presentation."

Prompt: I planned to give the WAIS-IV (10 subtests), WMS-IV Logical Memory and Visual Reproduction, WCST, BNT, CVLT-3, Grooved Pegboard, and the SCL-90. Make an order of tests such that the patient can have a break every 30 minutes without getting in the way of a memory delay.

Response

Proposed Test Order (approximate timing and break structure):

- **Block 1 (≈30 minutes)**
  WAIS-IV — Similarities, Vocabulary, Information (Verbal Comprehension tasks)
  WMS-IV Logical Memory I (Immediate recall)
- **→ 5-minute break**
- **Block 2 (≈30 minutes)**
  WAIS-IV — Block Design, Matrix Reasoning, Visual Puzzles (Perceptual Reasoning tasks)
  WMS-IV Visual Reproduction I (Immediate recall)

- **→ 5-minute break**
- **Block 3 (≈30 minutes)**
  CVLT-3 — Word List Learning and Immediate Recall Trials
  BNT — Boston Naming Test (short form if needed)
- **→ 5-minute break**
- **Block 4 (≈30 minutes)**
  WAIS-IV — Digit Span, Arithmetic (Working Memory tasks)
  WAIS-IV — Symbol Search, Coding (Processing Speed tasks)
- **→ 5-minute break**
- **Block 5 (≈30 minutes)**
  WMS-IV Logical Memory II (Delayed recall)
  WMS-IV Visual Reproduction II (Delayed recall)
  WCST — Wisconsin Card Sorting Test
  Grooved Pegboard (dominant and nondominant hands)*SCL-90*

Prompt: Try not to group together similar tests so closely.

Response

Proposed Test Order (Balanced by Modality and Timing):

- **Block 1 (≈30 minutes)**
  WAIS-IV Similarities
  WMS-IV Logical Memory I (Immediate recall)
  Grooved Pegboard (dominant hand only)—filler task during delay period
  WAIS-IV Block Design
- **→ 5-minute break**
- **Block 2 (≈30 minutes)**
  CVLT-3 (Word list learning and immediate recall trials)
  WAIS-IV Matrix Reasoning
  BNT (Boston Naming Test)
- **→ 5-minute break**
- **Block 3 (≈30 minutes)**
  WMS-IV Visual Reproduction I (Immediate recall)
  WAIS-IV Digit Span
  Grooved Pegboard (nondominant hand)
- **→ 5-minute break**
- **Block 4 (≈30 minutes)**
  WAIS-IV Coding
  WMS-IV Logical Memory II (Delayed recall)

WCST (Wisconsin Card Sorting Test)—executive task during delay period

- **→ 5-minute break**
- **Block 5 (≈30 minutes)**

WMS-IV Visual Reproduction II (Delayed recall)

WAIS-IV Vocabulary and *Information* (verbal reasoning and knowledge)

SCL-90—self-report questionnaire to conclude session

In these scenarios, AI functions as a support tool helping the clinician save time, locate resources, or organize workflow while ultimate test selection remains a matter of professional expertise. There are additional areas that can be further fixed (e.g., asking it not to split up the GPT or asking it not to use the BNT in the middle of the CVLT delay), but this is all up to the user.

Data Management and Analysis

Once testing is complete, the neuropsychologist faces the challenge of organizing and interpreting large volumes of numerical and narrative data. Raw scores must be converted, standardized, and presented coherently before interpretation can begin. This process can consume significant clinical time. AI can help by automating portions of this workflow, serving as a digital assistant that improves efficiency without displacing the clinician's judgment.

For instance, AI can extract test data from digital reports or scanned PDFs, identifying subtest names, standard scores, and classifications. A simple prompt such as *"Extract the subtest names and standard scores from this WAIS-IV report and list them in tabular format"* can save considerable time and reduce transcription errors. However, accuracy depends heavily on input quality. Even minor OCR errors can distort results, so clinicians must always verify extracted data against the source. Proprietary test materials should never be uploaded to third-party or nonsecure systems.

AI can also assist in organizing and converting scores. For example, *"Organize these results by domain and convert all scaled scores (mean = 10, SD = 3) to standard scores (mean = 100, SD = 15)."* It can help group data by cognitive domain and flag outliers or inconsistencies, aiding in quality control and table preparation. Nonetheless, psychometric oversight remains essential: AI may perform calculations but cannot determine which norms or conversions are appropriate for a given case.

Finally, AI can summarize structured data to facilitate interpretation, such as generating tables that display domain-level averages and percentile ranges. A prompt like *"Create a summary table showing each cognitive domain, average standard score, and highlight scores one or more standard deviations below the mean"* can provide a quick overview before detailed analysis.

Used judiciously, AI can make data management faster, cleaner, and less labor-intensive, freeing neuropsychologists to focus on synthesis and patient care. But efficiency does not absolve responsibility: the clinician remains the sole verifier of data accuracy, the guardian of test security, and the interpreter of clinical meaning.

Prompt: Create a table of test scores that can look nicely formatted into my medical record system, which does not accept tables so I need it to be free text. Start with IQ and then group tests in domains including processing speed, attention, language, memory, visuospatial, and executive functioning, followed by self-report measures. No need to use these labels, just use it for the order. No need to report raw scores unless there is no standardized score (I'll annotate as such with %ile). Otherwise report the test/subtest, convert all scores to standard scores (mean 100 sd 15) except self-report scales, which should be reported as T-scores. If I use the format "43T," it means t-score of 43. If I say something like "ss11," it means a scaled score of 11. Report scores using the format "Test/Standard Score/Percentile %ile (Adjust)" for the "Adjust" column; this is how the scores were adjusted. If I don't annotate it for a test, default to "A" for age. Other annotations might be some combination of Age "A," sex "S," education "E," and estimated Premorbid IQ "P"—so a test adjusted for all of those would be ASEP. Including a header column.

Here are the test scores:

Composite Score Summary Scale Sum of Scaled Scores Composite Score Percentile Rank 95% Confidence Interval Qualitative Description Verbal Comprehension 34 VCI 107 68 101–112 Average Perceptual Reasoning 32 PRI 104 61 98–110 Average Working Memory 20 WMI 100 50 93–107 Average Processing Speed 11 PSI 76 5 70–87 Borderline Full Scale 97 FSIQ 98 45 94–102 Average Subtest Raw Score Scaled Score Percentile Rank Reference Group Scaled Score SEM Similarities 30 12 75 13 1.04 Vocabulary 44 11 63 13 0.73 Information 16 11 63 12 0.73 Perceptual Reasoning Subtests Summary Subtest Raw Score Scaled Score Percentile Rank Reference Group Scaled Score SEM Block Design 41 10 50 9 0.95 Matrix Reasoning 21 13 84 12 0.95 Visual Puzzles 13 9 37 8 0.85 Working Memory Subtests Summary Subtest Raw Score Scaled Score Percentile Rank Reference Group Scaled Score SEM Digit Span 27 10 50 9 0.73 Arithmetic 14 10 50 10 0.9 Processing Speed Subtests Summary Subtest Raw Score Scaled Score Percentile Rank Reference Group Scaled Score SEM Symbol Search 7 1 0.1 1 1.56 Coding 66 10 50 9 1.2 WMS LM I—ss9, LM II—ss2, LM recognition 3–9%ile WMS VR 1—ss7, VR 2—ss2, VR recognition 3–9%ile BNT 51–60 WCST 4/6 categories >16%ile (AE) TMT A—43 T (ASE) TMT B—23 T (ASE) Verbal Fluency (FAS)—57T (ASE) Animal fluency—19T (ASE) grooved pegboard (dom)—34T (ASE) grooved pegboard (ndom)—41T (ASE) TOPF: standard score 114 SCL-90 SOM O-C I-S DEP ANX HOS PHOB PAR PSY GSI PSDI PST Nonpatient T Score: 73 81 63 70 79 73 59 74 75 74 68 69

Response

Test Results Summary

(All scores converted to standard scores unless otherwise noted. "Adjust" = A=Age; S=Sex; E=Education; P=Premorbid IQ.)

WAIS-IV Full Scale IQ/98/45%ile (A)
Verbal Comprehension/107/68%ile (A)

Similarities/110/75%ile (A)
Vocabulary/105/63%ile (A)
Information/105/63%ile (A)

Perceptual Reasoning/104/61%ile (A)

Block Design/100/50%ile (A)
Matrix Reasoning/115/84%ile (A)
Visual Puzzles/95/37%ile (A)

Working Memory/100/50%ile (A)

Digit Span/100/50%ile (A)
Arithmetic/100/50%ile (A)

Processing Speed/76/5%ile (A)

Symbol Search/55/<1%ile (A)
Coding/100/50%ile (A)

TOPF/114/82%ile (A)
WMS-IV Logical Memory I/85/16%ile (A)
WMS-IV Logical Memory II/70/2%ile (A)
WMS-IV Logical Memory Recognition/80/9%ile (A)
WMS-IV Visual Reproduction I/85/16%ile (A)
WMS-IV Visual Reproduction II/70/2%ile (A)
WMS-IV Visual Reproduction Recognition/80/9%ile (A)
BNT/55/40%ile (A)
WCST/4 of 6 categories/>16%ile (AE)
TMT-A/43T/24%ile (ASE)
TMT-B/23T/<1%ile (ASE)
Verbal Fluency (FAS)/57T/76%ile (ASE)
Category Fluency (Animals)/19T/<1%ile (ASE)
Grooved Pegboard (Dominant)/34T/5%ile (ASE)

Grooved Pegboard (Nondominant)/41T/18%ile (ASE)

SCL-90-R

SOM/73T/98%ile
O-C/81T/>99%ile
I-S/63T/90%ile
DEP/70T/98%ile
ANX/79T/>99%ile
HOS/73T/98%ile
PHOB/59T/82%ile
PAR/74T/98%ile
PSY/75T/>99%ile
GSI/74T/98%ile
PSDI/68T/95%ile
PST/69T/95%ile

Prompt: Now turn it into an actual table.

Response

Neuropsychological Test Results

Test/Subtest	Standard Score or T-Score	Percentile	Adjust
TOPF	114	82	A
WAIS-IV			
Full Scale IQ	98	45	A
Verbal Comprehension	107	68	A
Similarities	110	75	A
Vocabulary	105	63	A
Information	105	63	A
Perceptual Reasoning	104	61	A
Block Design	100	50	A
Matrix Reasoning	115	84	A
Visual Puzzles	95	37	A
Working Memory	100	50	A
Digit Span	100	50	A
Arithmetic	100	50	A
Processing Speed	76	5	A
Symbol Search	55	<1	A
Coding	100	50	A
WMS-IV			
Logical Memory I	85	16	A
Logical Memory II	70	2	A
Logical Memory Recognition	80	9	A

Test/Subtest	Standard Score or T-Score	Percentile	Adjust
Visual Reproduction I	85	16	A
Visual Reproduction II	70	2	A
Visual Reproduction Recognition	80	9	A
Other Measures			
BNT	55	40	A
WCST (4/6 categories)	—	>16	AE
TMT-A	43T	24	ASE
TMT-B	23T	<1	ASE
Verbal Fluency (FAS)	57T	76	ASE
Category Fluency (Animals)	19T	<1	ASE
Grooved Pegboard (Dom.)	34T	5	ASE
Grooved Pegboard (N-Dom.)	41T	18	ASE
SCL-90-R			
SOM	73T	98	—
O-C	81T	>99	—
I-S	63T	90	—
DEP	70T	98	—
ANX	79T	>99	—
HOS	73T	98	—
PHOB	59T	82	—
PAR	74T	98	—
PSY	75T	>99	—
GSI	74T	98	—
PSDI	68T	95	—
PST	69T	95	—

This illustrates how AI can generate various types of tables that fit various needs such as Electronic Medical Record constraints while maintaining clarity and alignment. A follow-up verification step (e.g., confirming conversions and percentiles) remains mandatory.

Caution: Clinicians must verify all extracted data manually against the source document before analysis. Raw data should never be entered into third-party systems that lack appropriate security and HIPAA compliance. Furthermore, test publishers generally prohibit uploading proprietary test content (such as item-level data, stimuli, or full protocols) into external AI tools without explicit permission.

Interpretation and Report Writing

Neuropsychological interpretation is an act of synthesis. It is also the stage where AI offers the greatest potential *and* the greatest risk. While AI can efficiently assist in drafting background narratives, organizing findings, and summarizing literature-based recommendations, it cannot replace the clinician's integrative reasoning, pattern recognition, or ethical responsibility for conclusions.

When used properly, AI serves as an editorial and organizational partner, helping transform raw clinical material into readable, structured text while the neuropsychologist remains the sole author and interpreter.

Drafting Background and Historical Sections

AI can streamline the most labor-intensive portion of report writing: converting detailed clinical notes, collateral interviews, and records into coherent background narratives. With careful prompting, a model can take structured notes or bullet-pointed timelines and produce grammatically polished prose while maintaining chronological logic and clinical neutrality.

For example:

Prompt: Turn the following clinical notes into a concise background section suitable for a clinical neuropsychological report. Maintain an objective tone and avoid interpretive language. Also use responses from the patient questionnaire that I provided earlier.

Interview Notes—Anna Garcia (DOB 01/01/1954)

- **Referral and Context:**
  - Evaluation referred by Dr. Emily Torres (primary care) for assessment of memory decline and cognitive changes.
  - Primary complaint: increasing forgetfulness, distractibility, and word-finding difficulty over the past 8 months.
- **Cognitive Concerns (Self-Reported):**
  - Reports difficulty remembering appointments and recent conversations.
  - Occasionally forgets her reason for entering a room or misplaces items.
  - Notes occasional written word substitutions (e.g., writing "coffee" instead of "computer").
  - Friends have commented that she seems more distracted or "spaced out."

- **Medical and Family Background:**
  - Medical conditions: htn, dm2 (diet-controlled), and osteoarthritis.
  - Past history of anxiety attacks in her 30s, currently resolved.
  - Father (a truck driver who mostly hauled eggs to Nashville) developed Alzheimer's disease in his late 70s.
  - Sister with a history of depression.
  - Denies other major psychiatric or neurological family history.
- **Trauma History:**
  - Described a past incident of being robbed at gunpoint, which she found deeply traumatizing.
  - Denies current nightmares or flashbacks but reports she "never quite forgot" the fear associated with the event.
- **Developmental and Educational History:**
  - No reported complications during birth or early development.
  - Completed high school without grade repetition.
  - Earned a BSN in Nursing and an MSN in Clinical Nursing Leadership.
- **Occupational History:**
  - Worked as a registered nurse for approximately 12 years in hospital and outpatient settings.
  - Later served as a nurse educator and clinical coordinator for a university-affiliated training program.
  - Before retirement, managed quality improvement projects for a regional health system.
  - Retired last year; noted mild difficulty juggling multiple deadlines and occasionally misplaced paperwork during her final year of employment.
- **Personal and Social History:**
  - Originally from Boston; met her husband, Joe, in Chicago.
  - Married for 24 years before Joe's passing 6 years ago.
  - The couple moved to Florida due to dissatisfaction with Chicago's weather.
  - Has four adult children; one local and three living out of state.

- Remains socially active: volunteers at the public library, attends a weekly book club and church group, and participates in her neighborhood association.
- Maintains regular contact with her children and close friends via phone and video calls.

- **Psychiatric and Substance Use History:**
  - No history of psychiatric hospitalization or substance misuse.
  - Denies current depression or active anxiety but acknowledges intermittent worry about her cognitive changes.

- **Current Medications:**
  - Metformin 500 mg qd
  - Lisinopril 10 mg qd
  - Atorvastatin 20 mg qd
  - Escitalopram 10 mg qd
  - Aspirin 81 mg qd
  - Vitamin D supplement

- **Additional Information:**
  - Denies involvement in litigation or disability applications.
  - Lives independently, manages finances and medications, and drives short distances.
  - Uses written reminders and a daily planner to compensate for memory lapses.

Response

Background

Ms. Anna Garcia is a 71-year-old, right-handed woman referred by her primary care physician, Dr. Emily Torres, for evaluation of reported memory decline and cognitive changes. Over the past 8 months, Ms. Garcia has experienced increasing difficulty recalling appointments and recent conversations. She described occasionally forgetting the purpose of entering a room, misplacing items, and substituting unintended words when writing (e.g., “coffee” instead of “computer”). Friends have commented that she appears more distracted than usual.

Her medical history is notable for hypertension, type 2 diabetes (diet-controlled), and osteoarthritis. She reported a past history of anxiety attacks in her 30s, which have since resolved. Family history is significant for Alzheimer's disease in her father, who worked as a truck driver transporting eggs to Nashville, and depression in her sister. Ms. Garcia also described a past experience of being robbed at gunpoint, which she characterized as highly distressing, though she denied persistent nightmares or intrusive recollections.

Developmental history was unremarkable, with no complications during birth or early childhood. She completed high school without grade repetition and later earned a bachelor of science in nursing and a master of science in clinical nursing leadership. Her occupational history includes approximately 12 years as a registered nurse in hospital and outpatient settings, followed by roles as a nurse educator and clinical coordinator for a university-affiliated program. Prior to retirement, she managed quality improvement projects for a regional health system. She retired last year, noting mild difficulty with organization and multitasking toward the end of her career.

Ms. Garcia was born in Boston and met her husband, Joe, while living in Chicago. The couple relocated to Florida after many years in the Midwest, citing a preference for warmer weather. They were married for 24 years prior to her husband's death 6 years ago. She has four adult children—one local and three living out of state—and remains socially engaged through volunteer work at the public library, participation in a neighborhood association, and involvement in a church book club. She maintains regular communication with her children and friends by phone and video calls.

Ms. Garcia denied any history of substance misuse or psychiatric hospitalization and reported no current depressive or anxiety symptoms, though she occasionally worries about her cognitive functioning. Current medications include metformin 500 mg daily, lisinopril 10 mg daily, atorvastatin 20 mg daily, escitalopram 10 mg daily, aspirin 81 mg daily, and a vitamin D supplement. Ms. Garcia lives independently, continues to drive short distances, and manages her own finances and medications. She uses written reminders and a daily planner to assist with organization and memory.

Although great detail still needs to be taken in analyzing for accuracy, this process allows clinicians to focus on substance and synthesis rather than sentence construction. When used with professional supervision, AI can also help maintain stylistic consistency across multiple reports or writers within a practice.

Caution: AI tools can inadvertently introduce errors, omit qualifiers, or subtly alter tone. Even small rephrasings can shift meaning. All AI-generated text must be treated as a draft, subject to full clinician review and editing. Moreover, clinicians should disclose the use of AI assistance in documentation where transparency is ethically warranted.

Summarizing and Interpreting Test Findings

AI can organize and summarize test findings into structured narratives or tables, helping the clinician maintain a coherent interpretive flow. For instance, see the following exchange:

Prompt: Summarize this table of test results into prose that highlights domains of relative strength and weakness, without making causal inferences or diagnostic statements.

Response

Brief Summary of Test Results

Anna Garcia demonstrated broadly average intellectual abilities, with balanced verbal comprehension, perceptual reasoning, and working memory. Processing speed was a relative weakness, falling well below her other cognitive skills. Verbal reasoning and general knowledge were average to above average, while visual reasoning and problem solving were adequate but somewhat variable. Memory performances showed a marked discrepancy between initial learning and delayed recall, affecting both verbal and visual materials. Language abilities were mixed, with average naming but low semantic fluency relative to phonemic fluency. Executive and motor tasks revealed uneven efficiency, with slower set-shifting and fine motor performance. Self-report data reflected significant psychological distress, most notably in obsessive-compulsive and anxiety-related symptoms.

The resulting draft can function as a scaffold upon which the clinician builds interpretive meaning, linking quantitative patterns to behavioral observations and case context. AI can also help check for logical consistency, ensuring that statements about test performance align with numerical data and normative ranges.

Nevertheless, interpretation remains a fundamentally *human* task. No model can weigh the nuanced interaction of motivation, emotional state, sociocultural factors, and neurological integrity. AI lacks clinical experience, awareness of base rates, or the ability to reconcile conflicting indicators. It can describe *what* appears in the data, but not *why* it matters.

Caution: Clinicians must never allow AI to draw diagnostic or etiological conclusions, explain test discrepancies, or infer brain–behavior relationships. Machine-generated explanations are speculative and risk ethical and significant misrepresentation if unverified.

Generating Evidence-Based Clinical Recommendations

AI can also serve as a rapid research assistant for developing clinical recommendations grounded in peer-reviewed literature. When asked appropriately, it can summarize interventions, accommodations, or management strategies for particular cognitive or emotional profiles. For example:

Prompt: Summarize evidence-based cognitive rehabilitation strategies for adults with traumatic brain injury showing impaired processing speed and executive dysfunction.

Response

Summary of Evidence-Based Cognitive Rehabilitation and Management Strategies for Adults with Mild Cognitive Impairment (MCI) due to Alzheimer's Disease

1. **Cognitive Stimulation and Engagement**
    - Structured cognitive activities—such as group-based cognitive stimulation therapy (CST), memory games, and problem-solving tasks—are associated with modest improvements in cognition and quality of life (Clare & Woods, 2004; Woods et al., 2012).
    - Activities that combine social interaction and mental engagement may help sustain cognitive function and emotional well-being.
2. **Strategy-Based Memory Training**
    - Focuses on compensatory approaches that strengthen functional memory use rather than restoring lost abilities.
    - Common methods include spaced retrieval, errorless learning, and visualization or association techniques to aid recall (Hampstead et al., 2012).

   - Training is most beneficial when linked to real-life applications such as remembering appointments or medication routines.
3. **External Memory and Organizational Aids**
   - Encourages consistent use of written planners, labeled reminders, smartphone alerts, and voice-activated assistants.
   - Collaboration with caregivers helps reinforce use of aids and maintain adherence to daily routines (Clare et al., 2010).
4. **Lifestyle and Multimodal Interventions**
   - Cognitive training combined with aerobic exercise, adequate sleep, and a Mediterranean-style diet supports general brain health and daily functioning (Ngandu et al., 2015).
   - Regular physical activity has shown additive benefits for attention and executive function in MCI.
5. **Pharmacologic Considerations**
   - Individuals with MCI attributed to Alzheimer's disease may benefit from a trial of cholinesterase inhibitors, such as donepezil, to support cognitive functioning.
   - Initiation should occur under physician supervision with ongoing monitoring for tolerability and side effects.
6. **Environmental Simplification and Routine Support**
   - Simplified, structured environments reduce cognitive load and facilitate independence.
   - Labeling key areas, minimizing clutter, and maintaining predictable routines can improve orientation and task completion.
7. **Psychosocial and Emotional Support**
   - Addressing anxiety, depression, or loss of confidence is critical for engagement in rehabilitation.
   - Psychoeducation and caregiver involvement promote coping, communication, and quality of life.

Key Practice Principles

- Prioritize compensatory over restorative strategies and tailor interventions to daily life.
- Combine cognitive, behavioral, and pharmacologic approaches when appropriate.
- Involve family or caregivers to promote strategy generalization and adherence.
- Regularly monitor emotional, behavioral, and cognitive status over time.

References

Clare, L., & Woods, R. T. (2004). Cognitive training and cognitive rehabilitation for people with early-stage Alzheimer's disease: A review. *Neuropsychological Rehabilitation, 14*(4), 385–401.

Clare, L. (2010). Goal-oriented cognitive rehabilitation for people with early-stage Alzheimer disease: A single-blind randomized controlled trial. *American Journal of Geriatric Psychiatry, 18*(10), 928–939.

Hampstead, B. M., Sathian, K., Phillips, P.A., Amaraneni, A., Delaune, W.R., & Stringer, A.Y. (2012). Mnemonic strategy training improves memory for object location associations in both healthy elderly and patients with amnestic mild cognitive impairment. *Neuropsychology, 26*(3), 385–399.

Ngandu, T., et al. (2015). A 2-year multidomain intervention of diet, exercise, cognitive training, and vascular risk monitoring in at-risk elderly people (FINGER): A randomized controlled trial. *The Lancet, 385*(9984), 2255–2263.

Woods, B., et al. (2012). Cognitive stimulation to improve cognitive functioning in people with dementia. *Cochrane Database of Systematic Reviews, 2*, CD005562.

This function can enhance both the thoroughness and specificity of recommendations, especially when clinicians must reference multiple domains (e.g., medical, educational, occupational). AI can also help adapt language to different audiences, tailoring technical recommendations into accessible summaries for patients, educators, or attorneys.

However, AI's ability to summarize literature depends entirely on the data it has been trained on and the recency of its information. Without real-time access to academic databases, models may misrepresent or fabricate references. In the above example, for instance, the second paper listed only the first author, when the correct citation was:

Clare, L., Linden, D. E., Woods, R. T., Whitaker, R., Evans, S. J., Parkinson, C. H., van Paasschen, J., Nelis, S.M., Hoare, Z., Yuen, K.S.L.,... Rugg, M. D. (2010). Goal-oriented cognitive rehabilitation for people with early-stage Alzheimer disease: A single-blind randomized controlled trial of clinical efficacy. *The American Journal of Geriatric Psychiatry, 18*(10), 928–939.

Caution: Clinicians must independently verify that cited studies exist, are peer-reviewed, and align with accepted evidence hierarchies. When drafting reports, AI-generated text should never be presented as expert opinion without the clinician's validation and revision. The neuropsychologist remains solely responsible for the accuracy and applicability of all recommendations.

Transparency, Authorship, and Professional Responsibility

The integration of AI into report writing requires ongoing reflection about authorship and accountability. Ethical documentation should clearly distinguish between machine-assisted drafting and clinician interpretation. This transparency not only protects professional integrity but also reinforces the neuropsychologist's central role as the final decision-maker and communicator of findings.

Professional bodies are beginning to articulate expectations around AI use in clinical documentation, emphasizing that human oversight is non-negotiable. The clinician must be able to attest that every statement in the report is accurate, appropriate, and personally reviewed.

In practice, this means viewing AI not as a coauthor but as a sophisticated editorial assistant. It can be useful for phrasing, organization, and literature retrieval, but never for judgment or inference. The ethical neuropsychologist integrates AI only to the extent that it amplifies clarity, efficiency, and evidence-based care without diluting human accountability.

Following is an example of part of the formulation written completely by the clinical neuropsychologist; it is a way in which AI can be helpful.

Clinician's Draft (Original)

Ms. Garcia presents with a pattern of mild cognitive ineffeciency affecting primarily attention and processing speed, along with notable difficulty recalling newly learned verbal and visuospatial material. These deficits appear consistent with early-stage neurocognative change. Emotional factors may also contribute modestly to the patient's cognitive perfomance, including mild anxiety and situational stress related to widwohood.

(Note: Spelling errors are intentional here to illustrate AI-assisted editing)

Prompt: Please review the following formulation for clarity, conciseness, and typographical errors. Suggest small edits to tighten the language while maintaining an objective, professional tone suitable for a neuropsychological report.

AI-Generated Revision (Example Output)

Ms. Garcia demonstrates mild cognitive inefficiency characterized by reduced processing speed and difficulties with new learning and memory for both verbal and visual information. The pattern is consistent with mild neurocognitive change. Emotional factors, including mild anxiety and stress related to recent life events, may modestly influence her cognitive performance.

Clinician Review and Integration

- Accepted AI's grammatical and stylistic edits for clarity.
- Reinstated clinical nuance where needed (e.g., specifying "appears consistent with" rather than "is consistent with").

- Verified that no interpretive meaning was added or altered.
- Documented that AI assistance was limited to stylistic refinement, not diagnostic inference.

This example illustrates appropriate transparency in AI-assisted authorship. The neuropsychologist retains full responsibility for clinical interpretation, explicitly limits AI input to editorial refinement, and verifies the accuracy of all content before inclusion in the final report. Such practices align with emerging professional guidelines emphasizing human oversight, disclosure, and accountability in AI-augmented documentation.

To maintain transparency, clinicians should clearly acknowledge any use of AI tools in documentation. A simple, professional statement may suffice, such as:

> *AI-assisted software was used to support editorial refinement of this report under clinician supervision. All clinical reasoning, interpretation, and conclusions remain the responsibility of the evaluating neuropsychologist.*

Such disclosure reinforces ethical practice by reminding both clinicians and readers that authorship in neuropsychology is inseparable from human judgment, accountability, and professional integrity.

The Balance Between Efficiency and Clinical Integrity

AI can help make report writing more efficient, structured, and consistent. But the ultimate measure of quality in neuropsychology is not speed; it is *thoughtfulness, precision, and integrity.* Clinicians must remain vigilant that technological efficiency does not erode reflective reasoning or narrative depth.

AI's greatest contribution to report writing lies not in replacing human cognition but in freeing it. By handling low-level editorial tasks and data organization, AI gives the neuropsychologist more bandwidth to think critically, reason deeply, and communicate meaningfully.

Used wisely, it can help clinicians produce clearer, more comprehensive reports and documents that reflect both scientific rigor and clinical humanity.

Ethical, Legal, and Professional Considerations

AI introduces profound ethical, legal, and professional challenges for clinical neuropsychology. While the technology offers clear advantages in efficiency and accessibility, it simultaneously raises complex questions about confidentiality, informed consent, data security, authorship, and professional accountability. These considerations are not secondary; they form the foundation of ethical AI integration.

The neuropsychologist's responsibility is not merely to *use* AI effectively but to *use it ethically*, upholding professional standards that safeguard patient welfare, scientific integrity, and public trust.

Confidentiality and Data Security

Neuropsychologists routinely handle highly sensitive health, educational, and legal records. Introducing AI into this workflow requires rigorous attention to data protection. Cloud-based AI platforms must meet the same privacy standards that govern all clinical documentation, including encryption, access control, and Business Associate Agreements (BAAs) under HIPAA.

Whenever possible, clinicians should de-identify data before submitting it to AI tools. Even then, residual contextual clues (such as rare injury descriptions or unique educational histories) may risk inadvertent re-identification. Models that store or train on user input pose additional risks, as data could theoretically be accessed or reproduced later.

> *Caution*: Protected health information (PHI) should never be entered into non–HIPAA-compliant systems. The responsibility for privacy rests entirely with the clinician, regardless of vendor assurances. Transparency with patients and referral sources about AI use is essential for maintaining trust and informed participation.

Informed Consent and Transparency

Incorporating AI into clinical work introduces a new dimension of *technological disclosure*. Patients and retaining parties should understand when, how, and to what extent AI tools are used in the evaluation process. For example, it may be appropriate to inform a patient that an AI-based system assisted in summarizing records or drafting parts of a report provided that the clinician maintains full authorship and oversight.

Transparency is not only ethical but protective. Clear documentation of AI involvement reduces the risk of misinterpretation in legal or disciplinary settings and demonstrates the clinician's adherence to professional standards.

> *Caution*: AI use must never blur authorship. The clinician, not the machine, is the author of all professional reports and is solely responsible for their accuracy, interpretation, and conclusions.

Bias, Fairness, and Cultural Competence

AI systems reflect the data on which they are trained. If those datasets are biased or incomplete, the outputs will reflect and potentially amplify those biases. In neuropsychology, this risk is particularly salient, given the field's historical challenges with cultural and linguistic fairness in testing and interpretation.

AI tools used to assist in summarization, question generation, or data analysis must therefore be scrutinized for potential bias in language, framing, or assumption. For instance, generative models might inadvertently produce culturally biased descriptions of behavior or pathologize normative variation. The neuropsychologist must remain vigilant, critically evaluating AI-generated text through the lens of multicultural competence and professional ethics.

> *Caution*: Do not assume neutrality in machine output. Bias can appear subtly (e.g., tone, word choice, or implicit framing) and may influence how information is interpreted by referral sources, courts, or patients. The clinician's ethical obligation to promote fairness extends fully to AI-assisted work.

Professional Competence and Continuing Education

Competent AI use requires more than technical familiarity; it demands digital literacy, critical reasoning, and ethical discernment. As AI becomes integrated into neuropsychological practice, clinicians must pursue continuing education in data privacy, prompt engineering, model limitations, and regulatory compliance. This evolving literacy will soon be as essential as familiarity with psychometrics or test interpretation.

Training programs and professional bodies should develop formal curricula addressing responsible AI use. Mastery involves not only knowing what AI can do but also recognizing what it *should not* do within professional boundaries.

> *Caution*: Using AI tools without understanding their constraints may constitute professional negligence. Competence includes knowing the limitations of one's tools, human or digital.

Conclusion

Compared to many scientific and clinical fields, neuropsychology has often been slow to embrace new technologies. This cautious stance reflects a deep respect for rigor and reliability. On one hand, established methods have earned that respect through decades of proven value. On the other hand, in protecting the field from premature innovation, we have at times overlooked opportunities to make our work more efficient, precise, and accessible. AI has entered neuropsychological practice not as a replacement for human expertise, but as an extension of it. It is a set of tools capable of amplifying organization, synthesis, and clarity. Across every phase of the neuropsychological workflow, from initial record review to final reporting, AI offers the potential to streamline information management and enhance analytic capacity. This promise is inseparable from responsibility; its value depends on the neuropsychologist's discernment. The quality and integrity of AI-assisted work depend entirely on the discernment of the neuropsychologist who uses it.

This chapter has outlined how AI can be integrated ethically and effectively from start to finish:

- *In pre-evaluation preparation*, AI assists with summarizing medical, educational, and legal records, enabling efficient data extraction while maintaining clinical oversight.
- *During intake and interviewing*, AI helps organize questionnaire data and generate structured, developmentally appropriate questions that support (but never dictate) the clinical encounter.
- *In test planning and selection*, AI can flag redundancies, anticipate fatigue or timing constraints, and suggest alternative measures when standard tools are impractical.
- *In data management and analysis*, it functions as an organizing assistant, extracting, converting, and tabulating data rapidly while the clinician remains the gatekeeper of accuracy, context, and security.
- *In interpretation and report writing*, AI supports synthesis and phrasing, helping transform raw notes into cohesive drafts under the neuropsychologist's authorship and ethical authority.

Across these applications, several guiding principles endure.

First, AI can improve, but not automate, clinical reasoning. The neuropsychologist's value lies not in processing data, but in interpreting it through empathy, contextual awareness, and ethical judgment.

Second, transparency and oversight are non-negotiable. Clinicians must disclose when and how AI tools are used, ensure data protection, and accept full accountability for all final content.

Third, digital literacy is now a core professional competency. Understanding both the capabilities and limitations of AI has become as essential as understanding psychometrics, cultural fairness, or evidence-based documentation.

Ultimately, AI may reshape how neuropsychologists work, but it cannot replace why they work. The human capacity for reasoning, compassion, and ethical reflection remains irreplaceable. Guided by these principles, AI becomes not a threat to the profession, but a reflection of its highest ideals, enhancing the clinician's work in the service of understanding, healing, and human dignity.

Author Note

Jonathan DeRight, PhD, ABPP-CN, is a board-certified clinical neuropsychologist and the founder of Precision Neuropsychology, PLLC, in Virginia. His practice specializes in clinical and forensic neuropsychological assessment, integrating traditional methods with emerging digital and AI-assisted tools to enhance efficiency, transparency, and patient-centered care. The views expressed in this chapter are intended for educational and professional discussion and do not represent opinions or conclusions related to any specific clinical or forensic case.

References

Butcher, J. N. (1987). The use of computers in psychological assessment: An overview of practices and issues. In J. N. Butcher (Ed.), *Computerized psychological assessment: A practitioner's guide* (pp. 1–24). Basic Books.

Conference Board of the Mathematical Sciences. (1975). *Overview and analysis of school mathematics, grades K–12.* National Advisory Committee on Mathematical Education, National Science Foundation.

DeRight, J. & Puente, A. N. (2026). Artificial intelligence in neuropsychological practice—Tool selection, privacy, and billing guidance. *The Clinical Neuropsychologist, 40*(3), 797–815.

Rubenzer, S. J. (1991). Computerized testing and clinical judgment: Cause for concern. *The Clinical Psychologist, 44*(5), 62–66.

4
Viewing Neurotech Through the Lens of the Ethical Principles

Considerations and Calls to Action

Robin C. Hilsabeck and Jared F. Benge

Introduction

Throughout this book, numerous examples of digital technologies for use by neuropsychologists and those we serve are discussed. In light of the changing technological landscape, it seems likely that digital technologies, amplified by the power of artificial intelligence (AI), will increasingly shape our understanding of, and indeed the very functioning of, the central nervous system. Further, these impacts will likely be evident across levels of analysis, from the functioning of individual neurons through that of nations.

As clinicians and researchers, we orient ourselves to these rapid changes and advancements with a few broad ideas. First, we do not assume that technological changes are inherently good or bad, but they are changes that we must adapt to. We also recognize that, given the intense interest in cognition and behaviors by society at large, neuropsychologists can either choose to participate in shaping this future or choose not to; the latter would, of course, run the risk of our profession becoming outdated as others leverage tech to understand real minds in the real world. Finally, in some ways the technological revolution is not a new experience for psychologists. Our ethical standards, for example, have long included references to the ethics of "automated reporting" since at least 1992, and the dramatic interest in telehealth that came about in the pandemic led the field to rapidly readjust to an ethics grounded in virtual appointments (Sugarman & Busch, 2023). A changing technological landscape is thus nothing new for the practicing neuropsychologist, but the rate of change does, at least in our estimation, seem to be increasing.

With all such dramatic changes, there are always gray areas and unknowns, and even as we write this chapter, numerous authors (Karimian et al., 2022; Naik et al., 2022; Parsons, 2019; Wang et al., 2023), professional organizations (American Psychological Association, n.d.; World Health Organization, n.d.), and even whole political entities (Directorate-General for Communications Networks,

Robin C. Hilsabeck and Jared F. Benge, *Viewing Neurotech Through the Lens of the Ethical Principles.*
In: *Technology and Neuropsychology*. Edited by: Jared F. Benge et al., Oxford University Press.
 DOI: 10.1093/9780197814116.003.0004

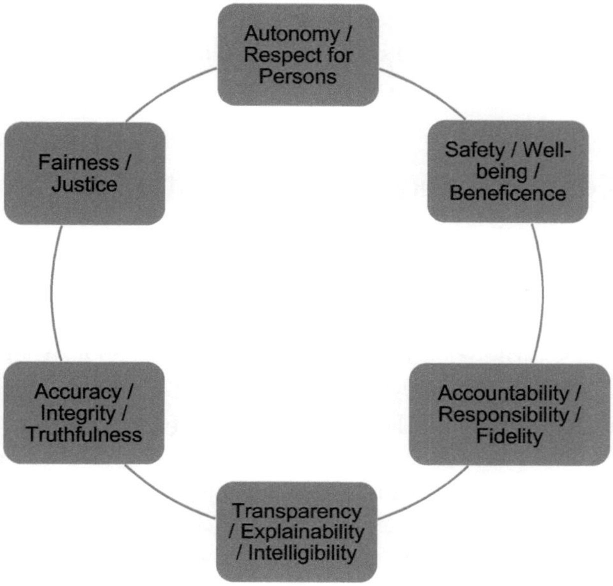

Figure 4.1 Core ethical principles for neurotechnology

Content and Technology, 2019; Office of the Director of National Intelligence Agency, n.d.) are grappling with creating ethical frameworks, evaluations, and guidelines for implementing new digital tools ethically. In fact, at the time of this writing, the American Psychological Association announced a call for public comment on revised Ethical Principles of Psychologists and Code of Conduct that includes technology as one of six standards that applies to all psychologists in their various professional activities (American Psychological Association, n.d.).

We do not use this chapter to replace these sources, and we recognize that there will undoubtedly be many more works that will come to help shape the ethics of neurotech by the time the reader engages with this text. Instead, we attempt to use this chapter to step back and take stock of how our existing ethical principles might apply to neurotech at this stage of development. There is much overlap in what many authorities, organizations, and entities consider core ethical principles for the development and use of neurotechnology (see Figure 4.1). We review what we, as practicing clinical neuropsychologists, researchers, and educators, view as key ethical considerations for a neurotech in its adolescence, and we end with a call to action to help promote ethical integration into neuropsychological spaces.

Beneficence and Nonmaleficence in the World of Neurotech

The fundamental goal of psychologists is to help, not hurt, those that we serve in clinical, educational, and research settings. At this stage in neurotech's development, we consider the most pressing ethical tension to be centered on using technology to expand access to critically needed services, while simultaneously protecting privacy and understanding implications for autonomy and self-determination.

Access: A Core, but Risky Benefit of Digital Technologies

There are not enough neuropsychologists, neurologists, psychiatrists, and mental health professionals to serve even well-developed countries like the United States (Health Resources and Service Administration, 2023), let alone the world at large. These access issues are dramatically amplified for underrepresented cultural, linguistic, and socioeconomic groups (Alegría et al., 2016). Technological advances could hold enormous potential for ameliorating these issues (Graham et al., 2021). In very pragmatic ways, telehealth services can bring providers to individuals far away from urban cores or bring specialists with cultural, linguistic, or disease-specific expertise anywhere around the globe. Large language models can instantly translate information into other languages (Zhu et al., 2024). Advances in psychometrics such as computer adaptive testing and item response theory may allow for shorter, more precise evaluations to be conducted, expanding the number and range of individuals we can serve (Bilder & Reise, 2019). In the future, AI agents and chatbots may be able to provide interactive behavioral interventions, advice, and guidance for managing behaviors and coping with cognitive problems in a way that does not require direct clinician time (Casu et al., 2024).

In these ways and more, we believe that expanding and automating neuropsychological services can benefit those we serve. Like all potential benefits, though, there are risks that need to be mitigated. Quality control in responses and services of automated services is only in its infancy, and such phenomena as AI hallucinations (though perhaps erroneously termed; Maleki et al., 2024) can become problematic in real-world use. In a related vein, a 1:1 replacement of words from one language to another is not a replacement for skilled and culturally aware translation of services (Nguyen et al., 2024). Beyond these concerns, automated services and services rendered remotely also raise security, data ownership, and pragmatic limitations that are not as obviously present in our standard in-person services today.

Automation, Detection, and Self-Determination

As neuropsychologists who have trained hundreds of students over the years, we are always impressed by how quickly trainees learn to observe the subtle mannerisms and behaviors of participants to arrive at very astute differential diagnoses even after brief conversations with patients or a review of the record. The ability to pattern match from small slices of behavior is a key skill for clinical neuropsychologists, and something our brains are well evolved to do (Mattson, 2014). In a similar vein, AI can take in vast swaths of small samples of behavior to derive at a categorical label (Shcherbiak et al., 2024). As many of our daily activities are inherently digital these days (Benge et al., 2024), digital behaviors provide robust data for such AI to potentially mine. For example, smartphones accompany most individuals in their day-to-day life, and their robust and continuous slices of daily activity hold potential to inform diagnostic decisions, even in the absence of active user inputs (Butler et al., 2025).

On the one hand, such algorithmic and passive activity detection may provide a unique and ecologically valid insight into the behavior of those we serve. For example, automated behavior patterns may allow for a valid window into daily activities and changes over time for patients and participants who do not have caregivers or collateral reports. Automation of such detection may identify individuals at high risk for developing cognitive decline or self-neglect before any issues occur. However, such automated identification holds risks as well. Did an individual consent to the use of data for this purpose? Who has access to the data? Might algorithmic-driven concerns be entered into records that could have unforeseen insurance or occupational outcomes in a manner similar to issues surrounding genetic testing and profiling (Chapman et al., 2020)?

Fidelity and Responsibility with Digital Tools

From a neurotech standpoint, the ethical principle of fidelity and responsibility highlights at least two core issues: ambiguity in data (analysis, interpretation, reporting) and the changing face of professional standards.

Typical neuropsychological training has a very hands-on approach to understanding human behavior. Data are obtained from record review, interview with collaterals and the patient, observation of behavior both in clinic and while performing standardized and observable tests, and the scores are still often computed based on relatively simple math (summing, norming, etc.). In this way, while not easy, most of the steps of the process are immediately observable by the clinician or researcher, and all those involved understand each step of the process.

How does this transparent process evolve with the new world of digital technology and tools? For example, if ubiquitous monitoring of behavior is coming from a broad array of sensors (i.e., imbedded technologies), can the psychologist take ownership for the quality and validity of the data that are collected? If an automated algorithm interprets a broad array of data points to come up with a diagnostic conclusion, but the opaque nature of the algorithm (or conversely the complexity of the model used to create the outcome) is beyond what the neuropsychologist can understand, how does the neuropsychologist ultimately take responsibility for the outcomes of the evaluation?

As we discuss in our conclusion, these sorts of questions require reconsideration of core professional standards for psychologists but also for considering our standards in the context of ethical codes of other professions we will need to work with in order to redefine the future of neuropsychology. As digital tools will sit in the crossroads of neuropsychology, computer science, engineering, data science, and more, we believe it is critical for neuropsychologists to be at the table to help shape the emerging standards of ethics for health-related technologies. Of particular importance in our opinion is the need to make tools and algorithms understandable and discoverable for clinicians, researchers, and the public to facilitate responsible use of these tools (Eke & Shuib, 2025). We also believe that transparent and informed consent becomes even more critical in the digital age, with patients being made aware of the relative weights and utility of these different tools in clinical practice and decision-making and being given the option to opt into and out these services (Farid et al., 2024).

Integrity: Accuracy and Truthfulness When Working with Smart Systems

Neurotech has the potential to impact the integrity of our work. At the basic transactional level, we increasingly see researchers and clinicians involved in the development of new tools and technologies and being open and honest about known or potential conflicts of interest, an idea that has sat at the core of ethical behavior for decades. But the broader issue of integrity hinges on the terms *accuracy* and *truthfulness*.

We are already living in an age where technological advances have changed some fundamental ways we communicate our results with accuracy and truthfulness. For example, in our space of dementia research and practice, the presence of ever more ubiquitous biomarkers is a notable example of how technology changes ground-level truth. For years, conditions such as Alzheimer's disease (AD) were defined by their neurobehavioral manifestations, but in these past few years the field has rapidly moved to a biological definition of AD informed by new diagnostic technologies (Jack et al., 2018, 2024). This technological development has changed the way we have to explain our tests, present our results (i.e., a more acute awareness that all that is amnestic is not AD, and that AD has myriad presenting forms), and talk about the implications of our findings (i.e., one can be intact cognitively but still have AD). More mundane tasks, such as the increasingly ubiquitous use of large language models like ChatGPT to generate, categorize, and summarize text, have been impacted by AI. While these tools can greatly enhance efficiency, one must be transparent when using one of these tools, appropriately documenting when and how it was used and ensuring the generated content is accurate and does not plagiarize or violate copyright rules in scientific writing (Sallam, 2023).

In these ways and more, we suspect that digital technologies will increasingly impact other such core pillars of our clinical and research practice. As these changes come online, we as a field more than ever have to update our assumptions, interpretations, and recommendations to be viewed as honest, accurate, and truthful in our practice and service to others. It will be critical for neuropsychologists to ensure they develop and maintain competence in the technologies they use and that the technologies they employ are accurate and appropriate for the intended use. Achieving these goals requires understanding of how technologies are developed, including their strengths and weaknesses, just like any nontechnological tool or test utilized. However, this understanding is difficult to accomplish when technologies include multiple layers of computation that are not transparent or accessible either due to the nature of how the computations are generated and/or intellectual property considerations (Eke & Shuib, 2025). These factors highlight some of the challenges facing neuropsychologists who want to engage with and use promising technologies yet may not have the training or knowledge needed to create or evaluate them.

Justice: Access, Quality for All, and Competence

Our existing APA ethics code focuses on justice through three critical issues: the call to allow all persons access and benefit to what psychology has to offer, to have equal quality in services, and for clinicians to function within the boundaries of their competence.

Extending Benefit to All

There remains a digital divide in the United States and around the world (Charness & Boot, 2022). For example, home broadband use in the United States hovers at about 70% among adults over age 65, much less than the 87% observed in midlife adults ("Internet, Broadband Fact Sheet," 2024). Beyond age, the divide is observed across a host of demographic and socioeconomic groups, groups that also face disparities in other social determinants of health (Braveman et al., 2011). The digital divide impacts how technologies are used in daily life. For example, podcasts, password managers, and sources of information online vary dramatically based on demographic factors such as age and education (Olmstead & Smith, 2017; Shearer et al., 2023).

With that being said, the digital divide appears to be closing. For example, while Internet use among older adults still lags that of younger generations, it has experienced nearly a fourfold increase since 2000—a trend seen in digitally disadvantaged groups as well (Pew Research, n.d.). Further, as neuropsychologists, we are moving from serving a generation of digital pioneers to a generation of digital natives. Around the world, economically disadvantaged regions such as sub-Saharan Africa that lacked early dial-up Internet and PC infrastructure have used increased access to smartphones and cellular networks to bootstrap mobile banking, commerce, and education paths, albeit with challenges (Lucero-Prisno et al., 2022; Scott et al., 2004). This is not to imply that digital inequities do not and will not remain. Rather we highlight that in addition to thinking of access to services being potentially hindered or helped by digital access, we have to remain aware of who is not seen in our digital data due to broader societal and economic trends. As neuropsychologists, we may need to develop and use tools that work across various degrees of digital access.

Equal Quality for All

Digital technologies rely on large datasets; given under-representation of minoritized groups is common in research settings, this can be problematic for the outcomes of digital diagnostic tools that are based on these datasets. For example, algorithmic machine learning diagnoses of AD progression may demonstrate more biased outcomes for members of under-represented groups than majority groups, perhaps due to inadequate sample size and representativeness of the samples in question (Yuan et al., 2023). Further, AI can inadvertently draw erroneous conclusions in decision-making based upon use of factors human raters would not apply, or whose use would be protected by law (Ajunwa & Greene, 2019). Thus, to meet our core goal addressing quality for all, it is more crucial than ever to develop databases that capture the rich complexity of cultural, linguistic, and economic factors that can train these tools.

Developing and Defining Digital Competence

At the time of this writing, the Minnesota Conference for Training in Neuropsychology has been underway (see www.minnesotaconference.org for details). Among a broader update to our training standards, we draw attention to the fact that training in technologies is being considered as an additional competency. We believe this change is sorely needed for neuropsychology to remain relevant in the 21st century and beyond. While it seems exceedingly unlikely that all neuropsychologists will become hardware engineers, computer programmers, or experts in neural network analysis, a working foundation of knowledge to update from will be key to practicing competently in the 21st century. What are these core skills? A proscriptive list of digital skills is likely to be outdated as soon as it is promulgated. Instead, we believe that foundational competencies are likely to include (1) providing a framework to know what sorts of questions to ask, considerations to make, and basic principles of large data and digital technology applications; (2) the foundational skills of teamwork and networking with other disciplines to enable bidirectional exchange of information, ideas, and ethical approaches to tech development and work; and (3) a flexible mindset so that new tools can be adopted and implemented over time. Curricula that address these core principles need to be tested, evaluated, and evolved over time. In this way, aspirational principles of justice, including knowing and working within one's boundaries of competence in a digital age, can be achieved.

Respect for People's Rights and Dignity

Psychologists strive to show respect for the fundamental rights of the individuals we serve. From a digital standpoint, we believe this principle gives a clarion call to consider the role of technologies toward privacy, confidentiality, and self-determination as well as the impacts of individual diversity factors on digital technology use and applicability.

What Do Privacy, Confidentiality, and Self-Determination Mean in the Age of Neurotech?

Digital technologies can capture who we talk to, where we go, and when we are awake and asleep. We bring digital tools with us everywhere, with their presence and sometimes passive monitoring occurring in areas of our lives that have historically been private. Electronic health records can unobtrusively provide information that can feed into complex algorithms even now to identify risk for cognitive impairment (Lyall et al., 2023). While at first blush, this reality can be seen as rather dystopian, it is the reality, and consumers seem to be readily exchanging data for conveniences enabled by digital technology and always-on connectivity. As these data points mesh with health care and research purposes, we believe there are several things to consider. First, clear and concise informed consent is critical when these data are going to be used for health or research purposes and when diagnostic or treatment decisions are assisted by AI algorithms, with a clear and easy ability to opt out of any particular data or health care element when possible (Farid et al., 2024). These principles align with the Health Insurance Portability and Accountability Act, which is the federal law that requires the patient's consent in order to disclose their health information (An Act to Amend the Internal Revenue Code of 1986 to Improve Portability and Continuity of Health Insurance Coverage in the Group and Individual Markets, to Combat Waste, Fraud, and Abuse in Health Insurance and Health Care Delivery, to Promote the Use of Medical Savings Accounts, to Improve Access to Long-Term Care Services and Coverage, to Simplify the Administration of Health Insurance, and for Other Purposes, 1996). Relatedly, we believe it is important for health- and research-related technologies to include education on how data elements can be turned on and off depending on the provider's preference, a feature rapidly being included in software research platforms currently (Srinivasa Rao, 2024). Also important is providing education about risks of data breach, protections in place, and what to do when those protections are suspected to have failed. Third, and as we have emphasized already several times, working with the teams and developers designing novel digital tools to ensure that data and algorithms are discoverable/transparent and widely applicable to users is critical as well. We believe that such factors help bridge some of the possible hindrances to self-determination and privacy in the digital age.

Summary and a Call to Action

Clearly, neurotech presents unique challenges but also opportunities to more fully realize our ethical principles as neuropsychologists. To maximize benefit and minimize harm, we believe that there are four broad steps that need to be taken: organize around a technology audit approach to novel tools, add technology competencies into our training, embrace working with teams, and pursue ethically grounded neurotech research, education, and practice programs.

Using Technology Audits to Understand and Shape Digital Neurotech

Landers and Behrend (2023) recently outlined a framework for evaluating fairness and bias in high-stakes AI predictive models in psychology more broadly, and we believe that with some modifications, such a technological audit approach may be of benefit for research and professional teams and organizations in neuropsychology to utilize when considering new technological approaches (see Table 4.1).

At the core of this approach is the need for and appreciation of the interdisciplinary nature of the work that is needed. In other words, with notable exceptions, evaluating and developing tools ethically will require the inclusion of technical, statistical, engineering, and neuropsychological experts, among others. Input from and

Table 4.1 Sample Technological Audit of Artificial Intelligence Model Components for Neuropsychological Uses

Component	Question	Neuropsychology Use Examples
Input Data	What data went into the model to begin with?	Was the sample representative of your clinical sample? Think of the questions we ask ourselves about normative data.
Model Design	What drove model choices?	Think of how we critique instruments and theory design. Were the original instruments appropriate? Why were certain markers included and not others? How might that influence outcomes? What happens with missing data?
Model Development	How was the model refined over time?	What variables were discarded and why? Were these decisions and their rationale documented so they can be reviewed?

Component	Question	Neuropsychology Use Examples
Model Features	How/what were the raw data entered?	Did speech to text work? What features from face/voice/other signals ended up in the model? Were potential sources of bias (i.e., hypophonia for voice) considered?
Model Processes	How is a score generated?	Did this process get "stress" tested in clinical settings, invalid/incomplete situations, etc.?
Model Outputs	How was predictive validity evaluated?	Reliability, validity, outputs across classes, etc.
First-Party Interpretation	How does marketing/ messaging flow from the original model questions?	Does this model claim to diagnose all cognitive impairment? A dementia? To replace the need for other tests?
Second-Party Effects	Who is directly impacted by this technology, and have their reactions been assessed? What are impacts of false positives/false negatives?	Were those with the condition of interest included in development/evaluation? How are results reported back to them?
Third-Party Understanding	How are regulators, insurers, advocacy groups, etc. viewing these results?	What do the Centers for Medicare and Medicaid Services, Federal Drug Administration, and neuropsychology specific groups say about this information?
Cultural Context	How was cultural context considered?	Did those who did not cross the digital divide get included? What assumptions about the condition of interest were made and considered in development?
Respect	How does this fit in with generally considered ethical codes (including outside of psychology)?	What evidence for consideration of these factors in development are present?
Research Design	How do research designs used in support of any claims impact the validity of the conclusions?	How did dropout rates get considered in looking at diagnostic accuracy models?

even co-designing with end users of the technology (e.g., patients, caregivers, health care professionals) is strongly encouraged. With the required expertise involved, the team can work together to understand issues around the data, ethics, and needs of consumers to evaluate impacts related to fidelity, adverse events, and model building. These conclusions can also be evaluated from a justice and access lens.

Clearly, such an undertaking cannot be performed for every new test, technology, or evaluation. This is also something that would be unlikely to be undertaken by a single professional in isolation. Rather, we suspect that there will be a need for neuropsychology organizations to take up this approach and move forward with facilitating these comprehensive evaluations, disseminating results to society members and the public at large to help identify the strengths and weaknesses of novel digital approaches.

Support for Incorporating Technology Competencies into Neuropsychological Training

As is outlined in Chapter 1, advances in neuropsychological training standards must include a grounding in technological innovation, and this cannot just be driven by using a particular publisher's testing platform. When viewed through the lens of our professional ethics, several training imperatives seem clear.

Learning to Work with Teams

Neuropsychologists are very familiar with working with patients, their families, and related medical disciplines. However, a neurotech-adept workforce means developing the skill sets necessary to work with a wide range of engineering, coding, and statistical professionals. Such learning is likely to encompass not only formal (i.e., courses and workshops hosted between organizations and disciplines to level set basic knowledge) but also informal relationship building. We call upon our professional organizations and working groups to start the process of bringing together experts in a proactive, not just a reactive manner. To meet the call of ethical technological developments, we must not stand alone as a profession.

A Neurotech Ethics Research Agenda

More research is needed to guide the ethics of technology use. Key research questions center on patients' and participants' understanding, use, and comfort with digital data tools, and means of increasing the security and privacy of such data. Understanding how digital tools work or react in situations where underserved, under-represented, cognitively impaired, or incomplete data streams are at play is also needed. Working to understand the sociocultural, psychological, and cognitive factors that drive the digital divide, and working with our patients and families to learn from the ingenuity of those we serve to make these tools more useful is key as well.

In summary, we believe that the future of neuropsychology is indeed digital, and we should embrace this emerging landscape with the ingenuity and close observation that has guided our field for generations. While many of the specifics are changed, the core ethical principles that have guided us for generations can continue to be relevant for the future of neurotech.

References

An Act to Amend the Internal Revenue Code of 1986 to Improve Portability and Continuity of Health Insurance Coverage in the Group and Individual Markets, to Combat Waste, Fraud, and Abuse in Health Insurance and Health Care Delivery, to Promote the Use of Medical Savings Accounts, to Improve Access to Long-Term Care Services and Coverage, to Simplify the Administration of Health Insurance, and for Other Purposes, 191, 191, 104, 104 (1996). https://www.govinfo.gov/app/details/PLAW-104publ191

Ajunwa, I., & Greene, D. (2019). Platforms at work: Automated hiring platforms and other new intermediaries in the organization of work. In Steven P. Vallas and Anne Kovalainen (Eds.), *Work and labor in the digital age* (pp. 61–91). Emerald. https://www.emerald.com/insight/content/doi/10.1108/S0277-283320190000033005/full/html

Alegría, M., Alvarez, K., Ishikawa, R. Z., DiMarzio, K., & McPeck, S. (2016). Removing obstacles to eliminate racial and ethnic disparities in behavioral health care. *Health Affairs (Project Hope), 35*(6), 991–999. https://doi.org/10.1377/hlthaff.2016.0029

American Psychological Association. (n.d.). *APA Public Comment Site—APA Public Comments Site.* https://apps.apa.org/APACommentingPortal/CommentSite?SiteNum=125&PersonID=0

Benge, J. F., Aguirre, A., Scullin, M. K., Kiselica, A., Hilsabeck, R. C., Paydarfar, D., Thomaz, E., & Douglas, M. (2024). Digital methods for performing daily tasks among older adults: An initial report of frequency of use and perceived utility. *Experimental Aging Research, 50*(2), 133–154. https://doi.org/10.1080/0361073X.2023.2172950

Bilder, R. M., & Reise, S. P. (2019). Neuropsychological tests of the future: How do we get there from here? *The Clinical Neuropsychologist, 33*(2), 220–245. https://doi.org/10.1080/13854046.2018.1521993

Braveman, P., Egerter, S., & Williams, D. R. (2011). The social determinants of health: Coming of age. *Annual Review of Public Health, 32*(1), 381–398. https://doi.org/10.1146/annurev-publhealth-031210-101218

Butler, P. M., Yang, J., Brown, R., Hobbs, M., Becker, A., Penalver-Andres, J., Syz, P., Muller, S., Cosne, G., Juraver, A., Song, H. H., Saha-Chaudhuri, P., Roggen, D., Scotland, A., Silveira, N., Demircioglu, G., Gabelle, A., Hughes, R., Erkkinen, M. G., ... Belachew, S. (2025). Smartwatch- and smartphone-based remote assessment of brain health and detection of mild cognitive impairment. *Nature Medicine, 31*(3), 829–839. https://doi.org/10.1038/s41591-024-03475-9

Casu, M., Triscari, S., Battiato, S., Guarnera, L., & Caponnetto, P. (2024). AI chatbots for mental health: A scoping review of effectiveness, feasibility, and applications. *Applied Sciences, 14*(13), Article 13. https://doi.org/10.3390/app14135889

Chapman, C. R., Mehta, K. S., Parent, B., & Caplan, A. L. (2020). Genetic discrimination: Emerging ethical challenges in the context of advancing technology. *Journal of Law and the Biosciences, 7*(1), 1–23.

Charness, N., & Boot, W. R. (2022). A grand challenge for psychology: Reducing the age-related digital divide. *Current Directions in Psychological Science, 31*(2), 187–193. https://doi.org/10.1177/09637214211068144

Directorate-General for Communications Networks, Content and Technology. (2019). *Ethics guidelines for trustworthy AI*. Publications Office of the European Union. https://data.europa.eu/doi/10.2759/346720

Eke, C. I., & Shuib, L. (2025). The role of explainability and transparency in fostering trust in AI healthcare systems: A systematic literature review, open issues and potential solutions. *Neural Computing and Applications, 37*(4), 1999–2034. https://doi.org/10.1007/s00521-024-10868-x

Farid, Y., Chang, C., Marcasciano, M., Di Meglio, F., Rodríguez-Mantilla, I., Nanni, J., Ortiz, S., & Chen, H.-C. (2024). Consent 2.0: Informed choices in the age of artificial intelligence. *Surgery, 175*(5), 1454–1455.

Graham, A. K., Weissman, R. S., & Mohr, D. C. (2021). Resolving key barriers to advancing mental health equity in rural communities using digital mental health interventions. *JAMA Health Forum, 2*(6), e211149. https://doi.org/10.1001/jamahealthforum.2021.1149

Health Resources and Service Administration. (2023). *Behavioral Health Workforce 2023 Brief.* https://bhw.hrsa.gov/sites/default/files/bureau-health-workforce/Behavioral-Health-Workforce-Brief-2023.pdf

Internet, Broadband Fact Sheet. (2024, November 13). Pew Research Center. https://www.pewresearch.org/internet/fact-sheet/internet-broadband/

Jack, C. R., Andrews, J. S., Beach, T. G., Buracchio, T., Dunn, B., Graf, A., Hansson, O., Ho, C., Jagust, W., McDade, E., Molinuevo, J. L., Okonkwo, O. C., Pani, L., Rafii, M. S., Scheltens, P., Siemers, E., Snyder, H. M., Sperling, R., Teunissen, C. E., & Carrillo, M. C. (2024). Revised criteria for diagnosis and staging of Alzheimer's disease: Alzheimer's Association Workgroup. *Alzheimer's & Dementia, 20*(8), 5143–5169. https://doi.org/10.1002/alz.13859

Jack Jr, C. R., Bennett, D. A., Blennow, K., Carrillo, M. C., Dunn, B., Haeberlein, S. B., Holtzman, D. M., Jagust, W., Jessen, F., & Karlawish, J. (2018). NIA-AA research framework: Toward a biological definition of Alzheimer's disease. *Alzheimer's & Dementia, 14*(4), 535–562.

Karimian, G., Petelos, E., & Evers, S. M. A. A. (2022). The ethical issues of the application of artificial intelligence in healthcare: A systematic scoping review. *AI and Ethics, 2*(4), 539–551. https://doi.org/10.1007/s43681-021-00131-7

Landers, R. N., & Behrend, T. S. (2023). Auditing the AI auditors: A framework for evaluating fairness and bias in high stakes AI predictive models. *American Psychologist, 78*(1), 36.

Lucero-Prisno, D. E., Olayemi, A. H., Ekpenyong, I., Okereke, P., Aldirdiri, O., Buban, J. M., Ndikumana, S., Yelarge, K., Sesay, N., Turay, F. U., Huang, J., & Kouwenhoven, M.

(2022). Prospects for financial technology for health in Africa. *Digital Health, 8*, 1–4. https://doi.org/10.1177/20552076221119548

Lyall, D. M., Kormilitzin, A., Lancaster, C., Sousa, J., Petermann-Rocha, F., Buckley, C., Harshfield, E. L., Iveson, M. H., Madan, C. R., McArdle, R., Newby, D., Orgeta, V., Tang, E., Tamburin, S., Thakur, L. S., Lourida, I., Network, T. D. D. P. (DEMON), Llewellyn, D. J., & Ranson, J. M. (2023). Artificial intelligence for dementia—Applied models and digital health. *Alzheimer's & Dementia, 19*(12), 5872–5884. https://doi.org/10.1002/alz.13391

Maleki, N., Padmanabhan, B., & Dutta, K. (2024). AI hallucinations: A misnomer worth clarifying. In *2024 IEEE Conference on Artificial Intelligence (CAI)* (pp. 133–138). IEEE. https://doi.org/10.1109/CAI59869.2024.00033

Mattson, M. P. (2014). Superior pattern processing is the essence of the evolved human brain. *Frontiers in Neuroscience, 8*. https://doi.org/10.3389/fnins.2014.00265

Naik, N., Hameed, B. M. Z., Shetty, D. K., Swain, D., Shah, M., Paul, R., Aggarwal, K., Ibrahim, S., Patil, V., Smriti, K., Shetty, S., Rai, B. P., Chlosta, P., & Somani, B. K. (2022). Legal and ethical consideration in artificial intelligence in healthcare: Who takes responsibility? *Frontiers in Surgery, 9*. https://doi.org/10.3389/fsurg.2022.862322

Nguyen, C. M., Rampa, S., Staios, M., Nielsen, T. R., Zapparoli, B., Zhou, X. E., Mbakile-Mahlanza, L., Colon, J., Hammond, A., & Hendriks, M. (2024). Neuropsychological application of the International Test Commission Guidelines for Translation and Adapting of Tests. *Journal of the International Neuropsychological Society, 30*(7), 621–634.

Office of the Director of National Intelligence Agency. (n.d.). *INTEL—Artificial Intelligence Ethics Framework for the Intelligence Community*. https://www.intelligence.gov/artificial-intelligence-ethics-framework-for-the-intelligence-community

Parsons, T. D. (2019). *Ethical challenges in digital psychology and cyberpsychology*. Cambridge University Press.

Pew Research, C. (n.d.). *Internet/Broadband Fact Sheet*. http://files/1174/internet-broadband.html

Sallam, M. (2023). ChatGPT utility in healthcare education, research, and practice: Systematic review on the promising perspectives and valid concerns. *Healthcare, 11*(6), 887. https://www.mdpi.com/2227-9032/11/6/887

Scott, N., Batchelor, S., Ridley, J., & Jorgensen, B. (2004). *The impact of mobile phones in Africa* (Contract ref: CNTR 026). Commission for Africa. http://gamos.org/publications/Impact%20of%20Mobile%20Phones%20in%20Africa_Commission%20for%20Africa_Report%202004.pdf

Shcherbiak, A., Habibnia, H., Böhm, R., & Fiedler, S. (2024). Evaluating science: A comparison of human and AI reviewers. *Judgment and Decision Making, 19*, e21.

Shearer, E., Liedke, J., Matsa, K. E., Lipka, M., & Jurkowitz, M. (2023, April 18). *Podcasts as a source of news and information*. Pew Research Center. https://www.pewresearch.org/wp-content/uploads/sites/20/2023/04/PJ_2023.04.18_Podcasts_FINAL.pdf

Olmestead, K. O., & Smith, A. (2017, January 26). *Password management and mobile security*. Pew Research Center. https://www.pewresearch.org/internet/2017/01/26/2-password-management-and-mobile-security/

Srinivasa Rao, A. (2024). The impact of iOS app development on mobile health solutions. *Journal of Recent Trends in Computer Science and Engineering, 12*(2), 54–72.

Sugarman, D. E., & Busch, A. B. (2023). Telemental health for clinical assessment and treatment. https://doi.org/10.1136/bmj-2022-072398

Wang, Y., Li, N., Chen, L., Wu, M., Meng, S., Dai, Z., Zhang, Y., & Clarke, M. (2023). Guidelines, consensus statements, and standards for the use of artificial intelligence in medicine: Systematic review. *Journal of Medical Internet Research, 25*, e46089. https://doi.org/10.2196/46089

World Health Organization. (n.d.). *Ethics and governance of artificial intelligence for health*. https://www.who.int/publications/i/item/9789240029200

Yuan, C., Linn, K. A., & Hubbard, R. A. (2023). Algorithmic fairness of machine learning models for Alzheimer disease progression. *JAMA Network Open, 6*(11), e2342203. https://doi.org/10.1001/jamanetworkopen.2023.42203

Zhu, W., Liu, H., Dong, Q., Xu, J., Huang, S., Kong, L., Chen, J., & Li, L. (2024). *Multilingual machine translation with large language models: Empirical results and analysis* (No. arXiv:2304.04675). arXiv. https://doi.org/10.48550/arXiv.2304.04675

5

Using Technology to Enhance Neuropsychological Tests

Early Mistakes and Lessons Learned in Developing the D-KEFS Advanced

Dean C. Delis, Lisa W. Drozdick, James Holdnack, Jennifer Puig, Ann M. Huber, and Miles L. Delis

Introduction

This chapter takes a different approach from the typical format of edited volumes that focus on summarizing and critically analyzing research studies within a specific domain. Instead, it tells the story behind the development of the all-digital D-KEFS Advanced. Digital technology is reshaping nearly every aspect of modern life, including medicine. Yet neuropsychological assessment instruments have been surprisingly slow to fully adopt digital formats. One reason for this reluctance, as we discovered, is that transitioning from all-print to all-digital is far more complex than it may initially appear.

Throughout this process, we encountered numerous challenges, setbacks, errors, and valuable lessons. By openly sharing both our missteps and insights, we aim to support and inform future researchers who undertake the important work of leveraging digital technology to advance neuropsychological assessment tools.

This chapter is organized into two parts. The first part recounts the long and demanding journey of transforming the original print-based D-KEFS into the fully digital D-KEFS Advanced. We discuss what worked, what didn't, and offer practical guidance to help others avoid the obstacles we faced. The second part outlines the final design goals of each of the six new D-KEFS Advanced tests and summarizes the clinical utility of the tests across various populations—including children with

Parts of this chapter are adaptations, tables, or figures taken from the *D-KEFS Advanced Manual* and are republished here with permission from Pearson Assessment. Dr. Delis is an author of the D-KEFS Advanced and receives royalties from the tests. Dr. Drozdick, Dr. Puig, and Ms. Huber are employees of Pearson Assessment, and Dr. Holdnack is a past employee and current consultant for Pearson Assessment.

Dean C. Delis et al., *Using Technology to Enhance Neuropsychological Tests*. In: *Technology and Neuropsychology*.
Edited by: Jared F. Benge et al., Oxford University Press. © Oxford University Press (2026).
DOI: 10.1093/9780197814116.003.0005

attention-deficit/hyperactivity disorder (ADHD), autism spectrum disorder (ASD), and specific learning disorder in mathematics; adults with traumatic brain injuries (TBIs); and older adults with mild cognitive impairment (MCI).

Going All In

In 2009, about 8 years after the publication of the original Delis-Kaplan Executive Function System (D-KEFS; Delis et al., 2001), the Pearson research team, headed by Dr. James Holdnack and Dr. Lisa Drozdick, and the senior author began discussing and planning the development of the second edition of the tests. At that time, the iPhone had been available only for about 1 year and the iPad had not been released, but it was clear the world was rapidly transforming into a mobile digital wonderland and there was no turning back. From our first meetings, we entertained the idea of embracing this technology and developing all-digital tests of executive functions without having the constraints of also developing paper-and-pencil (print) versions of the tests. Those discussions also occurred at Pearson for their legendary intelligence quotient (IQ) scales, but the legacy of those instruments, the uncertainty around digital development and adoption, and the passion and clinical experience that practicing psychologists had for the manipulatives of those tests (e.g., using blocks to make designs) made it clear that any revision of those scales had to include both a print version and digital-assist version, at least for the foreseeable future. But for the second edition of the D-KEFS, we were not tethered to over 100 years of legacy use like the IQ scales, freeing us to shed the constraints of paper-and-pencil tasks in order to fully harness the processing capacities of modern digital devices and develop new, more dynamic, sophisticated cognitive assessment instruments. For years, we witnessed the surge of digital technology in transforming the field of neuroimaging, revealing the structure and function of the brain in increasingly exquisite detail. And yet psychologists remained stuck with their clunky stopwatches, manipulatives, multipage record forms, lead pencils, and test administration manuals. So much invaluable process data was lost with this traditional approach to testing simply because it was not possible to capture scores at a micro-response level! Fortunately for us, the corporate side of Pearson loved the idea of using the D-KEFS as its first prototype of going from an all-print to an all-digital version of an assessment instrument. With their blessings, Dr. Holdnack, Dr. Drozdick, and the senior author embarked on our journey.

It was decided early on that, since a large percentage of psychologists still needed or wanted to administer print versions of the tests, the new all-digital D-KEFS tests would not replace the original D-KEFS; rather, we would design the new tests to complement the original version, and both versions would continue to be available for psychologists to use. For this reason, we decided to call the new tests the D-KEFS Advanced rather than the D-KEFS-2.

In the abstract, the idea of developing fully digital executive-function tests sounded so fun and easy. While the original D-KEFS tests took approximately 10 years to develop from start to finish, we were convinced that we would be able to develop the new all-digital tests and complete the national normative study in about half that time. After all, before and after we started this project, several excellent, all-digital cognitive screening tests were developed and successfully implemented, including the MicroCog Assessment of Cognitive Functioning (administration time: 15 to 60 minutes; Powell et al., 1993), the ImPACT (administration time: about 20 to 25 minutes; Lovell, 2004), and, after we started the D-KEFS Advanced project, the cognitive-domain tests of the NIH Toolbox for Assessment of Neurological and Behavioral Function (administration time: about 30 to 60 minutes; Weintraub et al., 2013). However, in trying to enhance neuropsychological tests by developing more complex, dynamic tests of multitasking and other executive functions that provide numerous new process scores, we had no idea of the difficulties and setbacks we would encounter. We quickly realized that we were navigating in uncharted waters, frequently blindsided by unforeseen obstacles and complications. But the silver lining of each setback was that we were able to regroup and make refinements to the tests to improve them. Even with the biggest setback of all, the worldwide pandemic, which struck near the end of our national tryout study and before the national standardization study, we were able to pivot and made changes that improved the tests, including eliminating pointing requirements by examiners during instructions so that the tests can be administered using social distancing (even in separate rooms with a large window in the adjoining wall). The tests were also designed for future adaptation for remote testing, although that feature is not available at this time. Further, in light of psychologists facing a growing battle to protect the validity of their assessment instruments for future uses by not releasing their raw paper test data to nonqualified individuals (e.g., attorneys), we were able to design the new, all-digital tests to offer the option of paper-free assessments, which eliminates print versions of the test stimuli, questions and answers that might have to be produced with a court order.

Lessons Learned in Developing the D-KEFS Advanced

Throughout the development of the D-KEFS Advanced, we gained valuable insights that may assist others in designing fully digital cognitive assessment tools. The following are the key lessons we learned.

From Paper to Pixels: No Cheap Seats

One of the first lessons we learned is that this would not be a low-budget journey. Pearson provided a very generous development budget, which we quickly exceeded multiple times. In the early stages, the D-KEFS Advanced was envisioned as a nine-test battery, including revisions to five original D-KEFS tests and the addition of three entirely new executive-function tasks. As development progressed, it became clear that our ambitions quickly outpaced our growing budget. While Pearson demonstrated remarkable patience, there eventually came a point where we had to make difficult decisions. Three tests were shelved—at least for the time being. It was a painful process, as each had been carefully designed and held promise. The only consolation was that, thanks to the fully digital platform, future additions could be integrated into the battery seamlessly, offering flexibility and room for growth.

The final selection of tests for the D-KEFS Advanced included the following:

- Trail Making Test (TMT)
    - Condition 1: Number Sequencing (NS)
    - Condition 2: Letter Sequencing (LS)
    - Condition 3: Number–Letter Switching (SW)
    - Condition 4: Switching–Distraction (SWD)
    - Condition 5: Switching–Working Memory (SWM)
- Verbal Fluency Test (VFT)
    - Condition 1: Letter Fluency (LF)
    - Condition 2: Category Fluency (CF)
    - Condition 3: Switching Fluency (SW)
        - Category–Letter Switching (CLS)
        - Letter–Category–Letter Switching (LCLS)
- Color–Word Interference Test (CWIT)
    - Condition 1: Color Identification (CI)
    - Condition 2: Word Identification (WI)
    - Condition 3: Inhibition (IN)
    - Condition 4: Inhibition/Switching (SW)
- Tower Test (TWR)
- Social Sorting Test (SST)
- Risk–Reward Decision Test (RISK)

Table 5.1 provides a brief description of the D-KEFS Advanced tests.

Rome Wasn't Built in a Day

While we learned this lesson from the original D-KEFS (which took 10 years to develop), we had to repeatedly remind ourselves of this lesson throughout the development of the D-KEFS Advanced. From start to finish, the development of the D-KEFS Advanced spanned a period of 16 years. Figure 5.1 shows a timeline of the development of the D-KEFS Advanced, which occurred across five stages and involved continuous review of the instrument by experts, examiners, and customers.

Table 5.1 Description of the D-KEFS Advanced Tests

Test	Description
Trail Making Test (TMT)	The TMT uses a visuomotor format to assess basic to complex multitasking. Two new switching conditions were developed to assist in assessing the contribution of cognitive shifting, response inhibition to distracting stimuli, and working memory to multitasking skills. There are five conditions: two baseline sequencing tasks that require the examinee to connect circles either in numerical or alphabetical order, and three switching tasks that require the examinee to shift between connecting numbers and letters under different executive function demands.
Verbal Fluency Test (VFT)	The VFT measures the ability to rapidly generate verbal responses according to either phonemic rules (i.e., initial letter) or semantic rules (i.e., superordinate category) and to perform verbal multitasking by switching between the phonemic and semantic rules. There are seven trials in which the examinee says as many words as possible in 60 seconds either according to an initial letter, a semantic category, or switching between the phonemic and semantic rules.
Color–Word Interference Test (CWIT)	The CWIT assesses the ability to inhibit a prepotent (i.e., overlearned or automatic) verbal response to generate a more difficult, conflicting response (i.e., the Stroop effect) and to engage in multitasking by switching between the automatic and more difficult verbal responses. There are four conditions: two baseline tasks that assess the fundamental skills of rapid color or word identification (which measure basic verbal processing speed), a test of verbal inhibition in which the examinee must inhibit the prepotent response of identifying the printed word (i.e., the name of a color) to identify the conflicting color of the word's letters, and a test of verbal multitasking in which the examinee must switch between the automatic and more difficult response.
Tower Test (TWR)	The TWR assesses spatial planning; rule learning; inhibition of impulsive, trial-and-error responses; and the ability to establish, maintain, and quickly switch between instructional sets. The examinee moves chips across three tables on the bottom of the stimulus to replicate the chip placements shown at the top of the stimulus while following several rules. The rules are to (a) use the fewest number of moves possible; (b) move only one chip at a time; (c) never place a larger chip on top of a smaller chip for solid chips; (d) never place a smaller chip on top of a larger chip for striped chips; and (e) complete the task within a liberal time frame rather than as quickly as possible, thereby placing greater emphasis on planning and accuracy over speed.

continued

Table 5.1 *continued*

Test	Description
Social Sorting Test (SST)	Modeled after the Wisconsin Card Sorting Test® (WCST®), which was developed by Grant and Berg (1948) and later normed by Heaton et al. (1993), the SST uses ecologically valid stimuli (i.e., photos of people with different emotional expressions and clothing) to measure problem-solving that requires facial and affect recognition, concept identification, use of feedback, conceptual flexibility, and inhibition of perseverative responses. The examinee is shown four key cards and a stack of sorting cards and then matches each of the sorting cards to a key card according to preestablished rules that are unknown to them. After each sort, the examinee is given correct/incorrect visual feedback according to these predefined rules. The rules change throughout the test without warning to the examinee, and the examinee must rely only on the feedback after each response to guide their next sorting response. For some sorts, two or three rules are simultaneously reinforced, which requires the examinee to adhere to the current conceptual rule despite the ambiguity in the feedback and the pull to be derailed to the other reinforced sorting rules. For other sorts, there is unambiguous feedback that a current sorting rule must be abandoned, which requires inhibition of perseverative responses and conceptual flexibility to implement a different sorting rule.
Risk–Reward Decision Test (RISK; ages 19–90 years only)	The RISK measures the hot executive function of risky decision-making in the context of a problem-solving task involving a horse-racing game. For each of 60 races, the examinee must pick one of three horses that vary in terms of their odds of winning and their payout. These parameters are well defined at the onset of the test, so the examinee does not have to learn them by trial and error like on other risk-taking tests. The examinee must choose between a horse that has the lowest chance of winning but pays the most money, a horse that is most likely to win but pays the least money, and a middle-odds horse that pays a middle-range amount. For each race, the examinee touches the horse they think will win, and the horses immediately race across the screen with the sounds of galloping hooves and chimes if they win. Pilot studies showed that this task often elicited animated responses in examinees as they root for their selected horse, which enhanced the "hot" executive function aspects of the tests. Money is earned or lost based on a predetermined outcome, and the examinee must use the win/loss feedback to adjust their level of risk-taking to maximize their winnings.

Stage 1: Proof of Concept

Our initial studies focused on whether an all-digital version of the standard print version of the tests was even viable. To be viable, the digital version needed to produce

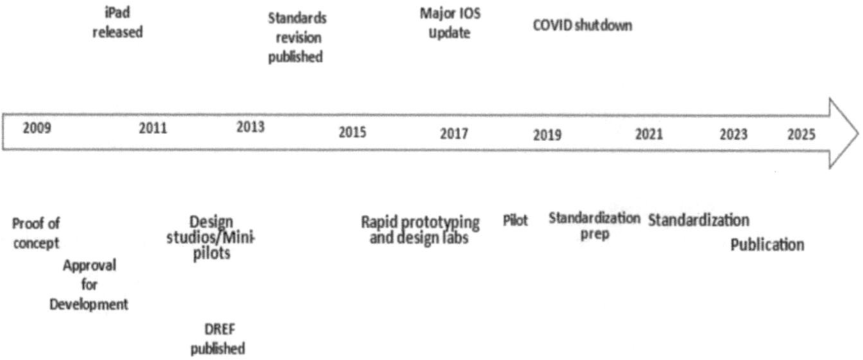

Figure 5.1 Timeline of the development of the D-KEFS Advanced

results without introducing significant technology effects on performance, improve ease of administration and scoring for examiners, decrease measurement error, produce results similar to the print versions, and yield useable results for children and adults ages 8—90 years. For this initial phase, usability and feasibility of the digital application was the focus, particularly for the youngest (i.e., ages 8–9 years) and oldest (i.e., ages 80–90 years) participants in the normative sample. In testing different digital devices, the focus was on capturing meaningful response data, improving usability for examiners and examinees, ensuring similar results to the print version, and exploring whether new conditions and process scores could be developed. Different technologies available at that time were examined during this phase, including laptops (both touchscreen and mouse entry), digital pens, and tablets (the iPad was released after this phase was completed). Based on these analyses, it was initially thought that a touchscreen laptop might be the best fit for the proof of concept. However, we quickly discovered that, once iPads were released, they were the best devices to use, one for the practitioner and one for the client; Pearson also chose to develop their Q-interactive platform on iPads, solidifying the decision.

Results from the proof-of-concept studies were generally positive: The digital versions were well tolerated by the youngest and oldest age ranges, desired data were captured for analysis, examiners reported the digital interface greatly improved ease of administration and scoring, and similar test results to the print versions were obtained.

Stage 2: Minipilots and Design Studios

Given the innovative nature of the D-KEFS Advanced, numerous aspects of digital administration and scoring needed to be vetted and validated before conducting large-scale research collections. Two types of studies were used throughout the initial development: minipilots and design studios. Minipilots focused on item and content development and tested small groups of examinees on print and/or digital prototypes to assess the viability, difficulty, and utility of items, conditions, or tests. Design studios focused on user interfaces and digital data collection; user experience specialists, engineering professionals, and research staff observed the interactions of examinees and examiners with the iPads. Small numbers of examinees were tested for these design studios, and sessions were recorded for further analysis of the interactions. Between 2011 and 2017, approximately 20 minipilot and design studio studies were conducted in an attempt to further develop and refine the new tests.

Stage 3: Pilot Studies

Two large pilot studies were completed as part of the D-KEFS Advanced development. The first pilot was conducted using a hybrid print/partially digitized version (with animation created in PowerPoint files) of the future all-digital tasks and focused on directions, item content, and testing new tests and conditions for the Trail Making Test, Verbal Fluency Test, Social Sorting Test, and Risk-Reward Decision Test. This pilot study was conducted from January 2012 to June 2012 and included approximately 120 typically developing children and adults, children with ADHD, and older adults with motor difficulties (e.g., hand tremors). This hybrid-version pilot study was collected before many of the design studios to determine which tests to include in digital development, to assess examiner and examinee usability, and to address general administration questions.

After the prototype and platform development, a second pilot version of the D-KEFS Advanced was designed for digital administration. The primary goal of this pilot study was to evaluate the tests in a national sample using external examiners with the goals of (1) producing a version for use in the subsequent national tryout phase and (2) evaluating the digital interface in a broad group of users. The pilot version was administered on the Q-interactive platform. This stage of development focused on such issues as item content and relevance, digital usability and fidelity, clarity of instructions to the examiner and examinee, administration procedures, capture of response processes, development of scoring criteria, evaluation of item bias, and analysis of other relevant psychometric properties. The nonclinical sample was collected in 2018 and included 139 children and adults. Emphasis was placed on recruiting individuals from the youngest and oldest age groups with minimal technological experience or with education levels of high school or less to ensure the interface was accessible and produced clinically useful results for these groups. Data from the pilot version and data on the functionality and stability of the interface were analyzed, and examiners were asked to provide feedback on their experience.

Stage 4: Expert, Examiner, and International Reviewers

Neuropsychologists, clinical psychologists, and school psychologists with expertise in the assessment of executive functioning were invited to review the prototypes and provide feedback on the design during all research stages, but with a particular emphasis before the national tryout study. Feedback was used to modify stimuli, instructions, response requirements, and scoring criteria.

Stage 5: National Tryout Study

The national tryout study used a version of the battery that consisted of seven of the originally planned nine tests. The Tryout study involved a sample of 346 participants that approximated the general makeup of the U.S. population on education level (self or parent) and race/ethnicity. Data collection for the tryout phase began in July 2019. In March 2020, the nearly complete national tryout data collection was paused because of the COVID-19 pandemic. Modifications were made to the tryout version based on the initial tryout data, and when data collection resumed from October 2021 to January 2022, the new version was used to verify the test and item decisions made based on data from the earlier sample.

Stage 6: National Standardization

After reviewing the accumulated evidence from the preceding research stages and the accumulated feedback, a standardization edition of the D-KEFS Advanced was created that included the final six tests. The final national normative sample of the D-KEFS Advanced consisted of 1,280 typically functioning participants ages 8:0–90:11 years matched to the demographic makeup of the U.S. population. The tests were also administered to 160 children and adults who met criteria for inclusion in one of various clinical groups, including children and adolescents with ADHD, specific learning disorder—mathematics, or ASD; adults with TBIs; and older adults with MCI.

Finger Versus Stylus

An early lesson we learned in our minipilot and pilot studies was that onscreen response capture was more reliable when examinees used a stylus rather than their finger. The stylus (1) kept the hand higher off the client's screen, which minimized issues with the examinee viewing the screen, (2) reduced variability in response capture caused by differences in finger conductivity or fingernail length, and (3) minimized accidental responding by touching the screen with the palm, wrist, or other fingers. The stylus also provided a helpful bridge for examinees who were not familiar with digital technology and who tended to use pencils and pens in their daily lives.

Drawing Versus Touching

During the proof-of-concept stage, we attempted to make the digital versions of the tests as equivalent as possible to the print version of the original D–KEFS, including using a stylus to draw the lines on the screen for the Trail Making Test (TMT). From our first study with a digital TMT (which occurred on a touch-screen laptop), we learned that drawing the connecting lines on-screen with a stylus was not going to work. The most significant problem occurred when the stylus went too close to a nontarget circle: The digital interface would sometimes code it as an error, resulting in a false high-error rate. Also, individuals with motor problems had difficulty drawing lines with the stylus, which also occurs when these individuals use a pencil or pen on print versions of these tests. We changed the response mode to improve usability by having the examinee simply touch the target circles and the digital interface automatically draw the connecting lines. This response mode was a gamechanger: It not only eliminated the problem of false error captures, but it also made the task significantly easier to perform for examinees with motor problems, especially for older individuals. In fact, from a motor perspective, we found that the touch-the-circle approach on a digital device was easier to perform than the draw-the-line approach on the print version for nearly all examinees. As a result, this response method afforded a more accurate assessment of both the fundamental processes and higher-level executive functions required to perform the TMT by reducing the confounding effects of the motor demands of the print version. The new touch method was refined throughout the minipilots and design studios to improve the accuracy of the touch captures (e.g., not counting rapid double-tapping; counting touches that were not made perfectly within a circle).

We discovered another advantage of using the touch method of responding on the TMT. On the original D-KEFS TMT, we wanted to increase the difficulty level of the task to enhance its sensitivity to mild decline in high-functioning individuals. One method we used to achieve this goal was to place the test stimuli (circled numbers or letters) across two pages instead of one. This feature increased the visual-scanning demands of the task, thereby drawing upon cognitive resources needed to perform the cognitive-shifting aspects of the task. However, on the iPad screen, our visual real estate was significantly reduced compared to the print version. But the touch-the-circle method saved the day. Because the lines are automatically drawn, we could place many of the consecutive target circles far apart, with connecting lines crossing and crisscrossing over existing lines and circles, making for a relatively dense, final roadmap of lines and circles. Our minipilot and pilot studies revealed that we could design the digital TMT to require a significant degree of visual scanning by requiring examinees to complete this complex roadmap of interconnecting lines.

Another advantage that we learned in using the touch method on a digital device was that it overcame the problem commonly seen on print versions of all trail making tests in which the examinee lays their nondominant hand on the paper to anchor it to the table while drawing the lines and, in the process, covers the next target circle. When this occurs, the examinee can spend a considerable amount of time searching for that circle, thereby creating a significant confound in interpreting a low score. The new touch method on the iPad essentially eliminated this problem.

Two Senses Are Better Than One

In our early research studies, we discovered that the digital procedures introduced unforeseen administration challenges; however, they also provided solutions to these issues and enhanced the tests in unexpected ways. For example, in using the stylus, some examinees made multiple rapid touches for each response on tests like the TMT, perhaps to ensure that their responses were being captured by the device. Adding a clicking sound marking the capture of each response greatly reduced this tendency. We also discovered that multisensory stimuli played a crucial role in enhancing the tests. For instance, as explained later, precisely timed auditory and visual stimuli made it possible to develop the new Switching–Distraction condition of the TMT, which systematically assesses the ability to multitask in a distracting environment. Combining visual and auditory feedback also proved effective for ensuring that examinees understood when they made errors. For example, on an earlier pilot version of the new Tower Test, only a visual red X was presented to mark a rule-violation error (e.g., when an examinee places a larger chip on a smaller chip for solid chips). However, some examinees moved the chips so quickly that they failed to notice their errors, even with the visual feedback. To address this, the feedback system was enhanced to incorporate visual, auditory, and motion cues. Now, when an examinee commits a rule-violation error on the Tower Test, a red "X" flashes, a distinct error sound plays, and the incorrectly placed chip briefly shakes to draw attention to the mistake. These additional cues significantly reduced the error rates in rapid responders. Multisensory presentations also played a key role in enhancing examinees' engagement during the tests. For instance, in the Risk-Reward Decision Test—which requires examinees to demonstrate emotional restraint within a horse-racing game—adding sound effects like galloping hooves and the chime of winning money significantly increased emotional involvement. It was not uncommon for examinees to cheer for their chosen horse as it raced across the screen, reflecting heightened immersion in the task. The use of these multisensory procedures was made possible solely by the all-digital format and the freedom to develop the tests without the constraint of also having to create equivalent print versions.

Let the Device Be the Bad Guy

One of the early lessons we learned during design studios and minipilot studies was that an all-digital platform could significantly reduce examiner burden, minimize measurement error, and shift the responsibility of error correction away from the examiner. For example, in all paper-and-pencil versions of the Trail Making Test—including the original D-KEFS—the examiner must remain highly vigilant: monitoring every response, stopping the examinee immediately upon an error, informing them of the mistake, and directing them where to resume. For fast, impulsive responders, it can be challenging to intervene quickly enough to prevent several errors in rapid succession, potentially compromising the standardized administration. Furthermore, repeated corrections from the examiner—especially for examinees who make frequent errors—can strain rapport. In the D-KEFS Advanced Trail Making Test, these issues were addressed by having the digital interface deliver immediate, automated feedback. When an error occurs, the incorrectly selected circle and connecting line turn red, and a white "X" briefly appears on the circle. The examinee is prevented from continuing from the incorrect point, and the last correctly selected circle remains highlighted in blue, indicating where to resume. Similar automated feedback features were incorporated into the D-KEFS Tower Test and Social Sorting Test. In each case, the device—not the examiner—handles all corrections. These changes substantially reduced the demands placed on examiners and helped preserve rapport with examinees.

Keeping Examinees on Track

One of the difficulties in administering print versions of tests like the original D-KEFS Color-Word Interference Test and the other print Stroop tests is keeping track of the items to which the examinee is responding. On these tests, the stimuli are presented on a single page, with rows of colors or printed words to name or read. If an examinee skips one or more item, and especially if they skip an entire row, it can be exceedingly difficult for the examiner to know which responses are correct or incorrect, which in turn can invalidate the entire results. Our first attempt to overcome this problem was to use voice capture to aid examiners in scoring; however, that technology yielded too many speech recognition errors and did not prevent examinees from skipping items or rows. We then conducted a minipilot study (about 30 participants) comparing the display of stimuli in rows on a single screen (the traditional method) versus presenting each stimulus individually and requiring a response before the next stimulus is displayed, an approach not feasible in a print test. The results were unequivocal: The single-stimulus presentation yielded equivalent findings as the single-page presentation and, more importantly, eliminated the problem of examinees skipping items or rows, resulting in a more precise assessment with significantly less measurement error.

Prompts for Prompting

Most examiners are not flawless in delivering standardized prompts precisely when they should be given, especially on complex tests like the original Tower Test where they must simultaneously track and record multiple aspects of the examinee's performance (e.g., first move time, number of moves, errors). With the fully digital format, we learned that this issue could be almost entirely eliminated. That is, on all tests that require a prompt to be read to the examinee at a precise moment (e.g., the first time the examinee makes a particular rule-violation error on the new Tower Test), a notification immediately appears on the practitioner's iPad screen with the exact words for the examiner to read to the examinee. In addition, for most prompts, the client's screen darkens and prevents the examinee from making further responses until the examiner reads the prompt and touches the OK button on the notification. This feature prevents impulsive examinees from continuing to respond and not focus on the prompt being read. In other words, the digital device automatically tracks all test responses, allowing the examiner to focus on other critical aspects of the assessment, such as behavioral observations. It was lessons like this that informed us that a fully digital approach to test development could deliver tasks with a level of precision that was not possible on print versions.

Test Multitasking Skills in the Examinee, Not the Examiner

Executive function tests can be among the most difficult assessment instruments to administer. The paradox is that these tests can require almost as many multitasking skills from the examiner as they do from the examinee. For example, the original D-KEFS Tower Test requires the examiner to record the first move time; count the number of moves as the examinee makes them (which is difficult for examinees who respond rapidly); keep in mind the possible rule-violation errors; spot rule-violation errors when they occur and stop the examinee from proceeding; explain the error the first time it occurs but not on subsequent errors; return the chip to its last location; count the number of rule-violation errors made; remember to read aloud the prompts verbatim when necessary; remember the different discontinuation times across items; and stop the examinee when the time limit is reached. The complexity of administering and scoring this type of task inherently introduces measurement error across examiners. In designing tests like the D-KEFS Advanced Tower Test, we learned that we could use technology to nearly eliminate the multitasking demands on the examiner. For example, we were able to program the D-KEFS Advanced Tower Test so that the vast majority of these administration tasks, and all the scoring, is done automatically, which again decreases measurement error across examiners. Ironically, one of the few drawbacks to the testing procedures that we developed is that they are so easy to administer, examiners sometimes get distracted doing other things during the assessment (e.g., looking at their mobile phones), which can cause them to miss things like reading a prompt when it appears on the practitioner's screen. However, because the examinee cannot respond until the examiner reads the prompt and touches the OK button, sometimes it is the examinee who prompts the examiner (e.g., "Is something supposed to happen here?").

Micro-Response Data Capture

The new, fully digital D-KEFS Advanced tests unveiled an assessment world that the senior author affectionately dubbed "process score heaven." On tests like the D-KEFS Advanced TMT and CWIT, the individual response times are captured to the millisecond and the raw scores for the core and process scores are rounded to the tenth of a second (which keeps the raw scores consistent across iPad models and upgrades). With this new metric at the individual response level, numerous new process scores could be developed, including standard deviation of response times, time to make correct versus incorrect responses, and first half versus second half performance.

These new process scores can aid interpretation. For example, if an examinee makes incorrect responses as fast or faster than correct responses, then this finding may reflect a problem with impulsive responding. In contrast, if an examinee makes incorrect responses significantly slower than correct responses, then this result might reflect a problem with confusion or loss of instructional set. On the CWIT, first-half versus second-half performance can reveal if an examinee exhibits problems with initiation versus sustained attention. Another advantage of this new metric was that the discontinue times of the tests could be significantly shortened. For example, because response times are captured at the individual connection level on the TMT, it was no longer necessary to have examinees complete all the connections on a condition, which allowed for shorter discontinue times. Whereas the discontinue time for the original D-KEFS Number-Letter Switching Condition is 240 seconds, and the discontinue time for the traditional "Trails B" switching condition is 300 seconds, the discontinue time for the new D-KEFS Advanced Number-Letter Switching condition was made significantly shorter (150 seconds) while increasing the range and distribution of the raw scores. The shorter discontinue times can decrease frustration in examinees who are struggling with the task and streamline the overall assessment.

The "Errors as Windows" Lesson

Of the numerous teachings and insights that Edith Kaplan imparted upon her students, this lesson is arguably the most important. Her lifelong work highlighted the importance of conducting careful analyses of the nature and frequency of errors that individuals make while solving cognitive tasks. As Edith often said, "Errors are the clearest windows into brain function." Her early research with Harold Goodglass demonstrated that a careful analysis of the type of paraphasic errors that an individual makes is essential for distinguishing between different language disorders, including Broca's versus Wernicke's aphasia (Goodglass & Kaplan, 1976). Similarly, intrusion analyses on list-learning tests like the CVLT are the key to distinguishing between individuals with different memory disorders, including Alzheimer disease versus Huntington disease (Delis et al., 1991). The same lesson applies to tests of executive functions. For example, on the original D-KEFS Trail Making Test, set-loss errors are more likely to reflect frontal involvement than sequencing errors (McDonald et al., 2005). In addition, on the original D-KEFS Tower Test, rule-violation errors were found to yield 83% sensitivity and 100% specificity in the detection of the presence or absence of frontal lesions (Carey et al., 2008). For these reasons, a key feature of all neuropsychological tests developed within the framework of Edith Kaplan's process approach is to include a careful and comprehensive scoring of the different types and frequency of errors made on the tests and to provide normative data for those scores.

Technology did not teach us this lesson, but early in our research with the D-KEFS Advanced we discovered that digital technology enabled the capture of numerous new error types, thereby opening more windows into brain function and dysfunction. A good example of this lesson comes from the D-KEFS Advanced Tower Test, which requires the examinee to follow several rules while recreating chip arrangements. The rules for the new Tower Test include moving only one chip at a time; never placing a larger chip on a smaller chip for solid-chip items; never placing a smaller chip on a larger chip for striped-chip items; and most importantly, using the fewest number of moves possible to recreate the arrangements. Our initial focus in developing this test was programming the digital interface to capture and score the different types of rule-violation errors (e.g., chip placement errors; moving two chips at a time). However, we then realized that we could go beyond scoring blatant errors and conduct a finer analysis of responses that were technically correct but counterproductive on the Tower Test. That is, the most important requirement of this test is to use spatial planning to recreate the chip arrangements using the fewest number of moves possible (which allows examinees to obtain bonus points). Examinees who are impulsive will often display a trial-and-error approach in which they make responses such as picking up a chip, placing it on a different peg, and then returning it to the original peg. These moves usually do not constitute rule violations because they adhere to the instructions of the test; however, they are always unproductive because they progressively decrease the ability to complete the item in the fewest number of moves possible. On the original (manual) version of the Tower Test, these types of responses are exceedingly difficult to record because the examiner is extremely busy recording so many other types of responses (i.e., first move time, number of moves, number of rule violations, total completion time). However, the new all-digital Tower Test automatically captures and provides three new process scores that reflect these impulsive, unproductive, trial-and-error moves including:

- 0-back moves: The examinee lifts a chip off a table and places it back on the same table.
- 1-back moves: The examinee lifts a chip off a table, places it on a different table, and then returns it to the original table.
- 2-back moves: The examinee lifts a chip off a table, places it on one table, lifts the same chip and places it on another table, and then returns it to the original table.

The new Tower Test also analyzes responses in terms of three levels of accuracy:

- Correct/productive responses: moves that adhere to the rules of the task *and* reduce the number of remaining moves needed to solve the item.
- Correct/unproductive responses: moves that adhere to the rules of the task (i.e., they are not rule violations) but either increase or keep the same number of remaining moves required to complete the target configuration.
- Incorrect/unproductive responses (i.e., rule-violation errors): moves that fail to follow one or more of the chip-moving rules *and* keep the number of remaining moves the same (because the incorrectly moved chip is automatically returned to its last location)

Collectively, these new error analyses can provide insights into why an examinee may be struggling on the test (e.g., poor spatial planning due to impulsive, trial-and-error responding).

Digital technology also enabled a more advanced level of error analysis by allowing us to examine the *relationship* between an examinee's error rate and their response speed. This relationship is referred to as the speed-accuracy tradeoff, which arises because the processing capacity of the human mind is limited when performing complex, timed cognitive tasks. That is, for many complex timed tasks, an inverse relationship exists between the speed and accuracy with which they are solved. Placing too much emphasis on speed when solving a complex task can result in a high error rate (i.e., sacrificing accuracy for speed), whereas placing too much emphasis on accuracy can result in an overly prolonged completion time (i.e., sacrificing speed for accuracy). For these types of tasks, a balance must be achieved between allocating cognitive resources toward speed versus accuracy for optimal performance. The digital interface of the D-KEFS Advanced provided the opportunity to automatically capture data reflecting not only speed and accuracy but also the relationship between them without adding more administration and scoring burden to the examiner.

To date, few neuropsychological tests have incorporated measures that capture speed–accuracy tradeoffs in their scoring systems. Two possible reasons for this are (a) many existing timed tests do not provide standardized scores for error rates (e.g., the Coding and Symbol Search subtests [e.g., Wechsler, 2024], the traditional Trails A and B test [Reitan, 1955]), thereby precluding their ability to measure the accuracy side of the speed–accuracy tradeoff, and (b) even for existing tests that do provide standardized scores for errors (e.g., the original D–KEFS Trail Making Test), those tests often do not elicit enough error responses in the normative sample to provide psychometrically adequate measures of accuracy (i.e., the error measures do not have sufficient range and adequate distribution of scores). However, in developing the D-KEFS Advanced, one of the main objectives was to design the tests to be more cognitively demanding, in part to elicit higher error rates in the normative sample. For example, as noted earlier, the new Trail Making Test has three switching conditions instead of one, and these conditions elicit higher error rates in the normative population, resulting in an overall error score that has a large range and distribution in the normative sample. As another example, the new Tower Test requires cognitive shifting in that examinees must switch between a different problem-solving rule depending on the item type (i.e., items with solid versus striped chips). This switching requirement increased the complexity of the task and yielded a wider range and better distribution of error rates than on the original D-KEFS (i.e., unproductive moves, rule violation errors). With the improved psychometric properties of the error rates on the D-KEFS Advanced, it was feasible to develop new measures of speed–accuracy tradeoff for the Trail Making Test, the Color–Word Interference Test, and the Tower Test. These scores can help assess whether an examinee sacrifices speed for accuracy, sacrifices accuracy for speed, or has impairments in both aspects of performance.

This information, in turn, can better inform recommendations for interventions (e.g., teaching a student with ADHD and impulsive responding to slow down and focus on accuracy).

Harnessing Technology to Probe Mechanisms of Impairment

One of the most exciting aspects of developing the D-KEFS Advanced was the opportunity to leverage digital technology to explore the underlying mechanisms of cognitive impairment. This was possible because we weren't merely transferring print-based tests to a digital format—we were taking full advantage of the processing power of digital platforms to design new, more dynamic assessments. Here, we did some things right, but we also made some notable mistakes.

The D-KEFS Advanced TMT now has three switching conditions instead of one: the standard Number-Letter Switching condition; a new Switching–Distraction condition (which assesses multitasking in a distracting environment); and a new Switching–Working Memory condition (which magnifies the working memory component of multitasking). Our objectives in developing the two new switching conditions were fourfold: (a) increase the cognitive demands of the tests to enhance their clinical sensitivity in detecting subtle to mild cognitive decline; (b) help elucidate the mechanism underlying an examinee's poor performance in multitasking; (c) increase the ecological validity of the tests (e.g., by systematically assessing the effects of distraction on multitasking performance), and (d) increase the error rates in typically functioning individuals so that we could develop new speed-accuracy tradeoff measures using the improved psychometric properties of the component scores.

Multitasking on the TMT can be thought of as having three executive-function components: cognitive shifting, response inhibition, and working memory. On the TMT, cognitive shifting is obviously needed to rapidly switch between two automatized (overlearned) sequences (numbers and letters). Response inhibition is needed to inhibit impulsive responding to prepotent stimuli. For example, after making a connection from 3 to C, the C response automatically activates the overlearned semantic network of letters and the thought of D is triggered, which must be inhibited to switch to the next correct number (i.e., 4). Working memory is needed on the TMT to hold several variables in mind simultaneously while performing the task (e.g., which number or letter in the sequence to touch next while visually scanning for that number or letter; holding both sequences in mind while switching between them). Accordingly, we wanted to include three switching conditions that would assist in identifying the underlying mechanism of a multitasking impairment on the TMT. The new Switching–Distraction condition selectively magnifies the next prepotent response that must be inhibited, which helps assess if an examinee has a disproportionate deficit in multitasking when the response inhibition demands of the task are increased. Similarly, the new Switching–Working Memory condition selectively magnifies the working memory demands of the test by having the connecting lines disappear as soon as each line is made. The senior author tested an individual who had suffered a severe TBI resulting in encoding/storage memory deficits for both verbal and nonverbal material and who, on the D-KEFS Advanced TMT, performed significantly worse on the Switching–Working Memory condition compared to the other two switching conditions. Thus, it could be concluded that a primary reason this individual struggled in multitasking was because of a deficit in working memory. Importantly, if we had to include an equivalent print version of the TMT, it would not have been possible to develop these two new, dynamic, switching tasks.

The "Glitz" Lesson

This lesson highlights one of the early mistakes we made. As noted earlier, we developed the new Switching–Distraction condition in part to address the common criticism of neuropsychological tests: They occur in a quiet, structured setting. An individual may perform normally in this setting and yet have difficulty in real-world settings that are replete with distractions (e.g., taking a test in a noisy classroom; remaining focused on work assignments in a busy office setting). To address this concern, we wanted to design a test that requires the same multitasking skills as the classic number-letter switching task, but with audio and visual distractions occurring during the task. But we also learned a very valuable lesson in designing this task. Digital technology allowed us to develop a test that, at face value, had ecological validity by including real-world distracting stimuli; however, what was "flashy" and "really cool" did not always translate to better clinical utility. Specifically, for our first year in trying to develop this task, we tried using a number of different real-world distracting stimuli, including people talking in the background, phones randomly ringing, traffic and construction sounds, even a voice saying a constant string of random numbers and letters while the examinee performed the switching task. A consistent finding from our early studies was that, when using these real-world distracting stimuli, examinees did not perform disproportionately worse on the Switching–Distraction condition compared to the classic number–letter switching task, indicating that the stimuli on the iPad screen were not significantly distracting. We then tried using more extreme forms of distracting stimuli, including visual images of flashing lights moving across the screen; fireworks bursting on the screen; cartoon figures flying across the screen; and images of objects and people appearing and disappearing on the screen. Again, our studies failed to find disproportionately lower performance when using these extreme distracting stimuli. There was one participant, an 83-year-old man, who, after taking an early version of the Switching–Distraction condition, said, "These things on the screen are kind of silly," and the group results confirmed his reaction. Ecologically realistic distracting stimuli (e.g., people talking, phones ringing; fireworks bursting) did not significantly impact performance and did not translate to more sensitive neuropsychological measures. At one point, we considered dropping the Switching–Distraction condition because the data did not support its inclusion as a more difficult or clinically useful task than the Number–Letter Switching condition.

Around this time, we discovered an invaluable lesson. We had been so enthralled by the glitz of digital technology that we forgot our roots: principles of brain–behavior relationships. The classic Stroop effect provided the insight that we needed. We developed a new distracting task in which, following each correct response, a single, precisely timed distracting stimulus is presented both auditorily and visually on the screen. The distracting stimuli are presented immediately after each correct connection is made, with each distracting stimulus preselected to magnify the next prepotent (i.e., incorrect) response that needs to be inhibited. For example, when an examinee touches the 3 circle, the examinee's semantic network automatically triggers the thought of 4 (i.e., the prepotent response), which must be inhibited to touch the C circle. In the Switching–Distraction condition, after the examinee correctly touches the 3 circle, a loud voice says the next prepotent (i.e., incorrect) response that should be inhibited (i.e., 4) and a 4 (that is not in a circle) also suddenly appears visually on the stimulus near the path for the next correct response. The examinee is instructed to ignore any numbers or letters they hear or that appear on the screen that are not in a circle and to continue switching between connecting the circled numbers and letters in order. Finally, the results from our subsequent research studies confirmed that this method of distraction made the Switching–Distraction condition significantly more difficult than the Number–Letter Switching condition.

In pilot studies involving this new Switching–Distraction task, a few high-ability participants adopted a strategy of mentally reframing the distracting stimuli as the next response *not* to make, thereby turning the distracting stimuli into a compensatory tool to help inhibit generating set-loss errors. Therefore, two distracting stimuli were added: one about one third of the way through the test and the other about two thirds of the way through in which the distracting stimulus *was* the next correct response to make. The subsequent pilot study confirmed that this change discouraged examinees from relying on the distracting stimuli as a cue of how not to respond; the final version incorporated these distracting stimuli.

The ultimate lesson that we learned here was that the dazzle of digital technology could lead us astray if we forgot what is most important: principles of brain–behavior relationships. However, technology combined with an appreciation of over 100 years of neuropsychological research could result in powerful new assessment instruments that would be impossible to develop using paper-and-pencil methods (e.g., presenting the precisely timed stimuli that magnified the next prepotent response that had to be inhibited).

The "Sweet Zone" Lesson

This lesson was arguably the most painful (and most expensive) one we learned. In developing the new tests, we quickly realized that digital technology allowed us to easily develop extraordinarily complex tasks. And it is always important to strive to develop more cognitively demanding tasks that have greater sensitivity in detecting subtle to mild cognitive decline, particularly in high functioning individuals. But we also learned that it is possible to go too far in developing complex tasks. Unfortunately, we learned this lesson the hard way when we tried to develop a fourth switching condition for the Trail Making Test. We called this task "Conditional Switching," and it was off the chart on the difficulty scale. It required examinees to switch between numbers and letters for some connections, and to go number to number or letter to letter for other connections depending on different stimulus features. The minipilot, pilot, and tryout studies revealed that examinees could perform the task with a generally good distribution of scores, albeit with considerable difficulty. Our earlier studies had fewer clinical cases, but the results generally suggested good psychometric properties, at least in typically developing individuals. Again, we were so enthralled with this new digital application that we overlooked the lack of clinical data to confirm the utility of this new testing procedure. In fact, we were so enthusiastic about this and the other new tasks we were developing that Pearson applied for—and was granted—patents for them.

This lesson was starkly delivered when, after the completion of the national normative study including testing of the special clinical groups, we closely examined the clinical data. The first two new switching conditions that we developed—Switching–Distraction and Switching–Working Memory—achieved our goal of making the tasks more difficult while also increasing their clinical sensitivity in the clinical groups. But we were dismayed to discover that, while we certainly increased the difficulty level with the Conditional Switching condition, it yielded low effect sizes in our clinical-group studies; that is, the clinical sensitivity of the Conditional Switching condition plummeted, making it appear that the clinical groups improved on the most difficult condition. This finding really hurt because this condition was our pride and joy. We then looked closely at the data, and we realized that the test was so difficult that, even for age groups that are at their peak of executive functioning (i.e., ages 18 to 29), not only did their mean raw completion times become significantly slower, but their standard deviations mushroomed. It was probably the very large standard deviations associated with this condition that dealt it a lethal blow in terms of its clinical sensitivity. Sadly, we had to let this task go in its current form, at least for the time being.

In retrospect, the excitement of digital possibilities again lured us from our roots. We forgot a basic principle of psychometrics in which there is a sweet zone between making a cognitive test too easy or too difficult for the general population to minimize both floor and ceiling effects. It is analogous to the Yerkes-Dodson law, where an inverted U-shaped curve exists between performance and arousal, with performance suffering with either too little or too much arousal. For test development, a similar inverted U-curve exists, with clinical sensitivity plotted on the Y-axis and task-difficulty level plotted on the X-axis (see Figure 5.2). Tasks that are either too easy or too difficult for the general population will both compromise clinical sensitivity. The sweet zone of test development is trying to increase both its difficulty level and clinical sensitivity while not falling off the right side of the inverted U-curve. And

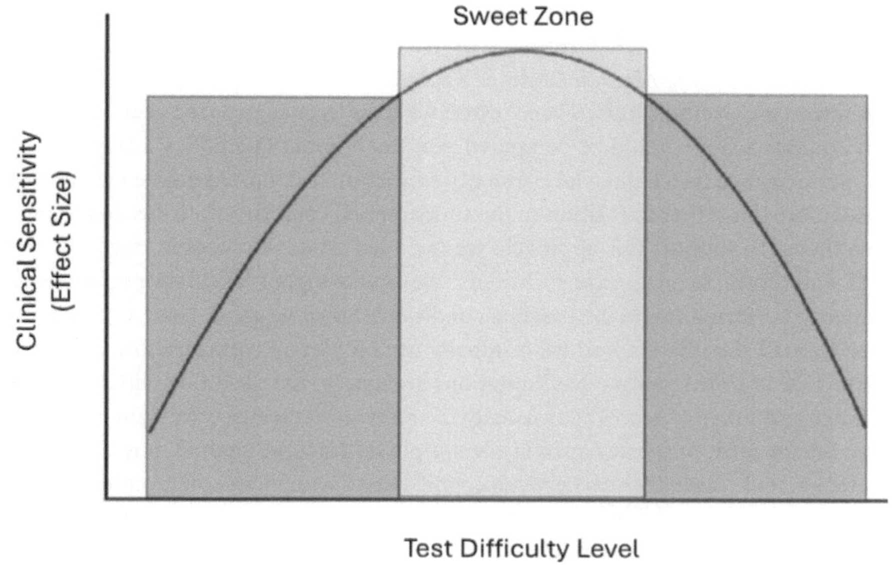

Figure 5.2 Relationship between test difficulty level and clinical sensitivity.

for most of the D-KEFS Advanced tests, we were able to accomplish this goal, resulting in larger effect sizes in our special clinical group studies. But for the Conditional Switching task, we went too far and fell completely off the right side of the inverted curve.

The "Keeping Up with the Norms" Lesson

For the original D-KEFS, only age-referenced scaled scores were provided. The invaluable contributions by Heaton and colleagues in demonstrating the utility of age/education-referenced standardized scores has had a profound influence on all cognitive tests published for the past 20 years, including IQ and memory tests (see Heaton et al., 2009). Accordingly, the D-KEFS Advanced provides age-referenced standardized scores as the default norms for all measures and the option to also generate age/education-referenced standardized scores for the core measures. However, it is important to be aware of the limitations of age/education-referenced scores. That is, some clinical questions are best addressed with age/education referenced scores, but other clinical questions should be addressed only with age-referenced scores and not age/education-referenced scores. For this reason, it is important for a cognitive assessment instrument to provide both types of adjusted standardized scores and for practitioners to be highly selective when using age-referenced versus age/education-referenced scores. It is beyond the score of this chapter to address these complex norming issues here; however, detailed guidance on the appropriate use of age-referenced versus age/education-referenced scores is provided in Chapter 2 of the *D-KEFS Advanced Manual* (Delis & Kaplan, 2025).

Another important norms-related lesson we have learned over the years concerns how contrast scores should be computed. For the original D-KEFS, we emphasized that performance on a higher-level executive function task should not be interpreted in isolation, but rather in relation to the fundamental cognitive skills needed to perform them. To support this approach, we included contrast scores in tasks like the TMT and CWIT to encourage examiners to evaluate higher-level task performance relative to performance on the baseline conditions. So far so good. However, we have since learned that the method we originally used to derive contrast scores—simple subtraction of scaled scores—has limitations because (a) the condition with the larger variance and range of scores (i.e., usually the more difficult executive-function task) accounts for most of the variance in the simple subtraction method, and (b) larger discrepancies in scaled scores between cognitive tasks are more common in the normative sample for individuals with overall above-average or below-average abilities than individuals with average-level abilities (McGee et al., 2009). While the individual scaled scores for each task help to correct some of these problems, a direct comparison of the two scores can be misleading, especially when performance on the baseline or less demanding task falls outside the average range. To empirically correct for these problems, the D-KEFS Advanced provides regression-based contrast scores. These scores yield a single scaled score that addresses the interpretive question: Given an examinee's level of performance (e.g., average, above average, below average) on the baseline (i.e., less demanding) cognitive task, is their performance on the more difficult (i.e., complex) task above, at, or below the predicted level? These contrast scores allow practitioners to empirically compare performance across tasks even for examinees whose overall ability levels reside at either end of the bell curve.

The "Connection Anxiety" Lesson

Range anxiety can make people hesitant to purchase an all-electric car. Similarly, connection anxiety can make psychologists hesitant to take the plunge in adopting all-digital cognitive tests into their practice for fear of losing test data. Ironically, the senior author was initially hesitant to incorporate the existing Q-interactive versions of tests like the WAIS-IV, WMS-IV, and original D-KEFS into his private practice due to connection anxiety. Meanwhile, our research group was striving to develop state-of-the-art digital tests for the Q-interactive platform. Fortunately, over the past several years, the Q-Interactive team has been successfully tackling this problem, consistently developing stronger functionality and connections between the practitioner's and client's iPads. For instance, if a disconnection occurs during administration, the client's iPad will continue to function and capture and store responses. Once the two devices are reconnected, all of the data in the client's iPad is synced back to the practitioner's iPad. Of course, it's impossible to fully prevent the client's iPad from shutting down—for example, due to a depleted battery. When this occurs, the tests can still be resumed once the problem has been fixed, although some items may need to be readministered and some data may be lost. Taking simple precautions like making sure the iPads are fully charged before a testing session helped to ensure connection. Precautions were also implemented to help avoid this situation, including a notification on the practitioner's iPad upon logging into the Pearson Assess app to let the examiner know of the connection status of the two iPads prior to the start of testing and alerts on the practitioner's iPad as soon as the battery on either device reaches a dangerously low percentage. Another helpful feature of the Q-Interactive platform is that the tests can be administered without the practitioner's and client's iPads being connected to a Wi-Fi network. Wi-Fi has to be turned on, but they do not need to be connected to a specific network during administration. A Wi-Fi tether is needed between the two iPads, but even if that connection is temporarily lost, the test data on the client's iPad are preserved. An encouraging lesson that we learned from our national normative study of the D-KEFS Advanced was that it was rare for a connection problem to occur, and in most cases the devices quickly reconnected without a loss of test data. There came a point when the senior author realized that print versions of tests can also trigger their fair share of anxiety in terms of losing valid test data (e.g., when an examinee skips items or rows on the Color-Word Interference Test; when an examinee sorts two cards stuck together on the Wisconsin Card Sorting Test; when an examinee covers the next target circle with their hand on the Trail Making Test; when an examiner is too late in stopping an examinee from making several rapid errors on the Trail Making Test or Tower Test; when an examiner is delayed in giving a prompt or stopping an examinee when the time limit is reached on a number of tests). The lesson that we learned here is that there is always some anxiety about losing test data, but the fully digital tests can provide a level of safety and precision that is at least comparable to if not better than their print counterparts.

The "Share the Love (aka Data)" Lesson

The advent of the Internet and cloud-based storage has ushered in a new era of research in which neuroscientists across disciplines can now gain access to massive databases containing cognitive, neuroimaging, and biomarker data from thousands of participants. These databases allow researchers who have limited access to clinical populations, including psychologists working in academic settings without medical schools or in private practice, to conduct sophisticated studies. One example of this approach is the current collaboration between the National Neuropsychology Network (NNN; supported by NIH [R01MH118514], Robert M. Bilder, PhD, Overall Principal Investigator) and Pearson Assessments. In this program, Pearson has created an application programming interface (API) that connects their portals for digital data collection through Q-interactive or Q-global with the NNN database, which in turn prepares these and other data collected at NNN sites and shares these data publicly via the NIMH Data Archive. As part of this collaboration with the NNN, Pearson created a "Research ID" field within Q-interactive that enables research data to be shared after removal of individually identifying information. Examples of tests currently available for this database are the Wechsler IQ and memory scales, CVLT3, and the original D-KEFS tests when they are administered and/or scored on Q-interactive. This model has been followed by the NNN to examine measurement invariance and compare the factor structures of WAIS-IV, WMS-IV, CVLT3, and original D-KEFS data from the NNN clinical samples with the original standardization sample results (see Bilder et al., 2023; Loring et al., 2021). The D-KEFS Advanced tests will soon be added to this program.

Objectives and Clinical Sensitivity of the Six Tests of the D-KEFS Advanced

For the remainder of this chapter, we present a summary of the specific objectives that we tried to achieve in developing each of the six tests of the D-KEFS Advanced. We also provide a brief summary of the results from our clinical group studies, which analyzed the effect sizes (clinical sensitivity) of the new tests in identifying deficits in children with ADHD, specific learning disorder—mathematics, or ASD; adults with moderate to severe TBIs; and older adults with MCI. For more details and results of these clinical group studies, see Chapter 3 of the *D-KEFS Advanced Manual* (Delis & Kaplan, 2025).

Objectives in Developing the D-KEFS Advanced Trail Making Test (TMT)

The D-KEFS Advanced presented an exciting opportunity to harness digital technology to provide a more sensitive and sophisticated assessment of multitasking. The goals in developing the new TMT included the following objectives.

Raise the Ceiling

We attempted to increase the cognitive demands of the new TMT to make it more sensitive to subtle to mild cognitive decline while also maintaining high clinical sensitivity. As discussed earlier, the Conditional Switching condition had to be dropped because we went too far on the difficulty level, compromising its clinical sensitivity.

However, the two other new switching conditions—Switching–Distraction and Switching–Working Memory—and the numerous new process scores that we added to the tests did achieve our sweet-zone goal of increasing both the difficulty level and clinical sensitivity of the tests (see Chapter 3 of the *D-KEFS Advanced Manual*).

Identify the Mechanism of Impaired Multitasking

As discussed previously, three key executive function skills are needed for multitasking: (1) cognitive shifting, (2) inhibition of responses to prepotent stimuli, and (3) working memory. The three switching conditions of the TMT were designed to assist the examiner in empirically assessing the relative integrity of these higher-level abilities and how they may be impacting multitasking skills.

Formally Assess Systematic Distraction

As noted earlier, a criticism of existing executive function tests is that the assessment occurs in a structured, quiet environment, whereas the real world often presents visual and auditory distractions. The new TMT Switching–Distraction condition systematically assesses the effect of visual and auditory distracting stimuli on the individual's ability to perform multitasking.

Elevate the Process Approach to Cognitive Assessment

On the TMT, new core and process scores were developed to enhance the measurement of both the fundamental abilities contributing to successful performance of the tasks and higher executive functions. The primary measure is the time to make each individual correct connection rather than the time to make all the connections on a condition (i.e., the measure used on the traditional print versions). This new scoring method resulted in several advantages: (a) more precise measurement of responses (i.e., 0.1 second), (b) a wider range of raw scores across the full ability range, which expanded both the floor and ceiling, and (c) development of new process scores (e.g., standard deviation of connection times, new error types).

Incorporate Speed–Accuracy Tradeoff Measures

Like many timed tasks, the instructions of the TMT emphasize the importance of responding both quickly and accurately (e.g., work as fast as you can without making mistakes). The fully digital format of the TMT enabled the development of scores that analyze the relationship between an examinee's speed and accuracy of responding. These scores can help assess whether an examinee sacrifices speed for accuracy, sacrifices accuracy for speed, or has impairments in both aspects of performance.

Decrease Motor Demands

On the new TMT, the examinee uses a stylus to touch circles on the client screen, and the lines are automatically generated. This procedure decreases the motor demands of the task, thereby minimizing the confounding effects that peripheral or central motor problems may exert on cognitive test performance.

Lower the Floor and Decrease Frustration

Because the primary measure is the time to make individual connections, the TMT uses significantly shorter discontinuation times than the original version while also lowering the floor (i.e., there is no longer a need to wait for an examinee to complete all the connections). The shorter discontinuation times on all conditions streamline the overall assessment time and also reduce the frustration that individuals who are struggling on the task often experience. In addition, after administration of each switching condition on the new TMT, the examiner is instantly provided with the examinee's core scaled score for that condition and all other completed conditions, which can help the examiner determine whether the more difficult switching conditions need to be administered.

Ease Administration and Scoring Requirements and Lower Measurement Error

As discussed earlier, on the print versions of traditional trail making tests, the examiner must be vigilant to stop an examinee as soon as they make an error and tell them to return to the last correct circle, which can be difficult for rapid impulsive responders. On the new TMT, the all-digital format prevents this problem from occurring. Examinees receive immediate visual feedback when they make an incorrect connection (i.e., the circle and connecting line turn red, and a white X briefly appears on the circle). All core and process scores, including individual response times scored to the tenth of a second (i.e., 0.1) level and error types, are automatically captured by the digital interface. The Score Report is fully automated; it provides instant raw and age-referenced standardized scores for the numerous core and process measures and includes optional age/education-referenced standard scores for several of the core and index measures.

The D-KEFS Advanced TMT Complements and Does Not Replace the Original D–KEFS TMT

An advantage of the original D–KEFS Trail Making Test is that it provides a direct assessment of two basic component skills needed to perform the switching task: visual scanning and motor speed. Because most examinees perform well on those two conditions, they were not included on the D-KEFS Advanced TMT (which helped to streamline the overall testing time for most examinees). However, if an examinee performs below expectations on the D-KEFS Advanced TMT Number Sequencing and Letter Sequencing conditions, one option is to use the original D–KEFS Visual Scanning and Motor Speed conditions to assess whether the examinee's basic sequencing difficulties may be related, at least in part, to an impairment in these fundamental skills.

Clinical Sensitivity of the D-KEFS Advanced TMT

The new TMT was administered to 160 children and adults as part of the D-KEFS Advanced special clinical group studies, and Cohen's d was used to analyze how many standard deviations apart the means of the two groups were controlling for sample variance. The studies revealed that the TMT yielded large effect sizes in identifying deficits in adults with moderate to severe TBIs and children with ASD. In addition, moderate effect sizes were found in children with ADHD or specific learning disorder–mathematics (SLD–Math). The finding of a moderate effect size in children with ADHD is notable, given the elusiveness of this clinical group in displaying consistent cognitive deficits. See Chapter 3 of the test manual for details of these studies and tables displaying the effect sizes and *p* values of these analyses for the TMT.

Objectives in Developing the D-KEFS Advanced Color-Word Interference Test (CWIT)

The all-digital format of the CWIT created exciting opportunities to enhance all aspects of this classic testing procedure. The goals in developing the CWIT included the following objectives.

Raise the Ceiling

As with all of the D-KEFS Advanced tests, we sought to increase the cognitive demands of the CWIT to be more sensitive to subtle to mild declines in individuals with high premorbid executive functions while maintaining high clinical sensitivity. For the CWIT, this goal was accomplished in two ways.

First, the response method was changed. The examinee no longer verbalizes the correct response but rather touches one of three words printed in black letters at the bottom of the client screen that denotes the correct response. Although this response method makes the two baseline conditions easier in terms of bypassing motor articulation and word-finding demands (and therefore helps to lower the floor), it also makes the Inhibition condition and half of the items on the Inhibition/Switching condition more difficult by increasing the prepotency of the stimulus that must be inhibited (i.e., the reading response). Specifically, for the Inhibition condition, the stimulus word at the top of the client screen, which must be inhibited, is also visually displayed at the bottom of the client screen as one of the three possible response choices. This visual display of the incorrect response, which does not occur on traditional Stroop tasks—including the original D-KEFS CWIT—magnifies the prepotency of that response and results in a greater stimulus pull, especially for individuals who are prone to make stimulus-bound responses.

Second, the Inhibition/Switching condition incorporates a new method to signal when the examinee should switch between identifying the color of the letters (the more demanding task because of the need for inhibition) versus identifying the printed word (the less demanding task because of the greater prepotency in reading words). This method was designed to create greater interference or difficulty when the examinee was responding to the less demanding task of identifying the printed word. In the original D-KEFS CWIT, the signal to switch response type was the presence or absence of a box surrounding the word. However, in the new CWIT, all the target stimuli are displayed inside a box at the top of the client screen. The signal developed for the new CWIT to switch response type is whether the box on top has a white interior (which signals to identify the color of the letters) or a red, green, or blue interior (which signals to identify the printed word). For example, if the target stimulus on top is the printed word red with blue letters and this stimulus is inside a blue box, the correct response is to identify the printed word red; however, the extra blue color shown in the box on top increases the prepotency of responding to blue in general and makes blue more difficult to inhibit in order to correctly select the word red at the bottom. Pilot studies confirmed the increased sensitivity of these new procedures in detecting problems in the Inhibition and Inhibition/Switching conditions (see also Chapter 3 of the *D-KEFS Advanced Manual*).

Lower the Floor and Decrease Frustration

On the new CWIT, the examinee uses a stylus to touch the correct response on the client screen. Early studies revealed that, for individuals with speech articulation or word-finding problems, this method was significantly easier than saying each response aloud (which is required by the other clinical Stroop tests, including the original D-KEFS CWIT). By bypassing articulation and word-finding problems, this method reduces floor effects caused by those problems and provides a more direct assessment of the higher-level executive functions required by the Inhibition and Inhibition/Switching conditions without the confounding effects of those difficulties. In addition, on the new CWIT, the primary measure (i.e., net correct responses) is the number of correct responses minus the number of incorrect responses made within a set time period for each condition. Because all examinees are administered the test items for the same amount of time (analogous to other tests, such as the Wechsler Coding and Symbol Search subtests [e.g., Wechsler 2014, 2024]), the discontinue times were made significantly shorter on three of the four conditions of the new CWIT compared to the original version. This can decrease frustration in examinees who are struggling on the test.

Elevate the Process Approach to Cognitive Assessment

The primary measure for the new CWIT is the number of correct responses minus the number of incorrect responses (i.e., net correct responses) made within a set time for each condition. Because this measure integrates accurate and inaccurate responses into a single score, it provides a better global performance measure by including important process data (i.e., error rate). In contrast, the original D–KEFS CWIT yields only separate scores for correct versus incorrect responses, and therefore it does not provide as sensitive a global measure. In addition, the digital interface of the CWIT captures the latency to make each response. New individual response-time process scores were developed to help uncover the reasons for a low overall performance on the test. For example, standard scores are derived for the mean time to make correct versus incorrect responses; these scores provide insight into why error responses are occurring (e.g., whether an incorrect response is related to impulsivity versus confusion). Process scores are also generated for first-half and second-half performance to provide an assessment of initiation and sustained attention over time.

Incorporate Speed–Accuracy Tradeoff Measures

Like many executive function tests, the CWIT requires the examinee to work quickly and accurately while adhering to complex instructional rules. The all-digital format of the CWIT enabled the development of new process measures that break down performance into speed and accuracy components. These scores can help assess whether an examinee sacrifices speed for accuracy, sacrifices accuracy for speed, or has weaknesses in both aspects of performance. This information, in turn, can better inform recommendations for interventions.

Provide a Screening Measure for Continuous Performance Testing (CPT)

The two baseline conditions of the CWIT require sustained rapid responding while completing a relatively easy, monotonous task similar to commonly used CPTs. The duration of the Color Identification and Word Identification conditions is significantly shorter than traditional CPTs (i.e., 120 seconds for the combined baseline conditions of the new CWIT compared to 10–15 minutes for traditional CPTs); however, the CWIT baseline conditions can serve as a brief sustained-attention screener. In fact, results from the clinical groups in the D-KEFS Advanced standardization revealed that the participants with ADHD scored significantly lower on the combined Color and Word Identification index measure compared to matched control participants, with moderate effect sizes (see Chapter 3). If an examinee obtains a below-average scaled score on the combined baseline conditions of the CWIT, then administering a formal CPT measure may be warranted.

Ease Administration and Scoring Requirements and Lower Measurement Error

As discussed earlier, on print versions of the various Stroop tests, including the original D–KEFS CWIT, stimuli are presented in several rows on a single page. This method can result in examinees skipping items or rows, which makes capturing, coding, and correcting responses very difficult for examiners (especially for examinees who respond rapidly) and can result in greater measurement error. On the new CWIT, because stimuli are presented individually, the problem of examinees skipping items or rows is eliminated, thereby reducing measurement error. In addition, responses are automatically captured and scored by the digital platform (i.e., correct responses, errors, error types, individual response times to the tenth of a second). This automated scoring also reduces measurement error and frees the examiner to observe the examinee's behavior while taking a complex test like the CWIT.

Clinical Sensitivity of the D-KEFS Advanced CWIT

The new CWIT was administered to children and adults as part of the D-KEFS Advanced special group studies, and Cohen's d was used to analyze how many standard deviations apart the means of the two groups were controlling for sample variance. The studies revealed that, although several of the D-KEFS Advanced tests were sensitive to the detection of cognitive deficits in children with ADHD, the CWIT was the most sensitive measure, with Condition 3 yielding a large effect size (which is an unusual finding in this clinical group when using performance-based cognitive tests). This result likely occurred because Condition 3 of the CWIT requires sustained attention, processing speed, and response inhibition, all of which can be affected in ADHD. The CWIT also yielded large to very large effect sizes in detecting cognitive deficits in adults with TBI and moderate to large effect sizes in children with ASD. See Chapter 3 of the *D-KEFS Advanced Manual* for details of these studies and tables displaying the effect sizes and *p* values of these comparisons for the various CWIT measures.

Objectives in Developing the D-KEFS Advanced Tower Test (TWR)

The D-KEFS Advanced presented an exciting opportunity to incorporate findings from over 20 years of research and clinical practice on the original D–KEFS Tower Test to improve the test. Although the original D–KEFS Tower Test was found to be sensitive to executive function deficits in several child and adult clinical groups, the test can have ceiling effects in high-functioning examinees, thereby limiting its ability to detect subtle to mild neurocognitive deficits in these individuals. The following objectives guided development of the new TWR.

Raise the Ceiling

For the TWR, this goal was accomplished in several ways:

- The original D–KEFS Tower Test items have the same final arrangement of chips (i.e., the shape of a tower with the largest chip on the bottom and the smallest chip on the top on a *single peg*). With this procedure, once an examinee learns some general heuristic rules of how to move the chips to create a tower, those rules can be easily transferred and implemented to build the larger towers on the more difficult items. In the new TWR, the final target arrangement of chips is scattered across the three different tables; no two items have the same type of final target chip arrangement. Early pilot studies revealed that this method increased the difficulty level of the items, in part because the same basic heuristic rules cannot be used to build the same type of tower across all items.
- A switching component was added to the test in which some items use solid chips and some use striped chips, and a key rule changes depending on the type of chip used on the item (i.e., never place a larger chip on a smaller one for solid chips; never place a smaller chip on a larger chip for striped chips). Early research revealed that this procedure increased the difficulty level and clinical sensitivity of the task.
- The original D–KEFS Tower Test contains only nine items, whereas the TWR consists of 17 items. This increase in items also increased the range of easier items (i.e., lowered the floor) and harder items (i.e., raised the ceiling).

Ease Administration and Scoring Requirements and Lower Measurement Error

As noted previously, the original D-KEFS Tower Test is one of the most challenging tasks for examiners to administer and score. The new fully digital TWR, in contrast, eliminates the need for the examiner to record and score any of the multiple measures. The digital interface automatically captures each move time, the number of moves made, and the type and number of rule violations made, and it scores all the core and process scores. It also automatically provides feedback to the examinee (i.e., with a red X, a shaking chip, and an error sound) each time they make a rule violation error, and, for size-placement errors, it prevents the examinee from making additional responses until the incorrectly placed chip is automatically returned to its last correct position. Additionally, the digital interface provides notifications to the examiner's iPad exactly when a prompt should be provided and what to say, and the examinee cannot respond until the prompt is read and the examiner touches the continue button. Further, the interface automatically stops the examinee from continuing to respond when either the time limit or move limit for each item is reached. Finally, the Score Report automatically provides raw and standardized scores for numerous core and process measures.

Elevate the Process Approach to Cognitive Assessment

The processing capabilities of the digital platform enabled the development of new process scores that illuminate the mechanisms of an examinee's difficulty on the TWR. Process variables that are recorded and scored automatically on the TWR include relative performance on solid chips versus striped chips (which reflects cognitive shifting); number of rule violations; types of rule violation errors (e.g., two-chip move, size-placement error); number of unproductive moves (i.e., moves that follow the rules but do not advance the examinee's arrangement of chips closer to the correct solution, which can reflect problems with spatial planning), and new measures that capture impulsive, trial-and-error responses (i.e., 0-back, 1-back, 2-back moves).

Incorporate Speed–Accuracy Tradeoff Measures

The instructions of most timed tests of processing speed or executive functions, including the TMT and the CWIT, impart equivalent weight to the importance of both the speed and accuracy aspects of the task (e.g., work as fast as you can without making mistakes). The new TWR provides a speed–accuracy tradeoff analysis on a task in which both speed and accuracy are important, but the instructions emphasize that accuracy is more important than speed. That is, for each item, the examinee is told that they should try to use the fewest number of moves possible to solve the task, and they are also told that they have a generous amount of time to accomplish that goal. An examinee's ability to modulate their allocation of cognitive resources to the varying speed versus accuracy demands of different tasks is, in itself, a higher-level cognitive skill. By including new speed–accuracy tradeoff measures on three of the D-KEFS Advanced tests (i.e., the TMT, the CWIT, the TWR), an examiner can assess whether an examinee changes their allocation of cognitive resources to the speed versus accuracy demands of the task depending on the test's instructions.

Decrease Motor Demands

On the original D–KEFS Tower Test, some examinees with motor deficits have difficulty placing the disks on the pegs. In studies with an early version of the all-digital TWR that also used virtual pegs, individuals with motor problems also had difficulty dragging the chips with a stylus and placing them on the pegs. To decrease the motor demands of the task, the interaction was modified so that examinees placed the chips on flat tables rather than pegs. In addition, the digital interface was designed to signal to an examinee when a chip could be placed on a table; when the examinee drags a chip in close proximity to a table, a blue highlight appears immediately above the table to signal that the chip can be released, and it will be automatically placed on the highlighted table. Subsequent studies revealed that these changes reduced the motor demands of the task, thereby providing a more accurate assessment of the cognitive aspects of the test.

Lower the Floor and Decrease Frustration

On the new TWR, a demonstration item and several easier items were added to ensure that examinees understand the basic requirements of the task. In addition, two trials were added to each of the first three items to provide additional practice and feedback. The new TWR, unlike the original D–KEFS Tower Test, incorporates error limits in addition to time limits to discontinue an item. Therefore, administration is discontinued based on either excessive unproductive moves (i.e., examinee reaches the move limit) or slow responding (i.e., examinee reaches the time limit), which provides a more streamlined assessment and decreases frustration for those who are struggling on the test.

Clinical Sensitivity of the D-KEFS Advanced Tower Test

The new TWR was administered to children and adults as part of the D-KEFS Advanced special clinical group studies, and Cohen's d was used to analyze its effect sizes. The findings revealed that the new TWR was the most sensitive measure among the D-KEFS Advanced tests in detecting executive function deficits in children with specific learning disorder–mathematics (SLD–Math), yielding large effect sizes and significant p values. The TWR requires spatial working memory, spatial planning, and spatial problem-solving, all of which are important for solving complex mathematic operations and may help explain why these children have difficulty with math. The TWR also yielded large effect sizes and significant p values in identifying executive function deficits in children with ASD and adults with TBIs.

Objectives in Developing the D-KEFS Advanced Social Sorting Test (SST)

The D-KEFS Advanced Social Sorting Test uses the testing procedures developed by David Grant and Esta Berg in the late 1940s for the Wisconsin Card Sorting Test (WCST) and applies them to real-world stimuli. The SST uses ecologically valid stimuli (i.e., photos of people with different emotional expressions and clothing) to measure problem-solving that requires facial and affect recognition, concept identification, use of feedback, conceptual flexibility, and inhibition of perseverative responses. The SST was developed with several goals in mind.

Raise the Ceiling

Ceiling effects in individuals with high premorbid executive function skills are commonly found on existing executive function tests (including the original D–KEFS Sorting Test and the WCST). For the WCST, the concepts are discrete, high frequency, and easy to identify. This reduces the cognitive demands on the concept identification aspects of the test, making it easier for examinees to focus on the other requirements of the task (e.g., using the right-wrong feedback to isolate which of the high-frequency concepts by which to sort). In contrast, the stimuli on the SST cards have numerous features from which several categories could be derived, making it more difficult to identify the key concepts by which to sort. Consequently, the three target categories on the SST are more difficult to identify than the target categories on the WCST. In addition, unlike the WCST key cards, the SST key cards display numerous incidental features that have the potential to entice examinees to try to sort by them, which results in increased errors (e.g., sorting by the concept of whether a person's mouth is open or shut). Thus, compared to the WCST, the SST places more processing demands on the concept identification aspect of the task, which can make it more difficult to perform the other executive function skills assessed by the test (e.g., feedback utilization, cognitive shifting, inhibition of perseverative responses).

Embrace Ecological Validity

The SST uses photos of real people with real emotional expressions wearing regular clothing. This feature measures how an individual may perform a complex task involving concept identification, feedback utilization, problem-solving, and inhibition in the context of real-world social situations.

Provide an Alternate Form for the WCST

Practice effects are a significant problem with a test like the WCST (Basso et al., 1999, 2001; Calamia et al., 2012). The first time an examinee takes the WCST, they may struggle throughout much of the test, but near the end they may figure out the general principles needed for successful performance (e.g., the rules change without warning). For these examinees, their performance can improve markedly the second time they take the test. This problem is accentuated by the fact that the WCST uses high-frequency categories that are easy to identify. Because one of the goals of the SST is to serve as an alternate form for the WCST, the SST was designed to closely mirror the same procedures developed by Berg and Grant. The SST uses three key categories, just like the WCST, involves 128 cards to sort and follows the same sequence of ambiguous and unambiguous sorts found in the deck of cards and the same sequence of categories reinforced as on the WCST. Practice effects may still occur when the SST is administered after the WCST; however, practice effects are attenuated relative to repeating the WCST across two testing sessions because (a) the sorting concepts are different, (b) the sorting concepts are more difficult to discern on the SST, and (c) the stimuli are so different it may not be recognized as the same task.

Develop a Standardized Score for Global Performance

The traditional scoring variables found on the WCST were developed and validated by researchers in the 1940s and 1950s (Fey, 1951; Grant et al., 1949; Grant & Cost, 1954; Grant & Patel, 1957), and the SST provides almost all those same variables. However, a significant problem with the existing WCST scores is that none of them function as a good measure of global performance. For example, the number of categories completed (i.e., categories that received 10 consecutive correct sorts) is sometimes used as the global measure for the WCST; however, this measure has a severely restricted range (i.e., 0–6). Therefore, the standardized score is best represented as a base rate measure, which has a significant ceiling effect. Sometimes the total number of correct sorts is used as the global measure for the WCST. The problem with this measure is that an examinee can obtain a high number of correct sorts and yet not complete a single series of 10 consecutive correct sorts (e.g., they repeatedly make eight or nine consecutive correct sorts and then switch to a different category). The perseverative error measure is sometimes employed as a global measure of performance, but it shares the same problem as the number of correct sorts (i.e., an examinee can make a high number of correct sorts, make few perseverative errors, but still not complete a single series of 10 consecutive correct sorts). To overcome this problem, a global performance score was created for the SST that integrates three scoring variables into a single measure: number of categories completed, total number of sorts made, and percentage of correct sorts (see Chapter 8 of the *D-KEFS Advanced Manual*). This new score variable, the Global Performance Index (GPI), better captures overall performance than the individual measures developed in the 1940s and 1950s. In addition, in the national normative study, this global measure usually had the highest clinical sensitivity, yielding moderate to large effect sizes in the various child and adult special clinical groups (see Chapter 3 of the *D-KEFS Advanced Manual*).

Ease Administration and Scoring Requirements and Lower Measurement Error

The traditional print version of the WCST is one of the most difficult and challenging cognitive tests to administer and score. During administration, the examiner must attend to multiple variables simultaneously, including tracking and coding the categories used for each sort made, determining whether each sort was correct or incorrect for the active sorting category, providing correct/incorrect feedback, keeping track of the number of consecutive correct sorts made, and remembering when and to which new category to switch when providing feedback. As noted earlier, the more complex a test is to administer and score, the greater the risk of examiner-introduced measurement error. The WCST also has a digital version of the test that is significantly easier to administer and score than the print version. However, normative data were not collected for the digital version but rather were taken from the manual version, and studies have found that the print and digital versions of the WCST yield significantly different results (Feldstein et al., 1999; Steinmetz et al., 2010). The all-digital format of the SST makes it an almost effortless test to administer and the scoring is done automatically; therefore, examiner-introduced measurement error is minimized. Further, there is only one version of the test (i.e., the all-digital SST), and the national normative data for the test were collected using that version.

Lower the Floor and Decrease Frustration

On the WCST, children and adults with moderate to severe executive function impairments sometimes fail to complete even one series of 10 consecutive correct sorts to the first category (i.e., Color). For these examinees, a floor effect can occur, making it difficult to assess levels of below-average performance on the test. In addition, these examinees often experience considerable frustration on the WCST because of frequently hearing the examiner say "wrong" or "incorrect" across the 128 cards. The SST addressed this problem in two ways. First, an instructional prompt was added that increases the likelihood that most examinees will complete at least one series of 10 consecutive correct sorts. If an examinee fails to make 10 consecutive correct sorts to the first target category by Sort 33, the examinee is read a prompt of the first category by which to sort. Pilot studies revealed that this change improved the range of the scores at the bottom of the distribution in the normative and clinical samples and decreased frustration in examinees. Second, another positive feature of the all-digital version of the SST is that the examiner never says to the examinee that they were wrong or incorrect after making a sort. Rather, this feedback is provided visually on the client screen as a red overlay with an X that appears over incorrect sorts and a green overlay with a checkmark that appears over correct sorts. Using visual corrective feedback on the client screen in place of verbal feedback from the examiner is less emotionally laden and reduces the examinees' frustration.

Provide a Test That Complements and Does Not Replace the Original D-KEFS Sorting Test

The original D–KEFS Sorting Test and the SST can be used together to assess different aspects of abstract thinking, problem-solving, and cognitive flexibility. The original D–KEFS Sorting Test was modeled after the sorting tasks developed by Vygotsky (1978) and Goldstein and Scheerer (1941) in the 1930s and 1940s in which the examinee not only performed conceptual sorts but also described the sorting principles they used. The examinee's explanations of how they made sorts usually revealed the reasons they had difficulty on the test, which is not a feature on either the WCST or the SST. The original D–KEFS Sorting Test is best used with examinees who likely have at least mild, and possibly moderate to severe, executive function impairments, and the clinical question is more focused on how the examinee is impaired in these abilities as opposed to whether they have an impairment. In contrast, the SST and the WCST are better suited for detecting whether an examinee has at least mild deficits in these areas of executive functioning. Although the SST and WCST provide numerous process scores that help elucidate the reasons why an examinee may have difficulty on the test, the fact that these procedures do not formally ask the examinee to describe how they made their sorts limits the examiner's ability to understand the examinee's thought process when attempting to solve the task.

Clinical Sensitivity of the D-KEFS Advanced SST

The new SST was administered to children and adults as part of the D-KEFS Advanced special clinical group studies, and Cohen's d was used to analyze the sensitivity of the test measures (effect sizes) in detecting executive function deficits in these clinical populations. Moderate effect sizes, indicating good sensitivity in the detection of cognitive deficits, were found for 10 of the 11 SST measures in children with ADHD. These findings are notable, given the elusiveness of this clinical group in displaying consistent cognitive deficits on performance-based measures. The SST was found to have good to very good sensitivity (moderate to large effect sizes) in identifying executive function deficits in children with SLD–Math; the new Global Performance Index yielded the largest effect size. Moderate effect sizes (good clinical sensitivity) were found when the SST was administered to children with ASD. Finally, the SST was found to have good to very good clinical sensitivity in detecting executive function deficits in adults with TBI; the new Global Performance Index again yielded the largest effect size, and the traditional card-sorting measures (e.g., perseverative errors) yielded moderate effect sizes. See Chapter 3 of the *D-KEFS Advanced Manual* for details of these results.

Objectives in Developing the D-KEFS Advanced Risk-Reward Decision Test (RISK)

The RISK is presented in the context of a virtual horse racing game that involves 60 races (i.e., trials) in which the examinee attempts to maximize gains while minimizing losses. For each race, the client's iPad displays three horses on the left side of the screen, with each horse in its own horizontal lane, a finish line on the right side, and the different amounts of money each horse can win. The three horses begin each race at varying distances from the finish line. The bottom horse always starts closest to the finish line and therefore has the greatest odds of winning but offers the least amount of money if it wins. The top horse always starts farthest from the finish line and therefore has the least chance of winning but offers the most money if it wins. The middle horse always starts in between the two other horses and offers an intermediate payout. This visual information, which conveys the gain-loss odds of the three bets, is also explained in the instructions provided to examinees. In the early years of developing this test, we also included an equivalent frog-racing game for children in which the examinee earns points rather than money. However, early pilot and tryout studies revealed that this type of risk-reward decision task yielded results that were difficult to explain in the child groups (i.e., they were highly variable); therefore, the RISK was developed for and normed only on adults, ages 19 to 90.

The goals in designing the RISK included the following objectives.

Expand Construct Coverage by Assessing Hot and Cold Executive Functions in the Same Task

The RISK expands the scope of the assessment of executive functioning in the D-KEFS by including a test that requires both cold and hot executive functioning for successful performance. That is, the RISK requires some skills that align closer to cold executive functions (i.e., primarily cognitive) and others that align closer to hot executive functions (i.e., they can be influenced by emotional factors).

Regarding the cold executive functions, the RISK has a problem-solving component in which the examinee must use the win/loss feedback provided after each race to figure out which risk-reward choice will ultimately yield the largest long-term gain. That is, at the beginning of the test, the examinee is unaware of which risk-reward strategy—the high-risk/high-reward, middle-risk/middle-reward, or low-risk/low-reward choice—will provide the best long-term outcome. The examinee must use the win/loss feedback provided after each race to decipher which strategy to adopt. The RISK also requires the cold executive function of abstract reasoning (i.e., trend analysis). This skill comes into play, given how feedback is provided on the RISK, which differs from the way feedback is provided on tasks like the SST and WCST. Although the feedback used on all three of these tests (i.e., the RISK, SST, and WCST) is often ambiguous, it is ambiguous for different reasons. On the SST and WCST, a single right/wrong feedback can reinforce up to three categories simultaneously, but the feedback is always accurate for at least one of the categories on the sorted card. The simultaneous reinforcement of up to three concepts is an intrinsic feature of those tests specifically designed to try to derail examinees from continuing to make sorts according to the active target principle and entice them to make sorts to an incorrect principle that just received reinforcement (which requires inhibitory skills to resist making those derailment responses). In contrast, on the RISK, the feedback always reinforces only one decision choice at a time (i.e., only one horse can win each race); however, feedback ambiguity is built into the RISK because the immediate positive and negative feedback (i.e., wins and losses) does not always align with the best (i.e., most profitable) long-term strategy. That is, even though one of the horse selections is the best choice to make consistently throughout the task, that selection sometimes yields losses. In addition, selecting one of the other two horses sometimes results in gains (i.e., positive feedback). The intermittent nature of this feedback requires abstract reasoning skills to realize that a key strategy for solving this task is to decipher *trends* in the feedback provided across multiple trials and to not be tempted to select a riskier horse simply because it was the last one to win.

The RISK also assesses components of hot executive functioning because an examinee's risk–reward decisions can be influenced by emotional factors. Two emotional factors that can influence decision-making performance on the RISK are emotional inhibition (to avoid making impulsive decisions) and risk aversion. The ability to flexibly modulate these two hot executive functions—emotional inhibition and risk aversion—is needed to make adaptive and successful decisions across a variety of risk–reward contingencies, including on the RISK. Process scores are provided that assist in assessing the hot executive function components of the test.

Explicitly Clarify the Risk-Reward Contingencies Up Front

One of the most important objectives in developing the RISK was to make the different risk-reward decisions as explicit as possible before examinees begin making decisions. On a test like the Iowa Gambling Test (IGT), examinees are presented with four decks of cards faced down, and they are given no information as to which decks yield high risk-reward outcomes versus low risk-reward outcomes. As a result, the IGT requires a significant, trial-and-error learning and memory component, which results in the test being more cognitively heterogeneous and therefore more difficult to parse the decision-making style from the learning and memory component. In contrast, the initial instructions of the RISK explicitly explain the risk-reward contingencies for each horse both visually (i.e., by the different distances of the horses from the finish line along with the different amounts of money each horse can win) and verbally (e.g., the relative odds of each horse winning and the amounts of money that each horse can win are explained at the start of the test). Early studies revealed that these explicit instructions were needed to ensure examinees understood the different risk-reward contingencies before making decisions, which resulted in a more homogeneous assessment of their risk-reward decision skills.

Increase the Visceral Reactions in the Examinees

In developing the RISK to maximize the hot executive function component, our early studies examined different types of risk-reward decision tasks. The horse-racing format was selected because it elicited strong, observable emotional reactions in many examinees as the horses raced to the finish line. For example, it was not uncommon for examinees to become quite animated and cheer their selected horse as the race unfolded. The visceral pull was enhanced throughout the development by adding sounds (e.g., the galloping hooves; the chime of winning money) and visual rewards (e.g., first-, second-, and third-place ribbons) designed to increase strong emotional reactions. These heightened emotional reactions, in turn, require greater emotional inhibition (i.e., hot executive functioning) in order to make more objective risk-reward decisions.

Enhance Examinee Engagement to Improve Assessment of Cold Executive Functions

As noted earlier, the RISK also assesses the cold executive functions of feedback utilization, problem-solving, and abstract thinking (trend analysis) in a task that is relatively quick to administer, is presented in a game-like format, and is enjoyable for most examinees to take. Other executive function tests like the SST and WCST, which also assess feedback utilization and problem-solving, can be frustrating, especially for examinees who have difficulty on the tasks and receive frequent incorrect (negative) feedback. However, from our early pilot studies to our final national standardization study, we discovered that the vast majority of examinees enjoyed taking the RISK regardless of whether they won or lost money. The test also takes significantly less time to administer than the SST or WCST. Importantly, the RISK was found to yield effect sizes in detecting executive function deficits that were comparable to other executive function tests (see Chapter 3 of the *D-KEFS Advanced Manual*). For this reason, the RISK can be a good test to administer as one of the last tasks in a battery of cognitive tests in order to have a positive end to the session for most examinees.

Embrace Ecological Validity

One of the many positive features of all of the existing risk-reward decision-making tests is that they involve common real-world tasks (e.g., playing cards, blowing up balloons, playing dice). The RISK extends and enhances this tradition by presenting a risk-reward decision test that involves a high degree of audio and visual animation that parallels a real-life experience.

Ease Administration and Scoring Requirements and Lower Measurement Error

Like all of the fully digital D-KEFS Advanced tests, the RISK is an almost effortless task to administer and yields a number of global performance and process scores that are computed automatically.

Clinical Sensitivity of the D-KEFS Advanced Risk-Reward Decision Test (RISK)

As noted earlier, the RISK was administered only to adults, ages 19 to 90 years; therefore, the test was not administered to the children in the D-KEFS Advanced special group studies (i.e., it was not administered to the ADHD, ASD, and LD-Mathematics groups). However, the RISK was found to yield high sensitivity (moderate effect sizes) in adults with TBI. See Chapter 3 of the *D-KEFS Advanced Manual* for details of this study.

Objectives in Developing the D-KEFS Advanced Verbal Fluency Test (VFT)

The D-KEFS Advanced provided an exciting opportunity to make improvements to the original D–KEFS Verbal Fluency Test. The goals in developing the new VFT included the following factors.

Raise the Ceiling by Developing a More Sensitive Switching Condition

Cognitive shifting is a quintessential feature of frontal-lobe functioning. Because of this finding, the original D–KEFS added switching procedures to several tests, including the Color-Word Interference Test, the Verbal Fluency Test, and the Design Fluency Test. Subsequent studies have found that these switching tasks are among the most sensitive clinical measures to brain dysfunction in general and frontal lobe dysfunction in particular (Baldo et al., 2001; Troyer et al., 1998). For example, on the original D-KEFS VFT, the category switching task (Condition 3) is more sensitive to brain dysfunction than single-category fluency (Condition 2). However, observations by the senior author in his clinical and research work and verified in subsequent pilot studies revealed that, while switching between two semantic categories resulted in an improvement in the assessment of verbal fluency over generating words from a single semantic category, the category-switching task had limited sensitivity to frontal involvement. When an examinee switches between two, common semantic categories, those categories reflect overlearned verbal knowledge (i.e., semantic memory); consequently, that verbal information can be accessed and retrieved in a more fluent, automatic way, which lessens the overall cognitive demands of the switching task. In other words, for the general population and most clinical groups, this task errs on being too easy and therefore hovers too much on the left side of the "sweet zone" of the inverted U curve of clinical sensitivity, which can result in a ceiling effect (see later for an exception to this finding). As a sidenote, when designing the original D-KEFS Verbal Fluency Test, the senior author entertained the idea of having examinees switch between semantic and phonemic fluency for the switching condition but then dismissed the idea because, intuitively, he thought the task would be too difficult for examinees. Here's another embedded lesson: in test development, relying solely on intuition can be misleading.

The opportunity to develop a new VFT offered the redemption that was needed to improve this test. On the new switching condition of the D-KEFS Advanced, examinees switch between phonemic fluency and category fluency (i.e., switching between saying words that start with a specific letter and words from a specific semantic category). This change significantly increases the cognitive demands of the switching task because the examinee must have the cognitive flexibility to generate words while shifting between two different mental search strategies (phonemic versus semantic). We also included two trials for the switching condition rather than one, which improves the psychometric properties of the switching scores (i.e., larger range and better distribution). In our minipilot, pilot, and tryout studies, we realized that, for examinees between the ages of 14 and 69, we could extend the sweet zone of test development even further to the right by having them switch between three rules—two letters and one semantic category—which further increased the cognitive demands of the task while improving clinical sensitivity.

Here's a lesson worth slipping in—one the senior author learned as a postdoctoral fellow in neuropsychology at the Boston V.A. Medical Center in the late 1970s. It can be called the "Remember the Classics" lesson and refers to the classic neurobehavioral syndromes that involve focal lesions and that sometimes defy typical patterns of spared and impaired cognitive functions found in other clinical groups. Examples of these syndromes include alexia without agraphia or left hemi-inattention. At that time, the Boston V.A. was the epicenter of neuropsychology and behavioral neurology, with an astonishing convergence of brilliant neuropsychologists and behavioral neurologists, including Edith Kaplan, Harold Goodglass, Nelson Butters, Norman Geschwind, Frank Benson, Jeffrey Cummings, and many others (see Delis, 2010). This lesson was learned when the senior author was presenting a case at neurobehavioral rounds and he casually used the word "easier" to describe a cognitive task. Norman Geschwind—the renowned behavioral neurologist who, with Edith Kaplan, discovered the first case of a human disconnection syndrome, immediately jumped up and declared, "I just don't like the word 'easier' to describe a cognitive task here! What may be easier for the general population and for most patients can be exceedingly difficult for a patient who has a lesion in a particular area of the brain." He was referring to copying versus spontaneously drawing a clock to command, and his point was that, while copying is easier for most patients, it can be harder for the patient who has the classic neurobehavioral syndrome of left hemi-inattention due to a lesion in the right parietal area. And in the case being presented, he was absolutely right: The patient successfully drew a complete clock to command (drawing from semantic memory), but when later asked to copy a clock model, exhibited left-sided neglect and reproduced only the right half of the clock face. Geschwind's direct and no-nonsense teaching style—characteristic of East Coast medical training—was strikingly effective. It wasn't personal, but it taught the interns and fellows neurobehavioral principles that they never forgot (i.e., it required only one-trial learning!). This lesson also applies to the switching condition of the original D-KEFS VFT versus the D-KEFS Advanced VFT. For most patients, the switching condition of the original D-KEFS VFT is easier because, again, it requires cognitive shifting between two overlearned semantic categories. However, for patients with involvement in left mesial temporal regions (e.g., due to a focal stroke or an early Alzheimer's process), which typically disrupts verbal semantic knowledge, they often have disproportionately greater difficulty switching between two semantic categories than switching between a semantic category and a phonemic rule (see Delis & Kaplan, 2025). Here is another example of how the original D-KEFS and D-KEFS Advanced can complement each other. For the early detection of preclinical Alzheimer's disease, the switching condition of the original D-KEFS VFT may be the most effective instrument. However, for most other clinical groups, the new D-KEFS Advanced VFT switching condition may be more sensitive to the detection of subtle to mild decline.

Improve Semantic Categories and Scoring Features

Lexical knowledge in the general population constantly evolves: New words are added, old words fade, nuanced meanings shift, and membership in semantic categories shuffles across cohorts. In addition, words from common categories (e.g., fruits, vegetables) are not only constantly evolving, but they can be especially difficult to precisely subsume within one or the other category because their use in everyday life may contradict their formal dictionary definition. For instance, avocados and tomatoes are often identified as vegetables and are used in a salad with other vegetables but are formally defined as fruits because they have seeds. As another example, zucchini is often served as a vegetable, even though it, too, is formally defined as a fruit because it contains seeds. In the original D–KEFS, Fruits and Vegetables were used as two separate categories on two separate trials, which often created difficulties in scoring. For the D-KEFS Advanced, closely related semantic categories are combined into a single category and used in a single trial, which significantly reduces the problem of how to score the responses.

Another limitation with the original D–KEFS was using Boys' Names (on the standard form) and Girls' Names (on the alternate form) as a type of semantic category. Edith Kaplan postulated that first names would be a clinically useful category to employ because it would minimize the effect of education level on category fluency compared to other semantic categories. However, subsequent research has found that examinees often adopt different response strategies when generating first names; that is, some examinees use a semantic strategy (e.g., people they know), others use a phonemic strategy (e.g., they cluster names that start with the same letter), and still others use a combination of semantic and phonemic strategies (Koren et al., 2005). Other problems with using first names as a semantic category include (1) names are increasingly difficult to score because of the broadening of naming conventions, (2) the distinction between boys' names and girls' names is increasingly fluid, making the scoring rules difficult to apply in a reliable and valid manner, and (3) changing gender naming conventions in the normative population must be addressed. For these reasons, the first name category was dropped completely from the D-KEFS Advanced, and only traditional semantic categories are employed.

The semantic categories used on the new VFT were selected because they (1) are common categories that contain a large range of higher to lower frequency words, and they (2) have been found to minimize scoring difficulties caused by ambiguity in category membership. Finally, rules were added to the VFT instructions that were designed to improve the scoring accuracy of the responses. For instance, for the Animals category, examinees are instructed to generate names of only real animals, whether living or once living, and not make-believe animals (e.g., dragons, unicorns). This instructional rule was added because animated movies, video games, and books frequently introduce names of new fictional animals into the English lexicon, which can be difficult for examiners to score.

Elevate the Process Approach to Cognitive Assessment

The new VFT, like the original version, continues to offer the only clinical version of word fluency tasks that provides normative data not only for total correct words generated but also for process scores (e.g., set-loss and repetition errors). New to the VFT are index scores that provide a global measure of verbal fluency performance including (a) an index score that reflects the combined performance across the Letter Fluency and Category Fluency conditions (which do not require cognitive shifting), (b) a new measure for the Switching Fluency condition that combines the total correct words generated scaled score and the switching accuracy scaled score into a single index score (which provides a better assessment of overall performance on the Switching Fluency condition compared to scoring only the number of the correct responses), and (c) a global index score that reflects performance across all three conditions (i.e., Letter Fluency, Category Fluency, and Switching Fluency).

Ease Administration and Scoring Requirements

The VFT is the only test among the six new measures of the D-KEFS Advanced that requires the examiner to enter the examinee's responses on the iPad and to code the type of response made (correct response; repeated correct response; set-loss error; repeated set-loss error). However, once the responses are entered and coded, the core and process scores are automatically computed and provided in the score report. This technology had already been developed for the original D-KEFS VFT in 2016 as part of the Q-Interactive platform, and it was easy to adopt those procedures for the D-KEFS Advanced. In 2022, before we started the national normative study, we revisited speech-to-text technology to see if it would be a viable tool to use to automatically capture examinees' verbal responses on the VFT, and it still resulted in an unacceptable error rate. However, since then, powerful AI tools have become available that should greatly improve speech-to-text capture. Another advantage of embracing digital technology in cognitive assessment instruments is that, as long as standardized administration procedures are not altered, software upgrades can be made to ease administration and scoring requirements. Hopefully, speech-to-text upgrades can be added to tests like the VFT and the CVLT3 in the future.

Use of an Alternate Form

The original D-KEFS VFT provides both a standard form and an alternate form. However, we discovered early in our work that the new VFT test has surprisingly minimal practice effects on repeat testing, which was confirmed in our standardization test-retest study. Specifically, the test–retest study of the new VFT found essentially no practice effects for the Category Fluency condition and only minimal practice effects (i.e., about 1/6 SD) for the Letter Fluency and Switching Fluency conditions (see Chapter 3 of the *D-KEFS Advanced Manual*). For this reason, the D-KEFS Advanced VFT provides only a standard form. However, if an alternate form is needed for verbal fluency, especially for the Letter Fluency condition, the alternate form from the original D–KEFS can be administered.

Clinical Sensitivity of the D-KEFS Advanced VFT

The new VFT was administered to children and adults as part of the D-KEFS Advanced special clinical group studies, and Cohen's d was used to analyze the clinical sensitivity of the test. The studies revealed that the VFT yielded large effect sizes in identifying deficits in children with ASD, adults with TBIs, and older adults with MCI. The findings from the MCI group were particularly interesting. These participants presented with deficits primarily in memory and not in other cognitive domains, which is a common profile seen in MCI and may reflect early mesial temporal involvement often seen in preclinical Alzheimer's disease (Salmon & Bondi, 2009). On the new VFT, the participants with MCI did not differ significantly from the matched normative group in their Letter Fluency performance, but they did differ significantly in their Category Fluency performance, with a large effect size. In addition, the new Switching Fluency condition yielded moderate effect sizes in distinguishing between the two groups, indicating that the Switching Fluency condition was sensitive but not as sensitive as the Category Fluency condition in identifying deficits in the participants with MCI. This finding may have occurred because the new Switching Fluency task involves in part phonemic fluency, which was found not to be impaired in this group. See Chapter 3 of the test manual for details of these studies and tables displaying the effect sizes and *p* values of these analyses for the VFT.

Conclusion

The development of the D-KEFS Advanced was a long journey replete with its fair share of early mistakes and countless setbacks that required constant regrouping and pivoting. Hopefully the lessons learned will prove helpful for future researchers who undertake the important task of embracing digital technology to enhance and refine our assessment instruments.

References

Baldo, J. V., Shimamura, A. P., Delis, D. C., Kramer, J., & Kaplan, E. (2001). Verbal and design fluency in patients with frontal lobe lesions. *Journal of the International Neuropsychological Society*, *7*(5), 586–596. https://doi.org/10.1017/S1355617701755063

Basso, M. R., Bornstein, R. A., & Lang, J. M. (1999). Practice effects on commonly used measures of executive function across twelve months. *The Clinical Neuropsychologist, 13*(3), 283–292. https://doi.org/10.1076/clin.13.3.283.1743

Basso, M. R., Lowery, N., Ghormley, C., & Bornstein, R. A. (2001). Practice effects on the Wisconsin Card Sorting Test–64 card version across 12 months. *The Clinical Neuropsychologist, 15*(4), 471–478. https://doi.org/10.1076/clin.15.4.471.1883

Bilder, R. M., Widaman, K. F., Bauer, R. M., Drane, D., Loring, D. W., Umfleet, L. G., Reise, S. P., Vannier, L. C., Wahlstrom, D., Fossum, J. L., Wong, E., Enriquez, K., Whelan, F., & Shih, S. (2023). Construct identification in the neuropsychological battery: What are we measuring? *Neuropsychology, 37*(4), 351–372. https://doi.org/10.1037/neu0000832

Calamia, M., Markon, K., & Tranel, D. (2012). Scoring higher the second time around: Meta-analyses of practice effects in neuropsychological assessment. *The Clinical Neuropsychologist, 26*(4), 543–570. https://doi.org/10.1080/13854046.2012.680913

Carey, C. L., Woods, S. P., Damon, J., Halabi, C., Dean, D., Delis, D. C., Miller, B. L., & Kramer, J. H. (2008). Discriminant validity and neuroanatomical correlates of rule monitoring in frontotemporal dementia and Alzheimer's disease. *Neuropsychologia, 46*(4), 1081–1087. https://doi.org/10.1016/j.neuropsychologia.2007.11.001

Delis, D. C. (2010). Edith Kaplan (1924–2009). *American Psychologist, 65*(2), 127–128.

Delis, D. C., & Kaplan, E. (2025). *Delis-Kaplan Executive Function System-Advanced.* NCS Pearson.

Delis, D. C., Kaplan, E., & Kramer, J. H. (2001). *Delis-Kaplan Executive Function System.* NCS Pearson.

Delis, D. C., Massman, P. J., Butters, N., Salmon, D. P., Cermak, L. S., & Kramer, J. H. (1991). Profiles of demented and amnesic patients on the California Verbal Learning Test: Implications for the assessment of memory disorders. *Psychological Assessment: A Journal of Consulting and Clinical Psychology, 3*(1), 19.

Feldstein, S. N., Keller, F. R., Portman, R. E., Durham, R. L., Klebe, K. J., & Davis, H. P. (1999). A comparison of computerized and standard versions of the Wisconsin Card Sorting Test. *The Clinical Neuropsychologist, 13*(3), 303–313. https://doi.org/10.1076/clin.13.3.303.1744

Fey, E. T. (1951). The performance of young schizophrenics and young normals on the Wisconsin Card Sorting Test. *Journal of Consulting Psychology, 15*(4), 311–319. https://doi.org/10.1037/h0061659

Goldstein, K., & Scheerer, M. (1941). Abstract and concrete behavior: An experimental study with special tests. *Psychological Monographs, 53*(2), i–151. https://doi.org/10.1037/h0093487

Goodglass, H., & Kaplan, E. (1976). The Assessment of Aphasia and Related Disorders. Philadelphia, PA: Lea & Febiger.

Grant, D. A., & Berg, E. (1948). A behavioral analysis of degree of reinforcement and ease of shifting to new responses in a Weigl-type card-sorting problem. *Journal of Experimental Psychology, 38*(4), 404–411. https://doi.org/10.1037/h0059831

Grant, D. A., & Cost, J. R. (1954). Continuities and discontinuities in conceptual behavior in a card sorting problem. *The Journal of General Psychology, 50*(2), 237–244. https://doi.org/10.1080/00221309.1954.9710121

Grant, D. A., Jones, O. R., & Tallantis, B. (1949). The relative difficulty of the number, form, and color concepts of a Weigl-type problem. *Journal of Experimental Psychology, 39*(4), 552–557. https://doi.org/10.1037/h0062126

Grant, D. A., & Patel, A. S. (1957). Effect of an electric shock stimulus upon the conceptual behavior of "anxious" and "non-anxious" subjects. *Journal of General Psychology, 57*(2), 247–256. https://doi.org/10.1080/00221309.1957.9920368

Heaton, R. K., Chelune, G. J., Talley, J. L., Kay, G. G., & Curtiss, G. (1993). *Wisconsin Card Sorting Test manual: Revised and expanded.* Psychological Assessment Resources.

Heaton, R. K., Ryan, L., & Grant, I. (2009). Demographic influences and use of demographically corrected norms in neuropsychological assessment. *Neuropsychological Assessment of Neuropsychiatric and Neuromedical Disorders, 3*, 127–155.

Koren, R., Kofman, O., & Berger, A. (2005). Analysis of word clustering in verbal fluency of school-aged children. *Archives of Clinical Neuropsychology, 20*(8), 1087–1104. https://doi.org/10.1016/j.acn.2005.06.012

Loring, D. W., Bauer, R. M., Cavanagh, L., Drane, D. L., Enriquez, K. D., Reise, S. P., Shih, K., Umfleet, L. G., Wahlstrom, D., Whelan, F., Widaman, K. F., Bilder, R. M., and The Nnn Study Group. (2021). Rationale and design of the National Neuropsychology Network. *Journal of the International Neuropsychological Society, 28*(1), 1–11.

Lovell, M. (2004). *ImPACT Version 2.0 clinical user's manual.* http://www.impacttest.com/clients.htm.

McDonald, C. R., Delis, D. C., Norman, M. A., Tecoma, E. S., & Iragui-Madoz, V. J. (2005). Is impairment in set-shifting specific to frontal lobe dysfunction? Evidence from patients with frontal-lobe or temporal-lobe epilepsy. *Journal of the International Neuropsychological Society, 11*(4), 477–481. https://doi.org/10.1017/S1355617705050484

McGee, C. L., Delis, D. C., & Holdnack, J. A. (2009). Cognitive discrepancies in children at the ends of the bell curve: A note of caution for clinical interpretation. *The Clinical Neuropsychologist, 23*(7), 1160–1172. https://doi.org/10.1080/13854040902794995

Powell, D. H., Kaplan, E. F., Whitla, D., Weintraub, S., Catlin, R., & Funkenstein, H. H. (1993). *MicroCog: Assessment of Cognitive Functioning.* The Psychological Corporation.

Reitan, R. M. (1955). The relation of the Trail Making Test to organic brain damage. *Journal of Consulting Psychology, 19*(5), 393–394. https://doi.org/10.1037/h0044509

Salmon, D. P., & Bondi, M. W. (2009). Neuropsychological assessment of dementia. *Annual Review of Psychology, 60*, 257–282. https://doi.org/10.1146/annurev.psych.57.102904.190024

Steinmetz, J.-P., Brunner, M., Loarer, E., & Houssemand, C. (2010). Incomplete psychometric equivalence of scores obtained on the manual and the computer version of the

Wisconsin Card Sorting Test? *Psychological Assessment*, *22*(1), 199–202. https://doi.org/10.1037/a0017661

Troyer, A. K., Moscovitch, M., Winocur, G., Leach, L., & Freedman, M. (1998). Clustering and switching on verbal fluency tests in Alzheimer's and Parkinson's disease. *Journal of the International Neuropsychological Society*, *4*(2), 137–143. https://doi.org/10.1017/s1355617798001374

Vygotsky, L. S., Cole, M., John-Steiner, V., Scribner, S., & Souberman, E. (1978). *Mind in society: The development of higher psychological processes.* Harvard University Press.

Wechsler, D. (2014). *Wechsler Intelligence Scale for Children* (5th ed.). NCS Pearson.

Wechsler, D. (2024). *Wechsler Adult Intelligence Scale* (5th ed.). NCS Pearson.

Weintraub, S., Dikmen, S. S., Heaton, R. K., Tulsky, D. S., Zelazo, P. D., Bauer, P. J., Carlozzi, N.E., Slotkin, J., Blitz, D., Wallner-Allen, K., Fox, N.A., Beaumont, J.L., Mungas, D., Nowinski, C.J., Richler, J., Deocampo, J.A., Anderson, J.E., Manly, J.J., Borosh, B., ... Gershon, R.C. (2013). Cognition assessment using the NIH Toolbox. *Neurology, 80*, S54–S64. DOI: 10.1212/WNL.0b013e3182872ded

6
Technology as an Activity of Daily Living

Conceptual Review and Practice Considerations

David Andrés González, Logan M. Tufty, Devin M. Ulrich, and Jared F. Benge

A neuropsychological evaluation involves more than just measuring cognitive status. Indeed, diagnostic criteria for psychiatric, neurodegenerative, and neurodevelopmental conditions all hinge on how cognitive abilities or difficulties are impacting real-world functional abilities (American Psychiatric Association, 2022; Jack et al., 2024; Litvan et al., 2012). Further, patients and families impacted by neuropsychological disorders frequently identify improving such functional abilities and improving independence and/or decreasing burden on others as key goals for medical and rehabilitative treatments (Tochel et al., 2019).

To these ends, in the 21st century, the ability to function independently and perform daily tasks increasingly requires consideration of technology. While other chapters in this volume focus on how technology can change the nervous system or allow for updated means of assessing cognition, in this section we instead look at how technology is being used in daily life by those we serve, as well as how our assessments of this critical aspect of human behavior are currently limited. We also hope to lay a path for clinicians and researchers to address technological activities of daily living as a routine part of clinical and research practice.

What Are Instrumental Activities of Daily Living?

Activities of daily living (ADLs) bear defining within a framework. Early models in gerontology, such as those of Lawton and Brody (1969), involved hierarchical formulations, ranging from life maintenance, physical self-maintenance, instrumental self-maintenance, effectance motivation (the desire to change our environment), and social engagement. The literature eventually coalesced around basic and instrumental activities of daily living (IADLs) as a focus in medicine, and these respectively entail

David Andrés González et al., *Technology as an Activity of Daily Living*. In: *Technology and Neuropsychology*.
Edited by: Jared F. Benge et al., Oxford University Press. © Oxford University Press (2026).
DOI: 10.1093/9780197814116.003.0006

activities that maintain bodily autonomy (also called physical self-maintenance tasks) and those that facilitate the ability to live independently (Katz, 1983; Lawton & Brody, 1969; Reuben & Solomon, 1989). These models had associated measures to better understand functioning in nursing homes, clinics, and the community. Interestingly, although these formulations acknowledged a higher level of functioning (what Lawton and Brody called effectance and social engagement, and what was later called advanced ADLs), this level of functioning has not been emphasized in medicine due to being considered "luxury" functioning (Reuben & Solomon, 1989). However, such advanced ADLs are critical to life quality and may correspond with earliest indications of cognitive change (Cornelis et al., 2019), such that advanced ADLs should regularly be considered in neuropsychological evaluations.

Although these hierarchical formulations have some heuristic utility in clinical practice, they do not provide a systematic framework to consider the interaction of functioning with health and the environment. The World Health Organization (WHO) approached this need from a biopsychosocial perspective and broadened the understanding of how diseases captured in their International Classification of Disease (ICD) contributed to disablement. This culminated in the International Classification of Functioning, Disability, and Health (ICF). Instead of a single hierarchy, the ICF considers multiple domains of function and context concurrently. The process of functional formulation involves first identifying the body structures and functions that are impaired. Subsequently, there is consideration of activity limitations and participation restrictions that result from those impairments. This consideration is aided by a checklist and core sets (see https://www.who.int/publications/m/item/icf-checklist) that delineate functional domains (e.g., communication, self-care, domestic life, occupation, interpersonal interactions, community and civic life) and activities within each of these domains and a scale for rating the extent of difficulty. Finally, the ICF considers environmental factors (e.g., services, attitudes, familial supports, technologies, climate factors) that either impede or facilitate functional performance.

For example, an individual may have a concern in a body structure and function: significant accumulation of phosphorylated tau in their brain with associated severe impairment in one cognitive domain, with mild-to-no cognitive impairment in other domains. This results in activity limitations and participation restrictions: moderate difficulty learning new software which mildly restricts their ability to participate as their church's treasurer. However, these restrictions may be buffered by environmental factors: This individual has a granddaughter facile in financial technology who has created an annotated guide which they review with the individual based on memory strategies learned during neuropsychological feedback. The ICF's approach shapes understanding functioning as the interaction of numerous factors. More recently, some authors have discussed approaches that integrate the instrumental and advanced ADL concepts with the ICF concept of technological facilitators, with emphasis on the role technology has in shaping daily activities (Rogers et al., 2020). Rogers and colleagues suggest that technology is not just a facilitator, but instead necessary for the performance of many so-called extended ADLs. A brief review of these impacts follows.

How Is Technology Shaping Instrumental Activities of Daily Living?

Technology has profoundly transformed daily functioning, particularly in adults' ability to complete IADLs. Namely, the widespread adoption of smartphones, the Internet, and related applications has revolutionized multiple aspects of life, including shopping, navigation, and financial management (e.g., paying bills). Within the field of neuropsychology, reviews of technology use among patients with dementia highlight a shared conclusion: Technology use can serve a primary purpose of compensation (Fabricatore et al., 2020; O'Neill & Gillespie, 2014). However, engaging with digital tools requires various cognitive abilities, such as working memory, executive functioning, and attentional control, which may present challenges for individuals with neurocognitive impairments. Additionally, factors such as digital literacy, socioeconomic disparities, and accessibility influence an individual's ability to effectively integrate technology into daily life. Understanding these complexities is critical for both research and clinical practice, as technology is increasingly embedded in assessments and interventions aimed at supporting functional independence. The following section explores trends in the intersection of technology and daily living, organized by key life domains.

Shopping and Commerce

One of the most striking changes to have occurred in both economically developed nations and developing countries is the transition to online shopping and e-commerce (Diaz-Gutierrez et al., 2024; Feng, 2022; Haji, 2021). This is particularly notable in a post-COVID-19 world, where rates of shopping virtually have remained high in the absence of quarantine guidelines and decreasing caution related to illness transmission (Benge, Aguirre, Scullin, Kiselica, Hilsabeck, Paydarfar, & Douglas, 2024; Feng, 2022; Galhotra & Dewan, 2020). Even as pandemic-related restrictions have eased, online shopping remains a dominant and preferred method for acquiring goods. As of early 2023, approximately 43% of U.S. consumers prefer to shop mostly online rather than in-store (Davies, 2025). Moreover, the way consumers interact with e-commerce platforms is evolving. Voice-activated shopping via smart assistants (e.g., Alexa, Google Assistant) and automated subscription-based purchases (e.g., Amazon Prime) are becoming increasingly common, reducing the need for effortful decision-making in routine purchases. A 2023 survey found that 30% of Gen Z engaged in voice shopping, compared to 7% of Baby Boomers (PYMNTS, 2024).

Though data are limited, trends of technology use, including online shopping, have increased even among older adults (aged 65+), who were initially hypothesized to be excluded from this trajectory (Weil et al., 2021). Relatedly, our understanding of how neuropsychological conditions can impact engagement with e-commerce is still in its infancy. This shopping modality theoretically possesses multiple advantages for individuals with physical or cognitive disabilities, eliminating the need for transportation, reducing physical and cognitive exertion, and allowing for home delivery. However, online shopping still requires a range of cognitive abilities, including working memory (e.g., remembering what has been added to a cart), attention (e.g., filtering out distractions from advertisements), and executive functioning (e.g., comparing products, evaluating costs, and making purchasing decisions) (Venkatesh et al., 2022). With online shopping now an integral part of daily life, more traditional measures of shopping independence (e.g., preparing change, navigating grocery store aisles to locate goods) are becoming less relevant. Instead, financial and digital literacy and the ability to navigate e-commerce platforms are emerging as essential skills for modern consumer engagement.

Finances

Related to commerce, the explosion of online banking, electronic account management, mobile wallets, and after-pay options has fundamentally reshaped how individuals handle their finances. The senior author remembers vividly on fellowship being instructed to take a blank fake check with him on the wards and to observe how patients could complete this task or label an envelope for mailing as independent predictors for how a patient may transition out of a highly structured medical facility into their home environment. Suffice it to say, this is no longer a practice most practitioners engage in, given limited ecological validity in these changing times. Today, the vast majority of financial transactions in the United States occur digitally, with online banking, automatic bill payments, and cashless transactions becoming the norm. As of 2023, upward of 66% of Americans utilize online banking, with projections suggesting this number will rise to 79% by 2029 (Statista Research Department, 2024). Similarly, autopay for bills is now utilized by approximately 40% of U.S. consumers, with adoption rates particularly high among younger demographics (MX, 2024; PYMNTS, 2025). The shift toward digital financial management extends beyond online banking. Mobile payment services, such as Apple Pay, Google Pay, and Venmo, have seen widespread adoption, with a 2022 survey reporting that 66% of Gen Z and 67% of Millennials in the United States have used a digital wallet at least once in the past year (PYMNTS, 2022). Additionally, a separate study found that 85% of Gen Z consumers use mobile wallets at least once a month, with 25% utilizing touchless payments five or more times per month (Billtrust, 2022). Credit card usage remains strong, but the ease of linking cards to mobile apps and subscription-based services further reinforces the trend of financial automation. New technologies (such as payment apps) are not as well studied in clinical populations, although research has linked adoption of integrated social media, communication, and payment apps (i.e., WeChat) with better cognitive function (Liu et al., 2023).

Mobility, Transportation, and Navigation

Technology has similarly had a dramatic impact on movement within a community. For car-based cultures, GPS-based navigation is frequently cited as the most common method of wayfinding and has been shown to support outdoor independence in individuals with mild dementia (Benge, Aguirre, Scullin, Kiselica, Hilsabeck, Paydarfar, Thomaz, et al., 2024; Kwan et al., 2020; Mis et al., n.d.). Additionally, automation of driving and automated safety features have steadily increased over time. These features, which include adaptive cruise control, automatic lane departure warnings and corrections, and increasingly full or partial self-driving capabilities, hold potential to shoulder some of the cognitive burden in transportation. However, research is mixed on the safety of autonomous vehicles (AVs), with some studies suggesting AVs reduce injury risk (Abdel-Aty & Ding, 2024) with others concluding that the utilization of AV technologies is unlikely to reduce crash frequency (McCarthy, 2021). Despite the outcomes of safety data, the availability of AVs may positively impact the lives of individuals with significant cognitive or physical challenges that limit their driving abilities. Though research has yet to investigate this explicitly, investigators have begun to survey caretakers of people with dementia on the perceived benefits and risks of using AVs for those in their care (Haghzare et al., 2022).

Beyond the availability of AVs, advancements in technology will transform how driving ability is assessed. Driving simulators, for example, provide a controlled method for evaluating how cognitive impairments impact reaction time, attention, and hazard detection in a structured environment. Research in this area has begun to explore how simulator performance correlates with real-world driving ability in individuals with impaired cognition with a wide range of etiologies (Blane et al., 2017; Stein & Dubinsky, 2011). Additionally, we anticipate investigative work will soon examine whether adaptive driving aids—such as lane-keeping assist and emergency braking—can help extend driving independence for individuals with early-stage cognitive decline. As these technologies continue to evolve, the intersection of neuropsychology, automated safety features, and AV development may soon redefine what it means to be a "safe driver."

Technology as a Cognitive Prosthetic

Smartphone ownership has increased drastically among U.S. adults over the past decade. Of those aged 65+, there has been a 369% increase in ownership between 2005 and 2021 (13% to 61%; Faverio, 2022). This trend is consistent internationally as well, with over 50% of the global population owning a smartphone as of October 2023 (Shanahan & Bahia, 2024). As more individuals across all age groups integrate smartphones into their daily lives, they gain closer proximity to built-in applications that function as "cognitive prosthetics." Pre-loaded features such as to-do lists, alarms, reminder systems, note-taking tools, and electronic calendars are now seamlessly embedded in operating systems like iOS and Android, providing users with an integrated digital support system for managing daily tasks. In addition to these default apps like Apple Reminders, Google Keep, and Microsoft To-Do, third-party applications such as Todoist, Evernote, and Notion allow for more complex task planning, habit tracking, and cross-device synchronization. Namely, Pomodoro and Kahoot have been cited as useful for assisting college students with attention-deficit/hyperactivity disorder (ADHD) to better manage their time and facilitate effective learning strategies, respectively (Fichten et al., 2022). Speech-to-text technology, available through applications like Google Assistant, Siri, and Bixby, also enables users to set reminders or jot down notes hands-free, making cognitive support more accessible for those with mobility or dexterity challenges.

Unlike arguably outdated memory aids—such as physical planners or sticky notes—these digital tools provide customizable, automated, and synchronized support across multiple devices, allowing users to manage tasks with greater efficiency. For individuals needing assistance with IADLs, and the individuals caring for them, these technologies can serve as essential aids in organization, time management, and daily routine adherence (Benge et al., 2020). Though empirical evidence is limited, initial studies have demonstrated effective adoption of smartphone use even in the context of mild cognitive impairment (MCI) and dementia (Bier et al., 2018; Hartin et al., 2014; Scullin et al., 2022). Collectively, the widespread adoption of smartphones ensures that such tools are no longer limited to specialized assistive technology but are instead becoming ubiquitous features of everyday devices, promoting cognitive support in both clinical and nonclinical populations.

Interpersonal Communication and Socialization

Over the past decade, digital communication methods such as social media platforms, texting, and virtual meeting tools have become dominant modes of interaction. In the United States, text messaging has seen widespread adoption; a 2022 survey revealed that 92% of adult respondents used texting as a primary communication method (Ceci, 2022). Further, the COVID-19 pandemic accelerated utilization of virtual meeting platforms like Zoom and Microsoft Teams for both corporate and personal use. Perhaps most strikingly, the percentage of adults using social media surged from 5% in 2005 to 79% in 2019 (Ortiz-Ospina, 2019). Among adults aged 65+ alone, social media use has increased from 11% to 45% (Faverio, 2022). These media applications, while often associated with recreational and personal use, have increasingly been recognized for their academic and practical benefits. Platforms like Discord have become widely used among college students for collaborative learning, group discussions, and coursework coordination, functioning as a digital workspace that extends beyond traditional classroom settings (Fichten et al., 2022). Similarly, Twitch, originally a gaming-focused streaming service, has gained popularity for its role in "body doubling"—a technique in which individuals stream themselves working or studying in real time, fostering accountability and motivation for viewers who engage in parallel tasks. This method has been particularly beneficial for neurodivergent individuals, as it creates a sense of shared focus and structured productivity, helping users maintain attention and complete tasks in a socially supportive environment (Eagle et al., 2023).

As digital communication becomes the default mode of social interaction, the ability to utilize these tools is emerging as a critical IADL. For older adults and those with cognitive impairments, proficiency in navigating digital communication may be a new marker of independence. Individuals who struggle with social media, messaging apps, or virtual meeting platforms may face (1) increased social isolation, (2) difficulty managing/coordinating appointments with caretakers, and (3) reduced access to telehealth or remote services. In contrast, individuals who can operate these technologies effectively have the potential to gain enhanced social connectivity and greater autonomy in managing their personal and professional lives.

Health-Related Self-Care Tasks

Technology is also playing an increasingly critical role in health-related self-care. Smart pill dispensers, such as Wisepill and MedMinder, release medication at scheduled times, provide reminders via alarms or text messages, and/or allow for remote adherence tracking (Oprea et al., 2021; Pellowski et al., 2014). Medication reminder apps, including MediSafe, PillPack, and CareZone, send push notifications or SMS reminders to help individuals take their medication on time (Dayer et al., 2013). Text message–based adherence programs have also been shown to be helpful for medication adherence, but they are often not followed (Buis et al., 2017). Beyond medication management, wearable devices have revolutionized self-monitoring of individual health status. Smartwatches and fitness trackers, such as Apple Watch and Fitbit, monitor heart rate, blood oxygen levels, sleep patterns, and physical activity while alerting users to potential health concerns, including falls. As of 2024, the global smartwatch user base reached approximately 454.69 million individuals, marking a 41% increase from 323.99 million users in 2023 (Kumar, 2025). Within the United States, 27.4% of the population (roughly 93.5 million people) were reported to use wearable devices in 2024 (Pawar, 2025).

Taken together, the ability to independently navigate health-related technologies—such as setting up medication reminders on a smartphone, interpreting data from a wearable device, or adjusting telehealth settings—could serve as a modern marker of functional independence. For example, an older adult who effectively uses an Apple Watch to monitor heart rate trends and fall risk alerts may demonstrate a higher level of digital and health literacy than one with limited exposure to such devices.

Conclusion

In sum, proficiency in navigating modern technology has become an integral component of IADLs, reshaping how individuals manage essential tasks across multiple life domains. While the primary role of technology in this context often revolves around compensation, its impact extends beyond mere assistance—it actively shapes autonomy, efficiency, and engagement with daily tasks. As research continues to explore the intersection of neurocognitive functioning and technology use, future studies may further clarify the cognitive demands, benefits, and barriers associated with the transition to a more virtually oriented world. Moreover, adapting existing ADL assessments—or developing new, technology-relevant measures—to align with the evolving digital landscape will enhance ecological validity, ultimately refining neuropsychological evaluations and informing more effective intervention strategies.

How Have Assessments of Activities of Daily Living Changed over the Past Century?

In contrast to the rapid changes in methods of performing daily activities over the past several decades, methods of capturing these daily activities in clinic have been slower to evolve.

Questionnaire-Based Assessments

Some of the most commonly used quantitative assessments of IADL functioning are caregiver-completed questionnaires. Many measures, such as the IADL Scale (Lawton & Brody, 1969), Functional Activities Questionnaire (Pfeffer et al., 1982), and Adaptive Behavior Scales (Sparrow et al., 1984), were developed well before such innovations as the personal computer revolution. As we explain in detail in a recent paper (Benge, Aguirre, Scullin, Kiselica, Hilsabeck, Paydarfar, Thomaz, et al., 2024), this mismatch between the content of the measures widely used to capture daily activities and the actual ways people are performing daily tasks can lead at a minimum to confusion but also introduces heterogeneity and difficulty interpreting items.

There are notable exceptions to the digital naivete in some measures, which include both creation of new measures and modification of heritage measures. For example, the Everyday Technology Use Questionnaire (ETUQ) was designed to explicitly assess competence in daily technology use with 86 items that cover technology in eight areas: kitchen activities, other home activities, personal care, power tools, home accessibility, data/telecommunication, finance, and transportation (Rosenberg et al., 2009). Scores can distinguish between cognitively unimpaired, MCI, and dementia groups, and a 32-item short form was subsequently published (Kottorp & Nygård, 2011; Rosenberg et al., 2009). Another measure, the 70-item Amsterdam IADL

Questionnaire (A-IADL-Q), assesses ADLs across seven domains, two of which focus on computer and digital device use (Sikkes et al., 2012). The A-IADL-Q is scored with item response theory (IRT) methods, which are facilitated by an online platform, and subsequent research with the A-IADL-Q has created a 30-item brief forms and demonstrated good classification properties between those with prodromal and mild Alzheimer's disease and ability to measure functional change (Dubbelman et al., 2022; Jutten et al., 2017; Sikkes et al., 2013; Teng et al., 2023).

Other approaches have modified older measures, such as the 10-item FAQ (González et al., 2022; Pfeffer et al., 1982), and created a bank of 11 additional items that explicitly assess technology-mediated ADL difficulties deemed applicable for older adults (Benge, Ali, et al., 2024). These items can be used in isolation with equivalent diagnostic properties to original FAQ, or in conjunction with the original FAQ as an expanded FAQ with improved psychometric properties (Benge, Ali, et al., 2024). Additionally, revisions to the Everyday Cognition scale (ECog-II), which captures five domains of cognitive concern with 41 items that contextualize cognition within daily functioning, have also added technology-mediated activities to the scale (Farias et al., 2021).

A final note regarding technology and ADL assessment centers on how we are scoring and administering these measures. Many neuropsychologists used fixed-form, hand-summed assessments. However, the panoply of daily activities that may be relevant to an individual are varied, and missing data are quite common when an activity simply did not apply to an individual (González & Benge, 2024). Given that increasing economic shifts, population trends, and other forces are likely to broaden the range of daily activities applicable to a given individual, and each person's context will guide how tools such as technology are used or not used, a more dynamic item bank of daily activities may be necessary to make IADL questionnaires relevant to all in the future (Fujii, 2023). We are hopeful that in future generations, neuropsychologists will take advantage of technologies such as computerized-based adaptive measure designs and item response theory to help create a wider range of activities with established item parameters that can be updated as daily demands change over time and allow for dynamic snapshots of daily activities as our daily task demands change.

Performance-Based Assessment

In contrast to questionnaire-based instruments, performance-based functional assessments (PBFAs) quantify individuals' task performance. PBFAs can broadly be grouped into those that quantify completion of (1) high-verisimilitude (e.g., appearing like a real world) tasks prompted by the examiner who actively monitors and rates performance, (2) actual tasks prompted by the examiner who actively monitors the performance in the environment, or (3) actual tasks whose initiation is unprompted and passively monitored. The first two do not typically measure technology use in the abstract. Instead, they focus on a particular activity, such as financial management, completed via a technological platform. Tasks in the latter two categories may also fall under the broader grouping of active and passive digital biomarkers (Ding et al., 2022; Teh et al., 2022).

Examples of high-verisimilitude tasks include the Harvard Automated Phone Task (HAPT; Marshall et al., 2015), Test of Online Pharmacy Skills (TOPS; Woods et al., 2016), Test of Online Health Records Navigation (TOHRN; Woods et al., 2016), Web-based Evaluation of Banking Skills (WEBS; Woods et al., 2017), Simulated Market Task (SMarT; Woods et al., 2017), and Computed-based Functional Skills Assessment and Training (CFSAT; Harvey et al., 2020). These tasks capture ADLs such as financial management (e.g., HAPT, WEBS, CFSAT), medication and health care management (e.g., HAPT, TOPS, TOHRN), transportation (e.g., CFSAT), and miscellaneous commerce (e.g., SMarT, CFSAT). These various ADLs are to be completed via a telephone portal (i.e., HAPT), with Internet navigation skills (i.e., TOPS, TOHRN, WEBS, SMarT, CFSAT), or miscellaneous technology like an ATM or transportation kiosk (e.g., CFSAT).

Instead of high-verisimilitude tasks, some authors have decided to quantify performance of actual ADLs. For example, the Actual Reality (AR) task directs individuals to complete tasks such as ordering food or completing travel arrangements on actual websites, with standardized ratings of performance (Goverover & DeLuca, 2018). Other approaches have included so-called serious games that are either on kiosks in living facilities (Yamada et al., 2024), or installed on tablets (Fukui et al., 2015), that individuals are prompted to engage with. Finally, passive monitoring of unprompted technologically mediated tasks such as leisure hobbies (e.g., Klondike Solitaire (Gielis et al., 2021), banking transactions (Wild et al., 2022), or keystroke and general smartphone usage patterns (Butler et al., 2025; Ding et al., 2022; Nguyen et al., 2023; Teh et al., 2022) holds promise for identifying cognitive change and distinguishing diagnostic groups. In fact, all three types of technological PBFAs hold promise in their relationships with cognition and neurocognitive diagnostic stages (Ding et al., 2022; Goverover et al., 2023; Harvey et al., 2021; Nguyen et al., 2023; Teh et al., 2022; Woods et al., 2019). However, most all of these tasks and metrics are not easily accessible to clinicians for the time being, although scalable interfaces may arrive in the future.

How Do Socioeconomic, Cultural, and Educational Factors Influence Technology Use in Daily Activities?

Although technology has become an integral part of daily life influencing how people communicate, shop, access information, and engage with the health care system, significant inequities remain in terms of access to and proficiency with these tools. This gap, referred to as the "digital divide," is shaped by various sociodemographic factors, including income, educational and occupational attainment, cultural context, and language. Psychologists and neuropsychologists have come to appreciate the importance of these sociodemographic factors across facets of neuropsychological and psychodiagnostic assessment from selection of instruments and normative comparison groups to interpretation of assessment results, and more. Similarly, these factors are crucial to consider when assessing individuals' ability to use technology, as they can influence both exposure to technology and the appropriateness of our functional assessments.

The use of technology for recreational, educational, or occupational purposes increases familiarity with technology overall, making it more seamless to use technology for health care or financial reasons. This can put individuals from certain demographic groups who have had limited exposure to technology at a disadvantage. Early on, access to technology like mobile phones, computers, and Internet were limited to those who were wealthy, White, and educated, living in urban areas (Gallardo, 2025; Vogels, 2021). Despite increased dissemination, this initial disparity has persisted, with factors such as educational attainment, occupation, rural-urban status, and race/ethnicity being strongly correlated with technology familiarity and technology use (Gallardo, 2025; Vogels, 2021). Indeed, data from the Pew Research Center have shown that technology, including smartphones and the Internet, is used less in rural than urban areas, and correlated with age, educational attainment, and income. Additionally, as of 2023, approximately 15% of adults in the United States were identified as "smartphone dependent," meaning they owned a smartphone but did not have home Internet. This percentage was larger for individuals with lower income, for individuals with lower levels of formal education, and for individuals who identified as Black or Hispanic than their White or Asian counterparts (Gelles-Watnick, 2024).

Using a social-drivers-of-health framework, we can ensure we are adequately considering sociodemographic variables that are likely to impact patients' exposure to technology and therefore impact our assessment of their functional status as it relates to technology. Additionally, this may help providers identify appropriate resources and compensatory strategies to provide recommendations to improve patients' overall quality of life and maximize their health and safety. This framework focuses on five factors (U.S. Department of Health and Human Services, Office of Disease Prevention and Health Promotion, 2024): (1) educational access and quality, (2) economic status, (3) social and community context, (4) neighborhood and built environment, and (5) health care access and quality.

Educational Access and Quality

The impact of educational background on exposure to and ability to use technology is, at least, two-fold, as both educational attainment *and* quality of education must be considered.

Higher levels of education are linked to increased digital literacy and comfort with using technology (Arias López et al., 2023; Li et al., 2025; Sualehi, 2023). Conversely, adults with lower educational attainment may face more challenges due to limited digital skills or unfamiliarity with technology, reducing their access to important technological tools. Furthermore, exposure to technology now often begins in school. However, wealthier school districts tend to have more resources, including technology access, digital literacy programs, and a focus on integrating technology into curricula. In contrast, schools in lower-income areas may lack these resources, leaving students without the same opportunities to develop digital literacy skills. This creates a disparity in how students are prepared to navigate digital tools and platforms, which can carry over into adulthood and impact their ability to access and use technology for health care and other purposes, further increasing the digital divide.

Economic Status

Income disparities influence both the age of initial technology exposure and the types of technology individuals can afford. Adults with higher incomes are more likely to own devices like smartphones or computers and have access to reliable Internet. In contrast, lower-income adults may face financial barriers that prevent them from accessing these technologies, exacerbating health inequities. That said, it is also true that individuals with lower educational or occupational attainment, from certain racial/ethnic backgrounds, and from rural settings are likely to have lower incomes resulting in a vicious cycle.

Similarly, exposure to technology in the workplace can vary greatly depending on the industry. Higher-paying jobs, especially in fields like technology, finance, and health care, often require digital skills and frequent use of technology, providing employees with regular exposure to digital tools. Conversely, blue-collar jobs in industries such as manufacturing, construction, or service work are less likely to require digital literacy, resulting in lower exposure to technology in these roles. This further entrenches the digital divide, as individuals in lower-paying jobs may have fewer opportunities to develop the skills necessary to navigate digital platforms in their personal and professional lives.

Social and Community Context

Culture

Cultural views on technology can influence how individuals from different racial or ethnic backgrounds use certain technologies. In some communities, there is a strong emphasis on face-to-face interaction, family ties, and traditional methods of communication, which can affect the adoption of technologies

(Antonucci et al., 2017; S.-G. Lee et al., 2013; Whitehead et al., 2023). Adults from these cultures might prefer direct, in-person communication and may view digital interactions as less authentic or less desirable. Thus, these individuals may be less likely to develop the technology literacy skills necessary to navigate our increasingly digital world not due to lack of ability but to lack of interest or motivation.

Cultural attitudes toward technology and its use in health care, specifically, can also vary widely. Communities that place a strong emphasis on face-to-face interaction and view digital health tools like telemedicine or online consultations with suspicion or as less authentic may be more resistant to adopting telemedicine or using digital health tools.

Language

Language is another important factor impacting technology use. For example, Fairlie (2007) found that a significant digital divide exists between Spanish-speaking and English-speaking Mexican or Mexican American families in the United States. At the time of the study, only 13.1% of "Spanish-only" Mexican or Mexican American families had home Internet access, compared to 40.1% of English-speaking Mexican or Mexican American families. This divide persists despite controlling for factors such as education, family income, and immigrant status (Fairlie, 2007). More recent data suggests that non-English-speaking Latino populations continue to have lower rates of Internet access and usage, further exacerbating the digital divide in these communities.

Rural-Urban Status

Adults living in rural or low-income urban areas may face challenges due to a lack of broadband Internet access or affordable devices, preventing them from engaging with telehealth, online health education, or digital health monitoring. Additionally, rural residents may face additional barriers such as poor Internet connectivity, which can limit their ability to use these technologies effectively (H. Y. Lee et al., 2021). Even when there is technology access in rural regions, the usage patterns may differ (Sapienza et al., 2023).

Health Care Access, Health Care Quality, and Health Status

Adults with limited access to health care services or those who are uninsured or underinsured may not be able to take full advantage of digital health technologies due to lack of access to providers offering telemedicine or insufficient health insurance coverage for digital health tools.

Adults with chronic health conditions or complex care needs may be more likely to use digital health tools to manage their health. For example, patients with diabetes, hypertension, or heart disease often benefit from wearable devices that track vital signs or telehealth consultations that allow them to monitor their conditions remotely.

Health status and well-being also affect adults' ability to use technology. For example, individuals with physical disabilities (e.g., limited mobility, vision or hearing impairments) may need adaptive devices or specialized technologies to use smartphones, computers, or other digital tools effectively.

Age and Technology Use

As the pervasiveness of technology is still a relatively new development, many sociodemographic variables, including income, educational attainment, occupation, and environmental context intersect with age in important ways, such that older adults are likely to be more impacted. Technology use varies across different age groups. Younger adults, particularly those aged 18–39, are generally more adept at using digital tools due to their familiarity with technology. In contrast, older adults (60+) may face challenges with digital literacy and adoption of new technologies, although this divide appears to be diminishing (Benge, Aguirre, Scullin, Kiselica, Hilsabeck, Paydarfar, Thomaz, et al., 2024). When asked about ability to perform activities of daily living without assistance, many older adults who have had little to no exposure to technology and/or little to no incentive to use technology may report requiring assistance from their children or other caregivers to manage daily tasks like appointments and finances due to the increasing necessity of using technology.

Clinical Considerations for Assessing Activities of Daily Living in the 21st Century and Beyond

Given the changes documented throughout this chapter, clinicians would do well to consider and integrate considerations of digital daily activities in their workflows. In our practice, ADL assessment begins with the interview. We routinely inquire about the role of technology in IADL completion. Starter questions may include "Do you/the patient have difficulties performing routine smartphone tasks, like sending a text message, making a call, or checking email?" We often find it useful when inquiring about financial management to follow up comments about bills being on autopay with "Can they log in and check activity?" or "Have there been any text or email frauds or scams?" For individuals with more impairments, we find it helpful to delineate between individuals who can't/shouldn't use the stove, versus those still able to microwave simple meals, as a method of tech facilitating a degree of independence for this domain. Though we know of no empirical literature to date on the topic, we increasingly note individuals who have given up driving due to motoric or sensory limitations but will use a rideshare app to facilitate community transportation. Documenting this adaptation, we feel, gives a better picture of independence than merely noting they cannot drive.

In this vein, clinicians should also consider whether technology skills are required to complete the activity, or merely facilitate the activity. For example, if an individual and their family report independence in managing their finances and, after follow-up inquiry, they note they have set up automatic payments to various accounts in their online banking portal and are not actively monitoring finances, this functional activity may be a less reliable marker of cognitive status, even if it accurately represents their functional status. To wit, research from our group showed that while traditional IADLs correlated with executive and memory measures, the technological IADLs correlated primarily with executive functioning, suggesting that individuals were able to maintain levels of functioning despite increasing cognitive impairment in certain domains (Benge, Ali, et al., 2024).

Given the literature reviewed previously, social drivers of health should be considered. These drivers may potentiate challenges with learning and adapting to digital tools. Furthermore, there may be a lack of access to technology, which contributes to reduced functioning. Recognizing that limitations in technology use may stem from barriers beyond cognitive function allows clinicians to make informed decisions and develop more effective, individualized care plans.

To standardize functional assessment in adults, clinicians should consider incorporating measures such as the ECog-II to assess cognitive complaints and measures such as the A-IADL-Q or expanded FAQ to assess a broader spectrum of IADLs. In children, scales such as the ABAS-3 include some items pertinent to technology use (e.g., sending emails, online academic resources), although there is not a domain specific to technology. Notably, when there are not items on a measure that capture technologically mediated functioning (as in the Lawton & Brody IADL Scale or traditional FAQ), respondents may implicitly consider technology use in their rating of pertinent activities. This may be of particular importance to those in the very early or prodromal stages of conditions, such as transitional cognitive decline (TCD; i.e., subjective cognitive decline (Jack et al., 2024). Research using item response theory has demonstrated that some of these tech enabled measures such as the A-IADL-Q and expanded FAQ, capture a broader range of functional ability, including better assessment of milder functional concerns in early stages (Dubbelman et al., 2020). Use of these measures bears the same caveats noted in interview regarding a cognitive-functional correlation. The impact of reporting bias—whether intentional or unintentional—on the accuracy of self and collateral functional ratings should always be considered.

Along those lines, neuropsychologists should ensure that assessment tools are culturally appropriate and sensitive to the patient's background, ensuring that tasks reflect the patient's real-world functioning rather than their ability to use technology that may be unfamiliar to them. This may involve adapting or modifying assessments to better suit the patient's cultural context and language, and considering how the use of technology may vary across different demographic groups. Some studies have applied differential item functioning and propensity score matching to identify biased items or items with limited applicability for certain groups (González et al., 2023; González & Benge, 2024).

Robust validation and dissemination of administration/scoring portals for the tech focused PBFAs noted earlier are still pending. As such, clinicians should consider informal assessment of technology-facilitated IADLs and advanced ADLs. This could include careful integration of information from the electronic medical record (EMR) when these are quantified (e.g., no-show rates, messaging read/response rates, medication refill dates, or inquiries with embedded medication compliance information). Expanding on this, clinicians can actively observe technology use in clinic (e.g., observe the facility with which they schedule a follow-up appointment, observe their response to notifications and general smartphone use) or even ask—with their consent—for them to demonstrate use, such as asking individuals to show you how they navigate EMR, map navigation, organization/scheduling, and messaging apps. We find such an approach elucidating, particularly for individuals who do not have a reliable informant to describe daily functioning.

The role of technology as a functional facilitator despite cognitive impairments should be heavily weighted in diagnosis. Diagnostic and staging criteria for cognitive disorders actively consider daily functioning, with some difficulty in IADLs and advanced ADLs being present in MCI, dependence in IADLs and advanced ADLs being present in transition to mild dementia (i.e., mild severity major neurocognitive disorder), and manifest assistance-dependence in basic ADLs and continued loss of functioning in IADLs and advanced ADLs being present in moderate-to-severe stages (American Psychiatric Association, 2022; Jack et al., 2024). However, as noted earlier, if there are enough technological facilitators in the environment, an individual may maintain IADL independence despite significant multidomain cognitive impairment that might otherwise be synonymous with dementia. In these cases, where multiple lines of evidence truly indicate functional independence due to technological facility, clinicians should clearly emphasize the role of environmental facilitators in maintenance of functioning. For certain referral questions where cognitive stage has predictive value, clinicians should emphasize the extent of cognitive impairment or consider rewording their diagnostic section and using other means of communication (e.g., active emphasis during team meetings, sending additional messages to referring provider) to reduce the likelihood that other clinicians heuristically scan for key words. Anecdotally, we have noticed worse cognitive outcomes for certain procedures (e.g., deep brain stimulation) in these individuals when teams placed more weight on the label (e.g., MCI) instead of the cognitive findings.

Additionally, neuropsychologists should be proactive in recommending interventions and resources that support patients' digital literacy and offering strategies to improve access to technology. This could include community continuing education classes offered by many municipalities and nonprofits (e.g., AARP's Digital Skills Ready@50+). For patients with low digital literacy, compensatory strategies can improve their ability to engage with technology, empowering individuals to use technology more effectively and integrate it into their daily lives.

Building Toward the Future

Neuropsychologists can be slow to change practice approaches over time (Rabin et al., 2016). While it can certainly be argued that this slow rate of change represents a maturation of the science in our field and the weight of evidence to support our practice and inferences, we must also acknowledge that the changes in the daily lives of those we serve have been dramatic and are likely to continue. Further, the core of what we do (understanding how an individual is thinking, feeling, and behaving in their own environment) is shaped by a broad array of factors that includes digital technology. So what is the path forward? We believe there are three core needs.

First, we believe that clinicians and researchers should consider auditing their own practice patterns. Sit with the questionnaires you give and ask yourself how you would answer these questions about yourself, your loved ones, your parents, and your children. Look closely at your interview and report templates. Do the daily activities assessed apply to you? How are the generations behind or ahead of you approaching this task? What aspects of daily life are you potentially missing? One does not need to have a wholesale abandonment of existing practices, but what new items, questions, and probes can you use to better understand the real-world functioning of the population you serve? Our interest in this field was driven by this approach: noticing discrepancies between what we were asking versus what patients were telling us, and noticing the number of times caregivers or patients wanted clarifications or explanations of survey items. There was much to be learned from listening to those we serve.

Second, we encourage the next generation of neuropsychologists to get involved in research and clinical practice groups. We are living through a time where the generation that brought us the Internet is facing age-related neurodegenerative diseases, while simultaneously a generation that has never known the world without Internet is entering the profession. As the baton is passed from generation to generation, the field will need the interest, enthusiasm, expertise, and lived experience of navigating a digital world to best understand and assess functional performance day to day.

Finally, we must consider daily functioning assessment among the most important things a neuropsychologist does but also one of the most uniquely individualized. While digital technologies touch on many aspects of daily life for many, the extent of this is uneven across our diverse populations. Neuropsychology should embrace the challenge of creating assessments applicable to all, recognizing the need to modernize our approaches and leverage technology in assessment of daily functioning.

References

Abdel-Aty, M., & Ding, S. (2024). A matched case-control analysis of autonomous vs human-driven vehicle accidents. *Nature Communications, 15*(1), 4931. https://doi.org/10.1038/s41467-024-48526-4

American Psychiatric Association. (2022). *Diagnostic and Statistical Manual of Mental Disorders, Fifth Edition, Text Revision (DSM-5-TR)* (5th ed., text revision). American Psychiatric Association.

Antonucci, T. C., Ajrouch, K. J., & Manalel, J. A. (2017). Social Relations and Technology: Continuity, Context, and Change. *Innovation in Aging, 1*(3), 1-9. https://doi.org/10.1093/geroni/igx029

Arias López, M. D. P., Ong, B. A., Borrat Frigola, X., Fernández, A. L., Hicklent, R. S., Obeles, A. J. T., Rocimo, A. M., & Celi, L. A. (2023). Digital literacy as a new determinant of health: A scoping review. *PLOS Digital Health, 2*(10), e0000279. https://doi.org/10.1371/journal.pdig.0000279

Benge, J. F., Aguirre, A., Scullin, M. K., Kiselica, A., Hilsabeck, R. C., Paydarfar, D., Thomaz, E., & Douglas, M. (2024). Digital methods for performing daily tasks among older adults: An initial report of frequency of use and perceived utility. *Experimental Aging Research, 50*(2), 133–154. https://doi.org/10.1080/0361073X.2023.2172950

Benge, J. F., Aguirre, A., Scullin, M. K., Kiselica, A. M., Hilsabeck, R. C., Paydarfar, D., & Douglas, M. (2024). Internet-enabled behaviors in older adults during the pandemic: Patterns of use, psychosocial impacts, and plans for continued utilization. *Work, Aging and Retirement, 10*(1), 6–13. https://doi.org/10.1093/workar/waac026

Benge, J. F., Ali, A., Chandna, N., Rana, N., Mis, R., González, D. A., Kiselica, A. M., Scullin, M. K., & Hilsabeck, R. C. (2024). Technology-based instrumental activities of daily living in persons with Alzheimer's disease and related disorders. *Alzheimer's & Dementia: Diagnosis, Assessment & Disease Monitoring, 16*(4), e70022. https://doi.org/10.1002/dad2.70022

Benge, J. F., Dinh, K. L., Logue, E., Phenis, R., Dasse, M. N., & Scullin, M. K. (2020). The smartphone in the memory clinic: A study of patient and care partner's utilisation habits. *Neuropsychological Rehabilitation, 30*(1), 101–115. https://doi.org/10.1080/09602011.2018.1459307

Bier, N., Paquette, G., & Macoir, J. (2018). Smartphone for smart living: Using new technologies to cope with everyday limitations in semantic dementia. *Neuropsychological Rehabilitation, 28*(5), 734–754. https://doi.org/10.1080/09602011.2015.1094395

Billtrust. (2022). *The future is now: Billtrust's 2022–23 Gen Z and digital payments study.* https://www.billtrust.com/-/media/assets/white-papers/2022-23-gen-z-digital-payments-white-paper-pm-pay-wp5.pdf

Blane, A., Lee, H. C., Falkmer, T., & Willstrand, T. D. (2017). Assessing Cognitive Ability and Simulator-Based Driving Performance in Poststroke Adults. *Behavioural Neurology, 2017*(1), 1378308. https://doi.org/10.1155/2017/1378308

Buis, L., Hirzel, L., Dawood, R. M., Dawood, K. L., Nichols, L. P., Artinian, N. T., Schwiebert, L., Yarandi, H. N., Roberson, D. N., Plegue, M. A., Mango, L. C., & Levy, P. D. (2017). Text Messaging to Improve Hypertension Medication Adherence in African Americans From Primary Care and Emergency Department Settings: Results From Two Randomized Feasibility Studies. *JMIR mHealth and uHealth, 5*(2), e6630. https://doi.org/10.2196/mhealth.6630

Butler, P. M., Yang, J., Brown, R., Hobbs, M., Becker, A., Penalver-Andres, J., Syz, P., Muller, S., Cosne, G., Juraver, A., Song, H. H., Saha-Chaudhuri, P., Roggen, D., Scotland, A., Silveira, N., Demircioglu, G., Gabelle, A., Hughes, R., Erkkinen, M. G., ... Belachew, S. (2025). Smartwatch- and smartphone-based remote assessment of brain health and detection of mild cognitive impairment. *Nature Medicine, 31*, 1–11. https://doi.org/10.1038/s41591-024-03475-9

Ceci, L. (2022, September 15). *Top communication methods in the U.S. 2022.* Statista. https://www.statista.com/statistics/1332443/us-users-top-communication-methods/

Cornelis, E., Gorus, E., Van Schelvergem, N., & De Vriendt, P. (2019). The relationship between basic, instrumental, and advanced activities of daily living and executive functioning in geriatric patients with neurocognitive disorders. *International Journal of Geriatric Psychiatry, 34*(6), 889–899. https://doi.org/10.1002/gps.5087

Davies, K. (2025, January 14). *Consumers shopping online vs. Offline worldwide 2023.* Statista. https://www.statista.com/statistics/1384193/mostly-online-vs-offline-shopping-worldwide/

Dayer, L., Heldenbrand, S., Anderson, P., Gubbins, P. O., & Martin, B. C. (2013). Smartphone medication adherence apps: Potential benefits to patients and providers. *Journal of the American Pharmacists Association, 53*(2), 172–181. https://doi.org/10.1331/JAPhA.2013.12202

Diaz-Gutierrez, J. M., Mohammadi-Mavi, H., & Ranjbari, A. (2024). COVID-19 Impacts on Online and In-Store Shopping Behaviors: Why they Happened and Whether they Will Last Post Pandemic. *Transportation Research Record, 2678*(12), 580–598. https://doi.org/10.1177/03611981231155169

Ding, Z., Lee, T.-L., & Chan, A. S. (2022). Digital Cognitive Biomarker for Mild Cognitive Impairments and Dementia: A Systematic Review. *Journal of Clinical Medicine, 11*(14), 4191. https://doi.org/10.3390/jcm11144191

Dubbelman, M. A., Jutten, R. J., Tomaszewski Farias, S. E., Amariglio, R. E., Buckley, R. F., Visser, P. J., Rentz, D. M., Johnson, K. A., Properzi, M. J., Schultz, A., Donovan, N., Gatchell, J. R., Teunissen, C. E., Van Berckel, B. N. M., Van der Flier, W. M., Sperling, R. A., Papp, K. V., Scheltens, P., Marshall, G. A., ... Alzheimer Disease Neuroimaging Initiative, National Alzheimer's Coordinating Center, the Harvard Aging Brain Study, the Alzheimer Dementia Cohort. (2020). Decline in cognitively complex everyday activities accelerates along the Alzheimer's disease continuum. *Alzheimer's Research & Therapy, 12*(1), 138. https://doi.org/10.1186/s13195-020-00706-2

Dubbelman, M. A., Verrijp, M., Terwee, C. B., Jutten, R. J., Postema, M. C., Barkhof, F., Berckel, B. N. M., Gillissen, F., Teeuwen, V., Teunissen, C., van de Flier, W. M., Scheltens, P., & Sikkes, S. A. M. (2022). Determining the minimal important change of everyday functioning in dementia. *Neurology, 99*(9), e954–e964. https://doi.org/10.1212/WNL.0000000000200781

Eagle, T., Baltaxe-Admony, L. B., & Ringland, K. E. (2023). Proposing Body Doubling as a Continuum of Space/Time and Mutuality: An Investigation with Neurodivergent Participants. *Proceedings of the 25th International ACM SIGACCESS Conference on Computers and Accessibility*, 1–4. https://doi.org/10.1145/3597638.3614486

Fabricatore, C., Radovic, D., Lopez, X., Grasso-Cladera, A., & Salas, C. E. (2020). When technology cares for people with dementia: A critical review using neuropsychological rehabilitation as a conceptual framework. *Neuropsychological Rehabilitation, 30*(8), 1558–1597. https://doi.org/10.1080/09602011.2019.1589532

Fairlie, R. W. (2007). Explaining differences in access to home computers and the Internet: A comparison of Latino groups to other ethnic and racial groups. *Electronic Commerce Research, 7*(3), 265–291. https://doi.org/10.1007/s10660-007-9006-5

Farias, S. T., Weakley, A., Harvey, D., Chandler, J., Huss, O., & Mungas, D. (2021). The measurement of Everyday Cognition (ECog): Revisions and updates. *Alzheimer Disease and Associated Disorders, 35*(3), 258–264. https://doi.org/10.1097/WAD.0000000000000450

Faverio, M. (2022, January 13). *Share of those 65 and older who are tech users has grown in the past decade.* Pew Research Center. https://www.pewresearch.org/short-reads/2022/01/13/share-of-those-65-and-older-who-are-tech-users-has-grown-in-the-past-decade/

Feng, Z. (2022). The review of online shopping trend during and After the Covid-19 Pandemic. *Proceedings of the 2022 International Conference on Economics, Smart Finance and Contemporary Trade*, 1556–1563. https://doi.org/10.2991/978-94-6463-052-7_172

Fichten, C., Havel, A., Jorgensen, M., Wileman, S., Harvison, M., Arcuri, R., & Ruffolo, O. (2022). What apps do postsecondary students with attention deficit hyperactivity disorder actually find helpful for doing schoolwork? An empirical study. *Journal of Education and Learning, 11*(5), Article 5. https://doi.org/10.5539/jel.v11n5p44

Fujii, D. (2023). Centering culture in neuropsychological training, research, and practice. *Archives of Clinical Neuropsychology: The Official Journal of the National Academy of Neuropsychologists, 38*(3), 301–303. https://doi.org/10.1093/arclin/acad025

Fukui, Y., Yamashita, T., Hishikawa, N., Kurata, T., Sato, K., Omote, Y., Kono, S., Yunoki, T., Kawahara, Y., Hatanaka, N., Tokuchi, R., Deguchi, K., & Abe, K. (2015). Computerized touch-panel screening tests for detecting mild cognitive impairment and Alzheimer's disease. *Internal Medicine (Tokyo, Japan), 54*(8), 895–902. https://doi.org/10.2169/internalmedicine.54.3931

Galhotra, B., & Dewan, A. (2020). Impact of COVID-19 on digital platforms and change in E-commerce shopping trends. *2020 Fourth International Conference on I-SMAC (IoT in Social, Mobile, Analytics and Cloud) (I-SMAC)*, 861–866. https://doi.org/10.1109/I-SMAC49090.2020.9243379

Gallardo, R. (2025). *Digital Divide Index (DDI)*. Purdue Center for Regional Development. http://pcrd.purdue.edu/ddi

Gelles-Watnick, R. (2024, January 31). *Americans' use of mobile technology and home broadband*. Pew Research Center. https://www.pewresearch.org/internet/2024/01/31/americans-use-of-mobile-technology-and-home-broadband/

Gielis, K., Vanden Abeele, M.-E., Verbert, K., Tournoy, J., De Vos, M., & Vanden Abeele, V. (2021). Detecting mild cognitive impairment via digital biomarkers of cognitive performance found in Klondike solitaire: A machine-learning study. *Digital Biomarkers*, *5*(1), 44–52. https://doi.org/10.1159/000514105

González, D. A., & Benge, J. F. (2024). Do we all do the same things? Applicability of daily activities at the intersection of demographics. *Neuropsychology*, *38*(5), 379–391. https://doi.org/10.1037/neu0000956

González, D. A., Clark, M. J., Gonzales, M. M., & Benge, J. (2023). An evaluation of item bias on the Functional Activities Questionnaire. *Archives of Clinical Neuropsychology: The Official Journal of the National Academy of Neuropsychologists*, *38*(2), 276–282. https://doi.org/10.1093/arclin/acac071

González, D. A., Gonzales, M. M., Resch, Z. J., Sullivan, A. C., & Soble, J. R. (2022). Comprehensive evaluation of the Functional Activities Questionnaire (FAQ) and its reliability and validity. *Assessment*, *29*(4), 748–763. https://doi.org/10.1177/1073191121991215

Goverover, Y., & DeLuca, J. (2018). Assessing everyday life functional activity using actual reality in persons with MS. *Rehabilitation Psychology*, *63*(2), 276–285. https://doi.org/10.1037/rep0000212

Goverover, Y., Salter, A., & DeLuca, J. (2023). Assessing everyday functional activity in cognitively impaired people with multiple sclerosis: The use of Actual RealityTM. *Multiple Sclerosis (Houndmills, Basingstoke, England)*, *29*(9), 1107–1117. https://doi.org/10.1177/13524585231185048

Haghzare, S., Delfi, G., Stasiulis, E., Mohamud, H., Dove, E., Rapoport, M. J., Naglie, G., Mihailidis, A., & Campos, J. L. (2022). Can automated vehicles be useful to persons living with dementia? The perspectives of care partners of people living with dementia. *The Gerontologist*, *62*(7), 1050–1062. https://doi.org/10.1093/geront/gnab174

Haji, K. (2021). E-commerce development in rural and remote areas of BRICS countries. *Journal of Integrative Agriculture*, *20*(4), 979–997. https://doi.org/10.1016/S2095-3119(20)63451-7

Hartin, P. J., Nugent, C. D., McClean, S. I., Cleland, I., Norton, M. C., Sanders, C., & Tschanz, J. T. (2014). A smartphone application to evaluate technology adoption and usage in persons with dementia. In *2014 36th Annual International Conference of the*

IEEE Engineering in Medicine and Biology Society, 5389–5392. https://doi.org/10.1109/EMBC.2014.6944844

Harvey, P. D., Forero, D. B., Ahern, L. B., Tibiriçá, L., Kallestrup, P., & Czaja, S. J. (2021). The computerized functional skills assessment and training program: Sensitivity to global cognitive impairment, correlations with cognitive abilities, and factor structure. *The American Journal of Geriatric Psychiatry: Official Journal of the American Association for Geriatric Psychiatry*, *29*(4), 395–404. https://doi.org/10.1016/j.jagp.2020.08.019

Harvey, P. D., Tibiriçá, L., Kallestrup, P., & Czaja, S. J. (2020). A computerized functional skills assessment and training program targeting technology based everyday functional skills. *Journal of Visualized Experiments: JoVE, 156*. https://doi.org/10.3791/60330

Jack, C. R., Andrews, J. S., Beach, T. G., Buracchio, T., Dunn, B., Graf, A., Hansson, O., Ho, C., Jagust, W., McDade, E., Molinuevo, J. L., Okonkwo, O. C., Pani, L., Rafii, M. S., Scheltens, P., Siemers, E., Snyder, H. M., Sperling, R., Teunissen, C. E., & Carrillo, M. C. (2024). Revised criteria for diagnosis and staging of Alzheimer's disease: Alzheimer's Association Workgroup. *Alzheimer's & Dementia: The Journal of the Alzheimer's Association*, *20*(8), 5143–5169. https://doi.org/10.1002/alz.13859

Jutten, R. J., Peeters, C. F. W., Leijdesdorff, S. M. J., Visser, P. J., Maier, A. B., Terwee, C. B., Scheltens, P., & Sikkes, S. A. M. (2017). Detecting functional decline from normal aging to dementia: Development and validation of a short version of the Amsterdam IADL Questionnaire. *Alzheimer's & Dementia (Amsterdam, Netherlands)*, *8*, 26–35. https://doi.org/10.1016/j.dadm.2017.03.002

Katz, S. (1983). Assessing self-maintenance: Activities of daily living, mobility, and instrumental activities of daily living. *Journal of the American Geriatrics Society*, *31*(12), 721–727. https://doi.org/10.1111/j.1532-5415.1983.tb03391.x

Kottorp, A., & Nygård, L. (2011). Development of a short-form assessment for detection of subtle activity limitations: Can use of everyday technology distinguish between MCI and Alzheimer's disease? *Expert Review of Neurotherapeutics*, *11*(5), 647–655. https://doi.org/10.1586/ern.11.55

Kumar, N. (2025, March 5). *Smartwatch statistics (2025)—Users & market share.* DemandSage. https://www.demandsage.com/smartwatch-statistics/

Kwan, R. Y. C., Cheung, D. S. K., & Kor, P. P.-K. (2020). The use of smartphones for wayfinding by people with mild dementia. *Dementia*, *19*(3), 721–735. https://doi.org/10.1177/1471301218785461

Lawton, M. P., & Brody, E. M. (1969). Assessment of older people: self-maintaining and instrumental activities of daily living. *The Gerontologist*, *9*(3_Part_1), 179–186. https://doi.org/10.1093/geront/9.3_Part_1.179

Lee, H. Y., Kanthawala, S., Choi, E. Y., & Kim, Y. S. (2021). Rural and non-rural digital divide persists in older adults: Internet access, usage, and attitudes toward technology. *Gerontechnology*, *20*(2), 1–9. https://doi.org/10.4017/gt.2021.20.2.32-472.12

Lee, S.-G., Trimi, S., & Kim, C. (2013). The impact of cultural differences on technology adoption. *Journal of World Business, 48*(1), 20–29. https://doi.org/10.1016/j.jwb.2012.06.003

Li, F., Cheng, L., Wang, X., Shen, L., Ma, Y., & Islam, A. Y. M. A. (2025). The causal relationship between digital literacy and students' academic achievement: A meta-analysis. *Humanities and Social Sciences Communications, 12*(1), 1–12. https://doi.org/10.1057/s41599-025-04399-6

Litvan, I., Goldman, J. G., Tröster, A. I., Schmand, B. A., Weintraub, D., Petersen, R. C., Mollenhauer, B., Adler, C. H., Marder, K., Williams-Gray, C. H., Aarsland, D., Kulisevsky, J., Rodriguez-Oroz, M. C., Burn, D. J., Barker, R. A., & Emre, M. (2012). Diagnostic criteria for mild cognitive impairment in Parkinson's disease: Movement Disorder Society Task Force guidelines. *Movement Disorders: Official Journal of the Movement Disorder Society, 27*(3), 349–356. https://doi.org/10.1002/mds.24893

Liu, X., Wang, X., Zhang, H., Pei, M., & Li, N. (2023). Relationship between digital exclusion and cognitive impairment in Chinese adults. *Frontiers in Aging Neuroscience, 15.* https://doi.org/10.3389/fnagi.2023.1194348

Marshall, G. A., Dekhtyar, M., Bruno, J. M., Jethwani, K., Amariglio, R. E., Johnson, K. A., Sperling, R. A., & Rentz, D. M. (2015). The Harvard Automated Phone Task: New performance-based activities of daily living tests for early Alzheimer's disease. *The Journal of Prevention of Alzheimer's Disease, 2*(4), 242–253. https://doi.org/10.14283/jpad.2015.72

McCarthy, R. L. (2021). Autonomous vehicle accident data analysis: California OL 316 Reports: 2015–2020. *ASCE-ASME J Risk and Uncert in Engrg Sys Part B Mech Engrg, 8*(034502). https://doi.org/10.1115/1.4051779

Mis, R. E., Benge, Jared F., Kamar, Jennifer L. Thompson, Webber, Troy A., & Woods, S. P. (n.d.). Digital and analog approaches for managing daily activities in younger and older adults. *The Clinical Neuropsychologist, 40*(1), 1–25. https://doi.org/10.1080/13854046.2025.2487151

MX. (2024, May 30). *MX's latest research reveals bill pay habits.* https://www.mx.com/news/manual-methods-consumer-research/

Nguyen, T. M., Leow, A. D., & Ajilore, O. (2023). A review on smartphone keystroke dynamics as a digital biomarker for understanding neurocognitive functioning. *Brain Sciences, 13*(6), Article 6. https://doi.org/10.3390/brainsci13060959

O'Neill, B., & Gillespie, A. (Eds.). (2014). *Assistive technology for cognition: A handbook for clinicians and developers.* Psychology Press. https://doi.org/10.4324/9781315779102

Oprea, F., Rosner, D., Popescu, F., & Scrab, A. (2021). Mediminder—Medication management and reminder application. In *2021 20th RoEduNet Conference: Networking in Education and Research (RoEduNet)*,1–6. https://doi.org/10.1109/RoEduNet54112.2021.9637712

Ortiz-Ospina, E. (2019, September 18). *The rise of social media.* Our World in Data. https://ourworldindata.org/rise-of-social-media

Pawar, P. (2025, February 5). *Wearable devices statistics by companies, products, shipment, users, demographics and region.* Coolest Gadgets. https://www.coolest-gadgets.com/wearable-devices-statistics/

Pellowski, J. A., Kalichman, S. C., White, D., Amaral, C. M., Hoyt, G., & Kalichman, M. O. (2014). Real-time medication adherence monitoring intervention: Test of concept in people living with HIV infection. *Journal of the Association of Nurses in AIDS Care, 25*(6), 646. https://doi.org/10.1016/j.jana.2014.06.002

Pfeffer, R., Kurosaki, T., Harrah, C., Chance, J., & Filos, S. (1982). Measurement of functional activities in older adults in the community. *Journal of Gerontology, 37*(3), 323–329. https://doi.org/10.1093/GERONJ/37.3.323

PYMNTS. (2022, November 29). *Digital wallets dominate surge in new payments use.* PYMNTS.com. https://www.pymnts.com/news/payments-innovation/2022/digital-wallets-dominate-surge-in-new-payments-use/

PYMNTS. (2024, July 18). *30% of Gen Z consumers shop by voice every week.* PYMNTS.com. https://www.pymnts.com/voice-activation/2024/30percent-of-gen-z-consumers-shop-by-voice-every-week/

PYMNTS. (2025, January 24). *Nearly 60% of Americans shun automatic bill payments, study reveals.* PYMNTS.com. https://www.pymnts.com/news/payment-methods/2025/nearly-60percent-of-americans-shun-automatic-bill-payments-study-reveals/

Rabin, L. A., Paolillo, E., & Barr, W. B. (2016). Stability in test-usage practices of clinical neuropsychologists in the United States and Canada over a 10-year period: A follow-up survey of INS and NAN members. *Archives of Clinical Neuropsychology, 31*(3), 206–230. https://doi.org/10.1093/arclin/acw007

Reuben, D. B., & Solomon, D. H. (1989). Assessment in geriatrics: Of caveats and names. *Journal of the American Geriatrics Society, 37*(6), 570–572. https://doi.org/10.1111/j.1532-5415.1989.tb05691.x

Rogers, W. A., Mitzner, T. L., & Bixter, M. T. (2020). Understanding the potential of technology to support enhanced activities of daily living (EADLs). *Gerontechnology, 19*(2), 125–137. https://doi.org/10.4017/gt.2020.19.2.005.00

Rosenberg, L., Nygård, L., & Kottorp, A. (2009). Everyday technology use questionnaire: Psychometric evaluation of a new assessment of competence in technology use. *OTJR: Occupational Therapy Journal of Research, 29*(2), 52–62. https://doi.org/10.3928/15394492-20090301-05

Sapienza, A., Lítlá, M., Lehmann, S., & Alessandretti, L. (2023). Exposure to urban and rural contexts shapes smartphone usage behavior. *PNAS Nexus, 2*(11), 1-9. https://doi.org/10.1093/pnasnexus/pgad357

Scullin, M. K., Jones, W. E., Phenis, R., Beevers, S., Rosen, S., Dinh, K., Kiselica, A., Keefe, F. J., & Benge, J. F. (2022). Using smartphone technology to improve prospective memory functioning: A randomized controlled trial. *Journal of the American Geriatrics Society, 70*(2), 459–469. https://doi.org/10.1111/jgs.17551

Shanahan, M., & Bahia, K. (2024). *The state of mobile internet connectivity 2024.* GSMA. https://www.gsma.com/r/somic/

Sikkes, S. A. M., de Lange-de Klerk, E. S. M., Pijnenburg, Y. A. L., Gillissen, F., Romkes, R., Knol, D. L., Uitdehaag, B. M. J., & Scheltens, P. (2012). A new informant-based questionnaire for instrumental activities of daily living in dementia. *Alzheimer's & Dementia: The Journal of the Alzheimer's Association, 8*(6), 536–543. https://doi.org/10.1016/j.jalz.2011.08.006

Sikkes, S. A. M., Knol, D. L., Pijnenburg, Y. A. L., de Lange-de Klerk, E. S. M., Uitdehaag, B. M. J., & Scheltens, P. (2013). Validation of the Amsterdam IADL Questionnaire©, a new tool to measure instrumental activities of daily living in dementia. *Neuroepidemiology, 41*(1), 35–41. https://doi.org/10.1159/000346277

Sparrow, S., Balla, D., & Cicchetti, D. (1984). *Vineland Adaptive Behavior Scales.* American Guidance Service.

Statista Research Department. (2024, June 27). *Online banking penetration in the U.S. 2019–2029.* Statista. https://www.statista.com/forecasts/1285979/digital-banking-penetration-rate-usa

Stein, A. C., & Dubinsky, R. M. (2011). Driving simulator performance in patients with possible and probable Alzheimer's disease. *Annals of Advances in Automotive Medicine. Association for the Advancement of Automotive Medicine. Annual Scientific Conference, 55*, 325–334.

Sualehi, S. H. (2023). (Some) adults left behind: Digital literacy and the working learner. *New Directions for Adult and Continuing Education, 2023*(179), 67–77. https://doi.org/10.1002/ace.20503

Teh, S.-K., Rawtaer, I., & Tan, H. P. (2022). Predictive accuracy of digital biomarker technologies for detection of mild cognitive impairment and pre-frailty among older adults: A systematic review and meta-analysis. *IEEE Journal of Biomedical and Health Informatics, 26*(8), 3638–3648. https://doi.org/10.1109/JBHI.2022.3185798

Teng, E., Li, Y., Manser, P. T., Pickthorn, K., Butcher, B. D., Blendstrup, M., Randolph, C., & Sikkes, S. A. M. (2023). Cross-sectional and longitudinal assessments of function in prodromal-to-mild Alzheimer's disease: A comparison of the ADCS-ADL and A-IADL-Q scales. *Alzheimer's & Dementia (Amsterdam, Netherlands), 15*(2), e12452. https://doi.org/10.1002/dad2.12452

Tochel, C., Smith, M., Baldwin, H., Gustavsson, A., Ly, A., Bexelius, C., Nelson, M., Bintener, C., Fantoni, E., Garre-Olmo, J., Janssen, O., Jindra, C., Jørgensen, I. F., McKeown, A., Öztürk, B., Ponjoan, A., Potashman, M. H., Reed, C., Roncancio-Diaz, E., … ROADMAP consortium. (2019). What outcomes are important to patients with mild cognitive impairment or Alzheimer's disease, their caregivers, and health-care professionals? A systematic review. *Alzheimer's & Dementia (Amsterdam, Netherlands), 11*, 231–247. https://doi.org/10.1016/j.dadm.2018.12.003

U.S. Department of Health and Human Services, Office of Disease Prevention and Health Promotion. (2024). *Social determinants of health—Healthy People 2030*. https://odphp.health.gov/healthypeople/priority-areas/social-determinants-health

Venkatesh, V., Speier-Pero, C., & Schuetz, S. (2022). Why do people shop online? A comprehensive framework of consumers' online shopping intentions and behaviors. *Information Technology & People*, *35*(5), 1590–1620. https://doi.org/10.1108/ITP-12-2020-0867

Vogels, E. A. (2021, June 22). *Digital divide persists even as Americans with lower incomes make gains in tech adoption*. Pew Research Center. https://www.pewresearch.org/short-reads/2021/06/22/digital-divide-persists-even-as-americans-with-lower-incomes-make-gains-in-tech-adoption/

Weil, J., Kamber, T., Glazebrook, A., Giorgi, M., & Ziegler, K. (2021). Digital inclusion of older adults during COVID-19: Lessons from a case study of older adults technology services (OATS). *Journal of Gerontological Social Work*, *64*(6), 643–655. https://doi.org/10.1080/01634372.2021.1919274

Whitehead, L., Talevski, J., Fatehi, F., & Beauchamp, A. (2023). Barriers to and facilitators of digital health among culturally and linguistically diverse populations: Qualitative systematic review. *Journal of Medical Internet Research*, *25*, e42719. https://doi.org/10.2196/42719

Wild, K., Marcoe, J., Mattek, N., Sharma, N., Loewy, E., Tischler, H., Kaye, J., & Karlawish, J. (2022). Online monitoring of financial capacity in older adults: Feasibility and initial findings. *Alzheimer's & Dementia (Amsterdam, Netherlands)*, *14*(1), e12282. https://doi.org/10.1002/dad2.12282

Woods, S. P., Iudicello, J. E., Morgan, E. E., Cameron, M. V., Doyle, K. L., Smith, T. V., Cushman, C., & HIV Neurobehavioral Research Program (HNRP) Group. (2016). Health-related everyday functioning in the Internet Age: HIV-associated neurocognitive disorders disrupt online pharmacy and health chart navigation skills. *Archives of Clinical Neuropsychology: The Official Journal of the National Academy of Neuropsychologists*, *31*(2), 176–185. https://doi.org/10.1093/arclin/acv090

Woods, S. P., Iudicello, J. E., Morgan, E. E., Verduzco, M., Smith, T. V., Cushman, C., & HIV Neurobehavioral Research Program (HNRP) Group. (2017). Household everyday functioning in the Internet Age: Online shopping and banking skills are affected in HIV-associated neurocognitive disorders. *Journal of the International Neuropsychological Society: JINS*, *23*(7), 605–615. https://doi.org/10.1017/S1355617717000431

Woods, S. P., Kordovski, V. M., Tierney, S. M., & Babicz, M. A. (2019). The neuropsychological aspects of performance-based Internet navigation skills: A brief review of an emerging literature. *The Clinical Neuropsychologist*, *33*(2), 305–326. https://doi.org/10.1080/13854046.2018.1503332

Yamada, Y., Okuda, T., Uchida, T., Ikenoue, T., & Fukuma, S. (2024). Monitoring reaction time to digital device in the very-old to detect early cognitive decline. *Npj Aging*, *10*(1), 1–7. https://doi.org/10.1038/s41514-024-00167-z

7

Teleneuropsychology in the 21st Century

Current Status and Future Promise

William Goette and C. Munro Cullum

Introduction

Teleneuropsychology (teleNP) refers to the use of "audiovisual technologies" to conduct neuropsychological assessments remotely with patients (Bilder et al., 2020, p. 648). The COVID-19 pandemic served as an unprecedented catalyst for the acceptance and practice of teleNP, necessitating widespread implementation of remote assessment services and generating substantial innovations in practice models, technological platforms, and assessment methodologies (Bilder et al., 2020) that continue to evolve. While the growth of teleNP is inextricably linked to the COVID-19 pandemic, the foundations of teleNP predate the pandemic by decades. Beyond the initial use of the telephone for remote cognitive screening in the 1980s (see review by Carlew et al., 2020), the first studies involving psychological services by videoconference were published in the late 1990s (Stamm, 1998). Around this same time, early studies comparing audiovisual versus in-person administration of psychometric measures were also occurring (Freir et al., 1999; Jacobsen et al., 2003; Montani et al., 1996). Schopp et al. (2000) provided some of the first evidence for the value, both financial and perceived, of teleNP. A decade later, our group (Grosch et al., 2011) suggested the first practice recommendations for teleNP, and the American Psychological Association (APA) published the first guidelines for the practice of telepsychology shortly thereafter (Joint Task Force for the Development of Telepsychology Guidelines for Psychologists, 2013).

The COVID-19 pandemic introduced a fundamental shift in telehealth interest, with telemedicine visits increasing nearly 700% in some areas (Mann et al., 2020), while the number of studies on telehealth doubled between 2019 and 2020 (Ali et al., 2024). Even still, telehealth services had already been a growing area of clinical practice before the pandemic. For example, the number of hospitals implementing telehealth systems had grown from 35% in 2010 to 76% by 2017 (American Hospital Association, 2019). Despite health services gradually increasing capacity for

William Goette and C. Munro Cullum, *Teleneuropsychology in the 21st Century*. In: *Technology and Neuropsychology*.
Edited by: Jared F. Benge et al., Oxford University Press. © Oxford University Press (2026).
DOI: 10.1093/9780197814116.003.0007

remote audiovisual visits, only about 10–25% of neuropsychologists had used telehealth services in their practice before the COVID-19 pandemic (Fox-Fuller et al., 2021; Hammers et al., 2020; Rochette et al., 2022). Similarly, even though evidence for the potential of teleNP had been gradually accumulating since the late 1990s, many neuropsychologists were initially hesitant to adapt their practices to meet the need for teleNP services during the pandemic (Hammers et al., 2020; Marra et al., 2020; Rochette et al., 2022). The slow adoption of teleNP practice largely reflects the fact that neuropsychologists had to rapidly navigate the nascent and shifting landscape of evidence-based practice, digital assessment tools, privacy regulations, test security considerations, and ethical challenges unique to remote practice. Now that the immediacy of transition from traditional, face-to-face neuropsychological services to teleNP practice has resolved, the field is in a position where we can ask what we want teleNP *to become* instead of simply how we can quickly convert to services to teleNP.

This chapter provides a comprehensive review of the current state of teleNP, emphasizing practical considerations for clinical implementation while identifying critical gaps and opportunities for future research. We examine the conceptual foundations of remote neuropsychological assessment, survey the technological infrastructure required for effective delivery, evaluate the empirical evidence supporting various assessment approaches, and explore applications across various clinical populations. Special attention is given to practical implementation challenges that clinicians may face routinely, including reimbursement policies, medical record integration, privacy regulations, and test security protocols. The chapter concludes with an examination of emerging technologies and methodologies poised to further transform neuropsychological practice in the digital age.

Barriers to TeleNP Adoption and Implementation

Before highlighting concerns specific to teleNP, it is worth noting that the adoption of telemedicine practices in general has been neither consistent nor easy. Kruse et al.'s (2016) prescient systematic review identified 33 specific barriers to the adoption of telemedicine worldwide. A recapitulation of Kruse and colleagues' findings is provided in Table 7.1. While progress toward the resolution of some of these barriers had clearly been made (e.g., American Hospital Association, 2019), the need to transition rapidly to a telemedicine-based health care model because of COVID-19 saw an almost immediate collective effort to find implementation strategies that cleared these barriers at a system or organizational level. As an example, by late March 2020, well over half (62%) of neuropsychologists reported that their practice was now fully remote (Marra et al., 2020), which is a substantial shift from the 10–25% of neuropsychologists who reported using telehealth services before the pandemic (Fox-Fuller et al., 2021; Hammers et al., 2020; Rochette et al., 2022).

With the abrupt pivot of health care systems to telemedicine services, some previous barriers were also necessarily addressed. For example, the transition of many clinic appointments to telehealth platforms inherently increased patients' awareness

Table 7.1 Barriers to Adopting Telemedicine Identified in Kruse et al. (2016)

Barrier	Level of Barrier	Examples
Financial	Organizational	Cost of infrastructure Maintenance and upkeep Reimbursement rates
Ethics	Organizational	Legal liability Privacy and confidentiality Data security
	Staff (clinical)	Licensing and training
Practicality	Organizational	Age of equipment Established workflow
	Patients	Access to audiovisual devices Awareness of service option Familiarity with technology Adequate internet connection
	Staff (programmers)	Interoperability of software Design of available software
	Staff (clinical)	Familiarity with technology
Perceptual	Patients	Preference for in-person visits Expectations from technology
	Staff (clinical)	Resistance to change Perception of impersonal care

of these services, and the need to continue with medical care resulted in increased experience and familiarity with virtual visits and technologies for both patients and clinicians. Additionally, an entire generation of young clinicians received much of their training and experience in the provision of telehealth services—albeit sometimes in a reactionary or post-hoc rather than standardized and carefully planned manner (Cena et al., 2023; Dzara et al., 2022; Triemstra et al., 2021; Wolff et al., 2020). Similarly, a number of webinars and continuing education resources on providing telehealth services quickly emerged to meet the demand from established clinicians for guidance, training, and current best practices (e.g., American Psychological Association, 2025; Cullum et al., 2019; Inter Organizational Practice Committee, n.d.; National Academy of Neuropsychology, n.d.).

The implementation and development of telehealth services as a product of necessity should not be confused with a comprehensive solution to the barriers of telemedicine more generally. The COVID-19 pandemic introduced the financial and systemic impetus needed for teleNP to become a realized model of neuropsychological care, but the increased provision of teleNP services in response to a global pandemic in many ways only added to the professional barriers to its long-term sustainability. To illustrate this point, one survey of neuropsychologists found that, while 95% of respondents endorsed interest in using video technology in their practice since the COVID-19 pandemic, only 45% actually had done so (compared to 24% who reported using video technology before the COVID-19 pandemic) (Hammers et al., 2020).

To understand the gap between interest in teleNP and its implementation, the remaining barriers specific to neuropsychology need to be considered. A number of published reports asked neuropsychologists about their experiences and beliefs related to transition to teleNP services (Chapman et al., 2020; Fox-Fuller et al., 2021; Hammer et al., 2020; Hewitt et al., 2020; Marra et al., 2020; Rochette et al., 2022; Scott et al., 2022), and several perspective papers provided examples of teleNP program and offered guidance and direction to neuropsychologists. Other papers highlighted a number of issues that require consideration in adopting teleNP services (Bilder et al., 2020; Postal et al., 2020; Sperling et al., 2024). Table 7.2 offers a synthesis of the barriers, problems, concerns, and open questions identified in these publications.

There is no single solution to telehealth barriers, and many are interrelated such that progress in addressing one will likely contribute to identifying meaningful

Table 7.2 Thematic Summary of TeleNP Barriers, Issues, and Concerns

Major Theme	Subthemes	Specific Concerns
Ethical and legal considerations	Test security	Copyright violations Limited control of test materials Legal/forensic precedent
	Privacy and confidentiality	HIPAA/privacy concerns Inability to control privacy of testing environment Potential for recording or unauthorized access
	Informed consent	Need for modified consent procedures Explaining limitations of teleNP Disclosure of potential technology failures
Technology-related barriers	Internet connectivity	Internet connectivity problems General connectivity problems Bandwidth limitations
	Technology access	Limited access by patients Digital divide of some populations
	Device/platform limitations	Screen sharing capabilities Lack of standardization across devices/platforms Technology interface impacting standardization
	Technical proficiency	Patient familiarity with technology Clinician familiarity with technology Time required for setup and troubleshooting

continued

Table 7.2 *continued*

Major Theme	Subthemes	Specific Concerns
Clinical and psychometric concerns	Test validity	Limited evidence for equivalence of teleNP Modifications to testing needed for teleNP Lack of teleNP norms
	Domain coverage	Limited ability to assess certain domains Limitations to motor and sensory assessment
	Behavioral observations	Reduced ability to observe behaviors Limited field of view Difficulty with rapport and alliance
	Environmental control	Distractions in patients' homes Inability to ensure optimal testing conditions
Administrative and institutional barriers	Reimbursement	Insurance reimbursement rates Billing challenges for teleNP Variable reimbursement policies across settings
	Organizational constraints	Institutional approval limitations Mandated telehealth platforms restrict testing Loss of support staff
	Licensing issues	State restrictions for cross-border practice Temporary nature of waivers during the pandemic International practice limitations
Population-specific challenges	Patient characteristics	Suitability for patients with impairment Behavioral dysregulation affecting test validity Language barriers and interpreter challenges
	Clinical populations	Specialized concerns for medicolegal cases Challenges with pediatric assessment Limitations for presurgical evaluations
	Equity and access	Digital divide affecting marginalized communities Rural/remote access challenges Socioeconomic factors affecting access
Training and competency	Provider knowledge	Limited formal training in teleNP Need for specific teleNP competencies Lack of standardized training
	Resources and guidance	Need for improved practice guidelines No centralized/comprehensive guidance document Lack of validation studies

solutions to others. Some of these barriers fall naturally in the purview of professional activities and development such as establishing ethical and legal guidance, accumulating empirical research regarding validity and test interpretation, and identifying new professional competencies and training. Other barriers reflect specific cases of broader, interprofessional challenges that emerged in the pandemic, such as licensing considerations and reimbursement rates for remote versus in-person health services. Individual neuropsychologists cannot directly control patient Internet reliability or software platform efficiency; however, clinicians must understand these limitations when planning and implementing teleNP services.

Digital Divide and Accessibility of TeleNP

The "digital divide" refers to disparities in accessibility to reliable, fast Internet connectivity and Internet-ready devices. This divide has persisted since commercial Internet services emerged in the late 1990s and early 2000s (van Dijk, 2019; Warschauer & Niiya, 2017; Witte et al., 2013). The COVID-19 starkly highlighted Internet dependency. During the pandemic, 90% of U.S. adults reported that Internet access was at least important to them personally, with 58% indicating it was *essential* (McClain et al., 2021). However, Internet access alone does not guarantee teleNP feasibility. Even among homes with high-speed Internet, 48% report frequent problems with connection speed, reliability, or quality (McClain et al., 2021). Financial barriers compound these technical challenges, with 26% of high-speed users expressing concern about affording their Internet bills (McClain et al., 2021).

Importantly, the quality of Internet and familiarity with technology ("tech readiness") is also associated with sociodemographic factors such as income, education, and age. For example, whereas 39% of high-speed Internet upper-income (at least twice the median family income) users reported problems related to speed, reliability, or quality of their connection, 47% of middle-income (two-thirds to twice the median family income) users and 60% of lower-income (less than two-thirds the median family income) users expressed the same concerns about their Internet connection (McClain et al., 2021). About 30% of adults in the United States indicated that they usually need someone else to help them with their electronic devices or lack confidence in their ability to do things they need to do on the Internet, but this percentage depends considerably on age, with just 16–17% of adults between the ages of 18 and 49 reporting this low tech readiness compared to 34% of adults between 50 and 64, 54% between 65 and 74, and 68% of adults older than 75 (McClain et al., 2021). Accessibility of Internet resources is further confounded by nearly half of adults in the United States having limited literacy skills and upward of 90% of adults having limited health literacy skills that can make navigating health-specific online content extraordinarily challenging, independent of connectivity or tech readiness (Office of Disease Prevention and Health Promotion, 2016).

The digital divide is not unique to United States, as similar issues with equitable Internet access are observed in Western (Zillien & Marr, 2013) and Eastern (Barbovschi & Balea, 2013; Radovanović, 2013) Europe, Russia (Deviatko, 2013), India (Ilavarasan, 2013), and China and Taiwan (Tseng & You, 2013), to name just a few countries and regions where this has been observed. The International Telecommunication Union and Office of the United Nations Secretary-General's Envoy on Technology (2022) released their aspirational targets for achieving universal and meaningful connectivity by 2030 with the aim of addressing the long-standing digital divide globally. The minimum target fixed-broadband Internet speed for individuals is 10 Mbit/s at a cost no more than 2% of monthly gross national income (GNI) per capita. As of 2022, the global median price for broadband services was 1.5% of GNI, but among low-income countries, the average cost was 9% of GNI (International Telecommunication Union, 2022).

In the United States, efforts to expand and ensure Internet connectivity are broadly overseen by the Federal Communications Commission (FCC). As a result of the Telecommunications Act of 1996, the FCC developed four programs within the Universal Service Fund to achieve the goals of increased access to affordable telecommunications and high-speed Internet (Universal Service Administrative Co., n.d.):

- Connect America Fund (formerly known as High-Cost Support): financial support services aimed at rural areas
- Lifeline: initiatives and support for low-income consumers and residents of Tribal lands
- E-Rate: financial support to cover equipment and services for increase access through schools and libraries
- Rural Health Care: financial support for health care providers to cover the telecommunication service costs needed to provide health care services

A number of additional initiatives managed through the FCC have emerged as part of the broader National Broadband Plan (FCC, 2010), which was developed following congressional order in 2009. Most notably, the Consolidated Appropriations Act passed by Congress in 2021 established the Emergency Broadband Benefit Program (FCC, 2025) specifically to assist low-income households with Internet connectivity during the COVID-19 pandemic, and later in 2021, Congress established the Affordable Connectivity Program that offered up to $30 monthly discounts for Internet services (up to $75 monthly discounts for households on Tribal lands) and up to $100 to assist in the purchase of a computer or tablet (FCC, 2024).

Again, any single neuropsychologist is unlikely to be equipped to solve accessibility-related concerns that exist at a broader societal level, but the recognition of these concerns is still a critical part of effectively implementing teleNP. In particular, the American Psychological Association's (2017) ethical principles D (Justice) and E (Respect for People's Rights and Dignity) come to bear on the practice of teleNP.

Justice, TeleNP, and the Digital Divide

The aspirational goal of justice encourages psychologists to "recognize that fairness and justice entitle all persons to access to and benefit from the contributions of psychology and to equal quality in the processes, procedures, and services being conducted by psychologists" (APA, 2017, General Principles section, para. 5). While teleNP can facilitate greater access to neuropsychological services for many individuals who otherwise would have difficulty receiving traditional in-person services, it should not be assumed that offering remote services is inherently fair or just simply because it expands accessibility. As emphasized throughout this section, the digital divide makes it such that there remains a portion of society across the world who lack the technological services necessary to participate in telehealth services. Similarly, even among those who have fast internet connections and electronic devices necessary to establish a remote assessment visit, the reliability and stability of these foundational teleNP tools may negatively impact the quality of the service they receive.

Neuropsychologists considering the implementation of teleNP for their own practice or research should reflect on the potential barriers in their setting or more general community. Barriers that could limit the accessibility of teleNP visits or those that could harm the quality of the teleNP service as a whole should be identified so that potential solutions can be implemented to maximize fairness and justice. While not traditionally emphasized in training programs (Alexander & Allo, 2021), neuropsychologists engaging in this evaluation of local needs relative to teleNP services may identify specific advocacy and public policy needs that would benefit from their unique experience or role in the community. Ultimately, if teleNP is to become a viable practice model, then public policy and sustained advocacy efforts to increase the availability of reliable high-speed internet and electronic devices with appropriate audiovisual capabilities is an essential prerequisite.

Respect for Rights and Dignity, TeleNP, and the Digital Divide

Closely related to the issues of obtaining equal quality of psychological services, the APA's aspirational goal for the respect of rights and dignity indicates that psychologists should be "aware of and respect cultural, individual, and role differences, including those based on age, gender, gender identity, race, ethnicity, culture, national origin, religion, sexual orientation, disability, language, and socioeconomic status, and consider these factors when working with members of such groups" (APA, 2017, General Principles section, para. 6). As noted earlier, the impact of the digital divide varies by age, education, and socioeconomic status (in the United States, at least). Recognizing that particular individuals may be at greater risk of inadequate technological resources, tech readiness, or digital health literacy ought to be part of the neuropsychologist's decision-making regarding the appropriateness of teleNP appointments with patients.

Failing to consider the potential impact of these factors with each individual patient would fall short of this aspirational ethical principle and certainly could increase the risk that the patient unfairly receives a poor quality of service. The potential financial advantage to a fully remote teleNP practice that might come from a reduction in overhead costs related to office space needs to be balanced against recognition that not every referral to that practice is appropriately served by such a model. At the same time, a referral for an 80-year-old patient who prefers a teleNP visit due to compromised immune function should not automatically be assumed to be inappropriate simply because of the individual's age or background. Neuropsychologists offering teleNP appointments ought to determine the most appropriate methods for making determinations about whether to proceed with teleNP or traditional in-person services (or a combination of both) for each patient. Preappointment triaging or scheduling interviews for telehealth before testing is scheduled may help clinicians assess a patient's appropriateness for teleNP services, but this additional clinical time on the front end of referrals introduces its own set of further considerations, ranging from billing of that time to the ethics of potentially denying a teleNP service that may be more affordable for a patient (e.g., no transportation costs, ability to take off less time from work due to the reduction in commute time).

Summary of Barriers to the Early Adoption of TeleNP

The groundwork for teleNP is now nearly 30 years old, and the adoption of telehealth methodologies by neuropsychologists has historically lagged that of other psychological and health professions. The fundamental change to so much of life in the wake of the COVID-19 pandemic in 2020 is ultimately what made the widespread implementation of teleNP a reality despite years of accumulating evidence and preceding encouragement, recommendation, and guidance to move in that direction. As explored throughout this section, the implementation of teleNP in response to the global pandemic should not be confused with the successful transition to teleNP-ready practices or even widespread acceptance of the potential for teleNP. The myriad barriers that we have highlighted thus far reflect the serious questions and doubts raised by neuropsychologists and contributed to the field's hesitancy to transition away from the well-established traditions of in-person assessments. Even then, while many neuropsychologists eventually transitioned to offering some form of teleNP services, as restrictions were lifted and public health guidance updated, much of the field returned to practice as usual with teleNP remaining a resource but less commonly a central practice.

The remainder of this chapter will review the current state of research and professional guidance on teleNP. Central to this review are the barriers that have been discussed here. The goal of these next sections is to dispel any misconceptions about the absence of empirical support for teleNP that may be lingering from the confusion and uncertainty experienced early in the pandemic. At the same time, we will emphasize open questions, gaps in the literature, and opportunities for future research on teleNP methods. At the very end of the chapter, we will present updated resources and guidance to help integrate this information and direct the field's next steps toward a robust, evidence-based teleNP practice.

Models and Approaches to TeleNP

To this point, we have not fully explained or broken down the elements of teleNP but instead have spoken more generally about the idea of conducting neuropsychological services with telecommunication/audiovisual technology. In reality, the scope of teleNP can include any aspect of the methods and procedures recognized as part of neuropsychological assessment and consultation (American Academy of Clinical Neuropsychology Board of Directors, 2007). The American Academy of Clinical Neuropsychology (AACN)'s practice guidelines outline 10 specific elements of a neuropsychological service, which are reproduced in Table 7.3 along with potential applications or uses of audiovisual technology for teleNP services. In this section, we will focus specifically on the previsit, appointment, and feedback procedures. Later in this chapter, we provide more focused attention on the topics of empirical research to support clinical practice decisions and post-assessment processes within the teleNP context.

Approaches to TeleNP

Before introducing some specific details regarding models for teleNP practices, it is important to clarify the difference between teleNP models and teleNP delivery approaches. A practice model is a comprehensive workflow that is designed intentionally to meet the specific clinical needs of a clinician or clinic. A fundamental element of a practice model is thus the delivery approach as this is, in effect, the medium by which the service described by the practice model is delivered. The literature on teleNP has traditionally focused on three main delivery approaches:

- Clinic-to-Clinic: both the neuropsychologist and patient are in a clinical setting but not in the same clinical location per se.
    - *Spoke-Hub Arrangement:* the neuropsychologist's clinical setting is located in a primary, high-volume area (e.g., urban hospital system, academic medical center) while the patient participates in the visit from a satellite location (e.g., rural outreach center, affiliated clinics).
    - *Point-to-Point Arrangement:* the neuropsychologist's clinical setting has arrangements with other clinical locations (e.g., primary care clinics, specialist clinics, hospitals) where patients can be scheduled to attend the visit.
    - *Intra-Office Arrangement:* the neuropsychologist and patient are present in the same clinical location but participate in the visit from different rooms (e.g., office to testing room).
- Clinic-to-Home: the neuropsychologist is located in a clinical setting while the patient attends the appointment from their home.
- Home-to-Home: both the neuropsychologist and patient participate in the appointment from their respective homes.

Table 7.3 Methods and Procedures of Neuropsychologists with TeleNP Opportunities and Concerns

Stage of Service	Method/Procedure	TeleNP Opportunities	TeleNP Concerns
Research to guide practice	Measurement procedures	Dedicated validation research	Reduced standardization of testing environment
	Assessment of motivation and effort	Digital assessment development	Maintenance of test security
	Assessment of concurrent validity	Novel assessment methods	Coverage of cognitive domains
Previsit preparation	Decision to evaluate	Previsit screening Integrated health records	Maintaining expectations of screening visit
	Review of records	"Warm" hand-offs from referring providers	Lack of guidance regarding appropriateness
Appointment	Interview of patient and significant others	More flexible scheduling options	Confidentiality, privacy, and call quality
	Test administration and scoring	Reduced opportunity costs for patients	Monitoring or viewing performance
Post-appointment	Interpretation	Automated scoring with computer-based tools	Availability of normative data
	Evaluation report	Direct integration with medical records	Limitations to conclusions or evaluation's scope
Feedback	Providing feedback	Flexible scheduling and inclusion of participants	Loss of personal dynamic or connection

In the survey by Fox-Fuller et al. (2021), the majority of neuropsychologists (81.6%) had conducted home-to-home teleNP evaluations during the COVID-19 pandemic. By comparison, nearly half (44.8%) had conducted clinic-to-home assessments and about a third (32.2%) had used a clinic-to-clinic approach for their evaluations (Fox-Fuller et al., 2022).

Another important consideration regarding the delivery approaches for teleNP is the potential for audiovisual technologies to be either focal or general in their utilization. To some extent, neuropsychological practice can be considered as being conducted across a spectrum of telehealth integration ranging from a fully face-to-face, in-person process to one conducted entirely remotely from start to finish. The clinic-to-clinic, clinic-to-home, and home-to-home delivery approaches are simply location-specific iterations of a fully remote (or completely teleNP) clinical practice. A more flexible teleNP approach would be to consider the specific neuropsychological services that the clinician plans to provide remotely versus in-person, which results in a *hybrid teleNP approach*. The survey of neuropsychologists by Hammers and colleagues (2020) illustrates the spectrum of hybrid teleNP approaches as shown in Figure 7.1.

Mirroring the results of this survey, Marra et al. (2020) found that neuropsychologists favored a hybrid teleNP approach, with just over half (51.7%) of their sample indicating that teleNP was being used for intakes and feedbacks but not for testing, while very few (2.6%) were utilizing a fully remote teleNP approach to their practice.

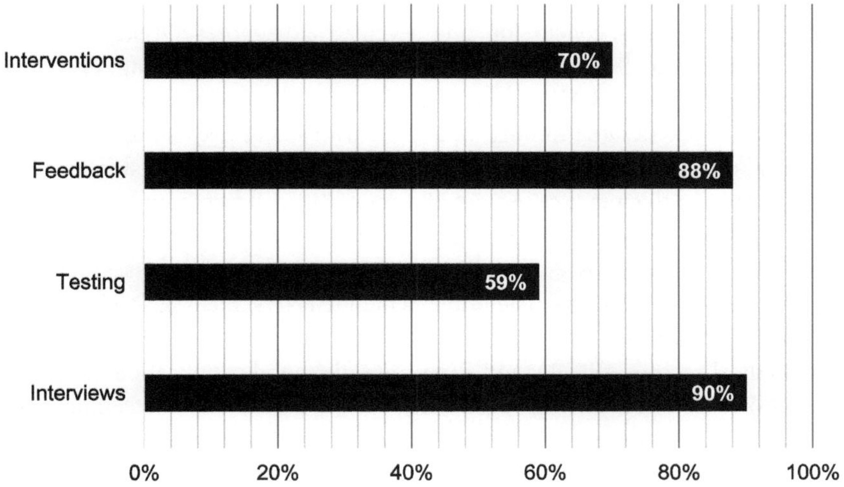

Figure 7.1 Percentage of neuropsychologists indicating they plan to use audiovisual technology for different parts of their evaluations

Hammers et al. (2020) surveyed neuropsychologists about their experiences with teleNP and plans for incorporating these technologies in their future practices. Shown in Figure 7.1 are the percentage of neuropsychologists in their survey who indicated that they planned to use audiovisual technology for each of the following four aspects of their clinical services: clinical interviews, cognitive testing, providing feedback, and providing interventions.

The preference of neuropsychologists to offer some services (particularly feedback or interventions) remotely but not others predates the widespread use of telehealth resources caused by the COVID-19 pandemic (Chapman et al., 2020). As we will review later in this section, the future of these hybrid teleNP approaches will likely be shaped greatly by reimbursement policies going forward. Billing and reimbursement limitations already influence prepandemic practice decisions among neuropsychologists (Sweet et al., 2021), so it would be unfortunate to see a return to similar financial decisions that may set teleNP interest and progress back to where we were 5 years ago.

Existing TeleNP Service Models

A variety of publications emerged in the first couple years of the COVID-19 pandemic aimed at describing how various practices transitioned to providing teleNP services. In some cases, the teleNP programs themselves had predated the pandemic, while in others they were developed directly in response to the practice changes needed at the time. Each of these example models of implemented teleNP services illustrates different ways of flexibly integrating telehealth and in-person modalities to meet specific clinical needs.

Salinas et al. (2020) described the development of a teleNP service in a private practice 2 years before the COVID-19 pandemic. The practice implemented a video-based teleNP screening process for the assessment of children with developmental and language disorders, concussion, and psychiatric diagnoses. Of particular value in the publication by Salinas and colleagues, the process of planning, developing, and implementing this teleNP practice was detailed in the methods. They describe the use of a 1-week "design thinking" bootcamp with a neuropsychologist and senior mechanical design engineer to determine the appropriate steps needed for teleNP services within in this practice. Across 68 (out of 70) children seen by the practice who were offered the teleNP screening, the practice had an 18% increase in profits and $67,000 savings in costs, all while reducing the length of the assessment from 5–11 hours to 75–90 minutes. The implemented teleNP screening service reported by Salinas et al. utilized Doxy as the video platform, Simple Practice for its electronic medical records (EMR), and Ring Central (mobile application) to monitor call duration and time receiving/organizing previous records. As a screening service, standardized history forms and questionnaires along with a targeted (20–30 minute) diagnostic interview were the primary assessment methods; however, for children suspected of having autism spectrum disorder, the Childhood Autism Rating Scale, NEPSY-II, DKEFS (verbal fluency), ADOS-II (cartoons, friends, and conversations), and Vineland-3 were also given. The neuropsychologist utilized two monitors for the visits with one used for videoconferencing and the other to access Q-global to assist in administering and scoring the Vineland-3. The neuropsychologist utilized screensharing with parents to provide feedback and diagnostic impressions as all materials were electronically available and thus accessible almost immediately after being uploaded to the EMR.

A consultation service model developed for rural outreach prior to the COVID-19 pandemic is described by Sherwood and MacDonald (2020). The goal of the service was to expand access to neuropsychological services for children with neurodevelopment and acquired disorders living in rural regions, and the implementation of this consultation-based service aligns with traditional spoke-hub arrangements with the neuropsychologists practicing out of urban areas while patients participated in the remote service from an outlying pediatric health clinic. As reviewed in their methods section, the development of this consultation service required coordination and planning in advance to work with participating rural pediatricians. Of primary note, the practical complexities of scheduling, billing, services provided by the pediatrician versus neuropsychologist, documentation responsibilities, sharing of records, and coordination of care are highlighted as part of the various challenges that the groups had to solve before implementing the consultation practice. As a consultation-based model rather than assessment- or intervention-based model, the primary endpoint of the outreach service was a clinical decision-making tree in which the neuropsychologist determined that the child either (1) has a medical condition that makes assessment an immediately necessary, (2) does not have a medical condition but likely a neurodevelopmental concern that makes an assessment indicated but not urgent, or (3) does not need a neuropsychological evaluation (e.g., diagnosis is psychiatric, previous/recent evaluation). While their pilot program was developed around a spoke-hub arrangement, Sherwood and MacDonald describe ongoing communication and work with the local pediatricians to identify private practice neuropsychologists, which illustrates the potential pivot to a point-to-point arrangement built around community relationships and centered on patient accessibility (e.g., private practices may have shorter waitlists or may be easier to access than the urban practices within medical centers).

Mietchen et al. (2025) provide a more longitudinal outcome study of their implementation of a telehealth triage consultation model similar in someways to the clinical decision-making tree used in Sherwood and MacDonald (2020). Children referred for neuropsychological evaluation who had learning concerns and no significant medical risk for cognitive or neurodevelopmental delays were provided a telehealth triage consultation appointment (TTCA) in order to clarify the possible differential diagnoses, clarify whether a neuropsychological evaluation was needed, and provide psychoeducation and/or resources to families as appropriate to meet short-term needs identified in the appointment. Based on the telehealth visit, the pediatric neuropsychologist would triage the scheduling of the referral by either closing it out (referral was not appropriate) or adding the referral to the appropriate wait list: standard (no known risk factors for cognitive deficits), priority (risk factors for cognitive deficits but no service line for the condition), or condition-specific (risk factors for cognitive deficits with a service line for the condition; e.g., epilepsy). The TTCAs were, on average, brief (45–75 minutes) and included the elements of a typical neurobehavioral examination, resulting in the billing of typically one unit of 96116 and one unit of 96121 CPT codes. As a result of the TTCA implementation, a quarter of referrals (25.5%) were determined to not need further neuropsychological evaluation. Over a 3-year period, the neuropsychological practice experienced a 12.9% increase in total referrals but also experienced a 19.3% decrease in the wait time of patients for neuropsychological assessment, which reduced the average waitlist time of patients from 608 days to 27.5 days. Follow-up satisfaction surveys sent to referring providers showed that they were largely satisfied with the neuropsychological services, and 66% of respondents indicated that they had received positive feedback from their patients about the TTCA service. The triaging model implemented by Mietchen et al. illustrates the significant practical benefits possible from a relatively simple telehealth implementation plan, with wait times for this single clinic dropping 95.9% at the same time that the clinic was receiving more referrals than before.

Thibodaux et al. (2021) describe their implementation of a home-to-home teleNP practice during the COVID-19 pandemic. Their clinic provides pediatric neuropsychological assessments in a large tertiary care hospital, and their transition to care to a teleNP model resulted in a manualized, four-part evaluation process. The first evaluation is the intake, which was conducted over the phone. In addition to the standard elements of a neuropsychological interview, the intake session included questions about the family's familiarity and experience with the videoconferencing software (Zoom). Based on the intake, the neuropsychologist determines whether to proceed with a connectivity visit or a health and behavior (CPT = 96150) assessment, which was used when the patient was determined to not be appropriate for teleNP evaluation. Patients seen for a health and behavior assessment may be scheduled for in-clinic testing if neuropsychological evaluation is determined to still be necessary. The connectivity visit involved both the neuropsychologist and psychometrist meeting with the caregiver and patient to review confidentiality, videoconference software security, risks of telehealth, and the goals of the evaluation. In effect, the connectivity visit provides an opportunity for rapport building and orientation to the expectations and experience of teleNP testing, which includes discussion of environmental considerations (e.g., sitting at a desk, reducing distractions/interruptions, availability of headphones), the device the child will be using to participate in the session (e.g., laptop, desktop, phone, tablet), and considerations specific to extended telehealth appointments (e.g., internet connection, accessibility of chargers). The next visit in Thibodaux and colleagues' practice is the evaluation itself. The neuropsychologist is on the video call for this visit with the psychometrist and patient so that the neuropsychologist can observe the testing and support the psychometrist as needed with modifications or adjustments needed to test administration that might arise because of the remote assessment. Thibodaux et al. provide a list of the tests they administered virtually for those interested in their selection. The final visit scheduled is the feedback visit either by telephone or videoconference.

Pritchard and colleagues (2020) outlined their pediatric neuropsychology department's transition to a three-tiered model of care in response to the pandemic.

The three tiers correspond generally to the complexity of the referral question and differential diagnosis. Tier 1 services included a comprehensive diagnostic interview of the patient and their family, a neurobehavioral status examination, review of available medical or academic records, and online questionnaire ratings from parents and teachers obtained prior to the visit. Tier 2 services add targeted assessment via videoconferencing to address specific questions or considerations that would otherwise not be adequately evaluated if the patient received Tier 1 services. Finally, Tier 3 services were recommended for referrals where face-to-face assessment was needed, though these patients may still receive a videoconference-based interview and record reviews as in Tier 1.

An important observation regarding these published examples of implemented teleNP practices is that all involved pediatric services, not adult. The fact that these examples were limited to pediatric populations is part of the reason that some neuropsychologists were hesitant or slow to integrate teleNP practices at the start of the COVID-19 pandemic (Hewitt et al., 2020). Much of the teleNP literature in adult populations has focused primarily on the comparison of testing results over the telephone or via videoconference to those obtained from traditional in-person administrations, though there are some exceptions to this (e.g., Barton et al., 2011). The comparative literature of teleNP to in-person neuropsychological testing is examined later in this chapter, so it is not presented here as part of the discussion on models of teleNP.

Consistent TeleNP Practice Recommendations and Considerations

While examples and descriptions of implemented teleNP models may be lacking in adult populations, there are a relatively large number of publications providing recommendations and considerations for adult teleNP services (Bilder et al., 2020; Kitaigorodsky et al., 2021; Postal et al., 2020; Serrano-Juárez et al., 2023; Wong et al., 2024). This kind of literature may not be the same as presenting evidence for a particular service model involving teleNP, but it does at least respond to the general lack of guidelines and recommendations that was present at the start of the pandemic and was one of the most commonly identified barriers to teleNP adoption by neuropsychologists (Marra et al., 2020; Rochette et al., 2022). A more detailed integration of the core practice recommendations and considerations across all of the studies reviewed for this chapter is provided in Appendix A. There are some specific elements of implemented and recommended teleNP models, however, that warrant direct comment outside of the more conceptual considerations synthesized in Appendix A.

As was emphasized in the documentation of implemented pediatric teleNP models, development of a teleNP practice begins with intentional reflection, consideration, problem-solving, and investment in determining the goals and role of telehealth services in the context of the neuropsychology clinic overall. Such consideration and planning were not available to clinicians at the start of the COVID-19 pandemic, and the potential flexibility of conducting specific services by telehealth but not others also did not exist for a variety of clinicians whose practices depended on specific workflows, resources, or clinical tools. Now that health care practices have transitioned to a postpandemic status quo, however, the adoption and implementation of teleNP can be undertaken thoughtfully again. Both Salinas et al. (2020) and Sherwood and MacDonald (2020) describe the planning stages of their teleNP implementations, and it is notable that, in both cases, the planning involved consultation and collaboration with others outside of the practice (and even outside of the field of neuropsychology).

Another specific reflection to undertake before implementing a teleNP model is the dynamic nature of the model. In the examples of Sherwood and MacDonald (2020), Mietchen et al. (2025), and Thibodaux et al. (2021), the teleNP implementation came with deliberate planning for continual monitoring of workflows and processes. Preparing a quality assessment and monitoring element of a teleNP model of care is a critical component. As mentioned earlier, teleNP services provide a significant amount of flexibility for clinicians, given the range of videoconference platforms that offer varying functionality and services, the level of integration between the telehealth software and EMR, and inherent considerations of necessary modifications to traditional neuropsychological services brought on by the change in delivery modality. The only way that this flexibility can be fully capitalized on is if there is monitoring of the teleNP process and corresponding outcome priorities that will be used to inform the success of the implemented practice model.

While certain professional standards may require some degree of modification when providing telehealth services (e.g., informed consent), teleNP models offer the potential for more fundamental shifts in the structure of neuropsychological service delivery. One example of this structural shift can be found in the implementation of referral triaging described in Sherwood and MacDonald (2020), Mietchen et al. (2025), and Thibodaux et al. (2021). In all three of these programs, the implementation of a teleNP service included a specific decision process regarding the most appropriate next step after a telehealth-administered neurobehavioral status examination. Thibodaux and colleagues introduced an entirely new telehealth visit specific to the teleNP model they implemented in the form of the connectivity visit while the rest of their service following the more traditional interview, testing, and feedback sequence of visits. An additional visit type may or may not be appropriate for all practices, but it is important to note that each of these models included a modification of some kind to their typical interviews specifically to evaluate the appropriateness and readiness of the patients for a telehealth appointment. The importance of setting aside time and being prepared to orient patients to the telehealth appointment, planning for potential disruptions or technical errors, and setting specific expectations for the environment, behavior, and engagement of patients during teleNP services is made abundantly clear in all of the literature related to teleNP.

TeleNP Considerations for Pediatric Populations

The literature on teleNP among pediatric populations has identified four broad areas of special consideration unique to this demographic. First is developmental appropriateness (e.g., Ransom et al., 2020; Thibodaux et al., 2021). This consideration is similar in nature to making decisions about a test battery for any child, but the telehealth context does introduce additional complexity since the neuropsychologist will have less direct oversight or accessibility to the child during the evaluation than would otherwise be needed to assist with behavioral management or redirection. Related directly to this consideration is the degree of caregiver involvement available, desired, or needed for the evaluation. The neuropsychologist may need to be prepared to work more closely with caregivers to prepare them for the session and brainstorm alternative solutions or options that could be needed during the evaluation. A third consideration for pediatric neuropsychologists engaging in teleNP services is related to the utilization and planning of engagement strategies (e.g., Harder et al., 2020; Thibodaux et al., 2021). Again, this is similar to what pediatric neuropsychologists already plan for, but the remote nature of the session adds further complexity in terms of establishing boundaries (e.g., maintaining a testing environment despite being at home), scheduling breaks, modifying presentation of stimuli, and providing positive reinforcement. Finally, pediatric teleNP evaluations should consider staging assessments into multiple shorter sessions.

TeleNP Considerations for Older Adult Populations

The specific considerations for teleNP services with older adults have been framed largely around technological familiarity and readiness. Just as with pediatric neuropsychologists, the literature has identified four specific considerations related to teleNP work with older adults. First is the need to consider what technology support may be needed. In offering teleNP services, the neuropsychologist should assess the additional technological support or even on-site assistance that may be needed for older adults (Bilder et al., 2020; Marra et al., 2020). A second consideration is related to sensory abilities and potential accommodations. The literature has generally emphasized visual and auditory acuity with recommendations including increasing stimuli size, utilizing higher-quality microphone equipment to minimize audio artifact, or connecting hearing assistive devices to the videoconference call (Kitaigorodsky et al., 2021; Serrano-Juárez et al., 2023). Third, as with earlier teleNP research (Cullum et al., 2006), Kitaigorodsky et al. (2021) designed their teleNP battery to be no longer than 120 minutes to avoid the potential influence of interruptions during the process as well as potential fatigue associated with teleconference meetings, which is not entirely different from considering test battery situation (e.g. in-hospital vs. in-clinic) and length with older adults in traditional neuropsychological evaluations. The final consideration is broadly related to using a simplified interface for the telehealth appointment and providing step-by-step guidance before the evaluation starts regarding the navigation of the relevant technology and determining what, if any, additional assistance may be needed during the exam (Kitaigorodsky et al., 2021; Nguyen et al., 2023).

Diverse Populations or Practice Settings

An important benefit of teleNP is the enhanced accessibility of neuropsychological services. For example, it has been reported that appointment attendance rates improved 24% when the service was conducted via telephone compared to in-person among a diverse, community hospital-based sample (Caze et al., 2020). At the same time, greater accessibility should not be confused with equitable access, which was reviewed earlier with respect to the digital divide. The consideration of socioeconomic factors has been raised by various authors, including Nguyen et al. (2021) and Serrano-Juárez et al. (2023) in their overview of teleNP considerations with Asian and Latin American populations. In addition to internet access, socioeconomic factors can influence the availability of technology, modernity of devices owned, and access to separate or private space for the assessment. Outside of socioeconomic status, individuals from diverse backgrounds may also have different cultural backgrounds that could impact their access, utilization, and comfort with technology (Crivelli et al., 2022; Nguyen et al., 2021). For example, individuals living in multigenerational homes may have adequate internet and technology required for a teleNP assessment, but the primary users of those materials may be children or grandchildren in the home. Preparing patients for the nature of the examination and carefully denoting the limitations of the help that they may be able to receive from others in the house may be more important for some individuals from different cultural and generational backgrounds. As with all neuropsychological services provided to individuals from diverse backgrounds, teleNP planning needs to include awareness of language-related barriers. Informed consent and any other informational materials provided as part of the practice should be culturally and linguistically adapted for the patient (Crivelli et al., 2022; Nguyen et al., 2021). Similarly, the teleNP services should be provided in the patient's primary language or using validated protocols for interpreter-mediated assessments whenever possible (Arias et al., 2020; Nguyen et al., 2021).

Reimbursement for TeleNP Services

The reimbursement for teleNP was a known limiter to its adoption even before the COVID-19 pandemic forced the question of how and whether remote health services should be reimbursed. For example, the 2020 professional survey of neuropsychologists in the United States was conducted just before the pandemic, and the majority of respondents indicated using facility-based billing, which excluded telephone-based feedback sessions, and even at that time, 60.9% of respondents reported that reimbursement of telehealth services would facilitate their ability to provide feedback sessions to their patients (Sweet et al., 2021).

Generally, the coverage of telehealth services has expanded since the COVID-19 pandemic secondary to federal policies affecting Medicare, but even at a federal level, not all of these changes expanding telehealth coverage have been made permanent (U.S. Department of Health and Human Services, 2025), resulting in ongoing uncertainty about the future of certain teleNP practice opportunities. Importantly, Medicare telehealth policy has intended to *permanently* allow for "interactive telecommunication systems" that must include, at a minimum, "audio and video equipment permitting two-way, real-time interactive communication" between the patient and clinician, with the important exception that "two-way, real-time audio-only communication technology" is allowable in the case that "the patient is not capable of, or does not consent to, the use of video technology" (U.S. Department of Health and Human Services, 2025). The trend in policies and utilization outcomes in the United States suggests that telehealth services will likely remain a reliable practice option, though these priorities may be subject to change between administrative priorities.

Given the ongoing uncertainty about what kind of coverage can be expected in the future as well as the range of coverage decisions that private insurers have made related to telehealth services in general, there is no uniform or standard guidance that can be provided at this time regarding reimbursement for teleNP. Some important considerations for U.S.-based neuropsychologists considering teleNP options, however, are worth highlighting as they relate to reimbursement and billing. Table 7.4 provides a side-by-side comparison of the CPT codes isolated by the American Psychological Association's (2024) billing and coding guide and their most recent status on the 2025 CMS list of telehealth services (CMS, 2024). Two observations from Table 7.4 merit further comment. First, only the CPT codes related to the neurobehavioral status exam services (96116 and 96121) are currently recognized as permanent telehealth services eligible for reimbursement through CMS. If this service remains the only one eligible for reimbursement, then the financial viability of most hybrid teleNP approaches will be significantly limited, as this excludes test administration (96136–96139) and interactive feedback (96132 and 96133). Second, the only CPT code in the table that is not currently included in the list of telehealth services is one associated with the administration of an automated clinical measure over an electronic platform. As emphasized later in this chapter, a potentially powerful advantage of teleNP practice is the ability to incorporate digital cognitive assessments that may go beyond the capabilities of traditional paper-and-pencil tests currently used by most neuropsychologists. While the potential for digital assessments is exciting, exclusion from reimbursement is likely to adversely affect any financial incentive there may be to further develop, validate, and integrate these tools for clinical practice, despite their promise.

In addition to these considerations recognizing the reimbursement eligibility of certain telehealth services, there are new modifiers associated with the indication of telehealth delivery approaches (Center for Connected Health Policy, 2024). There are three specific CPT modifiers likely of relevance to the majority of neuropsychologists: 93 (telehealth services delivered by audio-only telecommunications system), 95 (telehealth services delivered by audio *and* video telecommunications system), and FR (supervising practitioner present through two-way audio and video communication). Relatedly, neuropsychologists providing teleNP services may also be required to provide one of two place-of-service (POS) codes: 02 (Telehealth Provided Other than in Patient's Home) or 10 (Telehealth provided in Patient's Home). The POS code

Table 7.4 CPT Codes for Neuropsychological Services and Their Status on the CMS List of Telehealth Services

CPT Code	Service	CMS Telehealth Service	Status of CMS Service
96116	Neurobehavioral status exam (first hour)	Reimbursable	Permanent
96121	Neurobehavioral status exam (each additional hour)	Reimbursable	Permanent
96130	Psychological testing evaluation services (first hour)	Reimbursable	*Provisional*
96131	Psychological testing evaluation services (each additional hour)	Reimbursable	*Provisional*
96132	Neuropsychological testing evaluation services (first hour)	Reimbursable	*Provisional*
96133	Neuropsychological testing evaluation services (each additional hour)	Reimbursable	*Provisional*
96136	Psychological or neuropsychological test administration, nontechnician (first 30 minutes)	Reimbursable	*Provisional*
96137	Psychological or neuropsychological test administration, nontechnician (each additional 30 minutes)	Reimbursable	*Provisional*
96138	Psychological or neuropsychological test administration, technician (first 30 minutes)	Reimbursable	*Provisional*
96139	Psychological or neuropsychological test administration, technician (each additional 30 minutes)	Reimbursable	*Provisional*
96146	Psychological or neuropsychological test administration, automated instrument via electronic platform with automated results	Not Covered	—
96112	Developmental test administration (first hour)	Reimbursable	*Provisional*
96113	Developmental test administration (each additional 30 minutes)	Reimbursable	*Provisional*

for teleNP practices operating using a clinic-to-clinic delivery approach would be 02, while it would be 10 for either the clinic-to-home or home-to-home approaches.

Comparisons of TeleNP to Face-to-Face Neuropsychological Assessment

Equivalence of Interventions

Evidence supporting the equivalence of teleNP intervention services compared to in-person delivery has accumulated across multiple domains, including patient satisfaction, treatment effectiveness, assessment equivalence, and clinical outcomes. Research demonstrates that remotely delivered neuropsychological interventions can achieve comparable therapeutic benefits while maintaining high levels of patient acceptance and engagement.

Patient Satisfaction and Acceptability

Patient satisfaction studies consistently demonstrate high acceptance rates for teleNP services. Consistent with early findings within the context of TeleNP in research settings (e.g., Parikh et al., 2013), Lacritz et al. (2020) found that 97.7% of patients reported satisfaction with their teleNP visit and visit length, with 80% indicating the visit met their needs. This study of 43 diverse adult patients (30.2% Hispanic/Latinx, 32.6% Black) receiving telephone-based neuropsychological assessment found that 83.7% expressed interest in another "virtual visit" with their provider, despite 67.7% reporting a preference for in-person visits. Importantly, satisfaction levels showed no significant differences based on demographic factors, including age, race/ethnicity, sex, or education.

Comparable satisfaction rates have been documented for videoconference-based services. Appleman et al. (2021) reported that 90% of patients in their teleNP group agreed or strongly agreed with the statement "I was overall satisfied with this visit," compared to 98% in the in-person group—a statistically nonsignificant difference. This study of 67 teleNP and 64 in-person patients in a VA health care system demonstrated that self-reported satisfaction was high for all aspects of the patient experience, with no significant difference found between teleNP and in-person groups. These findings are similar to results in research settings wherein participants with or without cognitive impairment expressed general satisfaction with TeleNP as a medium for evaluation (Parikh et al., 2013). It is worth noting, however, that in the Parikh et al. study, almost 1/4 of participants who were cognitively normal expressed a preference for the TeleNP vs in-person test session, but none of those with cognitive impairment indicated such a preference.

Within a hybrid or mixed teleNP and in-person practice model, there has been long-standing evidence of patient acceptance for videoconference-based interview. Schopp et al. (2000) surveyed 49 neuropsychology clients who were interviewed via videoconference and 49 matched clients who were interviewed in-person, and they found that the telehealth clients were more likely to want to repeat the experience than their in-person peers. At the same time, there were no differences in the telehealth versus in-person ratings of satisfaction, ease of communication, degree of relaxation in the interview, or ratings of the psychologists' degree of caring. In contrast, the neuropsychologists gave significantly higher satisfaction ratings for in-person compared to telehealth interview.

Effectiveness of Remote Interventions

Systematic reviews of teleNP-based rehabilitation demonstrate promising evidence for intervention effectiveness, even when reviewing early tele-rehabilitation evidence (McCue & Cullum, 2013). Recently, Naamanka et al. (2024) conducted a systematic review of randomized controlled trials and concluded that remote interventions focused on computerized cognitive training are promising methods within teleNP-based rehabilitation. Their review found that telerehabilitation interventions could achieve cognitive improvements comparable to traditional approaches, though their impact on long-term meaningful, everyday functioning remained unclear. A recent meta-analysis by Hu et al. (2025) found that telehealth cognitive interventions significantly improved global cognitive function, memory, and quality of life among adults with neurological disorders compared to controls.

The study of telehealth-based intervention is an active and promising one. Martínez Canyazo et al. (2023) conducted a randomized, controlled study that demonstrated significant improvements in multiple cognitive domains following 10 weekly cognitive telerehabilitation sessions in patients with mild cognitive impairment. Compared to controls, the treatment group showed better scores in memory, phonological fluency, activities of daily living, satisfaction with memory performance, and use of memory strategies in addition to reporting significant reduction in depression, neuropsychiatric symptoms, forgetfulness, and stress. Additional research is underway to examine online/home-based cognitive stimulation interventions for individuals with dementia (e.g., Cintoli et al., 2025) and Parkinson's disease (e.g., Tagliente et al., 2025), with pilot data showing effectiveness of remote interventions.

Clinical Service Models and Outcomes

Real-world implementation studies support the viability of teleNP intervention services. Returning to the early work by Schopp and colleagues (2000), the use of a spoke-hub model for rural outreach with videoconference interviews was significantly cheaper than having patients commute to the primary neuropsychology clinic or having neuropsychologists travel to the outreach clinics, meaning that the hybrid teleNP implementation resulted in overall savings while also producing no differences in patient satisfaction. Pulsifer et al. (2021) found that teleNP services could be successfully integrated into clinical practice, with patient characteristics, especially age and referral categories, impacting feasibility. For adult patients, particularly older adults with neurodegenerative/memory disorders, teleNP provided an important option for delivering neuropsychological interventions. As previously reviewed, Salinas et al. (2020) experienced significant savings and reduced the assessment lengths in their private practice after starting a teleNP service, and they found that nearly all (98.5%) of those served received new interventions based on the recommendations of the video-based teleNP service. Mietchen et al. (2025) also documented their practice's ability to significantly reduce wait times despite an increase in referrals through a hybrid teleNP practice model, and notably, they found no evidence that satisfaction from referral sources was impacted by the change in practice.

Limitations and Considerations

While evidence supports the equivalence of teleNP interventions, several limitations warrant consideration. First, published reports often had relatively small sample sizes, particularly for cognitive training interventions, which can limit the generalizability of results. Additionally, few studies incorporated follow-up or emotional/psychosocial measures, and their impact on long-term meaningful, everyday functioning remained unclear. The heterogeneity of intervention approaches and outcome measures across studies also makes it challenging for systematic reviews like the one by Naamanka and colleagues (2024) or Hu et al. (2025) to draw definitive conclusions about optimal teleNP intervention protocols.

Equivalence of Assessments

A substantial body of research supports the equivalence of neuropsychological test scores obtained through teleNP compared to traditional in-person administration. Multiple investigations, meta-analyses, and systematic reviews demonstrate that teleNP assessment can yield comparable results across diverse cognitive domains and populations.

Meta-Analytic Evidence

The most comprehensive recent meta-analysis provides strong evidence for score equivalence. Alva et al. (2025) conducted a PRISMA-compliant systematic review and meta-analysis of 24 studies including 1,197 clinically and geographically diverse participants aged 18–96, examining 46 neuropsychological tests representing 11 cognitive domains. Their analysis revealed a statistically nonsignificant mean of true effect sizes, Cohen's d_z = .01, 95% CI [−0.01, .04], indicating that mean in-person test scores are, on average, only 0.01 standard deviations greater than teleNP scores. Importantly, examination of mean differences revealed 77% of tests/subtests with a difference of less than one raw point or second.

Earlier meta-analytic work established similar findings. Brearly et al. (2017) found that videoconference test scores were about 1/33 of a standard deviation less than on-site scores and were not significantly different. Test-specific analyses indicated that verbally mediated tasks including digit span, verbal fluency, and list learning were not affected by videoconference administration, while scores for the Boston Naming Test fell only 1/10 of a standard deviation below on-site scores.

Test-Specific Validity Evidence

Systematic reviews have identified specific measures with strong empirical support for remote administration. Marra et al. (2020) provided strong support for the remote administration of cognitive screeners such as the Mini-Mental State Examination (MMSE) and Montreal Cognitive Assessment (MoCA) for older adults 65 years and above, and moderate-to-strong evidence for remote administration of all aspects of Digit Span, the HVLT-R, the Clock Drawing Test, and the Boston Naming Test. For language-based tasks, letter fluency demonstrated excellent validity, while category fluency had moderate support. Additional tests showing promise included the Oral Trail Making Test—Parts A and B, Brief Visuospatial Memory Test—Revised, the Token Test, and Ponton-Satz Spanish Naming Test, though these were evaluated by only a few small studies.

Clinical Population Studies

Research in clinical populations supports assessment equivalence across diverse neurological conditions. Cullum et al. (2014) was the earliest large-scale study to demonstrate that a brief battery of measures administered via video teleconference could distinguish between cognitively impaired and nonimpaired older adults similar to traditional face-to-face assessment. Their study of approximately 200 older subjects found that all measures revealed significant main effects of group and nonsignificant interactions between group and administration condition, with nonsignificant main effects for administration condition except category fluency. Our group also explored the validity of teleNP, showing that diagnostic group differences on neuropsychological test scores were similar whether tests were administered in-person versus teleNP (Wadsworth et al., 2018).

It is important to note that, while the overall literature suggests that there are not significant differences in the test scores obtained in-person versus those obtained remotely, there are some tests and populations where this has not been consistently observed. Put another way, where the aggregation of data would suggest that there are not differences in test scores based upon test medium, clinicians will be best served by looking for the particular details that are more relevant to their patients and practice. To assist with this, we have listed studies or publications that focused on teleNP within a particular patient population in Table 7.5. Interested readers are encouraged to review these studies and treat Table 7.5 as an entry point into the literature base for a given population, but the studies listed are by no means comprehensive, and the field is in need of additional research.

Table 7.5 TeleNP References for Specific Clinical Populations

Clinical Population	Studies	Contents
Children and adolescents	Walker et al. (2023)	Systematic review summarizing teleNP research in pediatric populations
Neurodevelopemntal disorders	Moreau et al. (2023)	Comparison of in-person to in-home results on the WJ-IV
Demyelinating disorders	Harder et al. (2020)	Pre-COVID-19 counterbalanced study of in-home versus in-person testing
Older adults	Marra et al. (2020)	Systematic and critical review of teleNP literature specific to remote assessment with older adults
Epilepsy	Tailby et al. (2025)	Review of teleNP literature with attention to late-onset epilepsy and approaches to remote testing
Parkinson's disease	York et al. (2021)	Discussion of pre-DBS evaluations via teleNP
	Sperling et al. (2025)	Randomized crossover trial comparing in-home to in-person testing
Stroke and neurovascular disease	Chapman et al. (2021)	Randomized crossover study comparing in-home to in-person testing among stroke survivors
	Salvadori et al. (2023)	Critical review summarizing evidence for different cognitive measures for use in teleNP
Mixed dementias	Parks et al. (2021)	Archival study of clinic records for in-home versus in-person evaluations among patients with no impairment, Alzheimer's, Parkinson's, and vascular disease
	Wadsworth et al. (2018)	Pre-COVID-19 counterbalanced study of remote versus in-person testing of older adults with and without cognitive impairment using a brief neuropsychological battery

The equivalence findings must be interpreted within the context of study methodologies and technological constraints. Most of the pre-COVID-19 validity studies utilized subjects tested under controlled conditions of a remote clinic, oftentimes with the use of an assistant to establish videoconference connection and/or assist with task administration. This controlled environment may not fully reflect real-world, home-based teleNP conditions where environmental control is reduced. Similarly, studies have heterogeneous methods for managing potentially problematic cognitive domains with respect to remote assessment, with some adapting tests to make them more conducive to presentation via videoconference, while others omit these tasks/domains entirely. The preponderance of tests included in the meta-analyses are verbally mediated tasks, which is likely due to the relative ease in maintaining standardized administration methods via telehealth. In contrast, visuospatial tests and, perhaps most notably, motor tests where patients must manipulate stimuli (e.g., Block Design, Grooved Pegboard) are under-represented in these meta-analyses, so caution needs to be used in evaluating the scope of the evidence afforded by meta-analytic comparisons of face-to-face and remote neuropsychological test results. Another critical area of the cognitive evaluation that has been understudied and thus also underrepresented in these meta-analyses is that of performance validity.

Only recently has this topic received direct study, with Zakzanis et al. (2025) providing the first dedicated comparison of stand-alone and embedded performance validity measures between in-person and remote administrations. Prior to Zakzanis and colleagues' study, the only study providing comparison of in-person and teleNP performance validity results was from Krynicki et al. (2023), who found no significant difference between results on a stand-alone (Test of Memory Malingering Trial 1) or embedded (Logical Memory Recognition, Visual Reproduction Recognition, and Reliable Digit Span) validity measures. Importantly, while Krynicki and colleagues found no significant differences between these validity indicators, the meta-analysis by Alva et al. (2025) found that performance validity scores were higher in teleNP settings than in-person, but they note that this result was driven by a single effect size (TOMM Trial 1) and that the only study providing validity indicators for this meta-analysis was Krynicki and colleagues. In this context, the results of Zakzanis et al. provide critical additional context that points to the need for further investigation into the equivalency of teleNP and in-person performance validity indicators because they found that the Dot Counting Test and Judgement of Line Orientation Test as performance validity measures differed significantly by modality, while TOMM, 21 Item Test, and Reliable Digit Span did not. Compared to other cognitive measures and domains, performance validity remains understudied in the teleNP literature, and the couple of studies that have included these comparisons provide inconsistent evidence for the equivalence of in-person versus audiovisual teleconference results on these critical measures.

Future Directions and Opportunities for TeleNP

While the COVID-19 pandemic introduced a flood of necessary interest and sharp uptick in research on teleNP, there are still plenty of directions for the field to take this line of research. Some of these directions are sensible continuations of the typical progression of research in neuropsychology. Whereas the literature suggests relative equivalence of most of the neuropsychological tests studied to date in the teleNP context, suggesting no need for specialized teleNP norms, normative data specific to certain tests administered via teleNP may be needed, depending on test modifications (e.g., Rizzi et al., 2023). Similarly, we expect to see the development of cognitive test batteries designed specifically for teleNP (e.g., Wärn et al., 2025). This kind of research is needed and will benefit the field. Rather than going into the myriad possible testing paradigms and specific tasks for future consideration, we want to draw attention to two specific areas of focus that we can see benefiting all future teleNP research. The first of these areas is related to the research methods being used in teleNP studies, and we aim to highlight specific design and statistical opportunities that represent appropriate next steps for this line of research. The second area that we draw readers' attention to is that of collaborative potential, specifically with colleagues working on digital cognitive assessment tools. There are logical and mutually beneficial ways for teleNP research and computerized/digital cognitive test development to build off one another into a more modern approach to neuropsychological assessment development/practice altogether.

Research Methodologies for TeleNP

While the available literature has generally been supportive of the equivalence between cognitive testing results obtained through telehealth versus in-person assessment, the research methodology utilized thus far in the field suffers from some important limitations. Generally, these limitations can be categorized as those related to statistical methodology, psychometric characterization, and research design. We will briefly highlight these three limitation types and then provide suggestions for improved methodology to consider in future research.

Statistical Methodology: Moving Beyond Traditional Difference Testing

Starting with the statistical methodology, the inferential tests that have been used for meta-analytic evidence of the "equivalence" of administration modalities are all tests of difference and correlation, rather than tests of *equivalence*. In a standard paired samples t-test, such as may be used in the case of a counterbalanced study where participants complete both an in-person and videoconference assessment, the null hypothesis is typically that the average difference between participants' scores obtained in each administration modality is zero. The teleNP testing literature has relied on the assumption that a nonsignificant result from such a t-test would mean that the average difference between scores is not different from zero, or in other words, failing to reject the null hypothesis is taken as evidence supporting the null hypothesis. In reality, it is not statistically possible to support the hypothesis that the true effect of anything is exactly zero, so specialized tests of equivalence are needed to provide appropriate statistical evidence for whether sample data support the conclusion that the true effect is not meaningfully large—or not *clinically meaningful* in the case of most research in clinical neuropsychology. Läkens (2017) provides an accessible, practical overview of equivalence tests and how they differ from the default tests of difference typically used in research settings. The primary challenge of conducting equivalence testing is the need to determine the smallest effect size of interest

(SESOI). The SESOI allows the pivot from testing or asserting that the true effect size is (or is not) exactly zero to testing whether the true effect size is sufficiently close to zero as to be practically or pragmatically irrelevant (Läkens, 2017). There will not be a universal SESOI related to clinical decision-making since different settings will need to emphasize different utility statistics. Certain contexts would benefit from decisions that maximize sensitivity, while others may need an SESOI that preserves specificity. In the context of teleNP, a reasonable justification for SESOI can be made for setting a threshold that minimizes the discrepancy in false-positive rates between in-person and teleNP evaluations. Using the AACN consensus on labeling test performance, below-average scores occur at the 8th or lower percentile (Guilmette et al., 2020), so if test scores are normally distributed, then about 8% of cognitively normal individuals will obtain scores in this low range. Using this expectation for the false-positive rate, there will be one additional false positive for every 100 test scores from non-impaired individuals when the true difference in in-person and teleNP testing is just $d = 0.07$, which is considerably less than the traditional definition of $d = 0.20$ as a "small" effect.

Taking the SESOI as $d = 0.07$ since this is the smallest effect size before at least a 1% increase in the false-positive rate, power calculations can be completed to plan these equivalence tests. Läkens (2017) provides the methods for these power calculations, including the determination of equivalence based on meta-analytic results. The importance of planning research to conduct equivalence tests instead of standard tests of difference can be seen by conducting a power analysis using this SESOI. To obtain 80% power using a significance threshold $\alpha < 0.05$, a study needs $n = 1604$ pairs with $d = 0.07$ as the SESOI for equivalence. Utilizing the data extracted and provided as part of the meta-analysis by Alva et al. (2025), the average power of studies comparing teleNP and in-person test results was just 6.54% (range from 3.70% to 16.61%). Thus, the meta-analysis supports true equivalence between in-person and teleNP testing results, as the 95% confidence intervals for the combined effect ($d = 0.01$) fall entirely within the SESOI region. This conclusion is further supported by statistically significant formal equivalence test statistics ($Z = 4.13$). By comparison, the earlier meta-analysis by Brearly and colleagues (2017) found the difference between teleNP and in-person test scores to differ by $g = 0.03$, which resulted in limited support for true equivalence using the ±0.07 SESOI ($Z = 1.67$).

The proposed SESOI threshold of $d = 0.07$ requires careful consideration, however. This threshold assumes a 1% increase in false positive rates represents clinically meaningful change, but several critical assumptions underlie this calculation. First, the approach assumes approximately normal test score distributions. This assumption may hold for normative scores but becomes problematic for raw scores on bounded measures. For example, 12 of the effect sizes analyzed in Alva and colleagues' (2025) meta-analysis were for either the MMSE or MoCA, which both have bounded raw score distributions (scores range from 0 to 30) that often demonstrate marked skew in cognitively normal populations due to ceiling effects.

The second notable assumption in these SESOI calculations is the value of the correlation between scores obtained in-person and by teleNP. Alva and colleagues discuss the lack of correlations between assessment modalities and conducted sensitivity analyses using values of $r = 0.20$, 0.50, and 0.80 in the calculation of the d effect sizes for paired samples studies. Following the decision of Alva et al., all of the prior calculations using the SESOI assumed $r = 0.50$ between in-person and teleNP test scores.

Another assumption to acknowledge here is the implicit treatment of all of the meta-analysis' participants as representing samples from a cognitively normal population. The SESOI we suggested is centered on the false-positive rate, which can be derived only from the control population. Given the reporting of score differences within control and case samples, however, it would be possible to obtain both the sensitivity (true positive rate) from the case samples and specificity (true negative rate) from the controls, and this combination of information can be used to derive more clinically relevant SESOI decisions.

Finally, the decision to set the SESOI threshold at $d = 0.07$ is ultimately arbitrary, and our justification based on the false-positive rate is rooted in an implicit assumption about how many false positives need to occur before a clinical concern emerges. In the case where teleNP testing results in scores that are lower, on average, by $d = 0.07$ than in-person scores (and the distribution of these test scores is approximately normal), for every 100 scores obtained via videoconferencing there will be 1 additional false-positive test result than would have been obtained from standard in-person testing. Utilizing data from Rabin et al. (2016), neuropsychologists average three evaluations per week and use about 12 instruments per assessment, so if each of these instruments provided only one score each (which is an obvious underestimate), then over the course of a year, a neuropsychologist conducting only teleNP assessment will have observed nearly 20 spuriously below-average scores. Whether this rough approximation for error rate reaches the threshold of clinical significance is the primary question to answer before accepting $|d| \geq 0.07$ as a default SESOI for teleNP equivalence studies.

With more data and research in teleNP test administration, there are some novel approaches that could be used to establish appropriate SESOI bounds. One such approach is the net-benefit analysis for diagnostic tests (Vickers et al., 2016). The value of the net-benefit analysis is that it allows for the comparison of multiple diagnostic tools or indicators across a range of diagnostic probabilities, meaning that it is possible to compare several different diagnostic methods and select the one that maximizes the expected benefits at a clinician's specific level of diagnostic uncertainty. More tangibly, a clinician's decision to conduct an in-person versus telehealth cognitive assessment may be different depending on whether that clinician believes that the patient has a 10%, 50%, or 90% chance of having a cognitive disorder. Unlike more traditional diagnostic summaries like accuracy or the area under the curve, net-benefit analysis directly models the clinical decision-making process for case-by-case evaluations, not the long-run averages of correct versus incorrect conclusions a clinician can expect to have achieved by their retirement.

Psychometric Considerations: Reliability and Validity Evidence Gaps

Another methodological limitation of current teleNP research can be found in the supplemental materials for Alva et al.'s (2025) meta-analysis. Of all the studies that met their inclusion criteria, there was only a single study that provided a measure of reliability in the form of internal consistency. In contrast, 63% (100 of 160) of the test scores with data extracted for the meta-analysis reported test-retest reliability in the form of the intraclass correlation (ICC). Brown and Zakzanis (2023) review the published ICC values as evidence for the good-to-excellent test-retest reliability of several neuropsychological tests. As outlined in the joint publication on psychometric standards by the American Educational Research Association, American Psychological Association, and National Council on Measurement in Education (2014), this single focus on summarizing reliability in terms of test-retest consistency does not necessarily reflect the best practice. Demonstration that the relative ranking or ordering of individuals on tests administered in-person versus by teleNP with the ICC does not mean that other forms of reliability are also stable across the two modalities (Standard 2.6, p. 44). Similarly, whenever "any alteration in standard testing materials or procedures" is done, the reliability "for all versions of the test and testing procedures" should be examined (Standard 2.10, p. 45).

To an extent, the very question of whether test scores obtained by telehealth can be compared to those obtained during face-to-face assessment begs the question of whether reliability of the measures change over the modalities as well. Part of the concern regarding teleNP testing includes uncertainty about extraneous random error introduced by a less controlled testing environment when a patient completes an assessment from home, for example, and many neuropsychological tests would require some degree of modification in their standard administration in order to be conducive to telehealth-based presentation, which introduces potentially new sources of variation and error than were present in the standardization of test. The introduction of additional variability directly concerns traditional definitions of reliability as the ratio of true score variance to total (true score + error) variance that internal consistency coefficients approximate. Even though these kinds of concerns were among the most commonly reported by neuropsychologists with respect to selecting tests to administer via telehealth (e.g., Hewitt et al., 2020; Rochette et al., 2022), the preponderance of research has remained focused on the comparison of mean differences in testing and correlational strength while psychometric equivalence has been largely overlooked.

Where the reliability question in the existing research is particularly critical is in its compounding effect on effect sizes, power, and meta-analyses. An often-overlooked consequence of measurement error is that it attenuates the magnitude of effect sizes that can be detected (Baugh, 2002; Hunter & Schmidt, 1990; O'Connor, 2018). Since the measured effect size is smaller than the true effect size when one or more measure has imperfect reliability, a study's power to detect the true effect size of interest is reduced as the study must be powered according to the smaller detectable effect size that corresponds to the true effect size that would be of interest if there were no measurement error. To illustrate the impact of these effects, the disattenuated effect size for the difference in in-person versus remote scores on the RBANS Total Score as reported by McGoldrick (2015) was calculated based on the extracted data from Alva et al. (2025) for their meta-analysis. This particular effect size was selected since the correlation of scores between the two modalities was reported and the composite score has a desirably high reliability of 0.93 (Randolph, 2012). Ignoring measurement error, the difference in in-person (M = 105.42, SD = 12.22) and remote (M = 104.36, SD = 12.60) scores is small to negligible observed effect: $dz = 0.13$; using the reliability coefficient of 0.93 results in little change in the estimated true effect: $dz = 0.14$. Assuming that the in-person reliability coefficient remains 0.93 but the remote administration reliability declines to 0.90, then the estimated true effect becomes $dz = 0.16$, and in the unfavorable outcome where remote administration results in a more marked decline in reliability (say 0.85), the true effect becomes $dz = 0.18$. To highlight the importance of reliability in these handful of hypothetical examples, it is important to bear in mind that in all cases there is no change being made to the observed data, meaning that the observed effect size ($dz = 0.13$) is the same across all of these scenarios despite the true effects changing. Power analyses conducted to target the observable effect size will be misleading and require larger samples to obtain adequate power, and the more measurement error that exists in a measure, then the larger the sample size will need to be to achieve the desired power level.

Closely related to reliability evidence and still in the realm of psychometric comparisons is the relative dearth of studies examining factor models and factorial invariance of test batteries in teleNP. Alegret et al. (2021) seems to be, at present, the only study where measurement invariance between a test battery administered face to face versus home to home was explicitly and directly tested. Measurement invariance testing permits much richer information on the equivalence of measures across different groups. As a statistical model, measurement invariance incorporates and directly assesses comparison of means (at both the observed and latent variable levels) but also permits testing for equivalence (or noninvariance) of the relationships between measures, which can inform both reliability and validity of the administration methods. Certainly, one likely explanation for why measurement invariance testing has not been more common in teleNP research is related to the sample sizes typically being used in these studies, which we touched on earlier in the context of the generally low-powered studies that dominate this area of research. Alegret and colleagues, in contrast, had data for nearly 8000 face-to-face and 350 home-to-home assessments, which is more appropriate for these kinds of latent variable models.

Study Design Evolution: Enhancing Counterbalanced Designs

The final methodological improvement opportunity for future teleNP research is one related to general research design. Early influential teleNP studies capitalized on the use of counterbalanced designs in which participants were randomly assigned to receive either teleNP or face-to-face testing first (e.g., Cullum et al., 2014). This research design is particularly strong and well-suited to the kinds of head-to-head comparisons of videoconference to traditional testing that have established the evidence base behind teleNP, and as such, the first meta-analysis of teleNP studies included only studies that utilized this counterbalanced research design (Brearly et al., 2017). From a statistical standpoint, the counterbalanced study is efficient as its paired sample design results in more power with smaller samples sizes. In contrast, from a practical standpoint, a counterbalanced study is more cumbersome and time consuming as each participant must undergo the same evaluation twice within a relatively short time span, which often requires dedicated research funding and support since this is not a typical clinical practice. As the empirical support for teleNP is now much stronger and clearer than it was a decade ago, the opportunity for new kinds of data collection and study designs is more feasible. Since insurance policies started covering teleNP services following the COVID-19 pandemic, there will hopefully be additional observational studies emerging from various practice settings and neuropsychology clinics that may have archival records of their teleNP evaluations that can be added to the literature base. One such example of this archival, clinic-based research is that by Parks and colleagues (2021). To some extent, much of the ad hoc literature that emerged as practices were forced to transition to teleNP methods at the start of the pandemic followed this kind of archival sampling by necessity (e.g., Caze et al., 2020; Lacritz et al., 2020; Pritchard et al., 2020; Pulsifer et al., 2021; Thibodaux et al., 2021). While observational and retrospective studies like these may not provide the highest overall quality of evidence, they serve a valuable role in illustrating the kinds of real-world clinical scenarios that teleNP providers need to be able to respond to, so the results are often heterogenous but with the benefit of reflecting actual clinical practice rather than contrived research settings.

Another study design opportunity is the extension of the counterbalanced study to samples of individuals who have neurocognitive disorders such as that conducted recently by Sperling and colleagues (2025). This study is unique for two reasons: First, it is a randomized trial with a 4-week retest interval that involved both same and crossover group assignment, and second, it was conducted within a clinical sample of patients with Parkinson's disease. This builds upon earlier work by Wadsworth et al. (2018), which showed that neuropsychological test scores obtained via teleNP yielded diagnostic discriminability similar to in-person evaluations among participants with mild cognitive impairment and early dementia versus healthy aging controls. Further research into the validity and reliability of teleNP services with clinical populations is the next logical evolution in this area of neuropsychology that could not be started until it was relatively clear that teleNP was appropriate in healthy populations.

Digital Assessment and TeleNP

The transition away from the traditional paper-and-pencil tests that have dominated the neuropsychological assessment armamentarium has been both long predicted and slow to materialize (Bilder, 2010; Bilder & Reise, 2020; Casaletto & Heaton, 2017; Parsons, 2016; Schmand, 2019). As with the surge in interest for teleNP during the

COVID-19 pandemic, there was also a renewed hope among some for the broader adoption and acceptance of computerized and digital cognitive tools (Parsons & Duffield, 2020; Singh & Germine, 2021). Accordingly, the idea of "hybrid neuropsychology" has been posited to reflect the transition to a more technology-integrated clinical practice following the changes brought by the pandemic. TeleNP is a strong complement to this hybrid neuropsychology, but of course, it cannot be done without technological commitment and investment by clinicians. As emphasized in all of the reviewed models of teleNP, the successful implementation of a teleNP practice requires careful forethought, planning, and investment in the necessary technologies, services, and software that a specific practice model needs to operate smoothly.

An obvious benefit of computerized cognitive testing for teleNP is that the tests are, by design, amenable for administration over a screen. The direct integration of the technology into the administration and scoring of computerized tests solves one of the major methodological roadblocks for comprehensive teleNP: the presentation of stimuli. At the same time, being able to present a stimulus is often only part of the problem because, once the patient can see the item, there still needs to be an interface that allows the patient to respond and for their responses to be recorded. Again, computerized cognitive tests implicitly address this barrier as well, since some kind of user interface must be implemented to permit the response operation. This design model for computerized cognitive measures is, in effect, what has dominated this line of development. The workflow of computer-based tests has, historically at least, been the following: Take a popular and well-studied paper-and-pencil test, find a way to present it on a computer screen, and then make clicking or typing something as analogous as possible to the typical response method of the test. Examples of this line of work include computerization of measures like trail making (e.g., Fellows et al., 2017) and clock drawing (e.g., Souillard-Mandar et al., 2015). For additional context on this topic, Bauer and Bilder (2023) characterize the state of computerized and automated neuropsychological testing, and Bauer et al. (2012) provide a seminal statement aimed at defining the standards and conventions necessary for computerized assessment devices.

While that problem-solving approach is valuable for transitioning clinicians familiar with particular tests to these electronic *simulacra*, others are optimistic for a fundamentally different kind of truly *digital* assessment methodology. Harris and colleagues (2024) outline what such a "digital neuropsychology" might encompass. Much of the potential technologies that they discuss are far outside of current standard (and practical) cognitive assessment methods, including the collection of passive data from smartphones, wearable devices, and driving sensors. At the same time, a growing area of study in neuropsychology is in the development and collection of ecological momentary assessments (Aminikhanghahi et al., 2020; Parsey et al., 2019; Schmitter-Edgecombe et al., 2025), use of smart home data to assess functional health (Aramendi et al., 2018; Cook et al., 2019; Fritz et al., 2020; Ghods et al., 2019), integrated or multimethod assessments of everyday cognitive functioning (Fellows & Schmitter-Edgecombe, 2019; Schmitter-Edgecombe et al., 2022). In a world where significant amounts of rich, ecologically relevant data could be readily obtained by a clinician, it is easy to imagine how neuropsychological visits could be reduced in time by requiring less direct formal cognitive testing. In this same scenario, teleNP can become an appealing practice model since much of the challenge over the years in implementing teleNP evaluation has come from the technical issues encountered while trying to administer tests over a distance.

Another area of interest within the digital neuropsychology and teleNP nexus is in the collection and analysis of recorded voice biomarkers. Some such tasks record and analyze voice data being collected during standard neuropsychological tests such as verbal fluency and picture descriptions using machine learning. A growing number of studies have reported promising findings in terms of cognitive screening (e.g. Amini et al., 2024; Hajjar et al., 2023; Harris et al., 2024; Kaser et al., 2024). Going back to the recommendations for planning and starting a teleNP service, the selection and use of high-quality audio devices are important first steps, so those clinicians who already have an infrastructure in place to collect quality audio may also be particularly well situated to take advantage of future developments with voice biomarkers and natural language processing. The ability to collect diagnostic and clinically informative data while simultaneously conducting a standard interview provides a promising degree of efficiency that could help to reduce visit lengths and could help to produce a finalized report faster, depending on how well these natural language processing methods will be able to summarize their results.

Future Opportunities for TeleNP

The more that we study teleNP, the more we have to do to refine our understanding and competence in this area. While nearly four decades of research have built up a positive empirical base to support the validity of teleNP, more work is needed to more fully establish teleNP as an evidence-based, empirically supported general practice model for clinical neuropsychologists. Part of what is still needed in teleNP research is clear evidence that translates directly to stakeholders, especially those with financial investments such as insurance companies, as to what can be obtained from telehealth-based neuropsychological services. This kind of research requires special planning to ensure positive outcomes regarding factors such as time between referral and receipt of report, proportion of rural/underserved/under-resourced communities able to receive neuropsychological services after implementation of teleNP, service cost reductions, and so on.

For neuropsychologists or trainees looking for areas of research, teleNP is a rich vein poised to intersect with a number of other areas of interest in neuropsychology and health care more generally. The inclusion of training in technological advances as part of the updated Minnesota Conference Guidelines for Education and Training (Stringer et al., 2026) will hopefully spur further growth, development, curiosity, and research in teleNP. In fact, a recent survey of neuropsychology trainees revealed that one of the top three initiatives they would like to see prioritized in the next few years is the integration of advanced technology into clinical practice (Fox-Fuller et al., 2025), suggesting that there is already abundant interest in this area. Opportunities for relatively direct research projects include repeating existing study designs but utilizing more comprehensive statistical methods such as tests of equivalence and measurement invariance modeling. There is a clear need for studies that collect the necessary data to evaluate the reliability and similar psychometric properties of tests administered over videoconference. The teleNP literature is also to the point now where it is easy to justify its use with clinical populations, which is its own important area of research but also a valuable opportunity to expand accessibility to neuropsychological services.

Research on digital cognitive assessments has also gone hand in hand with teleNP research. There are natural integrative opportunities for studies validating or examining digital tests to do so through videoconferencing or even fully remotely and asynchronously. At the same time, teleNP research and adoption have been held back by the difficulty of conducting some tests over the internet, so it is reasonable to expect that more digital tests will be appearing in teleNP studies since these new testing platforms are designed in way far more conducive to telehealth than traditional paper-and-pencil tests. The growth of research in both of these areas is likely to be synergistic and will hopefully contribute to productive collaborations between those developing novel tests and those who will likely be using those tests regularly.

Appendix A: Proposed Core Guidance Principles for TeleNP

The following principles are derived from a broad synthesis of the literature reviewed and presented in the current chapter. The aim of these principles is to help establish narrow areas for clinicians to focus on as they evaluate their own teleNP practices. Similarly, these principles can serve as specific areas for focusing directions of research that will be needed to establish and inform evidence-based recommendations, standards, and guidelines for teleNP. Within each of these principles, we have collected the current state of practical guidance for clinicians. The hope is that this structure of pragmatic, actionable guidance within broader professional, ethical, and technical principles will facilitate future development, improvement, and maintenance of translational guidelines for teleNP.

Professional Competence

Clinicians offering teleNP services ought to take appropriate steps and engage in sufficient effort to obtain foundational training, supervision, and consultation in telepsychology generally. The empirical support, legal precedents, professional standards, and existing guidelines for telepsychology practice are a priori to the provision of teleNP services.

Once competency in telepsychology has been developed, neuropsychologists ought to then seek further specialized training, supervision, and consultation specific to teleNP. Prior experience and demonstrated competency in the provision of telepsychological services is not sufficient to establish a professional competence in teleNP as there are unique ethical, professional, and clinical challenges that do not generalize from other telepsychology practices. Appendix B provides proposed competency-based domains specific to teleNP that may be consulted for guidance in the process of evaluating one's own teleNP competency.

Continued professional competency in teleNP requires adherence to guidelines from the American Psychological Association, National Academy of Neuropsychology, Academy of Clinical Neuropsychology, International Neuropsychological Society, Inter Organizational Practice Committee, and similar established professional organizations as appropriate. Clinicians offering teleNP services ought to review any revisions or updates to previously published or released guidelines related to telepsychology or teleNP directly.

Specific skills that need to be cultivated for a true competency in teleNP are primarily influenced by the technological requirements inherent in telehealth services. Videoconferencing results in the patient having a restricted view of the clinician and the clinician a restricted view of the patient, and this restricted view carries implications for the development of rapport, monitoring of nonverbal clinical indicators, and particular aspects of a comprehensive mental status exam (e.g., evaluation of tremor, gait abnormalities). Videoconferencing also brings specific considerations related to visual and hearing acuity that the clinician must be prepared to assess and accommodate. The clinician must also develop requisite skills in attending to the environment and monitoring for threats to the internal and external validity of the telehealth-based assessment based on the limited view and interaction of the patient via a remote medium.

In addition to the translation of traditional clinical skills to telehealth settings just discussed, the neuropsychologist needs to also develop appropriate technological skills to maximize the utility and value of the telehealth resources being used. These skills include those necessary for troubleshooting connection or service issues as well as the ability to explain and guide patients with a range of technological experience through these potential issues. Additionally, the neuropsychologist should be able to leverage the features of their selected telehealth platform so as to maximally benefit or capitalize on opportunities such as screen sharing and integration with medical records/test administration platforms. Arguably, the choice to utilize teleNP over traditional neuropsychological services should be made only when there is sufficient benefit to the teleNP service that makes any of its limitations or drawbacks relative to the gold-standard, in-person service acceptable. Ease, accessibility, and patient preference are not sufficient justifications if the clinical neuropsychologist lacks sufficient competence and skill to make the teleNP service useful, informative, and supportive of the referral and patient needs. Even when a neuropsychologist is comfortable with certain features such as screen sharing, it is still important that they maintain awareness of the unique challenges that come with this kind of virtual workspace. For example, the neuropsychologist should be aware of potential risks associated with sharing the host's screen versus sharing particular windows open on the host's screen. Failing to thoughtfully separate windows and select appropriate screen-sharing options can lead to accidental sharing of protected health information belonging to other patients or communications with other providers or professionals that should not have been accessible to the patient on the call at that time.

An additional skill set necessary for neuropsychologists involved in teleNP at this time is that of flexibility and clinical judgment. There are very few neuropsychological measures validated explicitly for telehealth administration, and there are similarly very few normative references available for neuropsychological measures that have been adapted for telehealth. As a result, neuropsychologists opting to utilize teleNP need to have sufficient skill and experience in flexible test administration to be sufficiently confident in understanding the limitations of the assessment that they can still draw meaningful and appropriate conclusions from the service overall. With additional research and investment, this skill set will hopefully become less necessary as more tests become standardized or normed for teleNP purposes, but until then a deep understanding of psychometrics alongside extensive experience with the measures and thoughtful consideration of patient appropriateness are fundamental skills required of neuropsychologists offering teleNP services.

Technology and Equipment Standards

A robust teleNP practice requires support for videoconferencing because this is the only way of providing audiovisual services remotely. While use of purely audio services (e.g., telephone) can satisfy billing requirements under certain circumstances, it is important to recognize that billing compliance is the minimal standard and that teleNP practice should aim to exceed this minimal standard. Critical to reliable teleNP services are thus two considerations: videoconferencing platform and adequate bandwidth.

The landscape of videoconferencing software is dynamic and likely to change as financial incentives for telehealth services in general continue to stabilize in the post-pandemic health care environment. Fox-Fuller et al. (2022) found that Zoom was the most widely used (62.1% of their survey respondents) and recommended (M = 8.17 [out of 10], SD = 1.44, range = 5–10) videoconference platform followed by Doxy.Me (20.7%, M = 6.39, SD = 2.66, range = 1–10) and then MyChart (18.4%, M = 6.81, SD = 2.26, range = 1–10). Considerations that neuropsychologists need to be aware of while evaluating the choice of videoconferencing software include the following:

- Health Insurance Portability and Accountability Act (HIPAA) compliance and privacy practices of the software company

- Integration of software with other services (e.g., electronic medical records, test administration/scoring platforms)
- Popularity and/or familiarity of the software among patients
- Accessibility of the software to patients (e.g., browser-based access, previsit application download or installation required)
- Restrictions placed on software options by a clinician's institution
- Costs and limitations of features at certain account levels (e.g., time limits with free accounts, limits to number of calls per week/month for single-user accounts)
- Features available to users (e.g., screen sharing, interactive annotation while screen sharing, breakout rooms, waiting rooms)

Even the best and most thoughtful selection of a videoconferencing platform will not overcome challenges related to internet connections. For example, Fox-Fuller et al.'s (2022) survey revealed that just over 4 in 5 (82.8%) neuropsychologists experienced internet connectivity issues from their examinees' side while over half (58.6%) experienced some unknown source of connectivity problems. Some connectivity failures will be unpredictable or uncontrollable, but prescreening patients' internet connections should still be a standard part of teleNP practice. The International Telecommunication Union and Office of the United Nations Secretary-General's Envoy on Technology (2022) recommends a minimum speed of 10 Mbps for standard broadband globally, and this aligns with the FCC's (2022) recommendation to have a minimum download speed of 6 Mbps for high-definition videoconferencing. Notably, the FCC (2024) has recently updated its standard for high-speed fixed broadband from 25 Mbps (download speed) and 3 Mbps (upload speed) to 100 Mbps (download speed) and 20 Mbps (upload speed). While redefining the minimum necessary speeds for internet services to be considered high-speed broadband will likely cause internet service providers to continue developing infrastructure to support these higher speeds, care needs to be taken to consider whether these kinds of changes will further expand the digital divide with lower-income and less-advantaged communities potentially receiving less investment in necessary infrastructure to support these speeds and/or individual users electing to subscribe to budget plans that offer slower speeds that are adequate for most use cases but may be less reliable for telehealth services.

Neuropsychologists conducting teleNP services need to be aware of the recommended Internet speeds required for their selected videoconferencing software. As of the writing of this chapter, the following requirements are recommended for the highest quality videoconference services by three relatively common teleconferencing software options used by neuropsychologists (see Fox-Fuller et al., 2022):

- Zoom (2025): 3.8 Mbps (upload speed) and 3.0 Mbps (download speed) for 1080p high-definition video in 1:1 and group video calls
- Doxy.Me (2025): Above 15–20 Mbps

- Microsoft Teams (2024): 1.5 Mbps (upload and download speed) recommended for 1:1 video calls, 4 Mbps (upload and download speed) recommended for the best quality for 1:1 video calls, and 2.5 Mbps (upload and download speed) for group video calls with screen sharing

It is the neuropsychologist's responsibility and obligation to know the recommendations of their chosen videoconference software, and it is recommended that neuropsychologists strive to maintain Internet speeds necessary for the highest possible video and audio quality so that potential issues with visual and auditory acuity over the computer can be minimized as much as possible. It is also the responsibility and obligation of the neuropsychologist to screen the appropriateness of the patient's Internet connection to support these minimal requirements as well.

Compounding the determination of teleconferencing software and Internet speed are also the technological considerations that the teleNP service must evaluate. The devices that will be used by the neuropsychologist, psychometrist, and patient to access and participate in the evaluation require just as much forethought and consideration as any other part of the teleNP service. For example, if a patient's only Internet-accessible device is their smartphone, then the administration of tests via teleconference is likely inappropriate as the size of the device's screen will interfere with the presentation of visual stimuli during testing. Similarly, a phone or tablet may have hardware limitations that prevent them from fully utilizing the Internet speeds that may be accessed by a laptop or desktop computer. Similarly, it is important to review the minimum system requirements and supported operating services of the selected videoconferencing platform to ensure that the clinic and patient are both connecting through appropriate devices.

Outside of the device used to connect to videoconferencing, clinical neuropsychologists also need to evaluate whether supportive electronic devices are needed for their teleNP services. Obvious supportive devices would include a camera and microphone, which is necessary if the primary device (e.g., desktop) does not have either built in, or it may be needed if built-in cameras and/or microphones are low quality. In some cases, patients may need to rely on multiple devices such as using their phone for two-way audio on the call while they use an embedded camera on their primary device for video. On the clinic's side, there may be consideration for the addition of a document camera to facilitate the display of testing stimuli. Whereas each additional device offers potential enhancement to the services provided, they also lead to more coordination demands, potential for disconnection or service interruptions, software updating and management, and maintenance costs.

To support the neuropsychologist's awareness of and adherence to expected technological and Internet standards for telehealth services, the following resources are provided as starting points to incorporate into the planning and workflow of clinicians interested in teleNP services. First, the Department of the Health and Human Services has collected a series of resources to assist clinicians in planning their telehealth workflow: https://telehealth.hhs.gov/providers/planning-your-telehealth-workflow. Second, Telehealth Technology has assembled various toolkits aimed at helping clinicians start and maintain a telehealth program, select software support, and review technological considerations: https://telehealthtechnology.org/toolkits/. Finally, the two most consistently utilized Internet speed tests that can be used by neuropsychologists and shared with patients as part of prescreening are provided by M-Lab (https://speed.measurementlab.net/#/) and Ookla (https://www.speedtest.net/), which will provide both the upload and download speeds.

Patient Selection and Appropriateness

The aforementioned technological considerations are intrinsic considerations for the appropriateness of teleNP services for a patient or neuropsychological practice. Beyond these technical considerations, however, neuropsychologists should evaluate their patients individually before offering teleNP services. Note that some patients may be appropriate for certain kinds of teleNP services but not others; for example, a patient may be determined to be appropriate to receive an intake evaluation or feedback via telehealth but not necessarily be appropriate to complete neuropsychological testing virtually.

A neuropsychologist must consider the following factors in making a determination about a patient's appropriateness for teleNP:

- Referral question and needs of evaluation
- Clinical presentation
- Cognitive status
- Age and developmental level
- Access to and comfort with the necessary technology
- Availability of a suitable testing environment
- Ability to participate in the evaluation meaningfully without in-person support
- Whether sufficient breadth, depth, and range of cognitive domains can be sufficiently administered to answer the referral question and patient concerns
- Safety and risk considerations
- Whether test security can be managed and maintained

Hybrid teleNP services may be considered depending on the neuropsychologist's conclusions and impressions during the screening process. At any point in the screening process, the neuropsychologist needs to be prepared to adjust or adapt the teleNP plans, which requires considerable flexibility that can only be achieved with deliberate forethought and the development of competencies in teleNP as outlined throughout this appendix.

An ethical consideration that bears specific emphasis in this screening process is in respect to the handling of a patient who is receiving telehealth services after it is determined that teleNP is not appropriate. One way in which this ethical concern may arise is in the case of a neuropsychological practice where all services are provided only via teleNP. The neuropsychologist in this case should take time to consider whether they need a previsit screening or how a visit would proceed if teleNP is determined to be inappropriate. A previsit screening, for example, may be appropriate before agreeing to see a referred patient. This previsit screening will likely be unbillable time on behalf of the neuropsychologist. In the case where previsit screening is not being done, the neuropsychologist will need to consider the implications and costs of terminating a teleNP visit when it becomes clear that the patient is not appropriate for the service.

Informed Consent, Privacy, and Security

The American Psychological Association (2020) released a brief checklist for providing informed consent for telepsychological services, and Postal et al. (2020) expand on these general telepsychological components to provide guidance specific to teleNP services. The overlap between these resources is significant with the teleNP-specific elements largely relating to the issues and topics emphasized in this chapter. Certain elements of the informed consent that we want to highlight here are related to the limitations of teleNP and ensuring that the patient is aware of those limitations before continuing with the service. Patients need to be made aware during the consent process whether:

- Standardized test administration protocols will be modified
- Third parties are going to be involved (e.g., caregiver, technicians/facilitators)
- Privacy or security vulnerabilities, breaches, or limitations have been identified for the teleconferencing software being used

Associated with and informed by these specific considerations, the informed consent process must ensure that the patient understands whether and what alternative services are available to them in addition to the fact that the results of a teleNP evaluation may be impacted and possibly limited by nonstandard administration and loss of qualitative data/information usually obtained in in-person assessments. Any known or anticipated limitations with the acceptability of the teleNP report, conclusions, or recommendations by specific organizations for particular purposes like requesting accommodations or documenting a diagnosis should be shared during informed consent as well. An additional unique point of clarification to the teleNP informed consent is the establishment of emergency protocols and procedures in the event of service interruption, safety risk, environmental disruption or distraction, breach of test security, or other concerns.

Embedded in the informed consent process is the need for the neuropsychologist to be familiar with and prepared to discuss issues related to privacy and security. The selection of protocols and services that meet HIPAA compliance standards is the minimal expected clinical practice but not sufficient to ensure or guarantee the privacy and security of the services provided. The teleNP practice needs to take steps in advance to plan for potential privacy breaches that may arise in either a home-to-home or home-to-clinic delivery model. Similarly, the patient will need to be informed of who all will be present and participating in sessions since this can be less clear or obvious via telehealth than in in-person assessments. Typical security-related information such as how records are handled, stored, and shared will also need to be shared, although there is usually little difference in these considerations between telehealth and in-person services.

While telehealth standard and practice recommendations often prioritize the protection of privacy and security of patients, it is important that neuropsychologists also take steps to consider the protection of their own privacy and security during teleNP visits. The primary area of concern for this is in the form of managing test security, but any form of unauthorized or undisclosed recording of the session can present privacy and security concerns that affect the neuropsychologist. Some teleconference platforms include settings or options that prevent recording or screen capture while the application is open, which is a significant strength to consider in this respect. This being said, the neuropsychologist has little control or ability to detect when a patient or third party may be using a secondary device (e.g., cellphone) to video and/or audio-record parts or all of the assessment process. These risks are challenging to manage in any teleNP service model where the patient is completing the visit from home, so in particular practices or settings where there is sufficient worry or concern about the risk to privacy and security of the evaluation process or materials, a clinic-to-clinic model of service may be more preferred for teleNP services since this offers more control over the patient's environment. Similarly, the presence of a facilitator, technician, psychometrist, or proctor may be arranged in high-stakes assessment situations to provide further monitoring and security.

Test Selection, Administration, Interpretation, and Reporting

As has been stated throughout this chapter, the provision of teleNP services does not necessarily require the inclusion of cognitive testing as part of the remote evaluation. The administration of cognitive measures is a significant component of the neuropsychological profession and is typically the longest part of our evaluations, so the ability to provide testing remotely is often an area of focus for teleNP research and implementation. In the chapter, several example of triaging and screening teleNP models were described that emphasize the flexibility one may have in being able to recommend that a patient proceed with testing via telehealth or plan to be scheduled for traditional, in-person assessment instead. This decision-making framework has already been addressed by the practice guidelines around patient screening and appropriateness. For this particular core guideline principle, we intend for the focus to be on the administration of cognitive tests remotely.

Following the COVID-19 pandemic, guidance and information relevant to the selection of tests for teleNP cognitive assessments are more available than they were before. Capitalizing on this availability, neuropsychologists planning a teleNP cognitive battery should prioritize the selection of tests for which the following are true:

- Research has validated the test's administration via videoconference.
- The test publisher has released guidance and direction for its use via videoconference.
- Standardization or normative data are available for the test administered specifically via teleconference.

The list of tests that meet all of these priorities is currently limited, but this will hopefully change as digital assessment methods continue to emerge and test publishers see the market value behind the development of tests appropriate for teleNP.

Essential to the development of evidence bases for different tests in teleNP applications is the consistent documentation of modifications and adaptations made by researchers. It is critical that researchers who utilize teleNP assessments document and provide materials as transparently as copyright laws will permit them to do so that clinicians can (1) evaluate the significance or potential impact of these modifications to the measurement process and (2) implement these changes as closely as possible in their practice so as to maximize the generalizability of the results found in any given study. Just as with any other clinical assessment, if there is insufficient literature or available resources to strongly reinforce the selection or modification of a specific test, then the neuropsychologist needs to utilize their clinical judgment to evaluate the relative benefits of including the measure in the battery versus the associated limitations to its empirical evidence. All such decisions and their corresponding effect on the conclusions of the assessment must be clearly documented in the neuropsychological evaluation report.

In the documentation of any limits to results and interpretations related to modifications of tests or testing procedures for teleNP services, the neuropsychologist must be mindful of how this information is presented to the patient and referral source. A typical neuropsychological report is usually separated into multiple sections, and it is not uncommon that observations or comments related to the interpretability of particular tests may be provided in one such section. While this meets the professional standard to document these limitations and considerations, it is important to also recognize that consumers of a neuropsychological report, particularly referral sources, may not read the report in its entirety, which can result in this important contextual information not being readily accessible or obvious to others. Neuropsychologists conducting teleNP assessments should be thoughtful about whether certain factors related to the modification of tests or the lack of robust validity research are significant enough to merit inclusion in sections such as the "Summary and Conclusions" or "Impressions" in a report where it is much more likely that readers of the report will see and be able to appreciate these caveats.

Appendix B: Proposed Core Competency Domains for TeleNP Training

As teleNP continues to develop as a viable practice model, there is an increasing need to establish comprehensive competency-based training domains that prepare neuropsychologists to ethically and effectively deliver teleNP services (Bilder et al., 2020; Grosch et al., 2011). Heffelfinger et al. (2022) developed a detailed framework for competency-based assessment in clinical neuropsychology at the postdoctoral level, delineating stages, milestones, and benchmarks. While this framework was developed for traditional neuropsychology practice, it can be adapted and expanded to address the unique competencies required for teleNP. The following competency domains synthesize these frameworks to provide a comprehensive model for teleNP training. These domains align with existing competency frameworks while addressing the specific knowledge, skills, and attitudes needed for teleNP practice.

Core Competency Domains for TeleNP Training

Technical Competence

Definition: Knowledge of and proficiency with telecommunication technologies, hardware, software, and digital platforms used in teleNP

Elements:

- Understanding of teleconferencing platforms and their features (screen sharing, remote control, breakout rooms)
- Knowledge of technical specifications needed for reliable teleNP (bandwidth requirements, display resolution, audio quality)
- Ability to troubleshoot common technical issues
- Familiarity with security features and encryption standards
- Understanding of different technology platforms' strengths and limitations for specific assessment procedures

Milestones:

Basic/Intermediate	Intermediate	Intermediate/Proficient	Proficient
Demonstrates basic knowledge of relevant technology; requires supervision for platform setup and operation	Independently operates primary telehealth platform; recognizes when technical issues arise	Adapts testing procdures to accommodate technical limitations; proactively addresses potential technical issues	Independently navigates complex technical scenarios; implements advanced features to optimize assessment procedures

Assessment Methods:

- Direct observation of platform utilization
- Technical competency demonstration
- Case-based scenarios with technical challenges

Ethical and Legal Practice in TeleNP

Definition: Knowledge and application of ethical principles, legal requirements, and professional standards specific to teleNP practice

Elements:

- Knowledge of relevant laws and regulations governing telehealth across jurisdictions
- Understanding of licensure requirements for interjurisdictional practice
- Application of ethical principles to teleNP (e.g., informed consent, confidentiality, test security)
- Management of boundary issues in virtual environments
- Knowledge of billing and reimbursement considerations for teleNP services

Milestones:

Basic/Intermediate	Intermediate	Intermediate/Proficient	Proficient
Recognizes basic ethical and legal issues in teleNP; requires supervision to address them	Independently addresses common ethical issues; demonstrates knowledge of interjurisdictional practice requirements	Anticipates and proactively addresses complex ethical dilemmas; maintains consistent compliance with regulations	Applies sophisticated ethical reasoning to novel teleNP situations; contributes to development of practice policies

Assessment Methods:

- Ethics case discussions
- Development of teleNP-specific informed consent documents
- Analysis of complex ethical scenarios
- Case-based scenarios with technical challenges

Modified Assessment Procedures

Definition: Knowledge and skills related to the adaptation of standard neuropsychological assessment procedures for telehealth delivery

Elements:

- Understanding of how standardized test administration may need modification for telehealth
- Knowledge of research on equivalence between in-person and telehealth administration
- Skills in adapting test instructions, stimuli presentation, and response recording
- Ability to evaluate validity and reliability implications of modified procedures
- Competence in documenting modifications and their potential impact on interpretation

Milestones:

Basic/Intermediate	Intermediate	Intermediate/Proficient	Proficient
Follows established protocols for teleNP administration; recognizes basic differences from in-person testing	Independently administers common teleNP measures; makes appropriate basic modifications	Adapts complex assessment procedures for telehealth; considers validity implications	Develops innovative approaches to teleNP assessment; integrates research knowledge into practice decisions

Assessment Methods:

- Direct observation of teleNP test administration
- Case-based discussions of modifications
- Development of teleNP protocols for specific test batteries

Professional Identity and Interpersonal Skills in TeleNP

Definition: Development of professional identity as a teleNP provider and skills for effective therapeutic relationships in virtual environments

Elements:

- Ability to establish rapport and therapeutic alliance via telecommunication
- Skills in communicating empathy and professional presence virtually
- Adaptation of nonverbal communication for video-based interactions
- Management of the virtual "office" environment
- Integration of teleNP into professional identity and practice models

Milestones:

Basic/Intermediate	Intermediate	Intermediate/Proficient	Proficient
Demonstrates basic telehealth etiquette; requires supervision to establish rapport	Independently establishes working relationships with typical patients via telehealth	Effectively manages complex interpersonal dynamics virtually; adapts communication style to patient needs	Demonstrates excellence in virtual therapeutic relationships; serves as model for others

Assessment Methods:

- Patient feedback on telehealth experience
- Direct observation of telehealth interactions
- Reflective practice discussions

Cultural and Individual Diversity in TeleNP

Definition: Knowledge and skills related to cultural and individual factors that impact teleNP assessment and interpretation

Elements:

- Understanding of how cultural factors influence technology access and utilization
- Knowledge of digital literacy variations across populations
- Adaptation of teleNP procedures for diverse linguistic and cultural backgrounds
- Ability to address socioeconomic factors affecting telehealth access
- Skills in working with interpreters in virtual settings

Milestones:

Basic/Intermediate	Intermediate	Intermediate/Proficient	Proficient
Recognizes basic cultural and diversity factors in telehealth; requires supervision to address them	Independently incorporates cultural considerations into teleNP planning and execution	Adapts procedures for diverse populations; advocates for equitable telehealth access	Develops innovative approaches to cultural adaptation; contributes to reducing health care disparities

Assessment Methods:

- Case conceptualizations with diverse populations
- Development of culturally informed teleNP protocols
- Self-reflection on diversity factors in telehealth

Environmental Assessment and Optimization			
Definition: Skills in evaluating and optimizing the remote testing environment to ensure valid assessment			
Elements:			
• Ability to assess the suitability of remote environments for neuropsychological testing • Knowledge of environmental factors that may impact test performance • Skills in guiding patients to optimize their testing environment • Strategies for managing distractions and interruptions • Competence in documenting environmental factors relevant to interpretation			
Milestones:			
Basic/Intermediate	Intermediate	Intermediate/Proficient	Proficient
Conducts basic environmental checks; requires supervision to address problems	Independently assesses environmental suitability; implements basic modifications	Anticipates environmental challenges; develops creative solutions for complex situations	Expertly manages diverse remote environments; develops best practices for environmental optimization
Assessment Methods:			
• Environmental assessment checklists • Case examples of environmental problem-solving • Development of environmental protocols for specific assessment contexts			

Telehealth Documentation and Communication

Definition: Skills in telehealth-specific documentation, including informed consent, test modifications, and result communication

Elements:

- Knowledge of telehealth-specific documentation requirements
- Skills in documenting test modifications and their potential impact
- Ability to communicate assessment results effectively via telehealth
- Competence in secure electronic record-keeping
- Knowledge of telehealth-specific informed consent elements

Milestones:

Basic/Intermediate	Intermediate	Intermediate/Proficient	Proficient
Creates basic telehealth documentation; requires supervision for complex cases	Independently documents telehealth procedures; addresses common documentation issues	Produces comprehensive documentation addressing telehealth-specific factors; effectively communicates complex results	Develops innovative documentation approaches; serves as a model for ethical and comprehensive telehealth documentation

Assessment Methods:

- Review of telehealth documentation samples
- Development of telehealth-specific informed consent
- Feedback from referral sources on communication effectiveness

Research and Evidence-Based Practice in TeleNP

Definition: Knowledge of the teleNP research literature and skills in applying evidence-based practice principles to telehealth

Elements:

- Knowledge of current research on teleNP reliability and validity
- Understanding of gaps in the teleNP evidence base
- Ability to critically evaluate teleNP research findings
- Skills in implementing evidence-based teleNP practices
- Contribution to teleNP research and knowledge development

Milestones:

Basic/Intermediate	Intermediate	Intermediate/Proficient	Proficient
Demonstrates basic knowledge of teleNP literature; requires supervision to apply findings	Independently applies relevant research to common teleNP situations	Critically evaluates complex research questions; adapts practice based on emerging evidence	Contributes to teleNP knowledge development; implements sophisticated evidence-based practices

Assessment Methods:

- Literature reviews on teleNP topics
- Case conceptualizations integrating research evidence
- Participation in teleNP research or quality improvement projects

Interdisciplinary Collaboration in Telehealth

Definition: Skills in collaborating with other health care professionals in telehealth contexts

Elements:

- Knowledge of telehealth models across health care disciplines
- Skills in virtual consultation and collaboration
- Ability to communicate neuropsychological findings virtually to other professionals
- Understanding of roles and responsibilities in telehealth teams
- Knowledge of referral processes in telehealth systems

Milestones:

Basic/Intermediate	Intermediate	Intermediate/Proficient	Proficient
Participates in basic interdisciplinary telehealth activities; requires supervision for complex interactions	Independently collaborates with professionals from other disciplines in routine telehealth contexts	Effectively manages complex interdisciplinary situations; facilitates collaborative problem-solving	Demonstrates leadership in telehealth interdisciplinary teams; develops innovative collaborative approaches

Assessment Methods:

- Feedback from interdisciplinary team members
- Case examples of telehealth collaboration
- Development of telehealth collaboration protocols

Implementation Considerations

Assessment of Competencies

Consistent with Heffelfinger et al.'s (2022) recommendations, teleNP competencies should be assessed at regular intervals throughout training, with clear benchmarks for expected progress. The assessment should use multiple methods, including the following:

1. Direct observation of teleNP practice
2. Review of teleNP documentation
3. Case presentations and discussions
4. Feedback from patients and other professionals
5. Self-assessment and reflection

Developmental Progression

Training programs should establish clear expectations for competency development across training stages, recognizing that trainees will progress from basic knowledge to more advanced skills over time. The milestones provided for each domain reflect this developmental progression and can be used to track growth and identify areas needing additional focus.

Competency Development Plans

When trainees do not meet the expected benchmarks for a given stage, training programs should develop collaborative competency development plans with specific goals, training experiences, and timelines. These plans should be viewed as opportunities for growth rather than punitive measures.

Summary and Future Directions for Competency Domains in TeleNP

The teleNP competency domains reviewed here should be integrated with broader neuropsychology competency frameworks, recognizing that teleNP represents a specialized practice modality rather than an entirely separate discipline. Training programs may choose to embed teleNP competencies within their existing assessment structures or develop teleNP-specific supplements. By systematically addressing these domains, training programs can ensure that their graduates are equipped to provide ethical, effective, and accessible teleNP services.

As the field of teleNP continues to evolve, these competency domains will need ongoing refinement based on emerging research and practice innovations. Training programs are encouraged to adapt this framework to their specific contexts while maintaining the core focus on developing the knowledge, skills, and attitudes necessary for competent teleNP practice.

References

Alegret, M., Espinosa, A., Ortega, G., Pérez-Cordón, A., Sanabria, Á., Hernádez, I., Marquié, M., Rosende-Roca, M., Mauleón, A., Abdelnour, C., Vargas, L., de Antonio, E. E., López-Cuevas, R., Tartari, J. P., Alarcón-Martín, E., Tárraga, L., Ruiz, A., Boada, M., & Valero, S. (2021). From face-to-face to home-to-home: Validity of a teleneuropsychological battery. *Journal of Alzheimer's Disease, 81*(4), 1541–1553. https://doi.org/10.3233/JAD-201389

Alexander, A. A., & Allo, H. (2021). Building a climate for advocacy training in professional psychology. *The Counseling Psychologist, 49*(7), 1070–1089. https://doi.org/10.1177/00110000211027973

Ali, A., Zafar, R., Kumar, K. A., Shariq, K., Motiani, V., Ibrahim, S., & Farhat, H. (2024). Application of tele-neuropsychology and tele-mental health before and during COVID-19 era: A bibliometric analysis. *Annals of Medicine & Surgery, 86*(5), 2777–2785. https://doi.org/10.1097/MS9.0000000000001822

Alva, J. I., Brewster, R. C., Mahmood, Z., Harrell, K. M., Kaiser, N. C., Young-Sciortino, K., Brunet, H. E., Johnson, M. E., & Kovach, S. (2025). Are tele-neuropsychology and in-person assessment scores meaningfully different? A systematic review and meta-analysis. *The Clinical Neuropsychologist, 39*(5), 1037–1072. https://doi.org/10.1080/13854046.2025.2493343

American Academy of Clinical Neuropsychology Board of Directors. (2007). American Academy of Clinical Neuropsychology (AACN) practice guidelines for neuropsychological assessment and consultation. *The Clinical Neuropsychologist, 21*(2), 209–231. https://doi.org/10.1080/13825580601025932

American Educational Research Association, American Psychological Association, National Council on Measurement in Education. (2014). *Standards for educational and psychological testing.* American Educational Research Associates. https://www.testingstandards.net/uploads/7/6/6/4/76643089/standards_2014edition.pdf

American Hospital Association. (2019). *Fact sheet: Telehealth.* https://www.aha.org/system/files/2019-02/fact-sheet-telehealth-2-4-19.pdf

American Psychological Association. (2017). *Ethical principles of psychologists and code of conduct.* https://www.apa.org/ethics/code#:~:text=Psychologists%20respect%20the%20dignity%20and,with%20members%20of%20such%20groups.

American Psychological Association. (2020). *Informed consent checklist for telepsychological services.* https://www.apa.org/topics/disasters-response/informed-consent-checklist

American Psychological Association. (2025, April). *Telehealth continuing education resources.* https://www.apa.org/ed/ce/telehealth

Amini, S., Hao, B., Yang, J., Karjadi, C., Kolachalama, V. B., Au, R., & Paschalidis, I. C. (2024). Prediction of Alzheimer's disease progression within 6 years using speech: A novel approach leveraging language models. *Alzheimer's & Dementia, 20*(8), 5262–5270. https://doi.org/10.1002/alz.13886

Aminikhanghahi, S., Schmitter-Edgecombe, M., & Cook, D. J. (2020). Context-aware delivery of ecological momentary assessment. *IEEE Journal of Biomedical and Health Informatics, 24*(4), 1206–1214. https://doi.org/10.1109/jbhi.2019.2937116

Appleman, E. R., O'Connor, M. K., Boucher, S. J., Rostami, R., Sullivan, S. K., Migliorini, R., & Kraft, M. (2021). Teleneuropsychology clinic development and patient satisfaction. *The Clinical Neuropsychologist, 35*(4), 819–837. https://doi.org/10.1080/13854046.2020.1871515

Aramendi, A. A., Weakley, A., Goenaga, A. A., Schmitter-Edgecombe, M., & Cook, D. J. (2018). Automatic assessment of functional health decline in older adults based on smart home data. *Journal of Biomedical Informatics, 81*, 119–130. https://doi.org/10.1016/j.jbi.2018.03.009

Arias, F., Safi, D. E., Miranda, M., Carrión, C. I., Diaz Santos, A. L., Armendariz, V., Jose, I. E., Vuong, K. D., Suarez, P., Strutt, A. M., & The STAR Consortium. (2020). Teleneuropsychology for monolingual and bilingual Spanish-speaking adults in the time of COVID-19: Rationale, professional considerations, and resources. *Archives of Clinical Neuropsychology, 35*(8), 1249–1265. https://doi.org/10.1093/arclin/acaa100

Barbovschi, M., & Balea, B. (2013). Closing the gap, are we there yet? Reflections on the persistence of second-level digital divide among adolescents in central and eastern Europe. In M. Ragnedda & G. W. Muschert (Eds.), *The digital divide: The internet and social inequality in international perspective* (pp. 179–192). Routledge. https://doi.org/10.4324/9780203069769

Barton, C., Morris, R., Rothlind, J., & Yaffe, K. (2011). Video-telemedicine in a memory disorders clinic: Evaluation and management of rural elders with cognitive impairment. *Telemedicine and e-Health, 17*(10), 789–793. https://doi.org/10.1089/tmj.2011.0083

Bauer, R. M., & Bilder, R. M. (2023). Automated neuropsychological testing. In G. G. Brown, B. Crosson, K. Y. Haaland, & T. Z. King (Eds.), *APA handbook of neuropsychology: Neuroscience and neuromethods* (pp. 233–258). American Psychological Association. https://doi.org/10.1037/0000308-011

Bauer, R. M., Iverson, G. L., Cernich, A. N., Binder, L. M., Ruff, R. M., & Naugle, R. I. (2012). Computerized neuropsychological assessment devices: Joint position paper of the American Academy of Clinical Neuropsychology and the National Academy of

Neuropsychology. *The Clinical Neuropsychologist*, *26*(2), 177–196. https://doi.org/10.1080/13854046.2012.663001

Baugh, F. (2002). Corrcting effect size for score reliability: A reminder that measurement and substaintive issues are linked inextricably. *Educational and Psychological Measurement*, *62*(2), 254–263. https://doi.org/10.1177/0013164402062002004

Bilder, R. M. (2010). Neuropsychology 3.0: Evidence-based science and practice. *Journal of the International Neuropsychological Society*, *17*(1), 7–13. https://doi.org/10.1017/S1355617710001396

Bilder, R. M., Postal, K. S., Barisa, M., Aase, D. M., Cullum, C. M., Gillaspy, S. R., Harder, L., Kanter, G., Lanca, M., Lechuga, D. M., Morgan, J. M., Most, R., Puente, A. E., Salinas, C. M., & Woodhouse, J. (2020). Inter organizational practice committee recommendations/guidance for teleneuropsychology in response to the COVID-19 pandemic. *Archives of Clinical Neuropsychology*, *35*(6), 647–659. https://doi.org/10.1093/arclin/acaa046

Bilder, R. M., & Reise, S. P. (2019). Neuropsychological tests of the future: How do we get there from here? *The Clinical Neuropsychologist*, *33*(2), 220–245. https://doi.org/10.1080/13854046.2018.1521993

Brearly, T. W., Shura, R. D., Matindale, S. L., Lazowski, R. A., Luxton, D. D., Shenai, B. V., & Rowland, J. A. (2017). Neuropsychological test administration by videoconference: A systematic review and meta-analysis. *Neuropsychology Review*, *27*(2), 174–186. https://doi.org/10.1007/s11065-017-9349-1

Brown, T., & Zakzanis, K. K. (2023). A review of the reliability of remote neuropsychological assessment. *Applied Neuropsychology: Adult*, 1–7. https://doi.org/10.1080/23279095.2023.2279208

Carlew, A. R., Fatima, H., Livingstone, J. R., Reese, C., Lacritz, L., Pendergrass, C., Bailey, K. C., Presley, C., Mokhtari, B., Cullum, C. M. (2020). Cognitive assessment via telephone: A scoping review of instruments. *Archives of Clinical Neuropsychology*, *35*(8), 1215–1233. https://doi.org/10.1093/arclin/acaa096

Casaletto, K. B., & Heaton, R. K. (2017). Neuropsychological assessment: Past and future. *Journal of the International Neuropsychological Society*, *23*(9–10), 778–790. https://doi.org/10.1017/S1355617717001060

Caze, T., Dorsman, K. A., Carlew, A. R., Diaz, A., & Bailey, K. C. (2020). Can you hear me now? Telephone-based teleneuropsychology Improves utilization rates in underserved populations. *Archives of Clinical Neuropsychology*, *35*(8), 1234–1239. https://doi.org/10.1093/arclin/acaa098

Cena, E., Toner, P., McParland, A., Burns, S., & Dudgeon, K. (2023). Studying and learning psychology during the COVID-19 pandemic: A mixed-methods approach on students' perspectives of psychological well-being and adjustment to studying online. *Psychology Learning & Teaching*, *22*(2), 137–158. https://doi.org/10.1177/14757257231169938

Center for Connected Health Policy. (2024). *Medicare billing for telehealth encounters: An introductory guide for fee-for-service*. The National Telehealth Policy Resource Center. https://www.cchpca.org/2024/09/2024BillingGuide4FINAL.pdf

Centers for Medicare and Medicaid Services. (2024, September). *List of telehealth services for calendar year 2025* [Data set.]. https://www.cms.gov/medicare/coverage/telehealth/list-services

Chapman, J. E., Gardner, B., Ponsford, J., Cadilhac, D. A., & Stolwyk, R. J. (2021). Comparing performance across in-person and videoconference-based administrations of common neuropsychological measures in community-based survivors of stroke. *Journal of the International Neuropsychological Society, 27*(7), 697–710. https://doi.org/10.1017/S1355617720001174

Chapman, J. E., Ponsford, J., Bagot, K. L., Cadilhac, D. A., Gardner, B., & Stolwyk, R. J. (2020). The use of videoconferencing in clinical neuropsychology practice: A mixed methods evaluation of neuropsychologists' experiences and views. *Australian Psychologist, 55*(6), 618–633. https://doi.org/10.1111/ap.12471

Cintoli, S., Spadoni, G., Giuliani, V., Nicoletti, V., Del Prete, E., Frosini, D., Ceravolo, R., & Tognoni, G. (2025). A pilot study investigating the effectiveness, appreciation, and feasibility of a cognitive stimulation program in dementia patients: Online versus face-to-face. *Frontiers of Psychology, 16*, 1561157. https://doi.org/10.3389/fpsyg.2025.1561157

Cook, D. J., Schmitter-Edgecombe, M., Jonsson, L., & Morant, A. V. (2019). Technology-enabled assessment of functional health. *IEEE Reviews in Biomedical Engineering, 12*, 319–332. https://doi.org/10.1109/rbme.2018.2851500

Crivelli, L., Quiroz, Y. T., Calandri, I. L., Martin, M. E., Velilla, L. M., Cusicanqui, M. I., Yglesias, F. C., Llibre-Rodríguez, Armele, M., Román, F., Barceló, E., Dechent, C., Carello, M. A., ... & Allegri, R. F. (2022). Working group recommendations for the practice of teleneuropsychology in Latin America. *Archives of Clinical Neuropsychology, 37*(3), 553–567. https://doi.org/10.1093/arclin/acab080

Cullum, C. M., Weiner, M. F., Gehrmann, H. R., & Hynan, L. S. (2006). Feasibility of telecognitive assessment in dementia. *Assessment, 13*(4), 385–390. https://doi.org/10.1177/1073191106289065

Cullum, C. M., Hynan, L. S., Grosch, M., Parikh, M., & Weiner, M. F. (2014). Teleneuropsychology: Evidence for video teleconference-based neuropsychological assessment. *Journal of the International Neuropsychological Society, 20*(10), 1028–1033. https://doi.org/10.1017/S1355617714000873

Cullum, C. M., Gioia, G., & Podell, K. (2019, November 4). Taking neuropsychology out of the office: Extending our practice through telehealth technology [Webinar]. National Academy of Neuropsychology.

Deviatko, I. F. (2013). Digitizing Russia: The uneven pace of progress toward ICT equality. In M. Ragnedda & G. W. Muschert (Eds.), *The digital divide: The internet and social inequality in international perspective* (pp. 118–133). Routledge. https://doi.org/10.4324/9780203069769

Doxy.Me. (2025). *Minimum system requirements.* https://help.doxy.me/en/articles/95860-minimum-system-requirements

Dzara, K., Pusic, M., Carlile, N., Krupat, E., & Alexander, E. K. (2022). Educational adaptation to clinical training during the COVID-19 pandemic: A process analysis. *BMC Medical Education, 22*(1), 200. https://doi.org/10.1186/s12909-022-03237-6

Federal Communications Commission. (2010). *Connecting America: The national broadband plan.* https://transition.fcc.gov/national-broadband-plan/national-broadband-plan.pdf

Federal Communications Commission. (2022). *Broadband speed guide.* https://www.fcc.gov/consumers/guides/broadband-speed-guide

Federal Communications Commission. (2024). *Affordable connectivity program.* https://www.fcc.gov/acp

Federal Communications Commission. (2025). *Emergency broadband benefit program.* https://www.fcc.gov/emergency-broadband-benefit-program

Fellows, R. P., & Schmitter-Edgecombe, M. (2019). Multimethod assessment of everyday functioning and memory abilities in Parkinson's disease. *Neuropsychology, 33*(2), 169–177. https://doi.org/10.1037/neu0000505

Fellows, R. P., Dahmen, J., Cook, D., & Schmitter-Edgecombe, M. (2017). Multicomponent analysis of digital Trail Making Test. *The Clinical Neuropsychologist, 31*(1), 154–167. https://doi.org/10.1080/13854046.2016.1238510

Fox-Fuller, J. T., Rizer, S., Andersen, S. L., & Sunderaraman, P. (2021). Survey findings about the experiences, challenges, and practical advice/solutions regarding teleneuropsychological assessment in adults. *Archives of Clinical Neuropsychology, 37*(2), 274–291. https://doi.org/10.1093/arclin/acab076

Fox-Fuller, J. T., Wising, A. M., Koudys, J. W., DesRuisseaux, L. A., Cerny, B., Schmitt, T. R., Rahman-Filipiak, A., Votruba, K., L., & Clinical Neuropsychology Trainee Forum. (2025). Challenges and opportunities for a new era of neuropsychology training: A trainee survey study. *Journal of Clinical and Experimental Neuropsychology, 47*(9-10), 1025–1038. https://doi.org/10.1080/13803395.2025.2464654

Freir, V., Kirkwood, K., Peck, D., Robertson, S., Scott-Lodge, L., & Zeffert, S. (1999). Telemedicine for clinical psychology in the Highlands of Scotland. *Journal of Telemedicine and Telecare, 5*(3), 157–161. https://doi.org/10.1258/1357633991933567

Fritz, R. L., Wilson, M., Dermody, G., Schmitter-Edgecombe, M., & Cook, D. J. (2020). Automated smart home assessment to support pain management: Multiple methods analysis. *Journal of Medical Internet Research, 22*(11), e23943. https://doi.org/10.2196/23943

Ghods, A., Caffrey, K., Lin, B., Fraga, K., Fritz, R., Schmitter-Edgecombe, M., Hundhausen, C., & Cook, D. J. (2019). Iterative design of visual analytics for a clinician-in-the-loop smart home. *IEEE Journal of Biomedical and Health Informatics, 23*(4), 1742–1748. https://doi.org/10.1109/jbhi.2018.2864287

Grosch, M. C., Gottlieb, M. C., & Cullum, C. M. (2011). Initial practice recommendations for teleneuropsychology. *The Clinical Neuropsychologist, 25*(7), 1119–1133. https://doi.org/10.1080/13854046.2011.609840

Guilmette, T. J., Sweet, J. J., Hebben, N., Koltai, D., Mahone, E. M., Spiegler, B. J., Stucky, K., Westerveld, M., & conference participants. (2020). American Academy of Clinical Neuropsychology conference statement on uniform labeling of performance test scores. *The Clinical Neuropsychologist, 34*(3), 437–453. https://doi.org/10.1080/13854046.2020.1722244

Hajjar, I., Okafor, M., Choi, J. D., Moore, E., Abrol, A., Calhoun, V. D., & Goldstein, F. C. (2023). Development of digital voice biomarkers and associations with cognition, cerebrospinal biomarkers, and neural representation in early Alzheimer's disease. *Alzheimer's & Dementia: Diagnosis, Assessment & Disease Monitoring, 15*(1), e12393. https://doi.org/10.1002/dad2.12393

Hammers, D. B., Stolwyk, R., Harder, L., & Cullum, C. M. (2020). A survey of international clinical teleneuropsychology service provision prior to and in the context of COVID-19. *The Clinical Neuropsychologist, 34*(7–8), 1267–1283. https://doi.org/10.1080/13854046.2020.1810323

Harder, L., Hernandez, A., Hague, C., Neumann, J., McCreary, M., Cullum, C. M., & Greenberg, B. (2020). Home-based pediatric teleneuropsychology: A validation study. *Archives of Clinical Neuropsychology, 35*(8), 1266–1275. https://doi.org/10.1093/arclin/acaa080

Harris, C., Tang, Y., Birnbaum, E., Cherian, C., Mendhe, D., & Chen, M. H. (2024). Digital neuropsychology beyond computerized cognitive assessment: Applications of novel digital technologies. *Archives of Clinical Neuropsychology, 39*(3), 290–304. https://doi.org/10.1093/arclin/acae016

Heffelfinger, A. K., Janecek, J. J., Johnson, A., Miller, L. E., Nelson, A., & Pulsipher, D. T. (2022). Competency-based assessment in clinical neuropsychology at the post-doctoral level: Stages, milestones, and benchmarks as proposed by an APPCN work group. *The Clinical Neuropsychologist, 36*(6), 1209–1225. https://doi.org/10.1080/13854046.2020.1829070

Hewitt, K. C., Block, C., Bellone, J. A., Dawson, E. L., Garcia, P., Gerstenecker, A., Grabyan, J. M., Howard, C., Kamath, V., LeMonda, B. C., Margolis, S. A., McBride, W. F., Salinas, C. M., Tam, D. M., Walker, K. A., & Del Bene, V. A. (2022). Diverse experiences and approaches to tele neuropsychology: Commentary and reflections over the past year of COVID-19. *The Clinical Neuropsychologist, 36*(4), 790–805. https://doi.org/10.1080/13854046.2022.2027022

Hewitt, K. C., Rodgin, S., Loring, D. W., Pritchard, A. E., & Jacobson, L. A. (2020). Transitioning to telehealth neuropsychology service: Considerations across adult and pediatric care settings. *The Clinical Neuropsychologist, 34*(7–8), 1335–1351. https://doi.org/10.1080/13854046.2020.1811891

Hu, Y., Li, Y., Li, J., Liu, J. Y.W., Gustin, S. M., Li, M., & Leung, A.Y.M. (2025). Effectiveness of telehealth interventions on cognitive function and quality of life in adults with neurological disorders: A systematic review and meta-analysis. *Journal of the American Medical Directors Association, 26*(4), 105491. https://doi.org/10.1016/j.jamda.2025.105491

Hunter, J. E., & Schmidt, F. L. (1990). *Methods of Meta-Analysis: Correcting Error and Bias in Research Findings.* Newbury Park, CA: Sage.

Ilavarasan, P. V. (2013). The digital divide in India: Inferences from the information and communication technology workforce. In M. Ragnedda & G. W. Muschert (Eds.), *The digital divide: The internet and social inequality in international perspective* (pp. 134–146). Routledge. https://doi.org/10.4324/9780203069769

Inter Organizational Practice Committee (n.d.). *Tele-neuropsych training/webinars.* https://iopc.online/teleneuropsychology-training

International Telecommunication Union, & Office of the Secretary-Generals' Envoy on Technology. (2022). *Achieving universal and meaningful digital connectivity: Setting a baseline and targets for 2030.* https://www.itu.int/itu-d/meetings/statistics/wp-content/uploads/sites/8/2022/04/UniversalMeaningfulDigitalConnectivityTargets2030_BackgroundPaper.pdf

International Telecommunication Union. (2022). *Facts and figures 2022.* https://www.itu.int/itu-d/reports/statistics/facts-figures-2022/index/

Jacobsen, S. E., Sprenger, T., Stein, A., & Jan-Magne, K. (2003). Neuropsychological assessment and telemedicine: A preliminary study examining the reliability of neuropsychological services performed via telecommunication. *Journal of the International Neuropsychological Society, 9*(3), 472–478. https://doi.org/10.1017/S1355617703930128

Joint Task Force for the Development of Telepsychology Guidelines for Psychologists. (2013). Guidelines for the practice of telepsychology. *American Psychologist, 68*(9), 791–800. https://doi.org/10.1037/a0035001

Kaser, A. N., Lacritz, L. H., Winiarski, H. R., Gabirondo, P., Schaffert, J., Coca, A. J., Jiménez-Raboso, J., Rojo, T., Zaldua, C., Honorato, I., Gallego, D., Nieves, E. R., Rosenstein, L. D., & Cullum, C. M. (2024). A novel speech analysis algorithm to detect cognitive impairment in a Spanish population. *Frontiers in Neurology, 15*, 1342907. https://doi.org/10.3389/fneur.2024.1342907

Kitaigorodsky, M., Loewenstein, D., Cid, R. C., Crocco, E., Gorman, K., & González-Jiménez, C. (2021). A teleneuropsychology protocol for the cognitive assessment of older adults during COVID-19. *Frontiers in Psychology, 12*(1), 651136. https://doi.org/10.3389/fpsyg.2021.651136

Kruse, S. C., Karem P., Shifflett K., Vegi L., Ravi K., & Brooks M. (2016). Evaluating barriers to adopting telemedicine worldwide: A systematic review. *Journal of Telemedicine and Telecare, 24*(1), 4–12. http://doi.org/10.1177/1357633X16674087

Krynicki, C. R., Hacker, D., & Jones, C. A. (2023). An evaluation of the convergent validity of a face-to-face and virtual neuropsychological assessment counter balanced. *Journal of Neuropsychology, 17*(2), 319–334. https://doi.org/10.1111/jnp.12300

Lacritz, L. H., Carlew, A. R., Livingstone, J., Bailey, K. C., Parker, A., & Diaz, A. (2020). Patient satisfaction with telephone neuropsychological assessment. *Archives of Clinical Neuropsychology, 35*(8), 1240–1248. https://doi.org/10.1093/arclin/acaa097

Läkens, D. (2017). Equivalence tests: A practical primer for *t* tests, correlations, and meta-analysis. *Social Psychological and Personality Science, 8*(4), 355–262. https://doi.org/10.1177/1948550617697177

Mann, D. M., Chen, J., Chunara, R., Testa, P. A., & Nov, O. (2020). COVID-19 transforms health care through telemedicine: Evidence from the field. *Journal of the American Medical Informatics Association, 27*(7), 1132–1135. https://doi.org/10.1093/jamia/ocaa072

Marra, D. E., Hamlet, K. M., Bauer, R. M., & Bowers, D. (2020). Validity of teleneuropsychology for older adults in response to COVID-19: A systematic and critical review. *The Clinical Neuropsychologist, 34*(7–8), 1411–1452. https://doi.org/10.1080/13854046.2020.1769192

Marra, D. E., Hoelzle, J. B., Davis, J. J., & Schwartz, E. S. (2020). Initial changes in neuropsychologists clinical practice during the COVID-19 pandemic: A survey study. *The Clinical Neuropsychologist, 34*(7–8), 1251–1266. https://doi.org/10.1080/13854046.2020.1800098

Martínez Canyazo, C., Keller, G., Helou, B., et al. (2023). Effectiveness of cognitive rehabilitation on mild cognitive impairment using teleneuropsychology. *Dementia & Neuropsychologia, 17*, e20220082. https://doi.org/10.1590/1980-5764-DN-2022-0079

McClain, C., Vogels, E. A., Perrin, A., Sechopoulos, S., & Rainie, L. (2021). *The internet and the pandemic.* https://www.pewresearch.org/internet/2021/09/01/the-internet-and-the-pandemic/#fnref-92974-3

McCue, M., & Cullum, C. M. (2013). Telerehabilitation and teleneuropsychology: Emerging practices. In C. Noggle & R. Dean (Eds.), *Neuropsychological rehabilitation* (pp. 327–340). Springer.

McGoldrick, K. D. (2015). *Evaluating the repeatable battery for the assessment of neuropsychological status (RBANS) performance when administered via videoteleconference (VTC).* Fielding Graduate University.

Microsoft. (2024). *Prepare your organization's network for Microsoft Teams.* https://learn.microsoft.com/en-us/microsoftteams/prepare-network

Mietchne, J. J., Cleminksi, T. M., & Kessler-Jones, A. M. (2025). Your clinical interview *is* data: The benefit of telehealth appointments to triage referrals made to pediatric neuropsychology. *The Clinical Neuropsychologist, 39*(5), 1266–1285. https://doi.org/10.1080/13854046.2025.2456160

Montani, C., Billaurd, N., Couturier, P., Fluchaire, I., Lemaire, R., Malterre, C., Lauvernay, N., Piquard, J. F., Frossard, M., & Franco, A. (1996). "Telepsychometry": A remote psychometry consultation in clinical gerontology: Preliminary study. *Telemedicine Journal*, *2*(2), 145–150. https://doi.org/10.1089/tmj.1.1996.2.145

Moreau, J., Pollock, B., & Harrison, A. G. (2023). In-person and in-home teleneuropsychological assessments with youth with neurodevelopmental disorders: What's the difference? *Canadian Journal of School Psychology*, *38*(4), 317–332. https://doi.org/10.1177/08295735231199858

Naamanka, E., Salakka, I., Parkkila, M., Hotti, J., & Poutiainen, E. (2024). Effective of teleneuropsychological rehabilitation: Systematic review of randomized controlled trails. *Journal of the International Neuropsychological Society*, *30*(3), 295–312. https://doi.org/10.1017/S1355617723000565

National Academy of Neuropsychology. (n.d.). *Telehealth resources*. https://nanonline.org/Nanweb24/NAN/_ProfessionalResources/Telehealth_Resources.aspx

Nguyen, C. M., Tan, A., Nguyen, A., Lee, G. J., Qi, W., Thaler, N. S., & Fujii, D. (2023). Cross-cultural considerations for teleneuropsychology with Asian patients. *The Clinical Neuropsychologist*, *37*(5), 896–910. https://doi.org/10.1080/13854046.2021.1948104

O'Connor, B. (2018). An illustration of the effects of fluctuations in test information on measurement error, the attenuation of effect sizes, and diagnostic reliability. *Psychological Assessment*, *30*(8), 991–1003. https://doi.org/10.1037/pas0000471

Office of Disease Prevention and Health Promotion. (2016). *Health literacy online: A guide for simplifying the user experience* (2nd ed.). https://odphp.health.gov/healthliteracyonline/

Parikh, M., Grosch, M. C., Graham, L. L., Hynan, L. S., Weiner, M., Shore, J. H., & Cullum, C. M. (2013). Consumer acceptability of brief videoconference-based neuropsychological assessment in older adults with and without cognitive impairment. *The Clinical Neuropsychologist*, *27*(5), 808–817. https://doi.org/10.1080/13854046.2013.791723

Parks, A., C., Davis, J., Spresser, C. D., Stroescu, I., & Ecklund-Johnson, E. (2021). Validity of in-home teleneuropsychological testing in the wake of COVID-19. *Archives of Clinical Neuropsychology*, *36*(6), 887–896. https://doi.org/10.1093/arclin/acab002

Parsey, C. M., & Schmitter-Edgecombe, M. (2019). Using actigraphy to predict the ecological momentary assessment of mood, fatigue, and cognition in older adulthood: Mixed-methods study. *JMIR Aging*, *2*(1), e11331. https://doi.org/10.2196/11331

Parsons, T. D. (2016). *Clinical neuropsychology and technology: What's new and how we can use it*. Springer International/Springer Nature. https://psycnet.apa.org/doi/10.1007/978-3-319-31075-6

Parsons, T., & Duffield, T. (2020). Paradigm shift toward digital neuropsychology and high-dimensional neuropsychological assessments: Review. *Journal of Medical Internet Research*, *22*(12), e23777. https://doi.org/10.2196/23777

Postal, K. S., Bilder, R. M., Lanca, M., Aase, D. M., Barisa, M., Holland, A. A., Lacritz, L. H., Lechuga, D. M., McPherson, S., Morgan, J., & Salinas, C. (2020). Inter Organizational practice committee guidance/recommendation for models of care during the novel coronavirus pandemic. *The Clinical Neuropsychologist*, *35*(1), 81–98. https://doi.org/10.1080/13854046.2020.1801847

Pritchard, A. E., Sweeney, K., Salorio, C. F., & Jacobson, L. A. (2020). Pediatric neuropsychological evaluation via telehealth: Novel models of care. *The Clinical Neuropsychologist*, *34*(7–8), 1367–1379. https://doi.org/10.1080/13854046.2020.1806359

Pulsifer, M. B., Grieco, J. A., Burstein, S. M., Parsons, M. W., Gardner, M. M., & Sherman, J. C. (2021). The development and implementation of teleneuropsychology in an academic lifespan neuropsychology center: Lessons learned from the COVID-19 pandemic. *Journal of Clinical and Experimental Neuropsychology*, *43*(8), 774–785. https://doi.org/10.1080/13803395.2021.1963683

Rabin, L. A., Paolillo, E., & Barr, W. B. (2016). Stability in test-usage practices of clinical neuropsychologists in the United States and Canada over a 10-year period: A follow-up survey of INS and NAN members. *Archives of Clinical Neuropsychology*, *31*(3), 206–230. https://doi.org/10.1093/arclin/acw007

Radovanović, D. (2013). The internet and digital divide in south eastern Europe: Connectivity does not end the digital divide, skills do. In M. Ragnedda & G. W. Muschert (Eds.), *The digital divide: The internet and social inequality in international perspective* (pp. 167–178). Routledge. https://doi.org/10.4324/9780203069769

Randolph, C. (2012). *Repeatable Battery for the Assessment of Neuropsychological Status Update (RBANS Update)*. Bloomington, MN: Pearson.

Ransom, D. M., Butt, S. M., DiVirgilio, E. K., Cederberg, C. D., Srnka, K. D., Hess, C. T., Sy, M. C., & Katzenstein, J. M. (2020). Pediatric teleneuropsychology: Feasability and recommendations. *Archives of Clinical Neuropsychology*, *35*(8), 1204–1214. https://doi.org/10.1093/arclin/acaa103

Rizzi, E., Vezzoli, M., Pegoraro, S., Facchin, A., Strina, V., & Daini, R. (2023). Teleneuropsychology: Normative data for the assessment of memory in online settings. *Neurological Sciences*, *44*(2), 529–538. https://doi.org/10.1007/s10072-022-06426-9

Rochette, A. D., Rahman-Filipiak, A., Spencer, R. J., Marshall, D., & Stelmokas, J. E. (2022). Teleneuropsychology practice during COVID-19 within the United States. *Applied Neuropsychology: Adult*, *29*(6), 1312–1322. https://doi.org/10.1080/23279095.2021.1872576

Salinas, C. M., Bordes Edgar, V., Siervo, G. B., & Bender, H. A. (2020). Transforming pediatric neuropsychology through video-based teleneuropsychology: An innovative private practice model pre-COVID-19. *Archives of Clinical Neuropsychology*, *35*(8), 1189–1195. https://doi.org/10.1093/arclin/acaa101

Salvadori, E., Pantoni, L., & Societá Italiana di NeuroGeriatria (SINEG). (2023). Teleneuropsychology for vascular cognitive impairment: What tools do we have? *Cerebral Circulation – Cognitive and Behavior*, *5*(1), 100173. https://doi.org/10.1016/j.cccb.2023.100173

Schmand, B. (2019). Why are neuropsychologists so reluctant to embrace modern assessment techniques? *The Clinical Neuropsychologist, 33*(2), 1–11. http://doi.org/10.1080/13854046.2018.1523468

Schmitter-Edgecombe, M., Luna, C., Beech, B., Dai, S., & Cook, D. J. (2025). Capturing cognitive capacity in the everyday environment across a continuum of cognitive decline using a smartwatch n-back test and ecological momentary assessment. *Neuropsychology, 39*(1), 28–43. https://doi.org/10.1037/neu0000984

Schmitter-Edgecombe, M., McAlister, C., & Greeley, D. (2022). A comparison of functional abilities in individuals with mild cognitive impairment and Parkinson's disease with mild cognitive impairment using multiple assessment methods. *Journal of the International Neuropsychological Society, 28*(8), 798–809. https://doi.org/10.1017/s1355617721001077

Schopp, L., Johnstone, B., & Merrell, D. (2000). Telehealth and neuropsychological assessment: New opportunities for psychologists. *Professional Psychology: Research and Practice, 31*(2), 179–183. http://doi.org/10.1037//0735-7028.31.2.179

Scott, T. M., Marton, K. M. & Madore, M. R. (2022). A detailed analysis of ethical considerations for three specific models of teleneuropsychology during and beyond the COVID-19 pandemic. *The Clinical Neuropsychologist, 36*(1), 24–44. https://doi.org/10.1080/13854046.2021.1889678

Serrano-Juárez, C. A., Reyes-Méndez, C., Prieto-Corona, B., Seubert-Ravelo, A. N., Moreno-Villagómez, J., Cabañas-Tinajero, J.-A., Yáñez-Téllez, M. G., Quezada-Torres, R. A., Téllez-Rodríguez, M., Barrera-Rodríguez, B., Soto-Jiménez, M. P., González-Gutiérrez, F. A., & Castillo-Tejeda, E. (2023). A systematic review and a Latin American clinical model for teleneuropsychological assessment. *Archives of Clinical Neuropsychology, 38*(2), 283–300. https://doi.org/10.1093/arclin/acac077

Sherwood, A. R., & MacDonald, B. (2020). A teleneuropsychology consultation service model for children with neurodevelopmental and acquired disorders residing in rural state regions. *Archives of Clinical Neuropsychology, 35*(8), 1196–1203. https://doi.org/10.1093/arclin/acaa099

Singh, S., & Germine, L. (2021). Technology meets tradition: A hybrid model for implementing digital tools in neuropsychology. *International Review of Psychiatry, 33*(4), 382–393. https://doi.org/10.1080/09540261.2020.1835839

Souillard-Mandar, W., Davis, R., Rudin, C., Au, R., Libon, D. J., Swenson, R., Price, C. C., Lamar, M., & Penney, D. L. (2015). Learning classification models of cognitive conditions from subtle behaviors in the digital Clock Drawing Test. *Machine Learning, 102*(3), 393–441. https://doi.org/10.1007/s10994-015-5529-5

Sperling, S. A., Acheson, S. K., Fox-Fuller, J., Colvin, M. K., Harder, L., Cullum, C. M., Randolph, J. J., Carter, K. R., Espe-Pfeifer, P., Lacritz, L. H., Arnett, P. A., & Gillaspy, S. R. (2024). Tele-neuropsychology: From science to policy to practice. *Archives of Clinical Neuropsychology, 39*(2), 227–248. https://doi.org/10.1093/arclin/acad066

Sperling, S. A., Dong, J., Lapin, B., & Li, Y. (2025). Reliability and validity of in-home teleneuropsychological testing in patients with Parkinson's disease: A randomized trial. *The Clinical Neuropsychologist, 16*(1), 1–36. https://doi.org/10.1080/13854046.2025.2503374

Stamm, B. H. (1998). Clinical application of telehealth in mental health care. *Professional Psychology: Research and Practice, 29*(6), 536–542. https://doi.org/10.1037/0735-7028.29.6.536

Stringer, A., Fuchs, K., Bordes Edgar, V., Bristo T., Correia, S., Penna, S., Reyes A., Whiteside, D. M., Block, C., Bodin, D., Butt, K., Calamia, M., Didehbani, N., Dodzik, P., Dotson, V. M., Fernandes, M., Freece, K., Fuller, R., Getz, G., Harder, L., ... & Schmitter-Edgecombe, M. (2026). The Minnesota conference proposed guidelines for education and training in clinical neuropsychology. *The Clinical Neuropsychologist, 40*(2), 331–375. https://doi.org/10.80/13854046.2025.2520957

Sweet, J. J., Klipfel, K. M., Nelson, N. W., & Moberg, P. J. (2021). Professional practices, beliefs, and incomes of US neuropsychologists: The AACN, NAN, SCN 2020 practice and "salary survey." *The Clinical Neuropsychologist, 35*(1), 7–80. https://doi.org/10.1080/13854046.2020.1849803

Tagliente, S., Minafra, B., Aresta, S., Santacesaria, P., Buccoliero, A., Palmirotta, C., Lagravinese, G., Mongelli, D., Geloa, C., Macchitella, L., Pazzi, S., Scrutinio, D., Baiardi, P., & Battista, P. (2025). Effectiveness of a home-based computerized cognitive training in Parkinson's disease: A pilot randomized cross-over study. *Frontiers of Psychology, 15*, 1531688. https://doi.org/10.3389/fpsyg.2024.1531688

Tailby, C., Chapman, J. E., Pugh, R., Skogan, A. H., Helmstaedter, C., & Jackson, G. D. (2025). Applications of teleneuropsychology to the screening and monitoring of epilepsy. *Seizure, 128*(1), 54–58. https://doi.org/10.1016/j.seizure.2024.06.022

Telecommunications Act of 1996, 47 U.S.C. § 609 *et seq*. (1996). https://www.congress.gov/bill/104th-congress/senate-bill/652/text

Thibodaux, L. K., Breiger, D., Bledsoe, J., Sato, J., Hilsman, R., & Paolozzi, A. (2021). Teleneuropsychology: A model for clinical practice. *Practice Innovations, 6*(3), 189–198. https://doi.org/10.1037/pri0000150

Triemstra, J. D., Haas, M. R.C., Bhavsar-Burke, I., Gottlieb-Smith, R., Wolff, M., Shelgikar, A. V., Samala, R. V., Ruff, A. L., Kuo, K., Tam, M., Gupta, A., Stojan, J., Gruppen, L., & Ellinas, H. (2021). Impact of the COVID-19 pandemic on the clinical learning environment: Addressing identified gaps and seizing opportunities. *Academic Medicine, 96*(9), 1276–1281. https://doi.org/10.1097/ACM.0000000000004013

Tseng, S.-F., & You, Y.-C. (2013). The digital divide in China, Hong Kong, and Taiwan: The barriers of first order and second order digital divide. In M. Ragnedda & G. W. Muschert (Eds.), *The digital divide: The internet and social inequality in international perspective* (pp. 147–164). Routledge. https://doi.org/10.4324/9780203069769

Universal Service Administration Co. (n.d.). *Connecting millions to broadband services*. https://www.usac.org/

U.S. Department of Health and Human Services. (2025). *Telehealth policy updates.* https://telehealth.hhs.gov/providers/telehealth-policy/telehealth-policy-updates#extensions-of-telehealth-access-options

van Dijk, J. (2019). *The digital divide.* Wiley.

Vickers, A. J., van Calster, B., & Steyerberg, E. W. (2016). Net benefit approaches to the evaluation of prediction models, molecular markers, and diagnostic tests. *Research Methods & Reporting, 352*(16), 352. https://doi.org/10.1136/bmj.i6

Wadsworth, H. E., Dhima, K., Womack, K. B., Hart, J., Weiner, M. F., Hynan, L. S., & Cullum, C. M. (2018). Validity of teleneuropsychological assessment in older patients with cognitive disorders. *Archives of Clinical Neuropsychology, 33*(8), 1040–1045. https://doi.org/10.1093/arclin/acx140

Walker, E. J., Kirkham, F. J., Stotesbury, H., Dimitriou, D., & Hood, A. M. (2023). Teleneuropsychological assessment of children and young people: A systematic review. *Journal of Pediatric Neuropsychology, 9*(3), 113–126. https://doi.org/10.1007/s40817-023-00144-6

Wärn, E., Andersson, L, & Berginström, N. (2025). Remote neuropsychological testing as an alternative to traditional methods—A convergent validity study. *Archives of Clinical Neuropsychology, 40*(6), 1123–1132. https://doi.org/10.1093/arclin/acaf013

Warschauer, M., & Niiya, M. (2017). Digital divide and inclusion. In M. J. Bates, & M. N. Maack (Eds.), *Encyclopedia of library and information sciences* (4th ed., pp. 1279–1285). CRC Press. https://doi.org/10.1081/E-ELIS4

Witte, J., Kiss, M., & Lynn, R. (2013). The internet and social inequalities in the U.S. In M. Ragnedda & G. W. Muschert (Eds.), *The digital divide: The internet and social inequality in international perspective* (pp. 67–84). Routledge. https://doi.org/10.4324/9780203069769

Wolff, J., Angyal, B., Ameen, E., & Kay, T. S. (2020). *The impacts of COVID-19 on psychology education and training: Concerns, disparities & recommendations.* https://www.apadivisions.org/division-44/news-events/psychology-education-report/covid-19-psychology-report.pdf

Wong, D., Pike, K., Stolwyk, R., Allot, K., Ponsford, J., McKay, A., Longley, W., Bosboom, P., Hodge, A., Kinsella, G., & Mowszowski, L. (2024). Delivery of neuropsychological interventions for adult and older adult clinical populations: An Australian expert working group clinical guidance paper. *Neuropsychology Review, 34*(4), 985–1047. https://doi.org/10.1007/s11065-023-09624-0

York, M. K., Farace, E., Pollak, L., Floden, D., Lin, G., Wyman-Chick, K., Bobholz, J., Palmese, C. A., Racine, C., Tran, B., Turner, T. H., & Jimenez-Shahed, J., of the Parkinson Study Group Functional Neurosurgical Working Group. *Parkinsonism and Related Disorders, 86*(1), 135–138. https://doi.org/10.1016/j.parkreldis.2021.04.029

Zakzanis, K. K., Mascarenhas, M., Brown, T., Christidis, D., & Matic, O. (2025). Examining the impact of in-person and remote administration modality on free-standing and embedded performance validity test scores in neuropsychological assessment.

Psychological Injury and Law, 18(2), 165–172. https://doi.org/10.1007/s12207-025-09532-z

Zillien, N., & Marr, M. (2013). The digital divide in Europe. In M. Ragnedda & G. W. Muschert (Eds.), *The digital divide: The internet and social inequality in international perspective* (pp. 55–66). Routledge. https://doi.org/10.4324/9780203069769

Zoom. (2025). *Zoom system requirements: Windows, macOS, Linux.* https://support.zoom.com/hc/en/article?id=zm_kb&sysparm_article=KB0060748#h_d278c327-e03d-4896-b19a-96a8f3c0c69c

8

Technology to Facilitate Test Score Interpretation and Neuropsychological Report Writing

Andrew M. Bryant, Bryan M. Freilich, and Chris Gaskell

Introduction

Current Landscape

Neuropsychological assessment has historically centered on face-to-face administration of standardized test materials and subsequent multistep scoring (i.e., converting raw data into standardized scores). Advancements in technology have had an increasing influence on assessment over the late 20th and early 21st century. Beyond early computerized assessments first utilized in the military in the 1970s (Kane & Kay, 1992), major test publishers (e.g., Pearson and PAR Inc.) have developed more sophisticated platforms that offer digital assessment with automated scoring. Some clinicians supplement commercial offerings with homegrown scoring systems (e.g., Excel spreadsheets), especially for measures not offered by major publishers. The information-gathering phases of an assessment have similarly evolved through the widespread adoption of electronic medical record (EMR) systems. Such systems have dramatically improved access to patient's medical history while providing useful tools for documentation. All data are interpreted in the context of information gathered from a comprehensive biopsychosocial clinical interview with the patient and collateral. The primary output for a practicing neuropsychologist is the written report with summary of findings and clinical recommendations tailored to each patient. This traditional workflow, while effective, faces growing challenges in today's health care environment and does not fully leverage current technologies to enhance the process. As a result, it may not adequately position the field of neuropsychology to take advantage of rapidly advancing innovations.

Andrew M. Bryant, Bryan M. Freilich, and Chris Gaskell, *Technology to Facilitate Test Score Interpretation and Neuropsychological Report Writing*. In: *Technology and Neuropsychology*. Edited by: Jared F. Benge et al., Oxford University Press. © Oxford University Press (2026). DOI: 10.1093/9780197814116.003.0008

Technology in Test Scoring, Interpretation, and Report Writing

Technology has transformed nearly every sector from agriculture to manufacturing, academia to medicine, and the field of neuropsychology is no exception. Across disciplines, technological advancements have driven innovation, improved efficiency, and created unprecedented opportunities for growth and development. While the last several decades have brought about improvements across the study of brain–behavior relationships, integration of technology into the clinical practice of neuropsychology has lagged other medical disciplines. Given the rapid expansion of telemedicine and improved health care access for remote and underserved populations, the field of neuropsychology must continue to adapt and innovate its practices.

A comprehensive neuropsychological evaluation typically requires anywhere from several hours to multiple days of testing, depending on the complexity of the referral question and the extent of the assessment battery. As the length of the test battery increases, so does the amount of time and effort required to score the results and the likelihood of introducing human error in the process. Fortunately, digital scoring systems can significantly reduce calculation errors and streamline the conversion of raw scores to standardized scores. Automated scoring also opens the opportunity for more advanced analyses of test data.

Beyond scoring and analysis, technology significantly streamlines documentation and report writing, critical components of neuropsychological practice. Automated systems facilitate the rapid integration of information from diverse sources, such as clinical interviews, test results, and medical records, into comprehensive reports. This not only accelerates the documentation process but also enhances consistency and accuracy. Furthermore, digital platforms enable seamless sharing of these reports among health care providers, fostering collaborative patient care.

As outlined in this chapter, there are multiple opportunities for technology to be integrated at different stages of score interpretation and report writing (Figure 8.1).

Goals of the Chapter

The integration of technology in test score interpretation and report generation has the potential to significantly shift routine practice in clinical neuropsychology. The current chapter provides a brief overview of available technologies for these tasks, including consideration of the associated benefits of usage (e.g., improving efficiency, accuracy, quality) and barriers to implementation. In doing so, it is hoped that the current chapter builds upon the *role of technology for assessment and test administration*. The current chapter will also review integration of technology with clinical judgment of a well-trained clinician and provide practical frameworks for evaluating and implementing new technologies while adhering to ethical guidelines and professional standards. The chapter is divided into two main sections: test scoring

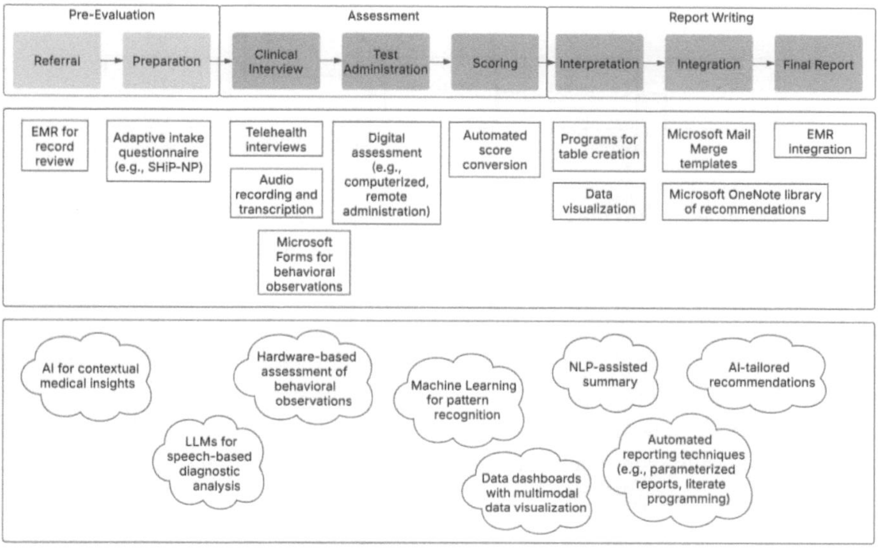

Figure 8.1 Neuropsychological evaluation workflow

and report writing with a case study at the end outlining how technology may be used in patient care. Throughout the chapter we seek to provide a practical guide for neuropsychologists seeking to optimize their assessment through technological integration and review of future directions. Where appropriate, technical details are included; however, the emphasis remains on clinical application and implementation.

Technology for Test Score Interpretation

Across the history of applied neuropsychology, cognitive test scores have consistently held a central place in the neuropsychologist's toolkit. As Crosson (2011) aptly stated, "The ultimate reason for conducting a neuropsychological assessment is that test results provide useful information to a consumer." These test scores serve as the backbone for neuropsychological assessments in which a qualified clinician gathers dependable and relevant information about an individual in order to answer a specific question (APA, 2000). Despite the significant emphasis and time dedicated to the scoring and interpretation of test scores in routine practice, little attention is paid to technologies or workflows that may aid (or hinder) neuropsychological assessment.

In essence, technologies used for test score interpretation, although varied, perform a unitary operation, as illustrated in Figure 8.2. They process numerical inputs through a set of functions to generate outputs. This principle can be applied to an endless number of use cases. For example, raw scores can be converted, coded, tabulated,

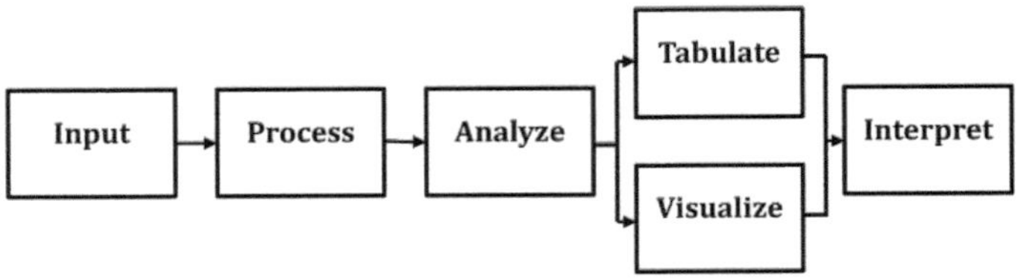

Figure 8.2 Flow diagram illustrating the general workflow of quantitative data in neuropsychology for the single case

predicted, and visualized using automated technologies. This opens many possibilities for neuropsychologists, as it allows for the delegation of tasks that, frankly, humans don't perform as well. Automated technologies can handle these highly sophisticated tasks efficiently and effectively. Although these ideas and applications are not new, it is our experience that they are yet to be fully embraced or implemented across neuropsychology.

Processing Test Scores

Converting neuropsychological test scores is a fundamental process in clinical neuropsychology as raw scores alone provide limited insight into cognitive performance. To allow for meaningful comparisons between scores, raw scores are typically converted into standard scores (e.g., z scores, t scores, etc.).[1] This allows for important contextual factors like age and education to be considered in performance. Moreover, manually converting scores can be time-consuming and prone to error, especially when dealing with large test batteries or intricate score systems.

When converting between standardized scores (e.g., z score to a t score), look-up tables are traditionally used to facilitate conversions, providing precomputed values for a range of scores. Although useful, these tables have limitations in precision and flexibility. Essentially, look-up tables are fundamentally constrained in that they are only as granular as the number of rows in the table. Alternatively, calculating a precise score is achievable using a straightforward formula for converting to or between standard scores. In practice, this is rarely performed as the increased time, complexity, and risk of error naturally deter clinicians, subsequently reverting to conventional look-up tables. For regression-based norms, which can be more sophisticated yet also error-prone when performed manually (multiple variables, sophisticated formula, polynomial and nonlinear terms), automated tools are essential for computation.

Fortunately, automated tools have become increasingly available to simplify the conversion process. These tools vary in terms of functionality and integration with

[1] For more information on the purpose of standardised scores, and an appraisal of the forms available, see Crawford (2012).

test administration. At one end, production-grade software packages and websites offer products that handle both the administration of tests and the immediate conversion of raw scores into standardized scores. These tools streamline the process and reduce the potential for errors. Alternatively, simpler solutions such as spreadsheets (e.g., Excel) and free web-based calculators provide a middle ground. These tools are typically less integrated with test administration but offer flexible and cost-effective options for conversion. They can either be test-specific (e.g., converting raw scores for a particular test to standard scores) or test-agnostic (e.g., tools that convert between different types of standard scores, such as z scores and t scores). These options are favorable when more integrated products are not available or when clinicians prefer greater control over data processing while still benefiting from automation.

Analyzing Scores

As discussed earlier, numerical output is an essential part of neuropsychological assessment, and that starts with the fundamentals (standardizing normally distributed test scores). However, there is a labyrinth of further analytical methods that can be applied to neuropsychological test data. For example, regression-based normative data (as outlined earlier), assessment of temporal stability (reliable change), profile analysis, diagnostic statistics, multivariate base rates, and dissociation analyses are among some of the more familiar statistical concepts that have high relevance for neuropsychological test data.

The statistical requirements for these methods surpass that of linear conversions, making computation impractical for calculating by hand—or at least with precision and efficiency. Automated tools are highly suited to this task; however, there are several considerations that users should be aware of before integrating statistical tools into routine practice. This includes suitability of the statistical method, the specific statistical approach, credibility, and reporting detail.

Considerations for Statistical Tools in Neuropsychological Test Score Interpretation

Suitability of Method

The availability of analytical tools can encourage their use; however, it is vital for users to have a sound understanding of the chosen approach and its suitability for the given situation. Many tools will make complex analyses more accessible, yet their outputs are only as valid as the clinician's knowledge of the underlying method and its application.

To support informed usage, software developers often provide resources such as manuals, peer-reviewed journal articles, and online walkthroughs/vignettes. These materials help users understand the tool's capabilities and limitations, allowing clinicians to consider the appropriateness for specific situations. When these are not available (or otherwise intuitive), then this could be a red flag for an underdeveloped tool. Foundational texts on statistical methods for computation and interpretation of test scores in neuropsychology can also help, particularly for those less familiar with specific statistical techniques and applications.[2]

Consider a spreadsheet implementing regression-based normative data. While the output from the software may appear consistent and precise, it may not necessarily guide the user on when the method is appropriate to apply. For example, linear-based methods assuming a normal distribution may provide misleading results if applied to data from a non-normally distributed test. In such cases, the clinician must recognize the statistical assumptions and limitations inherent in the method.

Best practice when using a software tool—or a new test—is to review the manual thoroughly. This not only helps in understanding the features but also ensures that the tool is correctly applied.

Specific Statistical Approach

When applying a statistical tool, it is important not only to understand why that approach is being used (e.g., regression) but also to understand the specific parameters being employed, to ensure their selection is justified and transparent. These parameters often have significant implications for interpretation of findings and future replication.

- Approach: Which regression-based method is being employed (e.g., linear, logistic, nonparametric, Bayesian). This should be supplemented by a reference to the methodological approach being used (see Table 8.1 for examples).
- Form of Standard Error: Understanding which type of standard error the tool uses (e.g., error of measurement, difference, estimate, or prediction) is necessary, as this can have an influence on the precision of the change estimate (Hinton-Bayre et al., 2010).
- Alpha Level: The choice of alpha level (e.g., 0.05 or 0.01) sets the threshold for statistical significance, directly impacting the interpretation of results.
- Threshold for Abnormality: The criterion used to define an abnormal change (e.g., a 1.65 SD cutoff) will influence whether the change is considered clinically meaningful.

These parameters should be chosen based on the context and the specific research or clinical question. Moreover, they must be documented clearly to ensure the procedure is replicable and that the findings can be interpreted accurately by others.

[2] We particularly recommend Crawford (2012) and Kiselica et al. (2024).

Table 8.1 Nonexhaustive List of Approaches for Converting and Analyzing Cognitive Test Data

Converting Scores	Reference	Tool Availability
Standardization		
Raw to Z	Ley, 1972	I
Raw to percentile (non-normal)	Crawford et al., 2009	I & II
Z to alternative standard score	Crawford, 2012	I
Z to percentile	Ley, 1972	I
Standard score to alternative standard score	Crawford, 2012	II
Regression		
Traditional regression-based techniques based on raw data	Cohen et al., 2003	I
Simple regression (single predictor) based on normative summary statistics (Mean and SD) of independent and dependent variables	Crawford & Garthwaite, 2007b	II
Multiple regression (several predictors) based on normative summary statistics (Mean and SD) of independent and dependent variables	Crawford et al., 2012a	II
Alternative regression-Based approaches, e.g., assuming distributions that are not normal	Lenhard et al., 2020	II & III
Analyzing Scores	**Reference**	**Tool**
Reliable Change		
Simple (single predictor) standardized regression-based estimation	Crawford & Garthwaite, 2006	II
Complex (multiple predictors) standardized regression-based estimation	Crawford & Garthwaite, 2006	II
Standard error of estimate	Cohen et al., 2003	I
Using standard error of prediction	Crawford & Garthwaite, 2006	II
Logistic regression	De Andrade Moral et al., 2022	III
Dissociation Analysis		
Analysis of deficit		
Classical approach	Ley, 1972	I
Modified *t*-test	Crawford & Howell, 1998	II
Bayesian	Crawford & Garthwaite, 2007a	II

continued

Table 8.1 *continued*

Analyzing Scores	Reference	Tool
Analysis of discrepancy		
Classical approach	Payne & Jones, 1957	I
Modified paired samples *t*-test	Crawford et al., 1998	II
Revised Standardized Difference Test (RSDT)	Crawford & Garthwaite, 2005	II
Analysis of dissociation	Crawford & Garthwaite, 2005	II
Profile Analysis		
Comparison of scores to the mean intercept	Crawford et al., 2012b	IV
Abnormality of *j* scores in a series of scores	Crawford et al., 2012b	IV
Abnormality of profile of scores using the Mahalanobis Distance Index	Crawford et al., 2012b	IV
Generate new composite score	Crawford et al., 2008	IV

Notes: I = Many test agnostic web-based calculators are available online; II = The author has provided a test agnostic stand-alone web/software application that is accessible to use; III = The author has provided code or syntax for test agnostic analyses to be applied or reproduced in existing software of programming environments; IV = No known test agnostic applications; however, statistical formulas are provided for users to apply.

Credibility

The reliability of automated tools largely depends on the source and transparency. Tools endorsed by professional organizations or subjected to peer review are generally considered more trustworthy; however, this trust should not necessarily be assumed without further scrutiny. In addition, tools developed by individuals (including clinicians) may lack the resources of production-grade products, but this does not necessarily make them less reliable. In many cases, individual developers are highly knowledgeable and transparent about their methods. A common practice among many developers is to store code in online repositories, such as *GitHub*, where the underlying code and methods can be reviewed and verified by others.

Reporting Detail

Clear and detailed reporting is essential for transparency and accurate interpretation. Automated tools should provide comprehensive outputs, including statistical parameters, assumptions, and limitations, with a time stamp of when the output was produced. Such detail enables clinicians to confidently interpret results and record the details required for replication within the patient's EMR. Clinicians and researchers should also provide full references to software used, including which version, within academic bibliographies.

Software Tools

As with tools for score conversion, analytical tools vary in their level of integration with test administration. Manual methods for performing some common analytical tasks are often provided within test manuals. For example, profiling strengths and weaknesses through pairwise comparisons between composite scores can be done manually using lookup tables from the *Wechsler Adult Intelligence Scale*®–fourth edition (WAIS®–IV; Wechsler, 2008) user manual or produced automatically when administering the test in digital form (e.g., via the *Q-interactive*® platform). It is often convenient when test developers include these solutions; however, such features are not available for all commonly used cognitive tests and, for those that are available, are often limited in the range of analytical approaches supported. For instance (continuing with the *WAIS*®*–IV* example), clinicians might wish to profile strengths and weaknesses against a mean intercept (Crawford et al., 2012b) or use an alternative statistical approach for detecting a dissociation. Unfortunately, these functions are not available in the current version of the *Q-interactive*® platform (Pearson, 2024). To conduct these analyses, users must seek alternative tools to perform the analysis (e.g., Crawford et al., 2012a), which is problematic for several reasons. It places additional reliance on clinician knowledge and expertise, requires access to other scoring programs, and increases the time needed to navigate multiple systems and tools. These additional barriers can discourage clinicians from applying more advanced techniques. To assist users, we have compiled a nonexhaustive list of statistical references (Table 8.1), of which many have available software applications to guide interested clinicians. Looking ahead, we hope to see more integrated solutions that remove the disjointed process of needing to navigate many test score interpretation applications.

Tabulating Scores

In neuropsychological assessments, the array of test scores collected for a patient are traditionally pooled into a table of results (patient summary table). Centralizing these scores offers several advantages, including ease of access, organization, aids comparisons, and supports communication of findings. Once finalized, the patient summary tables can be appended to the neuropsychological assessment report and included in the patient's EMR. This can be particularly useful when a patient requires serial assessment, as it provides a comprehensive and clear listing of their historic test results and procedures.

While the creation of patient summary tables is a routine part of neuropsychological practice, there is a notable lack of discussion surrounding the various approaches, tools, and best practices for tabulating scores. For example, several texts devoted to neuropsychological reports do not consider test score summary tables (e.g., Donders, 2001; King et al., 2022).

Clinicians typically use electronic word processors (e.g., Microsoft Word, Google Docs) to produce these tables, likely for their familiarity with these programs. While word processors can indeed create tables, they often fall short compared to spreadsheet-based software (e.g., Microsoft Excel, Google Sheets). Word processor tables can become cumbersome, are difficult to apply appropriate formatting, lack the capacity for complex data entry, and are static (i.e., no option for interactivity). Tables produced by word processors may also incur problems, such as inconsistent column usage (e.g., z scores and t scores in the same column), omission of key information, and a generally cluttered appearance.

We feel that the content of a neuropsychology table is of understated importance. Neuropsychologists must remain mindful of the possibility that a patient may require reassessment; therefore, sufficient detail should be provided to ensure that a close replication of the original assessment is possible. Important information often omitted from tables includes the normative data used (e.g., standardization vs. clinical sample), the statistical methods applied (e.g., when assessing temporal stability), the test form or edition employed, and frequently undefined acronyms. Omitting these details may threaten reproducibility and or potentially lead to inaccurate conclusions.

Equally important is the presentation of this content. Effective table organization should adhere to the principle of *tidy* data, ensuring that each subtest has its own row, and each variable (e.g., raw score, z score, percentile) is assigned a separate column. Combining multiple metrics in a single column may free up space; however, it can also significantly reduce clarity. Readability can be enhanced by reducing visual clutter, using consistent typesetting, and employing visual cues like zebra striping to help delineate between rows and columns.

Visualizing Scores

Although tabulation of test scores has much to offer, neuropsychologists commonly over-rely on tabulated test scores alone for interpretation. A problem with table reliance is that the process can be cognitively overloading (especially with large sets of scores and confidence intervals) and may fail to provide a clear, big-picture view. Visualization offers an alternative perspective, by illustrating test scores, providing a format that may be more intuitive and accessible for both clinicians, patients, and referrers. Neuropsychological test data for the individual patient can be shown in various types of plots, depending upon the use case (Figure 8.3). When single scores are to be shown, then bell curve plots are useful, whereas bar plots can be more suitable for larger batteries of scores. Radar plots can similarly show an array of scores, and they can be engaging for users, although they do not fare well for discriminating

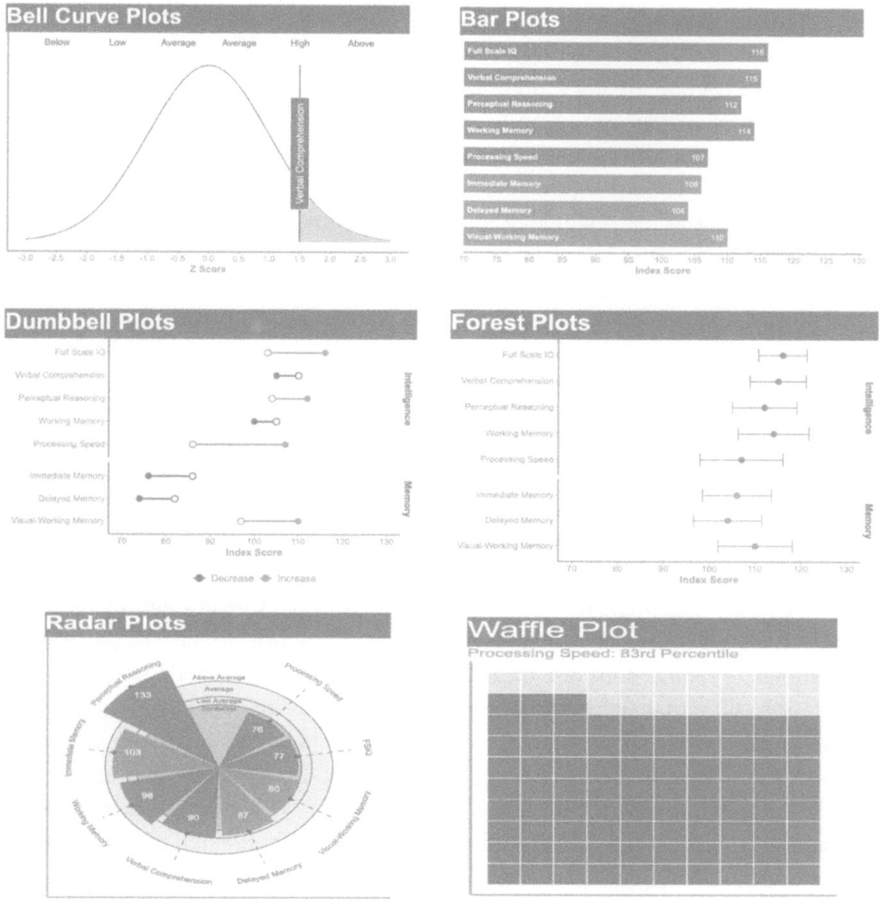

Figure 8.3 Examples of data visualizations as applied to neuropsychological test data for the single patient, including bell curve plots (top left), bar plots (top right), dumbbell plots (middle left), forest plots (middle right), radar plots (bottom left), and waffle plots (bottom right)

between scores. When uncertainty (e.g., confidence intervals) needs to be illustrated, forest plots are a strong choice, whereas dumbbell plots are more suited for showing change over time.

Software Platforms

Integrated Products

Generally speaking, products which integrate electronic administration and scoring have the highest potential benefits of automation. An ideal product would be a software platform that facilitates administration of all common neuropsychological tests, with processed scores (i.e., standard scores) made available immediately after administration, and providing the array of supplementary functions (visualization, tabulation, and supplementary analysis), to a high standard. Unfortunately, such a product is not available, and given the financial interests of competing proprietary test publishers, it is unlikely that such a product will become available anytime soon (we sincerely hope to be proven wrong about this). Some test publishers have developed integrated products that offer a range of functionalities; however, the quality of these products can be lacking, the features provided are overly general and inflexible, and each product will typically require a separate license fee.

Spreadsheets

Spreadsheet software (e.g., Microsoft Excel) has become a highly popular tool for developing simple data processors, largely due to its simplicity, availability, and familiarity among clinicians. Encryption can be embedded to secure normative data, while validation techniques can guide users on what type of data to input. Excel tools have been developed to facilitate a range of neuropsychological functions, including scoring, tabulating, and basic visualization.

Despite their widespread use, the primary drawbacks of spreadsheets include limitations on the types of tests that can be included (i.e., nonproprietary tests), the time and complexity required for design, and the lack of advanced functionality. It is also important to note that scoring systems developed by individuals may not undergo the same rigorous testing as production-grade products, increasing the risk of errors if the tool has not been sufficiently tested. Further limitations include the output being spreadsheet-based (unless integrated with a word processor), constraints imposed by the graphical user interface (GUI), and reduced flexibility compared to purpose-built tools or programming environments. Finally, scalability can be problematic, as users with local copies may not receive updates to newer versions.

Modular Calculators

Another approach involves purpose-built calculators designed to perform a unitary set of functions. These tools can serve specific purposes and may either be test-agnostic (i.e., without normative data) or come prepopulated with normative values for selected cognitive tests. They may be highly modular or consolidate a range of similar functions in one platform.

In terms of implementation, these calculators may take the form of downloadable software programs or online tools running through HTML. Web-based calculators have gained popularity with the rise of statistical programming environments (e.g., R, Python) that enable the development of scalable web applications. Alternatively, downloadable software remains an option, catering to users who prefer offline functionality and local computation over reliance on an Internet connection.

Despite their advantages, web calculators also have their limitations. They may lack flexibility, handling only a narrow set of functions, and can easily become outdated if not maintained. Downloadable versions, although without connectivity problems, may require ongoing updates, present compatibility issues, and may require additional layers of local governance.

Technology for Report Writing

Introduction

The neuropsychological report represents the culmination of the neuropsychologist's work and serves as the primary medium of communicating assessment findings to patients, families, and referring providers. Reports can vary in length, format, and content based on the clinical context and clinician preferences. However, they usually integrate information from multiple disciplines and are organized into key, structured sections. These sections typically include history and background, behavioral observations, test results, summary and impressions, and recommendations (Donders, 2016). Each section is crucial for interpreting assessment data and informing clinical decisions, contributing to a comprehensive understanding of the patient.

However, automated report writing systems come with important caveats. One major concern is the potential loss of clinical nuance. Neuropsychological assessments often involve complex cases where subtle differences in a patient's behavior, history, and symptom presentation require careful observation and interpretation. Automated systems may struggle to capture these crucial details, which could lead to less accurate conclusions and diagnoses. Another concern is the risk of overreliance on these technologies, which could reduce the critical thinking necessary for interpreting ambiguous or intricate findings. This reliance might inadvertently weaken a clinician's ability to adapt to unique cases that fall outside standardized patterns.

These challenges highlight the need to carefully balance the use of automation with the expertise of experienced neuropsychologists. Automated tools should be seen as supportive resources that enhance efficiency and consistency, not as replacements for clinical expertise. By using automation thoughtfully, clinicians can leverage its strengths while maintaining the crucial human element necessary for providing high-quality patient care.

The subsequent sections will explore how neuropsychologists can integrate automated tools into their clinical practice to streamline the report-writing process. The discussion is organized around the key sections of a neuropsychological report. For each section, existing tools will be reviewed, highlighting their potential to enhance efficiency, consistency, and accuracy, while also addressing their limitations and underscoring the indispensable role of the neuropsychologist in the evaluation process. Looking ahead, this section will explore how future technological developments can make it easier to integrate different data sources, create more individualized narratives, and further streamline report writing to meet the changing needs of clinical practice. The section will conclude with a practical example demonstrating how clinicians can create their own customizable report-writing systems using tools within commonly used productivity suites like Microsoft 365.

The following sections are organized according to the structure of the neuropsychological report.

History and Background

The history and background section is foundational to neuropsychological reports. It provides context for the evaluation by describing the reason for the referral, summarizing the patient's presenting problems and complaints, and detailing relevant background information. Such background information typically includes educational, occupational, medical, mental health, family, and pertinent personal history, all of which offer valuable insights for differential diagnosis and treatment planning. Accurate and thorough documentation in this section ensures the report serves as a meaningful tool for understanding the patient's unique circumstances and informing clinical decision-making.

Automated tools like the Structured History Protocol for Neuropsychology (SHiP-NP) can assist clinicians in systematically gathering and organizing this information. Developed as part of the National Neuropsychology Network (NNN), SHiP-NP is a structured, standardized tool designed to streamline the collection of comprehensive and relevant patient history across multiple domains, including medical, psychological, educational, and familial factors (Loring et al., 2022). A key feature of SHiP-NP is its use of common data elements (CDEs), which are standardized variables that ensure consistency and comparability across neuropsychological evaluations. These CDEs capture essential information about the patient's health history, cognitive function, and psychosocial context, and this helps improve the reliability and reproducibility of findings across different settings and clinicians. SHiP-NP also integrates cross-cutting questionnaires that screen for conditions such as mood disorders, neurological conditions, and substance use, guiding the diagnostic process. This cross-cutting approach increases efficiency by reducing the need for clinicians to create new forms for each patient. However, SHiP-NP has notable limitations. Currently, it is tailored exclusively for adult patients and offers limited options for customization, which may restrict its applicability in certain clinical settings.

To address these limitations and be efficient in gathering patient history, clinicians can develop their own customized intake forms using readily available digital tools. They can develop fillable PDFs (e.g., created with Adobe Acrobat) for convenient and secure electronic completion by patients. They can also use online tools like Google Forms or Microsoft Forms, which facilitate real-time data entry and integration with spreadsheets and word processing documents and can include branching logic to tailor the information gathered. For example, an intake form might ask a simple "yes/no" question about whether the patient has a history of mental health treatment (Figure 8.4). If the patient answers "no," the form could automatically

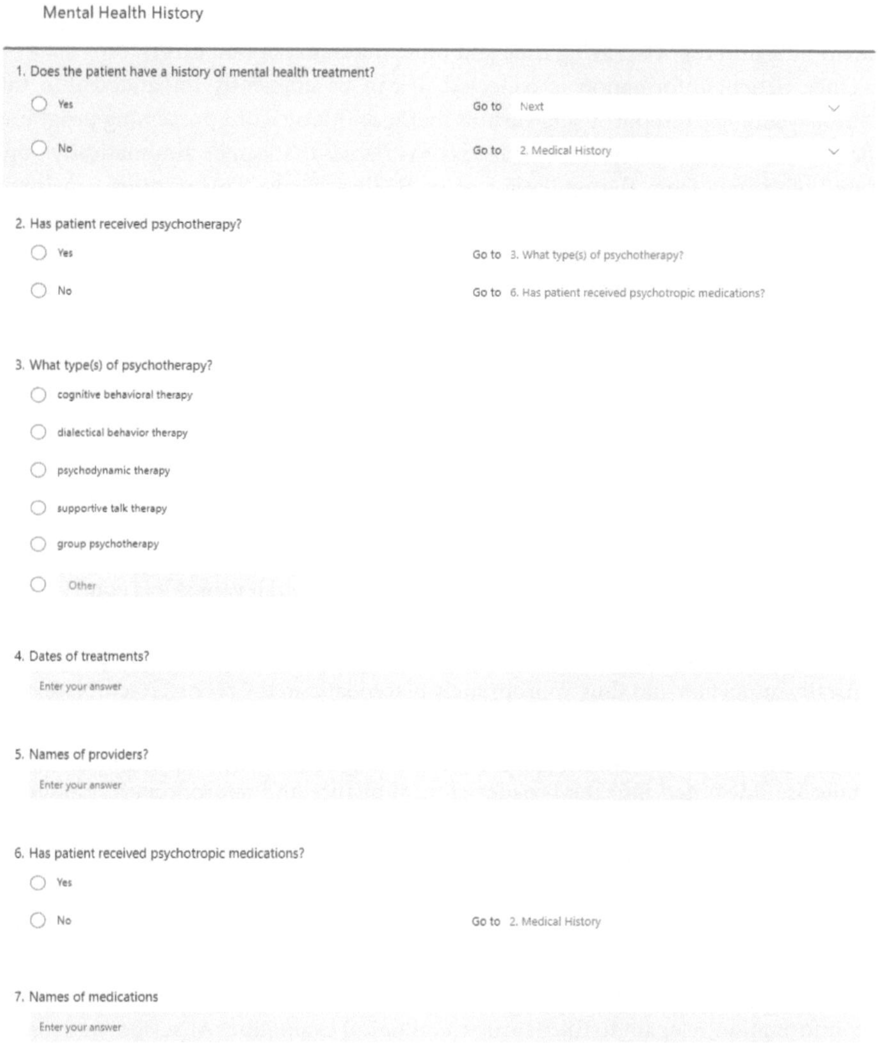

Mental Health History

1. Does the patient have a history of mental health treatment?
   - Yes — Go to Next
   - No — Go to 2. Medical History

2. Has patient received psychotherapy?
   - Yes — Go to 3. What type(s) of psychotherapy?
   - No — Go to 6. Has patient received psychotropic medications?

3. What type(s) of psychotherapy?
   - cognitive behavioral therapy
   - dialectical behavior therapy
   - psychodynamic therapy
   - supportive talk therapy
   - group psychotherapy
   - Other

4. Dates of treatments?
   Enter your answer

5. Names of providers?
   Enter your answer

6. Has patient received psychotropic medications?
   - Yes
   - No — Go to 2. Medical History

7. Names of medications
   Enter your answer

Figure 8.4 Example of Microsoft Forms with built in skip-logic to collect patient background information

skip ahead to the next section. If the patient answers "yes," a series of follow-up questions could appear, such as the type of treatment received (e.g., therapy, medication), the dates of treatment, and the names of treating providers. These customized options allow clinicians to tailor the intake process to specific referral questions and patient characteristics, ensuring efficient capture of relevant details. For clinicians using EMR systems like EPIC, further automation is possible. EPIC allows users to create customized templates that auto-populate relevant fields from patient records (e.g., demographic information, medical history, medications) and utilize features like SmartPhrases and SmartLinks to quickly insert standardized text or pull specific data points into reports, saving time and reducing transcription errors.

Once patient information is collected, it can be efficiently integrated into the neuropsychological report using various methods. Many word processing programs allow for the creation of predefined fields or variables that can be automatically populated with data from the intake forms or EMR systems. This ensures consistent and accurate transfer of information, minimizing the risk of transcription errors and streamlining the report-writing process. For example, a field for "Date of Birth" in the report template can be linked to the corresponding field in the intake form, automatically inserting the correct date into each report. Furthermore, tools like mail merge, which will be described in more detail later in this chapter in relation to building all-in-one report-writing systems, can be used to transfer captured information from spreadsheets into the neuropsychological report document.

While these automated and customizable tools offer clear benefits, they also have limitations. A key limitation is that predefined templates cannot fully capture the nuances of individual cases. The relative importance of historical details varies from patient to patient, making it impossible for a template to perfectly prioritize information. For example, a history of stroke could be highly relevant if it is contributing to the patient's current cognitive difficulties, warranting prominent discussion early in the report. However, a remote stroke with no residual symptoms might be less clinically important and thus appropriately placed later in the report. A template cannot make these clinical judgments. Therefore, neuropsychologists remain essential in reviewing the collected data and interpreting its significance, ensuring that historical details are integrated into the broader clinical picture and appropriately applied in the diagnostic process.

Recognizing these limitations of current automation, advancements in artificial intelligence (AI) offer the potential for significant improvement in history gathering. Natural language processing (NLP), which enables computers to understand and extract meaning from human language, could allow AI systems to analyze unstructured text from various sources (e.g., medical records, referral letters) and extract key information relevant to the neuropsychological evaluation. AI scribes and ambient listening technologies, designed to passively record and transcribe conversations, further enhance this process by organizing data from intake sessions in real time. These tools can passively capture clinician–patient interactions, extracting relevant historical details and categorizing them into structured report sections, thus reducing documentation burden. Moreover, machine-learning algorithms could be trained on large datasets of clinical data to identify patterns and correlations between historical factors and neuropsychological outcomes, enabling the system to prioritize information based on its predictive value. For instance, an AI system could learn that multiple concussions are a stronger predictor of cognitive difficulties than a single childhood head injury, thus prioritizing the former in a generated report. These advancements have the potential to transform automated history gathering from a simple data collection tool into a sophisticated clinical instrument.

However, the use of AI in handling sensitive patient data raises significant ethical and practical concerns. Many commercially available AI platforms designed for NLP or other purposes do not meet the stringent requirements of the Health Insurance Portability and Accountability Act (HIPAA). Therefore, clinicians should thoroughly vet any AI system to ensure it is HIPAA compliant and avoid inputting any personally identifiable information (PII), such as a patient's name, date of birth, or specific appointment details, into generative AI platforms that are not HIPAA compliant. It is also crucial for clinicians to understand how the AI systems they use handle the data they provide, specifically whether the data remain within the platform or are used for system development. Even if all identifiers and protected health information (PHI) are removed, using patient data with AI tools raises ethical concerns due to the lack of transparency regarding data utilization. It may be advisable for neuropsychologists to obtain informed consent from patients if they plan to provide their information to AI platforms, even in de-identified form. While it is less clear whether consent is strictly required if the data are only used within the system and not for further development, being open and transparent with patients about how their data are used is always a good ethical practice.

Behavioral Observations

The behavioral observations section of a neuropsychological report provides detailed insights into a patient's behavior during the assessment, offering a deeper understanding of their emotional and cognitive functioning that go beyond test scores. This section describes how the patient manages emotions, follows instructions, and engages with the evaluation. Observations may include aspects such as appearance, speech and language patterns, mood and affect, levels of engagement and cooperation, responsiveness, and how the patient handles frustration. These observations are crucial for interpreting test results, assessing the validity of test performance, and identifying emotional or psychological concerns. Additionally, they inform treatment planning by highlighting specific behavioral patterns that may guide interventions.

Automation can help streamline the documentation of behavioral observations. Tools like Microsoft Forms or Google Forms can provide standardized templates with dropdowns, checkboxes, and free-text fields, making it easier to capture data for integration into automated reporting systems. For example, when documenting a patient's mood and affect, clinicians can use a free-text field to describe the patient's mood and select from multiple-choice options to identify their affect (e.g., constricted, labile, or consistent with stated mood). The NNN also has a corollary to the SHiP-NP for behavioral observations: Behavioral Observations Assessment Tool (BOAT-NP) for standardized recording of behavioral observations. Although automation helps with consistency and streamlines data capture, it is still crucial for clinicians to use their expertise to interpret subtle nuances. For example, cultural influences, unusual problem-solving approaches, and complex emotions may not be fully captured by standard checklists but are essential for sound clinical judgments.

Looking ahead, advancements in technology could further enhance the documentation of behavioral observations. For instance, audio and video recordings of assessment sessions could be used to flag and capture key observations. These recordings could be analyzed by AI systems to identify patterns in speech, facial expressions, and body language that might indicate specific emotional or cognitive states. This could provide a more comprehensive and objective view of the patient's behavior during the assessment.

Additionally, smart pens and other digital writing tools could be used to capture fine motor skills and detect issues like tremors. These devices can record the pressure, speed, and rhythm of writing, providing detailed data that can be analyzed to identify motor difficulties. This information can be integrated into the behavioral observations section to offer a more complete picture of the patient's motor functioning.

While these technologies offer exciting possibilities, it is important to remember that they should complement, not replace, the clinician's expertise. The nuanced interpretation of behavioral observations requires a human touch to ensure that all relevant factors are considered and accurately reflected in the report.

Test Results

The test results section of a neuropsychological report presents the findings of the assessment. The format of this section can vary depending on the clinical context and preferences of the neuropsychologist. It may take the form of a narrative summary, describing the patient's performance across various domains, including cognitive, emotional, behavioral, and sometimes academic functioning. Alternatively, results might be displayed in a table, offering a concise overview of scores and other relevant metrics. Often, a combination of narrative and tabular presentation is used to provide both detailed descriptions and easily digestible summaries. Some neuropsychologists choose to include only interpretations of the test findings within the main body of the report, relegating the raw test data (e.g., scaled scores, standard scores, percentiles) to an appendix for reference.

Regardless of the chosen format, automation can significantly support clinicians in preparing the test results section. Technology for auto-generating narrative summaries of test performance has existed for several decades. Beginning in the late 1970s and early 1980s, computer report generators offering standardized narrative interpretations emerged, particularly for personality assessments like the Minnesota Multiphasic Personality Inventory (MMPI) and, later, the Personality Assessment Inventory (PAI). These programs used predetermined algorithms to generate text based on patterns in test responses. By the late 1990s and early 2000s, similar programs began appearing for cognitive tests, such as the WAIS-III–WMS-III–WIAT-II Writer and the CVLT-C Scoring Assistant with Report Writer. In general, these programs use templated fields, applying qualitative labels (e.g., average, below average, above average) to raw and normalized scores, and generating standardized text based on predetermined algorithms.

Neuropsychologists can also create their own systems to streamline the results section of their reports. They may opt to display data summary tables and visualizations, as described earlier in this chapter, or pair these with automated tools such as autofields and text templates within word processing or spreadsheet software. These tools allow clinicians to generate narrative descriptions relatively quickly while maintaining a desired level of customization and detail. For instance, they might incorporate templated descriptions of each test administered, along with the obtained scores, percentile ranks, and associated qualitative labels (e.g., average, below average, above average). This approach seeks to strike a balance between efficiency and personalization, enabling neuropsychologists to produce reports that are both clear and tailored to the specific needs and expectations of the referral source. It is important to note that, while rare, errors can occur in automated scoring and report generation, and clinicians should always review the output of these systems for accuracy. Furthermore, it is crucial for clinicians to adhere to copyright laws and licensing agreements with test publishers regarding the reproduction and use of proprietary test materials, including test items, scoring algorithms, and normative data. This is particularly relevant when developing or using automated reporting systems that incorporate such materials.

Summary and Impressions

The summary and impressions section of a neuropsychological report brings everything together, integrating all available data to provide a comprehensive understanding of the patient's cognitive and behavioral functioning. This section synthesizes test results, behavioral observations, patient history, and presenting concerns to highlight areas of strength and weakness, identify patterns of cognitive functioning, and determine the presence and nature of any impairment.

This section is typically the most complex and nuanced part of the report. It requires a deep understanding of the individual patient and an ability to interpret how various factors, from cognitive performance to medical history, fit together. Because of this, it is not easily automated. Even with available tools, the summary and impressions section remains an area where clinicians devote a significant amount of time, effort, and expertise, making judgments and crafting narratives that reflect the complexity of each case.

Nonetheless, advancements in AI and automation are beginning to provide more meaningful support for the summary and impressions section. For instance, automated tools can help by analyzing the variability in scores across the test battery and identify patterns or inconsistencies that might be clinically significant. These tools can quickly process large amounts of data, highlighting subtle trends that might be missed by human analysis alone. For example, AI algorithms can detect variations in performance across different cognitive domains, such as memory, attention, and executive function, and flag any discrepancies that warrant further investigation.

Looking ahead, AI holds considerable promise for enhancing the synthesis of clinical information in this section. AI algorithms, trained on large datasets of neuropsychological data, can be developed to recognize complex patterns of cognitive strengths and weaknesses associated with specific neurological conditions (e.g., Alzheimer's disease, traumatic brain injury, or attention-deficit/hyperactivity disorder [ADHD]), potentially offering valuable insights for differential diagnosis. These patterns could include specific profiles such as an amnestic profile, characterized by disproportionately poor encoding and retention of new information, or a frontal-subcortical profile, marked by deficits in attention, processing speed, and executive functioning coupled with difficulties in memory retrieval. AI systems can also synthesize background information, such as medical history and psychosocial factors, to help identify underlying causes of and contributors to cognitive performance. For example, AI might highlight factors such as sleep disturbances, chronic pain, or emotional symptoms that could be impacting test outcomes. Furthermore, AI tools can assess a patient's medication list, flagging potential side effects or harmful drug interactions, such as calculating the anticholinergic burden that can impact cognition, especially in older adults. However, it is important to acknowledge the current limitations of AI in this context. Rigorous validation of these technologies is essential to ensure their accuracy and reliability. Careful consideration must also be given to potential algorithmic biases and the ethical implications of using AI in clinical practice, including issues of data privacy and the essential role of clinician oversight. Critically, clinicians must use their professional judgment to determine which AI-generated information is relevant to the individual patient and how to interpret that information within the broader clinical context. Ultimately, the clinician's expertise, specifically their ability to integrate all available information, apply sound clinical judgment, and adhere to ethical practice, remains indispensable.

Recommendations

The recommendations section of a neuropsychological report translates the findings and conclusions into actionable steps for the patient, their family, and other professionals involved in their care. It typically includes guidance on managing identified issues, compensating for deficits, and leveraging strengths. Recommendations may address medical follow-up, rehabilitation strategies, educational interventions, work accommodations, or lifestyle adjustments, tailored to the individual's needs and circumstances. This section is critical for ensuring that the assessment leads to meaningful and practical outcomes.

It is already common practice for neuropsychologists to maintain a library of recommendations that they have collected over time and can deploy according to the unique factors of each case. These often include suggestions tailored to particular diagnoses, cognitive profiles, or identified challenges. This practice allows for greater consistency in recommendations, saves time in report writing, and provides a readily available starting point for developing individualized plans. Automated tools can streamline this process by auto-populating these prewritten recommendations into reports as they apply. For example, if a patient is found to have significant executive functioning deficits, the system might suggest strategies like using a planner, setting digital reminders, or seeking executive functioning coaching. Similarly, a diagnosis of ADHD might trigger recommendations for specific accommodations in educational or workplace settings. Clinicians can then review and edit these suggestions to ensure they are fully personalized for the individual patient.

Modern technology also allows neuropsychologists to include hyperlinks to valuable online resources directly within reports. These links can direct patients, families, and referring providers to patient-friendly websites, instructional videos, or mobile apps that support cognitive training or mental health. For instance, clinicians might include links to organizations such as the Alzheimer's Association, providing access to helpful information for caregivers and those affected by dementia. Similarly, hyperlinks to books or research articles can provide patients and families with more in-depth reading on relevant topics. For example, if the patient has a newly diagnosed learning disorder, the clinician might include a link to a book for parents about helping children with learning challenges or a reputable organization that offers tools for navigating educational systems.

In the future, AI could further enhance this process by suggesting recommendations based on patterns in the assessment data and synthesizing additional input, such as the patient's cultural background, personal goals, or available community resources. This could assist clinicians in generating recommendations that are not only evidence-based but also contextually sensitive and practical for the patient's unique situation. However, even with these advancements, the clinician's role remains paramount in ensuring that recommendations are appropriate, personalized, and effectively communicated to the patient and their family. This includes considering the patient's receptiveness to different types of interventions and their ability to access and implement recommended strategies. Ultimately, while technology offers significant support, the clinician's role in crafting recommendations that resonate with the patient and their family remains indispensable.

All-in-One Systems

Currently, a variety of commercially available all-in-one automated systems are available to assist clinicians with psychological and neuropsychological report writing. In general, these systems are designed to provide tables and/or a narrative of assessment results and, in some cases, offer interpretations based on test data, with certain platforms even incorporating aspects of AI. A few also leverage information from intake forms to help generate background history sections of reports. However, these systems come with notable limitations. While some offer a degree of customization, they rarely allow users to fully tailor the language, style, or overall format of the report. This often requires clinicians to accept phrasing or formats that may not align with their preferred style or the specific needs of the referral source. Furthermore, these systems often involve a financial investment, either through subscription fees or one-time purchases, which can be a consideration for some practices. Additionally, some platforms may present a significant learning curve, requiring clinicians to invest time and effort to become proficient in using the software and its various features.

Building Your Own Customizable System Using Productivity Suites

Fortunately, advancements in technology now enable neuropsychologists to create their own fully customizable report-writing systems with relative ease. Modern productivity suites like Microsoft 365 and Google Workspace offer a powerful collection of interconnected applications that can significantly enhance the efficiency and quality of neuropsychological report writing. These suites provide a versatile toolkit, including the following:

- Word Processing Programs (e.g., Microsoft Word, Google Docs): These applications facilitate the creation of the narrative sections of the report, allowing for rich text formatting, template creation, and the use of features like mail merge for automated data insertion.
- Spreadsheet Programs (e.g., Microsoft Excel, Google Sheets): These programs are invaluable for data management, calculations, and analysis. They can serve as a central repository for test scores, demographic information, and other relevant data, and they can be linked to report templates for automated data population.
- Form Creation Tools (e.g., Microsoft Forms, Google Forms): These tools allow for the creation of customized intake forms, questionnaires, and behavioral observation checklists. They can streamline data collection by allowing patients or clinicians to enter information directly into digital formats.
- Workflow Automation Services (e.g., Microsoft Power Automate, Google Apps Script): These services enable the automation of repetitive tasks, such as transferring data between applications, generating reports, and sending notifications. This automation can significantly reduce manual data entry and improve efficiency.

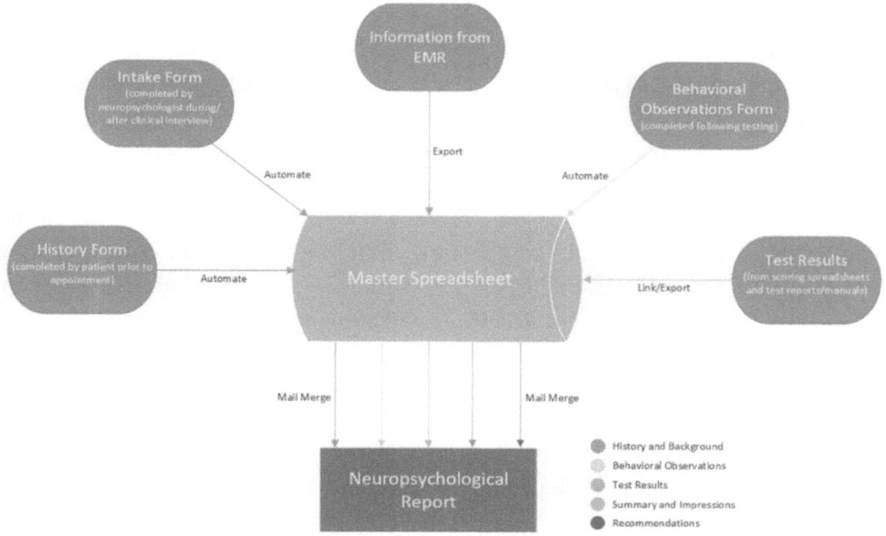

Figure 8.5 Diagram of a custom-built automated reporting system using Microsoft 365

- Cloud Storage and Collaboration Tools (e.g., OneDrive, Google Drive): Cloud-based storage allows for easy access to reports, templates, and data from any device, facilitating collaboration and sharing within a neuropsychological service or team.

Figure 8.5 illustrates how various data collection methods can be integrated into a custom-built automated reporting system using Microsoft 365. At the center of this system is a master spreadsheet (Microsoft Excel), which consolidates information from multiple sources.

History Form: Patients or caregivers complete this form (Microsoft Forms) before the appointment, providing essential details about medical, educational, and psychosocial histories, as well as presenting concerns. Upon submission, this information can be automatically populated into the master spreadsheet using Microsoft Power Automate. Specifically, a flow can be created in Power Automate that triggers when a new form is submitted and automatically adds a new row to the designated worksheet in the master spreadsheet, populating the corresponding cells with the submitted form data.

Intake Form: During or after the clinical interview, the neuropsychologist documents additional background details (Microsoft Forms). This information can also be automatically transferred to the master spreadsheet (via Power Automate).

EMRs: Relevant medical information, such as prior diagnoses, imaging findings, or lab results, can be exported directly into the master spreadsheet, ensuring that critical medical data are consolidated in one place.

Behavioral Observations Form: Following the evaluation, clinicians can record key qualitative observations of the patient's behavior during testing (Microsoft Forms). This information can be automatically transferred to the master spreadsheet (via Power Automate).

Test Results: Quantitative data, including raw scores and derived scores (e.g., standard scores, percentiles), from scoring spreadsheets or test administration software are linked or exported into the master spreadsheet. Many test reports are in Microsoft Word or rich text PDF formats, which allow clinicians to copy and paste data into Microsoft Excel. This data can then be linked to the master spreadsheet using lookup formulas (e.g., VLOOKUP, HLOOKUP). In cases where direct copy/paste is not feasible (e.g., image-based PDFs), clinicians can utilize the mobile version of Office 365 to extract data from tables in images directly into Excel, which can then be linked to the master spreadsheet.

Once all the necessary data have been consolidated in the master spreadsheet, mail merge, a feature originally developed for mass mailings (i.e., personalized letters), can be used to efficiently transfer this information into the neuropsychological report. Here's how:

1. Ensure your master spreadsheet has a dedicated worksheet with clear column headers (e.g., "PatientName," "Age," "FullScaleIQ") in the first row and individual patient data in subsequent rows. This worksheet will serve as the data source for your mail merge.
2. In Microsoft Word, create a template for your neuropsychological report. Insert merge fields (also sometimes called placeholders) where you want to insert data from the spreadsheet (e.g., ≪PatientName≫, ≪Age≫, ≪FullScaleIQ≫).
3. In Microsoft Word, start the mail merge process and connect your report template to the designated worksheet in your master spreadsheet. The data from each row will be inserted into the corresponding mail merge fields in the template.

This custom system balances efficiency and clinical nuance by putting clinicians in full control of report generation, seamlessly integrating data, and enhancing collaboration through platforms like Microsoft 365. This empowers clinicians to use technology effectively while maintaining the essential clinical judgment needed for comprehensive, individualized patient care. Importantly, a well-designed system must also prioritize data security and HIPAA compliance. This includes implementing strong security measures such as strong passwords, two-factor authentication, data encryption, access controls, and establishing Business Associate Agreements with third-party vendors as needed. However, it is important to acknowledge that this approach has limitations. These systems require ongoing maintenance, including updating templates and ensuring data integrity. Setting up these systems can also be complex initially and may require some technical proficiency.

Summary and Conclusions

This chapter has explored the multifaceted role of technology in enhancing neuropsychological assessment, from streamlining scoring and interpretation to revolutionizing report writing. We have demonstrated how automated tools can significantly improve efficiency and accuracy, allowing clinicians to focus on the nuanced aspects of patient care. By leveraging spreadsheets, databases, and AI-driven systems, neuropsychologists can transform raw data into meaningful clinical insights with greater speed and precision. Moreover, the ability to create custom, all-in-one systems using readily available productivity suites empowers clinicians to tailor their workflows to specific needs, ensuring both efficiency and adherence to ethical standards.

Looking forward, the integration of AI and machine learning holds immense promise for the field. These technologies have the potential to further refine diagnostic accuracy, personalize treatment recommendations, and even predict patient outcomes with greater precision. However, it is crucial to recognize that technology should augment, not replace, clinical expertise. The human element, including clinical judgment, empathy, and the ability to interpret subtle behavioral cues, remains indispensable in neuropsychological practice. As we continue to embrace technological advancements, we must remain vigilant in upholding ethical standards, ensuring data privacy, and prioritizing patient well-being. Future research should focus on validating AI-driven tools, exploring the impact of technology on patient outcomes, and developing best practices for integrating technology into clinical workflows. By doing so, we can harness the power of technology to advance the field of neuropsychology and improve the lives of those we serve.

References

American Psychological Association. (2000). *Report of the Task Force on Test User Qualification*. Author.

Cohen, J., Cohen, P., West, S. G., & Aiken, L. S. (2003). *Applied multiple regression/correlation analysis for the behavioral sciences* (3rd ed.). Routledge.

Crawford, J. R. (2012). Quantitative aspects of neuropsychological assessment. In L. H. Goldstein & J. E. McNeil (Eds.), *Clinical neuropsychology: A practical guide to assessment and management for clinicians* (2nd ed., pp. 129–158). John Wiley & Sons.

Crawford, J. R., Allum, S., & Kinion, J. E. (2008). An Index-based short-form of the WAIS-III with accompanying analysis of reliability and abnormality of differences. *British Journal of Clinical Psychology*, *47*, 215–237.

Crawford, J. R., & Garthwaite, P. H. (2005). Testing for suspected impairments and dissociations in single-case studies in neuropsychology: Evaluation of alternatives using Monte Carlo simulations and revised tests for dissociations. *Neuropsychology*, 19, 318–331.

Crawford, J. R., & Garthwaite, P. H. (2006). Comparing patients' predicted test scores from a regression equation with their obtained scores: A significance test and point estimate of abnormality with accompanying confidence limits. *Neuropsychology, 20*, 259–271.

Crawford, J. R., & Garthwaite, P. H. (2007a). Comparison of a single case to a control or normative sample in neuropsychology: Development of a Bayesian approach. *Cognitive Neuropsychology, 24*, 343–372.

Crawford, J. R., & Garthwaite, P. H. (2007b). Using regression equations built from summary data in the neuropsychological assessment of the individual case. *Neuropsychology, 21*(5), 611–620. https://doi.org/10.1037/0894-4105.21.5.611

Crawford, J. R., Garthwaite, P. H., Denham, K. A., & Chelune, G. J. (2012a). Using regression equations built from summary data in the psychological assessment of the individual case: Extension to multiple regression. *Psychological Assessment, 26*, 1154–1165. https://doi.org/10.1080/13854046.2012.720713

Crawford, J. R., Garthwaite, P. H., Longman, R. S., & Batty, A. M. (2012b). Some supplementary methods for the analysis of WAIS-IV Index scores in neuropsychological assessment. *Journal of Neuropsychology, 6*, 192–211. DOI: 10.1111/j.1748-6653.2011.02022.x

Crawford, J. R., Garthwaite, P. H., & Slick, D. J. (2009). On percentile norms in neuropsychology: Proposed reporting standards and methods for quantifying the uncertainty over the percentile ranks of test scores. *The Clinical Neuropsychologist, 27*, 1173–1195.

Crawford, J. R., & Howell, D. C. (1998). Comparing an individual's test score against norms derived from small samples. *The Clinical Neuropsychologist*, 12, 482–486.

Crawford, J. R., Howell, D. C., & Garthwaite, P. H. (1998). Payne and Jones revisited: Estimating the abnormality of test score differences using a modified paired samples *t* test. *Journal of Clinical and Experimental Neuropsychology*, 20, 898–905.

Crosson, B. (2011). *Application of neuropsychological assessment results* (R. D. Vanderploeg, Ed.; 2nd ed). Routledge.

De Andrade Moral, R., Díaz-Orueta, U., Oltra-Cucarella, J., & Alzheimer's Disease Neuroimaging Initiative. (2022). Logistic versus linear regression-based reliable change index: A simulation study with implications for clinical studies with different sample sizes. *Psychological Assessment, 34*(8), 731–741. https://doi.org/10.1037/pas0001138

Donders, J. (2001). A survey of report writing by neuropsychologists, I: General characteristics and content. *The Clinical Neuropsychologist, 15*(2), 137–149. https://doi.org/10.1076/clin.15.2.137.1893

Donders, J. (Ed.). (2016). *Neuropsychological report writing.* Guilford.

Hinton-Bayre, A. D. (2010). Deriving reliable change statistics from test–retest normative data: Comparison of models and mathematical expressions. *Archives of Clinical Neuropsychology, 25*(3), 244–256. https://doi.org/10.1093/arclin/acq008

Kane, R. L., & Kay, G. G. (1992). Computerized assessment in neuropsychology: A review of tests and test batteries. *Neuropsychology Review, 3*(1), 1–117. DOI: 10.1007/BF01108787

King, L., Hirst, R. E., Methley, A., Javed, H. M., Bowman, A. R., & Stevens, L. H. (2022). Improving the quality of neuropsychological assessment practice: The development of a self-assessment audit tool. *Archives of Clinical Neuropsychology, 37*(4), 814–825. https://doi.org/10.1093/arclin/acab099

Kiselica, A. M., Karr, J. E., Mikula, C. M., Ranum, R. M., Benge, J. F., Medina, L. D., & Woods, S. P. (2024). Recent advances in neuropsychological test interpretation for clinical practice. *Neuropsychology Review, 34*, 637–667. https://doi.org/10.1007/s11065-023-09607-5

Lenhard, W., & Lenhard, A. (2020). Improvement of norm score quality via regression-based continuous norming. *Educational and Psychological Measurement, 81*(2), 229–261. https://doi.org/10.1177/0013164420928457

Ley, P. (1972). *Quantitative aspects of psychological assessment.* Routledge.

Loring, D. W., Bauer, R. M., Cavanagh, L., Drane, D. L., Enriquez, K. D., Reise, S. P., Shih, K., Umfleet, L. G., Wahlstrom, D., Whelan, F., Widaman, K. F., Bilder, R. M., & NNN Study Group (2022). Rationale and design of the National Neuropsychology Network. *Journal of the International Neuropsychological Society, 28*(1), 1–11. https://doi.org/10.1017/S1355617721000199

Payne, R. W., & Jones, H. G. (1957). Statistics for the investigation of individual cases. *Journal of Clinical Psychology, 13*, 115–121.

Pearson. (2024). *Q-interactive®* (Version 2.0). Pearson. https://www.pearsonclinical.co.uk/digital-solutions/q-interactive

Wechsler, D. (2008). *Wechsler adult intelligence scale®.* 4th ed. Pearson.

9

Emerging Tools for Assessment

Laura M. Campbell, Katherine Hackett*, Emily W. Paolillo, Maria T. Schultheis, and Naomi S. Chaytor*

Introduction

Advances in technology over the last several decades have enhanced our traditional approach to neuropsychological assessment. For example, digitized cognitive test platforms have streamlined scoring procedures and facilitated automated capture of process-based scores, and advances in telehealth software have enabled remote administration of standard neuropsychological evaluations by trained professionals. This integration of technology into existing models of assessment represents a step forward. However, many have raised concerns that as a field we have not done enough to keep pace with rapid advances in technological innovation that other medical specialties have embraced (Miller & Barr, 2017; Parsons & Duffield, 2020).

To this end, a relatively nascent group of assessment approaches have emerged that serve to directly measure everyday function and capture cognition *in the wild* by leveraging the unique advantages of various technologies and devices. In this chapter, we cover a subset of these tools that appear particularly promising yet, at the time of writing, have not been widely implemented into clinical neuropsychological settings. We provide an overview of virtual reality (VR), cognitive ecological momentary assessment (EMA), and passive sensing approaches. We describe the unique advantages of each approach, consider the clinical relevance including preliminary evidence and clinical use cases, and discuss pragmatic concerns and open questions. We have chosen to highlight this subset of available tools based on their emerging relevance. Moreover, we present general concepts in this chapter that are applicable to other emerging technologies that may arise.

The new tools discussed herein share several advantages in terms of clinical relevance. First, they are geared toward improving our understanding of the patient's ability to perform everyday activities within everyday environments. This focus on ecological validity is a major priority among neuropsychologists, with calls to develop more clinically meaningful assessments of everyday function coming from researchers (Chaytor & Schmitter-Edgecombe, 2003), clinicians (Rabin et al., 2016), and funding agencies (Stoeckel et al., 2025). While VR technology enables us to

Note: *Laura M. Campbell and Katherine Hackett* contributed equally as first authors.

Laura M. Campbell et al., *Emerging Tools for Assessment*. In: *Technology and Neuropsychology*. Edited by: Jared F. Benge et al., Oxford University Press. © Oxford University Press (2026). DOI: 10.1093/9780197814116.003.0009

simulate everyday environments in which patients can perform or practice select activities that are deemed relevant, EMA allows us to measure cognitive abilities and fluctuations in complex environments at high frequencies, and passive sensing provides direct and continuous measurement of different domains of behavior as they naturally occur. Up until this point in time, it has not been technologically feasible to evaluate such a wide range of behaviors, settings, and outcomes. Insights from these approaches get us closer to understanding what happens when our patients leave the clinic and, ultimately, how we can devise more personalized and effective interventions. On a population level, findings from studies using these tools can inform new frameworks of cognitive risk and resilience and associated lifestyle factors, which can inform individual clinical recommendations. With decreasing costs and widespread availability of consumer devices, more and more individuals will own and use these tools in their day to day lives (e.g., smartphones, wearable fitness trackers, VR technology), enabling clinicians to harness what their patients already use as a complementary assessment or intervention tool.

The digital approaches discussed herein also yield rich, high-dimensional data compared to traditional approaches that use relatively "low-dimensional" paper-and-pencil tools. While well-validated to capture distinct cognitive constructs, traditional tools provide more limited insights into complex neuropsychological phenomena (Parsons & Duffield, 2020). For example, traditional assessment approaches cannot capture the dynamic interaction between a person and their environment and performance trends under varying timescales. The high-frequency nature of digital data also offers greater precision and sensitivity to subtle deficits that are more challenging to capture using conventional tools and may thus enable clinicians to more easily test the limits. Automated logging of such fine-grained data, such as mild performance decrements over time or in certain contexts, also offers a notable advantage to the burdensome and error-prone hand-scoring techniques that continue to be used by many practicing neuropsychologists (Rabin et al., 2016). When these digital data are captured on personal devices, patients should hypothetically be able to efficiently upload individual-level data to open-access normative networks if and when they exist (Bilder & Reise, 2019).

Nonetheless, there are many open questions and concerns about using these emerging methods in clinical care. In general, the development of psychometric and normative standards for VR, EMA, and passive sensing is still in the early stages and has yet to reach the rigorous standards of conventional assessment approaches, with no current "gold standard" for using these tools or interpreting results. This is partially due to the tradeoff between internal versus external validity, and the fact that these approaches intentionally sacrifice standardization for naturalistic assessment, rendering them potentially less appropriate for group-based norms. However, there is also potential to amass very large reference datasets from which to compare individual performance (S. Singh et al., 2021). Longitudinal approaches that focus on within-person change metrics are a unique advantage, however, and reduce the need to rely on normative datasets for clinical inference.

Best practices for developing and maintaining a working knowledge of these tools, their evidence base, and limitations is another major gap in clinical neuropsychology's training standards. As patients increasingly present with self-collected data from commercial health devices and mobile apps, we must strike a balance between remaining within our scope of practice while being open to the unique insights afforded by these data. The challenge will lie in how to stay informed, given the rapid pace of change and the ever-evolving number of hardware and software platforms. There are also a multitude of ethical considerations pertinent to emerging digital tools in neuropsychology, ranging from privacy and confidentiality issues that are particularly relevant for data captured from personal devices, to issues of equity related to differences in access to requisite devices and in digital literacy that may impact use behaviors and subsequent validity. These and other important issues are discussed further in the conclusion section.

Virtual Reality

Overview and Definition

Virtual reality (VR) includes technologies that allow the creation, presentation, and delivery of computer-generated simulation of a 3D image or environment that can be interacted with in a seemingly real or physical way by a person using special electronic equipment. VR comes in many forms, and while many associate this technology with a head-mounted display unit (HMD), a VR simulation is a combination of both hardware and software that can be delivered in a wider variety of platforms (i.e., display screens, haptic devices, sensory input devices.) VR simulated environments have been available since the early 2000s in several military and commercial applications (Lele, 2013). Back then, these technologies required significant computing power and significant cost. However, with the advancement of usable and accessible computer and information technologies, VR is now a household name, and there is an abundance of low-cost, readily available systems that can offer clinicians the opportunity to create and "immerse" users in the 3D simulated virtual environments of their choice. In the past 25 years, VR has become an accessible tool that many researchers have employed to better understand human behavior, both across clinical and nonclinical populations (Claudio & Maddalena, 2014; Schultheis & Rizzo, 2001).

Unique Advantages and Considerations of VR

The application of VR simulated environments to expand our understanding of brain–behavior relationships and to expand our cognitive assessment methodologies offers several unique advantages. The most notable is the ability to use VR to create 3D simulated environments that replicate real-world settings and uniquely allow the controlled selection and automatic recording of all stimuli and responses. What this means is that, in VR, you can build and simulate just about any environment and situation that happens in the real world. For clinicians, like neuropsychologists who study brain and behavior interactions, VR can offer a novel approach to objectively measure cognition and human behaviors in functionally relevant scenarios (e.g., at home, shopping in a store). Specifically, in scenarios or environments that may not be feasible in a hospital or clinic office, this provides the opportunity to assess cognition in a more dynamic and naturalistic manner (Pieri et al., 2023; Rizzo et al., 2004). The key benefit of offering more "realistic" or "real-life" environments for testing cognition is twofold.

First, through VR simulation neuropsychologists can more objectively measure how an individual will perform under more "natural" conditions—as VR immersion allows one to "enter" a simulated environment. This is in contrast to the presentation of "artificially" laden test-taking behaviors that may result from traditional test-taking environments (i.e., in the clinic). Second, this new objective measurement of cognition in simulated "real-world" environments can begin to answer questions regarding the ecological validity of our current assessments and interventions. VR allows full control of stimulus presentation and response measurement, which can include precise and specific measures of cognitive contributions to complex behaviors (T. D. Parsons, 2015; Schultheis & Mourant, 2001; Uswatte & Schultheis, 2010). For example, while current approaches allow for the examination of how specific cognitive constructs are correlated to functional behavior, neuropsychologists using VR simulation can provide a more precise understanding of where and how performance of specific cognitive domains can directly impact functional performance. For example, while it is well accepted that cognitive impairment is related to changes in driving behavior (Aschenbrenner et al., 2022; Schultheis & Chute, 1999; Wadley et al., 2021; Wolfe & Lehockey, 2016), using VR-based driving assessments allows for the safe examination of which specific cognitive constructs relate to specific risky driving behaviors or errors and could allow clinicians to better tailor both assessment and clinical recommendations.

Another unique advantage is the opportunity to directly examine cognition and brain–behavior relationships in hazardous situations that in the real world would neither be feasible nor safe for the individual or the clinician. For example, testing how cognition impacts an individual's cooking ability after neurological compromise (i.e., Alzheimer's dementia, stroke) by placing them in a kitchen under challenging conditions (i.e., hot pans, missing items, others in the room) would have significant safety risks. By contrast, in a VR environment, all of these stimuli could be safely and effortlessly presented, while automatically recording the individual's responses to provide the best assessment of cognition in real-life performance. As such, VR offers a new methodology for measuring verisimilitude, the degree to which tasks performed during testing resemble those performed in daily life, to establish ecological validity of cognitive assessments (Chaytor & Schmitter-Edgecombe, 2003; T. D. Parsons, 2015; Schultheis et al., 2002). However, it is important to note that VR applications may often result in incorrect interpretation of face validity and ecological validity, that is—because it "looks like" the real world does not mean that behaviors are equivalent to "real world" performance. Ultimately more research is needed to establish the psychometric evidence, including validity and reliability testing.

Some important considerations in the use of VR environments for cognitive assessment include ensuring that application aligns with the benefits of the technology, and not simply the digitization of an existing paper-and-pencil task. Developing an automated version of a task does not capitalize on the unique assets of VR. This also requires careful consideration of the program development, measurement design, and analysis. One unique consideration for VR use is the potential for "simulation sickness" as a result of exposure to the 3D simulated environments. Simulation sickness (SS) is a type of motion sickness, which can include symptoms such as nausea, dizziness, headache, and fatigue (Chang et al., 2020). While human factors studies have researched the causes of SS and identified some methods for reducing SS during VR exposure, most of these studies are conducted with nonclinical populations, therefore raising questions regarding the potential impact of SS to clinical populations (i.e., brain injury, dementia).

Finally, like the other emerging technologies highlighted in this chapter, VR has the ability to capture a wide range of data; however, this also serves as a potential disadvantage because it can result in an overabundance of metrics, some of which may or may not be relevant. As such, VR application development often benefits from including a variety of expertise in the team, including experts in programming, human factors, statistical analysis expertise, content expertise, and neuropsychologists. A multidisciplinary team can ensure that the application is not just a visual representation but rather a valid tool that will assess the cognitive construct of interest.

Preliminary Evidence

The potential contributions of clinical VR applications in the field of neuropsychology are evidenced by a growing body of literature demonstrating the application of VR in both assessment and intervention applications. Some early examples of VR programs that were developed to examine specific cognitive constructs include the evaluation of spatial navigation strategies in patients with vestibular loss using a virtual reality T-maze (Gammeri et al., 2022) and the assessment of spatial attention and neglect using a VR wheelchair navigation task (Buxbaum et al., 2008). In 2000, Rizzo et al. demonstrated the use of a VR Classroom to evaluate and rehabilitate attention deficits among children diagnosed with attention-deficit/hyperactivity disorder (ADHD) (Rizzo et al., 2000). Other virtual environments, such as a Virtual Office, a Virtual Kitchen, and a Virtual Grocery Store, have been employed to examine the cognitive constructs, such as learning, memory, and executive functioning in simulated complex scenarios (Matheis et al., 2007). Many of these early studies provided support of clinical utility and feasibility. More recent research has focused on demonstrating the validity of VR tools for the assessment of cognitive ability in comparison to traditional neuropsychological tools (Kirkham et al., 2024). In sum, there is a growing number of VR-based scenarios that have been explored as novel clinical tools for determining cognitive capacity.

Use Case Example: VR Driving Simulators to Safely Assess Driving Safety

One VR application that is already being used clinically in some settings is the use of VR to improve our knowledge of the cognitive demands of an important activity of daily living—in this case example VR driving simulators to assess and retrain driving ability. Specifically, returning to driving after neurological compromise such as traumatic brain injury or stroke, or maintaining safe driving during neurological disorders (i.e., multiple sclerosis, dementia), is a common clinical question. Current gold standard measures have focused on the visual and motor demands of driving ability, with less attention to the cognitive contributions (Fields & Unsworth, 2017; Korner-Bitensky et al., 2006). Furthermore, much of the existing literature examining cognition and driving has focused on individuals primarily within the moderate-to-severe range of cognitive impairment, thereby limiting our understanding of individuals in the mild impairment ranges, which often return to driving without assessment. The use of VR driving simulator offers the opportunity to provide a more precise measurement of the cognitive contributors to specific driving behaviors, including risky and cognitively challenging scenarios. To date, many researchers have demonstrated the utility of VR driving simulators, to demonstrate differences in simulated driving performance between clinical and nonclinical populations, such as stroke, HIV, multiple sclerosis, and autism (Chanmas et al., 2023; Krasniuk et al., 2022; Marcotte et al., 2004; Patrick et al., 2020). This research and the recent utilization of this technology by some clinicians highlight the value of translational research. The novelty of VR technology to generate new measures coupled with the neuropsychological expertise to clinically translate these new metrics both informs and expands our knowledge of cognition in this important human behavior (i.e., driving).

Future Directions

VR is now a usable and readily available technology that can offer novel approaches to move neuropsychology to the next phase of assessment and intervention (i.e., Neuropsychology 3.0; Bilder, 2011). VR applications can uniquely expand our understanding of cognition for complex behaviors (i.e., driving), as it offers a metric of the dynamic interplay of multiple cognitive constructs needed for successful functional performance.

In addition, it can be argued that VR applications are essential to leading the way to precision medicine within cognitive assessment by providing more specific and precise measurements of behavior. To benefit from this, the future generation of neuropsychologists must embrace the technological opportunities and challenges that come with new technologies. Playing a leading role in the development of the VR environments, defining the new metrics and their cognitive contributions to the targeted behavior, and supporting the safe utility of VR among clinically populations are some examples of new roles and opportunities for neuropsychologists. Similarly, these roles will require acquisition of new skills (i.e., higher-level statistics), but these can also represent the opportunity to collaborate with different experts and fields of knowledge (i.e., computer science, human factors, etc.).

Finally, as a field it is important to consider that while VR continues to evolve and offer a variety of benefits to improving cognitive assessment, the work still remains in research settings, with minimal transition into clinics. The challenge of clinical acceptance by neuropsychologist for VR technology will require further consideration.

Cognitive Ecological Momentary Assessment

Overview and Definition

EMA, also called experience sampling, is a method used to collect real-time data on individuals' self-reported behaviors and experiences repeatedly and within their natural environments (Shiffman et al., 2008). Traditional assessment methods rely on retrospective self-reports or laboratory-based observations, which research has repeatedly demonstrated are influenced by several biases such as recall and social desirability biases (Podsakoff et al., 2003). In comparison, EMA captures participants' responses in real time, offering a potentially more accurate and ecologically valid representation of the phenomena under study. From a historical perspective, EMA grew from a daily diary approach and began incorporating technology to lower participant burden and facilitate more continuous assessment. Currently, EMA is now commonly deployed via smartphones, and it has been used successfully in several different populations. An overview of EMA and current topics have been discussed in detail elsewhere (e.g., Shiffman et al., 2008; Stone et al., 2023; Wrzus & Neubauer, 2023).

The proliferation of smartphones with advanced displays and processing capacity has enabled more complex objective cognitive tests to be integrated into an EMA framework (Germine et al., 2019; Moore et al., 2017). Cognitive EMA, which is broadly defined as the integration of objective, performance-based, cognitive assessment into an EMA framework, is a more recent EMA approach and has evolved significantly in recent years as technology has advanced. Within this section we focus specifically on the unique advantages and considerations, preliminary evidence, and future directions of cognitive EMA. Of note, we will use the term "cognitive EMA" to describe the use of mobile devices (e.g., smartphones) to deploy objective cognitive testing in this chapter, but several different terms are used in the literature such as ecological momentary cognitive testing (EMCT), mobile or ambulatory cognitive assessment, and smartphone-based cognitive assessment/testing.

Unique Advantages and Considerations of Cognitive EMA

Traditional cognitive assessments are conducted in controlled environments, which may not accurately represent everyday cognitive functioning (Chaytor & Schmitter-Edgecombe, 2003). Transient factors like stress, sleep, and diet can affect single-occasion test results in some people more than others, leading to potentially inaccurate conclusions about neurocognitive status. Cognitive EMA offers a potential solution by collecting cognitive data frequently over time, in everyday environments, that can complement traditional neuropsychological assessment. Cognitive EMA offers numerous advantages, such as cognitive performance measurement in real-world settings, enhanced precision through digital tools, reduced costs, and improved accessibility (T. Parsons & Duffield, 2020). Intensive longitudinal cognitive EMA designs, which involve frequent assessments over time, can enhance reliability by averaging across repeated measurements. Similarly, longitudinal measurement burst designs, characterized by short periods of very frequent assessments embedded within longer study periods, may also improve sensitivity to important outcomes such as cognitive changes over time, real-world performance, or relevant biomarkers (e.g., brain magnetic resonance imaging, biomarkers associated with neurodegenerative pathology, genetic risk [Aschenbrenner et al., 2024; Staffaroni et al., 2024]), especially when combined with traditional neuropsychological evaluation (Allard et al., 2014; Sliwinski et al., 2010; Vaughan & Birney, 2024).

Relatedly, the amount of data captured due to the repeated measurement design approach paired with the ability to capture novel performance metrics (e.g., average, variability, best performance, etc.) allows for exploration into which metrics (both within a single test and across time; e.g., days to weeks) are most sensitive to a variety of important outcomes such as diagnosis, prognosis (e.g., future decline or improvement), and everyday function. For example, intraindividual cognitive variability, increasingly recognized as a sensitive early marker for brain dysfunction, is possible to measure via EMA designs both across time and within a single test (Anderson et al., 2016; Burton et al., 2006; Cerino et al., 2021). Other indicators from cognitive EMA such as practice effects, or lack thereof, may be a promising marker of risk of cognitive decline (Wilks et al., 2024). Overall, research into a myriad of data captured from this repeated design approach holds incredible promise for efficiently identifying persons in need of comprehensive neuropsychological assessment and tracking cognitive change over time.

Another advantage is that cognitive EMA designs can be paired with the assessment of other noncognitive variables that may affect, or vary with, cognition (e.g., sleep and circadian rhythms, mood, glucose, heart rate, temperature, noise). These can be collected either via traditional EMA or other devices (e.g., wearable devices, passive sensor data). These novel data streams can be used to answer questions about how cognition is influenced by internal states and external factors in daily life (Campbell et al., 2020; Hyun et al., 2019; Zlatar et al., 2022) that could in turn be used to help patients maximize their cognitive performance. This approach can not only improve predictions of daily functioning but also identify ways to enhance cognitive performance via modification of these variables (Chaytor & Fonseca, 2022).

There are also unique methodological and ethical considerations when it comes to cognitive EMA. As highlighted previously in the chapter, there are privacy and confidentiality concerns as well as the fast pace of smartphone and other technological advances that are relevant to cognitive EMA. Specific to cognitive EMA, testing completed in an unsupervised environment raises concerns about how to ensure valid performance and best account for contextual factors that may affect cognition (e.g., alcohol/substance use, distractors in the environment). Efforts to delineate best practices in these areas are ongoing. (Henneghan et al., 2025; Liao et al., 2016; N. B. Singh & Björling, 2019; Yang et al., 2019).

Preliminary Evidence

A 2017 review of mobile cognitive assessment studies (N = 12; age range: 14–83) concluded that the majority found cognitive EMA to be feasible with high levels of test–retest and internal reliability, as well as good convergent and divergent validity compared to lab-based assessments, although most studies reviewed were in nonclinical populations (Moore et al., 2017). Since this review, several additional studies have shown evidence of feasibility, reliability, and validity of cognitive EMA in adult and pediatric populations across a variety of cognitive domains. Illustrating the wide variety of potential clinical applications, it has been used in samples of older adults with and without neurodegenerative disorders (Moore et al., 2022; Nicosia et al., 2023; Schweitzer et al., 2017; Staffaroni et al., 2024; Weizenbaum et al., 2022), chronic health conditions (Henneghan et al., 2025; Moore et al., 2020; Ray et al., 2025; S. Singh et al., 2023), and substance and affective disorders (Bouvard et al., 2018; Parrish et al., 2021). Given the strong preliminary support among many populations, we anticipate that the evidence will continue to grow in other populations and settings. However, a 2020 systematic review did find that several app- and web-based tools for assessing cognition did not have published psychometric properties and were of uncertain quality (Charalambous et al., 2020). As with all cognitive tests, good psychometric properties are of the utmost importance, and we strongly encourage that when consuming the literature or choosing a cognitive EMA tool that the reader or consumer check to ensure that tests have good psychometric properties for their intended purpose.

That said, establishing the psychometric properties of cognitive EMA measures is complex, and there are no current gold standards for reporting of cognitive EMA studies, including psychometric properties. Validating new EMA cognitive tests is challenging, as many lack direct traditional neuropsychological counterparts or have been significantly modified to allow for brief, repeated administration. Cognitive EMA may require distinct approaches to validation, considering different clinical populations, age ranges, and devices (Germine et al., 2019).

Use Case Example: Cognitive EMA Coupled with Continuous Glucose Monitoring in Type 1 Diabetes

The Glycemic Variability and Fluctuations in Cognitive Status in Adults with Type 1 Diabetes Study (the GluCog study), a collaboration between Washington State University and McLean Hospital, investigated the dynamic impact of blood glucose fluctuations on cognitive performance in adults with type 1 diabetes. Here we present it as a use case, to highlight important study design considerations, such as the number of daily assessments, burst length, and pairing of devices. It also highlights the variety of questions that can be explored using cognitive EMA, such as dynamic associations (i.e., does cognition fluctuate in tandem with another variable), lagged models (i.e., do cognitive changes occur before or after another event), and associations with other variables of interest (i.e., in this case biomarkers) that may only be collected at one timepoint.

This study employed passive continuous glucose monitoring (CGM) coupled with self-administered mobile cognitive EMA using participants' own smartphones. The study used a commercial CGM device, Dexcom© G6, to measure glucose levels every 5 minutes over 10 days, with the ability to blind participants to their glucose readings to prevent bias. The EMA schedule involved three daily assessments, including cognitive tests and questions about noncognitive factors (e.g., interruptions during the cognitive tests, mood, anxiety, sleep quality, fatigue, recent substance use). The study included an optimization phase to determine the best EMA frequency to capture a wide range of glucose values and minimize missing data, as well as incentives for completing EMAs. The brief cognitive tasks in the EMA battery assessed processing speed and sustained attention using the TestMyBrain.org platform (participants received text messages with the testing link). To ensure valid data, EMAs were excluded when individual task characteristics indicated low task engagement and/or implausibly slow or fast responding. Additional details regarding the study design have been previously published (Fonseca et al., 2023).

It was determined that glucose values both lower and higher than participants' typical glucose level were associated with slower processing speed, but they did not impact momentary attention, with some participants being more vulnerable to the effects of glucose than others (Hawks et al., 2024). Results established the impact of glucose on processing speed in naturalistic environments, suggested that minimizing glucose fluctuations is important for optimizing processing speed, and identified several clinical characteristics that may exacerbate cognitive vulnerability to glucose fluctuations. This EMA based metric was also associated with plasma biomarkers of neurodegeneration, including pTau181 and pTau217 (Fonseca et al., 2025). This study also provided preliminary findings suggesting that nighttime hypoglycemia impacts next-day cognitive performance, independent of reported sleep quality (Zuniga-Kennedy et al., 2024). Overall, the GluCog study resulted in novel findings about the role of glucose on cognition in the daily lives of adults with type 1 diabetes that would not have been possible using other study designs or with traditional neuropsychological testing.

Future Directions

In addition to elucidating novel brain–behavior relationships that can inform clinical practice, cognitive EMA has multiple direct clinical applications. Some of the highest yield applications of this methodology include symptom tracking and assessing cognitive change in conjunction with traditional clinical assessments. For example, a patient who performs well during the controlled clinical testing environment while complaining of cognitive problems in daily life may benefit from EMA assessments that include both cognitive and noncognitive assessments to determine which factors impact cognition in daily life (e.g., cognitive performance is poorer when sleep duration is shorter, or when anxiety symptoms are higher). These data can provide documentation of everyday cognitive changes and also point to possible interventions patients can employ to maximize cognition, such as sleep or mood interventions. Despite the potential for useful clinical insights, practical use of cognitive EMA in psychology and neuropsychology will require training in these tools and user-friendly platforms for delivery and interpretation of data.

Cognitive EMA also could assist in efficient screening and monitoring of cognition over longer periods of time. As an example in the aging literature, recent studies indicate that smartphone-based EMA is feasible for older adults (Cerino et al., 2021; Ramsey et al., 2016), allowing repeated cognitive assessments over time. Thus, cognitive EMA could be used to help screen or identify early within-person cognitive changes and prompt clinical work-up, which could assist in early diagnosis before significant decline occurs and maximize the opportunity for cognitive rehabilitation, medication initiation, future planning, and establishing psychosocial and family support. EMA can also be used to monitor cognition following a mild cognitive impairment (MCI) diagnosis and determine when further clinical follow-up or new treatments are needed. Pharmacological and behavioral interventions can delay Alzheimer's symptoms when initiated early after diagnosis, and EMA can also monitor cognition and symptoms post-intervention.

Passive Activity Detection

Overview and Definition

Passive activity detection, also referred to as passive sensing, is an approach that involves the remote, continuous, and completely unobtrusive monitoring of activities and behaviors. The goal of passive sensing is to quantify objective, real-world behavior via sensor technology that provides insights into various clinical outcomes such as cognition, mood, and everyday functioning. Assessment of the latter has traditionally relied on flawed self- or informant-reports despite the crucial role of evaluating functional impact in a wide range of psychiatric and neurological diagnoses. These sensors may be intentionally placed on specific objects (e.g., in cars) or in homes (e.g., in doorways or room transitions) to track behaviors such as driving and in-home movement patterns. Alternatively, sensors that are already embedded within personal devices like smartphones and wearables can be used to infer a range of other behaviors such as community participation, gait function, social connectedness, or technology use. The term "digital phenotyping," first defined in 2016 by Torous et al. (2016) as "the moment-by-moment quantification of the individual-level human phenotype in situ using data from personal digital devices," can be conceptualized as a specific passive sensing approach that relies on personal devices with embedded sensors.

There is no single standardized definition of passive sensing in the context of neuropsychology, and the concept predates more recent applications in clinical research. For example, the digital traces captured by our smartphones when we move locations or browse the Internet have been tracked and aggregated by phone companies, Internet providers, and technology companies since these capabilities were introduced in the late 2000s (Bilder & Reise, 2019). Remote monitoring of vital signs (Wang et al., 2020; Yilmaz et al., 2010), falls (Melillo et al., 2015), and blood glucose or blood pressure (Or & Tao, 2016) has been used to capture biological measurements in health care for almost a decade now. Early work in digital phenotyping focused on smartphone-derived metrics to infer and predict mental health outcomes such as depression and psychosis relapse (Onnela & Rauch, 2016). The application of both digital phenotyping specifically and passive sensing more broadly to infer outcomes relevant to neuropsychology is a relatively novel concept, but it is increasingly recognized as a promising complementary tool to both traditional neuropsychological measures and other *active* digital approaches described earlier. While there are a range of sensor approaches that have been reviewed in detail elsewhere (Au, Lin, et al., 2023; Bufano et al., 2023; Giovannetti et al., 2022; Hackett & Giovannetti, 2022; Harris et al., 2024; Onnela, 2021), here we highlight a few specific examples with emerging evidence and discuss their clinical relevance to neuropsychological assessment. Of note, we do not cover speech and other digital (e.g., digital pen) biomarkers that, while passive to some degree, are usually captured during standardized neuropsychological test settings. This is an exciting area of work and is outlined elsewhere (Au, Popp, et al., 2023).

Unique Advantages and Considerations of Passive Sensing

Most existing neuropsychological paradigms require intentional engagement by the patient or person being evaluated. These *active* approaches typically involve standardized instructions to complete a task that aims to measure a discrete cognitive ability or psychological state. There are several drawbacks to this traditional active approach that passive sensing may uniquely address. One is the impact of language and cultural bias, which has been documented at length (e.g., see Brickman et al., 2006; Byrd & Rivera-Mindt, 2022; Tan et al., 2021). Briefly, individuals whose primary language and cultural background is different than the sample in which the test was created, validated, and normed are at a major disadvantage, as active tests with verbal instructions and/or items are significantly less valid and appropriate for these individuals. Passive approaches, however, do not require reading or following instructions or conforming to test taking practices; instead, they are completely unobtrusive and enable a naturalistic assessment of individually relevant tasks in multiple contexts (e.g., measuring what each person does in their day-to-day life within various settings). This does not mean that passive approaches are demographically or culturally agnostic; in fact, there are likely numerous ways in which culture, educational background, and other demographic factors influence the way in which people move through the world and the digital traces they leave. However, passive approaches represent a step in the right direction to improve some of the confounds inherent to active testing paradigms.

Second, active approaches are susceptible to practice effects—with repeated exposure to the test paradigm, healthy individuals are likely to improve on subsequent testing sessions which obscures our ability to measure clinically significant improvements or declines due to underlying neurological or medical causes. Because passive sensing occurs in the background without interference or active input, practice effects are essentially nonexistent. This makes passive approaches especially useful for longitudinal monitoring in situations where decline is expected due to the natural progression of a disease (e.g., neurodegenerative conditions) or when we hope to see true improvement as a result of intervention (e.g., cognitive rehabilitation in traumatic brain injury).

Third, active approaches, even high-frequency or burst designs used in EMA approaches, occur at discrete timepoints. Passive approaches enable near continuous monitoring, with data captured on interval (e.g., every X minutes) or event-based (e.g., every time someone unlocks their phone screen) schedules. This yields incredibly rich and high-volume data that can offer increased sensitivity and reduced sample size requirements to detect subtle behavioral manifestations of an underlying neurological issue or monitor treatment effectiveness in a clinical trial.

Preliminary Evidence

There are many different passive sensing approaches, and new technologies are constantly emerging, each with varying degrees of support for their feasibility and validity to measure what they intend to measure. Table 9.1 shows a select subset of passive sensing approaches that as of 2025 have the most support for their use in persons who have or are at risk for cognitive impairment. Because passive sensing technologies are designed to be multidomain, there are some overlaps in approaches (e.g., GPS can be measured through either wearable devices or smartphones). The most appropriate or optimal methodological choice should be made based on research design or clinical context (i.e., it may be preferable to leverage consumer smartphone devices that patients already own rather than account for the logistical and financial burden of introducing a new device; whereas if precision and guaranteed continuous monitoring are priorities, wearables would be more appropriate to assess mobility metrics). Evidence that these technologies are sensitive to clinically relevant constructs in neuropsychology continues to grow. The strongest

Table 9.1 Overview of Select Passive Sensing Approaches and Key Citations

Hardware	Data Type	Functional Domains Measured	Key Citations
Wearables	Accelerometry (+ gyroscope, magnetometer)	Physical activity, sedentary behavior, mobility, gait, sleep, circadian rest-activity rhythms (RAR), tremor	Smith et al., 2018; Winer et al., 2024
	Photoplethysmography	Cardiac health	Rykov et al., 2024
	GPS	Mobility, life space, community participation	Cullen et al., 2022
Smartphones	Phone use metadata (e.g., screen time, battery percentage, apps used)	Technology use	Paolillo et al., 2024; R. Chen et al., 2019
	Keystroke dynamics (from touchscreen keyboard typing)	Processing speed, executive functioning, language	M. H. Chen et al., 2022; R. Chen et al., 2019; Ross et al., 2021
	GPS	Mobility, life space, community participation	Hackett et al., 2024; Leaning et al., 2024
	Number of calls/text messages sent and received	Social activity	R. Chen et al., 2019
	Bluetooth signaling	Social activity	Boonstra et al., 2017

continued

Table 9.1 *continued*

Hardware	Data Type	Functional Domains Measured	Key Citations
In-home/ environment sensors	Motion detection and door open/close	In-home mobility, time out of home, daily routines	Bayat et al., 2021; Beattie et al., 2020
	Pillbox open/close	Medication use and timing	
	Bed movement and ballistography (from bed sensor)	Sleep, circadian rhythm activity, heart rate, respiratory rate	
	Vibration (from select items in the home, e.g., broom, dustpan)	Daily routines, household activities	
	Computer use	Technology use	
	Scale	Weight, body mass composition	
	GPS from car	Driving behavior	

support has been established for wearable accelerometers, as these devices have been implemented broadly for several decades now in large-scale studies such as UK Biobank, the Rush Alzheimer's Disease Research Center, Parkinson Progression Markers Initiative, WATCH-PD, the National Institute of Health All of Us study, and the Adolescent Brain Cognitive Development (ABCD) study (Adams et al., 2023; All of Us Research Program Investigators, 2019; Bagot et al., 2018; Bloem et al., 2019; Buchman et al., 2012; Doherty et al., 2017). Thus, here we review a use case from one recent wearable study (Case Example 1), as well as an innovative integrated in-home sensor approach (Case Example 2), to convey the range of available sensors and associated clinical findings.

Case Example 1: Using Wearable Accelerometry to Predict Incident Neurodegenerative Disease

The UK Biobank is a large longitudinal study of community-dwelling adults from mid- to late life across England, Scotland, and Wales. The UK Biobank implemented wearable accelerometer data collection from 2013 to 2016, resulting in over 100,000 participants who were asked to wear an AX3 Axivity wrist-worn triaxial accelerometer for 1 week and were followed longitudinally thereafter for an average of approximately 7 years. A recent study by Winer and colleagues (2024) leveraged these large-scale data to examine whether accelerometry-derived 24-hour activity patterns predicted incident Alzheimer's disease (AD) and Parkinson's disease (PD) diagnoses at follow up [6.8 ± 0.9 years later, on average], as well as longitudinal trajectories of cognitive decline (Winer et al., 2024). They examined data from 82,829 UK

Biobank participants with valid accelerometry data from at least 5 days and derived six well-established metrics that characterize patterns of circadian rest and activity. These included activity level during the most active 10 hours, intraday variability (fragmentation of activity within a given day), and interday stability (regularity of activity across days). Overall, results showed that participants with lower activity levels (quantified by several metrics) were at greater risk of both AD and PD, with higher interday stability (i.e., those with more regular movement patterns across days) also associating with greater risk of incident AD. Similarly, lower baseline activity levels prognosticated steeper longitudinal declines in processing speed while lower intraday variability (more consolidation of activity within days) prognosticated steeper declines in memory performance. This study highlights the power of using a scalable, passive sensing method to detect early and subtle signs of cognitive decline due to neurodegenerative disease.

Case Example 2: Using Integrated In-Home Sensor Systems Sensitive to Functional Impairment

This chapter highlights the multiple devices and methodologies that can be used to objectively quantify naturalistic, real-world cognitive and everyday functioning. Despite their feasibility to be implemented simultaneously, most published studies test each of these methods in isolation; however, the potential power of passive sensing tools comes from their combined ability to monitor multidomain functions. To highlight this potential, we present two existing in-home sensor platforms that are specifically designed to integrate multidomain sensor data for sensitive capture of functional changes. The Oregon Center for Aging and Technology (ORCATECH) group, spearheaded by Jeffrey Kaye, MD, has deployed their Collaborative Aging Research using Technology (CART) in-home sensor platform in numerous clinical populations across the globe (Thomas et al., 2021). The platform includes a technology back end, which stores and manages data, and a technology front end, which comprises the in-home sensors linked to a home hub computer that wirelessly receives all sensor data and transfers those data to the secure research server (Beattie et al., 2020). The CART platform currently includes motion sensors, door sensors, pillbox sensors, bed sensors, wrist-worn actigraphy, digital scales for weight and other cardiovascular metrics, software that monitors computer use, and GPS sensors placed in cars. The platform is designed to be able to flexibly integrate emerging sensor technology including those that are more mobile (e.g., smartphone). Since the CART platform was launched in 2015, numerous studies have reported relationships between individual sensors and outcomes related to cognitive aging in a wide variety of older adult samples. This includes the widely cited paper on in-home walking speed trajectories and their association with incident MCI (Dodge et al., 2012), as well as another important study showing that longitudinal changes in computer use habits associate with MCI status (Kaye et al., 2014).

Researchers from Washington State University (Cook et al., 2015) have also published advanced analytic methods to integrate data from multiple in-home and wearable sensors. In one study, they asked healthy older adults and adults with PD to perform a series of everyday activities in a "smarthome testbed," which is an experimental on-campus environment that closely resembles a home dwelling but is equipped with various sensors that can quantify behavior passively. The testbed is inclusive of the component sensors, software algorithms that notify researchers about events, and the ability to store all data locally or securely transmit them to cloud storage. Their goal was to see if automated machine learning algorithms could distinguish clinical groups based on differences in behavioral patterns picked up by a combination of ambient (e.g., light/temperature changes), object (e.g., door opening/closing), and wearable (e.g., accelerometer movement) sensors. After extracting features from the raw sensor data, they tested several machine learning classifiers and found that one model accurately distinguished healthy older adults from those with PD 97% of the time (accuracy = 0.97, with an area under the ROC curve of 0.97). These examples highlight powerful methodological approaches to integrating dense and high-dimensional data via multiple sensors, from data collection and storage to analytics.

Pragmatic Concerns and Open Questions

There are many challenges that must be addressed as we are faced with translating passive sensing methods from research to clinical environments. In terms of clinical relevance, additional development and validation in a wider range of patient populations are key. Passive sensing is a nascent approach with no gold-standard procedures in terms of the frequency, duration, and exact type of data that should be captured for particular populations and clinical questions. There are no existing normative databases to reference when attempting to interpret individual-level data. This is perhaps a moot point, given there are many more potential confounders when using a completely passive approach that cannot feasibly be adjusted for (i.e., idiosyncratic differences in daily habits, baseline differences in technology use, geographic regional differences in transportation and movement patterns, etc.). It is thus unclear whether group-level normative approaches are useful for clinical applications of this method or whether within-person approaches (i.e., monitoring someone's change over time or relative to their own baseline) are most appropriate. As in the other methods described in this chapter, clinicians will need to weigh the pros and cons of naturalistic versus controlled environments when determining which tool to use. A related question is whether passive sensing is in fact completely naturalistic, or whether knowledge of passive data collection affects individuals' behavior (i.e., Hawthorne effect).

Making sense of incredibly large, high-density datasets is also tantamount to clinical relevance and is a major methodological challenge. Clinicians and researchers engaging with passive methods should prioritize using clinically meaningful and replicable features from raw data so that "scores" or trends in these features are easy to interpret and can be integrated with other clinical data to inform prognosis and actionable recommendations. When using passive data for clinical prediction, it is critical to carefully consider whether to use bottom-up machine learning approaches that, while powerful, may pose issues of replicability and interpretability versus hypothesis-driven approaches. As with all new tools, we must continually evaluate the value-add and compare passive methods to existing tools we already have at our disposal to justify the added computational, analytic, and data storage burden.

When considering which passive sensing tool to use, there are several points to address. The first is which raw data type to collect depending on the construct you are interested in (i.e., if mobility, select a tool that allows you to capture GPS; if finer grained gait features, a wearable accelerometer is important; if social features, phone or text meta-data is useful). The next step is to ensure the tool you propose to use allows access to that data. This can be a challenge when relying on devices already owned by the patient (like smartphones), as privacy restrictions by commercial entities like Apple and Google are constantly evolving and may pose limitations on allowable data. In some cases, it may be necessary to install specific software on personal devices in order to capture certain data types (e.g., keystroke typing data may only be available if participants use a study-specific keyboard overlay), which may slightly alter the user experience and phone interface and thereby influence the behavior itself. Relatedly, when relying on personal device ownership, we need to be mindful of when users change hardware or software and remember that the same data type captured by different devices may not be comparable, both in terms of the technical features of the data (e.g., accuracy, quality, or amounts of missing data) and the latent differences between individuals who use different device types. For these reasons, sensor approaches that use a standardized, study-specific tool may afford greater control, although they will likely have lower ultimate clinical utility. As discussed earlier, it is critical to plan for how to store, manage, and process the incredibly high-volume data, and this step cannot be overlooked. For this reason, multidisciplinary collaboration is crucial, including with industry partners, data engineers, and biostatisticians with expertise in big data analytics.

Finally, researchers and clinicians using passive sensing technology must carefully consider ethical concerns of privacy, data security, and disparities in access. These issues are discussed in depth in the conclusion section of this chapter.

Future Directions

Cutting-edge passive sensing technology is gaining traction in many neuropsychological contexts as this method offers a comprehensive and fine-grained view into everyday functioning that complements our existing functional assessment tools. The power of this technology ultimately lies in the ability to monitor *multidomain within-person* change over time in person-specific behaviors that are not constrained by task instructions or limited to a set of activities that may or may not be relevant. With little to no added burden on patients/participants, this translates to a more efficient and individualized measurement approach for functional outcomes. Taking these passive sensing methods from research to clinical settings will require additional validation and development. Potential clinical applications include developing clinician portals where care teams can monitor patients' real-world behavior in real time to deliver just-in-time interventions. This would closely parallel existing infrastructures commonly used in other medical specialties, such as the routine integration of glucose, blood pressure, and sleep equipment monitoring metrics into electronic medical records (EMRs). In the context of early dementia detection, we may leverage advanced prediction algorithms that integrate passive data from commercially owned devices to upload a cognitive risk score into a patient's EMR, which could be used to flag individuals who would benefit from clinical referrals. If validated to have adequate sensitivity and specificity, this would yield an enormously beneficial, at-scale public health strategy to improve dementia screening. Additional future applications include using these real-time, real-world functional measurements as clinical trial endpoints to complement more conventional functional and cognitive outcome measures.

Conclusion

The integration of emerging technologies into neuropsychology represents a paradigm shift in how cognitive and everyday functioning is assessed, monitored, and treated. Emerging technologies such as VR, cognitive EMA, and passive sensing offer innovative approaches that address limitations of traditional neuropsychological methods, enhancing ecological validity, real-time tracking, and personalized assessment. We anticipate that with the fast pace of technology there will be additional emerging tools that neuropsychologists will need to be aware of, trained in, and potentially integrate into their practice. However, with these advancements come critical ethical considerations, challenges in clinical implementation, and questions about the future trajectory of neuropsychological practice. As technology continues to evolve rapidly, neuropsychologists must thoughtfully navigate issues of privacy, digital health equity, and training to maximize the benefits of these tools while ensuring responsible use.

Ethical Concerns: Balancing Innovation and Accessibility

Digital health equity remains a major challenge. Many emerging tools rely on personal device ownership, such as smartphones, and access to the Internet. Many studies have implemented a "bring your own device (BYOD)" paradigm, supplemented by provision of devices to those who do not have their own or whose device does not meet the standards necessary for the assessment technology. In these cases, we must be sensitive to disparities in access to technology and cautious about the conclusions we draw when using newly introduced and unfamiliar hardware. The most recent Pew Research from 2024 demonstrates that both Internet and smartphone use have increased with time, with 96% of U.S. adults reporting use of the Internet ("Internet, Broadband Fact Sheet," 2024), although this does not guarantee reliable access to the Internet, which is often required for more traditional teleneuropsychological assessments. Smartphone devices have become more universal, with 9 in 10 U.S. adults owning a smartphone ("Internet, Broadband Fact Sheet," 2024). However, other newer devices that may prove to be helpful in monitoring cognitive health are likely to have socioeconomic differences in accessibility. For example, there are clear trends for those who own a fitness tracker or smartwatch to be younger, have more education, and have higher socioeconomic status (Nagappan et al., 2024). These disparities highlight concerns that, without careful consideration, there will likely be inequalities among those who benefit from advancements in cognitive health monitoring.

Moreover, accessibility to technology does not equate to digital literacy or comfort with sharing of digital data. For example, the number of adults who are willing or interested in sharing digital data with their provider or for research varies widely and is associated with some sociodemographic factors (Shandhi et al., 2024; Tolentino et al., 2023). Some data types may be perceived as more invasive than others and may require higher levels of security assurance and explanation surrounding their clinical benefit. We highlight this to underscore again the clear need for discussion around privacy and confidentiality when it comes to emerging technologies and the need for clear consent for disclosure of this data. There are also unique data security concerns to prioritize on the back end. Compared with traditional neuropsychological data collected and stored locally during in person visits, real-world data captured from, for example, passive sensing and cognitive EMA are typically transferred wirelessly via Bluetooth and/or Internet. Beyond ensuring that these transfers utilize end-to-end encryption when implementing a new technology, a detailed protocol for secure data storage on device, data transfer, location of data storage after transfer, and data management (e.g., who has access) should be reviewed with and regularly updated by an IT/data security expert.

It is likely that there will continue to be sociodemographic differences in those with higher versus lower levels of digital literacy and comfort sharing digital cognitive data with providers. Thus, though technology may provide the ability to reach more people with cognitive concerns (e.g., screening, monitoring), it does not simply equate to equal use across groups. Without careful consideration of these differences, digital cognitive assessments risk exacerbating existing health disparities rather than reducing them. Furthermore, while technology could expand access to cognitive screening and remote monitoring and make neuropsychological assessment more efficient, it does not replace the expertise of a neuropsychologist in diagnosing and interpreting cognitive concerns. Importantly, access to neuropsychologists remains limited. Even if digital tools help identify individuals who may need further evaluation, they are only a first step in a process that still requires specialized clinical expertise—an area where access remains unequal. Thus, while emerging technologies hold promise for improving early detection and tracking of cognitive health, they must be implemented alongside broader efforts to expand access to neuropsychological services and ensure that those flagged for further assessment can receive the care they need.

Pace of Technological Development: Challenges for Clinical Practice and Training

The rapid evolution of technology presents both opportunities and challenges for neuropsychologists. While emerging tools have the potential to enhance cognitive assessment and intervention strategies, they also require clinicians to continually adapt to an ever-changing landscape. Historically, neuropsychology has relied on well-validated, standardized assessment tools, many of which have been in use for decades. The fast pace of technological change disrupts these traditional models, necessitating a shift in both clinical practice and training.

Even if neuropsychologists choose not to integrate these technologies into their own practice, they will still need to be well-informed as these tools become more mainstream. For instance, the rise of commercial online cognitive training programs has already required clinicians to evaluate the evidence base behind them and address patients' questions. Similarly, as digital tools for cognitive tracking and assessment become more accessible, patients may increasingly present self-collected data to their providers. Thus, neuropsychologists will need to determine whether such data have a strong scientific foundation, the advantages and potential risks or limitations, and whether it can be meaningfully incorporated into clinical decision-making.

Beyond working directly with patients, neuropsychologists must also educate their referral sources on the implications of these emerging technologies. Primary care and other health care providers may turn to neuropsychologists for guidance on interpreting new digital cognitive data, distinguishing between validated tools and unproven commercial products, and choosing new digital screening tools which may result in a referral for a neuropsychological assessment. Ensuring that health care professionals across disciplines are well-informed will be crucial in preventing misinterpretation or over-reliance on digital assessments that may lack clinical utility.

One of the key challenges in this technological shift is ensuring that neuropsychologists receive adequate training to interpret and integrate technologies relevant to neuropsychological practice. As emerging technologies become more prevalent, training programs must evolve to include training and hands-on experience in digital neuropsychology. Given the rapid pace of technological advancements, training may also need to be updated more frequently to keep pace with the field's changing landscape. This may include training in evaluation of a technology's evidence base; when they are and are not feasible, useful, and appropriate; risks and ethical considerations to promote privacy, confidentiality, and equitable cognitive health outcomes; and training in how to keep up with technological advances in general.

Beyond training, clinical adoption of new technologies is often hindered by logistical and financial constraints. Regulatory and reimbursement structures have not kept pace with technological advancements, leading to uncertainty about how digital assessments and interventions will be incorporated into standard clinical care. To address these barriers, future efforts should focus on demonstrating the added value of digital tools—both in terms of diagnostic accuracy and patient outcomes—to ensure their integration into health care is both feasible and beneficial.

Summary

Ultimately, emerging technologies to aid in cognitive assessment and intervention should complement, rather than replace, traditional neuropsychological testing. These tools hold promise for bridging the gap between clinical visits, more efficient and widespread cognitive screening, and allowing for real-time monitoring and earlier intervention before significant cognitive decline occurs. Additionally, technology could lead to the discovery of novel insights into factors impacting cognition in real-world environments, providing a more comprehensive understanding of patients' daily cognitive and functional challenges, thereby leading to more effective, individualized treatment plans. While the integration of emerging technologies into neuropsychology will require careful consideration, they offer an unprecedented opportunity to refine assessment methods and improve patient care in meaningful ways.

As technology continues to evolve, so, too, must neuropsychology. The challenge ahead is not merely to adopt new tools, but to do so in a way that maximizes their benefits while remaining firmly rooted in ethical, evidence-based practice. By embracing this shift with caution and curiosity, neuropsychologists can help shape a future in which digital tools enhance, rather than replace, the human-centered aspects of assessment and care.

References

Adams, J. L., Kangarloo, T., Tracey, B., O'Donnell, P., Volfson, D., Latzman, R. D., Zach, N., Alexander, R., Bergethon, P., Cosman, J., Anderson, D., Best, A., Severson, J., Kostrzebski, M. A., Auinger, P., Wilmot, P., Pohlson, Y., Waddell, E., Jensen-Roberts, S., ... Ray Dorsey, E. (2023). Using a smartwatch and smartphone to assess early Parkinson's disease in the WATCH-PD study. *NPJ Parkinson's Disease*, *9*(1), 1–10. https://doi.org/10.1038/s41531-023-00497-x

All of Us Research Program Investigators. (2019). The "All of Us" research program. *New England Journal of Medicine*, *381*(7), 668–676. https://doi.org/10.1056/NEJMsr1809937

Allard, M., Husky, M., Catheline, G., Pelletier, A., Dilharreguy, B., Amieva, H., Pérès, K., Foubert-Samier, A., Dartigues, J.-F., & Swendsen, J. (2014). Mobile technologies in the early detection of cognitive decline. *PLOS ONE, 9*(12), e112197. https://doi.org/10.1371/journal.pone.0112197

Anderson, E. D., Wahoske, M., Huber, M., Norton, D., Li, Z., Koscik, R. L., Umucu, E., Johnson, S. C., Jones, J., Asthana, S., Gleason, C. E., & Alzheimer's Disease Neuroimaging Initiative. (2016). Cognitive variability—A marker for incident MCI and AD: An analysis for the Alzheimer's Disease Neuroimaging Initiative. *Alzheimer's & Dementia: Diagnosis, Assessment & Disease Monitoring, 4*(1), 47–55. https://doi.org/10.1016/j.dadm.2016.05.003

Aschenbrenner, A. J., Hassenstab, J., Morris, J. C., Cruchaga, C., & Jackson, J. J. (2024). Relationships between hourly cognitive variability and risk of Alzheimer's disease revealed with mixed-effects location scale models. *Neuropsychology, 38*(1), 69–80. https://doi.org/10.1037/neu0000905

Aschenbrenner, A. J., Murphy, S. A., Doherty, J. M., Johnson, A. M., Bayat, S., Walker, A., Peña, Y., Hassenstab, J., Morris, J. C., & Babulal, G. M. (2022). Neuropsychological correlates of changes in driving behavior among clinically healthy older adults. *The Journals of Gerontology: Series B, 77*(10), 1769–1778. https://doi.org/10.1093/geronb/gbac101

Au, R., Lin, H., Christianson, K., & Brunner, D. (2023). Wearable and digital technology tools: Neuropsychological assessment, monitoring, and diagnosis in the digital era. In *APA handbook of neuropsychology: Neuroscience and neuromethods*, Vol. 2 (pp. 259–274). American Psychological Association. https://doi.org/10.1037/0000308-012

Au, R., Popp, Z. T., Low, S., Hwang, P. H., De Anda-Duran, I., Li, S., Rahman, S., Ding, H., Igwe, A., Karjadi, C., Ang, T. F. A., Devine, S. A., Gurnani, A. S., Mez, J. B., Farrer, L. A., Sunderaraman, P., Lin, H., & Kolachalama, V. B. (2023). Digital is the new blood: Enabling the present and the future. *Alzheimer's & Dementia, 19*(S21), e078220. https://doi.org/10.1002/alz.078220

Bagot, K. S., Matthews, S. A., Mason, M., Squeglia, L. M., Fowler, J., Gray, K., Herting, M., May, A., Colrain, I., Godino, J., Tapert, S., Brown, S., & Patrick, K. (2018). Current, future and potential use of mobile and wearable technologies and social media data in the ABCD study to increase understanding of contributors to child health. *Developmental Cognitive Neuroscience, 32*, 121–129. https://doi.org/10.1016/j.dcn.2018.03.008

Bayat, S., Babulal, G. M., Schindler, S. E., Fagan, A. M., Morris, J. C., Mihailidis, A., & Roe, C. M. (2021). GPS driving: A digital biomarker for preclinical Alzheimer disease. *Alzheimer's Research & Therapy, 13*(1), 115. https://doi.org/10.1186/s13195-021-00852-1

Beattie, Z., Miller, L. M., Almirola, C., Au-Yeung, W.-T. M., Bernard, H., Cosgrove, K. E., Dodge, H. H., Gamboa, C. J., Golonka, O., Gothard, S., Harbison, S., Irish, S., Kornfeld, J., Lee, J., Marcoe, J., Mattek, N. C., Quinn, C., Reynolds, C., Riley, T., ...

Kaye, J. (2020). The collaborative aging research using technology initiative: An open, sharable, technology-agnostic platform for the research community. *Digital Biomarkers, 4*(Suppl. 1), 100–118. https://doi.org/10.1159/000512208

Bilder, R. M. (2011). Neuropsychology 3.0: Evidence-based science and practice. *Journal of the International Neuropsychological Society, 17*(1), 7–13. https://doi.org/10.1017/S1355617710001396

Bilder, R. M., & Reise, S. P. (2019). Neuropsychological tests of the future: How do we get there from here? *The Clinical Neuropsychologist, 33*(2), 220–245. https://doi.org/10.1080/13854046.2018.1521993

Bloem, B. R., Marks, W. J., Silva de Lima, A. L., Kuijf, M. L., van Laar, T., Jacobs, B. P. F., Verbeek, M. M., Helmich, R. C., van de Warrenburg, B. P., Evers, L. J. W., intHout, J., van de Zande, T., Snyder, T. M., Kapur, R., & Meinders, M. J. (2019). The Personalized Parkinson Project: Examining disease progression through broad biomarkers in early Parkinson's disease. *BMC Neurology, 19*(1), 160. https://doi.org/10.1186/s12883-019-1394-3

Boonstra, T. W., Werner-Seidler, A., O'Dea, B., Larsen, M. E., & Christensen, H. (2017). Smartphone app to investigate the relationship between social connectivity and mental health. In *2017 39th Annual International Conference of the IEEE Engineering in Medicine and Biology Society (EMBC)* (pp. 287–290). https://doi.org/10.1109/EMBC.2017.8036818

Bouvard, A., Dupuy, M., Schweitzer, P., Revranche, M., Fatseas, M., Serre, F., Misdrahi, D., Auriacombe, M., & Swendsen, J. (2018). Feasibility and validity of mobile cognitive testing in patients with substance use disorders and healthy controls. *The American Journal on Addictions, 27*(7), 553–556. https://doi.org/10.1111/ajad.12804

Brickman, A. M., Cabo, R., & Manly, J. J. (2006). Ethical issues in cross-cultural neuropsychology. *Applied Neuropsychology, 13*(2), 91–100. https://doi.org/10.1207/s15324826an1302_4

Buchman, A. S., Boyle, P. A., Yu, L., Shah, R. C., Wilson, R. S., & Bennett, D. A. (2012). Total daily physical activity and the risk of AD and cognitive decline in older adults. *Neurology, 78*(17), 1323–1329. https://doi.org/10.1212/WNL.0b013e3182535d35

Bufano, P., Laurino, M., Said, S., Tognetti, A., & Menicucci, D. (2023). Digital phenotyping for monitoring mental disorders: Systematic review. *Journal of Medical Internet Research, 25*(1), e46778. https://doi.org/10.2196/46778

Burton, C. L., Strauss, E., Hultsch, D. F., Moll, A., & Hunter, M. A. (2006). Intraindividual variability as a marker of neurological dysfunction: A comparison of Alzheimer's disease and Parkinson's disease. *Journal of Clinical and Experimental Neuropsychology, 28*(1), 67–83. https://doi.org/10.1080/13803390490918318

Buxbaum, L. J., Palermo, M. A., Mastrogiovanni, D., Read, M. S., Rosenberg-Pitonyak, E., Rizzo, A. A., & and Coslett, H. B. (2008). Assessment of spatial attention and neglect with a virtual wheelchair navigation task. *Journal of Clinical and Experimental Neuropsychology, 30*(6), 650–660. https://doi.org/10.1080/13803390701625821

Byrd, D. A., & Rivera-Mindt, M. G. (2022). Neuropsychology's race problem does not begin or end with demographically adjusted norms. *Nature Reviews. Neurology, 18*(3), 125–126. https://doi.org/10.1038/s41582-021-00607-4

Campbell, L. M., Paolillo, E. W., Heaton, A., Tang, B., Depp, C. A., Granholm, E., Heaton, R. K., Swendsen, J., Moore, D. J., & Moore, R. C. (2020). Daily activities related to mobile cognitive performance in middle-aged and older adults: An ecological momentary cognitive assessment study. *JMIR mHealth and uHealth, 8*(9), e19579. https://doi.org/10.2196/19579

Cerino, E. S., Katz, M. J., Wang, C., Qin, J., Gao, Q., Hyun, J., Hakun, J. G., Roque, N. A., Derby, C. A., Lipton, R. B., & Sliwinski, M. J. (2021). Variability in cognitive performance on mobile devices is sensitive to mild cognitive impairment: Results from the Einstein Aging Study. *Frontiers in Digital Health, 3*, 758031. https://doi.org/10.3389/fdgth.2021.758031

Chang, E., Kim, H. T., & and Yoo, B. (2020). Virtual reality sickness: A review of causes and measurements. *International Journal of Human–Computer Interaction, 36*(17), 1658–1682. https://doi.org/10.1080/10447318.2020.1778351

Chanmas, G., Taveekitworachai, P., Paliyawan, P., Thawonmas, R., Thawonmas, R., Nukoolkit, C., & Dajpratham, P. (2023). Driving scenarios and environmental settings in simulator-based driving assessment systems for stroke: A systematic review. *Topics in Stroke Rehabilitation, 30*(8), 872–880. https://doi.org/10.1080/10749357.2023.2165273

Charalambous, A. P., Pye, A., Yeung, W. K., Leroi, I., Neil, M., Thodi, C., & Dawes, P. (2020). Tools for app- and web-based self-testing of cognitive impairment: Systematic search and evaluation. *Journal of Medical Internet Research, 22*(1), e14551. https://doi.org/10.2196/14551

Chaytor, N. S., & Mascarenhas Fonseca, L. (2022). Ambulatory assessment. In T.D. Marcottte, M. Schmitter-Edgecombe, & I. Grant (Eds.), *Neuropsychology of everyday functioning* (2nd ed., pp. 311–335). Guilford Press.

Chaytor, N., & Schmitter-Edgecombe, M. (2003). The ecological validity of neuropsychological tests: A review of the literature on everyday cognitive skills. *Neuropsychology Review, 13*(4), 181–197. https://doi.org/10.1023/B:NERV.0000009483.91468.fb

Chen, M. H., Leow, A., Ross, M. K., DeLuca, J., Chiaravalloti, N., Costa, S. L., Genova, H. M., Weber, E., Hussain, F., & Demos, A. P. (2022). Associations between smartphone keystroke dynamics and cognition in MS. *Digital Health, 8*, 20552076221143234. https://doi.org/10.1177/20552076221143234

Chen, R., Jankovic, F., Marinsek, N., Foschini, L., Kourtis, L., Signorini, A., Pugh, M., Shen, J., Yaari, R., Maljkovic, V., & others. (2019). Developing measures of cognitive impairment in the real world from consumer-grade multimodal sensor streams. In *Proceedings of the 25th ACM SIGKDD International Conference on Knowledge Discovery & Data Mining* (pp. 2145–2155).

Claudio, P., & Maddalena, P. (2014). Overview: Virtual reality in medicine. *Journal of Virtual Worlds Research, 7*(1). https://doi.org/10.4101/jvwr.v7i1.6364

Cook, D. J., Schmitter-Edgecombe, M., & Dawadi, P. (2015). Analyzing activity behavior and movement in a naturalistic environment using smart home techniques. *IEEE Journal of Biomedical and Health Informatics, 19*(6), 1882–1892. https://doi.org/10.1109/JBHI.2015.2461659

Cullen, A., Mazhar, M. K. A., Smith, M. D., Lithander, F. E., Ó Breasail, M., & Henderson, E. J. (2022). Wearable and portable GPS solutions for monitoring mobility in dementia: A systematic review. *Sensors, 22*(9), Article 9. https://doi.org/10.3390/s22093336

Dodge, H. H., Mattek, N. C., Austin, D., Hayes, T. L., & Kaye, J. A. (2012). In-home walking speeds and variability trajectories associated with mild cognitive impairment. *Neurology, 78*(24), 1946–1952. https://doi.org/10.1212/WNL.0b013e318259e1de

Doherty, A., Jackson, D., Hammerla, N., Plötz, T., Olivier, P., Granat, M. H., White, T., Hees, V. T. van, Trenell, M. I., Owen, C. G., Preece, S. J., Gillions, R., Sheard, S., Peakman, T., Brage, S., & Wareham, N. J. (2017). Large scale population assessment of physical activity using wrist worn accelerometers: The UK Biobank Study. *PLOS ONE, 12*(2), e0169649. https://doi.org/10.1371/journal.pone.0169649

Fields, S. M., & Unsworth, C. A. (2017). Revision of the competency standards for occupational therapy driver assessors: An overview of the evidence for the inclusion of cognitive and perceptual assessments within fitness-to-drive evaluations. *Australian Occupational Therapy Journal, 64*(4), 328–339. https://doi.org/10.1111/1440-1630.12379

Fonseca, L. M., Hawks, Z. W., Beeri, M. S., Jung, L., Kudva, Y., Rizvi, S., Bulger, J., Grinspoon, E., Janess, K., & Sliwinski, M. J. (2025). Cognitive vulnerability to glucose fluctuations: A digital phenotype of neurodegeneration. *Alzheimer's & Dementia, 21*(2), e70001.

Fonseca, L. M., Strong, R. W., Singh, S., Bulger, J. D., Cleveland, M., Grinspoon, E., Janess, K., Jung, L., Miller, K., Passell, E., Ressler, K., Sliwinski, M. J., Verdejo, A., Weinstock, R. S., Germine, L., & Chaytor, N. S. (2023). Glycemic variability and fluctuations in cognitive status in adults with type 1 diabetes (GluCog): Observational study using ecological momentary assessment of cognition. *JMIR Diabetes, 8*, e39750. https://doi.org/10.2196/39750

Gammeri, R., Léonard, J., Toupet, M., Hautefort, C., van Nechel, C., Besnard, S., Machado, M.-L., Nakul, E., Montava, M., Lavieille, J.-P., & Lopez, C. (2022). Navigation strategies in patients with vestibular loss tested in a virtual reality T-maze. *Journal of Neurology, 269*(8), 4333–4348. https://doi.org/10.1007/s00415-022-11069-z

Germine, L., Reinecke, K., & Chaytor, N. S. (2019). Digital neuropsychology: Challenges and opportunities at the intersection of science and software. *The Clinical Neuropsychologist, 33*(2), 271–286. https://doi.org/10.1080/13854046.2018.1535662

Giovannetti, T., Hackett, K., Tassoni, M., Mis, R., & Simone, S. (2022). APA handbook of neuropsychology. In *Assessing and predicting everyday function* (Vol. 2). American Psychological Association. https://www.apa.org/pubs/books/apa-handbook-of-neuropsychology?tab=2

Hackett, K., & Giovannetti, T. (2022). Capturing cognitive aging in vivo: Application of a neuropsychological framework for emerging digital tools. *JMIR Aging, 5*(3), e38130. https://doi.org/10.2196/38130

Hackett, K., Xu, S., McKniff, M., Paglia, L., Barnett, I., & Giovannetti, T. (2024). Mobility-based smartphone digital phenotypes for unobtrusively capturing everyday cognition, mood, and community life-space in older adults: Feasibility, acceptability, and preliminary validity study. *JMIR Human Factors, 11*(1), e59974. https://doi.org/10.2196/59974

Harris, C., Tang, Y., Birnbaum, E., Cherian, C., Mendhe, D., & Chen, M. H. (2024). Digital neuropsychology beyond computerized cognitive assessment: Applications of novel digital technologies. *Archives of Clinical Neuropsychology, 39*(3), 290–304. https://doi.org/10.1093/arclin/acae016

Hawks, Z. W., Beck, E. D., Jung, L., Fonseca, L. M., Sliwinski, M. J., Weinstock, R. S., Grinspoon, E., Xu, I., Strong, R. W., Singh, S., Van Dongen, H. P. A., Frumkin, M. R., Bulger, J., Cleveland, M. J., Janess, K., Kudva, Y. C., Pratley, R., Rickels, M. R., Rizvi, S. R., … Germine, L. T. (2024). Dynamic associations between glucose and ecological momentary cognition in type 1 diabetes. *NPJ Digital Medicine, 7*(1), 59. https://doi.org/10.1038/s41746-024-01036-5

Henneghan, A. M., Paolillo, E. W., Van Dyk, K. M., Franco-Rocha, O. Y., Bang, S., Tasker, R., Kaufmann, T., Haywood, D., Hart, N. H., & Moore, R. C. (2025). Feasibility and psychometric quality of smartphone administered cognitive ecological momentary assessments in women with metastatic breast cancer. *Digital Health, 11*, 20552076241310474. https://doi.org/10.1177/20552076241310474

Hyun, J., Sliwinski, M. J., & Smyth, J. M. (2019). Waking up on the wrong side of the bed: The effects of stress anticipation on working memory in daily life. *The Journals of Gerontology: Series B, 74*(1), 38–46. https://doi.org/10.1093/geronb/gby042

Internet, Broadband Fact Sheet. (2024, November 13). *Pew Research Center*. https://www.pewresearch.org/internet/fact-sheet/internet-broadband/

Kaye, J., Mattek, N., Dodge, H. H., Campbell, I., Hayes, T., Austin, D., Hatt, W., Wild, K., Jimison, H., & Pavel, M. (2014). Unobtrusive measurement of daily computer use to detect mild cognitive impairment. *Alzheimer's & Dementia, 10*(1), 10–17. https://doi.org/10.1016/j.jalz.2013.01.011

Kirkham, R., Kooijman, L., Albertella, L., Myles, D., Yücel, M., & Rotaru, K. (2024). Immersive virtual reality–based methods for assessing executive functioning: Systematic review. *JMIR Serious Games, 12*(1), e50282. https://doi.org/10.2196/50282

Korner-Bitensky, N., Bitensky, J., Sofer, S., Man-Son-Hing, M., & Gelinas, I. (2006). Driving evaluation practices of clinicians working in the United States and Canada. *The American Journal of Occupational Therapy, 60*(4), 428–434. https://doi.org/10.5014/ajot.60.4.428

Krasniuk, S., Knott, M., Bagajati, R., Azizderouei, M., Sultania, R., & Alvarez, L. (2022). Utilizing driving simulators for persons with multiple sclerosis: A scoping review.

Transportation Research Part F: Traffic Psychology and Behaviour, 85, 103–118. https://doi.org/10.1016/j.trf.2021.12.006

Leaning, I. E., Ikani, N., Savage, H. S., Leow, A., Beckmann, C., Ruhé, H. G., & Marquand, A. F. (2024). From smartphone data to clinically relevant predictions: A systematic review of digital phenotyping methods in depression. *Neuroscience & Biobehavioral Reviews, 158*, 105541. https://doi.org/10.1016/j.neubiorev.2024.105541

Lele, A. (2013). Virtual reality and its military utility. *Journal of Ambient Intelligence and Humanized Computing, 4*(1), 17–26. https://doi.org/10.1007/s12652-011-0052-4

Liao, Y., Skelton, K., Dunton, G., & Bruening, M. (2016). A systematic review of methods and procedures used in ecological momentary assessments of diet and physical activity research in youth: An adapted STROBE Checklist for reporting EMA studies (CREMAS). *Journal of Medical Internet Research, 18*(6), e4954. https://doi.org/10.2196/jmir.4954

Marcotte, T. D., Wolfson, T., Rosenthal, T. J., Heaton, R. K., Gonzalez, R., Ellis, R. J., Grant, I., & the HIV Neurobehavioral Research Center Group. (2004). A multimodal assessment of driving performance in HIV infection. *Neurology, 63*(8), 1417–1422. https://doi.org/10.1212/01.WNL.0000141920.33580.5D

Matheis, R. J., Schultheis, M. T., Tiersky, L. A., DeLuca, J., Millis, S. R., & and Rizzo, A. (2007). Is learning and memory different in a virtual environment? *The Clinical Neuropsychologist, 21*(1), 146–161. https://doi.org/10.1080/13854040601100668

Melillo, P., Orrico, A., Scala, P., Crispino, F., & Pecchia, L. (2015). Cloud-based smart health monitoring system for automatic cardiovascular and fall risk assessment in hypertensive patients. *Journal of Medical Systems, 39*(10), 109. https://doi.org/10.1007/s10916-015-0294-3

Miller, J. B., & Barr, W. B. (2017). The technology crisis in neuropsychology. *Archives of Clinical Neuropsychology, 32*(5), 541–554. https://doi.org/10.1093/arclin/acx050

Moore, R. C., Ackerman, R. A., Russell, M. T., Campbell, L. M., Depp, C. A., Harvey, P. D., & Pinkham, A. E. (2022). Feasibility and validity of ecological momentary cognitive testing among older adults with mild cognitive impairment. *Frontiers in Digital Health, 4*. https://doi.org/10.3389/fdgth.2022.946685

Moore, R. C., Campbell, L. M., Delgadillo, J. D., Paolillo, E. W., Sundermann, E. E., Holden, J., Schweitzer, P., Heaton, R. K., & Swendsen, J. (2020). Smartphone-based measurement of executive function in older adults with and without HIV. *Archives of Clinical Neuropsychology, 35*(4), 347–357. https://doi.org/10.1093/arclin/acz084

Moore, R. C., Swendsen, J., & Depp, C. A. (2017). Applications for self-administered mobile cognitive assessments in clinical research: A systematic review. *International Journal of Methods in Psychiatric Research, 26*(4), e1562. https://doi.org/10.1002/mpr.1562

Nagappan, A., Krasniansky, A., & Knowles, M. (2024). Patterns of ownership and usage of wearable devices in the United States, 2020–2022: Survey study. *Journal of Medical Internet Research, 26*, e56504.

Nicosia, J., Aschenbrenner, A. J., Balota, D. A., Sliwinski, M. J., Tahan, M., Adams, S., Stout, S. S., Wilks, H., Gordon, B. A., Benzinger, T. L. S., Fagan, A. M., Xiong, C., Bateman, R. J., Morris, J. C., & Hassenstab, J. (2023). Unsupervised high-frequency smartphone-based cognitive assessments are reliable, valid, and feasible in older adults at risk for Alzheimer's disease. *Journal of the International Neuropsychological Society*, *29*(5), 459–471. https://doi.org/10.1017/S135561772200042X

Onnela, J.-P. (2021). Opportunities and challenges in the collection and analysis of digital phenotyping data. *Neuropsychopharmacology*, *46*(1), 45–54. https://doi.org/10.1038/s41386-020-0771-3

Onnela, J.-P., & Rauch, S. L. (2016). Harnessing smartphone-based digital phenotyping to enhance behavioral and mental health. *Neuropsychopharmacology*, *41*(7), 1691–1696. https://doi.org/10.1038/npp.2016.7

Or, C., & Tao, D. (2016). A 3-month randomized controlled pilot trial of a patient-centered, computer-based self-monitoring system for the care of type 2 diabetes mellitus and hypertension. *Journal of Medical Systems*, *40*(4), 81. https://doi.org/10.1007/s10916-016-0437-1

Paolillo, E. W., Casaletto, K. B., Clark, A. L., Taylor, J. C., Heuer, H. W., Wise, A. B., Dhanam, S., Sanderson-Cimino, M., Saloner, R., Kramer, J. H., Kornak, J., Kremers, W., Forsberg, L., Appleby, B., Bayram, E., Bozoki, A., Brushaber, D., Darby, R. R., Day, G. S., ... ALLFTD Consortium. (2024). Examining associations between smartphone use and clinical severity in frontotemporal dementia: Proof-of-concept study. *JMIR Aging*, *7*, e52831. https://doi.org/10.2196/52831

Parrish, E. M., Kamarsu, S., Harvey, P. D., Pinkham, A., Depp, C. A., & Moore, R. C. (2021). Remote ecological momentary testing of learning and memory in adults with serious mental illness. *Schizophrenia Bulletin*, *47*(3), 740–750. https://doi.org/10.1093/schbul/sbaa172

Parsons, T. D. (2015). Virtual reality for enhanced ecological validity and experimental control in the clinical, affective and social neurosciences. *Frontiers in Human Neuroscience*, 9. https://doi.org/10.3389/fnhum.2015.00660

Parsons, T., & Duffield, T. (2020). Paradigm shift toward digital neuropsychology and high-dimensional neuropsychological assessments: Review. *Journal of Medical Internet Research*, *22*(12), e23777. https://doi.org/10.2196/23777

Patrick, K. E., Schultheis, Maria T., Agate, F. Taylor, McCurdy, Mark D., Daly, Brian P., Tarazi, Reem A., Chute, Douglas L., & Hurewitz, F. (2020). Executive function "drives" differences in simulated driving performance between young adults with and without autism spectrum disorder. *Child Neuropsychology*, *26*(5), 649–665. https://doi.org/10.1080/09297049.2020.1713311

Pieri, L., Tosi, G., & Romano, D. (2023). Virtual reality technology in neuropsychological testing: A systematic review. *Journal of neuropsychology*, *17*(2), 382–399. https://doi.org/10.1111/jnp.12304

Podsakoff, P. M., MacKenzie, S. B., Lee, J.-Y., & Podsakoff, N. P. (2003). Common method biases in behavioral research: A critical review of the literature and recommended remedies. *Journal of Applied Psychology, 88*(5), 879–903. https://doi.org/10.1037/0021-9010.88.5.879

Rabin, L. A., Paolillo, E., & Barr, W. B. (2016). Stability in test-usage practices of clinical neuropsychologists in the United States and Canada over a 10-year period: A follow-up survey of INS and NAN members. *Archives of Clinical Neuropsychology, 31*(3), 206–230. https://doi.org/10.1093/arclin/acw007

Ramsey, A. T., Wetherell, J. L., Depp, C., Dixon, D., & Lenze, E. (2016). Feasibility and acceptability of smartphone assessment in older adults with cognitive and emotional difficulties. *Journal of Technology in Human Services, 34*(2), 209–223. https://doi.org/10.1080/15228835.2016.1170649

Ray, M. K., Fleming, J., Aschenbrenner, A., Hassenstab, J., Redwine, B., Burns, C., Arbelaez, A. M., Vajravelu, M. E., & Hershey, T. (2025). Assessing dynamic cognitive function in the daily lives of youths with and without type 1 diabetes: Usability study. *JMIR Formative Research, 9*, e60275.

Rizzo, A. A., Buckwalter, J. G., Bowerly, T., Van Der Zaag, C., Humphrey, L., Neumann, U., Chua, C., Kyriakakis, C., Van Rooyen, A., & Sisemore, D. (2000). The virtual classroom: A virtual reality environment for the assessment and rehabilitation of attention deficits. *CyberPsychology & Behavior, 3*(3), 483–499. https://doi.org/10.1089/10949310050078940

Rizzo, A. A., Schultheis, M., Kerns, K. A., & Mateer, C. (2004). Analysis of assets for virtual reality applications in neuropsychology. *Neuropsychological rehabilitation, 14*(1-2), 207-239. https://doi.org/10.1080/09602010343000183

Ross, M. K., Demos, A. P., Zulueta, J., Piscitello, A., Langenecker, S. A., McInnis, M., Ajilore, O., Nelson, P. C., Ryan, K. A., & Leow, A. (2021). Naturalistic smartphone keyboard typing reflects processing speed and executive function. *Brain and Behavior, 11*(11), e2363. https://doi.org/10.1002/brb3.2363

Rykov, Y. G., Patterson, M. D., Gangwar, B. A., Jabar, S. B., Leonardo, J., Ng, K. P., & Kandiah, N. (2024). Predicting cognitive scores from wearable-based digital physiological features using machine learning: Data from a clinical trial in mild cognitive impairment. *BMC Medicine, 22*(1), 36. https://doi.org/10.1186/s12916-024-03252-y

Schultheis, M. T., & Chute, D. L. (1999). An ecologically valid driving assessment program: The neurocognitive driving test. *Archives of Clinical Neuropsychology, 14*(8), 794–795. https://doi.org/10.1093/arclin/14.8.794a

Schultheis, M. T., Himelstein, J., & Rizzo, A. A. (2002). Virtual reality and neuropsychology: Upgrading the current tools. *The Journal of Head Trauma Rehabilitation, 17*(5), 378.

Schultheis, M. T., & Mourant, R. R. (2001). Virtual reality and driving: The road to better assessment for cognitively impaired populations. *Presence, 10*(4), 431–439. https://doi.org/10.1162/1054746011470271

Schultheis, M. T., & Rizzo, A. A. (2001). The application of virtual reality technology in rehabilitation. *Rehabilitation psychology, 46*(3), 296. https://doi.org/10.1037/0090-5550.46.3.296

Schweitzer, P., Husky, M., Allard, M., Amieva, H., Pérès, K., Foubert-Samier, A., Dartigues, J.-F., & Swendsen, J. (2017). Feasibility and validity of mobile cognitive testing in the investigation of age-related cognitive decline. *International Journal of Methods in Psychiatric Research, 26*(3), e1521. https://doi.org/10.1002/mpr.1521

Shandhi, M. M. H., Singh, K., Janson, N., Ashar, P., Singh, G., Lu, B., Hillygus, D. S., Maddocks, J. M., & Dunn, J. P. (2024). Assessment of ownership of smart devices and the acceptability of digital health data sharing. *NPJ Digital Medicine, 7*(1), 44.

Shiffman, S., Stone, A. A., & Hufford, M. R. (2008). Ecological momentary assessment. *Annual Review of Clinical Psychology, 4*, 1–32. https://doi.org/10.1146/annurev.clinpsy.3.022806.091415

Singh, N. B., & Björling, E. A. (2019). A review of EMA assessment period reporting for mood variables in substance use research: Expanding existing EMA guidelines. *Addictive Behaviors, 94*, 133–146. https://doi.org/10.1016/j.addbeh.2019.01.033

Singh, S., Strong, R., Xu, I., Fonseca, L. M., Hawks, Z., Grinspoon, E., Jung, L., Li, F., Weinstock, R. S., Sliwinski, M. J., Chaytor, N. S., & Germine, L. T. (2023). Ecological momentary assessment of cognition in clinical and community samples: Reliability and validity study. *Journal of Medical Internet Research, 25*(1), e45028. https://doi.org/10.2196/45028

Singh, S., Strong, R. W., Jung, L., Li, F. H., Grinspoon, L., Scheuer, L. S., Passell, E. J., Martini, P., Chaytor, N., Soble, J. R., & and Germine, L. (2021). The TestMyBrain digital neuropsychology toolkit: Development and psychometric characteristics. *Journal of Clinical and Experimental Neuropsychology, 43*(8), 786–795. https://doi.org/10.1080/13803395.2021.2002269

Sliwinski, M., Hoffman, L., & Hofer, S. (2010). Modeling retest and aging effects in a measurement burst design. In P. C. M. Molenaar & K. M. Newell (Eds.), *Individual pathways of change: Statistical models for analyzing learning and development* (pp. 37–50). American Psychological Association. https://doi.org/10.1037/12140-003

Smith, M. T., McCrae, C. S., Cheung, J., Martin, J. L., Harrod, C. G., Heald, J. L., & Carden, K. A. (2018). Use of actigraphy for the evaluation of sleep disorders and circadian rhythm sleep-wake disorders: An American Academy of Sleep Medicine systematic review, meta-analysis, and GRADE assessment. *Journal of Clinical Sleep Medicine, 14*(7), 1209–1230. https://doi.org/10.5664/jcsm.7228

Staffaroni, A. M., Clark, A. L., Taylor, J. C., Heuer, H. W., Sanderson-Cimino, M., Wise, A. B., Dhanam, S., Cobigo, Y., Wolf, A., Manoochehri, M., Forsberg, L., Mester, C., Rankin, K. P., Appleby, B. S., Bayram, E., Bozoki, A., Clark, D., Darby, R. R., Domoto-Reilly, K., … ALLFTD Consortium. (2024). Reliability and validity of smartphone cognitive testing for frontotemporal lobar degeneration. *JAMA Network Open, 7*(4), e244266. https://doi.org/10.1001/jamanetworkopen.2024.4266

Stoeckel, L. E., Fazio, E. M., Hardy, K. K., Kidwiler, N., McLinden, K. A., & Williams, B. (2025). Clinically meaningful outcomes in Alzheimer's disease and Alzheimer's disease related dementias trials. *Alzheimer's & Dementia: Translational Research & Clinical Interventions, 11*(1), e70058. https://doi.org/10.1002/trc2.70058

Stone, A. A., Schneider, S., & Smyth, J. M. (2023). Evaluation of pressing issues in ecological momentary assessment. *Annual Review of Clinical Psychology, 19*, 107–131. https://doi.org/10.1146/annurev-clinpsy-080921-083128

Tan, Y. W., Burgess, G. H., & Green, R. J. (2021). The effects of acculturation on neuropsychological test performance: A systematic literature review. *The Clinical Neuropsychologist, 35*(3), 541–571. https://doi.org/10.1080/13854046.2020.1714740

Thomas, N. W., Beattie, Z., Riley, T., Hofer, S., & Kaye, J. (2021). Home-based assessment of cognition and health measures: The Collaborative Aging Research Using Technology (CART) Initiative and international collaborations. *IEEE Instrumentation & Measurement Magazine, 24*(6), 68–78. https://doi.org/10.1109/MIM.2021.9513638

Tolentino, D. A., Costa, D. K., & Jiang, Y. (2023). Determinants of American adults' use of digital health and willingness to share health data to providers, family, and social media: A cross-sectional study. *CIN: Computers, Informatics, Nursing, 41*(11), 892. https://doi.org/10.1097/CIN.0000000000001025

Torous, J., Kiang, M. V., Lorme, J., & Onnela, J.-P. (2016). New tools for new research in psychiatry: A scalable and customizable platform to empower data driven smartphone research. *JMIR Mental Health, 3*(2), e16. https://doi.org/10.2196/mental.5165

Uswatte, G., & Schultheis, M. T. (2010). Real and virtual tools for objectively measuring function during everyday activities. In *Rehabilitation and health assessment: Applying ICF guidelines* (pp. 121–139). Springer.

Vaughan, A. C., & Birney, D. P. (2024). Ecological cognitive assessment has incremental validity for predicting academic performance over and above single occasion cognitive assessments. *Intelligence, 107*, 101869. https://doi.org/10.1016/j.intell.2024.101869

Wadley, V. G., Bull, T. P., Zhang, Y., Barba, C., Bryan, R. N., Crowe, M., Desiderio, L., Deutsch, G., Erus, G., Geldmacher, D. S., Go, R., Lassen-Greene, C. L., Mamaeva, O. A., Marson, D. C., McLaughlin, M., Nasrallah, I. M., Owsley, C., Passler, J., Perry, R. T., ... Kennedy, R. E. (2021). Cognitive processing speed is strongly related to driving skills, financial abilities, and other instrumental activities of daily living in persons with mild cognitive impairment and mild dementia. *The Journals of Gerontology: Series A, 76*(10), 1829–1838. https://doi.org/10.1093/gerona/glaa312

Wang, H., Zhao, Y., Yu, L., Liu, J., Zwetsloot, I. M., Cabrera, J., & Tsui, K.-L. (2020). A personalized health monitoring system for community-dwelling elderly people in Hong Kong: Design, implementation, and evaluation study. *Journal of Medical Internet Research, 22*(9), e19223. https://doi.org/10.2196/19223

Weizenbaum, E. L., Fulford, D., Torous, J., Pinsky, E., Kolachalama, V. B., & Cronin-Golomb, A. (2022). Smartphone-based neuropsychological assessment in Parkinson's disease: Feasibility, validity, and contextually driven variability in cognition. *Journal of the International Neuropsychological Society*, *28*(4), 401–413. https://doi.org/10.1017/S1355617721000503

Wilks, H. M., Welhaf, M. S., Aschenbrenner, A. J., Cruchaga, C., Morris, J. C., & Hassenstab, J. J. (2024). Examining practice effects at multiple retest intervals in older adults at risk for Alzheimer's disease. *Alzheimer's & Dementia*, *20*(S3), e086319. https://doi.org/10.1002/alz.086319

Winer, J. R., Lok, R., Weed, L., He, Z., Poston, K. L., Mormino, E. C., & Zeitzer, J. M. (2024). Impaired 24-h activity patterns are associated with an increased risk of Alzheimer's disease, Parkinson's disease, and cognitive decline. *Alzheimer's Research & Therapy*, *16*(1), 35. https://doi.org/10.1186/s13195-024-01411-0

Wolfe, P. L., & Lehockey, K. A. (2016). Neuropsychological assessment of driving capacity. *Archives of Clinical Neuropsychology*, *31*(6), 517–529. https://doi.org/10.1093/arclin/acw050

Wrzus, C., & Neubauer, A. B. (2023). Ecological momentary assessment: A meta-analysis on designs, samples, and compliance across research fields. *Assessment*, *30*(3), 825–846. https://doi.org/10.1177/10731911211067538

Yang, Y. S., Ryu, G. W., & Choi, M. (2019). Methodological strategies for ecological momentary assessment to evaluate mood and stress in adult patients using mobile phones: Systematic review. *JMIR mHealth and uHealth*, *7*(4), e11215. https://doi.org/10.2196/11215

Yilmaz, T., Foster, R., & Hao, Y. (2010). Detecting vital signs with wearable wireless sensors. *Sensors*, *10*(12), Article 12. https://doi.org/10.3390/s101210837

Zlatar, Z. Z., Campbell, L. M., Tang, B., Gabin, S., Heaton, A., Higgins, M., Swendsen, J., Moore, D. J., & Moore, R. C. (2022). Daily level association of physical activity and performance on ecological momentary cognitive tests in free-living environments: A mobile health observational study. *JMIR mHealth and uHealth*, *10*(1), e33747. https://doi.org/10.2196/33747

Zuniga-Kennedy, M., Wang, O. H., Fonseca, L. M., Cleveland, M. J., Bulger, J. D., Grinspoon, E., Hansen, D., Hawks, Z. W., Jung, L., Singh, S., Sliwinski, M., Verdejo, A., Miller, K. M., Weinstock, R. S., Germine, L., & Chaytor, N. (2024). Nocturnal hypoglycemia is associated with next day cognitive performance in adults with type 1 diabetes: Pilot data from the GluCog study. *The Clinical Neuropsychologist*, *38*(7), 1627–1646. https://doi.org/10.1080/13854046.2024.2315749

10
Psychometric Properties of Emerging Disruptive Technologies

Examining Reliability and Validity of Digital Tools and Platforms in Clinical Neuropsychology

Brittany Wolff and Alexandra Davis

Introduction

Neuropsychological services play a crucial role in diagnosing and managing neurological disorders and injuries. However, compared with other medical specialties, clinical neuropsychology has seen relatively limited technological progress over the last century (Bilder & Reise, 2019). Today, the most commonly used measures remain paper-and-pencil tests developed before the era of personal computing. With advances in computerized cognitive assessments and novel digital health approaches, including ecological momentary assessment, smartphone-based assessment and sensors, wearable devices, passive driving sensors, smart homes, voice biomarkers, and electronic health record mining, there are ample opportunities for the field of neuropsychology to rapidly improve patient care and outcomes (Harris et al., 2024). However, some worry that increased automation could marginalize the clinician's role, reducing the neuropsychologist to a technician role. Highlighting the stagnation, a 10-year follow-up survey on test usage patterns of clinical neuropsychologists found the top five most commonly used tests were identical and the same order of use as those from the prior survey (the Wechsler Adult Intelligence Scales, the Wechsler Memory Scales, Trail Making Test, California Verbal Learning Test, and Wechsler Intelligence Scale for Children), with respondents noting lack of ecological validity and difficulty comparing standardized scores as greatest obstacles to progress (Rabin et al., 2016).

As personal computing has become widespread, certain paper-and-pencil neuropsychological measures have been adapted into computerized formats that address several limitations of conventional testing. For instance, computer-based assessments can boost efficiency by lessening examiner workload and shortening test batteries through computerized adaptive testing. Streamlined assessments can free up

Brittany Wolff and Alexandra Davis, *Psychometric Properties of Emerging Disruptive Technologies*.
In: *Technology and Neuropsychology*. Edited by: Jared F. Benge et al., Oxford University Press.
 DOI: 10.1093/9780197814116.003.0010

the neuropsychologist's schedule and increase the number of patients evaluated, thereby improving access to care. Automated scoring not only conserves time but also simplifies generating various scores, such as comparisons with different normative samples, reliable change indices, regression-based formulas, and process scores to better understand patients' test-taking behaviors. As results are recorded digitally, it is easier to build large normative databases (e.g., the National Neuropsychology Network; Loring et al., 2022). Additionally, computerized tests can deliver stimuli with a degree of timing precision that is hard to replicate using human examiners, although this depends on hardware, software, and connectivity factors. Digital platforms can also produce almost unlimited alternate versions by drawing randomly from a broad stimulus pool, minimizing the influence of practice effects. Finally, instructions in computerized tests can be translated into multiple languages without requiring multilingual administrators, thereby enhancing accessibility for non-English-speaking patients (Harris et al., 2024).

By incorporating technology, neuropsychologists can expand assessment methods and improve treatment approaches. Yet, as with any new methodology, questions arise regarding the psychometric properties, particularly reliability and validity, of these emerging tools. This chapter provides a focused review addressing the question, "What is ready for clinical prime time?" We explore key applications of commercial and research-based platforms employing digital forms of traditional neuropsychological tests that have shown promising psychometric support. First, we evaluate establish platforms and software most commonly used in neuropsychology. Second, we highlight selected novel yet primarily research-based technological approaches we predict will be integrated into neuropsychological practice in the future.

Neuropsychological Assessment Software Platforms

There are several established online or technology-based platforms which have expanded beyond experimental studies as discussed earlier. We now highlight several candidates already used in practice, or which we believe are ready for neuropsychological prime time.

NIH Toolbox

The NIH Toolbox assesses a broad range of functions across the lifespan (ages 3–85) in cognition, motor function, sensory perception, and emotional state. Evidence has emerged that the normative assessments of the NIH Toolbox have reliability and validity for the diagnosis of mild cognitive impairment (MCI) and dementia, as well as reliability and predictability from the reviews of the motor and sensory batteries of the NIH Toolbox. Evidence has emerged for the validity and usefulness of the NIH Toolbox in detecting changes in function in various populations (Mather et al., 2024).

Age range	3–85 + years
Device required	iOS (iPad)
Domains assessed	Cognitive function, motor skills, sensory perception, emotional health
Test duration	Varies by test, typically 5–30 minutes per test
Test format	Computerized, touch-screen-based, and manual tasks
Reliability	High test-retest and inter-rater reliability
Primary use	Clinical and research
Applications	Neurological disorders, cognitive development, psychological assessment, aging, Alzheimer's disease, and health-related studies
Reference	https://nihtoolbox.org/

Validity

Recent studies have evaluated the construct validity and reliability of the NIH Toolbox Cognition Battery (NIHTB-CB). For example, the validity of the NIHTB-CB cognitive domains has been provided by a study from Carlozzi et al. (2017), which found the cognitive constructs to have varying levels of validity for different constructs. To also assess the reliability of the measures, researchers (Taylor et al., 2022) examined the test-retest reliability of the NIHTB-CB in children and adolescent across 3 years and reported that the measures were lower in reliability than anticipated, which raises concerns about their usage for longitudinal studies of youth populations. While the NIHTB-CB measures have been administered to multiple groups in varied clinical and research environments, that validity and reliability function differently for groups and constructs, and more research is needed to ensure its validity for groups and constructs in research and clinical settings.

Reliability

Substantial research has repeatedly confirmed the robust reliability of the NIH Toolbox across numerous domains. In an investigation of the NIHTB-CB construct validity, Ott et al. (2022) determined that each subtest displayed moderate construct validity, indicating effective measurement of targeted cognitive constructs. Moreover, Wei et al. (2025) conducted a systematic review of 22 studies across 33 assessments, evaluating the validity and reliability of the NIH Toolbox in healthy children aged 3 to 17. This review further substantiates the tool's applicability across diverse populations. These findings highlight the utility of the NIH Toolbox in both research and clinical contexts, providing reliable and valid assessments across cognitive, emotional, motor, and sensory domains.

Version 3

Version 3 of the NIH Toolbox introduces several enhancements to improve its psychometric properties and usability. These updates include an improved user interface and user experience, streamlined test instructions, and updated scoring algorithms, all aimed at enhancing the precision of cognitive assessments. This version also emphasizes improved clinical utility by integrating more effectively with electronic health record (EHR) systems, enabling efficient data sharing and longitudinal tracking, which is crucial for monitoring cognitive changes over time, particularly in neurodegenerative diseases (*What Changes Were Made from NIH Toolbox V2 to V3?, 2024*).

Application in Neurodegenerative Diseases

The NIH Toolbox is particularly valuable for early dementia detection. Studies in Alzheimer's disease and dementia show its utility in identifying subtle cognitive function changes in individuals with prodromal Alzheimer's, primarily through tools like the Picture Sequence Memory Test, which correlates with early Alzheimer's episodic memory impairments (Hackett et al., 2018). This feature is instrumental in clinical settings for monitoring cognitive decline before significant symptoms manifest. Recent studies and national research priorities support the NIH Toolbox for assessing various forms of dementia, including frontotemporal, vascular, and Lewy body dementia. Though less validated for non-Alzheimer's dementias, the Toolbox shows promise in distinguishing subtypes through biomarkers, cognitive tests, and unique symptomatology (Hackett et al., 2018). For instance, the National Institute of Neurological Disorders and Stroke (NINDS) has recently prioritized research on frontotemporal dementia (FTD), including the identification of biomarkers and the validation of diagnostic tools such as the NIH Toolbox (Schor et al., 2022). This agenda also emphasizes longitudinal tracking to detect cognitive and behavioral changes over time, crucial for conditions like vascular dementia, where symptom progression is variable. Research presented at the Alzheimer's Disease-Related Dementias (ADRD) Summit, convened by the NINDS and the National Institute on Aging, is fostering the advancement of diagnostic and therapeutic instruments that integrate NIH Toolbox metrics. These initiatives underscore the utility of NIH Toolbox assessments within clinical investigations and applied dementia research, thereby enriching the diagnostic paradigm beyond Alzheimer's disease (Hackett et al., 2018).

Limitations

The NIH Toolbox exhibits certain limitations in its construct validity across various cognitive domains. Recent studies have found that the attention and executive function, episodic memory, and processing speed domains demonstrate poor-to-adequate construct validity. In contrast, the working memory, language, and motor dexterity domains and the fluid composite show poor-to-good construct validity (Ott et al., 2022). In addition, the Toolbox's normative sample is limited to a range of ages 3–85, presenting challenges to its feasibility with an ever-growing oldest-old population (85+) (Nolin et al., 2023). Moreover, the difference between the test stage and scoring may introduce false inflated or deflated scores longitudinally within participants, increasing or decreasing the magnitude of change (Shields et al., 2023).

DANA

Age range	18 years and older
Device required	Smartphones or tablets (Android or iOS)
Domains assessed	Memory, attention, reaction time, processing speed, executive function
Test duration	Individual tasks typically take 1–5 minutes; full assessment durations vary based on protocol
Test format	Computerized tasks administered via a mobile application
Reliability	High test-retest reliability (coefficients above 0.80 for most subtests)
Primary use	Cognitive and neurobehavioral assessment in military, clinical, and research contexts
Applications	Traumatic brain injury, concussion, fatigue, neurocognitive monitoring, stress evaluation
Reference	https://danabrainvital.com/

The Defense Automated Neurobehavioral Assessment (DANA) is a portable, computerized cognitive testing tool for neurobehavioral evaluation in diverse settings, suitable for ages 18 and above. It assesses attention, memory, reaction time, and executive function.

Reliability

Several recent studies showed the DANA cognitive test is reliable. Reference values for DANA tasks are now established based on age and sex, which improves consistency. For instance, the median response times for the Go-No-Go format showed significant age-related differences, which further supports the tests validity for measuring cognitive processes in diverse populations (Ding et al., 2024).

Furthermore, empirical evidence supports the efficacy of DANA in field environments, particularly during military deployments. A study involving deployed U.S. Marines demonstrated consistent correlations between DANA scores and standard concussion screening tools such as the Military Acute Concussion Evaluation (MACE), thereby confirming the tool's robust psychometric properties in practical settings (Pryweller et al., 2020). Ongoing research continues to validate DANA's reliability in identifying cognitive changes associated with stress, fatigue, and traumatic brain injury, underscoring its significance in both military and clinical settings (Ding et al., 2024).

Validity

Recent studies have also suggested that DANA be valid across multiple applications. Its concurrent validity has been shown through studies of age-related changes in cognitive performance. A 2023 study in the Framingham Heart Study cohort established age- and sex-specific reference values for DANA tasks, showing reliability across multiple populations. For example, median response times for the Go-No-Go task showed age-related changes, proving DANA can measure cognitive processes (Ding et al., 2024).

The criterion validity of DANA has been demonstrated through its alignment with established clinical evaluation tools. In a study conducted with deployed U.S. Marines, DANA Brief Cognitive Test performance showed significant correlations with Military Acute Concussion Evaluation (MACE) cognitive scores, suggesting that DANA can effectively identify cognitive impairments associated with mild traumatic brain injury and other conditions in field settings (Pryweller et al., 2020). These findings reinforce DANA's potential for broader health monitoring applications beyond traditional neuropsychological testing.

Limitations

DANA, while proficient, has several disadvantages and criticisms. The biggest concern is that it relies on touch screen devices, which undoubtedly adds variability to response times from participant differences in screen sensitivity, latency due to different device settings, and user experience with similar technology. This variability would adversely affect the consistency of results across devices/platforms (Ding et al., 2024). DANA has been established to be both valid and reliable with military and clinical populations, yet investigations into its use in the healthy civilian population have yet to be developed. The tasks within a DANA battery are not static; rather, they vary based on the client's age, level of education, and tech savviness—all of which could impact performance metrics. Furthermore, DANA task design is beneficial for use in the field because the tasks are minimalist and uncomplicated, yet might not capture nuanced cognitive deficits or provide as rigorous of a neuropsychological assessment as other batteries (Pryweller et al., 2020). More work is needed to improve DANA scoring algorithms to accommodate individual differences so that maximum precision and relevance can be achieved.

CANTAB

Age range	18+
Device required	iOS (iPad and iPhone) and Android devices
Domains assessed	Attention, memory, executive function, working memory, spatial memory
Test duration	Varies by task, typically 10–30 minutes per session
Test format	Computerized, touch-screen-based tasks
Reliability	High test-retest and inter-rater reliability
Primary use	Cognitive assessment in clinical and research settings
Applications	Neurodegenerative diseases, cognitive disorders, psychiatric conditions
Reference	https://cambridgecognition.com/digital-cognitive-assessments/

The Cambridge Neuropsychological Test Automated Battery (CANTAB) is a computerized suite of tests developed at the University of Cambridge. It assesses various cognitive domains, including memory, attention, executive function, and decision-making, and is used in clinical and research settings to detect cognitive impairment in all populations. Recent research has shown that CANTAB is effective in many applications. For example, a study of 23,004 people in the United States used the CANTAB for core cognitive assessments and demonstrated its scalability and sensitivity across the lifespan (Mak, 2025). Another study showed the CANTAB can discriminate between cognitive impairment in multiple sclerosis patients, and the results are comparable to traditional assessment batteries (Talebi et al., 2020). These findings demonstrate the CANTAB as a robust tool for cognitive assessment and early detection and intervention in many neurological and psychiatric conditions.

Validity

Working memory, attention, and executive functions are just a few of the many cognitive domains that CANTAB has proven reliable in evaluating. Numerous studies have indicated that CANTAB is appropriate for clinical and research settings because it can distinguish between people with neurological disorders and healthy controls. Concurrent validity was supported, for instance, by a study by Siew et al. (2022) that provided normative data for various CANTAB measures in Singaporean older adults who lived in the community and discovered strong correlations with conventional neurocognitive tests. CANTAB's ability to monitor cognitive function across diverse populations is supported by research that evaluated its test-retest reliability and emphasized the importance of maintaining a balance between reliability, sensitivity, and relevance.

Reliability

CANTAB has undergone considerable research regarding its ability to reliably assess cognitive functions. Research has shown that CANTAB scores are stable over time, and it provides high test-retest reliability (Gonçalves et al., 2016; Skirrow et al., 2022). It has been evaluated for its test-retest reliability across various cognitive domains. Karlsen et al. (2022) assessed the 3-month test-retest reliability of nine CANTAB tests in 75 healthy adults, focusing on visual learning and memory, executive function, and visual attention. With correlation coefficients ranging from 0.39 to 0.79, the study showed sufficient test-retest reliability for the Rapid Visual Processing, Attention Switching Task, and Spatial Working Memory tests. Inter-rater reliability and the tool's consistency across populations with neurological and psychiatric disorders, however, were not covered in the study. Even though CANTAB shows promise in some areas, more investigation is required to validate its inter-rater reliability and suitability for a range of clinical populations.

Limitations

One of the concerns is the variable test-retest reliability that has been shown in some CANTAB subtests. For example, a study by Karlsen et al. (2020) examined the 3-month test-retest reliability of nine CANTAB tests among healthy adults. While some subtests showed good reliability, other subtests did not achieve the acceptable levels. Such variability implies that the temporal stability of CANTAB test scores will be unreliable at times, thus diminishing their utility when it comes to longitudinal cognitive assessment. Furthermore, there are issues with CANTAB's generalizability to diverse and multicultural populations. Cross-validation is required to ascertain the battery's suitability in multiculturally diverse contexts, according to early validity studies using non-Western samples. These results raise questions about the validity of CANTAB subtests with diverse populations since they show that performance on them is culture-sensitive (Kim et al., 2014). Additional research needs to be done to overcome the noted limitations and increase the validity and reliability of CANTAB.

CNSVS

Age range	8 years and older
Device required	Desktop or laptop computer with Windows operating system
Domains assessed	Memory, attention, processing speed, executive function, visual perception, motor skills
Test duration	Typically 30–45 minutes for a full battery; individual subtests range from 2 to 10 minutes
Test format	Computerized tasks administered via software download
Reliability	Moderate to high test-retest reliability (coefficients ranging from 0.65 to 0.85)
Primary use	Neurocognitive assessment in clinical, educational, and research settings
Applications	attention-deficit/hyperactivity disorder, traumatic brain injury, neurodegenerative conditions, cognitive impairment, research studies
Reference	https://www.cnsvs.com/

CNS Vital Signs (CNSVS) is also a widely used computerized neurocognitive assessment tool in clinical and research settings. CNSVS appears to yield good test-retest reliability according to the literature on the measure, notably higher reliability between the second and third repeated testing than between the first and second. Nevertheless, reliability coefficients have been shown to vary across populations and cognitive domains. This emphasizes the importance of accounting for domain-specific variability and practice effects when using CNSVS in longitudinal assessments (Rijnen et al., 2018).

Validity

Recent research has provided evidence supporting the validity of CNSVS in assessing executive functioning among older adults. A study examined the CNSVS executive functioning scores in a sample of community-dwelling older adults and found significant correlations with established neuropsychological measures, indicating that CNSVS is a valid tool for evaluating executive functions in this population (DesRuisseaux et al., 2025).

Reliability

CNSVS's dependability has been assessed across a range of demographics. Test-retest reliability was found to be acceptable in a study by Littleton et al. (2015), with better reliability between the second and third test administrations than between the first and second. The reliability of some subtests varied, though, which may indicate that some cognitive domains are more prone to inconsistencies over time. The significance of cautious interpretation when using CNSVS for repeated assessments is highlighted by this variability.

Limitations

While CNSVS is beneficial, it has disadvantages. For instance, less computer-savvy individuals—such as older people—may experience the computerized nature of the assessment as difficult, which could affect the accuracy of the outcome of the assessment. Although CNSVS has age-adjusted normative data available, its ability to detect subtle cognitive changes—that are seen with mild traumatic brain injury or neurodegenerative disease in the early stage—has been questioned. Jung et al. (2023) stated that more research is needed to establish the predictive validity of CNSVS in these situations. There have also been practice effects with CNSVS, as participants performed better the second or subsequent time the test was administered, simply because they were familiar with the task and not because they demonstrated improvement in their cognitive capabilities. This again underlines the need for alternative forms, or alternative tests, as it can bias longitudinal data analysis.

CogState

Age range	6 years and older
Device required	Desktop, laptop, or tablet with internet access
Domains assessed	Processing speed, attention, working memory, visual learning, executive function
Test duration	Typically, 10–15 minutes for a brief battery; individual subtests range from 2 to 5 minutes
Test format	Computerized tasks administered via a web-based platform or downloadable software
Reliability	High test-retest reliability (coefficients often exceeding 0.80 for most cognitive domains)
Primary use	Cognitive screening and monitoring in clinical, research, and educational settings
Applications	Alzheimer's disease, mild cognitive impairment, traumatic brain injury, psychiatric conditions, sports-related concussion
Reference	https://www.cogstate.com/

The CogState is a computerized cognitive assessment, and it is widely used in clinical and research settings for its efficiency and sensitivity in detecting cognitive changes.

It evaluates processing speed, attention, working memory, and executive function through brief, computerized tasks. Several studies have confirmed its validity by comparing it to traditional neuropsychological tests and its reliability through consistent performance over time.

Validity

Recent studies further support the efficacy of the CogState computerized cognitive assessment among diverse populations and settings. For example, a 2025 study examined the CogState Brief Battery's (CBB) ability to differentiate between MCI and dementia; the CBB was successful at distinguishing between the two classifications, and this shows its validity for clinical assessment (Kuan et al., 2025). In a different study, Perin et al. (2020) studied the acceptability and validity of a web-based version of the CBB among adult participants in the Healthy Brain Project; they found that participants responded positively to the version of the CBB, and this indicated that web-based adminsitration for assessing cognition is valid and acceptable (Perin et al., 2020).

Additionally, studies presented at the Alzheimer's Disease/Parkinson's Disease (AD/PD) 2024 conference examined the utility and validity of collected data remotely utilizing the CBB. The findings demonstrated that remote assessments correlated well with standardized neuropsychological assessments in-clinic as well as Alzheimer's disease biomarkers, providing support for the validity of an unsupervised remote test for cognitive assessment (Maruff et al., 2026). These recent studies provide more support for the CogState battery's validity and adaptability, showing potential usability in traditional clinical settings as well as novel remote assessment contexts.

Reliability

Recent research has further supported the stability of the CBB across various groups and contexts. In a study by Rigby et al. (2024), the test-retest reliability of the CBB was assessed with community-dwelling Black/African American older adults both with and without MCI. Results suggested that the CBB had fairly stable measurement over a 4-month period, and intraclass correlation coefficients indicated generally moderate to high reliability. However, differences between MCI participants and healthy controls were noted to further underscore the importance of cognitive status when interpreting results (Rigby et al., 2024).

The Alzheimer's Disease/Parkinson's Disease (AD/PD) 2024 conference presented research regarding the validation of data acquired through remote, unsupervised administration of CBB. The study showed that remote assessments correlated well with standardized in-clinic neuropsychological assessments and Alzheimer's disease biomarkers, suggesting that unsupervised remote testing could be a valid assessment process for cognitive assessments (Maruff et al., 2026). Altogether, the new evidence supports the reliability and validity of the CogState cognitive assessment and adds further support for its use as a comprehensive evaluation tool for cognition across populations and contexts.

Limitations

While CogState cognitive has become popular, it has experienced several drawbacks. There are important cultural and educational biases where differences in computer familiarity could influence usability with more diverse populations. Moreover, some practice effects may influence reliability with repeated testing, as improvements can occur for familiarity to the task, not for neurocognitive differences or changes. While CogState is beneficial for identifying cognitive decline, it is less sensitive to subtle or more advanced neurodegenerative changes. Remote assessments may also introduce limitations, such as environmental distractions and variations in technology hardware, to which the testing response may not capture the cognitive capability or assessment accuracy. Financial accessibility also limits CogState, as not all resources are available in remote settings (Polk et al., 2024). Additionally, although CogState is a helpful screening option, it is not diagnostic, meaning cognitive diagnostic options need to follow increased testing results to reach a definitive diagnosis. Technological reliance might also not reach populations that do not have access to reliable hardware and reliable internet. Recognizing these limitations may enhance the application of CogState by customizing the assessment to culture and technology and integrating other cognitive assessment instruments.

ImPACT

Age range	12 years and older
Device required	Desktop or laptop with Internet access
Domains assessed	Memory (verbal and visual), processing speed, reaction time, attention
Test duration	Typically 20–30 minutes
Test format	Computerized tasks administered via a secure web-based platform
Reliability	Moderate test-retest reliability (coefficients range from 0.60 to 0.80 depending on the domain)
Primary use	Concussion baseline testing, postinjury cognitive assessment, and recovery monitoring
Applications	Sports-related concussion, return-to-play decision-making, and clinical and research settings
Reference	https://impacttest.com/

Immediate Post-Concussion Assessment and Cognitive Testing (ImPACT) is a computerized neurocognitive assessment instrument that can measure cognitive function following a concussion. It measures cognitive components, including memory, attention, reaction time, and processing speed. A large body of research on validity and reliability supports its use in clinical and research contexts.

Reliability

Recent investigations were done to examine the test-retest reliability and practice effects of the tool called ImPACT. Overall, visual motor speed and reaction time showed more excellent reliability than verbal and visual memory. A comprehensive approach to assessing concussions includes integrated clinical examinations, symptom reports, cognitive tests, and balance assessments. However, test intervals that are too long may ultimately decrease reliability due to practice effects, which may occur when someone is repeatedly exposed to cognitive tests, with improved performance on the repeated testing (Resch et al., 2013). As practice effects would affect cognitive assessments, it is necessary to consider practice effects to track cognitive changes accurately. The ImPACT should be utilized every year before the first day of the season to prepare for clinical decision-making. Considering ImPACT within a comprehensive concussion management program, including clinical evaluations and balance assessments, leads to an enhanced understanding of an individual's cognitive status.

Validity

Recent studies have been assessing the reliability of ImPACT. A paper published by Abeare and colleagues (2018) documented significant variability in invalid baseline performances across age groups, with invalidity rates ranging from 6.4% to 47.6%, depending on the measure of invalidity. This suggests that baselines might not be reliable for testing purposes (Abeare et al., 2018). A systematic review showed ImPACT to have moderate sensitivity but high specificity, supporting its use alongside other assessments for accurate concussion management (Higgins et al., 2023). Additionally, another study demonstrated that sleep deprivation has negative effects on ImPACT scores, which indicates the necessity for practitioners to consider the influence of noncognitive variables (Hrabarchuk et al., 2024). Taken together, the body of literature demonstrate the necessity of comprehensive evaluation models that examine ImPACT as part of a package of assessment including other clinical measures and judgment to better advance the accuracy of management decisions related to concussion.

Limitations

Concerns have been raised about how sufficient normative data are, specifically in understanding demographic factors like age, education, and culture. A study contrasting urban high school athletes to age-dependent normative scores provided by ImPACT also found significant differences and emphasized the need for specific population norms for accurate assessment (Hunt & Byrd, 2024). Experts caution against relying solely on ImPACT for information when making decisions about concussion management. Including the results from ImPACT within a comprehensive clinical evaluation framework that involves clinical examinations, symptom reports, and a balance assessment can provide a full picture of an individual's cognitive status (Graham et al., 2014). Overall, ImPACT can be a useful tool despite some limitations in both clinical and research settings. In both a sports environment and concussion clinics, ImPACT is a common tool used to monitor recovery and inform return-to-play decisions. Again, the combined use of ImPACT with other clinical evaluation tools and assessments will lead to greater information and is part of a multidisciplinary approach to concussion management.

Q-Interactive (WAIS-V)

Age range	16 to 90 years and 11 months
Device required	Two iPads (one for the examiner and one for the examinee) connected via Bluetooth or Wi-Fi
Domains assessed	Verbal comprehension, perceptual reasoning, working memory, processing speed, and fluid reasoning
Test duration	Varies by assessment; typically 45–90 minutes for full-scale intelligence tests
Test format	Digitally administered tasks with real-time scoring and automated reporting
Reliability	High test-retest reliability (coefficients above 0.90 for most subtests)
Primary use	Comprehensive cognitive assessments for clinical, educational, and research purposes
Applications	Diagnostic evaluations, learning disability assessments, neuropsychological testing, research studies
Reference	https://www.pearsonassessments.com/

The WAIS administered via Q-interactive has been evaluated for validity and reliability across digital formats. Research on the WISC-V (the most extensively studied Wechsler scale on Q-interactive) indicates that digital versions produce raw scores largely consistent with traditional paper-based formats, with small effect sizes (mean $|d| = 0.09$), supporting digital-paper equivalence when tests are designed with that goal (Daniel & Wahlstrom, 2019). However, an independent examination found significant format effects for Full Scale IQ and Processing Speed on Q-interactive, particularly for the Coding subtest ($d = 0.69$), suggesting that equivalence may not be complete across all subtests (Gilbert et al., 2021). Similarly, Young (2020) found evidence supporting score equivalency for WAIS-IV core subtests administered via iPad in routine clinical practice with healthy young adults. Regarding the WAIS-5 specifically, Canivez et al. (2026) conducted an independent structural validity assessment and found that the purported five-factor structure was not supported; instead, a four-factor model dominated by a general intelligence (g) factor — similar to the WAIS-IV structure — provided the best fit. Despite these findings, further research is needed to explore potential impacts of digital administration on certain populations and settings, particularly given that most equivalence studies have been conducted with the WISC-V rather than the WAIS-5.

Reliability

The Wechsler Adult Intelligence Scale has demonstrated strong reliability across editions. The WAIS-IV Full Scale IQ has an internal consistency (split-half reliability) of 0.98 and a test–retest reliability of 0.96 based on 298 individuals assessed with a mean interval of 22 days (van Esch et al., 2020). Regarding digital administration, research on the Q-interactive platform supports score consistency across formats. Young (2020) found that iPad administration of the WAIS-IV produced scores equivalent to the traditional paper format across all 10 core subtests in routine clinical practice with healthy young adults, with Bayesian analyses supporting equivalence. Similarly, Bartholomaeus et al. (2025) found that telehealth administration of the WAIS-IV yielded scores similar to face-to-face administration, with observed differences smaller than those expected due to measurement error, though formal statistical equivalence was not established for all indices. However, Gilbert et al. (2021) found significant format effects for the WISC-V on Q-interactive, particularly for the Coding subtest ($d = 0.69$), suggesting that digital-paper equivalence may not be complete across all subtests. Additionally, Estevis et al. (2012) demonstrated that WAIS-IV scores improve approximately 7 points on Full Scale IQ upon retesting at 3- or 6-month intervals due to practice effects, which should be considered when interpreting longitudinal assessments.

Validity

Research has established the construct validity of the Wechsler scales through extensive factor analytic studies. For the WAIS-IV, factor analytic research supports a well-fitting measurement model aligned with the Cattell-Horn-Carroll (CHC) theory of cognitive abilities, with five factors (acquired knowledge, fluid intelligence, short-term memory, visual processing, and processing speed) demonstrating metric invariance between clinical and standardization samples (Sudarshan & Bowden, 2023). However, Gignac and Watkins (2013) found that while the bifactor model-based reliability for Full Scale IQ was respectably high ($\omega h = .86$), the unique internal consistency reliabilities for the individual index scores were very low ($\omega s = .13$ to $.47$), raising concerns about the justifiability of clinical index score interpretations. For the WAIS-5 specifically, an independent structural validity assessment by Canivez et al. (2026) found that the purported five-factor structure — with separate Visual Spatial and Fluid Reasoning factors — was not supported; instead, a four-factor model dominated by a general intelligence (g) factor, similar to the WAIS-IV structure, provided the best fit. These findings suggest that the Full Scale IQ should be prioritized as the primary interpretive metric, with caution applied to index-level interpretations.

Limitations

One limitation is that the Q-interactive assessment is a technology-based assessment, which makes it subject to some risks related to technical problems, software malfunctions, or loss of internet connection during assessment (Schneider et al., 2021).

Although generally, equivalency studies have provided appropriately tested reliability and validity for digital assessment, there is some concern about performance anxiety among test takers in remote digital settings, with over one-third of older adults in one study reporting performance anxiety during unsupervised computerized testing (Kochan et al., 2022). The APA Guidelines for Psychological Assessment and Evaluation (2020) further note that older adults have less technology experience and proficiency, and that the acceptability of technology-based measures must be examined in diverse populations. Furthermore, WAIS-5's newly designed format aligns with recent cognitive models; however, the new index scoring and subtest formatting may present a challenge related to longitudinal comparisons with prior versions of the WAIS (Wechsler, 2024). These limitations demonstrate the need for continued research and training of practitioners to optimize the use of the assessments and supplementary interpretation of results.

Emergent and Research-Based Technological Innovations

Boston Process Approach Technologies

As any complex neurocognitive operation can be completed through multiple strategies, analyzing the process (i.e., examining and quantifying real-time neurocognitive activities as tasks progress) can reveal information about brain function and behavior. Within the total time required to complete a task are essential indicators of when and how different neurocognitive resources are recruited and synchronized for successful performance. Along with process, examining errors on neuropsychological tests provides insight into underlying brain–behavior connections. The Boston Process Approach (BPA), largely credited to Edith Kaplan, emphasizes the qualitative analysis of cognitive processes rather than simply focusing on final test scores (Kaplan, 1988). Kaplan's collaboration with Heinz Werner, PhD, laid the foundation for the BPA by emphasizing that cognition and behavior arise from multiple cognitive processes, each tied to distinct neuroanatomical pathways. Werner, considered one of the most influential developmental psychologists of the 20th century, argued that children's cognitive growth is not merely an expansion of problem-solving capacity but a qualitative shift in how problems are solved, highlighting the multifactorial nature of cognition (Werner, 1937). In his seminal work on education, Werner cautioned against relying on a single achievement score to draw conclusions about cognitive abilities, noting that the same final outcome can emerge from different processes, potentially involving different brain regions. Kaplan applied these insights to her work with brain-injured patients, observing that two individuals might earn the same score through fundamentally different strategies, as revealed by their errors. For instance, one patient might misplace only one block on a challenging Block Design item, while another might discard or even try to eat the blocks, yet both would receive a zero (Bauer & Bowers, 2013). Kaplan's assertion that *how* someone arrives at a solution is as important as *how much* they achieve was a paradigm shift in American clinical neuropsychology.

Widespread adoption of the BPA has been limited by the substantial time and labor needed to accurately quantify behavior, as well as the specialized training required. However, evolving digital technologies for capturing eye movements, postural and facial expressions, and drawing, written, and spoken output, combined with automated scoring tools, offer new approaches. Digital approaches to neuropsychological assessment using the BPA can record, capture, and quantify behavior and errors in real time (i.e., "en route") to detect subtle but potentially significant neurocognitive impairments. As Kaplan illustrated, analyzing visuoconstructional behavior (e.g., block-matching or copying complex figures) can be enhanced by using "flow charts" that capture the step-by-step process within the total time needed to produce a final response. Such detailed observation can highlight errors and the strategies guiding performance, thereby offering a deeper understanding of a patient's overall cognitive profile. In this way, process and error analysis may help identify neurocognitive biomarkers before individuals meet formal criteria. There are three core criteria for using digital technology with BPA methods: (1) Enhanced behavioral insights: Digitally administered tests should uncover and measure behaviors that are not observable with standard paper-and-pencil assessments. (2) Operational definition of neurocognitive constructs: The newly captured data should be used to define key cognitive processes known to underlie predementia and dementia syndromes. For instance, measuring the time needed to generate a correct response may predict the onset of neurodegenerative disease, and tracking prosody or speech metrics can yield novel ways to characterize word-finding difficulties. (3) Translation into action: Abnormalities detected via digital BPA-based scoring should lead to actionable recommendations to help mitigate the impact of emerging neurological conditions (Libon et al., 2022).

Psychometric Evidence

In the context of the Framingham Heart Study, researchers integrated technology to capture in-depth process-oriented data on a large scale, thereby providing more nuanced insights into cognitive functioning. Digital platforms allow for real-time capture of error patterns, response latencies, and other indicators of cognitive strategy. The DCTclock, a digital clock drawing test, was evaluated as a biomarker for Alzheimer's disease susceptibility, by examining effects of Apolipoprotein E (APOE) ε4 allele carrier status and a polygenic risk score (PRS) on DCTclock composite outcomes, in the Framingham Heart Study, which represents the largest repository of digital clock drawing data to date (Thompson et al., 2024). The analysis included 2,398 older adults (mean age 72.3, range 60–94; 55% female, 92% White). PRS was constructed using 38 variants identified in a recent large genome-wide association study (GWAS) and meta-analysis of late-onset alzheimer's disease (LOAD). Digital clock drawing performance declined with advancing age, lower education, and possession of one or more APOE ε4 alleles. Lower total scores, as well as lower Information Processing Speed (command and copy conditions) and Drawing Efficiency (command condition) composite scores, correlated with higher PRS levels and APOE ε4 allele counts. The effects of APOE and PRS were similar across both men and women. Findings suggest that Alzheimer's disease genetic risk is associated with digital clock drawing performance. The digital clock drawing task (dCDT) in Framingham was further supported by an association between digital metrics and global amyloid burden (Ding et al., 2025). Specifically, initiation speed (speed of the pen when beginning to draw the command clock face), average speed (of the pen for all pen strokes used during drawing the clock face), termination speed (speed of the pen when finishing the clock face), maximum speed (maximum speed of the pen on the page during drawing), percent ink time (percentage of the test time spent actively drawing with the pen on paper for the copy clock), and percent thinking time (percentage of test time spent "thinking" with pen off the page on the copy clock) predicted amyloid positivity and tau biomarkers.

Accurate figure copying is widely recognized as a sensitive indicator of visuoconstructional skill. However, drawing tasks also rely on other cognitive and motor processes that can influence the final product, factors not typically captured by conventional scoring methods. A study introduced a novel tablet-based assessment of the Rey Complex Figure copy task (T-RCF), which continuously records data throughout the drawing process, yielding 12 indices that reflect different facets of drawing ability (Petilli et al., 2021). A total of 102 healthy adults completed the T-RCF; among them, 35 individuals also finished a paper-based drawing battery that measured constructional, procedural, and motor aspects. Principal component analysis of the T-RCF indices revealed three distinct dimensions (spatial, procedural, and kinematic), and a composite score was generated. Correlational analyses supported the validity of these composite scores by showing that the spatial, procedural, and kinematic dimensions were linked to constructional, organizational, and motor measures, respectively. Importantly, overall copy accuracy was associated with all three components, underscoring the multifaceted nature of complex figure copying. The T-RCF capitalizes on continuous data collection to provide three critical dimension-specific scores for a more comprehensive understanding of drawing execution, capitalizing on technology to enhance cognitive evaluation findings beyond that obtained through clinical observation of paper-and-pencil drawing.

Mobile Cognitive Testing Platforms—Application in Dementia

Frontotemporal dementia (FTD/FTLD) is a progressive neurodegenerative disorder characterized by changes in behavior, language, and executive function. Early detection is crucial, yet traditional office-based testing can be burdensome for patients and caregivers. Recent work has developed mobile applications to evaluate executive, language, and social cognition functions in at-risk individuals and diagnosed patients. Work by the ALL-FTD consortium has made initial steps in characterizing FTD using mobile technology. Staffaroni and colleagues (2024) aimed to evaluate whether unsupervised smartphone-based tests of executive function and memory can reliably and validly assess individuals with FTLD in remote settings. In this cohort study, participants from the North American ALLFTD consortium (across 18 research centers) completed the ALLFTD mobile application (ALLFTD-mApp) on their own smartphones, three times over 2 weeks. Among 1,163 eligible individuals, 360 enrolled and were divided into a discovery (n = 258) and validation (n = 102) cohort. Participants completed both standard in-clinic tests and a remote smartphone battery via the ALLFTD-mApp. Of the 360 participants, smartphone-based executive and memory tasks demonstrated moderate-to-excellent reliability (intraclass correlation coefficients: 0.77–0.95). Their performance correlated with FTLD disease severity (r = 0.38–0.59), traditional neuropsychological measures (r = 0.40–0.66), and brain volume (β = 0.34–0.50). Smartphone tests effectively distinguished individuals with FTLD dementia from controls (AUC = 0.93 [95% CI, 0.90–0.96]) and outperformed the Montreal Cognitive Assessment in detecting early FTLD symptoms (AUC = 0.82 vs. 0.68; p = .01). Findings were consistent in both discovery and validation cohorts. Notably, participants carrying pathogenic variants performed significantly worse on three app tasks even when asymptomatic (e.g., 2-back task $\beta = -0.49$; $p < .001$), but they did not show deficits on a composite of conventional neuropsychological measures ($\beta = -0.14$; $p = .32$).

These promising early findings indicate that smartphones provide a feasible, reliable, valid, and scalable approach for remote cognitive evaluations in FTLD, potentially enabling earlier detection. This represents a key advance in neuropsychological research and clinical practice, showing that smartphone-based tools can complement and, in some cases, exceed traditional in-person assessments. Future studies should confirm these findings in more diverse populations and explore their utility for ongoing monitoring. Smartphones are gaining attention across neurological conditions, and preliminary data have underscored the feasibility, reliability, and validity of unsupervised smartphone assessments in Alzheimer's disease, Parkinson's disease, and Huntington's disease. Given the clinical heterogeneity of FTLD, the ALLFTD-mApp was designed to comprehensively measure cognition, behavior, language, and motor function. Previous research confirmed its feasibility and acceptability, while this study expands on that work by demonstrating robust reliability and validity in a large, clinically well-characterized FTLD cohort. These findings highlight the potential for remote digital technologies to enhance neuropsychological evaluations, reduce barriers to clinical trial enrollment, and ultimately improve patient outcomes.

The NeuroUX Mobile Cognitive Tests

The first NeuroUX study examined how adults across the United States perform on eight smartphone-based tasks delivered through the proprietary NeuroUX platform, with the overarching goal of clarifying the psychometric and contextual factors that influence remote cognitive assessment in clinical neuropsychology (Paolillo et al., 2024). A total of 393 English-speaking participants, ranging in age from 20 to 79 years, installed NeuroUX on their own iOS or Android devices and completed one ecological momentary assessment survey and one cognitive test each day for 10 consecutive days, resulting in five administrations of every test. Most outcomes demonstrated strong psychometric qualities: Nine of the 12 primary scores displayed good-to-excellent stability across repeated administrations, with intraclass correlation coefficients exceeding 0.76, while only a third of the scores showed measurable practice-related gains, indicating modest learning effects over the 10-day protocol. As expected, increasing age predicted slower or less accurate performance on nine of the 12 indices and greater day-to-day fluctuation on three of four reaction-time measures, confirming the sensitivity of the mobile tests to well-established lifespan trends. Device characteristics also mattered: iPhone users and participants running up-to-date Android software outperformed those with older Android versions. Contextual factors exerted discernible, domain-specific influences; completing assessments at home corresponded to better processing-speed performance, whereas being alone conferred advantages for recognition- and working-memory tasks. Usability findings were highly favorable: The vast majority of respondents described the app as easy to learn, enjoyable, and potentially useful for tracking cognitive health; fewer than 5% expressed privacy concerns, and more than three-quarters indicated they would share their results with a health care professional. Only older age, not sex, race, or education, was linked to perceiving the tasks as more difficult.

The mobile battery itself was deliberately broad, covering processing speed, working memory, recognition memory, executive control, reaction time, and cognitive flexibility. Memory List required participants to study 12 words for 30 seconds, complete a distractor task, and then identify the original words among 24 probes; performance reflected correct recognitions and correct rejections across five alternate word lists. Memory Matrix assessed visual working memory by displaying highlighted tiles within an expanding grid and scoring the number of tiles correctly reproduced. Matching Pair gauged processing speed as users located identical shapes within increasingly larger arrays under a 90-second limit. Quick Tap 1 measured simple reaction time and processing speed via rapid taps on intermittently appearing targets, whereas Quick Tap 2 employed a Go/No-Go format to index response inhibition alongside reaction time. Odd One Out combined visual working memory with speed by asking participants to identify the subtly different symbol among six alternatives as quickly as possible. CopyKat, modeled after the game Simon, evaluated sequential visual working memory by having users replicate progressively longer sequences of flashing tiles. Finally, Hand Swype tested cognitive flexibility by instructing participants, under continuously visible, shifting rules, to swipe in either the direction indicated by pointing hands or the direction in which those hands moved, recording both accuracy and reaction time. Minimal-effort thresholds were enforced for each task to exclude implausibly low scores or implausibly fast responses.

Taken together, the findings demonstrate that NeuroUX delivers dependable, repeatable cognitive performance metrics, shows only limited susceptibility to practice effects, and captures meaningful variation related to age and moment-to-moment context. Coupled with overwhelmingly positive user feedback and negligible privacy concerns, these qualities position mobile cognitive testing as a practical, scalable complement to traditional in-clinic assessment, one that can support individualized clinical decision-making, facilitate ecological monitoring of cognitive change, and advance research on cognition in everyday environments (Paolillo et al., 2024).

Research with the Mayo Test Drive and the Strikker Learning Test

The ability to efficiently and affordably identify individuals at risk for preclinical and prodromal Alzheimer's disease is critical for ongoing clinical trials, newly emerging decentralized research efforts, and for determining who may benefit most from existing and future treatments, whether pharmacologic or behavioral. One key element of early detection strategies involves remotely administered cognitive tests that people can complete on their own, for example at home, since these require fewer logistical resources and provide greater access to screening compared to in-person evaluations. To broaden accessibility, particularly for those with limited ability to visit research centers, or out of necessity during the COVID-19 pandemic, tests originally designed for in-person clinic settings have often been adapted for remote use. However, this "conversion" approach lacks a foundational focus on self-administration, sometimes producing inconsistent performance across different settings. Hence, there remains a call for validated cognitive assessment tools developed from the ground up with remote use in mind. This is especially important for verbal memory measures, which are highly sensitive to early Alzheimer's disease changes but can be challenging to adapt to self-administered, off-site (Stricker et al., 2024)

Self-administered digital cognitive measures may improve access to testing compared with traditional, in-person screening and assessment. However, their successful implementation and widespread use hinge on usability, feasibility, and acceptability. Many digital tools, though aimed at broad populations, still require close supervision or involve steep technological demands, outcomes that can ultimately resemble the resource requirements of paper-and-pencil tests (Patel et al., 2025). Following Patel et al. (2025), usability can be defined as the extent to which self-administered measures can actually be used by their intended population, here evaluated through completion rates and user feedback. Feasibility refers to the factors influencing successful implementation in the target group, including session duration, testing context (e.g., location, noise, interruptions), and the type of device employed. Acceptability refers to elements affecting individuals' willingness to use self-administered digital tests, such as participation, adherence, retention, and user feedback. Identifying potential obstacles to scaling these technologies is crucial. For instance, Hackett et al. (2018) found that the NIH Cognition Toolbox Picture Sequence Memory and List Sorting Working Memory subtests were overly difficult for individuals with cognitive impairments, resulting in low completion rates and eventual removal from their study. Ultimately, digital assessments may have limited utility if the target population cannot or will not complete it.

The Stricker Learning Span (SLS) is a digital computer-adaptive word list memory test designed for remote assessment (Stricker et al., 2022). It administered through an Internet-based multidevice platform which facilitates unsupervised self-administration of digital cognitive tests, called the Mayo Test Drive (MTD), grounded in previous evidence of validity and reliability. The SLS's unique feature is its ability to present stimuli adaptively, offering additional exposures to items that the examinee struggles to recall. This adaptive approach is hypothesized to provide a more nuanced view of learning capacity and strategy use. The MTD also includes the Symbols Test, a measure of processing speed, executive functioning, and visual discrimination. These measures correlate with the Mayo Preclinical Alzheimer's disease Cognitive Composite (Mayo-PACC), Alzheimer's disease PET biomarkers, hippocampal volume, and show large effect sizes for detecting cognitive impairment (Boots et al., 2024). Initial findings in an all-remote pilot with 96 women (aged 55–79) without dementia revealed that 98% completed a test session once started (Stricker et al., 2022). Moreover, remote, unsupervised normative data for MTD demonstrate sensitivity to MCI and dementia.

Psychometric Evidence

A recent study assessed MTD's usability, defined by session completion rates, with an expectation that completion would exceed 90% (Patel et al., 2025). A total of 1,950 participants (97% White, 99% non-Hispanic) were recruited from the Mayo Clinic Study of Aging and the Mayo Alzheimer's Disease Research Center to take part in an uncompensated, remote ancillary study. Of these, 1,769 were cognitively unimpaired (CU) and 181 had cognitive impairment (CI). Among 1,217 participants who started the baseline session, 1199 (98.5%) successfully finished (mean age 71 years, range 35–100). Completion rates were statistically comparable between CU (98.7%) and CI (95.0%) groups and did not differ significantly by age. Individuals aged 80+ also had high completion rates (97.3%). Feedback from 36.4% of participants addressed topics such as usability, acceptability, perceived face validity, and contextual factors.

Another study evaluated the SLS's criterion validity by comparing its capacity to distinguish individuals with amyloid and tau PET-defined Alzheimer's disease pathology against the in-person, experimenter-administered Rey's Auditory Verbal Learning Test (AVLT). A total of 353 participants (mean age 71 years, SD = 11; 93%

CU) completed both the AVLT in person and the SLS remotely (within 3 months). All had amyloid and tau PET scans available (within 3 years). Two overlapping biomarker-based groupings were formed: (1) amyloid-positive (A+) versus amyloid-negative (A–), and (2) Alzheimer's disease pathology (amyloid- and tau-positive, A+T+) versus no Alzheimer's disease pathology (A–T–). Analyses were replicated among CU participants only. Both the SLS and AVLT showed a similar ability to separate individuals by biomarker status, as indicated by comparable AUROCs. In logistic regression models, SLS scores remained significant predictors of biomarker group beyond age, education, and sex, including within the CU subgroup. Effect sizes for both the SLS and AVLT ranged from medium (A– vs A+) to large (A–T– vs A+T+). Learning and delayed-recall scores from the SLS demonstrated comparable power to the AVLT in differentiating these biomarker-defined groups (Stricker et al., 2024).

A further study aimed to determine appropriate variables for inclusion in normative models of MTD to develop normative data, and to validate these norms (Stricker et al., 2025). The sample comprised 1,240 CU adults aged 32–100 (96% White) from the Mayo Clinic Study of Aging and the Mayo Alzheimer's Disease Research Center, all with a Clinical Dementia Rating of zero. The study used a predetermined cutoff of 1% variance improvement beyond the base model to evaluate additional potential predictors (e.g., device type, response input source, or session interference). Validation included examining rates of low test performance (< –1 SD) in independent CU (n = 167), MCI (n = 64), and dementia (n = 14) samples. No variables surpassed the 1% threshold for added variance beyond the base model, including device type, response input source, or session interference. Normative data showed the expected prevalence of low scores in CU participants and higher rates in those with MCI or dementia, confirming their validity. Standard regression-based normative models appear sufficient for remotely administered MTD measures and effectively detect cognitive impairment. While device type and response input method did not add enough explanatory power to warrant inclusion in normative equations, they remain important for interpreting individual outcomes.

iPad-Based Trail Making Test Part B

The Trail Making Test (TMT) is a widely used assessment of processing speed, visual scanning, and executive functioning, commonly split into Part A (TMT-A) and Part B (TMT-B). TMT-B specifically evaluates cognitive flexibility and set-shifting by requiring the individual to alternate between numbers and letters in ascending order. The advent of touchscreen tablets offers a convenient platform for digitizing the TMT. An iPad-based version promises automated scoring, reduced administration time, and immediate feedback for clinicians and researchers. Meta-analytic data suggest that TMT-B accounts for the largest share of functional variance in mild cognitive impairment (McAlister et al., 2016), and it is associated with real-world behaviors, for instance, walking characteristics in Parkinson's disease

(Piet et al., 2024). Despite TMT-B's consistent association with real-world outcomes, the cognitive mechanisms driving that relationship remain unclear. Individuals may arrive at similar TMT-B total scores via different underlying challenges, for example, visuospatial sequencing issues versus inhibitory control deficits, each of which could influence clinical decision-making and recommendations. Deconstructing TMT-B into its core processes may thus provide a clearer picture of cognitive functioning and its connection to everyday abilities.

Psychometric Evidence

Studies have attempted to translate Trails B to the digital sphere. One example is the tablet-based digital TMT (dTMT), designed to capture precise, component-level data to better isolate the cognitive abilities that contribute to TMT performance. Mirroring the traditional paper-and-pencil TMT, this digital version includes two parts: Part A and Part B. However, beyond recording total time to completion and error counts, the dTMT automatically collects additional component-level information, such as number of pauses, pause duration, number of lifts, lift duration, time spent inside each circle, and time between circles. Community-dwelling older adults participated in this study and underwent a standard neuropsychological evaluation measuring processing speed, inhibitory control, visual working memory/sequencing, and set-switching. Multiple regression analyses were conducted to relate these traditional neuropsychological measures to the dTMT's component scores (Fellows et al., 2017). Correlations between the traditional paper-based TMT and the new dTMT were significant for both Part A ($r = .541, p < .001$) and Part B ($r = .799, p < .001$). Regression models indicated that Part A performance was most strongly associated with speeded processing, whereas select Part B components were predicted by inhibitory control and visuospatial sequencing measures. Exploratory analyses also revealed a link between specific dTMT-B components and performance on a medication management task. These findings highlight how digitally isolating TMT subcomponents can clarify the distinct cognitive processes underlying test performance, particularly regarding speeded processing, inhibitory control, and sequencing. The results support the dTMT's potential to retain the established clinical utility of the TMT while offering more nuanced insights that may enhance functional predictions and individualized treatment planning.

Further research has been conducted into computerized versions of the TMT (cTMT) and analyzing eye-tracking and hand movements, to derive "internal" measures of working memory and inhibitory control (Linari et al., 2022). This study has found that computerized versions have similar performance profiles to the classic TMT, while providing additional information on patient pathology by parsing three stages of the TMT process: exploratory, planning, and monitoring; and facilitating improved control of spatial configuration bias for more robust results. Finally, extensions have been applied to virtual reality, such as the TMT-VR, a 360-degree virtual environment with numbered cubes distributed across a three-dimensional space to mirror real-world spatial challenges, has been validated against standard

TMT and symptomatology in adults with attention-deficit/hyperactivity disorder (Gounari et al., 2025). These approaches emphasize ecological validity, enable fine-grained analysis of patient characteristics, and have potential for real-time feedback for personalized interventions.

General Challenges and Limitations

Despite evidence of good psychometric properties in these emerging tools, challenges persist. Tablet versions may introduce variability due to unfamiliarity with touch-screen devices, particularly in older adults with limited technology experience. As with any digital measure, one must ensure that software updates and hardware differences do not inadvertently alter test parameters. Access to touchscreen devices is not uniform across socioeconomic and cultural groups, potentially creating biases if the test becomes widely adopted without consideration of digital literacy. Additionally, normative data stratification by race, ethnicity, education level, and age is critical to avoid misinterpretation of performance in underrepresented populations. From an ethical standpoint, data security is important; electronic data must be encrypted and stored in compliance with relevant privacy regulations (e.g., the Health Insurance Portability and Accountability Act).

A potential challenge of mobile cognitive testing involves the variability in device types and operating systems. While the studies validated the app on specific tablets or smartphones, differences in screen size, touch sensitivity, and processing speed might affect performance metrics. Another limitation is the novelty of the tasks, though derived from established measures, the tasks themselves require ongoing normative data collection to improve clinical utility. Mobile cognitive testing can improve access for individuals who have limited mobility or live far from specialized centers. However, this advantage is offset by the "digital divide" in which certain populations (e.g., older adults of lower socioeconomic status) have less familiarity with or access to smartphones and tablets. Data security is again a significant concern, as test scores and potentially sensitive health information are transmitted wirelessly. In addition, validated translations and culturally appropriate norms are required before using the app with linguistically and culturally diverse individuals.

Although the SLS shows promising psychometric properties, its adaptive nature can complicate interpretation. Clinicians must distinguish between genuine cognitive deficits and difficulties in navigating the adaptive format. Moreover, limited normative data exist for older adults, individuals from various linguistic backgrounds, and clinical populations beyond MCI. Adaptive testing approaches can enhance fairness by tailoring difficulty levels, but they also risk cultural bias if the content has not been validated across diverse groups. The test's reliance on verbal material underscores the need for careful translation and norming in multiple languages. Additionally, data privacy and the secure handling of adaptive algorithms must be considered, particularly if remote testing becomes commonplace.

Future Directions and Conclusion

Traditional clinical neuropsychology has long relied on streamlined, low-dimensional assessment tools (i.e., pencil-and-paper tests with static 2D stimuli and manual response logging) that, although rigorously validated for basic cognitive constructs, fall short in capturing the complexity of human behavior. This conservative approach, which has persisted since the early 1900s, mirrors the limitations articulated in the Flatland fallacy—that by confining our models to simplified, linear interpretations, there is the risk of diminishing and misinterpreting the multidimensional nature of cognitive deficits (Parsons & Duffield, 2020). The convergence of neuropsychology and digital technologies is reshaping clinical practice, offering opportunities to enhance test accuracy, streamline data collection, and potentially improve ecological validity. Across the technologies reviewed, there is growing evidence of reliable and valid measurement of core neuropsychological constructs. Studies generally show strong correlations with established paper-and-pencil tests, indicating that these digital measures assess similar cognitive domains effectively. Test-retest reliability and internal consistency metrics have also been encouraging, suggesting that many of these tools are nearing "clinical prime time." However, several unresolved issues warrant caution. Normative data remain limited for diverse demographic groups, and questions remain about how cultural, linguistic, and socioeconomic factors may influence performance in technology-based measures. Data security, privacy, and ethical considerations must be addressed to protect sensitive health information. Moreover, the potential for hardware or software obsolescence necessitates ongoing technological support and updates, a considerable investment in many clinical settings. To further establish these tools in clinical neuropsychology, future research should focus on large-scale normative studies, cross-cultural validation, and longitudinal designs that track sensitivity to cognitive change over time. Additionally, integrating these tools into telehealth platforms could enhance their accessibility and impact, especially in rural or underserved areas. With thoughtful deployment and continued empirical scrutiny, technology-based assessments have the potential to revolutionize neuropsychological testing and improve outcomes for diverse patient populations.

References

Abeare, C. A., Messa, I., Zuccato, B. G., Merker, B., & Erdodi, L. (2018). Prevalence of invalid performance on baseline testing for sport-related concussion by age and validity indicator. JAMA Neurology, 75(6), 697–703. https://doi.org/10.1001/jamaneurol.2018.0031

Bartholomaeus, V., Chronowski, N. H., Santiago, P. H. R., Kuring, J. K., & Sawyer, A. (2025). Equivalence of telehealth and face-to-face administration of the Wechsler Adult

Intelligence Scale Fourth Edition (WAIS-IV). The Clinical Neuropsychologist, 39(5), 1073–1096. https://doi.org/10.1080/13854046.2024.2335117

Bauer, R. M., & Bowers, D. (2013). In L. Ashendorf, R. Swenson, & D. Libon (Eds.), The Boston process approach to neuropsychological assessment: A practitioner's guide. Oxford University Press.

Bilder, R. M., & Reise, S. P. (2019). Neuropsychological tests of the future: How do we get there from here? Clinical Neuropsychologist, 33(2), 220–245. https://doi.org/10.1080/13854046.2018.1521993

Boots, E. A., Frank, R. D., Fan, W. Z., Christianson, T. J., Kremers, W. K., Stricker, J. L., Machulda, M. M., Fields, J. A., Hassenstab, J., Graff-Radford, J., Vemuri, P., Jack, C. R., Knopman, D. S., Petersen, R. C., & Stricker, N. H. (2024). Continuous associations between remote self-administered cognitive measures and imaging biomarkers of Alzheimer's disease. The Journal of Prevention of Alzheimer's Disease, 11(5), 1467–1479. https://doi.org/10.14283/jpad.2024.99

Boyle, G. J., Golden, C. J., Stein, D. J., & Stern, Y. (2023). The Sage handbook of clinical neuropsychology: Clinical neuropsychological assessment and diagnosis. Sage.

Canivez, G. L., Watkins, M. W., McGill, R. J., & Dombrowski, S. C. (2026). Construct validity of the WAIS-5: Complementary exploratory and confirmatory factor analyses of the 20 primary and secondary subtests. Assessment. Advance online publication. https://doi.org/10.1177/10731911251412219

Carlozzi, N. E., Tulsky, D. S., Wolf, T. J., Goodnight, S., Heaton, R. K., Casaletto, K. B., Wong, A. W. K., Baum, C. M., Gershon, R. C., & Heinemann, A. W. (2017). *Construct validity of the NIH Toolbox Cognition Battery in individuals with stroke. Rehabilitation Psychology*, *62*(4), 443–454. https://doi.org/10.1037/rep0000195

Corcoran, S. (2022). Q-interactive: Training implications for accuracy and technology integration. Contemporary School Psychology, 26(1), 90–99. https://doi.org/10.1007/s40688-021-00368-3

Daniel, M., & Wahlstrom, D. (2019). Raw-score equivalence of computer-assisted and paper versions of WISC-V. Psychological Services, 16(2), 213–220. https://doi.org/10.1037/ser0000295

DesRuisseaux, L. A., Gereau Mora, M., & Suchy, Y. (2025). Computerized assessment of executive functioning: Validation of the CNS Vital Signs executive functioning scores in a sample of community-dwelling older adults. The Clinical Neuropsychologist, 39(1), 159–181. https://doi.org/10.1080/13854046.2024.2354953

Ding, H., Kim, M., Searls, E., Sunderaraman, P., De Anda-Duran, I., Low, S., Popp, Z., Hwang, P. H., Li, Z., Goyal, K., Hathaway, L., Monteverde, J., Rahman, S., Igwe, A., Kolachalama, V. B., Au, R., & Lin, H. (2024). Digital neuropsychological measures by defense automated neurocognitive assessment: Reference values and clinical correlates. Frontiers in Neurology, 15, 1340710. https://doi.org/10.3389/fneur.2024.1340710

Ding, H., Lyu, C., Karjadi, C., Sunderaraman, P., Young, C. B., Mormino, E. C., Low, S., Devine, S., Gifford, K., Au, R., & Lin, H. (2025). Association of the digital clock drawing test with amyloid and tau PET biomarkers in low age risk adults. Scientific Reports, 15(1), 11104. https://doi.org/10.1038/s41598-025-95852-8

Estevis, E., Basso, M. R., & Combs, D. (2012). Effects of practice on the Wechsler Adult Intelligence Scale-IV across 3- and 6-month intervals. The Clinical Neuropsychologist, 26(2), 239–254. https://doi.org/10.1080/13854046.2012.659219

Fellows, R. P., Dahmen, J., Cook, D., & Schmitter-Edgecombe, M. (2017). Multicomponent analysis of a digital Trail Making Test. The Clinical Neuropsychologist, 31(1), 154–167. https://doi.org/10.1080/13854046.2016.1238510

Gamaldo, A. A., Tan, S. C., Sardina, A. L., Henzi, D., Guest, R., Ross, L. A., & Andel, R. (2020). Older Black adults' satisfaction and anxiety levels after completing alternative versus traditional cognitive batteries. The Journals of Gerontology: Series B, 75(7), 1462–1474. https://doi.org/10.1093/geronb/gby095

Gignac, G. E., & Watkins, M. W. (2013). Bifactor modeling and the estimation of model-based reliability in the WAIS-IV. Multivariate Behavioral Research nudge, 48(5), 639–662. https://doi.org/10.1080/00273171.2013.804398

Gilbert, K., Kranzler, J. H., & Benson, N. (2021). An independent examination of the equivalence of the standard and digital administration formats of the Wechsler Intelligence Scale for Children–5th Edition. Journal of School Psychology, 85, 113–124. https://doi.org/10.1016/j.jsp.2021.01.002

Gonçalves, M. M., Pinho, M. S., & Simões, M. R. (2016). Test–retest reliability analysis of the Cambridge Neuropsychological Automated Tests for the assessment of dementia in older people living in retirement homes. Applied Neuropsychology: Adult, 23(4), 251–263. https://doi.org/10.1080/23279095.2015.1053889

Gounari, K. A., Giatzoglou, E., Kemm, R., Beratis, I. N., Nega, C., & Kourtesis, P. (2025). The Trail Making Test in Virtual Reality (TMT-VR): Examination of the ecological validity, usability, acceptability, and user experience in adults with ADHD. Psychiatry International, 6(1), Article 1. https://doi.org/10.3390/psychiatryint6010031

Graham, R., Rivara, F. P., Ford, M. A., & Spicer, C. M. (Eds.). (2014). Concussion recognition, diagnosis, and acute management. In Sports-related concussions in youth: Improving the science, changing the culture. National Academies Press. https://www.ncbi.nlm.nih.gov/books/NBK185340/

Hackett, K., Krikorian, R., Giovannetti, T., Melendez-Cabrero, J., Rahman, A., Caesar, E. E., Chen, J. L., Hristov, H., Seifan, A., Mosconi, L., & Isaacson, R. S. (2018). Utility of the NIH Toolbox for assessment of prodromal Alzheimer's disease and dementia. Alzheimer's & Dementia: Diagnosis, Assessment & Disease Monitoring, 10, 764. https://doi.org/10.1016/j.dadm.2018.10.002

Harris, C., Tang, Y., Birnbaum, E., Cherian, C., Mendhe, D., & Chen, M. H. (2024). Digital neuropsychology beyond computerized cognitive assessment: Applications of novel digital technologies. Archives of Clinical Neuropsychologywidget, 39(3), 290–304. https://doi.org/10.1093/arclin/acae016

Higgins, K. L., Bouchard, H. C., Maietta, J. E., Laing-Young, J. M., & Schultz, D. H. (2023). Valid, invalid, or somewhere in between? Baseline ImPACT and stand-alone performance validity testing in collegiate athletes. bioRxiv. https://doi.org/10.1101/2023.05.03.538988

Hrabarchuk, E. I., Kalagara, R., Ezzat, B., Rentzeperis, F., Leska, T. M., Schupper, A. J., Rodriguez, B., Ali, M., Quinones, A., McCarthy, L., Carr, M. T., Lehman, A. B., Gometz, A., Lovell, M., & Choudhri, T. F. (2024). Effects of hours of sleep on ImPACT concussion testing: Comparing baseline with postinjury scores. Journal of Neurosurgery: Pediatrics. Advance online publication. https://doi.org/10.3171/2024.2.PEDS23437

Hunt, T. N., & Byrd, M. (2024). Comparison of urban versus industry normative values of immediate post-concussion assessment and cognitive testing (ImPACT™). International Journal of Environmental Research and Public Health, 21(3), 247. https://doi.org/10.3390/ijerph21030247

Jung, S. O., Kim, J. E. E., & Kim, H.-J. (2023). Assessing objective cognitive impairments in cancer survivors: Features and validity of measures for research and clinical applications. Asia-Pacific Journal of Oncology Nursing, 10(11), 100309. https://doi.org/10.1016/j.apjon.2023.100309

Kaplan, E. (1988). A process approach to neuropsychological assessment. In T. Boll & B. K. Bryan (Eds.), Clinical neuropsychology and brain function: Research, measurement, and practice (pp. 129–167). American Psychological Association.

Karlsen, R. H., Karr, J. E., Saksvik, S. B., Lundervold, A. J., Hjemdal, O., Olsen, A., Iverson, G. L., & Skandsen, T. (2022). Examining 3-month test-retest reliability and reliable change using the Cambridge Neuropsychological Test Automated Battery. Applied Neuropsychology: Adult, 29(2), 146–154. https://doi.org/10.1080/23279095.2020.1722126

Kim, H. S., An, Y. M., Kwon, J. S., & Shin, M.-S. (2014). A preliminary validity study of the Cambridge Neuropsychological Test Automated Battery for the assessment of executive function in schizophrenia and bipolar disorder. Psychiatry Investigation, 11(4), 394–401. https://doi.org/10.4306/pi.2014.11.4.394

Kochan, N. A., Heffernan, M., Valenzuela, M., Sachdev, P. S., Lam, B. C. P., Brodaty, H.,... & Lampit, A. (2022). Reliability, validity, and user-experience of remote unsupervised computerized neuropsychological assessments in community-living 55- to 75-year-olds. Journal of Alzheimer's Disease, 90(4), 1629–1645. https://doi.org/10.3233/JAD-220665

Kuan, Y.-C., Jhang, K.-M., Wang, W.-F., Yeh, Y.-C., Chen, C.-S., Yang, C.-C., & Hu, C.-J. (2025). Cogstate Brief Battery performance in assessing cognitive impairment in Taiwan: A prospective, multi-center study. Journal of the Formosan Medical Association. Advance online publication. https://doi.org/10.1016/j.jfma.2025.02.025

Libon, D. J., Swenson, R., Lamar, M., Price, C. C., Baliga, G., Pascual-Leone, A., Au, R., Cosentino, S., & Andersen, S. L. (2022). The Boston process approach and digital neuropsychological assessment: Past research and future directions. Journal of Alzheimer's Disease, 87(4), 1419–1432. https://doi.org/10.3233/JAD-220096

Linari, I., Juantorena, G. E., Ibáñez, A., et al. (2022). Unveiling Trail Making Test: Visual and manual trajectories indexing multiple executive processes. Scientific Reports, 12, 14265. https://doi.org/10.1038/s41598-022-16431-9

Littleton, A. C., Register-Mihalik, J. K., & Guskiewicz, K. M. (2015). Test-retest reliability of a computerized concussion test. Sports Health, 7(5), 443–447. https://doi.org/10.1177/1941738115586997

Loring, D. W., Bauer, R. M., Cavanagh, L., Drane, D. L., Enriquez, K. D., Reise, S. P., Shih, K., Umfleet, L. G., Wahlstrom, D., Whelan, F., Widaman, K. F., Bilder, R. M., & National Neuropsychology Network Study Group. (2022). Rationale and design of the National Neuropsychology Network. Journal of the International Neuropsychological Society, 28(1), 1–11. https://doi.org/10.1017/S1355617721000199

Mak, Y. (2025, March 6). CANTAB® demonstrates substantial value in one of the largest brain health studies ever conducted. Cambridge Cognition. https://cambridgecognition.com/cantab-demonstrates-substantial-value-in-one-of-the-largest-brain-health-studies-ever-conducted/

Maruff, P., Albala, B., Harvey, D., Saito, N., Kanoria, S., Aisen, P., Petersen, R., Weiner, M. W., Beckett, L., & Alzheimer's Disease Neuroimaging Initiative. (2026). Remote, unsupervised assessment of cognitive impairment and decline in Alzheimer's disease using the Cogstate Brief Battery in ADNI-3. Alzheimer's & Dementia: The Journal of the Alzheimer's Association, 22(5), e71357. https://doi.org/10.1002/alz.71357

Mather, M. A., Ho, E. H., Bedjeti, K., Karpouzian-Rogers, T., Rogalski, E. J., Gershon, R., & Weintraub, S. (2024). Measuring multidimensional aspects of health in the oldest old using the NIH Toolbox: Results from the ARMADA study. Archives of Clinical Neuropsychology, 39(5), 535–546. https://doi.org/10.1093/arclin/acad105

Mcalister, C., Schmitter-Edgecombe, M., & Lamb, R. (2016). Examination of variables that may affect the relationship between cognition and functional status in individuals with mild cognitive impairment: A meta-analysis. Archives of Clinical Neuropsychology, 31(2), 123–147. https://doi.org/10.1093/arclin/acv089

Nolin, S. A., Cowart, H., Merritt, S., McInerney, K., Bharadwaj, P. K., Franchetti, M. K., Raichlen, D. A., Jessup, C. J., Hishaw, G. A., Etten, E. J. V., Trouard, T. P., Geldmacher, D. S., Wadley, V. G., Porges, E. S., Woods, A. J., Cohen, R. A., Levin, B. E., Rundek, T., Alexander, G. E., & Visscher, K. M. (2023). Validity of the NIH toolbox cognitive battery in a healthy oldest-old 85+ sample. Journal of the International Neuropsychological Society, 29(6), 605–614. https://doi.org/10.1017/S1355617722000443

Ott, L. R., Schantell, M., Willett, M. P., Johnson, H. J., Eastman, J. A., Okelberry, H. J., Wilson, T. W., Taylor, B. K., & May, P. E. (2022). Construct validity of the NIH Toolbox cognitive domains: A comparison with conventional neuropsychological assessments. Neuropsychology, 36(5), 468–481. https://doi.org/10.1037/neu0000813

Paolillo, E. W., Bomyea, J., Depp, C. A., Henneghan, A. M., Raj, A., & Moore, R. C. (2024). Characterizing performance on a suite of English-language NeuroUX mobile cognitive tests in a US adult sample: Ecological momentary cognitive testing study. Journal of Medical Internet Research, 26, e51978. https://doi.org/10.2196/51978

Parsons, T., & Duffield, T. (2020). Paradigm shift toward digital neuropsychology and high-dimensional neuropsychological assessments: Review. Journal of Medical Internet Research, 22(12), e23777. https://doi.org/10.2196/23777

Patel, J. S., Christianson, T. J., Monahan, L. T., Frank, R. D., Fan, W. Z., Stricker, J. L., Kremers, W. K., Karstens, A. J., Machulda, M. M., Fields, J. A., Hassenstab, J., Jack, C. R., Jr., Botha, H., Graff-Radford, J., Petersen, R. C., & Stricker, N. H. (2025). Usability of the Mayo Test Drive remote self-administered web-based cognitive screening battery in adults aged 35–100 with and without cognitive impairment. Journal of Clinical and Experimental Neuropsychology, 47(1–2), 67–89. https://doi.org/10.1080/13803395.2025.2464633

Perin, S., Buckley, R. F., Pase, M. P., Yassi, N., Lavale, A., Wilson, P. H., Schembri, A., Maruff, P., & Lim, Y. Y. (2020). Unsupervised assessment of cognition in the Healthy Brain Project: Implications for web-based registries of individuals at risk for Alzheimer's disease. Alzheimer's & Dementia (New York, N. Y.), 6(1), e12043. https://doi.org/10.1002/trc2.12043

Petilli, M. A., Daini, R., Saibene, F. L., & Rabuffetti, M. (2021). Automated scoring for a Tablet-based Rey Figure copy task differentiates constructional, organisational, and motor abilities. Scientific Reports, 11(1), Article 1. https://doi.org/10.1038/s41598-021-94247-9

Piet, A., Geritz, J., Garcia, P., et al. (2024). Predicting executive functioning from walking features in Parkinson's disease using machine learning. Scientific Reports, 14, 29522. https://doi.org/10.1038/s41598-024-80144-4

Polk, S. E., Öhman, F., Hassenstab, J., König, A., Papp, K. V., Schöll, M., & Berron, D. (2024). A scoping review of remote and unsupervised digital cognitive assessments in preclinical Alzheimer's disease. medRxiv. Advance online publication. https://doi.org/10.1101/2024.09.25.24314349

Pryweller, J. R., Baughman, B. C., Frasier, S. D., O'Conor, E. C., Pandhi, A., Wang, J., Morrison, A. A., & Tsao, J. W. (2020). Performance on the DANA Brief Cognitive Test correlates with MACE cognitive score and may be a new tool to diagnose concussion. Frontiers in Neurology, 11, 839. https://doi.org/10.3389/fneur.2020.00839

Rabin, L. A., Paolillo, E., & Barr, W. B. (2016). Stability in test-usage practices of clinical neuropsychologists in the United States and Canada over a 10-year period: A follow-up survey of INS and NAN members. Archives of Clinical Neuropsychology, 31(3), 206–230. https://doi.org/10.1093/arclin/acw007

Resch, J., Driscoll, A., McCaffrey, N., Brown, C., Ferrara, M. S., Macciocchi, S., Baumgartner, T., & Walpert, K. (2013). ImPact test-retest reliability: Reliably unreliable? Journal of Athletic Training, 48(4), 506–511. https://doi.org/10.4085/1062-6050-48.3.09

Rigby, T., Kavcic, V., Shair, S. R., Hill-Jarrett, T. G., Garcia, S., Reader, J., Persad, C., Bhaumik, A. K., Pal, S., Hampstead, B. M., & Giordani, B. (2024). Retest reliability and reliable change of community-dwelling Black/African American older adults with and without mild cognitive impairment using NIH Toolbox-Cognition Battery and Cogstate Brief Battery for laptop. Journal of the International Neuropsychological Society, 1–11. https://doi.org/10.1017/S1355617724000444

Rijnen, S. J. M., van der Linden, S. D., Emons, W. H. M., Sitskoorn, M. M., & Gehring, K. (2018). Test-retest reliability and practice effects of a computerized neuropsychological battery: A solution-oriented approach. Psychological Assessment, 30(12), 1652–1662. https://doi.org/10.1037/pas0000618

Schor, N. F., Scott, P., Litvina, E. Y., Torborg, C., Kim, J. L., Zalutsky, R., Adams, A. B., & Taskforces on Science, Scientific Training and Workforce Diversity, Communications and Dissemination, and Workforce Culture. (2022). Planning and implementing strategically: Year 1 of the NINDS 2021-2026 Strategic Plan. Neurology, 99(24), 1099–1107. https://doi.org/10.1212/WNL.0000000000201380

Shields, R. H., Kaat, A., Sansone, S. M., Michalak, C., Coleman, J., Thompson, T., McKenzie, F. J., Dakopolos, A., Riley, K., Berry-Kravis, E., Widaman, K. F., Gershon, R. C., & Hessl, D. (2023). Sensitivity of the NIH Toolbox to detect cognitive change in individuals with intellectual and developmental disability. Neurology, 100(8), e778–e789. https://doi.org/10.1212/WNL.0000000000201528

Siew, S. K. H., Han, M. F. Y., Mahendran, R., & Yu, J. (2022). Regression-based norms and validation of the Cambridge Neuropsychological Test Automated Battery among community-living older adults in Singapore. Archives of Clinical Neuropsychology, 37(2), 457–472. https://doi.org/10.1093/arclin/acab073

Skirrow, C., Cashdollar, N., Granger, K., Jennings, S., Baker, E., Barnett, J., & Cormack, F. (2022). Test-retest reliability on the Cambridge Neuropsychological Test Automated Battery: Comment on Karlsen et al. (2020). Applied Neuropsychology: Adult, 29(5), 889–892. https://doi.org/10.1080/23279095.2020.1860987

Staffaroni, A. M., Clark, A. L., Taylor, J. C., et al. (2024). Reliability and validity of smartphone cognitive testing for frontotemporal lobar degeneration. JAMA Network Open, 7(4), e244266. https://doi.org/10.1001/jamanetworkopen.2024.4266

Stricker, N. H., Frank, R. D., Boots, E. A., Fan, W. Z., Christianson, T. J., Kremers, W. K., Stricker, J. L., Machulda, M. M., Fields, J. A., Lucas, J. A., Hassenstab, J., Aduen, P. A., Day, G. S., Graff-Radford, N. R., Jack, C. R., Jr., Graff-Radford, J., & Petersen, R. C. (2025). Mayo normative studies: Regression-based normative data for remote self-administration of the Stricker Learning Span, Symbols Test, and Mayo Test Drive Screening Battery Composite and validation in individuals with mild cognitive impairment and dementia. The Clinical Neuropsychologist, 1–30. https://doi.org/10.1080/13854046.2025.2469340

Stricker, N. H., Stricker, J. L., Frank, R. D., Fan, W. Z., Christianson, T. J., Patel, J. S., Karstens, A. J., Kremers, W. K., Machulda, M. M., Fields, J. A., Graff-Radford, J., Jack,

C. R., Jr., Knopman, D. S., Mielke, M. M., & Petersen, R. C. (2024). Stricker Learning Span criterion validity: A remote self-administered multi-device compatible digital word list memory measure shows similar ability to differentiate amyloid and tau PET-defined biomarker groups as in-person Auditory Verbal Learning Test. Journal of the International Neuropsychological Society, 30(2), 138–151. https://doi.org/10.1017/S1355617723000322

Stricker, N. H., Stricker, J. L., Karstens, A. J., Geske, J. R., Fields, J. A., Hassenstab, J., Schwarz, C. G., Tosakulwong, N., Wiste, H. J., Jack, C. R., Jr., Kantarci, K., & Mielke, M. M. (2022). A novel computer adaptive word list memory test optimized for remote assessment: Psychometric properties and associations with neurodegenerative biomarkers in older women without dementia. Alzheimer's & Dementia, 14(1), e12299. https://doi.org/10.1002/dad2.12299

Sudarshan, N. J., & Bowden, S. C. (2023). Common factor structure of the ten subtest Wechsler Adult Intelligence Scale–Fourth Edition in a clinical sample and 15 subtest version in the standardization sample. Archives of Clinical Neuropsychology, 38(8), 1646–1658. https://doi.org/10.1093/arclin/acad035

Talebi, M., Majdi, A., Kamari, F., & Sadigh-Eteghad, S. (2020). The Cambridge Neuropsychological Test Automated Battery (CANTAB) versus the Minimal Assessment of Cognitive Function in Multiple Sclerosis (MACFIMS) for the assessment of cognitive function in patients with multiple sclerosis. Multiple Sclerosis and Related Disorders, 43, 102172. https://doi.org/10.1016/j.msard.2020.102172

Taylor, B. K., Frenzel, M. R., Eastman, J. A., Wiesman, A. I., Wang, Y. P., Calhoun, V. D., Stephen, J. M., & Wilson, T. W. (2022). Reliability of the NIH toolbox cognitive battery in children and adolescents: A 3-year longitudinal examination. Psychological Medicine, 52(9), 1718–1727. https://doi.org/10.1017/S0033291720003487

Thompson, L. I., Cummings, M., Emrani, S., Libon, D. J., Ang, A., Karjadi, C., Au, R., & Liu, C. (2024). Digital clock drawing as an Alzheimer's disease susceptibility biomarker: Associations with genetic risk score and APOE in older adults. The Journal of Prevention of Alzheimer's Disease, 11(1), 79–87. https://doi.org/10.14283/jpad.2023.48

van Esch, A. Y. M., de Vries, J., & Masthoff, E. D. M. (2020). Screening for intellectual disability in Dutch psychiatrically disturbed detainees: Assessing the psychometric properties of the Screener for Intelligence and Learning Disability (SCIL). Journal of Applied Research in Intellectual Disabilities, 33(6), 1418–1427. https://doi.org/10.1111/jar.12769

Wei, X., McKinlay, C. J. D., Harding, J. E., Wouldes, T. A., Rogers, J., Brown, G. T. L., & Franke, N. (2025). NIH Toolbox for assessment of neurocognitive, motor and emotional-behavioral function in childhood: A systematic review. Child Neuropsychology, 31(6), 948–983. https://doi.org/10.1080/09297049.2024.2447444

Werner, H. (1937). Process and achievement: A basic problem of education and developmental psychology. Harvard Educational Review, 7, 353–368.

NIH Toolbox. (2024, November 20). What changes were made from NIH Toolbox V2 to V3? NIH Toolbox Zendesk. https://nihtoolbox.zendesk.com/hc/en-us/articles/12645131226644-What-changes-were-made-from-NIH-Toolbox-V2-to-V3

Young, S. R. (2020). Format effects of iPad administration of Wechsler Adult Intelligence Scale–Fourth Edition: Cross-sectional evidence for score equivalency in routine clinical practice. Archives of Clinical Neuropsychology, 35(8), 1283–1287. https://doi.org/10.1093/arclin/acaa040

11
Technology in Diverse Populations
Issues of Inclusion, Accessibility, and Bias

April Thames and Lucia Cavanagh

Introduction

The advancement and integration of technology in clinical neuropsychology hold great promise for increasing efficiency, expanding access, and enhancing the precision of cognitive assessment and intervention. The deployment of digital tools can help bridge the gap for minoritized populations who have historically remained underrepresented. However, as technology becomes increasingly embedded in neuropsychological procedures, issues of equitable access, applicability, and representative research become evident. In this chapter, we explore the multifaceted issues of inclusion, equity, and accessibility as they pertain to the digital transformation of clinical neuropsychology. While research in this regard is nascent within the field of neuropsychology, there are many insights to be gained from other disciplines, which consider diversity-related factors that directly influence and shape current brain health disparities. Considerations are made not only at the individual level but also within community, institutional, and societal spheres. We will critically examine existing barriers and opportunities for inclusive practice in testing, research, and intervention, and offer recommendations for culturally informed integration of technology.

The Digital Divide in Clinical Neuropsychology

Currently used neuropsychological protocols present many difficulties that would benefit from technological advancements, including remote and computerized testing procedures, incorporation of technological wearable devices, aggregation of large-scale databases, and application of modern psychometric approaches (Bilder & Reise, 2019). Such advances can make remote testing more widely available and increase efficiency of neuropsychological testing (i.e., to increase the number of patients that can be seen). However, diverse populations that have historically faced systemic barriers to health care are at increased risk of being left behind in

April Thames and Lucia Cavanagh, *Technology in Diverse Populations*. In: *Technology and Neuropsychology*.
Edited by: Jared F. Benge et al., Oxford University Press.
DOI: 10.1093/9780197814116.003.0011

this digital transition (Brearly et al., 2017; Marra et al., 2020). The "digital divide" refers to disparities in access to and proficiency with digital technology. Populations with limited digital access, such as older adults, individuals from lower socioeconomic backgrounds, rural-dwelling individuals, and certain racial and ethnic minorities, may face barriers to receiving equitable care and exacerbate pre-existing disparities in health care access and cognitive health outcomes. This is particularly true when digital platforms are assumed to be universally available or understood.

Indeed, some of the exciting technological applications discussed in this book necessarily require that both patients and providers have ready access to reliable Internet service, computers, and/or other mobile devices. However, for many, these assumptions are prohibitive due to cost and availability (Fernandez, 2019).

Inequalities linked to the digital divide have been associated with more pronounced cognitive decline among older adults (Li et al., 2024) and lower quality of life and poorer health outcomes among marginalized women in the United States (Philbin et al., 2019). Stigmas and challenges related to technology use among older adults can further hinder their participation in digital brain health research (Nicosia et al., 2022). Differences in technological literacy, defined as an individual's familiarity and comfort with using digital tools, can also impact testing validity. For example, a lack of experience with digital devices or testing platforms may impair test engagement or introduce unintended cognitive load, leading to inaccurate assessment results (Alhussein et al., 2023). These factors underscore the importance of contextualizing test results within the individual's lived experience, including their exposure to and comfort with technology. Addressing these issues is crucial to ensuring that technological advancements do not inadvertently widen gaps in care and research participation among already underserved populations.

To this end, technological deployment must be done with care and intention toward inclusivity and accessibility, ensuring broad reach across patient populations. Exactly how to go about doing this, however, is demonstrably less clear, although some guidance on this topic exists. For example, the U.S. Department of Defense has developed practice guidelines for integrating technology into clinical care that includes cultural considerations (Armstrong et al., 2018). Integrating cultural responsivity in the deployment of technology-enabled services (TES) to effectively address existing disparities may also be helpful (Eustis et al., 2023; Willis et al., 2022). For example, Eustis and colleagues (Eustis et al., 2023) propose a framework that provides specific recommendations both at the technological level (e.g., involving individuals in program development, tailoring content and delivery formats) and the individual level (e.g., providing culturally responsive support services to increase engagement and relevance). Integrating culturally responsive considerations into the development of novel tools as well as the application of existing models can facilitate accessibility for a broad range of patients.

In the following sections, we will discuss relevant considerations for culturally informed application of more specific technological applications, as it pertains to data aggregation, testing protocols, treatment/intervention work, and continuity of care.

Data Aggregation and Testing Considerations

Teleneuropsychology

Teleneuropsychology (tele-NP) has emerged as a useful tool for delivering cognitive assessment services, most notably in response to the COVID-19 pandemic. A growing body of research supports the feasibility, reliability, and clinical utility of tele-NP across a range of populations and cognitive domains (Marra et al., 2020; Munro Cullum et al., 2014). However, when applied to diverse populations, tele-NP presents unique benefits and challenges that require careful consideration to ensure equitable and valid application (Arias et al., 2020; Hilty et al., 2020). A growing body of literature demonstrates that tele-NP can enhance service accessibility and improve utilization rates, promote cultural responsiveness, and reduce health disparities for a range of patients, including those from culturally and linguistically diverse backgrounds and those in rural and underserved areas (Hilty et al., 2020; Messler et al., 2023). For example, when coupled with cultural and linguistic competencies, tele-NP can facilitate more equitable health care for rural and minoritized communities by reducing travel burdens and aligning services with patients' cultural norms (Hilty et al., 2020).

Despite its potential reach, the application of tele-NP services among diverse populations can pose unique challenges. In a review of tele-NP with culturally and linguistically diverse populations in the United States, Messler et al. (2023) underscore concerns about technological access, environmental distractions, clinician preparedness to address cultural differences remotely, and a lack of standardized guidelines for test adaptation in diverse contexts. Language barriers can also present a risk to validity when assessments rely on translated materials or are conducted by clinicians with limited cultural training (Arias et al., 2020).

Together, these findings suggest that while Tele-NP offers significant opportunities to expand neuropsychological services to diverse communities, it must be implemented with intentional cultural and structural accommodations. Best practices include ensuring technological accessibility (and using hybrid models when full remote assessment is not feasible), adapting assessment materials, employing bilingual/bicultural staff whenever possible, and engaging in ongoing training to enhance cross-cultural telehealth competence (Arias et al., 2020; Hilty et al., 2020; Messler et al., 2023). Larger structural barriers, such as varying insurance coverage for tele-NP services, can be more challenging to overcome and require ongoing advocacy and collaboration with institutional stakeholders.

Wearables and Smart Technology

Mobile Health Tools

Mobile health (m-health) refers to the use of mobile devices, including smartphones, wearable devices, wireless sensors, and other portable technologies, to support health care services, patient education, and public health interventions (Bhavnani et al., 2016; D. Kumar et al., 2023). This definition encompasses a wide range of digital tools that facilitate diverse aspects of health care delivery, such as remote patient monitoring, telemedicine, and health information management (Mumtaz et al., 2023). With the pervasive adoption of smartphones and wearable technologies, m-health has emerged as a cornerstone of modern health care strategies, transforming patient–provider interactions, health monitoring, and the management of health data (Boulos et al., 2011; Wall et al., 2023). In particular, the integration of wearable devices with mobile platforms has enabled real-time data collection and personalized care, while also facilitating more efficient communication between patients and health care providers (A. Kumar et al., 2020; S. Kumar et al., 2020). This paradigm shift in health care delivery has been driven by technological advancements and the increasing accessibility of mobile devices, which together have reduced barriers to care and improved both the accuracy and efficiency of health data management (Okolo et al., 2024).

Types of M-Health Technologies

M-health technologies encompass a variety of tools (Shaw et al., 2016):

- Wearable activity trackers: Devices such as fitness bands and smartwatches that monitor physical activity, sleep patterns, and vital signs
- Wireless health monitors: Includes scales, blood pressure cuffs, glucometers, and pulse oximeters connected via Bluetooth or Internet connections for real-time monitoring and reporting
- Health apps: Smartphone applications designed to manage medication, track diet and exercise, provide mental health resources, and facilitate telehealth consultations

While these technologies offer substantial potential, current evidence on their efficacy is mixed (Istepanian, 2022), highlighting the need for further rigorous investigation and standardized evaluation methods.

In neurocognitive health, systematic reviews have identified m-health applications targeting modifiable lifestyle behaviors associated with reduced dementia risk, notably emphasizing mental stimulation (Ali et al., 2024). Given the increasing cost burden associated with chronic neurological conditions, integrating digital solutions into traditional clinical practices represents a valuable strategy to empower patients, enhance adherence to medical recommendations, and improve overall health management (Varshney, 2014).

M-Health Implementation in Diverse Populations

The integration of emerging smart technologies (e.g., wearable sensors, smartphone-based applications, ecological momentary assessments [EMA], passive driving monitors, smart home systems, etc.) can expand the scope of neuropsychological assessment and intervention, especially for diverse and historically marginalized populations. These tools offer real-time, contextually rich data that can not only improve ecological validity but also overcome traditional access barriers, particularly in geographically isolated or underserved areas. For instance, Cook et al. (2023) demonstrated the feasibility of using wearable devices to monitor physiological and behavioral markers of cognitive risk in rural, multicultural older adults, offering a promising pathway for early detection in a higher-risk population. Similarly, Butler et al. (2025) used smartphone and smartwatch sensing to identify mild cognitive impairment in diverse participants. In this large longitudinal study, overall adherence was slightly lower across participants of racial/ethnic minority groups (i.e., compared to non-Hispanic White), but data capture over time remained robust, demonstrating an ability to overcome retention issues in this line of research.

The application of wearable smart technology can also allow for novel and more nuanced understanding of the intersection between culture/language and neuropsychology. For example, Jylkkä et al. (2020) used EMA to capture bilingual language-switching behavior, revealing the method's utility in understanding complex, context-dependent behaviors among bilingual individuals in real-world settings.

Despite the promising capabilities of m-health, its uptake remains uneven among disadvantaged and culturally diverse groups, such as racial minorities, immigrants, refugees, and Indigenous populations (Nouri et al., 2020; Whitehead et al., 2023). For example, studies in the United States have demonstrated lower m-health utilization among African American and Latino individuals compared to their White counterparts (Buis et al., 2017; Chen et al., 2023; Mitchell et al., 2018), attributed to cultural mistrust, resource disparities, and access challenges (Hoagland & Kipping, 2024). Kim et al. (2023) found that socioeconomic status (SES) significantly predicted wearable device use among children, suggesting that disparities in digital access begin early and persist across the lifespan. In adults, similar patterns likely impact the uptake and utility of wearable and smart technologies, particularly among individuals who may also face language, cultural, and mistrust-related barriers. Immigrant groups also experience barriers due to linguistic and cultural misalignments, which negatively influence their acceptance and use of digital health technologies (Radu et al., 2023; Whitehead et al., 2023). Indigenous populations encounter further challenges, including limited digital literacy, insufficient culturally relevant content, and technological access barriers, underscoring the critical need for culturally tailored and responsive strategies (Intahchomphoo, 2018; Jones et al., 2017). Without addressing these culturally specific requirements, digital health interventions risk exacerbating existing health disparities. Cultural mistrust significantly influences m-health adoption, reflecting historical and ongoing experiences of discrimination within health care systems. Skepticism toward digital health tools arises from perceptions that these technologies perpetuate marginalization and bias against minority groups (Hernandez-Green et al., 2024; James et al., 2017). Experiences of racial microaggressions and discrimination contribute to pervasive mistrust, affecting the willingness of racial minority populations to engage with digital platforms for health management (Villanueva, 2019).

Past practices—where surveillance data were misappropriated or used in ways that marginalized vulnerable groups—have contributed to an enduring legacy of mistrust (Gilman & Green, 2018). In several instances, systemic abuses and breaches of privacy in health care systems have been documented, reinforcing perceptions among minority populations that modern wearable technologies could perpetuate similar harms (Marfo & Obeng-Gyasi, 2024; Walter et al., 2024). Such historical misuses are often compounded by broader sociopolitical contexts, where communities that have faced discrimination are particularly wary of continuous monitoring, fearing that sensitive data might be exploited to undermine their interests or infringe on civil liberties (Colvonen et al., 2020). Undocumented immigrants in the United States face risks of discrimination, surveillance, and deportation (Guberek et al., 2018). In some cases, undocumented immigrants avoid risks that come with their vulnerable legal status by limiting contact with authorities and institutions, even nongovernmental ones offering heath care and social services (Hacker et al., 2015).

Thus, the reluctance to adopt wearables is not solely a matter of apprehension regarding privacy. It also reflects a broader narrative of disillusionment with health care technologies that were once envisioned as liberatory but have, in some cases, been co-opted into surveillance regimes (Kang et al., 2023). This sentiment is particularly pronounced among minority and underserved populations, as evidenced in studies where historical misuse has led to a persistent digital divide, stymieing the adoption of otherwise beneficial health technologies (Nittas et al., 2024).

When wearable and sensor-based technologies are not designed with diverse users in mind, poor interoperability, nonrepresentative datasets, and biased algorithms can reduce data quality and reinforce health inequities (Canali et al., 2022). This being said, the acceptability of wearable technology among diverse groups is not universally negative. In fact, some research suggests greater openness to passive monitoring and wearable use among Spanish-speaking individuals and individuals outside of the United States (Britton et al., 2023; Josephy-Hernandez et al., 2021).

Overcoming M-Health Implementation Challenges

Potential solutions to overcome these barriers involve a multifaceted approach aimed at rebuilding trust and ensuring that wearable health technologies are designed with explicit safeguards and culturally sensitive frameworks (Canali et al., 2022). For example, enhancing transparency through decentralized data management approaches, such as blockchain technology, can offer a promising avenue for re-establishing confidence among skeptical user groups (Chafiq et al., 2024). Additionally, interventions that incorporate community engagement and participatory design methodologies have been shown to improve the cultural relevance and trustworthiness of m-health and wearable platforms (Ceasar et al., 2019; Willis et al., 2022). A number of scholars advocate for integrating end-user perspectives in early design phases to ensure that the systems address historical grievances while meeting contemporary health needs (Farao et al., 2020; Song et al., 2021).

Other proposed solutions include educational outreach and collaborative policymaking that prioritize digital inclusion for underserved communities, thereby reducing the structural inequities that contribute to mistrust (Koehle et al., 2022). Research on older adults and other vulnerable subpopulations reveals that tailoring technological solutions to the social context of users is critical for mitigating the legacy of historical surveillance misuse (Sartori et al., 2022).

Thus, to ensure equitable and effective implementation, recommendations may include co-designing tools with target populations to ensure cultural appropriateness (Canali et al., 2022), providing linguistic customization and low-literacy interfaces (Lipio Brothers, 2023), emphasizing linguistic sensitivity in the design and interpretation of EMA approaches (Jylkkä et al., 2020), and incorporating hybrid assessment models that combine digital monitoring with human support (Eustis et al., 2023). Ultimately, intentional design, inclusive validation, and equitable deployment strategies are essential to maximize benefits and minimize disparities in the application of these devices.

In conclusion, m-health technologies hold significant promise for transforming health care delivery through personalized, accessible, and efficient services. However, to fully realize their potential, future development must prioritize cultural relevance, address barriers rooted in mistrust and accessibility, and ensure inclusivity to bridge existing health care disparities.

Large-Scale Data Mining and Modern Psychometrics

The development and use of large-scale databases in clinical neuropsychology offer great opportunities to enhance our understanding of brain–behavior relationships across the lifespan by enabling more robust and advanced modeling, greater statistical power, and the potential to generalize findings across more diverse populations. However, there are several critical concerns about these approaches as they pertain to diverse populations. Most notably, many large-scale datasets frequently lack representativeness, especially for individuals from minoritized backgrounds (Kamikubo et al., 2022; White et al., 2023). Large neuroimaging and behavioral data repositories often skew toward higher socioeconomic status, better-educated, and majority racial/ethnic groups, limiting the applicability of normative models to broader populations (Bethlehem et al., 2022). Similarly, neuropsychological test data can also be harmonized without accounting for linguistic, educational, and cultural variability (Merkley et al., 2023). Such under- and misrepresentation can compromise the validity and fairness of artificial intelligence (AI)-driven tools or predictive models that draw on these large-scale datasets and risk the propagation of bias and misinterpretation in cross-cultural contexts.

Using an exemplary case of American Indian individuals in the Adolescent Brain and Cognitive Development (ABCD) Study^{SM}, White et al. (2023) demonstrated the effects of underrepresentation and misrepresentation in large datasets. They call for culturally grounded approaches to data use, offering key recommendations that consider (1) the heterogeneity of the communities represented, (2) the importance of focusing on advancing the health and well-being of underrepresented groups, (3) engagement of relevant communities and community leaders at each step of the research process, (4) consideration of historical and ongoing injustices on study variables, and (5) engagement with representative regulatory agencies or review boards. Other recommendations to promote inclusive and valid use of large-scale neuropsychological data include intentional sampling strategies, greater demographic transparency, culturally sensitive variable selection, and the application of fairness metrics in model evaluation (White et al., 2023). Community involvement and data governance frameworks are also essential to foster trust and ethical use of data among marginalized and underrepresented groups. Perhaps most importantly, researchers and clinicians must advocate for increased representation of diverse groups in normative datasets and algorithm training samples to enhance fairness and accuracy in interpretation.

A major benefit of increasing access to large-scale datasets is to facilitate the application of modern psychometric approaches (e.g., machine learning [ML], item response theory [IRT], measurement invariance, large language modeling, etc.) that can advance testing paradigms to enhance diagnostic precision, efficiency, and scalability, especially for diverse populations that have historically been underrepresented in neuropsychology research. These tools can be used to empirically tailor assessments to individual linguistic, cultural, socioeconomic, and other backgrounds, offering more equitable alternatives to our current static, one-size-fits-all testing approaches. For example, computerized adaptive tests grounded in IRT can adjust question difficulty in real time, potentially reducing cultural and educational biases associated with floor and ceiling effects that disproportionately affect certain individuals on select tests. ML techniques have been employed to identify cognitive phenotypes in people with HIV, who are often disproportionately affected by social and structural inequities (Bowe et al., 2023), and to predict neurodevelopmental outcomes in children from large, heterogeneous datasets (Bowe et al., 2023).

Another promising approach to improve equity and equivalence in testing is the application of measurement invariance analyses, which can empirically detect item- and trait-level differences in test performance among individuals. While studies in this regard are increasing, some researchers suggest measurement invariance is often not adequately tested in modern test development, raising questions about the validity of inferences across cultures, languages, and socioeconomic contexts (Wicherts, 2016).

Large language models (LLMs) are also helpful tools for mining and uncovering unique differences in cross-cultural neuropsychology applications. While powerful, LLMs can be particularly prone to encoding and perpetuating biases present in training data. Disparities in performance across racial, linguistic, and disability groups have been documented in multiple LLM applications in health care (Omar et al., 2025), with demonstrated underperformance and biased outputs for racial, linguistic, or neurodivergent populations (Gallegos et al., 2023). To mitigate these risks, researchers advocate for the intentional inclusion of diverse populations in training datasets, the application of fairness metrics and bias audits, and greater transparency in model development (Abdurahman et al., 2024; Romano et al., 2023).

These approaches, when developed with representative data and equity-focused frameworks, can enhance the inclusivity, efficiency, and diagnostic accuracy of neuropsychological assessments across cultural and demographic boundaries. However, as these technologies evolve, careful attention to cultural validity and equitable access will be essential to ensure they serve, rather than exacerbate, disparities in neuropsychological practice and research.

Digitized Interventions in Neuropsychological Care

Historically, clinical neuropsychologists primarily focused on the identification, assessment, and diagnosis of cognitive impairments and neurological disorders. However, contemporary developments, such as digital health tools, virtual reality (VR), AI, and telehealth platforms, have facilitated a shift toward a more holistic, intervention-driven approaches. These emerging technologies enable clinical neuropsychologists to actively engage in the direct delivery of personalized therapeutic interventions (Wong et al., 2024). Nevertheless, despite technological advancements and opportunities, substantial efforts remain necessary to ensure effective implementation and equitable access to these advancements among culturally and linguistically diverse populations. In this section, we examine technologies including VR, mobile health applications, and AI.

VR Intervention

VR creates an immersive, interactive experience that bridges humans and computers, placing users in computer-generated environments (Heesen, 2012; Wohlgenannt et al., 2020). Effective VR experiences are often the result of integrating sophisticated interaction devices, sensory displays, and intentionally designed content to simulate realistic, three-dimensional settings (Jerald, 2015; Slater & Sanchez-Vives, 2016). Users can actively explore and engage with these simulated environments, closely mirroring real-world experiences (Kim, 2005).

Clinically, VR is widely utilized in exposure therapy but has also emerged as a potent tool for cognitive and neurorehabilitation (Yondjo & Siette, 2024). It offers customized environments tailored to therapeutic goals for neurologic conditions such as stroke, Parkinson's disease, dementia, and traumatic brain injury (Alashram et al., 2019; Gamito et al., 2020; Maggio et al., 2022; Oliveira et al., 2022; Yondjo & Siette, 2024). Research indicates that VR not only supports motor recovery in patients with Parkinson's disease but also fosters cognitive and behavioral improvement by stimulating cognitive processing and possibly slowing cognitive decline (Maggio et al., 2018, 2022). Emerging technologies, notably brain-computer interfaces (BCIs), further enhance VR's effectiveness by providing personalized, real-time feedback, allowing for adaptive rehabilitation strategies (Drigas & Sideraki, 2024; J. Kumar et al., 2023; Tang et al., 2023). Nevertheless, the lack of standardized protocols and consistent outcome metrics remains a significant barrier, complicating cross-study comparisons and evaluations of long-term effectiveness (Aminov et al., 2018). Furthermore, the lack of diverse samples in VR research limits understanding in potential demographic differences that may emerge in the VR setting and experience (Martingano et al., 2023).

VR Applications for Fostering Inclusivity

Digital technologies have significantly contributed to narrowing opportunity gaps, particularly for underserved and disadvantaged groups (Dick, 2021; Mavangere et al., 2022). For example, VR technology might help people with neurodevelopmental disorders to develop communication abilities, as these persons can "navigate" in an easier way in a virtual environment that provides challenges similar to the real world (Bailey et al., 2022). VR has potential to promote health care and educational access for populations previously lacking such opportunities (Chițu et al., 2023; Kouijzer et al., 2023). Collectively, these technological innovations have fostered novel approaches to addressing inequities.

Clinical neuropsychology is a field that is evolving with respect to addressing the field's history of noninclusive practices and understanding the impact this has had on health equity. Neuropsychologists have worked toward mitigating health disparities and inequities through exploration of biases and prejudices in our instruments and interactions as providers (Bordes Edgar et al., 2025; Burton et al., 2024).

VR provides an innovative and promising method for investigating and intervening in experiences related to discrimination faced by racial minority groups, particularly in the context of health care. By immersing users in realistic, computer-generated scenarios, VR can replicate instances of racial bias and discriminatory encounters, making it an effective tool for research, education, and psychological intervention (Franks, 2017; Lui et al., 2023; Roswell et al., 2020).

A key advantage of using VR in this context is its ability to simulate both overt discrimination and subtle microaggressions, offering valuable insights into the psychological effects of such stressful experiences, which significantly impact brain health (Berger & Sarnyai, 2015; Lui et al., 2023; Williams et al., 2025). Moreover, VR fosters empathy among individuals who may not personally experience racial discrimination, enabling them to virtually experience scenarios reflective of everyday biases encountered by racial minority groups (Beti et al., 2019; Nakamura, 2020). This immersive perspective-taking approach enhances users' understanding of discrimination's pervasive and harmful impacts, thereby contributing to greater awareness and potentially reducing implicit biases (Higgins et al., 2024).

In neuropsychological settings, the role of stereotype threat—a paradigm that explains why minoritized groups may underperform on testing—illustrates the impact of how discriminatory experiences may lead to further health inequities (e.g., inaccurate conclusions made about cognitive performance) (Thames et al., 2013; VanLandingham et al., 2022). VR can provide safe and controlled environments to train students, faculty, administrators, and health care professionals including neuropsychologists to recognize potential discriminatory practices that may elucidate stereotype threat. By participating in simulated discriminatory interactions, neuropsychologists can develop skills necessary to challenge and address biases, fostering more inclusive and equitable environments (Edgar et al., 2024).

VR Implementation in Diverse Populations

Implementing VR in diverse clinical populations brings unique challenges. Issues such as the lack of standardized administration procedures and normative data for VR platforms pose substantial hurdles, particularly when working with diverse cultural groups (Kourtesis et al., 2019; Parsons et al., 2018). Ethical considerations, including balancing patient benefits against potential harms (such as simulator sickness or dissociative experiences), further complicate clinical use (Parsons, 2021; Schulteis & Rothbaum, 2002; Zhou et al., 2023). Hence, informed consent, clarifying the procedures and anticipated outcomes of VR interventions, is critical to maintaining ethical integrity and patient safety (Parsons, 2021).

Economically, the implementation of VR is impeded by high development costs driven by the need for advanced hardware and software. Initially cumbersome designs and usability challenges further constrained widespread adoption, particularly in limited resource settings (Fares et al., 2024; Singha & Singha, 2023). Additionally, VR content requires specialized programming skills and multidisciplinary collaboration, significantly inflating development expenses (Chamusca et al., 2023).

The digital divide represents another crucial challenge, with disparities in economic resources, digital literacy, and cultural appropriateness limiting VR's accessibility and exacerbating existing socioeconomic inequities (Ma et al., 2016; Saeed & Masters, 2021). To address these disparities, VR systems should be customizable, adapting to the specific physical, cognitive, and cultural requirements of diverse user groups. Stanica et al. (2020) describe an adaptive VR system that dynamically adjusts to users' capabilities, enhancing usability and therapeutic outcomes. Ecological validity, aligning virtual tasks with users' cultural and environmental contexts, significantly enhances VR engagement and effectiveness. For instance, Jimenez et al. (2025) assessed the effectiveness of a language-concordant, VR-guided meditation on inpatient caregiver anxiety among English- and Spanish-speaking participants. VR-guided meditation effectively reduced caregiver anxiety in pediatric inpatient settings for both linguistic groups.

In sum, VR presents an innovative approach to therapeutic interventions, offering immersive, customizable environments beneficial for cognitive and neurorehabilitation across various clinical conditions, such as stroke, Parkinson's disease, and traumatic brain injury. Beyond clinical applications, VR also addresses societal inequities by fostering empathy and understanding regarding racial discrimination through realistic simulations of discriminatory experiences. These tools enable users to identify, confront, and address implicit biases and structural inequalities effectively. Despite its promise, VR faces challenges, including economic costs, lack of standardized protocols, and accessibility barriers driven by the digital divide. Addressing these challenges through adaptive, culturally relevant, and ethically mindful VR implementations can enhance therapeutic effectiveness and inclusivity, ultimately promoting greater equity in health care and social contexts.

Augmented Clinical Care with AI

AI refers to computer systems designed to perform tasks traditionally requiring human cognitive and physical capabilities, such as sensing, perception, problem-solving, and recognizing subtle patterns in language and behavior (Graham et al., 2019, 2020). Within mental health care, AI technologies facilitate enhanced patient care by enabling clinicians to prioritize their interactions and relationships with patients, ultimately making therapeutic interventions more effective (Kellogg & Sadeh-Sharvit, 2022). In health care, AI's capabilities—including automation, patient engagement, and decision support—are reviewed by domain experts before integration into clinical practice. This approach allows AI to complement clinician efforts, thereby enhancing patient experiences, improving professional satisfaction, and reducing health care costs (Crigger et al., 2022).

AI-driven engagement tools, particularly natural language processing (NLP)-based chatbots and intelligent virtual assistants, are significantly enhancing the interactions between patients and health care providers (Wilson & Marasoiu, 2022). These tools allow communication to be immediate, context-specific, and responsive, thus elevating patient satisfaction and engagement levels (Sarella & Mangam, 2024).

AI enables automation of health care management processes, through the application of computer vision and machine learning (ML) systems (Alowais et al., 2023). ML algorithms and neural networks to conduct extensive analyses of structured health care data, facilitating early detection, accurate diagnosis, and ultimately improved clinical outcomes (Krishnan et al., 2023).

Bias in AI

Bias may be introduced into an ML algorithm throughout all steps of the development process, which involves data collection, data selection, model training, and model deployment (Davy van de et al., 2022; Mehrabi et al., 2021). Such algorithms may be shaped by various factors such as social determinants of health that can influence health outcomes (Chelak & Chakole, 2023). Racial bias in clinical ML is one such challenge arising from these limitations and must be addressed to ensure fairness in clinical implementation of ML (Cary et al., 2023). As ML is premised on prediction of novel outcomes based on previously seen examples, unintended discrimination is a natural consequence of algorithm development involving training data that reflect real-world inequities (Huang et al., 2022). The lack of diversity in datasets leads to inaccuracies, especially for marginalized groups whose health issues are often overlooked. Therefore, creating balanced datasets and employing diverse metrics are crucial for developing accurate and equitable AI models (Afrose et al., 2022). In response to growing concerns regarding algorithmic bias, various federal agencies and nonprofit organizations have recently initiated regulatory actions or supported governance and oversight efforts to ensure algorithms are safe, fair, and transparent (Forrest, 2023; Schwartz et al., 2022). Cary et al. (2023) reviewed 109 articles describing empirical applications, frameworks, reviews and perspectives, and tools related to mitigating racial and ethnic bias in algorithms used to guide health care decisions. From their review, they provided the following recommendations for bias mitigation in clinical algorithms: (1) ensure professional diversity; (2) require auditable clinical algorithms; (3) foster transparent organizational culture; (4) implement health equity by design; (5) accelerate research in mitigation methodologies; (6) establish government structures and evaluation schemes; and (7) amplify patient voices by engaging diverse patients and local communities in the design and preprocessing of clinical algorithms to inform patient-centered and culturally affirming care.

AI holds considerable promise for transforming care in neuropsychological health care by augmenting clinical decision-making, enhancing patient engagement, and streamlining care delivery. From NLP chatbots to ML algorithms for early detection and diagnosis of cognitive impairment, AI technologies are redefining how clinicians interact with patients and manage health information. However, the growing reliance on AI also necessitates critical attention to issues of bias, fairness, and transparency. Addressing algorithmic bias, particularly its impact on marginalized populations, requires a concerted effort among developers, clinicians, regulatory bodies, and community stakeholders. As the field advances, integrating ethical frameworks, inclusive design principles, and oversight mechanisms will be critical to ensure that AI aligns with the goal of delivering culturally responsive and high-quality care for all.

References

Abdurahman, S., Atari, M., Karimi-Malekabadi, F., Xue, M. J., Trager, J., Park, P. S., Golazizian, P., Omrani, A., & Dehghani, M. (2024). Perils and opportunities in using large language models in psychological research. *PNAS Nexus, 3*(7), 245. https://doi.org/10.1093/pnasnexus/pgae245

Afrose, S., Song, W., Nemeroff, C. B., Lu, C., & Yao, D. D. (2022). Subpopulation-specific machine learning prognosis for underrepresented patients with double prioritized bias correction. *Community Medicine (London), 2,* 111. https://doi.org/10.1038/s43856-022-00165-w

Alashram, A. R., Annino, G., Padua, E., Romagnoli, C., & Mercuri, N. B. (2019). Cognitive rehabilitation post traumatic brain injury: A systematic review for emerging use of virtual reality technology. *Journal of Clinical Neuroscience, 66,* 209–219. https://doi.org/10.1016/j.jocn.2019.04.026

Alhussein, M., Patel, B., & Liu, X. (2023). Closing the gap: Technology access and telehealth use among older adults in the U.S. Medicare beneficiaries. *Telematics and Informatics Reports, 12,* 100–103. https://doi.org/https://doi.org/10.1016/j.teler.2023.100103

Ali, S., Alizai, H., Hagos, D. J., Rubio, S. R., Calabia, D., Serrano Jimenez, P., Senthil, V. A., & Appel, L. (2024). mHealth apps for dementia, Alzheimer disease, and other neurocognitive disorders: Systematic search and environmental scan. *JMIR Mhealth Uhealth, 12,* e50186. https://doi.org/10.2196/50186

Alowais, S. A., Alghamdi, S. S., Alsuhebany, N., Alqahtani, T., Alshaya, A. I., Almohareb, S. N., Aldairem, A., Alrashed, M., Bin Saleh, K., Badreldin, H. A., Al Yami, M. S., Al Harbi, S., & Albekairy, A. M. (2023). Revolutionizing healthcare: The role of artificial intelligence in clinical practice. *BMC Medical Education, 23*(1), 689. https://doi.org/10.1186/s12909-023-04698-z

Aminov, A., Rogers, J. M., Middleton, S., Caeyenberghs, K., & Wilson, P. H. (2018). What do randomized controlled trials say about virtual rehabilitation in stroke? A systematic literature review and meta-analysis of upper-limb and cognitive outcomes. *Journal of Neuroengineering and Rehabilitation, 15*(1), 29. https://doi.org/10.1186/s12984-018-0370-2

Arias, F., Safi, D. E., Miranda, M., Carrión, C. I., Diaz Santos, A. L., Armendariz, V., Jose, I. E., Vuong, K. D., Suarez, P., & Strutt, A. M. (2020). Teleneuropsychology for monolingual and bilingual Spanish-speaking adults in the time of COVID-19: Rationale, professional considerations, and resources. *Arch Clin Neuropsychol, 35*(8), 1249–1265. https://doi.org/10.1093/arclin/acaa100

Armstrong, C. M., Ciulla, R. P., Edwards-Stewart, A., Hoyt, T., & Bush, N. (2018). Best practices of mobile health in clinical care: The development and evaluation of a competency-based provider training program. *Professional Psychology: Research and Practice, 49*(5–6), 355–363. https://doi.org/10.1037/pro0000194

Bailey, B., Bryant, L., & Hemsley, B. (2022). Virtual reality and augmented reality for children, adolescents, and adults with communication disability and neurodevelopmental disorders: A systematic review. *Review Journal of Autism and Developmental Disorders, 9*(2), 160–183. https://doi.org/10.1007/s40489-020-00230-x

Berger, M., & Sarnyai, Z. (2015). "More than skin deep": Stress neurobiology and mental health consequences of racial discrimination. *Stress, 18*(1), 1–10. https://doi.org/10.3109/10253890.2014.989204

Bethlehem, R. A. I., Seidlitz, J., White, S. R., Vogel, J. W., Anderson, K. M., Adamson, C., Adler, S., Alexopoulos, G. S., Anagnostou, E., Areces-Gonzalez, A., Astle, D. E., Auyeung, B., Ayub, M., Bae, J., Ball, G., Baron-Cohen, S., Beare, R., Bedford, S. A., Benegal, V., . . . Alexander-Bloch, A. F. (2022). Brain charts for the human lifespan. *Nature, 604*(7906), 525–533. https://doi.org/10.1038/s41586-022-04554-y

Beti, R. A., Al-Khatib, F., & Cook, D. M. (2019). The efficacy of using virtual reality for job interviews and its effects on mitigating discrimination. In Unger, H., Sodsee, S., Meesad, P. (Eds.), *Recent Advances in Information and Communication Technology 2018: Proceedings of the 14th International Conference on Computing and Information Technology (IC2IT 2018)*. Advances in Intelligent Systems and Computing, vol 769 (pp. 43–52). Springer, Cham. https://doi.org/10.1007/978-3-319-93692-5_5

Bhavnani, S. P., Narula, J., & Sengupta, P. P. (2016). Mobile technology and the digitization of healthcare. *European Heart Journal, 37*(18), 1428–1438. https://doi.org/10.1093/eurheartj/ehv770

Bilder, R. M., & Reise, S. P. (2019). Neuropsychological tests of the future: How do we get there from here? *Clinical Neuropsychology, 33*(2), 220–245. https://doi.org/10.1080/13854046.2018.1521993

Bordes Edgar, V., MacDonald, B., Thames, A. D., & McClintock, S. M. (2025). The time has come: discussing the clinical neuropsychology provider's role in cultural respect and inclusion. *Journal of Clinical and Experimental Neuropsychology, 47*(6), 531–548. https://doi.org/10.1080/13803395.2025.2455126

Boulos, M. N., Wheeler, S., Tavares, C., & Jones, R. (2011). How smartphones are changing the face of mobile and participatory healthcare: an overview, with example from eCAALYX. *Biomedical Engineering Online, 10*, 24. https://doi.org/10.1186/1475-925X-10-24

Bowe, A. K., Lightbody, G., Staines, A., & Murray, D. M. (2023). Big data, machine learning, and population health: Predicting cognitive outcomes in childhood. *Pediatric Research, 93*(2), 300–307. https://doi.org/10.1038/s41390-022-02137-1

Brearly, T. W., Shura, R. D., Martindale, S. L., Lazowski, R. A., Luxton, D. D., Shenal, B. V., & Rowland, J. A. (2017). Neuropsychological test administration by videoconference: A systematic review and meta-analysis. *Neuropsychology Review, 27*(2), 174–186. https://doi.org/10.1007/s11065-017-9349-1

Britton, G. B., Huang, L. K., Villarreal, A. E., Levey, A., Philippakis, A., Hu, C. J., Yang, C. C., Mushi, D., Oviedo, D. C., Rangel, G., Ho, J. S., Thompson, L., Khemakhem, M., Ross, M., Carreira, M. B., Kim, N., Joung, P., Albastaki, O., Kuo, P. C., . . . Au, R. (2023). Digital phenotyping: An equal opportunity approach to reducing disparities in Alzheimer's disease and related dementia research. *Alzheimer's Dementia (Amsterdam), 15*(4), e12495. https://doi.org/10.1002/dad2.12495

Buis, L., Hirzel, L., Dawood, R. M., Dawood, K. L., Nichols, L. P., Artinian, N. T., Schwiebert, L., Yarandi, H. N., Roberson, D. N., Plegue, M. A., Mango, L. C., & Levy, P. D. (2017). Text messaging to improve hypertension medication adherence in African Americans from primary care and emergency department settings: Results from two randomized feasibility studies. *JMIR Mhealth Uhealth, 5*(2), e9. https://doi.org/10.2196/mhealth.6630

Burton, C. Z., Katz, L. A., Schmitt, T. R., Trittschuh, E. H., Correro, A. N., II, Rahman-Filipiak, A., & Richard, A. E. (2024). Perceptions in neuropsychology about non-inclusivity in testing materials: Preliminary results from a small-scale survey. *Clinical Neuropsychology*, 1–13. https://doi.org/10.1080/13854046.2024.2430549

Butler, P. M., Yang, J., Brown, R., Hobbs, M., Becker, A., Penalver-Andres, J., Syz, P., Muller, S., Cosne, G., Juraver, A., Song, H. H., Saha-Chaudhuri, P., Roggen, D., Scotland, A., Silveira, N., Demircioglu, G., Gabelle, A., Hughes, R., Erkkinen, M. G., . . . Belachew, S. (2025). Smartwatch- and smartphone-based remote assessment of brain health and detection of mild cognitive impairment. *Nature Medicine, 31*(3), 829–839. https://doi.org/10.1038/s41591-024-03475-9

Canali, S., Schiaffonati, V., & Aliverti, A. (2022). Challenges and recommendations for wearable devices in digital health: Data quality, interoperability, health equity, fairness. *PLOS Digital Health, 1*(10), e0000104. https://doi.org/10.1371/journal.pdig.0000104

Cary, M. P., Jr., Zink, A., Wei, S., Olson, A., Yan, M., Senior, R., Bessias, S., Gadhoumi, K., Jean-Pierre, G., Wang, D., Ledbetter, L. S., Economou-Zavlanos, N. J., Obermeyer, Z., & Pencina, M. J. (2023). Mitigating racial and ethnic bias and advancing health equity in clinical algorithms: A scoping review. *Health Affairs (Millwood), 42*(10), 1359–1368. https://doi.org/10.1377/hlthaff.2023.00553

Ceasar, J. N., Claudel, S. E., Andrews, M. R., Tamura, K., Mitchell, V., Brooks, A. T., Dodge, T., El-Toukhy, S., Farmer, N., Middleton, K., Sabado-Liwag, M., Troncoso, M., Wallen, G. R., & Powell-Wiley, T. M. (2019). Community engagement in the development of an mHealth-enabled physical activity and cardiovascular health intervention (Step It Up): Pilot focus group study. *JMIR Form Research*, *3*(1), e10944. https://doi.org/10.2196/10944

Chafiq, T., Azmi, R., Fadil, A., & Mohammed, O. (2024). Investigating the potential of blockchain technology for geospatial data sharing: Opportunities, challenges, and solutions. *Geomatica*, *76*(2), 100026. https://doi.org/ https://doi.org/10.1016/j.geomat.2024.100026

Chamusca, I. L., Ferreira, C. V., Murari, T. B., Apolinario, A. J. r., & Winkler, I. (2023). Towards sustainable virtual reality: Gathering design guidelines for intuitive authoring tools. *Sustainability*, *15*(4), 2924. https://doi.org/10.3390/su15042924

Chelak, K., & Chakole, S. (2023). The role of social determinants of health in promoting health equality: A narrative review. *Cureus*, *15*(1), e33425. https://doi.org/10.7759/cureus.33425

Chen, Y., Kruahong, S., Elias, S., Turkson-Ocran, R. A., Commodore-Mensah, Y., Koirala, B., & Himmelfarb, C. R. D. (2023). Racial disparities in shared decision-making and the use of mHealth technology among adults with hypertension in the 2017–2020 Health Information National Trends Survey: Cross-sectional study in the United States. *Journal of Medical Internet Research*, *25*, e47566. https://doi.org/10.2196/47566

Chițu, I. B., Tecău, A. S., Constantin, C. P., Tescașiu, B., Brătucu, T. O., Brătucu, G., & Purcaru, I. M. (2023). Exploring the opportunity to use virtual reality for the education of children with disabilities. *Children (Basel)*, *10*(3), 436. https://doi.org/10.3390/children10030436

Colvonen, P. J., DeYoung, P. N., Bosompra, N. A., & Owens, R. L. (2020). Limiting racial disparities and bias for wearable devices in health science research. *Sleep*, *43*(10), 159. https://doi.org/10.1093/sleep/zsaa159

Cook, D., Wiese, L., Luna, C., & Schmitter-Edgecombe, M. (2023). Testing the feasibility of tracking behavior and physiology patterns using wearable technology to detect potential cognitive risk among rural, multicultural older adults. *Alzheimer's & Dementia*, *19*(S19), e077802. https://doi.org/10.1002/alz.077802

Crigger, E., Reinbold, K., Hanson, C., Kao, A., Blake, K., & Irons, M. (2022). Trustworthy augmented intelligence in health care. *Journal of Medical Systems*, *46*(2), 12. https://doi.org/10.1007/s10916-021-01790-z

Davy van de, S., Michel, E. V. G., Jim, M. S., Joost, H., Jacob, J. V., Robert, E. R. V., Edwin van, U., Oliver Hilgers, B. A., Diederik, G., & Jasper van, B. (2022). Developing, implementing and governing artificial intelligence in medicine: A step-by-step approach to prevent an artificial intelligence winter. *BMJ Health & Care Informatics*, *29*(1), e100495. https://doi.org/10.1136/bmjhci-2021-100495

Dick. (2021). Current and potential uses of AR/VR for equity and inclusion. In *Information Technology and Innovation Foundation* (Vol. 2025, pp. 1–14). Retrieved from: https://itif.org/publications/2021/06/01/current-and-potential-uses-arvr-equity-and-inclusion/

Drigas, A., & Sideraki, A. (2024). Brain neuroplasticity leveraging virtual reality and brain-computer interface technologies. *Sensors (Basel), 24*(17). https://doi.org/10.3390/s24175725

Edgar, A. K., Tai, J., & Bearman, M. (2024). Inclusivity in health professional education: How can virtual simulation foster attitudes of inclusion? *Advances in Simulation (London), 9*(1), 15. https://doi.org/10.1186/s41077-024-00290-7

Eustis, E. H., LoPresti, J., Aguilera, A., & Schueller, S. M. (2023). Cultural responsivity in technology-enabled services: Integrating culture into technology and service components. *Journal of Medical Internet Research, 25*, e45409. https://doi.org/10.2196/45409

Farao, J., Malila, B., Conrad, N., Mutsvangwa, T., Rangaka, M. X., & Douglas, T. S. (2020). A user-centred design framework for mHealth. *PLoS One, 15*(8), e0237910. https://doi.org/10.1371/journal.pone.0237910

Fares, O. H., Aversa, J., Lee, S. H., & Jacobson, J. (2024). Virtual reality: A review and a new framework for integrated adoption. *International Journal of Consumer Studies, 48*(2), e13040. https://doi.org/https://doi.org/10.1111/ijcs.13040

Fernandez, A. L. (2019). Modern neuropsychological tests for a diversity of cultural contexts. *Clinical Neuropsychology, 33*(2), 438–445. https://doi.org/10.1080/13854046.2018.1560501

Forrest, S. (2023). *Artificial intelligence/machine learning (AI/ML)-enabled medical devices: Tailoring a regulatory framework to encourage responsible innovation in AI/ML.* Food and Drug Administration.

Franks, M. A. (2017). The desert of the unreal: Inequality in virtual and augmented reality. *UCDL Review, 51*, 499.

Gallegos, I., Rossi, R., Barrow, J., Tanjim, M. M., Kim, S., Dernoncourt, F., Yu, T., Zhang, R., & Ahmed, N. (2023). Bias and fairness in large language models: A survey. *Compuational Linguistics, 50*(3), 1097–1179. https://doi.org/10.48550/arXiv.2309.00770

Gamito, P., Oliveira, J., Alves, C., Santos, N., Coelho, C., & Brito, R. (2020). Virtual reality-based cognitive stimulation to improve cognitive functioning in community elderly: A controlled study. *Cyberpsychology Behavior and Social Network, 23*(3), 150–156. https://doi.org/10.1089/cyber.2019.0271

Gilman, M., & Green, R. (2018). The surveillance gap: The harms of extreme privacy and data marginalization. *NYU Review Law & Social Change, 42*, 253.

Graham, S., Depp, C., Lee, E. E., Nebeker, C., Tu, X., Kim, H. C., & Jeste, D. V. (2019). Artificial intelligence for mental health and mental illnesses: An overview. *Current Psychiatry Report, 21*(11), 116. https://doi.org/10.1007/s11920-019-1094-0

Graham, S. A., Lee, E. E., Jeste, D. V., Van Patten, R., Twamley, E. W., Nebeker, C., Yamada, Y., Kim, H. C., & Depp, C. A. (2020). Artificial intelligence approaches to predicting and detecting cognitive decline in older adults: A conceptual review. *Psychiatry Research, 284*, 112732. https://doi.org/10.1016/j.psychres.2019.112732

Guberek, T., McDonald, A., Simioni, S., Mhaidli, A. H., Toyama, K., & Schaub, F. (2018). Keeping a low profile? Technology, risk and privacy among undocumented immigrants. In Mandryk, R., Hancock, M., Cox, A. & Dey, A. (Eds.), *Proceedings of the 2018 CHI conference on human factors in computing systems*. Association for Computing Machinery, New York, NY. Paper No. 114, pp. 1–15. https://dl.acm.org/doi/10.1145/3173574.3173688

Hacker, K., Anies, M., Folb, B. L., & Zallman, L. (2015). Barriers to health care for undocumented immigrants: A literature review. *Risk Management and Healthcare Policy*, *8*, 175–183. https://doi.org/10.2147/rmhp.S70173

Heesen, J. (2012). Computer and information ethics. In R. Chadwick (Ed.), *Encyclopedia of applied ethics* (2nd ed.) (pp. 538–546). Academic Press. https://doi.org/https://doi.org/10.1016/B978-0-12-373932-2.00059-4

Hernandez-Green, N., Davis, M. V., Beshara, M. S., Hernandez-Spalding, K., Francis, S., Parker, A., Farinu, O., & Chandler, R. (2024). Examining the perceptions of mHealth on racial and ethnic disparities in postpartum health for Black women: A scoping review. *Health Promotion Practice*, *25*(6), 1116–1128.

Higgins, S., Alcock, S., Aveiro, B. D., Daniels, W., Farmer, H., & Besharati, S. (2024). Perspective matters: A systematic review of immersive virtual reality to reduce racial prejudice. *Virtual Reality*, *28*(3), 125. https://doi.org/10.1007/s10055-024-01024-w

Hilty, D. M., Gentry, M. T., McKean, A. J., Cowan, K. E., Lim, R. F., & Lu, F. G. (2020). Telehealth for rural diverse populations: Telebehavioral and cultural competencies, clinical outcomes and administrative approaches. *Mhealth*, *6*, 20. https://doi.org/10.21037/mhealth.2019.10.04

Hoagland, A., & Kipping, S. (2024). Challenges in promoting health equity and reducing disparities in access across new and established technologies. *Canadian Journal of Cardiology*, *40*(6), 1154–1167. https://doi.org/https://doi.org/10.1016/j.cjca.2024.02.014

Huang, J., Galal, G., Etemadi, M., & Vaidyanathan, M. (2022). Evaluation and mitigation of racial bias in clinical machine learning models: Scoping review. *JMIR Medical Information*, *10*(5), e36388. https://doi.org/10.2196/36388

Intahchomphoo, C. (2018). Indigenous peoples, social media, and the digital divide: A systematic literature review. *American Indian Culture and Research Journal*, *42* (4), 85–111. https://doi.org/http://dx.doi.org/10.17953/aicrj.42.4.intahchomphoo

Istepanian, R. S. H. (2022). Mobile health (m-Health) in retrospect: The known unknowns. *International Journal of Environmental Research and Public Health*, *19*(7), 3747. https://doi.org/10.3390/ijerph19073747

James, D. C., Harville, C., Sears, C., Efunbumi, O., & Bondoc, I. (2017). Participation of African Americans in e-Health and m-Health studies: A systematic review. *Telemedicine and e-Health*, *23*(5), 351–364.

Jerald, J. (2015). *The VR book: Human-centered design for virtual reality*. Association for Computing Machinery and Morgan & Claypool.

Jimenez, R. T., Zuniga-Hernandez, M., Suen, M. Y., Feng, R., Pinedo, K., Arshad, F., Collins, F., Ganesan, A., Jackson, C., Wang, E. Y., Rodriguez, S. T., & Caruso, T. J. (2025). Culturally sensitive treatment of caregiver anxiety with virtual reality: A prospective, pragmatic, randomized study. *Journal of Patient Experience, 12*, 23743735251326671, 1–12. https://doi.org/10.1177/23743735251326671

Jones, L., Jacklin, K., & O'Connell, M. E. (2017). Development and use of health-related technologies in Indigenous communities: Critical review. *Journal of Medicine and Internet Research, 19*(7), e256. https://doi.org/10.2196/jmir.7520

Josephy-Hernandez, S., Norise, C., Han, J. Y., & Smith, K. M. (2021). Survey on acceptance of passive technology monitoring for early detection of cognitive impairment. *Digital Biomarker, 5*(1), 9–15. https://doi.org/10.1159/000512207

Jylkkä, J., Soveri, A., Laine, M., & Lehtonen, M. (2020). Assessing bilingual language switching behavior with ecological momentary assessment. *Bilingualism: Language and Cognition, 23*(2), 309–322. https://doi.org/10.1017/S1366728918001190

Kamikubo, R., Wang, L., Marte, C., Mahmood, A., & Kacorri, H. (2022). Data representativeness in accessibility datasets: A meta-analysis. In *Proceedings of the 24th international ACM SIGACCESS conference on computers and accessibility*, Athens, Greece. https://doi.org/10.1145/3517428.3544826

Kang, D., Park, J., & Eun, S. D. (2023). Home-based virtual reality exergame program after stroke rehabilitation for patients with stroke: A study protocol for a multicenter, randomized controlled trial. *Life (Basel), 13*(12), 2256. https://doi.org/10.3390/life13122256

Kellogg, K. C., & Sadeh-Sharvit, S. (2022). Pragmatic AI-augmentation in mental healthcare: Key technologies, potential benefits, and real-world challenges and solutions for frontline clinicians. *Frontiers in Psychiatry, 13*, 990370. https://doi.org/10.3389/fpsyt.2022.990370

Kim, E. H., Jenness, J. L., Miller, A. B., Halabi, R., de Zambotti, M., Bagot, K. S., Baker, F. C., & Pratap, A. (2023). Association of demographic and socioeconomic indicators with the use of wearable devices among children. *JAMA Network Open, 6*(3), e235681. https://doi.org/10.1001/jamanetworkopen.2023.5681

Kim, G. J. (2005). A SWOT analysis of the field of virtual reality rehabilitation and therapy. *Presence, 14*(2), 119–146.

Koehle, H., Kronk, C., & Lee, Y. J. (2022). Digital Health Equity: Addressing Power, Usability, and Trust to Strengthen Health Systems. *Yearbook of Medical Informatics, 31*(1), 20–32. https://doi.org/10.1055/s-0042-1742512

Kouijzer, M., Kip, H., Bouman, Y. H. A., & Kelders, S. M. (2023). Implementation of virtual reality in healthcare: A scoping review on the implementation process of virtual reality in various healthcare settings. *Implement Sci Commun, 4*(1), 67. https://doi.org/10.1186/s43058-023-00442-2

Kourtesis, P., Collina, S., Doumas, L. A. A., & MacPherson, S. E. (2019). Technological competence is a pre-condition for effective implementation of virtual reality head mounted displays in human neuroscience: A technological review and meta-analysis. *Frontiers in Human Neuroscience, 13*, 342. https://doi.org/10.3389/fnhum.2019.00342

Krishnan, G., Singh, S., Pathania, M., Gosavi, S., Abhishek, S., Parchani, A., & Dhar, M. (2023). Artificial intelligence in clinical medicine: catalyzing a sustainable global healthcare paradigm. *Frontiers in Artificial Intelligence, 6*, 1227091. https://doi.org/10.3389/frai.2023.1227091

Kumar, S., Buckley, J. L., Barton, J., Pigeon, M., Newberry, R., Rodencal, M., Hajzeraj, A., Hannon, T., Rogers, K., Casey, D., O'Sullivan, D., & O'Flynn, B. (2020). A wristwatch-based wireless sensor platform for IoT health monitoring applications. *Sensors (Basel), 20*(6), 1675. https://doi.org/10.3390/s20061675

Kumar, J., Patel, T., Sugandh, F., Dev, J., Kumar, U., Adeeb, M., Kachhadia, M. P., Puri, P., Prachi, F., Zaman, M. U., Kumar, S., Varrassi, G., & Syed, A. R. S. (2023). Innovative approaches and therapies to enhance neuroplasticity and promote recovery in patients with neurological disorders: A narrative review. *Cureus, 15*(7), e41914. https://doi.org/10.7759/cureus.41914

Li, Y., Liu, C., Sun, J., Zhang, J., Li, X., & Zhang, Z. (2024). The digital divide and cognitive disparities among older adults: Community-based cohort study in China. *Journal of Medical Internet Research, 26*, e59684. https://doi.org/10.2196/59684

Lipio Brothers, S. (2023). Application of novel technological solutions in the assessment of culturally diverse older adults. *Practice Innovations, 8*(1), 1–22. https://doi.org/10.1037/pri0000206

Lui, P. P., Stringer, E., & Jouriles, E. N. (2023). Advancing knowledge on the health consequences of discrimination: The potential of virtual reality. *Cultural Diversity & Ethnic Minority Psychology, 29*(1), 96.

Ma, D., Du, J., Cen, Y., & Wu, P. (2016). Exploring the adoption of mobile internet services by socioeconomically disadvantaged people: A qualitative user study. *Aslib Journal of Information Management, 68*, 670–693. https://doi.org/10.1108/AJIM-03-2016-0027

Maggio, M. G., De Cola, M. C., Latella, D., Maresca, G., Finocchiaro, C., La Rosa, G., Cimino, V., Sorbera, C., Bramanti, P., De Luca, R., & Calabro, R. S. (2018). What about the role of virtual reality in Parkinson disease's cognitive rehabilitation? Preliminary findings from a randomized clinical trial. *Journal of Geriatric Psychiatry and Neurology, 31*(6), 312–318. https://doi.org/10.1177/0891988718807973

Maggio, M. G., Luca, A., D'Agate, C., Italia, M., Calabro, R. S., & Nicoletti, A. (2022). Feasibility and usability of a non-immersive virtual reality tele-cognitive app in cognitive rehabilitation of patients affected by Parkinson's disease. *Psychogeriatrics, 22*(6), 775–779. https://doi.org/10.1111/psyg.12880

Marfo, A., & Obeng-Gyasi, E. (2024). Empowering communities: The role of wearable devices in environmental justice. *Authorea Preprints*. [Preprint]. https://doi.org/10.22541/au.170965072.20316399/v1

Marra, D. E., Hamlet, K. M., Bauer, R. M., & Bowers, D. (2020). Validity of teleneuropsychology for older adults in response to COVID-19: A systematic and critical review.

Clinical Neuropsychology, 34(7–8), 1411–1452. https://doi.org/10.1080/13854046.2020.1769192

Martingano, A. J., Duane, JN., Brown, E. Persky, S. (2023). Demographic differences in presence across seven studies. *Virtual Reality*. https://doi.org/10.1007/s10055-023-00805-z

Mavangere, N., Edfor, E. E., Adedovin, F., Apeh, E., & Owusu, A. (2022). Education inequality in underserved regions: Exploring the role of technology to promote diversity and inclusivity. In *IEEE International Conference on e-Business Engineering, ICEBE 2022*. The Institute of Electrical and Electronics Engineers, Inc., (pp. 288–293). https://doi.org/10.1109/ICEBE55470.2022.00057.

Mehrabi, N., Morstatter, F., Saxena, N., Lerman, K., & Galstyan, A. (2021). A Survey on Bias and Fairness in Machine Learning. *ACM Computing Surveys, 54*(6), Article 115. https://doi.org/10.1145/3457607

Merkley, T. L., Esopenko, C., Zizak, V. S., Bilder, R. M., Strutt, A. M., Tate, D. F., & Irimia, A. (2023). Challenges and opportunities for harmonization of cross-cultural neuropsychological data. *Neuropsychology, 37*(3), 237–246. https://doi.org/10.1037/neu0000818

Messler, A. C., Kane, K. D., & Serrano, Y. (2023). Tele-neuropsychology in culturally and linguistically diverse populations within the U.S. and U.S. territories: A scoping review. *The Clinical Neuropsycholist*, 39(5), 1345–1367. https://doi.org/10.1080/13854046.2023.2215954

Mitchell, U. A., Chebli, P. G., Ruggiero, L., & Muramatsu, N. (2018). The Digital Divide in Health-Related Technology Use: The Significance of Race/Ethnicity. *The Gerontologist, 59*(1), 6–14. https://doi.org/10.1093/geront/gny138

Mumtaz, H., Riaz, M. H., Wajid, H., Saqib, M., Zeeshan, M. H., Khan, S. E., Chauhan, Y. R., Sohail, H., & Vohra, L. I. (2023). Current challenges and potential solutions to the use of digital health technologies in evidence generation: a narrative review. *Frontiers in Digital Health, 5*, 1203945. https://doi.org/10.3389/fdgth.2023.1203945

Munro Cullum, C., Hynan, L. S., Grosch, M., Parikh, M., & Weiner, M. F. (2014). Teleneuropsychology: evidence for video teleconference-based neuropsychological assessment. *Journal of International Neuropsychology Society, 20*(10), 1028–1033. https://doi.org/10.1017/s1355617714000873

Nakamura, L. (2020). Feeling good about feeling bad: Virtuous virtual reality and the automation of racial empathy. *Journal of Visual Culture, 19*(1), 47–64.

Nicosia, J., Aschenbrenner, A. J., Adams, S. L., Tahan, M., Stout, S. H., Wilks, H., Balls-Berry, J. E., Morris, J. C., & Hassenstab, J. (2022). Bridging the technological divide: Stigmas and challenges with technology in digital brain health studies of older adults. *Frontiers in Digital Health, 4*, 1–10. https://doi.org/10.3389/fdgth.2022.880055

Nittas, V., Daniore, P., Chavez, S. J., & Wray, T. B. (2024). Challenges in implementing cultural adaptations of digital health interventions. *Communications Medicine, 4*(1), 7. https://doi.org/10.1038/s43856-023-00426-2

Nouri, S. S., Adler-Milstein, J., Thao, C., Acharya, P., Barr-Walker, J., Sarkar, U., & Lyles, C. (2020). Patient characteristics associated with objective measures of digital health tool use in the United States: A literature review. *Journal of the Americal Medical Information Association, 27*(5), 834–841. https://doi.org/10.1093/jamia/ocaa024

Okolo, C., Babawarun, O., & Olorunsogo, T. (2024). Mobile Health (mHealth) Innovations for public health feedback: A global perspective. *International Medical Science Research Journal, 4*, 235–246. https://doi.org/10.51594/imsrj.v4i3.915

Oliveira, J., Gamito, P., Lopes, B., Silva, A. R., Galhordas, J., Pereira, E., Ramos, E., Silva, A. P., Jorge, A., & Fantasia, A. (2022). Computerized cognitive training using virtual reality on everyday life activities for patients recovering from stroke. *Disability and Rehabilitation: Assistive Technology, 17*(3), 298–303. https://doi.org/10.1080/17483107.2020.1749891

Omar, M., Sorin, V., Agbareia, R., Apakama, D. U., Soroush, A., Sakhuja, A., Freeman, R., Horowitz, C. R., Richardson, L. D., Nadkarni, G. N., & Klang, E. (2025). Evaluating and addressing demographic disparities in medical large language models: A systematic review. *International Journal of Equity in Health, 24*(1), 57. https://doi.org/10.1186/s12939-025-02419-0

Parsons, T. D. (2021). Ethical challenges of using virtual environments in the assessment and treatment of psychopathological disorders. *Journal of Clinical Medicine, 10*(3), 378. https://doi.org/10.3390/jcm10030378

Parsons, T. D., McMahan, T., & Kane, R. (2018). Practice parameters facilitating adoption of advanced technologies for enhancing neuropsychological assessment paradigms. *Clinical Neuropsychology, 32*(1), 16–41. https://doi.org/10.1080/13854046.2017.1337932

Philbin, M. M., Parish, C., Pereyra, M., Feaster, D. J., Cohen, M., Wingood, G., Konkle-Parker, D., Adedimeji, A., Wilson, T. E., Cohen, J., Goparaju, L., Adimora, A. A., Golub, E. T., & Metsch, L. R. (2019). Health disparities and the digital divide: The relationship between communication inequalities and quality of life among women in a nationwide prospective cohort study in the United States. *Journal of Health Communication, 24*(4), 405–412. https://doi.org/10.1080/10810730.2019.1630524

Radu, I., Scheermesser, M., Spiess, M. R., Schulze, C., Händler-Schuster, D., & Pehlke-Milde, J. (2023). Digital health for migrants, ethnic and cultural minorities and the role of participatory development: A scoping review. *International Journal of Environmental Research and Public Health, 20*(20), 6962. https://doi.org/10.3390/ijerph20206962

Romano, M. F., Shih, L. C., Paschalidis, I. C., Au, R., & Kolachalama, V. B. (2023). Large language models in neurology research and future practice. *Neurology, 101*(23), 1058–1067. https://doi.org/10.1212/wnl.0000000000207967

Roswell, R. O., Cogburn, C. D., Tocco, J., Martinez, J., Bangeranye, C., Bailenson, J. N., Wright, M., Mieres, J. H., & Smith, L. (2020). Cultivating empathy through virtual reality: advancing conversations about racism, inequity, and climate in medicine. *Academic Medicine, 95*(12), 1882–1886.

Saeed, S. A., & Masters, R. M. (2021). Disparities in health care and the digital divide. *Current Psychiatry Report, 23*(9), 61. https://doi.org/10.1007/s11920-021-01274-4

Sarella, P. N. K., & Mangam, V. T. (2024). AI-driven natural language processing in healthcare: Transforming patient-provider communication. *Indian Journal of Pharmacy Practice, 17*(1), 21–26.

Sartori, F., Savi, M., & Talpini, J. (2022). Tailoring mHealth apps on users to support behavior change interventions: Conceptual and computational considerations. *Applied Sciences, 12*(8), 3782. https://www.mdpi.com/2076-3417/12/8/3782

Schulteis, M., & Rothbaum, B. O. (2002). Ethical issues for the use of virtual reality in the psychological sciences. *Ethical Issues in Clinical Neuropsychology, 243*(80), 5.

Schwartz, R., Schwartz, R., Vassilev, A., Greene, K., Perine, L., Burt, A., & Hall, P. (2022). *Towards a standard for identifying and managing bias in artificial intelligence* (Vol. 3). US Department of Commerce, National Institute of Standards and Technology.

Shaw, R. J., Steinberg, D. M., Bonnet, J., Modarai, F., George, A., Cunningham, T., Mason, M., Shahsahebi, M., Grambow, S. C., Bennett, G. G., & Bosworth, H. B. (2016). Mobile health devices: Will patients actually use them? *Journal of American Medical Information Association, 23*(3), 462–466. https://doi.org/10.1093/jamia/ocv186

Singha, R., & Singha, S. (2023). The challenges and opportunities of virtual reality in marketing and advertising. In Kunnumpurath, B. & Stephen, C. (Eds.). Virutal Reality and New Media vol I., The Native Tribe. (pp. 154–165). https://doi.org/10.17605/OSF.IO/GNHC6

Slater, M., & Sanchez-Vives, M. V. (2016). Enhancing our lives with immersive virtual reality. *Frontiers in Robotics and AI, 3*, 74.

Song, T., Yu, P., Bliokas, V., Probst, Y., Peoples, G. E., Qian, S., Houston, L., Perez, P., Amirghasemi, M., Cui, T., Hitige, N. P. R., & Smith, N. A. (2021). A clinician-led, experience-based co-design approach for developing mHealth services to support the patient self-management of chronic conditions: Development study and design case. *JMIR Mhealth Uhealth, 9*(7), e20650. https://doi.org/10.2196/20650

Stanica, I. C., Moldoveanu, F., Portelli, G. P., Dascalu, M. I., Moldoveanu, A., & Ristea, M. G. (2020). Flexible virtual reality system for neurorehabilitation and quality of life improvement. *Sensors (Basel), 20*(21), 6045. https://doi.org/10.3390/s20216045

Tang, Z., Wang, H., Cui, Z., Jin, X., Zhang, L., Peng, Y., & Xing, B. (2023). An upper-limb rehabilitation exoskeleton system controlled by MI recognition model with deep emphasized informative features in a VR scene. *IEEE Trans Neural Syst Rehabil Eng, 31*, 4390–4401. https://doi.org/10.1109/TNSRE.2023.3329059

Thames, A. D., Hinkin, C. H., Byrd, D. A., Bilder, R. M., Duff, K. J., Mindt, M. R., Arentoft, A., & Streiff, V. (2013). Effects of stereotype threat, perceived discrimination, and examiner race on neuropsychological performance: simple as black and white? *Journal of International Neuropsychology Society, 19*(5), 583–593. https://doi.org/10.1017/S1355617713000076

VanLandingham, H., Ellison, R. L., Laique, A., Cladek, A., Khan, H., Gonzalez, C., & Dunn, M. R. (2022). A scoping review of stereotype threat for BIPOC: Cognitive effects and intervention strategies for the field of neuropsychology. *Clinical Neuropsychology, 36*(2), 503–522. https://doi.org/10.1080/13854046.2021.1947388

Varshney, U. (2014). Mobile health: Four emerging themes of research. *Decision Support Systems, 66*, 20–35. https://doi.org/ https://doi.org/10.1016/j.dss.2014.06.001

Villanueva, A. (2019). Associations between mental health, racial discrimination, and racial identity on mHealth for African Americans. [Honors thesis, Univeristy of North Carolina at Chapel Hill]. Carolina Digital Repository. https://doi.org/10.17615/yewq-e445

Wall, C., Hetherington, V., & Godfrey, A. (2023). Beyond the clinic: The rise of wearables and smartphones in decentralising healthcare. *NPJ Digital Medicine, 6*(1), 219. https://doi.org/10.1038/s41746-023-00971-z

Walter, J. R., Xu, S., & Rogers, J. A. (2024). From lab to life: How wearable devices can improve health equity. *Nature Communications, 15*(1), 123. https://doi.org/10.1038/s41467-023-44634-9

White, E. J., Demuth, M. J., Wiglesworth, A., Coser, A. D., Garrett, B. A., Kominsky, T. K., Jernigan, V., Thompson, W. K., Paulus, M., & Aupperle, R. (2023). Five recommendations for using large-scale publicly available data to advance health among American Indian peoples: The Adolescent Brain and Cognitive Development (ABCD) Study(SM) as an illustrative case. *Neuropsychopharmacology, 48*(2), 263–269. https://doi.org/10.1038/s41386-022-01498-9

Whitehead, L., Talevski, J., Fatehi, F., & Beauchamp, A. (2023). Barriers to and facilitators of digital health among culturally and linguistically diverse populations: Qualitative systematic review. *Journal of Medical Internet Research, 25*, e42719. https://doi.org/10.2196/42719

Wicherts, J. M. (2016). The importance of measurement invariance in neurocognitive ability testing. *Clinical Neuropsychology, 30*(7), 1006–1016. https://doi.org/10.1080/13854046.2016.1205136

Williams, C. D., Bravo, D. Y., Santana, A., Paige, R., 2nd, Wise, C., Leslie, C. E., & Sullivan, T. N. (2025). Racial discrimination and adverse childhood experiences predicting depressive symptoms and developmental assets: Testing cultural socialization and preparation for bias as moderators among Black adolescents and caregivers. *Journal of Research in Adolescents, 35*(1), e13056. https://doi.org/10.1111/jora.13056

Willis, H. A., Gonzalez, J. C., Call, C. C., Quezada, D., Scholars for Elevating Equity and Diversity (SEED), & Galán, C. A. (2022). Culturally responsive telepsychology & mHealth interventions for racial-ethnic minoritized youth: Research gaps and future directions. *Journal of Clinical Child and Adolescent Psychology, 51*(6), 1053–1069. https://doi.org/10.1080/15374416.2022.2124516

Wilson, L., & Marasoiu, M. (2022). The development and use of chatbots in public health: Scoping review. *JMIR Human Factors, 9*(4), e35882. https://doi.org/10.2196/35882

Wohlgenannt, I., Simons, A., & Stieglitz, S. (2020). Virtual reality. *Business & Information Systems Engineering, 62*, 455–461.

Wong, D., Pike, K., Stolwyk, R., Allott, K., Ponsford, J., McKay, A., Longley, W., Bosboom, P., Hodge, A., Kinsella, G., & Mowszowski, L. (2024). Delivery of neuropsychological interventions for adult and older adult clinical populations: An Australian expert working group clinical guidance paper. *Neuropsychology Review, 34*(4), 985–1047. https://doi.org/10.1007/s11065-023-09624-0

Yondjo, J., & Siette, J. (2024). "VR is the future": Perspectives of healthcare professionals on virtual reality as a diagnostic tool for dementia status in primary care. *BMC Medical Informatics and Decision Making, 24*(1), 9.

Zhou, S., Gromala, D., & Wang, L. (2023). Ethical challenges of virtual reality technology interventions for the vulnerabilities of patients with chronic pain: Exploration of technician responsibility. *Journal of Medical Internet Research, 25*, e49237. https://doi.org/10.2196/49237

12
Technology in Clinical Neuropsychological Feedback
Emerging Evidence for Innovative Methods

Brittany Wolff, Diana C. Hereld, and Amanda D. Ball

Introduction

Neuropsychological assessment plays a critical role in identifying an individual's cognitive strengths and weaknesses, informing diagnostic clarity, treatment planning, and educational or occupational recommendations. Yet a key, and often underemphasized, component of this process is the feedback session, during which these findings are communicated to patients, families, and other stakeholders. The primary goal in delivering feedback is to help the patient and others involved understand the testing results, along with implications for their care and daily function (Gruters et al., 2021). While this definition is a commonly accepted one, patient access to health care data and records (including mental health records), how feedback is delivered, and who our audience is have radically shifted in recent years. Dr. Karen Postal's pioneering work in *Feedback That Sticks* has underscored the importance of structuring feedback in a manner that is both understandable and memorable, thereby enhancing patient engagement and adherence to subsequent recommendations (Postal, 2013). Postal's emphasis on tailoring the "message" to the recipient's cognitive, emotional, and cultural context has served as a catalyst for reshaping how neuropsychologists approach the communication of complex test findings.

In tandem with these shifts in communication style, emerging technologies are offering innovative channels for delivering impactful and continuous feedback. Telehealth platforms now enable real-time and remote feedback sessions, especially vital for patients in rural or underserved regions. Automated summarization tools, often leveraging artificial intelligence (AI), can transform dense reports into more digestible summaries for varied audiences, such as educators, psychiatrists, primary care providers, or the patients themselves. Wearable devices and smartphone applications, meanwhile, generate ongoing data streams that can guide "just-in-time" interventions to help patients manage cognitive, psychiatric, or behavioral challenges in

Brittany Wolff, Diana C. Hereld, and Amanda D. Ball, *Technology in Clinical Neuropsychological Feedback*. In: *Technology and Neuropsychology*. Edited by: Jared F. Benge et al., Oxford University Press. © Oxford University Press (2026).
DOI: 10.1093/9780197814116.003.0012

daily life (Hanssen et al., 2020). Further, secure messaging systems and video recordings of feedback sessions may show promise in reinforcing patient comprehension and extending the "therapeutic window" for learning.

These new opportunities for technologically mediated feedback dovetail with broader trends in integrated and stepped care models. As health systems increasingly adopt interprofessional teams, neuropsychologists are finding themselves in close collaboration with psychiatrists, nurse practitioners, social workers, and other allied professionals. Digital platforms that store neuropsychological results and generate user-friendly feedback summaries can ensure that each team member has rapid access to relevant information, promoting coordinated care, improving adherence to recommendations, and helping tailor pharmacological or psychoeducational interventions. For instance, a patient's cognitive profile can be instantly shared with a speech-language pathologist or a special education coordinator, enabling individualized academic accommodations or targeted rehabilitative strategies.

Looking ahead, futuristic applications of technology in feedback sessions may include immersive virtual reality (VR) demonstrations, allowing patients to experience simulations of their cognitive challenges in safe, controlled settings (Parsons, 2015). Further, natural language processing (NLP) algorithms might provide dynamic, on-the-fly translations of highly technical feedback into patient-friendly language, potentially bridging linguistic or health literacy gaps. Neuropsychologists might also integrate machine learning–based predictive models to forecast a patient's risk of deterioration in specific cognitive domains, prompting timely re-evaluations or referrals. Taken together, these advancements exemplify how technology can extend and enhance Postal's foundational principles of effective feedback: clarity, personalization, cultural sensitivity, and a collaborative spirit (Postal, 2013). By embracing these tools in tandem with empathetic, person-centered communication, neuropsychologists are poised to deliver more meaningful and actionable insights to patients and the broader care team. As such, this chapter will explore the landscape of emerging feedback methods, ranging from AI-assisted summaries to passive data monitoring, offering a vision of how neuropsychologists can remain at the forefront of integrated, technology-enhanced clinical services. In this chapter, we discuss innovative feedback methods that may be ready for clinical prime time. Specifically, we review the main domains in which technology has begun to transform how neuropsychological feedback is structured and delivered:

1. The use of digital applications, commonly used technology platforms, and visual representation tools to provide accessible feedback and recommendations for specialized audiences
2. Capitalizing on advances in AI to use novel techniques such as audio generation and NLP for enhanced feedback in neuropsychology
3. Providing feedback through passive and active data monitoring for just-in-time interventions and ongoing monitoring of cognitive and psychiatric status

4. Case examples illustrating how a patient can benefit from these technological advances in feedback
5. Emerging techniques, including virtual reality, digital education, biofeedback, and digital twins

Collectively, these innovations herald a shift toward more dynamic, personalized, and continuous neuropsychological feedback, positioning the field to better meet the diverse needs of patients and collaborate effectively with interdisciplinary teams.

History of Feedback and COVID-19 Pandemic Shifts

Historically, neuropsychological feedback was paternalistic and typically given to physicians or referring providers rather than directly to the patient. Additionally, previous models of provision of neuropsychological feedback often included specifics around handing the patient a completed report, turning the pages and pointing out specific sections, that assumed the in-person delivery model (Carone, 2017). In recent years, the field has shifted to collaborative models along the impact of the arrival of open notes. In 2016, the bipartisan passing of the 21st century Cures Act in the United States required health organizations to make medical information available to patients and that this information would be readily available without delay (Hudson & Collins, 2017). Providers could only block this information if releasing it would cause the patient substantive harm, protect the privacy of another individual mentioned in the note, or by patient request. In this world of open notes, clients are often able to access notes in real time immediately after posting them in their medical record. This change made some providers rethink the contents of the report and how to approach feedback, as the option of not sharing the report is no longer available. Additionally, this increased access creates a greater necessity to communicate the findings to our clients in feedback in a way that is accessible, understandable, and transparent. Additionally, feedback is not only the provision of results but is increasingly viewed as an opportunity for therapeutic intervention (Gruters et al., 2021). Recent review by Gruters et al. (2022) noted that while feedback is an increasingly vital piece of the neuropsychological evaluation, information retention and adherence to recommendations by patients and family are often poor. They noted more research is needed to establish best communication aids that can improve these areas and that research into neuropsychological feedback continues to be limited.

More recently, particularly since the COVID-19 pandemic in 2020, the provision of virtual sessions via live video teleconference (e.g., Zoom, Microsoft Teams, Epic visits) is increasingly the norm rather than the exception. At the start of the pandemic in 2020, when we were all forced to stay home and begin virtual care, clinical neuropsychologists had to adapt to a new way of work. Test publishers rapidly began the process of providing electronic versions of stimulus books and protocols for providers who continued virtual neuropsychological assessments in a more limited scope during this initial pandemic period.

Since this time, many neuropsychologists continue to provide virtual feedback and work from a hybrid model (i.e., virtual intakes/feedback with in person testing). Recent surveys, however, indicated that feedback sessions in the United States remain brief, usually verbally delivered by telephone, and that training in conducting high-quality feedback is lacking (4). Nonetheless, some neuropsychologists provide almost all feedback and intakes with patients in virtual format for pediatric neuropsychological evaluations in a university hospital setting. Virtual care delivery through a hybrid model can be particularly advantageous in provision of feedback for pediatric patients who may have multihousehold family members and stakeholders who can join virtually (Lichtenstein et al., 2022). While there are many benefits of use of virtual platforms for feedback (e.g., allowing patients from rural areas greater access to care without multiple trips to a care center, saving time for providers and patients/family members to be able to join from home), there are things we lose when go to screens. Our ability to fluidly discuss findings can be interrupted by a multitude of factors, such as glitches in technology, audio/video interruptions, loss of Internet connection, devices losing battery power, distractions in the patient's home environments, along with the loss of the richness of in person behavioral observations. Nonetheless, virtual care delivery endures and will likely continue to persist in health care. In this, we as neuropsychologists must continue to adapt our methods and "pearls" of wisdom, to work for virtual formats. For instance, we have had to take what used to be a handout to the patient, to a screen share or discussion during the feedback session. There is a greater need to tailor our feedback to be engaging and meaningful.

Digital Tools to Enhance Feedback Delivery

In the use of these virtual platforms for provision of feedback, we have at our fingertips access to a variety of digital tools that can greatly enhance our ability to explain the results of the testing to our patients. Various test publishers, such as Pearson, offer comparative charts for examining differences between normative samples (e.g., the Behavior Assessment Scale for Children [BASC]), and these can be useful visuals to share in feedback. These comparative charts are valuable for providers, yet they were designed for the clinician, not the patients, and as such, they can be confusing and misinterpreted when provided as isolated data points.

There are various emerging technologies using large language models (LLMs) for use in medical settings, including some programs designed for adjacent work such as progress note writing. LLMs are being investigated for use in various settings and applications, including for generation of educational feedback (Zhang et al., 2024). For application in neuropsychological feedback, one of the major challenges in integration of these technologies is data security and regulations as in Health Insurance Portability and Accountability Act (HIPAA) regarding storage and transmission of health-related information via the Internet. For those working in large organizations such as hospitals and universities, our ability as individual providers to radically change the technology we integrate into our daily work may seem difficult in the face of red tape and administrative approvals needed to access new technologies. Hurdles individual providers can face even to integrate an established technology or software into their practice can take months if not years due to the layers of approvals, lack of funding to push the project forward, and/or the lack of impetus on the administration of the department to make changes which may appear unnecessary prima facie. Providers vary widely in their familiarity, comfort level, and desire to transition to virtual platforms versus traditional paper-and-pencil methods of administering and describing tests. By furthering our development and availability of tools specifically designed for our specialty, we can increase ease of use and availability of training to implement tools such as AI for report writing or programs for the creation of visuals, as we discuss in the next section. This will assist in removing or reducing barriers for provider-specific learning edges to encourage and facilitate their use of emerging technologies in the provision of feedback and other aspects of the evaluation process.

It is also important to note that our patients are increasingly from diverse backgrounds and range in their own comfort level with use of technology. For some patients, use of the following may be inappropriate depending on their comfort level accessing care via telehealth and devices they have available to them to join virtual feedback. Anecdotally, some clinicians note that when patients join virtual feedback on a phone, the use of screen sharing features, while possible, greatly decreases the usefulness, given the small size of the screen and the difficulty toggling between the screen share and video platform. It is vital that as providers we consider the multitude of specific factors such as age, gender, racial background, technology savviness, education level, and stated preference when we approach provision of feedback using video conferencing. Given this common experience of difficulty making changes related to technology, it can seem daunting to use a new software or program without training, education, and support. Provision of feedback is a unique opportunity for us to do so.

Visualization and Monitoring Change over Time

As many have transitioned to virtual feedback via platforms such as Zoom or Epic video visits, clinicians are deciding how to present virtually to replace paper handouts. Sharing our screen is a commonly used way to provide this information to patients, but the question becomes, What do we share? Due to the complexity of the information we present, ways to effectively and clearly demonstrate how the patient performed is vital in feedback. There are some groups working on creating visual tools specific for neuropsychology. For example, a pilot study of an interactive visual tool for memory clinics found the visualizations were received positively by patients and families and assisted in understanding their results (Gruters et al., 2021).

Patients and families still expressed difficulty with information retention, the insights gained into seeing their cognitive profile with daily life function had benefits overall. While the provision of patient feedback in neuropsychology has often relied upon predominantly verbal explanations, the incorporation of multimedia aids has become a salient tool for enhancing comprehension of testing data. For example, visual representations of a child's age- or grade-based scores in the context of performance in comparison to a normative reference group may be particularly helpful when communicating with parents, who may not have a background in psychometrics. Incorporating visual structures such as bell curves at the outset of feedback can ground these discussions in a context that is both empirically valid and ecologically meaningful.

Another clinical application that can benefit from visual aids involves explaining change over time. Patients who are evaluated cross multiple timepoints can clarify whether observed performance changes reflect meaningful neurocognitive development, stability, or decline. In this type of feedback, one particularly effective strategy involves illustrating cognitive change using reliable change indices (RCIs). By incorporating tools and applications that visually depict these differences (e.g., line graphs, bar charts, or animated progressions, whether together in clinic or through a shared Zoom screen), clinicians can break down statistical concepts into a more easily digestible and accessible format for families.

For example, sharing a profile graph of a Woodcock Johnson IV (WJ-IV) Achievement test shows grey bars with grade level number and a dotted line representing grade level. Some clinicians report this is an easy-to-understand method to demonstrate to parents how their child performed on achievement batteries in discussion of possible learning disorders.

One important question asked to neuropsychologists in referrals can be, "Has the patient demonstrated any change in their cognitive function since [event] (e.g., surgery, traumatic brain injury, transplant, device implantation)?" For example, a repeat neuropsychological evaluation can often be during monitoring of treatment of recurrent brain tumors. In pediatric clinic settings, for example, this can be used to monitor the child's response to treatment and need for updated accommodations or therapies in response to such findings. Schools use similar models such as response to intervention (RTI) in measuring change over time. One future direction for AI and software development is a program that can take scores from evaluation 1 and scores from evaluation 2 and create a graph which shows not only point scores but also confidence intervals (e.g., a bar as in the WJ profile report example) showing overlap and divergence from each evaluation set. For example, the Adaptive Behavior Assessment Scale (ABAS, 3rd ed.) is a popular measure of functional abilities across the lifespan. Creating a graph which compares dataset one to the follow-up evaluation would allow clinicians to easily demonstrate change in function over time important for cases such as follow-up evaluation on brain tumor as noted earlier. Automated reports overcome the limitations and time-consuming nature of manually entering scores, which for many providers makes this type of process for each evaluation untenable. Many work in settings where time for each evaluation is already limited, and we are spending more time than insurance allots for the evaluation. Progress toward normalizing and standardizing use of a program to analyze these numbers for us and create visualizations would open up significant options for providing simple and compelling methods of displaying key data such as change over time and general comparisons to normative groups (e.g., grade level/typically developing peers, normal aging).

One area that can be challenging in discussion in virtual feedback sessions is that of personality, and in particular, sensitive discussion of results of personality tests. The results of personality tests are typically discussed in either a narrative or bullet-pointed format, while in some settings, the score report may also contain T-scores as in the MMPI-3. Use of visualizations in discussion of personality dysfunction intuitively makes sense, given the continuous nature of personality traits. For example, discussion of introversion or extroversion is a concept many if not most of our patients have heard in popular culture. Providing a visual displaying introversion or avoidant personality on this continuum could assist in demonstrating how the patient scores on that domain area. Use of other graphics or diagrams may also be relevant; for example, the overlap of social anxiety and avoidant personality traits is another prime opportunity for use of a visualization. Further, discussion of the defined clusters in the DSM-5-TR could be improved with visuals such as Venn diagrams. In review of available literature, this area of use of technology in discussion of personality testing is under-researched and underdeveloped. It is an area we recommend for future development and integration into our discussion of cognitive testing results.

Clinicians have employed this visual feedback model by developing and compiling engaging animations and customizable slideshows tailored for pediatric populations. Through her Brain Building framework, for example, Liz Angoff uses child-friendly metaphors and visuals to improve understanding and reduce confusion that can lead to anxiety during feedback sessions (Angoff, 2022). These resources, including a spreadsheet of child-friendly videos, graphics, and books, serve as robust tools in facilitating positive and productive conversations with both children and their caregivers. Other tools such as MindMup for creating mind maps of assessment findings, or digital interactive whiteboards may be further helpful for more synchronous visual explanations. Canva is another useful tool for creating visuals like infographics, animations such as GIF exports, and more custom slide decks. By adapting feedback methods to the developmental context of patients and families, these technologies can promote increased engagement and clarity in communicating assessment results.

AI-Assisted Summaries, Audio Feedback, and NLP

Neuropsychological evaluation reports can be lengthy, replete with complex terminology, and primarily tailored to other mental health professionals. Yet different stakeholders (patients, psychiatrists, educators, social workers, and family members) require unique forms of these reports, ranging from simplified summaries to specialized jargon for academic or clinical contexts. Traditionally, clinicians manually generate separate versions, which is laborious and prone to inconsistencies. Recent advancements in AI, specifically in NLP and text summarization, offer avenues to automate parts of this process (Clay et al., 2025). AI systems designed for summarization can "scrape" or extract salient information (e.g., diagnoses, recommended interventions, test scores) from a lengthy neuropsychology report and reframe it to match the linguistic and conceptual needs of specific audiences. For example, an AI tool might generate a succinct, clinically precise outline for a psychiatrist (detailing relevant medications, comorbidities, and risk factors), while creating a plain-language version for a high school's special education team, focusing on learning accommodations and behavioral strategies. These tools can leverage LLMs trained on medical and educational corpora, enabling them to "translate" specialized neuropsychological language into comprehensible, audience-targeted narratives.

A growing trend in clinical practice is the provision of recorded feedback sessions, either audio or video, allowing patients to revisit the discussion of their assessment results on their own time. Audio-based feedback has been shown to improve patient recall and satisfaction in medical settings (Smith et al., 2022). In neuropsychology, the complexity of findings, from subtle memory deficits to explanations of executive dysfunction, often challenges patients' immediate comprehension. Recording feedback sessions can help patients and families absorb information at a comfortable pace. Concurrently, NLP can analyze these audio recordings to extract key points, highlight frequently mentioned concerns, or automatically annotate the session for swift review by both clinicians and patients. NLP algorithms can identify patterns in the patient's speech, detect emotional cues (e.g., frustration, confusion), and guide the neuropsychologist to clarify misunderstood aspects in follow-up communications. Audio archives can be shared, securely and with consent, with other providers, including psychiatrists and case managers, facilitating coordinated care.

One major challenge lies in ensuring the accuracy and fidelity of AI-generated summaries. Automatic summarization tools can occasionally omit nuanced but critical details, for instance, subtle personality dynamics or context-specific recommendations that a specialized professional would require (Rohil & Magotra, 2022). Additionally, commercial AI tools vary in their ability to handle domain-specific terminology in neurology, psychiatry, and education, risking oversimplification or misinterpretation of vital findings. Another concern is user oversight. Clinicians may over-rely on AI output, reducing their engagement in the interpretive process that is so integral to translating neuropsychological findings into actionable feedback. This underscores the continued need for professional judgment: AI-driven text summaries should be reviewed and refined by the clinician rather than being accepted at face value.

There is a risk of algorithmic bias in AI-driven summaries (Olawade et al., 2024). Language models can inadvertently propagate stereotypes or produce recommendations that do not reflect a patient's cultural, linguistic, or socioeconomic context if they were trained primarily on data from a narrow demographic. This problem can exacerbate health disparities if the AI tailoring does not account for cultural nuances. From a privacy standpoint, the use of AI to scrape and store personal health information increases the security risk, necessitating stringent data protection measures (e.g., encryption, restricted access) to comply with HIPAA and GDPR regulations. Moreover, for certain populations, such as individuals with limited English proficiency, AI-based summaries must be carefully validated to ensure that translation or language simplification does not compromise the accuracy of crucial recommendations.

New Evidence for the Value of LLMs

In a rapidly evolving health care landscape, there is an opportunity for neuropsychologists to harness the potential of AI to assist clinicians in delivering tailored recommendations based on patients' unique neuropsychiatric and demographic profiles. In the first author's (BW) proof-of-concept study, we applied NLP and LLMs to generate personalized neuropsychological feedback and recommendations from a dataset of 114 deidentified neuropsychological reports (patients aged 24 to 69 years) which had the clinician-written recommendation sections removed. Most (70, 61.4%) patients had some level of comorbidity with more than one diagnosis. Most (40 of 63, 62.5%) were diagnosed with mild and major neurocognitive disorders were due to multiple etiologies (see Tables 12.1 and 12.2).

Table 12.1 Examples of Recommendations by Diagnosis, Using Basic Demographics Extracted via NLP Pipelines in Python and Fed into the LLM

Diagnosis	Recommendations Derived from LLM with NLP Data Input
Major neurocognitive disorder	1. Implement a structured daily routine with visual aids and written reminders to support basic activities of daily living and medication management. 2. Arrange for regular safety evaluations of the home environment and driving abilities to ensure appropriate supervision and support levels. 3. Consider placement of durable power of attorney and advanced directives while cognitive abilities allow for informed decision-making. 4. Patient must relinquish independent medication management and transition to a supervised medication dispensing system within 30 days.
Mild neurocognitive disorder	1. Engage in cognitive stimulation activities like puzzles, reading, and structured memory exercises for 30 minutes daily. 2. Maintain a memory notebook or digital calendar system to track appointments and important information.

Diagnosis	Recommendations Derived from LLM with NLP Data Input
	3. Participate in regular physical exercise and social activities to maintain cognitive function and emotional well-being. 4. Patient must complete cognitive rehabilitation sessions twice weekly for a minimum of 12 weeks.
Major depression	1. Initiate combination treatment with both psychotherapy (CBT or IPT) and consultation with psychiatry for medication management. 2. Develop a crisis safety plan including emergency contacts and coping strategies for periods of severe symptoms. 3. Establish regular sleep-wake cycles and daily structure to support mood regulation and treatment engagement. 4. Patient must attend weekly psychotherapy sessions and maintain a daily mood log for review at each appointment.
Anxiety	1. Learn and practice relaxation techniques such as deep breathing, progressive muscle relaxation, and mindfulness meditation. 2. Work with a therapist skilled in exposure therapy and anxiety management strategies. 3. Identify and gradually confront anxiety-provoking situations using a hierarchical approach under therapeutic guidance. 4. Patient must complete assigned exposure exercises between sessions and document anxiety ratings daily.
Substance dependence	1. Complete a medically supervised detoxification program if physically dependent, followed by intensive outpatient or residential treatment. 2. Attend regular support group meetings (e.g., AA/NA) and establish a relationship with a sponsor or recovery mentor. 3. Develop a comprehensive relapse prevention plan identifying triggers, coping strategies, and support resources. 4. Patient must submit to random drug screenings twice weekly and attend a minimum of three support group meetings per week.
Trauma	1. Engage in trauma-focused psychotherapy (e.g., EMDR, PE, or CPT) with a qualified mental health professional. 2. Practice grounding techniques and emotional regulation skills to manage trauma-related symptoms. 3. Build a strong support network including both professional and personal relationships that understand trauma impacts. 4. Patient must complete standardized trauma symptom measures at baseline and every 4 weeks to track treatment progress.
ADHD	1. Implement organizational systems using planners, reminders, and breaking tasks into smaller manageable steps. 2. Consider a combination of behavioral strategies and medication management through consultation with psychiatry. 3. Create a structured work/study environment with minimal distractions and regular breaks for optimal focus. 4. Patient must schedule monthly medication management appointments and provide documentation of medication compliance.

Notes: The fourth recommendation for each diagnosis was considered the most prescriptive. The locations, patient data, specific websites, or product names have been removed from these exemplar recommendations.

Table 12.2 Categories Derived from NVivo Thematic Analysis with Examples of LLM Recommendations

Category (NVivo)	Recommendations Examples
Cognitive rehabilitation strategies	1. Implement spaced retrieval training for memory enhancement, gradually increasing the delay interval between learning and recall. 2. Utilize errorless learning techniques when acquiring new skills or information, with systematic fading of prompts. 3. Practice dual-task training exercises to improve divided attention and processing speed. 4. Engage in computerized cognitive training programs targeting specific domains (attention, memory, executive function) for 30 minutes, 3× weekly.
Behavioral interventions	1. Implement token economy system with clearly defined target behaviors and reinforcement schedule. 2. Practice progressive muscle relaxation and deep breathing exercises twice daily, with documentation of anxiety levels. 3. Utilize functional behavior analysis to identify triggers and maintain ABC (Antecedent-Behavior-Consequence) logs. 4. Establish behavioral contracts for medication adherence and appointment attendance with specified rewards and consequences.
Lifestyle modifications	1. Maintain a structured sleep hygiene routine with consistent bed/wake times and pre-sleep ritual. 2. Engage in moderate cardiovascular exercise for 30 minutes daily, adapting intensity to individual capacity. 3. Follow Mediterranean-style diet with emphasis on omega-3 fatty acids and antioxidant-rich foods. 4. Participate in social activities or community groups at least twice weekly to prevent isolation.
Home and environment modification	1. Install motion-sensor lighting in bathrooms and hallways to prevent falls during nighttime mobility. 2. Remove throw rugs and secure electrical cords to reduce fall risks; install grab bars in bathrooms. 3. Create designated stations for important items (medications, keys, wallet) with visual cues and labels. 4. Modify work/study space to minimize visual and auditory distractions, incorporating noise-canceling options if needed.
Planning for future care	1. Complete advance health care directives and durable power of attorney documentation within 60 days. 2. Develop written plan for transition to higher level of care, including specific triggers for implementation. 3. Establish emergency contact protocol with hierarchy of decision-makers and their specific roles. 4. Create financial planning document outlining current resources and projected care costs with monthly review.

Category (NVivo)	Recommendations Examples
Pharmacological suggestions	1. Consult with psychiatry regarding initiation of acetylcholinesterase inhibitors for cognitive symptoms. 2. Consider trial of stimulant medication with baseline testing and monthly monitoring of vital signs. 3. Evaluate current medication regimen for anticholinergic burden and potential cognitive side effects. 4. Implement medication timing schedule to optimize cognitive functioning during peak performance periods.

Note: The locations, patient data, specific websites, or product names have been removed from these exemplar recommendations.

At the first step, reports were cleaned and preprocessed using Python libraries, and an NLP pipeline was employed using the spaCy library to perform tokenization, lemmatization, and entity recognition, to extract relevant clinical and cognitive data from the reports. Second, we fed the limited report data into OpenAI's GPT-4, an advanced LLM, to generate personalized feedback and recommendations based on the extracted data. The model was trained on a domain-specific dataset to enhance its understanding of neuropsychological terminology and concepts. Third, the generated feedback was then categorized into themes using qualitative thematic analysis, facilitated by the NVivo software. Finally, the themes were cross-validated in R (packages tidytext and topicmodels) to derive topic-based categories.

On average, the LLM generated four recommendations per patient diagnosis. Each patient had an average of eight recommendations. A total of 877 unique neuropsychological recommendations were generated. Comparative analysis of AI-generated feedback indicated patterns of recommendations by type of neuropsychiatric condition; for example, reports for patients with depressive disorders predominantly included behavioral interventions and cognitive restructuring, while those for neurodegenerative conditions focused on cognitive rehabilitation and caregiver support. We assessed the style and tone of the recommendations generated by the LLM, noting that some diagnoses elicited more direct and prescriptive advice, while others resulted in more supportive and exploratory feedback. Categorization indicated that, of the 877 recommendations, 412 (49.2%) may have been overly prescriptive or outside of scope for neuropsychologists. All feedback included "actions," "resources" (e.g., with links to webpages or apps), and "timeline" (e.g., when and how to implement the recommendation). The thematic analysis identified key recommendation categories, including cognitive rehabilitation strategies, behavioral interventions, lifestyle modifications, home and environment modification, planning for future care, and pharmacological suggestions.

The findings suggest that NLP and LLMs can be effectively used to augment the process of generating personalized neuropsychological recommendations, offering a scalable approach to enhance clinical practice. Future research will focus on refining these models with more diverse datasets, developing ethical guidelines for AI use in clinical settings, and exploring the integration of these tools into existing health care workflows.

Challenges and Limitations

Although audio recording is relatively straightforward, the application of NLP in live or recorded feedback remains in early stages. Accuracy of transcription is crucial, yet background noise, accents, or technical problems can degrade voice recognition. Furthermore, the interpretive aspect of a feedback session, where the psychologist navigates dynamic emotional and cognitive responses from the patient, may be difficult to capture in textual form, potentially limiting the algorithm's ability to glean meaningful insights. Additionally, patients might be reluctant to have their sessions recorded due to privacy concerns or discomfort in sharing personal cognitive and emotional information, leading to reticence or reduced candor during the session.

Informed consent is paramount when employing audio recording. Patients and families must fully understand why the session is being recorded, how the data will be used, who will have access, and how long it will be stored. Fear of surveillance could exacerbate mistrust in health care, especially among historically marginalized groups. Linguistic and cultural diversity also influences the reliability of NLP. Speech recognition tools perform best on widely used languages (e.g., English, Spanish) and can falter with less common languages or dialectical variations. This presents a barrier to equitable care if effective NLP-based feedback remains limited to certain linguistic or cultural groups.

Feedback Through Passive and Active Data Monitoring for Just-in-Time Interventions

Just-in-time adaptive interventions (JITAI) leverage real-time data from mobile devices, wearables, or environmental sensors to identify the optimal timing and content of an intervention (Nahum-Shani et al., 2018). In neuropsychology, passive data streams (e.g., step count, heart rate variability, smartphone usage patterns) can yield insights into a patient's stress levels, sleep quality, or medication adherence (Harris et al., 2024). Active data, such as brief ecological momentary assessments (EMAs) where patients report mood or cognition multiple times a day, can help detect fluctuations in executive or emotional functioning (Heron & Smyth, 2010).

When integrated into a feedback system, these data allow the neuropsychologist to provide near real-time advice. For instance, if an adolescent with attention-deficit/hyperactivity disorder (ADHD) logs consistent afternoon lapses in focus during distance learning, the system could trigger a timely alert or micro-intervention via text or app notification. Over time, these micro-interventions can serve as feedback loops, reinforcing strategies learned during the formal assessment feedback session (Baumel et al., 2020).

Despite the allure of real-time feedback, technical feasibility varies. Patients must reliably carry or wear devices (e.g., smartwatches, fitness trackers) and consistently respond to app prompts. Noncompliance or device attrition can impair data completeness. Moreover, raw sensor data often require advanced analytics, such as machine learning techniques, to interpret. Neuropsychologists may find themselves ill-equipped to handle these technical demands, necessitating collaboration with data scientists or specialized software (Nahum-Shani et al., 2018). Signal noise is another concern. Environmental factors, device errors, or random events can produce spurious data that might lead to false alarms or missed detections of clinically relevant changes. The continuous flow of data can also overwhelm providers if dashboards and alerts are not carefully optimized, risking "alert fatigue" and undermining the intervention's efficacy.

Passive and active monitoring inevitably raises privacy questions. Individuals may find it intrusive to have their daily movements, sleep patterns, or phone usage so closely tracked. Clinicians must secure informed consent that outlines the scope of monitoring and the nature of data sharing. Digital equity issues also arise: Not all patients can afford smartphones or wearables, nor may they feel comfortable with technology. Low-income or rural communities could be disproportionately excluded, widening the care gap. It is crucial to develop JITAI protocols that are culturally sensitive, incorporate user-friendly interfaces, and accommodate varying levels of digital literacy.

Case Example: A Psychiatric Patient Benefiting from Technological Feedback

Clinical Background

Mr. A is a 35-year-old patient with a history of recurrent major depressive disorder and mild executive function challenges, as identified in a prior neuropsychological evaluation. He was referred to a neuropsychologist by his psychiatrist for re-evaluation after reporting increased difficulty in managing daily tasks and a growing sense of hopelessness about his cognitive decline. Mr. A's initial testing revealed mild deficits in planning, inhibitory control, and working memory, likely exacerbated by depressive symptoms.

Implementation of Technology in Assessment and Feedback

AI-Generated Summaries for Psychiatrist and Employer

After completing the neuropsychological testing, the clinician used an AI-assisted summarization tool to transform a comprehensive 15-page report into the following:

1. A clinician-oriented version for Mr. A's psychiatrist, emphasizing diagnostic impressions, medication considerations, and the interplay between depressive symptoms and cognitive functioning
2. An employer-friendly version focusing on recommendations for mild workplace accommodations, such as flexible deadlines or reduced distractors in his work environment

Mr. A appreciated that he did not need to spend time explaining his condition to his employer in detail; the AI-summarized report was succinct, verified by the neuropsychologist to ensure clinical accuracy.

Audio-Recorded Feedback Session with NLP Insights

During the feedback session, the neuropsychologist used a secure application to record the conversation. Mr. A granted consent, understanding he could replay the session at home. Post-session, an NLP module transcribed the audio, highlighting key concepts (e.g., "executive function," "planning strategies," "medication adherence"). The module flagged confusion on Mr. A's part when discussing medication schedules. A follow-up alert prompted the neuropsychologist to send Mr. A additional clarifications, thus ensuring he fully understood the recommended regimen.

Passive and Active Monitoring for Just-in-Time Support

Given Mr. A's struggles with daily planning, the clinician introduced a wearable device and a smartphone app that tracked his sleep duration and triggered brief morning EMAs about his mental state. The system also correlated his sleep data with daily self-reports of executive failures at work, such as forgetting tasks or missing deadlines. When patterns suggested an elevated risk for depressive ruminations or cognitive slips, the system provided "just-in-time" text messages containing coping prompts (e.g., mindful breathing exercises, a quick planning checklist). Over 6 weeks, Mr. A reported feeling more aware of his early warning signs (e.g., multiple nights of short sleep correlated with next-day mental fatigue) and found the short, automated prompts helpful in managing stress. His psychiatrist also used weekly summary logs to fine-tune Mr. A's medication regimen and therapy sessions.

Challenges, and Ethical and Diversity Considerations

Mr. A's willingness to engage with technology was influenced by his relatively high digital literacy. Patients with lower technological familiarity might have found the monitoring overwhelming. Additionally, Mr. A's strong rapport with both his psychiatrist and neuropsychologist made it easier to address any concerns over data privacy and the perceived "intrusiveness" of continuous monitoring. Culturally, Mr. A was from a background that placed trust in medical professionals, easing the process of obtaining informed consent for data sharing. In different cultural contexts, such technology-driven processes might be met with greater skepticism or ethical concerns regarding autonomy and confidentiality. Despite these caveats, Mr. A's case underscores how an integrated technological feedback system, encompassing AI summaries, audio-based feedback, and real-time monitoring, can empower patients to actively participate in their care, inform collaborating professionals, and enhance overall treatment outcomes.

Case Example: A Neurologic Patient Benefits from Targeted Psychoeducation in Context

Clinical Background

Mr. N is a 52-year-old man with a 5-year medical history of Parkinson's disease (akinetic-rigid), with worsening gait and fatigue and new onset of amotivation and procrastination observed by him and his wife. This new lack of motivation contributed to decreased physical activity and socialization both in his home and externally. He was referred by his neurosurgeon for a neuropsychological assessment to characterize his cognitive functioning and assist with treatment planning in consideration of candidacy for deep brain stimulation (DBS) surgery. His cognitive evaluation was solidly intact and notable for mild inefficiencies in executive function, specifically his ability to plan and organize his approach to learning when presented with large amounts of information at once.

Implementation of Technology in Assessment: Feedback as Intervention

AI-Generated Summaries for Patient and Family

Following the neuropsychological evaluation, the clinician used an AI-assisted summarization tool to create a plain language outline of the assessment findings in the setting of expected weaknesses typically seen in Parkinson's disease. The summary used NLP to form an easy-to-digest, condensed version of the evaluation results to be easily understood and retained by the patient and his wife. The feedback session was held over HIPAA-compliant Zoom telehealth to allow the clinician to meet with and observe the patient operating in his natural environment. Following the feedback session, the patient and family also received an NLP-enhanced version of the report recommendations, integrating personalized psychoeducation heavily into the summary.

Personalized Psychoeducation and Treatment Plan

As part of the feedback session, the clinician illustrated the types of initiation deficits commonly seen in Parkinson's disease (McGregor & Nelson, 2019). This was appreciated by his wife, given she was not aware of the likely cause of her husband's decreased socialization and physical activity. The clinician solicited information from the patient and his wife regarding his daily activities and schedule, providing insight into the context where he might benefit from targeted intervention. As a result of the discussion occurring in the patient's environment, together the clinician and family were able to collaboratively devise a highly individualized treatment plan that could be implemented right away.

Integration of Environmental Cues Through Visuals and Music

When it was learned that gardening and yard work were until recently a main source of enjoyment and physical activity, the clinician provided information on the benefits of external cues in the environment to propel and "bypass" the weakened internal initiation system. They were encouraged to set up Mr. N's environment to respond to external cues versus having to initiate actions and behaviors internally, for example:

1. Place items required for exercise, chores, or other daily tasks within close view where they are easily accessible to simplify and minimize any preparation needed to initiate the task.
2. Experiment with setting alarms to signify doing tasks at the same time every day.
3. Pair activities such as exercise or yard work with listening to music, which acts as an external cue and motivator to help with both initiation and stamina.

Given Mr. N's reduced ability to intrinsically initiate activities, the use of multimedia was introduced as an additional motivator in his daily surroundings. Environmental cues of both visuals around the house (e.g., a graphic reminder within easy view of his living room recliner; placing his outside shoes and gardening tools near the door) and music via his phone (e.g., not only an enjoyable alarm song that would ring to remind him to get up but a playlist alert to keep him moving once there) were implemented. Mr. N was debriefed on the benefits of listening to music while working and going about his normal physical activity, especially for disorders of initiation where "getting started" is often a challenge (Wu et al., 2015).

Challenges, and Ethical and Diversity Considerations

Despite concerns that technology-based interventions may inadvertently exclude certain groups of individuals (e.g., those in low-income brackets), research indicates that there are high smartphone penetration rates (U.S. Census Bureau, 2024) and that technology-based home care is patient-centered (Dorsey et al., 2016; Spear et al., 2019). This stated, people from older generations or communities of less digital literacy are at times more comfortable with in-person visits, citing the challenges of new telehealth technology as a confusing obstacle. It is important to note that at the same time, a hybrid care model that provides the option for both in-clinic and remote sessions can reduce geographic and financial barriers for rural, low-income, and mobility-limited individuals. Moreover, as mentioned earlier, it can provide a unique glimpse into a patient's daily context and related potential challenges they may face. In the case of Mr. N, it is believed he benefitted from this feedback session's introduction to telehealth as he expressed an openness to attending brief family psychotherapy remotely with his wife for coping and adjustment to illness. Upon follow-up, it was learned Mr. N and his wife successfully attended and completed a course of remote psychotherapy, with improvements noted. Overall, Mr. N communicated feeling highly supported by this feedback as intervention, combining accessible summaries and a targeted psychoeducation and treatment plan which emphasized matching his own contextual needs to the appropriate technical supports.

Innovative and Emerging Tools: Future Directions and Translation to Neuropsychology

Technology for Education

Using technology for education in feedback is another avenue, expanded on with a summary of a recent study as follows (see Fusunyan et al., 2024). Educational interventions grounded in contemporary neuroscience have proven valuable in the management of chronic pain, and the growing elucidation of functional neurological disorder (FND) suggests that comparable strategies could improve clinician knowledge and patient care for this condition. To meet the clear public-health need for broader provider expertise, the investigators produced a 20-minute web-based module for clinicians that delivers neuroscience-informed psychoeducation about FND; the module incorporates an 8-minute scripted role-play that demonstrates best practices for conveying the diagnosis. Embedded pre- and post-module surveys evaluated participants' self-rated attitudes and knowledge about FND, as well as objective retention of the scientific content through multiple-choice items.

Nonparametric Wilcoxon signed-rank tests and McNemar tests were applied to the paired data. Among the 103 clinicians who initiated the surveys, 40 completed both the baseline and follow-up assessments. After viewing the module, participants reported markedly greater confidence in discussing the diagnosis and treatment options, alongside a significant reduction in negative perceptions toward patients with FND. Their accuracy on questions probing the functional neuroanatomy of FND also rose appreciably. These findings indicate that a brief, online neuroscience-based tutorial can meaningfully enhance clinicians' factual knowledge and comfort with FND care. More broadly, web-delivered training appears to be an efficient and cost-effective vehicle for disseminating essential information and practical skills to health care providers managing FND, which could be incorporated into neuropsychology feedback for psychoeducation with patients.

Virtual Reality

Virtual reality (VR) has shown promise as a pedagogical aid for training clinicians and students in dementia care, yet its value in educating the general public remains underexplored. VR could be applied in neuropsychology feedback via hands-on educational interventions at a large scale, as summarized in the following exemplar study (see Li et al., 2025). Researchers analyzed 12,754 YouTube comments posted beneath the VR film series "A Walk-Through Dementia," which immerses viewers in everyday challenges faced by people with Alzheimer's disease and related dementias (ADRD). Leveraging a Bidirectional Encoder Representations from Transformers (BERT) model, they converted the comments into vector embeddings and applied topic modeling to uncover the principal thematic structures. Part-of-speech tagging of the 300 most frequent words guided the extraction of eight initial topics, which were subsequently distilled into five overarching themes. The largest theme, encompassing 2,917 comments, captured personal narratives describing the impact of ADRD on patients and caregivers. The remaining commentary clustered around positive reactions to the VR experience, recognition of the daily obstacles imposed by ADRD, reflections on caregiver roles, and lessons users felt they had learned from the videos. These findings indicate that VR-based social-media content can provide an engaging, experiential platform for broad public education about dementia, and they underscore the potential of future VR deployments on social networks to extend the reach and impact of ADRD awareness initiatives.

Biofeedback

The example of biofeedback will be briefly discussed in the context of music as intervention. Mental-health–related morbidity and age-associated cognitive decline continue to outpace the reach of traditional pharmacotherapies, sharpening interest in non-drug interventions that can recalibrate emotion, memory, and underlying neural circuitry. Three modalities have surfaced as particularly compelling: (1) music-based interventions, (2) brain-wave entrainment techniques such as binaural beats, isochronic tones, and broader multisensory pulsing, and (3) their fusion into a single, closed-loop therapeutic ecosystem (Jiao, 2025). Accumulating data show that purposefully designed music can engage limbic, prefrontal, and dopaminergic reward networks, reducing stress reactivity and improving executive and mnemonic performance. This aligns with neural resonance theory (NRT), which is postulated to explain variability in affect, the influence of music on interpersonal relationships, and brain health (Harding et al., 2025). Other work on auditory and audiovisual entrainment demonstrates that driving cortical oscillations, especially in the gamma band (30–100 Hz, with 40 Hz most frequently studied), promotes states of relaxed vigilance and augments memory consolidation, although interindividual differences in resonance frequency and subjective response remain substantial. When auditory and visual pulses are synchronized at gamma rates, preliminary Alzheimer's disease trials report not only transient cognitive gains but also putative neuroprotective effects on microglial function and amyloid dynamics (Chan et al., 2022). Each approach is impacted by heterogeneous patient responses, the absence of universally accepted stimulation protocols, and practical hurdles to broad dissemination. A convergent strategy may be to embed music therapy and entrainment stimuli within an adaptive, AI-driven biofeedback loop that continuously samples physiological (e.g., heart-rate variability, EEG phase-locking) and behavioral markers, then retunes musical complexity, carrier frequencies, or multisensory timing in real time. Such personalization could standardize delivery while maximizing durability of benefit (Ingendoh et al., 2023).

In the feedback phase of a neuropsychological evaluation, where the goal is to translate test scores into actionable insight, this adaptive biofeedback model offers multiple advantages. First, real-time visualizations of a client's heart-rate coherence or gamma synchrony while different musical passages or entrainment protocols are presented can make otherwise abstract cognitive findings tangible, deepening the patient's understanding of brain–behavior links. Second, clinicians can use the system to demonstrate how self-regulation strategies (paced breathing, attentional reframing) immediately modify neural and autonomic metrics, reinforcing a sense of agency. Third, session-specific data can seed bespoke "home programs" that stream optimized musical or entrainment content calibrated to the individual's resonance profile, thus extending therapeutic momentum beyond the clinic and enabling objective monitoring of adherence and response trajectories. Finally, because the same platform can log cognitive-performance probes (e.g., n-back tasks) alongside physiological feedback, it creates an integrated dataset that can inform longitudinal treatment planning and research on brain–behavior change mechanisms. Although still nascent, the synthesis of music, entrainment, and AI-guided biofeedback heralds a shift toward patient-centered, scalable, and neurobiologically grounded interventions. Further, biofeedback is now being applied in many other contexts and syndromes; for instance, heart rate variability biofeedback treatment for traumatic brain injury (Talbert et al., 2023).

Digital Twins in Health Care

Within the medical field, a digital twin (DT) can be conceptualized as a patient-specific, computational avatar that integrates multimodal information, ranging from neuroimaging, genomics, and metabolomics to electronic health-record data, environmental exposures, and social determinants of health, to simulate, forecast, and optimize brain-related outcomes across the lifespan (Katsoulakis et al., 2024). For neuropsychological applications, the DT should embody the "5 I" attributes (individualized, interconnected, interactive, informative, and impactful) to ensure that simulation outputs translate into tangible benefits such as precision treatment selection, mitigation of adverse cognitive effects, and proactive surveillance of neurodegenerative trajectories (Katsoulakis et al., 2024). Deep phenotyping is extended here to include digital phenotypes: continuously streaming metrics from smartphones, wearables, and other connected devices that reveal everyday behavior, cognitive performance fluctuations, affective states, and contextual factors that modulate treatment response. A recent review classified DT interventions into three domains: tailored health management, individualized therapeutic precision, and personal risk prediction, evaluating 45 outcome metrics, of which over 80% demonstrated favorable effects at the population level indicating clinical utility (Shen et al., 2024).

In oncology for example, DT frameworks already guide image-based adaptive radiotherapy for high-grade gliomas, illustrating how iterative model-patient feedback loops can personalize care. Analogous approaches in neuropsychology could leverage structural and functional brain imaging, cognitive task performance, and ecological momentary assessment to predict progression from mild cognitive impairment to dementia or to fine-tune pharmacological regimens for mood and psychotic disorders. Platforms such as Babylon and IBM already incorporate sensor data to support clinician–patient engagement, while MindBank AI aims to enhance mental well-being through introspective feedback cycles. Research toolkits including Beiwe and MindLAMP facilitate real-time behavioral monitoring and just-in-time psychological interventions. These platforms are optimized for building DTs and facilitating use in clinical neuropsychology as part of dynamic feedback processes.

Recent work highlights two distinct complementary DT models (Drummond & Gonsard, 2024). Simulation DTs achieve high anatomical and physiological fidelity by melding mechanistic models with hospital-acquired data, typically structural or functional magnetic resonance imaging (MRI), conmputerized tomography (CT), or intraoperative hemodynamic recordings. These twins are static snapshots: They enable one-off, in-silico experiments that test surgical options, pharmacological regimens, or lesion placements but are not continuously refreshed with new data. A neuropsychological analog would be an individualized connectome-based model of a patient's brain used to predict cognitive or behavioral changes after deep-brain stimulation or tumor resection. In contrast, monitoring DTs are dynamic, real-time reflections of the individual created by integrating streaming data from wearables, smartphones, smart home sensors, and cloud-linked medical devices (Drummod & Gonsard, 2024). Machine-learning pipelines detect anomalies and can trigger just-in-time interventions, such as adaptive cognitive-behavioral prompts when a change in gait, speech prosody, or sleep pattern signals heightened relapse risk in mood or psychotic disorders.

Hybrid twins may combine mechanistic brain simulations with 24/7 phenotypic streams. At present, only a minority of clinical DT prototypes fully integrate multidimensional data, advanced analytics, and immersive visualization; those that do tend to reside in surgical navigation suites where real-time updates can guide intraoperative decisions. Extending similar capabilities to neuropsychology could, for instance, combine diffusion-tensor–based structural models with continuous cognitive-performance metrics captured via mobile games. Such patient-centric twins would elevate precision care by (1) tailoring pharmacologic or neuromodulatory treatments to an individual's genetic profile, comorbidities, and predicted cognitive side-effect burden; (2) optimizing rehabilitative strategies based on simulated responses to task difficulty or stimulus modality; and (3) enhancing patient engagement, as individuals visualize how lifestyle choices (sleep hygiene, physical activity, substance use) dynamically reshape their own neurocognitive trajectories. This real-world monitoring promises a step-change toward personalized neuropsychological assessment and intervention.

Conclusions

Technological innovation in clinical neuropsychology is swiftly moving beyond assessment to transform the feedback process itself. AI-driven text summarization and rewriting can streamline communication across multiple stakeholders, audio recording integrated with NLP can enhance patient comprehension and clinician follow-through, and just-in-time interventions informed by passive and active data can deliver timely support that aligns with the patient's daily life. In the case examples provided, leveraging these tools led to more nuanced, accessible, and continuous care, potentially improving both cognitive and psychiatric outcomes. Feedback is considered key to scalability and translatability of assessment findings to real-world patient functioning. Indeed, recent efforts have designed a feedback competency evaluation tool (the PsyCET-F) resulting in four categories integral to all feedback sessions as considered by Delphi consensus (Wong et al., 2024). This tool included several items within which technology could be integrated, including addressing how key strategies could be implemented in daily life, adapting the information to suit the feedback scenario, supplementing with assistive tools, and providing summaries during or after the session in writing or audio format. At any stage in this process, the feedback competencies could be enhanced through technology use. However, these emerging techniques are not without challenges and ethical considerations. The risk of oversimplification or misinterpretation in AI summaries, concerns about data security in audio recordings, the digital divide limiting access to wearable devices, and issues of algorithmic bias all require thoughtful attention. Finally, promising innovations in biofeedback, digital twins, and virtual reality have demonstrated efficacy in neighboring medical fields, which could be extended to clinical neuropsychology applications in the future. As neuropsychologists integrate these technologies, interdisciplinary collaboration with data scientists, software developers, ethicists, and cultural consultants is critical. By doing so, the field can ensure that disruptive feedback technology genuinely serves its promise: to make neuropsychological findings more comprehensible, actionable, and equitable for every patient and partner involved in their care.

References

Angoff, L. (2022, January 22). *Tools for talking to kids about their brains* [Blog post]. Dr. Liz Angoff. https://drlizangoff.com/2022/01/22/tools-spreadsheet/

Baumel, A., Fleming, T., & Schueller, S. M. (2020). Digital micro interventions for behavioral and mental health gains: Core components and conceptualization of digital micro intervention care. *Journal of Medical Internet Research, 22*(10), e20631. https://doi.org/10.2196/20631

Carone, D. (2017). But the scores don't show how I really function: A feedback method to reveal cognitive distortions regarding normal neuropsychological test performance. *Applied Neuropsychology: Adult, 24*(2), 160–168.

Chan, D., Suk, H. J., Jackson, B. L., Milman, N. P., Stark, D., Klerman, E. B., Kitchener, E., Fernandez Avalos, V. S., de Weck, G., Banerjee, A., Beach, S. D., Blanchard, J., Stearns, C., Boes, A. D., Uitermarkt, B., Gander, P., Howard, M., 3rd, Sternberg, E. J., Nieto-Castanon, A., Anteraper, S., ... Tsai, L. H. (2022). Gamma frequency sensory stimulation in mild probable Alzheimer's dementia patients: Results of feasibility and pilot studies. *PloS One, 17*(12), e0278412. https://doi.org/10.1371/journal.pone.0278412

Clay, B., Bergman, H. I., Salim, S., Pergola, G., Shalhoub, J., & Davies, A. H. (2025). Natural language processing techniques applied to the electronic health record in clinical research and practice—An introduction to methodologies. *Computers in Biology and Medicine, 188*, 109808. https://doi.org/10.1016/j.compbiomed.2025.109808

Dorsey, E. R., Vlaanderen, F. P., Engelen, L. J., Kieburtz, K., Zhu, W., Biglan, K. M., & Bloem, B. R. (2016). Moving Parkinson care to the home. *Movement Disorders, 31*(9), 1258–1262. https://doi.org/10.1002/mds.26744

Drummond, D., & Gonsard, A. (2024). Definitions and characteristics of patient digital twins being developed for clinical use: Scoping review. *Journal of Medical Internet Research, 26*(1), e58504. https://doi.org/10.2196/58504

Fusunyan, M., Medina, M., Giambarberi, L., & Bajestan, S. (2024). A web-based educational module using clinical neuroscience to deliver the diagnosis of functional neurological disorder. *Journal of Neuropsychiatry and Clinical Neurosciences, 36*(2), 166–171. https://doi.org/10.1176/appi.neuropsych.20230060

Gruters, A. A. A., Ramakers, I. H. G. B., Stiekema, A. P. M., Verhey, F. R. J., Kessels, R. P. C., & de Vugt, M. E. (2021). An exploratory study of the development and pilot testing of an interactive visual tool of neuropsychological test results in memory clinics. *Journal of Alzheimer's Disease, 79*(3), 1157–1170. https://doi.org/10.3233/JAD-201128

Gruters, A. A., Ramakers, I. H., Verhey, F. R., Kessels, R. P., & de Vugt, M. E. (2022). A scoping review of communicating neuropsychological test results to patients and family members. *Neuropsychology Review, 32*(2), 294–315. https://doi.org/10.1007/s11065-021-09507-2

Hanssen, E., Balvert, S., Oorschot, M., Borkelmans, K., van Os, J., Delespaul, P., & Fett, A.-K. (2020). An ecological momentary intervention incorporating personalised feedback to improve symptoms and social functioning in schizophrenia spectrum disorders. *Psychiatry Research, 284*, 112695. https://doi.org/10.1016/j.psychres.2019.112695

Harding, E. E., Kim, J. C., Demos, A. P., Roman, I. R., Tichko, P., Palmer, C., & Large, E. W. (2025). Musical neurodynamics. *Nature Reviews Neuroscience, 26*(5), 293–307. https://doi.org/10.1038/s41583-025-00915-4

Harris, C., Tang, Y., Birnbaum, E., Cherian, C., Mendhe, D., & Chen, M. H. (2024). Digital neuropsychology beyond computerized cognitive assessment: Applications of novel digital technologies. *Archives of Clinical Neuropsychology, 39*(3), 290–304. https://doi.org/10.1093/arclin/acae016

Heron, K. E., & Smyth, J. M. (2010). Ecological momentary interventions: incorporating mobile technology into psychosocial and health behaviour treatments. *British journal of health psychology, 15*(Pt 1), 1–39. https://doi.org/10.1348/135910709X466063

Hudson, K. L., & Collins, F. S. (2017). The 21st Century Cures Act—A view from the NIH. *The New England Journal of Medicine, 376*(2), 111–113. https://doi.org/10.1056/NEJMp1615745

Ingendoh, R. M., Posny, E. S., & Heine, A. (2023). Binaural beats to entrain the brain? A systematic review of the effects of binaural beat stimulation on brain oscillatory activity, and the implications for psychological research and intervention. *PloS One, 18*(5), e0286023. https://doi.org/10.1371/journal.pone.0286023

Jiao, D. (2025). Advancing personalized digital therapeutics: Integrating music therapy, brainwave entrainment methods, and AI-driven biofeedback. *Frontiers in Digital Health, 7*, 1552396. https://doi.org/10.3389/fdgth.2025.1552396

Katsoulakis, E., Wang, Q., Wu, H., Shahriyari, L., Fletcher, R., Liu, J., Achenie, L., Liu, H., Jackson, P., Xiao, Y., Syeda-Mahmood, T., Tuli, R., & Deng, J. (2024). Digital twins for health: A scoping review. *NPJ Digital Medicine*, *7*(1), 1–11. https://doi.org/10.1038/s41746-024-01073-0

Li, X., Liu, X., Yin, C., Collins, S., & Alanazi, E. (2025). Impact of a virtual reality video ("A walk-through dementia") on YouTube users: Topic modeling analysis. *JMIR Formative Research*, *9*, e67755. https://doi.org/10.2196/67755

Lichtenstein, J. D., Amato, J. T., Holding, E. Z., Grodner, K. D., Pollock, E. N., Marschall, K. P., & Scull, S. (2022). How we work now: Preliminary review of a pediatric neuropsychology hybrid model in the era of COVID-19 and beyond. *Archives of Clinical Neuropsychology*, *37*(1), 40–49. https://doi.org/10.1093/arclin/acab041

McGregor, M. M., & Nelson, A. B. (2019). Circuit mechanisms of Parkinson's disease. *Neuron*, *101*(6), 1042–1056. https://doi.org/10.1016/j.neuron.2019.03.004

Nahum-Shani, I., Smith, S. N., Spring, B. J., Collins, L. M., Witkiewitz, K., Tewari, A., & Murphy, S. A. (2018). Just-in-Time Adaptive Interventions (JITAIs) in mobile health: Key components and design principles for ongoing health behavior support. *Annals of Behavioral Medicine*, *52*(6), 446–462. https://doi.org/10.1007/s12160-016-9830-8

Olawade, D. B., Wada, O. Z., Odetayo, A., David-Olawade, A. C., Asaolu, F., & Eberhardt, J. (2024). Enhancing mental health with artificial intelligence: Current trends and future prospects. *Journal of Medicine, Surgery, and Public Health*, 3, 100099. https://doi.org/10.1016/j.glmedi.2024.100099

Parsons T. D. (2015). Virtual reality for enhanced ecological validity and experimental control in the clinical, affective and social neurosciences. *Frontiers in Human Neuroscience*, *9*, 660. https://doi.org/10.3389/fnhum.2015.00660

Postal, K., & Armstrong, K. (2013). *Feedback that sticks: The art of effectively communicating neuropsychological assessment results.* Oxford University Press.

Rohil, M. K., & Magotra, V. (2022). An exploratory study of automatic text summarization in biomedical and healthcare domain. *Healthcare Analytics*, 2, 100058. https://doi.org/10.1016/j.health.2022.100058

Shen, M., Chen, S., & Ding, X. (2024). The effectiveness of digital twins in promoting precision health across the entire population: A systematic review. *NPJ Digital Medicine*, *7*(1), 1–10. https://doi.org/10.1038/s41746-024-01146-0

Smith, S. M., Stelmar, J., Lee, G., Carroll, P. R., & Garcia, M. M. (2022). Use of voice recordings in the consultation of patients seeking genital gender-affirming surgery: An opportunity for broader application throughout surgery? *Journal of Surgery and Research*, *5*(4), 618–625. https://doi.org/10.26502/jsr.10020269

Spear, K. L., Auinger, P., Simone, R., Dorsey, E. R., & Francis, J. (2019). Patient views on telemedicine for Parkinson disease. *Journal of Parkinson's Disease*, *9*(2), 401–404. https://doi.org/10.3233/JPD-181557

Talbert, L. D., Kaelberer, Z., Gleave, E., Driggs, A., Driggs, A. S., Steffen, P. R., Baldwin, S. A., & Larson, M. J. (2023). A systematic review of heart rate variability (HRV) biofeedback treatment following traumatic brain injury (TBI). *Brain Injury*, *37*(7), 635–642. https://doi.org/10.1080/02699052.2023.2208880

U.S. Census Bureau. (2024, January). *Computer and internet use in the United States: 2021.* U.S. Department of Commerce. https://www.census.gov/newsroom/press-releases/2024/computer-internet-use-2021.html

Varela, J. L., Sperling, S. A., Block, C., O'Leary, K., Hart, E. S., & Kiselica, A. M. (2024). A survey of neuropsychological assessment feedback practices among neuropsychologists. *The Clinical Neuropsychologist, 38*(3), 529–556. https://doi.org/10.1080/13854046.2023.2233738

Wong, D., Pinto, R., Price, S., Watson, L., & McKay, A. (2024). What does competently delivered neuropsychological assessment feedback look like? Development and validation of a competency evaluation tool. *The Clinical Neuropsychologist, 38*(1), 116–134. https://doi.org/10.1080/13854046.2023.2200205

Wu, T., Hallett, M., & Chan, P. (2015). Motor automaticity in Parkinson's disease. *Neurobiology of Disease, 82*, 226–234. https://doi.org/10.1016/j.nbd.2015.06.014

Zhang, D. W., Boey, M., Tan, Y. Y., & Jia, A. H. S. (2024). Evaluating large language models for criterion-based grading from agreement to consistency. *NPJ Science of Learning, 9*(1), 79–84. doi:10.1038/s41539-024-00291-1

13
The Impact of Everyday Technology Use on Cognitive Health

Rachel E. Mis, Cecilia K. Zuniga, Kelsey K. Amon, Zoe R. Anthos, Andrew M. Kiselica, Michael K. Scullin, and Jared F. Benge

Introduction

> "We shape our tools and thereafter our tools shape us."
>
> —**John Culkin in McLuhan (1967)**

One of the defining characteristics of the human brain is the ability to make and use sophisticated tools, and, as Culkin implied, successful use of these tools seems to reciprocally shape and select traits associated with a broad range of cognitive, psychomotor, and social skills (Vaesen, 2012) to form the society in which we live. As more complex hand tools developed over evolutionary history, use of these tools conferred an evolutionary advantage, such that individuals with superior motor planning and execution abilities (and brains set up to effectively utilize these abilities) were more likely to survive and reproduce. Even over the lifespan of a single human, use of tools shapes brain structure and function. For instance, individuals who more frequently use transportation tools (cars or trucks) have superior spatial navigation skills and correspondingly increased brain volumes in hippocampal regions necessary for spatial memory (Maguire et al., 2000). Over the past century, digital technologies such as the computer, Internet, and smartphones, have reshaped the landscape of many of the daily cognitive tasks that humans perform. These digital tools now permeate most activities of day-to-day life, impacting how we shop, interact with others, access information, and engage in leisure; it is challenging to find an aspect of life digital technology does not touch.

In the context of neuropsychology, digital technologies are most commonly discussed as methods of assessment (e.g., computerized tests) or means of rehabilitation (e.g., computerized cognitive training). While these uses are certainly important and are explored elsewhere in this volume (for example, see Chapters 8, 10, 12, and 17), a more central question regarding the human experience of technology has received relatively less attention from neuropsychologists: What is the impact of the everyday,

Rachel E. Mis et al., *The Impact of Everyday Technology Use on Cognitive Health*. In: *Technology and Neuropsychology*.
Edited by: Jared F. Benge et al., Oxford University Press. © Oxford University Press (2026).
DOI: 10.1093/9780197814116.003.0013

real-world, digital technology use on human cognition? This chapter seeks to review research relevant to this critical question.

Impact of Everyday Digital Technology Use on the Developing Brain

Early development is a time of rapid change in the brain, and a time where there is exquisite sensitivity to environmental influences. In recent years, overstimulation from digital tools (Christakis et al., 2018) has emerged as a significant health concern. Despite recommendations from the American Academy of Pediatrics to avoid screen use in infants younger than 18 months for all purposes except video chatting (Hill et al., 2016), many children are now regularly exposed to digital devices within the first few months of life (Hish et al., 2021; Kılıç et al., 2019; Perrin et al., 2014), and digital device usage only increases as children grow (Duch et al., 2013a). In this section, we review the emerging literature on this digital technology exposure on the developing brain.

What Do Longitudinal Studies Reveal About the Impact of Screen Time in Infancy and Toddlerhood?

The literature examining digital technology exposure in the first years of life has focused on the concept of "screen time," defined as the time spent viewing digital devices, including televisions, computers, video game consoles, and smartphones (Kaye et al., 2020). Concern about the deleterious impact of screen exposure on children's cognition dates to at least the 1970s (e.g., Halpern, 1975), with proposed mechanisms including screen use displacing more cognitively beneficial activities such as in-person social interactions ("displacement hypothesis;" Neuman, 1988) as well as the direct impact of excess stimulation on the developing brain (Christakis et al., 2018). Studies have since demonstrated a link between increased screen time and adverse outcomes, including worse language development (Duch et al., 2013b), attentional difficulties (Lingineni et al., 2012; Tong et al., 2016), and other deleterious psychological and physical health outcomes (Danner, 2008; Thompson & Christakis, 2005; Tomopoulos et al., 2007). Many of the aforementioned studies were cross-sectional and therefore limited in ability to draw causal inferences. However, large, longitudinal studies of screen exposure during infancy and toddlerhood have also indicated a relationship with multiple detrimental cognitive and behavioral outcomes in later childhood. For example, Christakis et al. (2004) found in a longitudinal sample of American youth born in the late 1980s to early 1990s, daily hours of television watched during the toddler years (ages 1 and 3 years) predicted presence of attentional problems at age 7 years on a behavioral rating scale. Similarly, Madigan et al. (2019) found that among a sample of Canadian children born in the late 2000s, higher weekly screen times at ages 2 and 3 years predicted subsequent worse performance on a developmental screener at ages 3 and 6 years. While these studies relied on parent-report of attentional and developmental outcomes, increased screen time during toddlerhood has also been found to predict worse performance on cognitive tests of executive functions 1 year later (McHarg et al., 2020).

Over time, the link between increased screen time and negative cognitive outcomes has been shown to vary based on several factors, including age of screen exposure, type of content viewed, and the context in which screen use occurs. For example, in a cross-sectional study of children ages 8–24 months, an association between screen time and poorer language development was only seen for exposure at ages 8–16 months and only with videos marketed for babies, but not other types of media content intended for older children or adults (Zimmerman et al., 2007). One account for why negative associations are found for some, but not all, types of digital media content, called the "overstimulation hypothesis," posits that the fast pace of visual and auditory stimulation from screens conditions the developing brain to expect this high rate of sensory input, which leads to attentional problems as children grow and fail to adapt to the slower pace of sensory input from real-world environments (Christakis et al., 2018). Consistent with this hypothesis, Zimmerman and Christakis (2007) found that viewing noneducational children's media content at age 3 years predicted attentional problems at age 8, while no such association was demonstrated for viewing of the slower paced, educational children's content. Similarly, a meta-analysis of 64 observational studies of screen use in children under age 6 found that while some forms of screen time, such as passive media viewing and background television exposure, were negatively associated with cognitive outcomes, co-viewing with caregivers was associated with a small positive effect on cognition (Mallawaarachchi et al., 2024). These findings underscore the need to move beyond unidimensional measures of screen time to fully capture when digital exposure may be helpful versus harmful to the developing brain. In sum, while there is certainly evidence from large-scale, longitudinal studies to support an overall link between screen exposure during the first few years of life and worse brain health outcomes, this relation does not hold for all types and conditions of digital media exposure, and additional research is required to understand the contexts in which screen time may lead to benign versus harmful outcomes during this critical developmental window. We next consider whether a similarly detrimental relation between digital exposure and neurodevelopmental outcomes exists for later stages of childhood and adolescence.

What Is the Impact of Screen Exposure on Older Children and Adolescents?

In contrast to the early life studies, later childhood and adolescent exposures of screen time in representative samples suggest more mixed or neutral effects on cognition and other psychological outcomes (Mills, 2016). Among a large, representative sample of adolescents in England, Przybylski and Weinstein (2017) found a quadratic relation between digital screen use and mental well-being, demonstrating that moderate levels of digital screen exposure do not inherently negatively affect psychological outcomes in youth. Studies using the United States nationally representative Adolescent Brain Cognitive Development (ABCD) Study have similarly demonstrated relations between screen use and imaging measures of brain structure and function, but the significance of these findings in terms of behavioral and cognitive outcomes has been mixed (Miller et al., 2023; Paulus et al., 2019). Perhaps unsurprisingly, Paulus et al. (2019) found that screen use was associated most strongly with occipital regions, though associations with other brain regions such as prefrontal and temporal regions were also demonstrated. However, relations with cognition were mixed, with, for example, brain structural patterns associated with gaming demonstrating a positive relation with cognitive abilities, while brain structural patterns associated with social media and general screen use demonstrating worse cognitive outcomes, particularly for crystallized verbal abilities. Similarly, brain structural characteristics associated with social media and general screen use were also associated with higher levels of externalizing pathologies, while no associations were found with internalizing pathologies (Paulus et al., 2019). Also using the ABCD study, Miller et al. (2023) reported that digital screen use by children ages 9–12 years old was not associated with poorer reading, memory, executive, fluid intelligence, or mental health outcomes. A statistically significant relation with a test of vocabulary comprehension was found, though the effect was small and perhaps not clinically meaningful. Though the authors did identify two patterns of screen activity associated with brain functional connectivity patterns, there were not meaningful relations with the cognitive or mental health outcomes examined in the study (Miller et al., 2023).

Moreover, some forms of digital screen use may have *beneficial* effects on adolescents' cognition. Literature examining video games has demonstrated positive associations with spatial skills (Uttal et al., 2013), attentional and executive functions (Dye et al., 2009; Moisala et al., 2017), problem-solving (Adachi & Willoughby, 2013), and creativity (Jackson et al., 2012), among other motivational, emotional, and social outcomes (for reviews, see Connolly et al., 2012; Granic et al., 2014; Powers et al., 2013). However, many of these studies are subject to small sample sizes and other limitations that warrant a more cautious interpretation. In another study using the ABCD data from children aged 9–10 years old, Chaarani et al. (2022) indeed found an association between video game play and better performance on tasks of cognitive control, but the effect was small and of questionable clinical significance. Furthermore, the children who spent more time playing video games had higher behavioral scores related to attentional and hyperactivity symptoms (Chaarani et al., 2022). Notably though, the ABCD Study does not differentiate between types of video games played, which has implications for their effects on cognition, with some researchers hypothesizing that the complex visual spaces and fast-paced nature of action video games have more pronounced beneficial effects on cognition (see Granic et al., 2014).

Overall, the period of late childhood and adolescence does not appear as vulnerable to deleterious effects of digital screen exposure as that of infancy and toddlerhood, with a mixed pattern of risks and potential for benefits to some aspects of cognitive health in these older youth. This nuanced position stands in contrast to the oftentimes alarming reporting in popular news media and perhaps may alleviate some concern, given the high rates of digital screen use among children and adolescents. However, further research is required to understand which forms of screen use are most beneficial to youth and who may be most at risk for harms such as disordered technology use (e.g., "Internet/social media addiction"; Bickham, 2021; Chou et al., 2005; Sun & Zhang, 2021).

Impact of Everyday Digital Technology Use on the Adult Brain

The effect of digital technology on the adult brain is a topic that has received considerable attention from lay audiences, with popular press articles frequently espousing a pessimistic view on digital technology's impact on the brain and highlighting research that aligns with this viewpoint. But does empirical literature truly support the view that digital technology is overwhelmingly harmful for the adult brain? In fact, concern about the deleterious effects of technology on human cognition arose as early as the time of Socrates, who lamented that people will "cease to exercise memory because they rely on that which is written" (Cecutti et al., 2021), though literacy is generally considered to have a positive impact on cognitive performance in modern neuropsychological literature (Barnes et al., 2004; Manly et al., 1999). While the relation between digital technology use and cognition has been explored for a variety of cognitive abilities (for reviews, see Marsh & Rajaram, 2019; Wilmer et al., 2017), we consider next three domains of cognition of frequent interest to the neuropsychologist: attention, memory, and spatial navigation.

What Is the Impact of Digital Technology on Younger Adults' Attention?

Interacting with a cell phone while simultaneously engaged in another task negatively impacts performance of activities such as driving (Caird et al., 2008) or walking (Hyman Jr et al., 2010; Nasar & Troyer, 2013; Stavrinos et al., 2011). The presence of a cell phone, even when not currently in use, may be sufficient to disrupt adults' attention (Thornton et al., 2014; Skowronek et al., 2023). For example, Thornton et al. (2014) found that adults performed worse on a test of cognitive shifting (i.e., Trail Making Test-Part B) when either their own or the experimenter's cell phone was within view on the table, though presence of a cell phone did not impact performance on two tasks considered less cognitively demanding (Trail Making Test-Part A and a digit cancellation task). These technology-related distractions may have significant negative impacts on adults' real-world functioning, including academic performance (Junco & Cotton, 2012; Sana et al., 2013).

However, whether digital technology use is affecting adults' attentional abilities in and of themselves, beyond being a source of distraction, is less clear. Some studies have sought to examine this question by studying a behavior known as *media multitasking*, defined as simultaneously consuming media content from more than one source, such as a television and a smartphone (Ophir et al., 2009). Adults who engage in more frequent media multitasking have been found in some studies to be more susceptible to interference during attentional and working memory tasks and exhibit worse task-switching performance than the less frequent media multitaskers (Cain & Mitroff, 2011; Moisala et al., 2016; Ophir et al., 2009). However, other studies have found either no relation between media multitasking and attentional performance decrements (Ralph et al., 2015) or even stronger cognitive abilities in heavy media multitaskers (Alzahabi & Becker, 2013). In either case, given the correlational nature of these studies, it remains unclear whether media multitasking itself alters these cognitive abilities.

What Is the Impact of Digital Technology on Younger Adults' Memory?

In a high-profile series of experiments published in the journal *Science*, Sparrow et al. (2011) examined the impact of digital technology on younger adults' memory by having participants type trivia statements on a computer under several experimental manipulations. In one experiment, half of the participants were informed that the computer would save the information typed, while half were told this information would be erased; participants who believed the computer erased the information were found to have better recall for the trivia statements. In another experiment, all participants were informed for each statement that it was either (a) erased, (b) saved by the computer, or (c) saved by the computer in a specified location. Participants again better recognized the accuracy of statements they believed were erased by the computer but had better memory for whether or not a statement was saved for statements they were told were saved by the computer. In the final experiment, participants were given a specific folder name where the information would be stored for each statement; under this condition, participants had better memory for the location of the folder where each statement was stored than for the content of the trivia statement itself. The authors interpreted their findings as suggesting that when individuals expect to be able to later access information, they have worse recall for the information itself and stronger recall for where the information can be accessed (Sparrow et al., 2011). However, a later study using a similar saved-versus-erased paradigm did not find an association with memory performance (Marsh & Rajaram, 2019), and cognitive offloading of information to computers or other digital tools may improve ability to learn and remember some types of information presented later (Storm & Stone, 2015).

Digital photography has also been used as a paradigm for examining the impact of digital technology on memory. Henkel (2014) found that young adults had worse memory for museum objects they photographed with a digital camera than objects they simply viewed without photographing, demonstrating a "photo-taking impairment effect." However, when participants were instructed to focus the photograph on a particular element of the object, memory performance was no longer impaired, and recall was equally strong for both the element in focus as well as other elements of the same object that were not photographed. The author hypothesized that the greater attentional and cognitive processes required for the focused condition eliminated the photo-taking impairment effect (Henkel, 2014). Similarly, Barasch et al. (2017) found that allowing young adults to volitionally choose which objects in a museum to photograph *boosted* visual memory. While both cognitive offloading and attentional disengagement have been proposed as mechanisms for the photo-taking impairment effect, Soares and Storm (2018) found the effect persisted even when participants used the application Snapchat in which photos are deleted after a limited time, which would not support the cognitive offloading hypothesis.

What Is the Impact of Digital Technology on Younger Adults' Spatial Navigation Abilities?

As we mentioned at the beginning of this chapter, individuals who drive more frequently have better spatial navigation abilities, as well as corresponding increases in hippocampal regions underlying spatial memory (Maguire et al., 2000). Perhaps unsurprisingly, the proliferation of GPS navigation systems has been accompanied by concerns that their use is negatively impacting our brains' abilities to navigate our environments. However, the literature on this topic has been mixed, with some studies indeed demonstrating a negative association of GPS usage with spatial navigation abilities (e.g., Dahmani & Bohbot, 2020; Ruginski et al., 2019), while others indicate a neutral or even positive relation (e.g., Cochran & Dickerson, 2019; Yavuz et al., 2024). A recent meta-analysis on this topic found that while higher GPS usage demonstrated a small-to-moderate relation with reduced environmental knowledge, there was no significant association with wayfinding ability, and over two-thirds of the included studies had a moderate-to-high risk of bias (Miola et al., 2024). Indeed, as in the attention and memory literature discussed earlier, it seems most likely that the relation between GPS use and spatial navigation abilities is more complex than a simple "good versus bad" relationship, and the association with cognition may depend more on *how* GPS is used rather than simply *if* it is used, with some indication that using GPS for turn-by-turn directions is more harmful to cognitive health than using GPS for route planning or traffic updates (Topete et al., 2024).

In sum, as in the childhood and adolescence literature, the relation between digital technology use and cognition in younger adults is again complex and is likely to have both positive and negative effects depending on factors including intended purpose of digital technology use. Unlike the developmental literature reviewed earlier or aging literature discussed later, much of the young adult literature is based on experimental paradigms that are highly controlled and artificial, and thus bear little resemblance to digital technology use and cognition in everyday life. As demonstrated with the photo-taking impairment literature, simple manipulations of the experimental paradigm can result in disparate relations with cognition.

Impact of Everyday Digital Technology Use on the Aging Brain

In contrast to the critical developmental windows reviewed earlier, the aging brain faces its own unique and intersecting challenges when it comes to technology use. First, there are age-related changes in cognition, particularly with speeded and executive processes (Salthouse, 1996). Second, over and above these normal age-related changes, older adults face mounting risks for neurodegenerative conditions, particularly Alzheimer's disease and vascular-related cognitive impairments (Lanctôt et al., 2024; Manly et al., 2022; Rizzi et al., 2014). Third, these cognitive changes seem to intersect with larger attitudinal, societal, and habitual factors that have historically led to lower rates of technology adoption and challenges utilizing technology (Charness & Boot, 2022). For example, individuals with lower formal educational attainment are both less likely to make use of technologies (Gell et al., 2015) and more likely to demonstrate cognitive decline (Arce Rentería et al., 2019).

Despite these challenges, technology adoption has increased rapidly among older adults in the United States and around the world (Wike et al, 2022). The Pew Research Center has tracked Internet and smartphone use for more than 20 years, with surveys indicating Internet use among older adults in the United States has risen from below 20% in the year 2000 to nearly 90% in 2024 ("Internet, Broadband Fact Sheet," 2024). Mobile device use has similarly seen a rapid uptake among older adults: At the time of this writing, it is estimated that 94% of those over age 65 have a cell phone, and 79% use a smartphone ("Mobile Fact Sheet," 2024). Thus, despite persistent myths and ageist stereotypes, the fact is that older adults are increasingly engaging with digital technologies (Johnson, 2022; Mace et al., 2022; Wilson et al., 2022).

What Do We Know About the Impact of Everyday Digital Technology Use on the Aging Brain from Epidemiological Literature?

We consider the current generation of older adults to be digital pioneers because they are the first to reach late age with significant exposure to computers, the Internet, and other important digital developments. As such, our group was interested in the net effect of general technology use on older adults' cognitive health and well-being. To this end, we recently published a meta-analysis of over 410,000 adults from 57 different studies across the globe to specifically address the question of whether everyday digital technology use was associated with better or worse cognitive outcomes (Benge & Scullin, 2025). Our findings suggested that older adults who engage more with daily technologies such as the Internet, computers, and smartphones demonstrate better cognitive outcomes and less risk of dementia than those who engage less with these technologies (OR = 0.42, $p < .0001$). These effects remained even when adjusting for factors that might have led to a healthy user effect, such as limiting analyses to studies that included adjustments for socioeconomic, health, educational, and occupational factors that are known in their own right to impact cognition and risk of dementia (Huang et al., 2020; Menegon et al., 2024; A.-Y. Wang et al., 2023).

While encouraging, these epidemiological cohort studies demonstrate a correlational, rather than causal, relationship between technology use and older adult cognitive health. We hypothesize that the overall relation between cognition and technology use among older adults is complex, with available data supporting a bidirectional relationship between technology use and cognition. In this vein, Choi and colleagues (2021) reviewed 4 years of data from a representative national sample from the National Health and Aging Trends study. In cross lagged analyses, they reported that older adults with greater use of Internet communication technologies showed better memory and executive functioning performance in subsequent years of the study, even after controlling for factors such as baseline cognitive performance and education. Conversely, participants with lower memory (but not executive) scores at baseline subsequently demonstrated less Internet communication technology use in subsequent waves.

Experimental designs on digital technology use in older adults yield greater opportunities for understanding causality but are challenging to divorce from other factors such as baseline technology familiarity, length of technology exposure, and what aspects of technology training are targeted. With these caveats in mind, experimental studies also tend to support a bidirectional relationship between digital technology use and cognition in aging. For example, experiments training older adults to use a tablet have yielded generally positive results on short-term cognitive outcomes. These interventions typically involve structured training sessions where participants learn to use digital devices and applications, with improvements noted in domains such as processing speed (Chan et al., 2016; Vaportzis et al., 2017) as well as global cognitive outcomes (Givon Schaham et al., 2024; Harvey et al., 2020, 2022, 2024; D.-R. Kim et al., 2021). However, while encouraging, not all experimental trials of digital technology use have proven beneficial, with other well-designed studies of initial internet training (Slegers et al., 2008) and later general use computing applications (S. Zhang et al., 2022) failing to show any demonstrable benefit to cognition.

What explains these discrepancies? First, we note that some of the studies occurred before the age of widespread mobile device use. For example, the Slegers et al. (2008)

study was conducted well before the proliferation of tablet computers that may be easier and more interesting for some older adults to use (Chan et al., 2016; Givon Schaham et al., 2024; Vaportzis et al., 2017). We also note a wide variety in design, sample size ranges, outcome measures, and duration of training, all of which can introduce heterogeneity to outcomes. That being said, we believe that the strength of the evidence, which is largely observational but increasingly supported with experimental designs, supports the notion that technology can play a role in promoting beneficial cognitive outcomes in older adults, with technology use being reciprocally influenced by cognitive status.

What Are the Possible Mechanisms by Which Digital Technology Use May Promote Cognition Functioning?

We hypothesize at least three mechanisms by which digital technology engagement can benefit cognition in older adults: connection, compensatory behaviors, and cognitive complexity.

With regard to connection, loneliness is recognized as a common problem in older adults (Cacioppo & Cacioppo, 2018) and is linked with increased risk of cognitive decline (Kang & Oremus, 2023). As digital technology is increasingly used for social interactions among older adults, it may provide a means of reducing loneliness and its deleterious effects on cognition (Zhang et al., 2021, 2024). An elegant example of using technology to reduce loneliness was reported by Dodge et al. (2015), who found that older adults who engaged in video chats demonstrated improved cognitive functioning relative to control particiapnts, particularly for language-based tasks such as semantic and phonemic fluency. Similarly, social media use by older adults has been linked to better executive functioning (Khoo & Yang, 2020). Thus, digital technology may help foster social connections that reduce loneliness, in turn promoting cognitive health among older adults. Future research, however, is required to evaluate how technology-mediated approaches to social interaction perform relative to face-to-face interactions, and to understand how the likelihood of engaging successfully with these digital technologies is impacted by factors such as personality and mood.

In addition to social connection, digital tools may be powerful ways of facilitating cognitive compensation, allowing individuals to function more effectively in their environments and reducing cognitive load and stress. Cognitive offloading, the process of using external, rather than internal, systems for tracking prospective memory tasks, may facilitate greater independence and daily task performance in some older adults (Scullin et al., 2022). For example, digital automatic bill pay may help to avoid financial errors, and GPS may help older adults to navigate more effectively (Benge et al., 2024).

Finally, everyday use of digital technology may help promote more cognitively complex activities, particularly compared to other passive forms of leisure. For example, Raichlen et al. (2022) evaluated dementia risk in the UK Biobank cohort in relation to watching TV versus using a computer. These two seemingly passive, non–physically active behaviors had diametrically opposite impacts on dementia risk, with computer use associated with decreased risk and television consumption associated with increased risk. Relatedly, Small et al. (2009) found that searching the web relative to reading text produced greater cortical activation among older adults. Critically, this finding was most pronounced for older adults who were not "net naïve," suggesting that longer term, repeated exposure to evolving or different digital technology is may be needed to see altered brain responses. While this is an area that requires more research, the cognitive complexity of digital interactions may be an important variable to monitor in older adults' cognitive health.

As illustrated earlier, there are several potential mechanisms and supportive evidence indicating a role of digital technology use in promoting cognitive health in aging. However, any tool powerful enough to help a brain can also be powerful enough to harm it. Next, we review the potential cognitive harms of digital technology use in older adults.

Are There Potential Cognitive Harms for Everyday Digital Technology Use for Older Adults?

Similar to the childhood developmental literature reviewed earlier, is it possible to "overdose" on digital technologies as an older adult? While this phenomenon has not been as well characterized in older adults, in one study a U-shaped association was observed with digital technology use and cognition, where both nonusers and the most excessive digital users demonstrated increased risk of cognitive decline, though these findings failed to reach statistical significance due to small sample size (Cho et al., 2023). Additionally, higher social media use among older adults has been linked to more frequent daily memory failures (Sharifian & Zahodne, 2020). In these ways, excessive use of everyday digital technologies may not be universally favorable for cognition, though additional work is required to replicate these outcomes, understand appropriate dosing and the most beneficial types of digital activities, and identify those at risk for overuse.

In addition, neuropsychologists should consider the difference between cognition as a "trait" (a relatively static variable) versus a "state" (how a person's cognition is performing in the moment). As most readers have probably experienced, a computer notification while concentrating, the allure of the smartphone while driving, or a deluge of text messages occurring simultaneously can easily have detrimental and even catastrophic impacts on transient concentration and other cognitive processes. These "state-based" cognitive errors may be magnified in older adults. For example, texting while driving, while problematic for drivers of all ages, more significantly impacted older relative to younger drivers' ability to stay in the lane (Thompson et al., 2012). Texting may also create balance issues in drivers, making it harder to keep steady while driving (Sanjani et al., 2020). Even outside the context of driving, Lino et al. (2023) found that older adults using a smartphone when engaged in a balance test performed at a deficit compared to those not concurrently using a smartphone. In short, under conditions that require multiple tasks to be completed simultaneously, even when one of the tasks is purely motor, multitasking with digital technology may increase risk of harm.

Use of digital technology may also place older adults at greater risk of fraud, scams, and misinformation, posing an additional threat to the cognitive health and well-being of older adults. Factors such as social isolation, health problems, lack of technological skills, and more (Burton et al., 2022) seem to increase the susceptibility of older adults to online fraud. Similar factors can also promote older adults' risks for being taken in by false information and influence in online environments (Brashier & Schacter, 2020).

As the earlier review highlights, the rapidly evolving technological environment does seem to be influencing cognition in older adults. Our read of the evidence to date is that everyday digital technology use seems to be a net positive for older adults' cognitive well-being thus far, without widespread evidence of digital dementia among the first generation exposed to these devices. However, further work is required to complete careful experimental studies with long-term follow-ups to better understand this phenomenon, understand the mechanisms by which technology may promote cognitive well-being, and develop methods of understanding and ultimately ameliorating potential harms from digital technology use, particularly in terms of reducing distractions and multitasking demands. Neuropsychologists are uniquely equipped to inform this important research, and we hope this selective review highlights these opportunities. We turn next to reviewing the available literature on how patients and their families are using digital technologies in their daily lives.

Impact of Everyday Digital Technology Use on Those with Neurocognitive Disorders and Care Partners

As we argue elsewhere in this volume (see Chapter 9), technology use is increasingly considered a part of everyday functioning for everyone, even those impacted by neurocognitive disorders. In this section, we turn to reviewing how those impacted by neurocognitive disorders, both themselves and their care partners, are using technologies to assist with cognition.

How Are Individuals with Neurocognitive Disorders Using Digital Technologies for Compensation?

Digital technologies have the potential for reducing some of the everyday difficulties experienced by those with neurological disorders (Chen et al., 2023; Kiselica et al., 2024; Moyle, 2019). For example, digital technologies offer mobile tracking and fall detection for monitoring safety, GPS guidance and ride-sharing application for navigation, and home delivery of goods and groceries for shopping. However, in the context of neurocognitive disorders, the key word is "potential," as most of these digital activities are well used by young healthy adults but have not been directly tested in persons with neurological disorders. Furthermore, there is a concern that the age-related digital divide could prevent persons with cognitive impairment from learning to effectively use digital technologies (Charness & Boot, 2022; Johnson, 2022). Neurodegenerative disease is indeed associated with reduced technology engagement, including lower rates of smartphone ownership, less frequent use, and failure to take advantage of helpful device features (Benge et al., 2020). Nevertheless, investigations of using digital technologies to address everyday cognitive demands are emerging. For this review we consider just one of the myriad possible ways everyday technology use can help those with neurocognitive disorders: specifically, the case of prospective memory.

Prospective memory is the ability to remember to complete intended tasks in the future (i.e., remembering to remember), such as taking one's medication, wishing a family member happy birthday, and picking up milk at the grocery store (McDaniel & Einstein, 2007). Prospective memory abilities are impaired, sometimes severely, in neurological disorders (Henry, 2021). Cognitive training and mnemonic strategies have been attempted in persons with neurological disorders, but these interventions only produce mild to moderate improvements in prospective memory performance (Jones et al., 2021). Digital technologies, such as digital calendars, digital voice recorders, and personal assistant reminder systems have the potential to improve everyday prospective memory functioning via cognitive offloading (Gilbert, 2015), or "taking the memory out of prospective memory." However, at present most older adults with neurological disorders do not habitually use these technology-based strategies (Benge et al., 2020).

McDonald et al. (2011) demonstrated proof of principle that individuals with neurological disorders could learn how to use a digital calendar. In a 5-week study, 12 individuals with acquired brain injury, ages 19–65, showed better prospective memory performance when using Google Calendar (82%) than when using a standard diary (55%). El Haj and colleagues observed similar positive outcomes of digital calendar usage in a case study of a patient with mild Alzheimer's disease (El Haj et al., 2017) and in a nonrandomized study in which 22 patients with mild Alzheimer's disease self-selected into using paper-based or smartphone-based calendars (El Haj et al., 2021). A meta-analysis of the literature on prospective memory in persons with neurological disorders indicated that electronic memory aides produce large-sized ($g = .81$) improvements in performance (Jones et al., 2021).

Randomized controlled trials are also emerging in this field. Scullin et al. (2022) enrolled 52 older adults with mild cognitive impairment (MCI) or mild dementia who had minimal experience using smartphones (corresponding to once monthly average use of smartphone features). In a single 1- to 2-hour session, these participants were trained to use iPhone or Samsung Galaxy phones to offload prospective memory intentions to either a digital recorder application or a personal assistant reminder application (Cortana). Ninety percent of participants completed all study procedures, and participants averaged using their app approximately once each day. Prospective memory was measured objectively via remembering to perform experimenter-assigned tasks at appropriate times (call laboratory phone) and locations (take photo of location). Participants using the reminder app initially produced better prospective memory performance (week 1), but the effect declined over time, potentially indicating a decrease in use of the Cortana app. Prospective memory functioning was also measured via a structured interview on personally relevant daily prospective memory tasks, and this measure indicated that two-thirds of participants experienced improved functioning across the month, in both conditions. Correlational analyses demonstrated that participants who used their apps more also showed better prospective memory functioning as well as improved caregiver-reported instrumental activities of daily living. These associations persisted even when controlling for condition, age, baseline cognitive functioning, and prior smartphone experience. These findings indicated that persons with geriatric neurological disorders who had low prior experience with smartphones could effectively learn to use apps that can help support daily prospective memory functioning.

The work by McDonald et al., El Haj et al., our author team, and others in the field suggests that persons with neurological disorders can effectively use new digital technologies in a compensatory manner for prospective memory. However, several questions remain concerning selection biases and long-term usage. While some studies have targeted recruitment at individuals who lacked prior experience with digital devices, clinic-recruited participants may be more motivated to learn new approaches that may be beneficial to their health than the general population. Furthermore, existing studies have typically monitored digital device usage and prospective memory over a few weeks, and therefore it is unknown whether devices are abandoned (and prospective memory suffers) over months and years in the absence of booster training sessions (Luna et al., 2023). Larger-scale randomized controlled trials using more extensive longitudinal designs are therefore necessary to further advance this field.

How Are Digital Technologies Being Used in the Care of Persons with Cognitive Disorders?

While much of this chapter has focused on the cognitive impacts of digital technology use by an individual on their own cognition, caregivers of those with neurocognitive disorders are increasingly employing everyday digital technologies to help the health and cognitive well-being of those they care for (Kaser et al., 2024; Kiselica et al., 2024). In the following section, we present results of a rapid review of the literature on these indirect impacts of technology use on cognitive well-being of those with neurocognitive disorders. We focus on these impacts through the lens of older adults, but we hope the overall framework is useful for caregivers across broader classes of neurocognitive disorder.

In our work, we think about how we can build technology that CARES (see Figure 13.1 and Table 13.1). This model is built upon the observations that caregivers

Figure 13.1 The technology that CARES framework

Table 13.1 Care Technologies in Development or Testing Organized by the CARES Framework

	Number of Studies	Example	Additional Studies
Cognitive offloading	1	Lacob et al. (2022) developed Time for Living and Caring, used by care partners to offload scheduling to better incorporate respite activities into their routines.	—
Automated task management	0	—	—
Remote monitoring and intervention	17	Matthews et al. (2015) investigated a wearable camera system to for bias-free recall of activities of people with dementia.	Amabili et al., 2022; Anderson et al., 2021; Bankole et al., 2020; Gaugler et al., 2019, 2021; Guisado-Fernandez et al., 2019, 2020; Kernebeck et al., 2019; K. Kim et al., 2020; Lauriks MSc et al., 2020; Lindauer et al., 2017; Liu et al., 2017; Malmgren Fänge et al., 2017; Matthews et al., 2015, 2016; Smith et al., 2025; Sung et al., 2022
Emotional and social support	9	Digital journals for care partners help facilitate social support online, increasing emotional and social support (Pickett et al., 2024).	Beentjes et al., 2023; Bosco et al., 2025; Fan et al., 2024; Kwok et al., 2023; Monnet et al., 2023; Oostra et al., 2023; Pickett et al., 2024; Rose et al., 2021; Williams et al., 2019
Symptom treatment	13	Digital reminiscence therapy has been found to increase quality of life for the care partner and improve neuropsychiatric symptoms for people with dementia.	Aguirre et al., 2024; Arthanat et al., 2020; Brown et al., 2016; Cheng & Ng, 2025; Elfrink et al., 2021; Gustafson Jr. et al., 2019; Han et al., 2022; Hou et al., 2022; Kales et al., 2018; Meßmer et al., 2024; Potts et al., 2020; Wilkerson et al., 2018; K. Williams et al., 2018
Multiple	5	Stara et al. (2021) explored the use of a virtual agent, Anne, who could support communication, personal calendars, digital reminders, and relaxation.	Ghani et al., 2022; Raharjo et al., 2024; Rashid et al., 2022; Stara et al., 2021; Zuschnegg et al., 2023

frequently use technologies for *c*ognitive offloading, *a*utomated task management, *r*emote monitoring and intervention, *e*motional/social support, and direct *s*ymptom treatment. To provide some concrete examples, caregivers use digital technology for cognitive offloading, in which they delegate tasks associated with care to a digital device or software. For example, they may create calendar events reminders for doctor's appointments, medication times, and other care-related appointments and tasks, instead of relying on memory (Block et al., 2020; Kristiansen et al., 2022; Lariviere et al., 2021; Larnyo et al., 2022; Mo et al., 2021; Ruggiano et al., 2019; Wilson et al., 2024). Similarly, care partners report automating tasks, such as setting up autopay for a loved one's bills, ordering groceries to be delivered through online portals, and setting medications to auto-refill (Mikula et al., 2024). Care partners frequently describe automation as a way to reduce the number of tasks they have to complete, alleviating some of the stress of providing care and allowing them to focus on more meaningful activities. Remote monitoring, whether with in-home cameras or fall sensors, can also mitigate concerns regarding their loved one. Emotional and social support can also be facilitated by technology, with care partners using social media to connect with family members and other care partners for support and communication (Block et al., 2020; Iribarren et al., 2018; Kristiansen et al., 2022; Leszko, 2020; Mikula et al., 2024; Mo et al., 2021; Tang et al., 2023; Wójcik et al., 2021). Further, informational support frequently comes through technology. For example, surveys and interviews repeatedly identify care partners as using technologies (particularly smartphones) to search for care-related topics, such as health information, care strategies, and legal advice (Guzman-Parra et al., 2020; Kales et al., 2017; Wójcik et al., 2021). Finally, direct symptom treatment can be facilitated by technology. For example, digital technologies to track symptom changes (Dunn et al., 2022; Guzman-Parra et al., 2020; Ruggiano et al., 2019), manage medications (Kristiansen et al., 2022; Mo et al., 2021; Ruggiano et al., 2019), and actually treat symptoms (e.g., improving memory and mood through reminiscence apps) are all in use. Extending beyond the CARES framework, new technologies (artificial intelligence agents, virtual assistants; Table 13.1) are emerging that will continue to facilitate caregiving of those with neurocognitive disorders.

What Are the Facilitators and Barriers to Digital Technology Use in Care?

Further research has investigated barriers and facilitators to the use of technologies in care of which neuropsychologists should be aware. Similar to the digital divide literature reviewed elsewhere in this volume (see Chapter 14), Chary et al. (2024) found that people from minoritized ethnic and racial backgrounds reported less comfort with virtual formats in health appointments, potentially influenced by the costs of purchasing digital technologies to access virtual appointments. Spanish-speaking care partners identified more barriers to technology use in care (Iribarren et al., 2018), such as a lack of resources available in their language. Care partners with less education have been found to use technology in care less often as well (Amiri et al., 2023; Efthymiou et al., 2020; H. Kim, 2015; Oh et al., 2024; Wójcik et al., 2021), perhaps due to a lack of awareness of the technologies available. Older age is also associated with less technology use in care (Amiri et al., 2023; Arighi et al., 2021; Efthymiou et al., 2020; Guzman-Parra et al., 2020; H. Kim, 2015; Oh et al., 2024; Teles et al., 2022; Wójcik et al., 2021). Some studies suggested that women are more accepting of and knowledgeable about the use of technology in care (Xiong et al., 2018, 2020), while men may be willing to pay more for digital technologies (Xiong et al., 2020). Finally, perceived self-efficacy for digital technology use, such as high health and digital literacy, may facilitate care partners' use of technologies (Peterson et al., 2020; Werner et al., 2017; Wrede et al., 2023).

Beyond demographic factors, there are multiple other influences on technology adoption in caregiving. Higher perceived usefulness of a particular technology predicted actual use of the technology, over and above other factors in one study (Nasrun et al., 2024), suggesting it is important to identify specific goals for which care partners will perceive the technology as useful to aide adoption within care (Kaser et al., 2024). Ease of use is also a critical factor affecting actual use of a technology (Amiri et al., 2023; Liu et al., 2018; Werner et al., 2017; Xiong et al., 2018, 2020; Zhong et al., 2025). Interventionalists can increase ease of use in a variety of ways, such as adjusting device settings for sensory limitations of the users (Amiri et al., 2023; Chary et al., 2024). Also, multiple studies found that if a device had a complicated interface or required users to log in each time they used it, care partners were less likely to want to adopt the technology (Feeney Mahoney et al., 2016; Holthe et al., 2018; Kowe et al., 2023; Mikula et al., 2024; Oh et al., 2024; Peterson et al., 2020). Thus, simple design changes like increasing text size and limiting sign in requirements may expand technology use by care partners.

Care partners also weigh specific aspects of the digital technology itself when considering adoption. The most commonly reported barrier to digital technology use in care is financial cost (Feeney Mahoney et al., 2016; Mikula et al., 2024; Stavropoulos et al., 2021; Van Assche et al., 2024; R. H. Wang et al., 2017; Xiong et al., 2018, 2020). Perceived reliability of the technology or the information it provides was noted as another factor influencing use (Van Assche et al., 2024; Werner et al., 2017); for example, if a remote monitoring device was likely to give false alarms, care partners were skeptical about using it (Liu et al., 2017). Finally, care partners noted that they must feel confident in the privacy of their data if they are going to adopt a technology (Amiri et al., 2023; Gris et al., 2023; Kowe et al., 2023; Mao et al., 2015; Mikula et al., 2024; Mulvenna et al., 2017; Oh et al., 2024; Stavropoulos et al., 2021; Wilson et al., 2024; Wrede et al., 2021, 2023).

How Can Neuropsychologists Expand Use of Digital Technology for Care Partners?

As increasing technological approaches emerge, practitioners may be looking for ways to support the use of digital technology-based strategies in care right now. Kaser et al. (2024) developed the Technology Assistance in Dementia (Tech-AiD) framework as a resource for currently practicing clinicians hoping to incorporate digital technology-based strategies into their behavioral interventions. Their approach involves (1) assessing disease severity to determine whether patients can use technologies on their own versus relying more on a care partner; (2) evaluating the technological environment to guide technology-related recommendations; (3) providing psychoeducation on the benefits of technology-based strategies; (4) identifying goals that can be addressed via technologies; (5) using problem-solving approaches to implement technologies; and (6) developing a maintenance plan to main technology-supported gains beyond the treatment phrase. Such models have preliminary support, but we believe a future area of research is to rigorously test such frameworks to identify what interaction of digital tools and metacognitive strategies best help caregiving.

Summary: Digital Technology Is Changing the Brain

While much is yet to be discovered, we believe the literature reveals three broad themes relating to digital technology and cognition: (1) technology does seem to have a measurable impact on developing brains, though whether this is a net positive or a net negative may be both dependent on both the type of digital exposure and at what age the exposure occurs; (2) in older adults, there is increasing epidemiological (though more mixed experimental) evidence that engaging with everyday digital technologies may provide a cognitive health benefit to some; and (3) spontaneous and trained use of everyday technologies by those with neurocognitive disorders and those who care for them may be beneficial for aspects of cognition and real-world functioning, though this is the space least well characterized.

These themes suggest that neuropsychologists should attend carefully to the technological environment of those we serve. How might this look? First, because we tend to only "see" as professionals what we measure, developing, refining, and expanding measures of everyday activities to include digital technologies may help guide clinical hypotheses and better clarify technology's impact on the cognitive health of populations. Further, neuropsychologists should work both in clinical and research settings to understand how spontaneous use of compensatory strategies may be effective or ineffective at serving others, consistent with long-standing principles of neurorehabilitation. Finally, we encourage neuropsychologists to recognize that technologies can be a part of caring, and we leverage these habits to help those that we serve.

References

Adachi, P. J. C., & Willoughby, T. (2013). More than just fun and games: The longitudinal relationships between strategic video games, self-reported problem solving skills, and academic grades. *Journal of Youth and Adolescence*, *42*(7), 1041–1052. https://doi.org/10.1007/s10964-013-9913-9

Aguirre, A., Hilsabeck, R., Smith, T., Xie, B., He, D., Wang, Z., & Zou, N. (2024). Assessing the quality of ChatGPT responses to dementia caregivers' questions: Qualitative analysis. *JMIR Aging*, *7*(1), e53019. https://doi.org/10.2196/53019

Alzahabi, R., & Becker, M. W. (2013). The association between media multitasking, task-switching, and dual-task performance. *Journal of Experimental Psychology: Human Perception and Performance*, *39*(5), 1485–1495.

Amabili, G., Cucchieri, G., Margaritini, A., Benadduci, M., Barbarossa, F., Luzi, R., Riccardi, G. R., Pelliccioni, G., Maranesi, E., & Bevilacqua, R. (2022). Social robotics and dementia: Results from the eWare Project in supporting older people and their informal caregivers. *International Journal of Environmental Research and Public Health*, *19*(20), Article 20. https://doi.org/10.3390/ijerph192013334

Amiri, P., Pirnejad, H., Bahaadinbeigy, K., Baghini, M. S., Khazaee, P. R., & Niazkhani, Z. (2023). A qualitative study of factors influencing ePHR adoption by caregivers and care providers of Alzheimer's patients: An extension of the unified theory of acceptance and use of technology model. *Health Science Reports*, *6*(7), e1394. https://doi.org/10.1002/hsr2.1394

Anderson, M. S., Bankole, A., Homdee, N., Mitchell, B. A., Byfield, G. E., & Lach, J. (2021). Dementia Caregiver Experiences and Recommendations for Using the Behavioral and Environmental Sensing and Intervention System at Home: Usability and Acceptability Study. *JMIR Aging*, *4*(4), e30353. https://doi.org/10.2196/30353

Arce Rentería, M., Vonk, J. M. J., Felix, G., Avila, J. F., Zahodne, L. B., Dalchand, E., Frazer, K. M., Martinez, M. N., Shouel, H. L., & Manly, J. J. (2019). Illiteracy, dementia risk, and cognitive trajectories among older adults with low education. *Neurology*, *93*(24), e2247–e2256. https://doi.org/10.1212/WNL.0000000000008587

Arighi, A., Fumagalli, G. G., Carandini, T., Pietroboni, A. M., De Riz, A., Galimberti, D., & Scarpini, E. (2021). Facing the digital divide into a dementia clinic during COVID-19 pandemic: Caregiver age matters. *Neurological Sciences*, *42*, 1247–1251. https://doi.org/10.1007/s10072-020-05009-w

Arthanat, S., Begum, M., Gu, T., LaRoche, D. P., Xu, D., & Zhang, N. (2020). Caregiver perspectives on a smart home-based socially assistive robot for individuals with Alzheimer's disease and related dementia. *Disability and Rehabilitation: Assistive Technology*, *15*(7), 789–798. https://doi.org/10.1080/17483107.2020.1753831

Bankole, A., Anderson, M. S., Homdee, N., Alam, R., Lofton, A., Fyffe, N., Goins, H., Newbold, T., Smith-Jackson, T., & Lach, J. (2020). BESI: Behavioral and Environmental Sensing and Intervention for dementia caregiver Empowerment—Phases 1 and 2.

American Journal of Alzheimer's Disease & Other Dementias, 35. https://doi.org/10.1177/1533317520906686

Barasch, A., Diehl, K., Silverman, J., & Zauberman, G. (2017). Photographic memory: The effects of volitional photo taking on memory for visual and auditory aspects of an experience. *Psychological Science, 28*(8), 1056–1066. https://doi.org/10.1177/0956797617694868

Barnes, D. E., Tager, I. B., Satariano, W. A., & Yaffe, K. (2004). The relationship between literacy and cognition in well-educated elders. *The Journals of Gerontology Series A: Biological Sciences and Medical Sciences, 59*(4), M390–M395.

Beentjes, K. M., Neal, D. P., Kerkhof, Y. J. F., Broeder, C., Moeridjan, Z. D. J., Ettema, T. P., Pelkmans, W., Muller, M. M., Graff, M. J. L., & Dröes, R.-M. (2023). Impact of the FindMyApps program on people with mild cognitive impairment or dementia and their caregivers; an exploratory pilot randomised controlled trial. *Disability and Rehabilitation: Assistive Technology, 18*(3), 253–265. https://doi.org/10.1080/17483107.2020.1842918

Benge, J. F., Aguirre, A., Scullin, M. K., Kiselica, A., Hilsabeck, R. C., Paydarfar, D., Thomaz, E., & Douglas, M. (2024). Digital methods for performing daily tasks among older adults: An initial report of frequency of use and perceived utility. *Experimental Aging Research, 50*(2), 133–154. https://doi.org/10.1080/0361073X.2023.2172950

Benge, J. F., Dinh, K. L., Logue, E., Phenis, R., Dasse, M. N., & Scullin, M. K. (2020). The smartphone in the memory clinic: A study of patient and care partner's utilisation habits. *Neuropsychological Rehabilitation, 30*(1), 101–115. https://doi.org/10.1080/09602011.2018.1459307

Benge, J. F., & Scullin, M. K. (2025). A meta-analysis of technology use and cognitive aging. *Nature human behaviour, 9*(7), 1405–1419. https://doi.org/10.1038/s41562-025-02159-9

Bickham, D. S. (2021). Current research and viewpoints on internet addiction in adolescents. *Current Pediatrics Reports, 9*(1), 1–10. https://doi.org/10.1007/s40124-020-00236-3

Block, L., Gilmore-Bykovskyi, A., Jolliff, A., Mullen, S., & Werner, N. E. (2020). Exploring dementia family caregivers' everyday use and appraisal of technological supports. *Geriatric Nursing, 41*(6), 909–915. https://doi.org/10.1016/j.gerinurse.2020.06.019

Bosco, C., Otenen, E., Torres, J. O., Nguyen, V., Chheda, D., Peng, X., Jessup, N. M., Himes, A. K., Cureton, B., Lu, Y., Hill, C. V., Hendrie, H. C., Barnes, P. A., & Shih, P. C. (2025). Designing a multimodal and culturally relevant Alzheimer disease and related dementia generative artificial intelligence tool for Black American informal caregivers: Cognitive walk-through usability study. *JMIR Aging, 8*(1), e60566. https://doi.org/10.2196/60566

Brashier, N. M., & Schacter, D. L. (2020). Aging in an era of fake news. *Current Directions in Psychological Science, 29*(3), 316–323.

Brown, E. L., Ruggiano, N., Page, T. F., Roberts, L., Hristidis, V., Whiteman, K. L., & Castro, J. (2016). CareHeroes web and Android™ apps for dementia caregivers: A feasibility study. *Research in Gerontological Nursing, 9*(4), 193–203. https://doi.org/10.3928/19404921-20160229-02

Burton, A., Cooper, C., Dar, A., Mathews, L., & Tripathi, K. (2022). Exploring how, why and in what contexts older adults are at risk of financial cybercrime victimisation: A realist review. *Experimental Gerontology, 159*, 111678.

Cacioppo, J. T., & Cacioppo, S. (2018). The growing problem of loneliness. *The Lancet, 391*(10119), 426. https://doi.org/10.1016/S0140-6736(18)30142-9

Cain, M. S., & Mitroff, S. R. (2011). Distractor filtering in media multitaskers. *Perception, 40*(10), 1183–1192. https://doi.org/10.1068/p7017

Caird, J. K., Willness, C. R., Steel, P., & Scialfa, C. (2008). A meta-analysis of the effects of cell phones on driver performance. *Accident Analysis & Prevention, 40*(4), 1282–1293. https://doi.org/10.1016/j.aap.2008.01.009

Cecutti, L., Chemero, A., & Lee, S. W. S. (2021). Technology may change cognition without necessarily harming it. *Nature Human Behaviour, 5*, 973–975. https://doi.org/10.1038/s41562-021-01162-0

Chaarani, B., Ortigara, J., Yuan, D., Loso, H., Potter, A., & Garavan, H. (2022). Association of video gaming with cognitive performance among children. *JAMA Network Open, 5*(10), e2235721. https://doi.org/doi:10.1001/jamanetworkopen.2022.35721

Chan, M. Y., Haber, S., Drew, L. M., & Park, D. C. (2016). Training older adults to use tablet computers: Does it enhance cognitive function? *The Gerontologist, 56*(3), 475–484. https://doi.org/10.1093/geront/gnu057

Charness, N., & Boot, W. R. (2022). A grand challenge for psychology: Reducing the age-related digital divide. *Current Directions in Psychological Science, 31*(2), 187–193. https://doi.org/10.1177/09637214211068144

Chary, A., Hernandez, N., Rivera, A. P., Ramont, V., Obi, T., Santangelo, I., Ritchie, C., Singh, H., Hayden, E., Naik, A. D., Liu, S., & Kennedy, M. (2024). Perceptions of acute care telemedicine among caregivers for persons living with dementia: A qualitative study. *Journal of Applied Gerontology, 43*(1), 69–77. https://doi.org/10.1177/07334648231198018

Chen, C., Ding, S., & Wang, J. (2023). Digital health for aging populations. *Nature Medicine, 29*, 1623–1630. https://doi.org/10.1038/s41591-023-02391-8

Cheng, S.-T., & Ng, P. H. F. (2025). The PDC30 Chatbot—Development of a psychoeducational resource on dementia caregiving among family caregivers: Mixed methods acceptability study. *JMIR Aging, 8*(1), e63715. https://doi.org/10.2196/63715

Cho, G., Betensky, R. A., & Chang, V. W. (2023). Internet usage and the prospective risk of dementia: A population-based cohort study. *Journal of the American Geriatrics Society, 71*(8), 2419–2429. https://doi.org/10.1111/jgs.18394

Choi, E. Y., Wisniewski, K. M., & Zelinski, E. M. (2021). Information and communication technology use in older adults: A unidirectional or Bi-directional association with cognitive function? *Computers in Human Behavior, 121*, 106813. https://doi.org/10.1016/j.chb.2021.106813

Chou, C., Condron, L., & Belland, J. C. (2005). A review of the research on internet addiction. *Educational Psychology Review, 17*(4), 363–388. https://doi.org/10.1007/s10648-005-8138-1

Christakis, D. A., Ramirez, J. S. B., Ferguson, S. M., Ravinder, S., & Ramirez, J.-M. (2018). How early media exposure may affect cognitive function: A review of results from observations in humans and experiments in mice. *Proceedings of the National Academy of Sciences of the United States of America, 115*(40), 9851–9858. https://doi.org/10.1073/pnas.1711548115

Christakis, D. A., Zimmerman, F. J., DiGiuseppe, D. L., & McCarty, C. A. (2004). Early television exposure and subsequent attentional problems in children. *Pediatrics, 113*(4), 708–713. https://doi.org/10.1542/peds.113.4.708

Cochran, L. M., & Dickerson, A. E. (2019). Driving while navigating: On-road driving performance using GPS or printed instructions. *Canadian Journal of Occupational Therapy, 86*(1), 61–69.

Connolly, T. M., Boyle, E. A., MacArthur, E., Hainey, T., & Boyle, J. M. (2012). A systematic literature review of empirical evidence on computer games and serious games. *Computers & Education, 59*(2), 661–686. https://doi.org/10.1016/j.compedu.2012.03.004

Culkin, J. M. (1967, March). *A schoolman's guide to Marshall McLuhan.* https://static1.squarespace.com/static/5a6135761f318d1d719bd5d9/t/5b2536342b6a288644 1759d5/1529165365116/JOHN_CULKIN.pdf

Dahmani, L., & Bohbot, V. D. (2020). Habitual use of GPS negatively impacts spatial memory during self-guided navigation. *Scientific Reports, 10*(1), 6310.

Danner, F. W. (2008). A national longitudinal study of the association between hours of TV viewing and the trajectory of BMI growth among US children. *Journal of Pediatric Psychology, 33*(10), 1100–1107. https://doi.org/10.1093/jpepsy/jsn034

Dodge, H. H., Zhu, J., Mattek, N., Bowman, M., Ybarra, O., Wild, K., Loewenstein, D. A., & Kaye, J. A. (2015). Web-enabled conversational interactions as a means to improve cognitive functions: Results of a 6-Week randomized controlled trial. *Alzheimer's & Dementia (New York, N. Y.), 1*(1), 1–12. https://doi.org/10.1016/j.trci.2015.01.001

Duch, H., Fisher, E. M., Ensari, I., Font, M., Harrington, A., Taromino, C., Yip, J., & Rodriguez, C. (2013a). Association of screen time use and language development in Hispanic toddlers: A cross-sectional and longitudinal study. *Clinical Pediatrics, 52*(9), 857–865. https://doi.org/10.1177/0009922813492881

Duch, H., Fisher, E. M., Ensari, I., & Harrington, A. (2013b). Screen time use in children under 3 years old: A systematic review of correlates. *International Journal of Behavioral Nutrition and Physical Activity, 10*(1), 102. https://doi.org/10.1186/1479-5868-10-102

Dunn, T., Howlett, S. E., Stanojevic, S., Shehzad, A., Stanley, J., & Rockwood, K. (2022). Patterns of symptom tracking by caregivers and patients with dementia and mild cognitive impairment: Cross-sectional study. *Journal of Medical Internet Research, 24*(1), e29219. https://doi.org/10.2196/29219

Dye, M. W. G., Green, C. S., & Bavelier, D. (2009). The development of attention skills in action video game players. *Neuropsychologia, 47*(8), 1780–1789. https://doi.org/10.1016/j.neuropsychologia.2009.02.002

Efthymiou, A., Papastavrou, E., Middleton, N., Markatou, A., & Sakka, P. (2020). How caregivers of people with dementia search for dementia-specific information on the Internet: Survey study. *JMIR Aging, 3*(1), e15480. https://doi.org/10.2196/15480

El Haj, M., Gallouj, K., & Antoine, P. (2017). Google calendar enhances prospective memory in Alzheimer's disease: A case report. *Journal of Alzheimer's Disease, 57*(1), 285–291. https://doi.org/10.3233/JAD-161283

El Haj, M., Moustafa, A. A., Gallouj, K., & Allain, P. (2021). Cuing prospective memory with smartphone-based calendars in Alzheimer's disease. *Archives of Clinical Neuropsychology, 36*(3), 316–321. https://doi.org/10.1093/arclin/acaa060

Elfrink, T. R., Ullrich, C., Kunz, M., Zuidema, S. U., & Westerhof, G. J. (2021). The online life story book: A randomized controlled trial on the effects of a digital reminiscence intervention for people with (very) mild dementia and their informal caregivers. *PLOS ONE, 16*(9), e0256251. https://doi.org/10.1371/journal.pone.0256251

Fan, Q., Hoang, M.-N., DuBose, L., Ory, M. G., Vennatt, J., Salha, D., Lee, S., & Falohun, T. (2024). The Olera.care digital caregiving assistance platform for dementia caregivers: Preliminary evaluation study. *JMIR Aging, 7*(1), e55132. https://doi.org/10.2196/55132

Feeney Mahoney, D., Coon, D. W., & Lozano, C. (2016). Latino/Hispanic Alzheimer's caregivers experiencing dementia-related dressing issues: Corroboration of the preservation of self model and reactions to a "smart dresser" computer-based dressing aid. *Digital Health, 2*, 2055207616677129. https://doi.org/10.1177/2055207616677129

Gaugler, J. E., Zmora, R., Mitchell, L. L., Finlay, J. M., Peterson, C. M., McCarron, H., & Jutkowitz, E. (2019). Six-month effectiveness of remote activity monitoring for persons living with dementia and their family caregivers: An experimental mixed methods study. *The Gerontologist, 59*(1), 78–89. https://doi.org/10.1093/geront/gny078

Gaugler, J. E., Zmora, R., Mitchell, L. L., Finlay, J., Rosebush, C. E., Nkimbeng, M., Baker, Z. G., Albers, E. A., & Peterson, C. M. (2021). Remote activity monitoring for family caregivers of persons living with dementia: A mixed methods, randomized controlled evaluation. *BMC Geriatrics, 21*(1), 715. https://doi.org/10.1186/s12877-021-02634-8

Gell, N. M., Rosenberg, D. E., Demiris, G., LaCroix, A. Z., & Patel, K. V. (2015). Patterns of technology use among older adults with and without disabilities. *The Gerontologist, 55*(3), 412–421. https://doi.org/10.1093/geront/gnt166

Ghani, Z., Saha, S., Jarl, J., Andersson, M., Berglund, J. S., & Anderberg, P. (2022). Short term economic evaluation of the digital platform "Support, Monitoring and Reminder Technology for Mild Dementia" (SMART4MD) for people with mild cognitive impairment and their informal caregivers. *Journal of Alzheimer's Disease, 86*(4), 1629–1641. https://doi.org/10.3233/JAD-215013

Gilbert, S. J. (2015). Strategic offloading of delayed intentions into the external environment. *Quarterly Journal of Experimental Psychology, 68*(5), 971–992. https://doi.org/10.1080/17470218.2014.972963

Givon Schaham, N., Buckman, Z., & Rand, D. (2024). TECH preserves global cognition of older adults with MCI compared with a control group: A randomized controlled trial. *Aging Clinical and Experimental Research, 36*(1), 1.

Granic, I., Lobel, A., & Engels, R. C. M. E. (2014). The benefits of playing video games. *American Psychologist, 69*(1), 66–78. https://doi.org/10.1037/a0034857

Gris, F., D'Amen, B., Lamura, G., Paciaroni, L., Socci, M., & Melchiorre, M. G. (2023). Personalized technological support for informal caregivers of older people with dementia: A co-design approach involving potential end users and healthcare professionals in three focus groups in Italy. *Healthcare, 11*(19), Article 19. https://doi.org/10.3390/healthcare11192640

Guisado-Fernandez, E., Blake, C., Mackey, L., Silva, P. A., Power, D., O'Shea, D., & Caulfield, B. (2020). A smart health platform for measuring health and well-being improvement in people with dementia and their informal caregivers: Usability study. *JMIR Aging, 3*(2), e15600. https://doi.org/10.2196/15600

Guisado-Fernandez, E., Caulfield, B., Silva, P. A., Mackey, L., Singleton, D., Leahy, D., Dossot, S., Power, D., O'Shea, D., & Blake, C. (2019). Development of a caregivers' support platform (connected health sustaining home stay in dementia): Protocol for a longitudinal observational mixed methods study. *JMIR Research Protocols, 8*(8), e13280. https://doi.org/10.2196/13280

Gustafson Jr., D. H., GustafsonSr., D. H., Cody, O. J., Chih, M.-Y., Johnston, D. C., & Asthana, S. (2019). Pilot test of a computer-based system to help family caregivers of dementia patients. *Journal of Alzheimer's Disease, 70*(2), 541–552. https://doi.org/10.3233/JAD-190052

Guzman-Parra, J., Barnestein-Fonseca, P., Guerrero-Pertiñez, G., Anderberg, P., Jimenez-Fernandez, L., Valero-Moreno, E., Goodman-Casanova, J. M., Cuesta-Vargas, A., Garolera, M., Quintana, M., García-Betances, R. I., Lemmens, E., Berglund, J. S., & Mayoral-Cleries, F. (2020). Attitudes and use of information and communication technologies in older adults with mild cognitive impairment or early stages of dementia and their caregivers: Cross-sectional study. *Journal of Medical Internet Research, 22*(6), e17253. https://doi.org/10.2196/17253

Halpern, W. I. (1975). Turned-on toddlers. *Journal of Communication, 25*(4), 66–70. https://doi.org/10.1111/j.1460-2466.1975.tb00640.x

Han, S. S., White, K., & Cisek, E. (2022). A feasibility study of individuals living at home with Alzheimer's disease and related dementias: Utilization of visual mapping assistive technology to enhance quality of life and reduce caregiver burden. *Clinical Interventions in Aging, 17*, 1885–1892. https://doi.org/10.2147/CIA.S387255

Harvey, P. D., Chirino, M., Mueller, A., Rivera-Molina, A., Zayas-Bazan, M., Kallestrup, P., & Czaja, S. J. (2024). Improvements in performance based measures of functional capacity and cognition after computerized functional skills training in older people with mild cognitive impairment and healthy comparators. *Psychiatry Research, 334*, 115792. https://doi.org/10.1016/j.psychres.2024.115792

Harvey, P. D., Tibiriçá, L., Kallestrup, P., & Czaja, S. J. (2020). A computerized functional skills assessment and training program targeting technology based everyday functional skills. *Journal of Visualized Experiments, 156*, 10.3791/60330. https://doi.org/10.3791/60330

Harvey, P. D., Zayas-Bazan, M., Tibiriçá, L., Kallestrup, P., & Czaja, S. J. (2022). Improvements in cognitive performance with computerized training in older people with and without cognitive impairment: Synergistic effects of skills-focused and cognitive-focused strategies. *The American Journal of Geriatric Psychiatry, 30*(6), 717–726. https://doi.org/10.1016/j.jagp.2021.11.008

Henkel, L. A. (2014). Point-and-shoot memories: The influence of taking photos on memory for a museum tour. *Psychological Science, 25*(2), 396–402. https://doi.org/10.1177/0956797613504438

Henry, J. (2021). Prospective memory impairment in neurological disorders: Implications and management. *Nature Reviews Neurology, 17*, 297–307. https://doi.org/10.1038/s41582-021-00472-1

Hill, D., Ameenuddin, N., Reid Chassiakos, Y. (Linda), Council on Communications and Media, Cross, C., Hutchinson, J., Levine, A., Boyd, R., Mendelson, R., Moreno, M., & Swanson, W. S. (2016). Media and young minds. *Pediatrics, 138*(5), e20162591. https://doi.org/10.1542/peds.2016-2591

Hish, A. J., Wood, C. T., Howard, J. B., Flower, K. B., Yin, H. S., Rothman, R. L., Delamater, A. M., Sanders, L. M., Bian, A., Schildcrout, J. S., & Perrin, E. M. (2021). Infant television watching predicts toddler television watching in a low-income population. *Academic Pediatrics, 21*(6), 988–995. https://doi.org/10.1016/j.acap.2020.11.002

Holthe, T., Jentoft, R., Arntzen, C., & Thorsen, K. (2018). Benefits and burdens: Family caregivers' experiences of assistive technology (AT) in everyday life with persons with young-onset dementia (YOD). *Disability and Rehabilitation: Assistive Technology, 13*(8), 754–762. https://doi.org/10.1080/17483107.2017.1373151

Hou, Y.-J., Zeng, S.-Y., Lin, C.-C., Yang, C.-T., Huang, H.-L., Chen, M.-C., Tsai, H.-H., Liang, J., & Shyu, Y.-I. L. (2022). Smart clothes-assisted home-nursing care program for family caregivers of older persons with dementia and hip fracture: A mixed-methods study. *BMC Geriatrics, 22*(1), 104. https://doi.org/10.1186/s12877-022-02789-y

Huang, L.-Y., Hu, H.-Y., Wang, Z.-T., Ma, Y.-H., Dong, Q., Tan, L., Yu, J.-T., & Zhu, L.-Q. (2020). Association of occupational factors and dementia or cognitive impairment: A systematic review and meta-analysis. *Journal of Alzheimer's Disease, 78*(1), 217–227. https://doi.org/10.3233/JAD-200605

Hyman Jr, I. E., Boss, S. M., Wise, B. M., McKenzie, K. E., & Caggiano, J. M. (2010). Did you see the unicycling clown? Inattentional blindness while walking and talking on a cell phone. *Applied Cognitive Psychology, 24*(5), 597–607. https://doi.org/10.1002/acp.1638

Iacob, E., Caserta, M., Donaldson, G., Sparks, C., Terrill, A., Thompson, A., Wong, B., & Utz, R. L. (2024). Evaluating the Efficacy of Time for Living and Caring: An Online Intervention to Support Dementia Caregivers' Use of Respite. *Innovation in aging, 8*(5), igae043. https://doi.org/10.1093/geroni/igae043

Internet, Broadband Fact Sheet. (2024, November 13). Pew Research Center.https://www.pewresearch.org/internet/fact-sheet/internet-broadband/

Iribarren, S., Stonbraker, S., Suero-Tejeda, N., Granja, M., Luchsinger, J. A., Mittelman, M., Bakken, S., & Lucero, R. (2018). Information, communication, and online tool needs of Hispanic family caregivers of individuals with Alzheimer's disease and related dementias. *Informatics for Health and Social Care, 44*(2), 115–134. https://doi.org/10.1080/17538157.2018.1433674

Jackson, L. A., Witt, E. A., Games, A. I., Fitzgerald, H. E., von Eye, A., & Zhao, Y. (2012). Information technology use and creativity: Findings from the Children and Technology Project. *Computers in Human Behavior, 28*(2), 370–376. https://doi.org/10.1016/j.chb.2011.10.006

Johnson, J. A. (2022). Myths about digital technology and older adults. *Nature Aging, 2*(12), 1073–1076. https://doi.org/10.1038/s43587-022-00319-4

Jones, W. E., Benge, J. F., & Scullin, M. K. (2021). Preserving prospective memory in daily life: A systematic review and meta-analysis of mnemonic strategy, cognitive training, external memory aid, and combination interventions. *Neuropsychology, 35*(1), 123–140. https://doi.org/10.1037/neu0000704

Junco, R., & Cotten, S. R. (2012). No A 4 U: The relationship between multitasking and academic performance. *Computers & Education, 59*(2), 505–514.

Kales, H. C., Gitlin, L. N., Stanislawski, B., Marx, K., Turnwald, M., Watkins, D. C., & Lyketsos, C. G. (2017). WeCareAdvisor™: The development of a caregiver-focused, web-based program to assess and manage behavioral and psychological symptoms of dementia. *Alzheimer Disease & Associated Disorders, 31*(3), 263. https://doi.org/10.1097/WAD.0000000000000177

Kales, H. C., Gitlin, L. N., Stanislawski, B., Myra Kim, H., Marx, K., Turnwald, M., Chiang, C., & Lyketsos, C. G. (2018). Effect of the WeCareAdvisor™ on family caregiver outcomes in dementia: A pilot randomized controlled trial. *BMC Geriatrics, 18*(1), 113. https://doi.org/10.1186/s12877-018-0801-8

Kang, J. W., & Oremus, M. (2023). Examining the combined effects of social isolation and loneliness on memory: A systematic review. *Archives of Gerontology and Geriatrics, 104*, 104801. https://doi.org/10.1016/j.archger.2022.104801

Kaser, A. N., Mikula, C. M., & Kiselica, A. M. (2024). Technology assistance in dementia (Tech-AiD): A framework for care in the digital age. *Journal of Health Service Psychology, 50*(1), 37–46. https://doi.org/10.1007/s42843-024-00101-7

Kaye, L., Orben, A., A. Ellis, D., C. Hunter, S., & Houghton, S. (2020). The conceptual and methodological mayhem of "screen time." *International Journal of Environmental Research and Public Health, 17*(10), Article 10. https://doi.org/10.3390/ijerph17103661

Kernebeck, S., Holle, D., Pogscheba, P., Jordan, F., Mertl, F., Huldtgren, A., Bader, S., Kirste, T., Teipel, S., Holle, B., & Halek, M. (2019). A tablet app- and sensor-based assistive technology intervention for informal caregivers to manage the challenging behavior of people with dementia (the insideDEM Study): Protocol for a feasibility study. *JMIR Research Protocols, 8*(2), e11630. https://doi.org/10.2196/11630

Khoo, S. S., & Yang, H. (2020). Social media use improves executive functions in middle-aged and older adults: A structural equation modeling analysis. *Computers in Human Behavior, 111*, 106388.

Kim, D.-R., Song, S., Kim, G.-M., Chang, J. H., Tak, Y. J., Huh, U., Cho, J. S., Liao, Y., Han, K.-S., Ko, M.-H., & Park, J.-H. (2021). Effects of ICT-based multicomponent program on body composition and cognitive function in older adults: A randomized controlled clinical study. *Clinical Interventions in Aging, 16*, 1161–1171. https://doi.org/10.2147/CIA.S306894

Kim, H. (2015). Understanding internet use among dementia caregivers: Results of secondary data analysis using the US Caregiver Survey Data. *Interactive Journal of Media Research, 4*(1), e1. https://doi.org/10.2196/ijmr.3127

Kim, K., Lee, S., Kim, S., Kim, J., Shin, D., & Shin, D. (2020). Sensor-based deviant behavior detection system using deep learning to help dementia caregivers. *IEEE Journals & Magazine, 8*, 136004–136013. https://doi.org/10.1109/ACCESS.2020.3011654

Kiselica, A. M., Lin, S. S. H., Ranum, R., Mikula, C. M., Hermann, G., Boone, A., Scullin, M., Mechanic-Hamilton, D., Wolf, T., Stevens, A., & Benge, J. F. (2024). The Technology in Caring Questionnaire: Development and psychometric properties. *Alzheimer Disease & Associated Disorders, 38*(1), 77. https://doi.org/10.1097/WAD.0000000000000604

Kılıç, A. O., Sari, E., Yucel, H., Oğuz, M. M., Polat, E., Acoglu, E. A., & Senel, S. (2019). Exposure to and use of mobile devices in children aged 1–60 months. *European Journal of Pediatrics, 178*(2), 221–227. https://doi.org/10.1007/s00431-018-3284-x

Kowe, A., Köhler, S., Görß, D., & Teipel, S. (2023). The patients' and caregivers' perspective: In-hospital navigation aids for people with dementia—a qualitative study with a value sensitive design approach. *Assistive Technology, 35*(3), 248–257. https://doi.org/10.1080/10400435.2021.2020378

Kristiansen, S., Beck, M., Kabir, Z. N., & Konradsen, H. (2022). Providing dementia care using technological solutions: An exploration of caregivers' and dementia coordinators' experiences. *Journal of Clinical Nursing, 31*(13–14), 1874–1883. https://doi.org/10.1111/jocn.15440

Kwok, I., Lattie, E. G., Yang, D., Summers, A., Grote, V., Cotten, P., & Moskowitz, J. T. (2023). Acceptability and feasibility of a socially enhanced, self-guided, positive emotion regulation intervention for caregivers of individuals with dementia: Pilot intervention study. *JMIR Aging, 6*(1), e46269. https://doi.org/10.2196/46269

Lanctôt, K. L., Hahn-Pedersen, J. H., Eichinger, C. S., Freeman, C., Clark, A., Tarazona, L. R. S., & Cummings, J. (2024). Burden of illness in people with Alzheimer's disease: A systematic review of epidemiology, comorbidities and mortality. *Journal of Prevention of Alzheimer's Disease, 11*(1), 97–107. https://doi.org/10.14283/jpad.2023.61

Lariviere, M., Poland, F., Woolham, J., Newman, S., & Fox, C. (2021). Placing assistive technology and telecare in everyday practices of people with dementia and their caregivers: Findings from an embedded ethnography of a national dementia trial. *BMC Geriatrics, 21*(1), 121. https://doi.org/10.1186/s12877-020-01896-y

Larnyo, E., Dai, B., Larnyo, A., Nutakor, J. A., Ampon-Wireko, S., Nkrumah, E. N. K., & Appiah, R. (2022). Impact of actual use behavior of healthcare wearable devices on quality of life: A cross-sectional survey of people with dementia and their caregivers in Ghana. *Healthcare, 10*(2), Article 2. https://doi.org/10.3390/healthcare10020275

Lauriks Msc, S., Meiland Phd, F., Osté Msc, J. P., Hertogh Phd, C., & Dröes Phd, R.-M. (2020). Effects of assistive home technology on quality of life and falls of people with dementia and job satisfaction of caregivers: Results from a pilot randomized controlled trial. *Assistive Technology, 32*(5), 243–250. https://doi.org/10.1080/10400435.2018.1531952

Leszko, M. (2020). The role of online communication among spousal caregivers of individuals with Alzheimer's disease. *Journal of Women & Aging, 32*(4), 462–480. https://doi.org/10.1080/08952841.2020.1754119

Lindauer, A., Seelye, A., Lyons, B., Dodge, H. H., Mattek, N., Mincks, K., Kaye, J., & Erten-Lyons, D. (2017). Dementia care comes home: Patient and caregiver assessment via telemedicine. *The Gerontologist, 57*(5), e85–e93. https://doi.org/10.1093/geront/gnw206

Lingineni, R. K., Biswas, S., Ahmad, N., Jackson, B. E., Bae, S., & Singh, K. (2012). Factors associated with attention deficit/hyperactivity disorder among US children: Results from a national survey. *BMC Pediatrics, 12*(50). https://doi.org/10.1186/1471-2431-12-50

Lino, T. B., Scarmagnan, G. S., Sobrinho-Junior, S. A., Tessari, G. M. F., Gonçalves, G. H., Pereira, H. M., & Christofoletti, G. (2023). Impact of using smartphone while walking or standing: A study focused on age and cognition. *Brain Sciences, 13*(7), 987. https://doi.org/10.3390/brainsci13070987

Liu, L., Miguel Cruz, A., & Juzwishin, D. (2018). Caregivers as a proxy for responses of dementia clients in a GPS technology acceptance study. *Behaviour & Information Technology, 37*(6), 634–645. https://doi.org/10.1080/0144929X.2018.1470672

Liu, L., Miguel Cruz, A., Ruptash, T., Barnard, S., & Juzwishin, D. (2017). Acceptance of global positioning system (GPS) technology among dementia clients and family caregivers. *Journal of Technology in Human Services, 35*(2), 99–119. https://doi.org/10.1080/15228835.2016.1266724

Luna, C., Cook, D. J., & Schmitter-Edgecombe, M. (2023). But will they use it? Predictors of adoption of an electronic memory aid in individuals with amnestic mild cognitive impairment. *Neuropsychology, 37*(8), 955–965. https://doi.org/10.1037/neu0000898

Mace, R. A., Mattos, M. K., & Vranceanu, A.-M. (2022). Older adults can use technology: Why healthcare professionals must overcome ageism in digital health. *Translational Behavioral Medicine, 12*(12), 1102–1105. https://doi.org/10.1093/tbm/ibac070

Madigan, S., Browne, D., Racine, N., Mori, C., & Tough, S. (2019). Association between screen time and children's performance on a developmental screening test. *JAMA Pediatrics, 173*(3), 244–250. https://doi.org/10.1001/jamapediatrics.2018.5056

Maguire, E. A., Gadian, D. G., Johnsrude, I. S., Good, C. D., Ashburner, J., Frackowiak, R. S. J., & Frith, C. D. (2000). Navigation-related structural change in the hippocampi of taxi drivers. *Proceedings of the National Academy of Sciences, 97*(8), 4398–4403. https://doi.org/10.1073/pnas.070039597

Mallawaarachchi, S., Burley, J., Mavilidi, M., Howard, S. J., Straker, L., Kervin, L., Staton, S., Hayes, N., Machell, A., Torjinski, M., Brady, B., Thomas, G., Horwood, S., White, S. L. J., Zabatiero, J., Rivera, C., & Cliff, D. (2024). Early childhood screen use contexts and cognitive and psychosocial outcomes: A systematic review and meta-analysis. *JAMA pediatrics, 178*(10), 1017-1026. https://doi.org/10.1001/jamapediatrics.2024.2620

Malmgren Fänge, A., Schmidt, S. M., Nilsson, M. H., Carlsson, G., Liwander, A., Dahlgren Bergström, C., Olivetti, P., Johansson, P., Chiatti, C., & on behalf of the TECH@HOME Research Group. (2017). The TECH@HOME study, a technological intervention to reduce caregiver burden for informal caregivers of people with dementia: Study protocol for a randomized controlled trial. *Trials, 18*(1), 63. https://doi.org/10.1186/s13063-017-1796-8

Manly, J. J., Jacobs, D. M., Sano, M., Bell, K., Merchant, C. A., Small, S. A., & Stern, Y. (1999). Effect of literacy on neuropsychological test performance in nondemented, education-matched elders. *Journal of the International Neuropsychological Society, 5*(3), 191–202.

Manly, J. J., Jones, R. N., Langa, K. M., Ryan, L. H., Levine, D. A., McCammon, R., Heeringa, S. G., & Weir, D. (2022). Estimating the prevalence of dementia and mild cognitive impairment in the US: The 2016 Health and Retirement Study Harmonized Cognitive Assessment Protocol Project. *JAMA Neurology, 79*(12), 1242–1249. https://doi.org/10.1001/jamaneurol.2022.3543

Mao, H.-F., Change, L.-H., Yao, G., Chen, W.-Y., & Wennie Huang, W.-N. (2015). Indicators of perceived useful dementia care assistive technology: Caregivers' perspectives—Mao—2015-. *Geriatrics & Gerontology International, 15*(8), 1049–1057. https://doi.org/10.1111/ggi.12398

Marsh, E. J., & Rajaram, S. (2019). The digital expansion of the mind: Implications of Internet usage for memory and cognition. *Journal of Applied Research in Memory and Cognition, 8*(1), 1–14. https://doi.org/10.1016/j.jarmac.2018.11.001

Matthews, J. T., Campbell, G. B., Hunsaker, A. E., Klinger, J., Mecca, L. P., Hu, L., Hostein, S., & Lingler, J. H. (2016). Wearable technology to garner the perspective of dementia family caregivers. *Journal of Gerontological Nursing, 42*(4), 16–22. https://doi.org/10.3928/00989134-20151008-65

Matthews, J. T., Lingler, J. H., Campbell, G. B., Hunsaker, A. E., Hu, L., Pires, B. R., Hebert, M., & Schulz, R. (2015). Usability of a wearable camera system for dementia family caregivers. *Journal of Healthcare Engineering, 6*(2), 120149. https://doi.org/10.1260/2040-2295.6.2.213

McDaniel, M. A., & Einstein, G. O. (2007). *Prospective memory: An overview and synthesis of an emerging field.* Sage.

McDonald, A., Haslam, C., Yates, P., Gurr, B., Leeder, G., & Sayers, A. (2011). Google Calendar: A new memory aid to compensate for prospective memory deficits following acquired brain injury. *Neuropsychological Rehabilitation, 21*(6), 784–807. https://doi.org/10.1080/09602011.2011.598405

McHarg, G., Ribner, A. D., Devine, R. T., & Hughes, C. (2020). Screen time and executive function in toddlerhood: A longitudinal study. *Frontiers in Psychology, 11*. https://doi.org/10.3389/fpsyg.2020.570392

Menegon, F., De Marchi, F., Aprile, D., Zanelli, I., Decaroli, G., Comi, C., & Tondo, G. (2024). From mild cognitive impairment to dementia: The impact of comorbid conditions on disease conversion. *Biomedicines, 12*(8), Article 8. https://doi.org/10.3390/biomedicines12081675

Meßmer, L.-M., Held, P., Bejan, A., Kunze, C., & Reich, C. (2024). Designing a dementia caregiver-centered recommendation and context-aware AI media analytical application: A comprehensive system requirements analysis. *International Journal of Human–Computer Interaction, 41*(7), 3974-3993.https://doi.org/10.1080/10447318.2024.2344913

Mikula, C. M., Perry, C., Boone, A. E., Benge, J. F., Scullin, M. K., & Kiselica, A. M. (2024). Dementia caregiver insights on use of assistive technologies. *Work, Aging and Retirement, 10*(1), 14–24. https://doi.org/10.1093/workar/waac027

Miller, J., Mills, K. L., Vuorre, M., Orben, A., & Przybylski, A. K. (2023). Impact of digital screen media activity on functional brain organization in late childhood: Evidence from the ABCD study. *Cortex, 169*, 290–308. https://doi.org/10.1016/j.cortex.2023.09.009

Mills, K. L. (2016). Possible effects of internet use on cognitive development in adolescence. *Media and Communication, 4*(3), 4–12. https://doi.org/10.17645/mac.v4i3.516

Miola, L., Muffato, V., Sella, E., Meneghetti, C., & Pazzaglia, F. (2024). GPS use and navigation ability: A systematic review and meta-analysis. *Journal of Environmental Psychology, 99*,102417.

Mo, G. Y., Biss, R. K., Poole, L., Stern, B., Waite, K., & Murphy, K. J. (2021). Technology use among family caregivers of people with dementia. *Canadian Journal on*

Aging/La Revue Canadienne Du Vieillissement, *40*(2), 331–343. https://doi.org/10.1017/S0714980820000094

Mobile Fact Sheet. (2024, November 13). Pew Research Center. https://www.pewresearch.org/internet/fact-sheet/mobile/

Moisala, M., Salmela, V., Hietajärvi, L., Carlson, S., Vuontela, V., Lonka, K., Hakkarainen, K., Salmela-Aro, K., & Alho, K. (2017). Gaming is related to enhanced working memory performance and task-related cortical activity. *Brain Research*, *1655*, 204–215. https://doi.org/10.1016/j.brainres.2016.10.027

Moisala, M., Salmela, V., Hietajärvi, L., Salo, E., Carlson, S., Salonen, O., Lonka, K., Hakkarainen, K., Salmela-Aro, K., & Alho, K. (2016). Media multitasking is associated with distractibility and increased prefrontal activity in adolescents and young adults. *NeuroImage*, *134*, 113–121. https://doi.org/10.1016/j.neuroimage.2016.04.011

Monnet, F., Dupont, C., Smets, T., Vleminck, A. D., Audenhove, C. V., Block, L. V. den, & Pivodic, L. (2023). Advance care planning website for people with dementia and their family caregivers: Protocol for a development and usability study. *JMIR Research Protocols*, *12*(1), e46935. https://doi.org/10.2196/46935

Moyle, W. (2019). The promise of technology in the future of dementia care. *Nature Reviews Neurology*, *15*, 353–359. https://doi.org/10.1038/s41582-019-0188-y

Mulvenna, M., Hutton, A., Coates, V., Martin, S., Todd, S., Bond, R., & Moorhead, A. (2017). Views of caregivers on the ethics of assistive technology used for home surveillance of people living with dementia. *Neuroethics*, *10*, 255–266. https://doi.org/10.1007/s12152-017-9305-z

Nasar, J. L., & Troyer, D. (2013). Pedestrian injuries due to mobile phone use in public places. *Accident Analysis & Prevention*, *57*, 91–95. https://doi.org/10.1016/j.aap.2013.03.021

Nasrun, M. W. S., Kusumaningrum, P., Malik, K., Kusumaningsih, W., Harimurti, K., Prawiroharjo, P., Mardhiyah, F. S., Matanta, R. H., Lalenoh, L. A. P., & Kiasati, S. K. (2024). Technological acceptance and features needed in mobile health apps development for people living with dementia and their caregivers in Indonesia. *Informatics for Health and Social Care*, *49*(2), 99–115. https://doi.org/10.1080/17538157.2024.2328029

Neuman, S. B. (1988). The displacement effect: Assessing the relation between television viewing and reading performance. *Reading Research Quarterly*, *23*(4), 414–440. https://doi.org/10.2307/747641

Oh, K. M., Inoue, M., Koizumi, N., Beran, K., & Lee, J.-A. (2024). Chronic health conditions and patient portal use in caregivers of people with Alzheimer's disease and related dementias. *Journal of Applied Gerontology*, *43*(4), 363–373. https://doi.org/10.1177/07334648231210677

Oostra, D. L., Vos, W. L., Olde Rikkert, M. G. M., Nieuwboer, M. S., & Perry, M. (2023). Digital resilience monitoring of informal caregivers of persons with dementia for early detection of overburden: Development and pilot testing. *International Journal of Geriatric Psychiatry*, *38*(1), e5869. https://doi.org/10.1002/gps.5869

Ophir, E., Nass, C., & Wagner, A. D. (2009). Cognitive control in media multitaskers. *Proceedings of the National Academy of Sciences*, *106*(37), 15583–15587. https://doi.org/10.1073/pnas.0903620106

Paulus, M. P., Squeglia, L. M., Bagot, K., Jacobus, J., Kuplicki, R., Breslin, F. J., Bodurka, J., Morris, A. S., Thompson, W. K., Bartsch, H., & Tapert, S. F. (2019). Screen media activity and brain structure in youth: Evidence for diverse structural correlation networks from the ABCD study. *NeuroImage*, *185*, 140–153. https://doi.org/10.1016/J.NEUROIMAGE.2018.10.040

Perrin, E. M., Rothman, R. L., Sanders, L. M., Skinner, A. C., Eden, S. K., Shintani, A., Throop, E. M., & Yin, H. S. (2014). Racial and ethnic differences associated with feeding- and activity-related behaviors in infants. *Pediatrics*, *133*(4), e857–e867. https://doi.org/10.1542/peds.2013-1326

Peterson, C. M., Mikal, J. P., McCarron, H. R., Finlay, J. M., Mitchell, L. L., & Gaugler, J. E. (2020). The feasibility and utility of a personal health record for persons with dementia and their family caregivers for web-based care coordination: Mixed methods study. *JMIR Aging*, *3*(1), e17769. https://doi.org/10.2196/17769

Pickett, A. C., Valdez, D., White, L. A., Loganathar, P., Linden, A., Boutilier, J. J., Caldwell, C., Elliott, C., Zuraw, M., & Werner, N. E. (2024). The CareVirtue digital journal for family and friend caregivers of people living with Alzheimer disease and related dementias: Exploratory topic modeling and user engagement study. *JMIR Aging*, *7*(1), e67992. https://doi.org/10.2196/67992

Potts, C., Bond, R., Ryan, A., Mulvenna, M., McCauley, C., Laird, E., & Goode, D. (2020). Ecological momentary assessment within a digital health intervention for reminiscence in persons with dementia and caregivers: User engagement study. *JMIR mHealth and uHealth*, *8*(7), e17120. https://doi.org/10.2196/17120

Powers, K. L., Brooks, P. J., Aldrich, N. J., Palladino, M. A., & Alfieri, L. (2013). Effects of video-game play on information processing: A meta-analytic investigation. *Psychonomic Bulletin & Review*, *20*(6), 1055–1079. https://doi.org/10.3758/s13423-013-0418-z

Przybylski, A. K., & Weinstein, N. (2017). A large-scale test of the Goldilocks hypothesis. *Psychological Science*, *28*(2), 204–215. https://doi.org/10.1177/0956797616678438

Raharjo, A. P., Amalia, A. H., Aulia, S. Z., Zhafirah, A. A., Evitananda, S., Prabaningtyas, F. D., & Elga Hamiseno Putri, I. N. (2024). Effectiveness of community-based psychosocial crisis intervention in elderly and future research directions: Scoping review. *Buletin Psikologi*, *32*(1), 56. https://doi.org/10.22146/buletinpsikologi.94751

Raichlen, D. A., Klimentidis, Y. C., Sayre, M. K., Bharadwaj, P. K., Lai, M. H. C., Wilcox, R. R., & Alexander, G. E. (2022). Leisure-time sedentary behaviors are differentially associated with all-cause dementia regardless of engagement in physical activity.

Proceedings of the National Academy of Sciences of the United States of America, 119(35), e2206931119. https://doi.org/10.1073/pnas.2206931119

Ralph, B. C., Thomson, D. R., Seli, P., Carriere, J. S., & Smilek, D. (2015). Media multitasking and behavioral measures of sustained attention. *Attention, Perception, & Psychophysics, 77*, 390–401.

Rashid, N. S. A., Chen, X. W., Mohamad Marzuki, M. F., Takshe, A. A., Okasha, A., Maarof, F., & Yunus, R. M. (2022). Development and usability assessment of a mobile app (demensia KITA) to support dementia caregivers in Malaysia: A study protocol. *International Journal of Environmental Research and Public Health, 19*(19), Article 19. https://doi.org/10.3390/ijerph191911880

Rizzi, L., Rosset, I., & Roriz-Cruz, M. (2014). Global epidemiology of dementia: Alzheimer's and vascular types. *BioMed Research International, 2014*(1), 908915. https://doi.org/10.1155/2014/908915

Rose, K. M., Coop Gordon, K., Schlegel, E. C., Mccall, M., Gao, Y., Ma, M., Lenger, K. A., Ko, E., Wright, K. D., Wang, H., & Stankovic, J. (2021). Smarthealth technology study protocol to improve relationships between older adults with dementia and family caregivers. *Journal of Advanced Nursing, 77*(5), 2519–2529. https://doi.org/10.1111/jan.14714

Ruggiano, N., Brown, E. L., Shaw, S., Geldmacher, D., Clarke, P., Hristidis, V., & Bertram, J. (2019). The potential of information technology to navigate caregiving systems: Perspectives from dementia caregivers. *Journal of Gerontological Social Work, 62*(4), 432–450. https://doi.org/10.1080/01634372.2018.1546786

Ruginski, I. T., Creem-Regehr, S. H., Stefanucci, J. K., & Cashdan, E. (2019). GPS use negatively affects environmental learning through spatial transformation abilities. *Journal of Environmental Psychology, 64*, 12–20.

Salthouse, T. A. (1996). The processing-speed theory of adult age differences in cognition. *Psychological Review, 103*(3), 403–428. https://doi.org/10.1037/0033-295X.103.3.403

Sana, F., Weston, T., & Cepeda, N. J. (2013). Laptop multitasking hinders classroom learning for both users and nearby peers. *Computers & Education, 62*, 24–31.

Sanjani, F. M., Bahram, A., Bahmani, M., Arvin, M., & van der Kamp, J. (2020). The effects of texting, sitting surface stability, and balance training on simulated driving performance and perceived workload in young and older drivers. *Motor Control, 25*(1), 1–18.

Scullin, M. K., Jones, W. E., Phenis, R., Beevers, S., Rosen, S., Dinh, K., Kiselica, A., Keefe, F. J., & Benge, J. F. (2022). Using smartphone technology to improve prospective memory functioning: A randomized controlled trial. *Journal of the American Geriatrics Society, 70*(2), 459–469. https://doi.org/10.1111/jgs.17551

Sharifian, N., & Zahodne, L. B. (2020). Social media bytes: Daily associations between social media use and everyday memory failures across the adult life span. *The Journals of Gerontology: Series B, 75*(3), 540–548. https://doi.org/10.1093/geronb/gbz005

Skowronek, J., Seifert, A., & Lindberg, S. (2023). The mere presence of a smartphone reduces basal attentional performance. *Scientific Reports, 13*(1), 9363.

Slegers, K., van Boxtel, M. P. J., & Jolles, J. (2008). Effects of computer training and internet usage on the well-being and quality of life of older adults: A randomized, controlled study. *The Journals of Gerontology: Series B, 63*(3), P176–P184. https://doi.org/10.1093/geronb/63.3.P176

Small, G. W., Moody, T. D., Siddarth, P., & Bookheimer, S. Y. (2009). Your brain on Google: Patterns of cerebral activation during internet searching. *The American Journal of Geriatric Psychiatry, 17*(2), 116–126. https://doi.org/10.1097/JGP.0b013e3181953a02

Smith, M. L., Wilson, A. D., Knebl, J., Hilsabeck, R. C., Reuter, K., Aguirre, A., Harty, B., Lin Kew, C., Lee, S., & Ory, M. G. (2025). Utilization and perceived usefulness of monitoring technology for family caregivers of people living with Alzheimer's disease and related dementias. *Journal of Alzheimer's Disease, 103*(1), 127–132. https://doi.org/doi:10.1177/13872877241300078

Soares, J. S., & Storm, B. C. (2018). Forget in a flash: A further investigation of the photo-taking-impairment effect. *Journal of Applied Research in Memory and Cognition, 7*(1), 154–160. https://doi.org/10.1016/j.jarmac.2017.10.004

Sparrow, B., Liu, J., & Wegner, D. M. (2011). Google effects on memory: Cognitive consequences of having information at our fingertips. *Science, 333*(6043), 776–778. https://doi.org/10.1126/science.1207745

Stara, V., Vera, B., Bolliger, D., Rossi, L., Felici, E., Rosa, M. D., Jong, M. de, & Paolini, S. (2021). Usability and acceptance of the embodied conversational Agent Anne by people with dementia and their caregivers: Exploratory study in home environment settings. *JMIR mHealth and uHealth, 9*(6), e25891. https://doi.org/10.2196/25891

Stavrinos, D., Byington, K. W., & Schwebel, D. C. (2011). Distracted walking: Cell phones increase injury risk for college pedestrians. *Journal of Safety Research, 42*(2), 101–107. https://doi.org/10.1016/j.jsr.2011.01.004

Stavropoulos, T. G., Lazarou, I., Diaz, A., Gove, D., Georges, J., Manyakov, N. V., Pich, E. M., Hinds, C., Tsolaki, M., Nikolopoulos, S., Kompatsiaris, I., & The RADAR-AD Consortium. (2021). Wearable devices for assessing function in Alzheimer's disease: A European public involvement activity about the features and preferences of patients and caregivers. *Frontiers in Aging Neuroscience*, 13. https://doi.org/10.3389/fnagi.2021.643135

Storm, B. C., & Stone, S. M. (2015). Saving-enhanced memory: The benefits of saving on the learning and remembering of new information. *Psychological Science, 26*(2), 182–188.

Sun, Y., & Zhang, Y. (2021). A review of theories and models applied in studies of social media addiction and implications for future research. *Addictive Behaviors, 114*, 106699. https://doi.org/10.1016/j.addbeh.2020.106699

Sung, Y.-L., Huang, H.-L., Lin, C.-C., Kröger, T., Hsu, W.-C., Hsu, J.-L., Lin, Y.-E., & Shyu, Y.-I. L. (2022). Experiences of family caregivers of persons living with dementia with and without a smart- clothes assisted home nursing program during the heightened COVID-19 alert. *BMC Geriatrics, 22*(1), 697. https://doi.org/10.1186/s12877-022-03379-8

Tang, A. Y., Kwak, J., Xiao, L., Xie, B., Lahiri, S., Flynn, O. A., & Murugadass, A. (2023). Online health information wants of caregivers for persons with dementia in social media. *SAGE Open, 13*(4), 21582440231205367. https://doi.org/10.1177/21582440231205367

Teles, S., Paúl, C., Costa-Santos, C., & Ferreira, A. (2022). Use of dementia and caregiving-related internet resources by informal caregivers: A cross-sectional study. *Frontiers in Medicine*, 9. https://doi.org/10.3389/fmed.2022.978635

Thompson, D. A., & Christakis, D. A. (2005). The association between television viewing and irregular sleep schedules among children less than 3 years of age. *Pediatrics, 116*(4), 851–856. https://doi.org/10.1542/peds.2004-2788

Thompson, K. R., Johnson, A. M., Emerson, J. L., Dawson, J. D., Boer, E. R., & Rizzo, M. (2012). Distracted driving in elderly and middle-aged drivers. *Accident; Analysis and Prevention, 45*(2), 711–717. https://doi.org/10.1016/j.aap.2011.09.040

Thornton, B., Faires, A., Robbins, M., & Rollins, E. (2014). The mere presence of a cell phone may be distracting. *Social Psychology, 45*(6), 479–488. https://doi.org/10.1027/1864-9335/a000216

Tomopoulos, S., Dreyer, B. P., Valdez, P., Flynn, V., Foley, G., Berkule, S. B., & Mendelsohn, A. L. (2007). Media content and externalizing behaviors in Latino toddlers. *Ambulatory Pediatrics, 7*(3), 232–238. https://doi.org/10.1016/j.ambp.2007.02.004

Tong, L., Xiong, X., & Tan, H. (2016). Attention-deficit/hyperactivity disorder and lifestyle-related behaviors in children. *PLOS ONE, 11*(9), e0163434. https://doi.org/10.1371/journal.pone.0163434

Topete, A., He, C., Protzko, J., Schooler, J., & Hegarty, M. (2024). How is GPS used? Understanding navigation system use and its relation to spatial ability. *Cognitive Research: Principles and Implications, 9*(1), 16.

Uttal, D. H., Meadow, N. G., Tipton, E., Hand, L. L., Alden, A. R., Warren, C., & Newcombe, N. S. (2013). The malleability of spatial skills: A meta-analysis of training studies. *Psychological Bulletin, 139*(2), 352–402. https://doi.org/10.1037/a0028446

Vaesen, K. (2012). The cognitive bases of human tool use. *Behavioral and Brain Sciences, 35*(4), 203–218. https://doi.org/10.1017/S0140525X11001452

Van Assche, M., Petrovic, M., Cambier, D., Calders, P., Van Gelder, P., & Van de Velde, D. (2024). The perspectives of older adults with mild cognitive impairment and their caregivers on the use of socially assistive robots in healthcare: Exploring factors that influence attitude in a pre-implementation stage. *Disability and Rehabilitation: Assistive Technology, 19*(1), 222–232. https://doi.org/10.1080/17483107.2022.2075477

Vaportzis, E., Martin, M., & Gow, A. J. (2017). A tablet for healthy ageing: The effect of a tablet computer training intervention on cognitive abilities in older adults. *The American Journal of Geriatric Psychiatry, 25*(8), 841–851.

Wang, A.-Y., Hu, H.-Y., Ou, Y.-N., Wang, Z.-T., Ma, Y.-H., Tan, L., & Yu, J.-T. (2023). Socioeconomic status and risks of cognitive impairment and dementia: A systematic review and meta-analysis of 39 prospective studies. *The Journal of Prevention of Alzheimer's Disease, 10*(1), 83–94. https://doi.org/10.14283/jpad.2022.81

Wang, R. H., Sudhama, A., Begum, M., Huq, R., & Mihailidis, A. (2017). Robots to assist daily activities: Views of older adults with Alzheimer's disease and their caregivers. *International Psychogeriatrics, 29*(1), 67–79. https://doi.org/10.1017/S1041610216001435

Werner, N. E., Stanislawski, B., Marx, K., Watkins, D. C., Kobayashi, M., Kales, Helen, & Gitlin, L. N. (2017). Getting what they need when they need it. *Applied Clinical Informatics, 8*(1), 191–205. https://doi.org/10.4338/ACI-2016-07-RA-0122

Wike, R., Silver, L., Fetterolf, J., Huang, C., Austin, S., Clancy, L., & Gubbala, S. (2022, December 6). *Internet, smartphone and social media use in advanced economies 2022.* Pew Research Center. https://www.pewresearch.org/global/2022/12/06/internet-smartphone-and-social-media-use-in-advanced-economies-2022/

Wilkerson, D. A., Brady, E., Yi, E.-H., & Bateman, D. R. (2018). Friendsourcing peer support for Alzheimer's caregivers using Facebook social media. *Journal of Technology in Human Services, 36*(2–3), 105–124. https://doi.org/10.1080/15228835.2018.1449709

Williams, K., Blyler, D., Vidoni, E. D., Shaw, C., Wurth, J., Seabold, D., Perkhounkova, Y., & Van Sciver, A. (2018). A randomized trial using telehealth technology to link caregivers with dementia care experts for in-home caregiving support: FamTechCare protocol. *Research in Nursing & Health, 41*(3), 219–227. https://doi.org/10.1002/nur.21869

Williams, K. N., Perkhounkova, Y., Shaw, C. A., Hein, M., Vidoni, E. D., & Coleman, C. K. (2019). Supporting family caregivers with technology for dementia home care: A randomized controlled trial. *Innovation in Aging, 3*(3), igz037. https://doi.org/10.1093/geroni/igz037

Wilmer, H. H., Sherman, L. E., & Chein, J. M. (2017). Smartphones and cognition: A review of research exploring the links between mobile technology habits and cognitive functioning. *Frontiers in Psychology*, 8. https://doi.org/10.3389/fpsyg.2017.00605

Wilson, S. A., Byrne, P., & Rodgers, S. E. (2024). "I'd be lost without my smartphone": A qualitative analysis of the use of smartphones and tablets by people living with dementia, mild cognitive impairment, and their caregivers. *Aging & Mental Health, 28*(4), 595–603. https://doi.org/10.1080/13607863.2023.2205585

Wilson, S. A., Byrne, P., Rodgers, S. E., & Maden, M. (2022). A systematic review of smartphone and tablet use by older adults with and without cognitive impairment. *Innovation in Aging, 6*(2), igac002. https://doi.org/10.1093/geroni/igac002

Wójcik, D., Szczechowiak, K., Konopka, P., Owczarek, M., Kuzia, A., Rydlewska-Liszkowska, I., & Pikala, M. (2021). Informal dementia caregivers: Current technology use and acceptance of technology in care. *International Journal of Environmental Research and Public Health*, *18*(6), Article 6. https://doi.org/10.3390/ijerph18063167

Wrede, C., Braakman-Jansen, A., & van Gemert-Pijnen, L. (2021). Requirements for unobtrusive monitoring to support home-based dementia care: Qualitative study among formal and informal caregivers. *JMIR Aging*, *4*(2), e26875. https://doi.org/10.2196/26875

Wrede, C., Braakman-Jansen, A., & van Gemert-Pijnen, L. (2023). Understanding acceptance of contactless monitoring technology in home-based dementia care: A cross-sectional survey study among informal caregivers. *Frontiers in Digital Health*, *5*, 1257009. https://doi.org/10.3389/fdgth.2023.1257009

Xiong, C., Astell, A., Mihailidis, A., & Colantonio, A. (2018). Needs and preferences for technology among Chinese family caregivers of persons with dementia: A pilot study. *Journal of Rehabilitation and Assistive Technologies Engineering*, *5*, 2055668318775315. https://doi.org/10.1177/2055668318775315

Xiong, C., Ye, B., Cameron, J. I., Astell, A., Nalder, E., & Colantonio, A. (2020). Sex and gender differences in technology needs and preferences among informal caregivers of persons with dementia. *BMC Geriatrics*, *20*, 176. https://doi.org/10.1186/s12877-020-01548-1

Yavuz, E., He, C., Gahnstrom, C. J., Goodroe, S., Coutrot, A., Hornberger, M., Hegarty, M., & Spiers, H. J. (2024). Video gaming, but not reliance on GPS, is associated with spatial navigation performance. *Journal of Environmental Psychology*, *96*, 102296. https://doi.org/10.1016/J.JENVP.2024.102296

Zhang, K., Burr, J. A., Mutchler, J. E., & Lu, J. (2024). Pathways linking information and communication technology use and loneliness among older adults: Evidence from the health and retirement study. *The Gerontologist*, *64*(4), gnad100. https://doi.org/10.1093/geront/gnad100

Zhang, K., Kim, K., Silverstein, N. M., Song, Q., & Burr, J. A. (2021). Social media communication and loneliness among older adults: The mediating roles of social support and social contact. *The Gerontologist*, *61*(6), 888–896. https://doi.org/10.1093/geront/gnaa197

Zhang, S., Boot, W. R., & Charness, N. (2022). Does computer use improve older adults' cognitive functioning? Evidence from the personal reminder information and social management trial. *The Gerontologist*, *62*(7), 1063–1070. https://doi.org/10.1093/geront/gnab188

Zhong, T., Tian, H., Wen, X., Ma, D., Cui, H., Zhang, L., Zhu, X., Wang, Y., & Chen, L. (2025). Perspectives of persons with mild cognitive impairment, caregivers and healthcare professionals on computer-assisted cognitive training: A multi-perspective qualitative study. *Geriatric Nursing*, *61*, 560–567. https://doi.org/10.1016/j.gerinurse.2024.12.009

Zimmerman, F. J., & Christakis, D. A. (2007). Associations between content types of early media exposure and subsequent attentional problems. *Pediatrics*, *120*(5), 986–992. https://doi.org/10.1542/peds.2006-3322

Zimmerman, F. J., Christakis, D. A., & Meltzoff, A. N. (2007). Associations between media viewing and language development in children under age 2 years. *The Journal of Pediatrics, 151*(4), 364–368. https://doi.org/10.1016/j.jpeds.2007.04.071

Zuschnegg, J., Schoberer, D., Häussl, A., Herzog, S. A., Russegger, S., Ploder, K., Fellner, M., Hofmarcher-Holzhacker, M. M., Roller-Wirnsberger, R., & Paletta, L. (2023). Effectiveness of computer-based interventions for community-dwelling people with cognitive decline: A systematic review with meta-analyses. *BMC Geriatrics, 23*(1), 229.

14
Digital Rehabilitation
Bridging Technology and Neuropsychology in Aging Care

Maureen Schmitter-Edgecombe and Tania Giovannetti

Cognitive deficits can hinder an individual's ability to perform daily living tasks critical for maintaining independence, such as shopping, home maintenance, and meal preparation. For older adults, such impairments can lead to reduced quality of life, increased health care utilization, and nursing home placement (Björkstedt et al., 2023; Howard et al., 2021; Nagarkar et al., 2022). This chapter will review some of the recent advances in digital health technologies, machine learning applications, and artificial intelligence that have shown potential to prevent or mitigate cognitive impairments to maintain or improve functional health and quality of life for older adults (Clay et al., 2022).

This chapter will focus on the advances neuropsychologists have made in incorporating technology into treatment services (Block et al., 2017). Incorporating digital technologies into the rehabilitation process has been called digital rehabilitation (Arntz et al., 2023). For older adults with cognitive impairment, digital tools can aid in regaining or maintaining cognitive or functional abilities through practice (i.e., training). Digital technologies can also serve as a retrieval aid or memory cue for prospective memory failures (i.e., prompting) and as a prosthetic for lost memories, knowledge, and abilities (i.e., compensation). Several novel intervention tools have combined these important functions into powerful, multifaceted digital health technologies that may be adapted to meet the specific needs of older adult users and enable clinicians to track outcomes in real time and improve care access. This chapter begins with a review of the development and use of new technologies for cognitive training, prompting, and compensation with a focus on older adults as summarized in Figure 14.1. Challenges to the use of digital health technologies also will be reviewed for researchers and clinicians working in this arena. The chapter closes with suggestions for future directions in research and clinical practice emphasizing the promises of digital rehabilitation for transforming the landscape of functional health for older adults.

Maureen Schmitter-Edgecombe and Tania Giovannetti, *Digital Rehabilitation*. In: *Technology and Neuropsychology*.
Edited by: Jared F. Benge et al., Oxford University Press. © Oxford University Press (2026).
DOI: 10.1093/9780197814116.003.0014

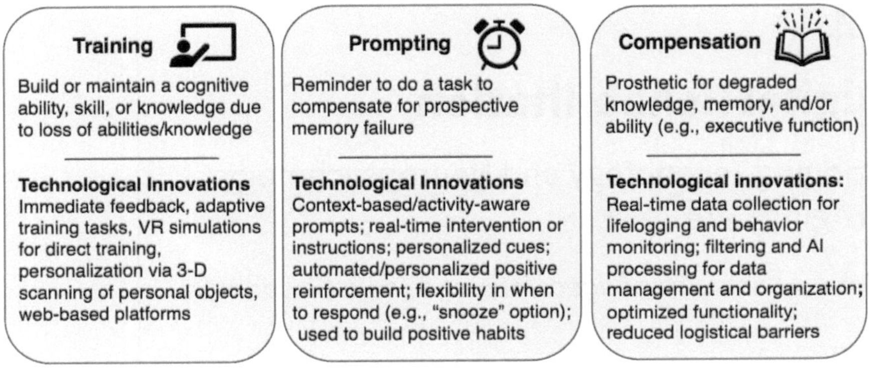

Figure 14.1 Summary of digital rehabilitation approaches reviewed in this chapter and the technological innovations applied to each approach. Many new multifaceted digital tools combine aspects of all three approaches.

Cognitive Training

There is a long history of repeated practice, or cognitive training, as a restorative technique to improve cognition after brain damage or disease, beginning with Paul Broca's efforts of retraining language abilities in people following stroke (Lazar & Mohr, 2011). Over time, cognitive training has evolved through several innovations. One major innovation has been the use of computers to deliver training with immediate feedback and adaptive tasks that increase or decrease in difficulty according to the patient's ability (Ge et al., 2018); these features have been shown to increase engagement and efficacy. A second innovation is the application of computer cognitive training for older adults to *maintain* cognitive abilities in the context of typical cognitive aging or neurodegenerative disease (Kueider et al., 2012). Third, there has been a push to show empirical evidence that cognitive training effects generalize to everyday life tasks, and more recent cognitive training studies include functional outcome measures (Lintern & Boot, 2021).

These three innovations were incorporated in the longest and largest randomized clinical trial for cognitive training in older adults, the Advanced Cognitive Training for Independent and Vital Elderly (ACTIVE) study (Ball et al., 2002; Rebok et al., 2014). The ACTIVE study began in 1996 and enrolled 2,832 people aged 65 years and older who were followed for 10 years. Participants were randomly assigned to a control group or one of three computerized cognitive training groups: processing speed, reasoning/executive function, or episodic memory. The theoretical model guiding the ACTIVE study proposed that cognitive training would improve the targeted cognitive skills (reasoning, processing speed, memory; proximal outcomes), which would consequently lead to benefits in everyday (activity of daily living [ADL]/individual activity of daily living [IADL]) functioning (primary outcome). Primary outcome measures of everyday function were included at each study timepoint with expectation of observing greater decline in the control group. The results at the 10-year timepoint showed persistent effects on the trained cognitive process for participants in the groups that underwent processing speed and reasoning training. All three training groups self-reported fewer difficulties in everyday function than the control group at 10 years; effect sizes were small to medium, and no training effects were observed on performance-based tests of everyday problem-solving or everyday speed of processing.

The ACTIVE trial results clearly support the efficacy for computerized training for long-term maintenance of reasoning and processing speed, though the effects on everyday function were relatively modest, suggesting weak support for the conceptual model. In fact, using a structural equation modeling technique called latent score change modeling, Farias and colleagues (2018) showed that among the ACTIVE study participants, decline in self-reported everyday function preceded declines in tests of specific cognitive processes and not the other way around (Farias et al., 2018). Thus, it may be faulty to conceptualize the cognitive demands of everyday tasks as the sum of specific cognitive abilities. Rather, everyday activities may be better understood as distinct and highly complex cognitive tasks that may be especially sensitive to cognitive decline, possibly even more sensitive than conventional tests of specific cognitive abilities. This view may explain the mixed results regarding the benefits of conventional cognitive training for functioning in everyday life (Gómez & Rodríguez, 2021; Richmond et al., 2011) and suggests direct practice of everyday tasks may be a more efficacious approach to cognitive training.

Procedural stimulation therapy, based on the rationale that everyday tasks are procedural skills, involves the repeated practice of everyday tasks to improve everyday function. Studies of procedural memory stimulation show significant benefits (e.g., faster completion time) for repeated tasks in older adults with moderate dementia (Avila, Bottino et al. 2004; Farina, Fioravanti et al. 2002; Josephsson et al., 1995; Zanetti et al., 2001). Although effective, traditional procedural memory stimulation is not practical or efficient. In a fraction of the time required to set up objects for a practice session and to do and redo a daily task, a care partner could just simply do the daily task themself. Virtual reality (VR) simulations offer a technological solution to the drawbacks of conventional functional training, and pilot studies support the efficacy of VR training and shed light on how repeated practice improves everyday task performance.

Foloppe and colleagues (2018) developed VR simulations of everyday tasks to test the hypothesis that repeated practice with VR simulations (e.g., bake cake, make soup) would improve performance just as well as repeated practice with real objects (e.g., make coffee, prepare breakfast). Results from a single case report of a 79-year-old woman with moderate dementia showed that training with the VR simulation was just as good as training with real objects and that the benefits from training in both real and VR conditions remained stable 6 months after the training had ended. Both real and VR training led to more accurate and independent everyday task performance.

Following the work of Fallope and colleagues, two recent pilot studies (Divers et al., 2025; Kaplan et al., 2026) have used an updated VR platform with touchscreen and advanced graphics (see Figure 14.2) to evaluate transfer of VR task training to real tasks in older adults with a range of cognitive ability levels from subjective cognitive decline to mild dementia. To preclude basic motor/procedural learning and emphasize the strengthening of task knowledge, VR objects were rearranged on the screen before each training session. Across a series of six cases, Divers and colleagues reported that VR training led to a significant improvement in the time required to complete task steps in five of the six participants. Similarly, Kaplan et al., 2026 showed VR training led to a specific increase in the number of task steps that were accomplished in a group of 16 participants with mild cognitive impairment (MCI) or mild dementia. Though neither study showed a significant difference in the total number of errors committed before versus after training. Results on the maintenance of training effects over 1 month were mixed, with Divers et al (2025) showing persistence of training benefits but Kaplan et al. (2025) showing that training effects diminished over 1 month. Taken together, these studies suggest that VR training of everyday tasks may strengthen representations of everyday tasks so that task steps are more likely to be performed and performed quickly (i.e., due to rapid retrieval/access to task representations). However, repeated task practice in VR may not sufficiently improve executive control over task performance to prevent errors. Future studies are needed to determine whether lengthier VR training is needed to reduce everyday task errors.

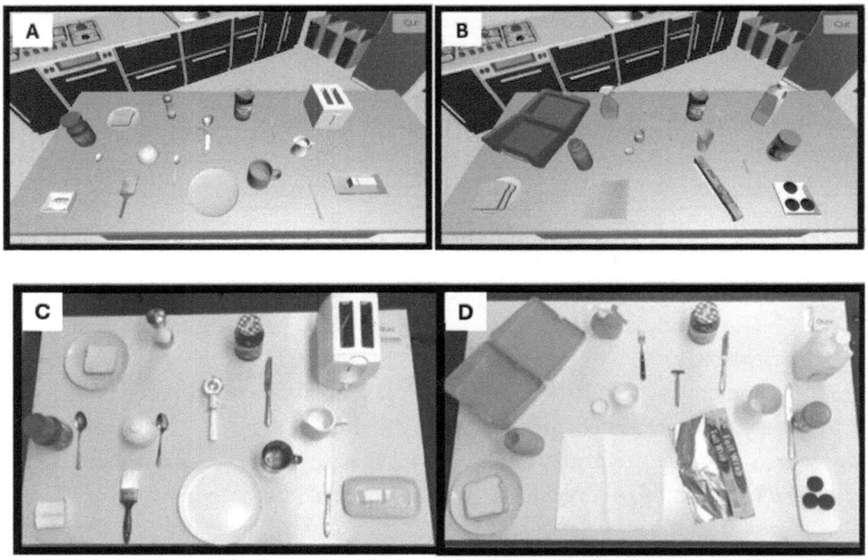

Figure 14.2 Screenshots of VR-simulated tasks in A and B above photos of real objects presented on tabletop used for pre- and post-testing (C and D). Images show the visual similarity between simulated and real environments achieved through 3D scanning and digitization of real objects.

Another important conclusion of the recent data on VR training is that training effects do not generalize to untrained tasks; thus, the VR simulation must be personalized to an individual's specific task. Such personalization is not prohibitive, as 3D scanners are capable of digitizing objects and AI may be used to efficiently program VR systems to simulate specific tasks.

Finally, another important development in computerized cognitive training is the use of web-based training platforms. Web-based training addresses the time constraints faced by clinicians in delivering intensive interventions and training (Jamieson et al., 2014) and offers alternative or adjunctive training sessions through scalable, independent instruction and practice that clients can access outside the clinic. Web-based restorative cognitive training platforms have been utilized for over a decade (Cruz et al., 2013) and are well-accepted by users (Sanz et al., 2023). These web-based technologies have also been used to enhance the scalability of memory strategies training (Pike et al., 2023) and can be used for training to use other forms of digital rehabilitation, such as prompting tools and cognitive prosthetics (described later).

Summary: Cognitive Training

In summary, technological advances have made computerized cognitive training widely available to older adults, as evidenced by the growing number of commercially available programs, such as Lumosity and CogniFit. Most studies show benefits from training specific cognitive processes, such that compared to control groups, older adults who complete cognitive training show less decline in the trained processes. Transfer to everyday tasks has been reported but varies across outcome measures and cognitive training paradigm. Empirical data and novel conceptualizations of the relations between specific cognitive abilities and everyday tasks suggest direct training of everyday tasks is more likely to lead to improvement in everyday function and is made more efficient through VR simulations, which appear to be effective, even in older adults with dementia. Future directions for further improved training will incorporate highly personalized tasks using new methods for rapid object digitation and VR programming. VR training may be improved through incorporation of gaming features and adaptive tasks to promote attention and adherence, as training effects may be time-limited, requiring sustained adherence to practice.

Prompting Technologies in Cognitive Rehabilitation

Prospective memory failures (i.e., failing to remember to do something in the future) are among the earliest and most common complaints among older adults experiencing cognitive decline (Woods et al., 2015). In such cases, cognitive training may not be immediately necessary, as there is no difficulty in performing everyday tasks once the intention to do the task is recalled. Here, prompting or memory cues may be sufficient to enhance independence and engagement in everyday activities (Jamieson et al., 2014; McDonald et al., 2011). Analog prompts, like sticky notes and paper calendars, are useful if they are in sight, but personal digital devices offer a wide array of advantages for prompting. NeuroPage, one of the first digital devices specifically designed to prompt individuals to assist with everyday memory impairment, is a pager device that people could carry and would sound an alarm and provide instruction when a task needed to be completed. Results with Neuropage showed significant improvements in task completion among cognitively impaired adults (Wilson et al., 1997). Building on the success of NeuroPage, prompting has been effectively integrated into new personal digital devices (Annese et al., 2023; El Haj et al., 2017; Jamieson et al., 2019, 2024), incorporating smartphones, smartwatches, electronic reminder pill boxes, and virtual assistants like Alexa and Google Calendar. Smart homes and other context-aware prompting technologies have also been used to deliver prompts to support everyday task completion (Schmitter-Edgecombe et al., 2022; Yaddaden et al., 2020). Since Neuropage, the prompting itself has evolved beyond simple reminders, notifications, and alerts to more sophisticated systems powered by machine learning algorithms that monitor behavior and provide highly specific prompts based on time, location, task, and other features (Lancioni et al., 2021; Seelye et al., 2012).

Prompting systems that include time-based cues alone may demand a great deal of time and attention from care partners who are needed to oversee the prompt programming (Olsson et al., 2018) and to check that prompts are attended to and tasks are performed and finished accurately. To address some of these challenges, conceptual frameworks and cognitive rehabilitation principles have been incorporated into the development of smart prompting technologies, paving the way for more intuitive and user-friendly solutions (Hackett et al., 2022, 2026; Seelye et al., 2012). For example, prompting systems have been extended to also support the retrospective aspect of activity completion by inclusion of information about the purpose of the prompt or by logging completed tasks (i.e., compensation features; described in detail in the next section). The SmartPrompt was designed according to neuropsychological principles, pilot data, and user feedback to deliver highly personalized prompts, including audio alerts stating the participants' name, photos of the tasks that they had to recall, and text reminding them of their daily task. The SmartPrompt also includes the option to delay prompts, like a snooze button, if the user is occupied. After a delay, the prompt will repeat until the user logs a photo of a completed task. A personalized reward (e.g., favorite song) plays at the end of the day after all tasks were complete in an attempt to engage the user and promote app adherence (Braley et al., 2019). Pilot data from older adults with MCI or dementia who used the SmartPrompt showed that compared to a control period, task completion improved, and caregiver burden decreased when using the app, with no rise in user frustration and high usability ratings from participants and care partners (Hackett et al., 2022, 2025). The SmartPrompt also includes a task log that stores photos of completed tasks to prevent repeating tasks already completed. See Table 14.1 for list of all the features included in the SmartPrompt.

Table 14.1 Theoretically Guided SmartPrompt Features

SmartPrompt Feature	Description	Cognitive Target
Reminder alert with nudges	Personalized auditory alarm and text of goal. The auditory alert included the participant's first name and instructed them to look at their phone. (e.g., "Hey Joe look at your phone!"). The participant also had the option to submit a recording by someone close to them (e.g., grandchild). If the participant did not respond to the alert, then it was deployed again 15 minutes later.	Prospective memory impairment, goal decay, distractibility
Choice	Participants were given the choice to delay task completion in case they were occupied and were not able to direct their full attention. When participants selected "do it later" the reminder alert was deployed again 15 minutes later.	Distractibility/ multitasking
Instructions	Screen showed customized photo of the objects needed or the scene where the target task must be completed. A written reminder of the task goal was presented along with the photo.	Semantic knowledge degradation
Activity log	Participant is instructed to take a photo of the completed activity (e.g., for "take medication" the participant takes a photo of their pillbox). The photo is logged into the system and may be viewed by the participant or caregiver at any time.	Episodic memory impairment
Progress bar and reward for task completion	Points are awarded as photos are collected into the photo log and shown in a progress bar after each task. After completing the last task of each day, a reward song, which was selected by the participant was played for several seconds.	Apathy
Task list	Tasks appeared on a task list screen when it was time to be completed. After the task was logged then it was crossed off in the list. If a task was not logged, then it would not be crossed off. At any time after the task appeared on the list, the participant could tap on the task and receive prompts to complete and log the task from the task list.	Episodic memory impairment

New technologies also have enabled prompting systems to evolve beyond time-based prompts to more sophisticated methods of prompt delivery. Even with the option to "snooze" a prompt, interrupting a cognitively impaired individual at an inopportune time, forcing them to shift to a new task, can disrupt performance on both the current task and the prompted activity (Woods et al., 2020). This may increase cognitive load (Okoshi et al., 2015), reduce willingness to engage with the technology (Morrison et al., 2017), and potentially introduce task errors (Adamczyk & Bailey, 2004). Prompts delivered during important, lengthy activities, such as taking a shower, may go unnoticed or unaddressed. An alternative to time-based prompting is location-based prompting, which depends on the user's location. Location-based prompts occur in the context that may be most conducive for task completion (e.g., when entering the kitchen or approaching the medicine cabinet; Seelye et al., 2012). Transition-based, activity-aware prompting is even more sophisticated by adapting to users' activity patterns and identifying ideal moments for intervention based on context, leading to improved response rates and task completion. Smart homes with activity-aware algorithms have the potential to recognize typical routines, predict when activities should occur (e.g., exercising after lunch), and issue timely prompts if deviations are detected. Further, these systems can detect if the prompted task is not initiated and then reissue prompts to ensure activity completion. Both testbed and in-home smart home studies demonstrated that participants responded to more task prompts and to the first prompt if they were prompted during transition between activities (Aminikhanghahi et al., 2020; Robertson et al., 2015). Context-aware prompting technologies have also been applied to everyday behaviors, including meal preparation (Yaddaden et al., 2020) and handwashing (Czarnuch et al., 2013).

Much of the research on the best methods for delivering prompts when an error occurs during task completion has been conducted in controlled settings due to the challenges of recognizing errors in real time and providing appropriate prompts. One study found that audible verbal instructions were more effective for task completion compared to tone-based or visual prompts (Cannings et al., 2024). Graded cue hierarchies, which provide increasing levels of directive assistance based on an individual's cognitive or functional status, have also proven successful (Milhaidis et al., 2008). Test-bed smart home studies have shown that less directive prompts are effective for individuals with milder impairments, while more detailed prompts (e.g., "Turn the stove off now") are often required for those with greater needs (Greber et al., 2007; Seelye et al., 2013). This graded approach can help maintain a sense of autonomy and independence, although one study found that older adults preferred directive prompts (Van Etten et al., 2016). A qualitative analysis of the observed behaviors of people with dementia responding to a smart home auto-prompting system highlighted the importance of considering contextual factors, such as the individual characteristics and the environment (Braley et al., 2019). In some cases, effective prompts may require communication with another person

(Braley et al., 2019; Cannings et al., 2024). Additionally, prompting systems should provide positive reinforcement to encourage adjustments and successful task completion (Braley et al., 2019), as well as adapt to the individual's changing cognitive level (Hammink et al., 2023).

Prompting technologies can also support rehabilitation goals by fostering habit formation (Zhu, Long et al., 2024). Traditionally, for individuals with cognitive impairments, reminder prompts to use a memory notebook or other compensatory aids are provided by a care partner, a time-based alarm, or routine cue (e.g., check the memory notebook at mealtimes; Schmitter-Edgecombe et al., 2009). Digital technologies now integrate prompting features such as vibrations, text messages, or alarm reminders, which can alert individuals to use an app and assist in habit development. For instance, a recent study trained individuals with amnestic MCI to use a digital memory aid, EMMA (electronic memory and management aid) by combining app usage training with transition-based, context-aware smart home prompts (i.e., "partnered" condition; Schmitter-Edgecombe et al., 2022). App use training included 1 week of hourly alarms from the digital aid (EMMA) itself to facilitate habit formation. In the partnered condition, context-aware smart home prompts continued to encourage app use after periods of nonuse. By week four, participants in the partnered condition engaged with the app more frequently and were utilizing more basic and advanced app features than the group that did not receive the transition-based, context-aware smart home prompts. The benefits of the advanced prompts were sustained throughout the post-training phase, with less decline in app usage over time in the partnered condition. In addition to smart home prompts, wearables (e.g., smartwatches) also hold promise for delivering context-based prompts to support everyday activities (Fang et al., 2025), further expanding the potential of digital tools to promote independence and long-term behavior change through advanced, sophisticated prompting strategies.

Summary: Prompting Technologies

In summary, prompting technologies have proven to be an important tool for supporting individuals with cognitive impairments, enhancing independence, and promoting engagement in everyday activities. From early innovations like NeuroPage to work with advanced context-aware systems, these technologies have evolved and offer the potential to deliver tailored interventions, enhancing healthy lifestyle behaviors (e.g., exercise), supporting task completion and independence, and promoting habit formation. Transition-based and activity-aware prompting systems address limitations of time- and location-based approaches by adapting to users' activity patterns, delivering timely assistance, and, in some cases, detecting errors during tasks. Research demonstrates that graded cue hierarchies and verbal instructions improve task accuracy. For degenerating conditions, personalized and adaptable cues that evolve alongside the individual's changing cognitive and functional needs are essential (Hammink et al., 2023). While there is still significant progress needed to fully realize these systems, adaptive auto-prompting technologies that adjust directive assistance based on cognitive levels, monitor performance, and deliver positive reinforcement in real time when needed hold great promise for enhancing independent functioning and extending individuals' ability to manage tasks at home over longer periods. As prompting technologies continue to evolve, future research should focus on optimizing the timing and presentation of prompts within the real-world environment to maximize their potential for enhancing independence and improving the quality of life for individuals with cognitive impairments.

Digital Cognitive Compensation

Digital technologies serving as a compensatory strategy or cognitive prosthetic are increasingly being utilized in neuropsychology to support individuals with memory loss, enhancing their ability to perform daily activities, recollect events, and maintain independence (e.g., Annese et al., 2023). These tools span a range of complexity, from simple devices like smart pens for subsequent audio replay of written notes to advanced technologies such as smartphones equipped with sensors to monitor location, track activities, and suggest healthy behaviors. Commercially available applications, such as Cozi, Touch Calendar, Medisafe, MemoCook, and Calendar Clock, exemplify the wide range of tools available for managing memory tasks, goal setting, and daily responsibilities. While both digital and nondigital (e.g., paper and pencil) memory strategies can be effective (Beech et al., 2024), technology-based methods often offer superior solutions, such as enabling simultaneous recording of tasks and reminders while reducing the risk of losing information. Increased reliance on digital cognitive prosthetics among older adults has been associated with slower cognitive decline and improved functional outcomes (Farias et al., 2020), supporting the technological reserve hypothesis (Benge & Scullin, 2020). This theory posits that regular use of technology enhances independence by providing cognitive support and helping older adults adapt to age-related changes (Benge & Scullin, 2020; Wolff et al., 2021). Though the following brief review focuses on memory-assistive technologies, digital compensatory tools also address a variety of needs for older adults, including wayfinding (Kwan et al., 2020), wandering prevention (Kim et al., 2024), communication enhancement (Derbring et al., 2023; Hoel et al., 2021), fostering socialization (Sawik et al., 2023), word finding (Bier et al., 2018; Joubert, 2024; Repetto, 2021), and goal management (Ertas-Spantgar et al., 2024: Kringle et al., 2020).

A variety of digital technologies have emerged to support memory for past events and improve recollection, ranging from audio recorders and smart pens that digitize written documents to more advanced tools like digital memory notebooks and life-logging devices. The SenseCam, a small wearable camera that captures still images from an egocentric point of view automatically every 30 seconds or in response to environmental sensors, was one of the first digital tools available for lifelogging in neurological rehabilitation (Berry et al., 2007). The rationale is that reviewing images of weak episodic memories can reinitiate associated thoughts, feelings, and nonvisual sensory inputs that will ultimately enrich the representation of the episode and strengthen the memory (Dubourg et al., 2016). Others have extended the use of the SenseCam to individuals with poor self-regulation in attempt to promote insight offline, when reviewing past events (Cuberos-Urbano et al., 2018). There are significant challenges associated with life-logging approaches, including privacy concerns, social acceptability, and the overwhelming volume of images generated by continuous recordings (Barnard et al., 2011). Newer methods incorporating computer vision, activity recognition, and natural language processing are being applied to streamline data filtering and process the unlabeled, unstructured data generated by life-logging devices (Allé et al., 2017; Ksibi et al., 2021). Despite these challenges, life-logging techniques have shown promising, though limited, evidence in improving subjective and objective memory in individuals with memory deficits (Alle et al., 2017; Dubourg et al., 2016; van Teijlingen et al., 2021). Other tools, such as MyMemory (Chang et al., 2018) and Our Story (Critten & Kucerkova, 2019), also provide memory support through personalized approaches. MyMemory allows users to record memory cues—such as location, people, and activities—to facilitate autobiographical recall, while Our Story combines personalized multimedia creation with integrated camera functionality and audio recordings, allowing users to craft narratives that support reminiscence and connection. These tools highlight the growing potential of digital technologies to enhance recall of memories, with artificial intelligence poised to further optimize their functionality and effectiveness (Ksibi et al., 2021).

A variety of apps are also being used in rehabilitation to support memory, with low-cost, off-the-shelf devices increasing accessibility for patients (Evald, 2015). A review of the traumatic brain injury literature found that most studies (12 of 19) supported the efficacy of technology in improving memory-related functioning, particularly through preprogrammed reminders that aid in the retrieval and execution phases of memory (Ownsworth et al., 2023). For example, a case study of A.V. demonstrated how digital technology apps, combined with regular schedule reviews with a family member, enabled independent living despite severe amnesia (Annese et al., 2023). Similarly, an intensive, tailored intervention for a 65-year-old woman with Alzheimer's disease showed that she was able to progressively learn how to use a calendar app on a tablet computer to support her daily activities (Imbeault et al., 2018). In another 4-week randomized controlled trial, individuals with MCI or mild dementia learned to use smartphone-based memory strategies, such as app reminders or digital recorders, after just one training session, resulting in improved prospective memory functioning (Scullin et al., 2022).

Historically, technology development overlooked the needs of older adults and individuals with cognitive impairment. However, the past decade has seen a shift toward user-centered and co-design approaches, prioritizing the needs of these populations (Cagiltay et al., 2008). Research highlights a preference for all-in-one apps with customizable features (Osborne et al., 2021), leading to the creation of tools like ApplTree (Jamieson et al., 2017, 2024), EMMA (Schmitter-Edgecombe et al., 2022), and I-Care (Weakley et al., 2021). Designed collaboratively with individuals with cognitive impairment, these apps follow well-established best practices in rehabilitation sciences. For example, ApplTree is a smartphone app for individuals with brain injuries, offering customizable push prompts (e.g., "Do you need to set any reminders?") and a simplified interface for creating reminders (Jamieson, 2024). EMMA is a digital memory notebook offering prospective memory aids (e.g., calendar and to-do list alarms), retrospective memory support (e.g., note-taking/journaling), health tracking (e.g., exercise, blood pressure), and goal-setting tools (Schmitter-Edgecombe et al., 2022). Designed for remote caregiving of older adults, I-Care integrates daily activity scheduling, list making, brain health tracking, and collaborative communication features (e.g., text messaging, video chat) (Weakley et al., 2021). Pilot feasibility and effectiveness studies suggest that these apps are user-friendly and effective in enhancing everyday coping and memory ability (Chudoba et al., 2020; Jamieson et al., 2024; Schmitter-Edgecombe et al., 2022; Weakley et al., 2021). These tools also allow for optimized device functionality, integration of prompting technologies, and real-time collection of digital markers that can be used to personalize training and improve device adoption and intervention efficacy. Future development of such apps will require academic-industry partnerships to balance scientific rigor with the rapid pace of technological advancement. AI also offers opportunities to enhance flexibility in app design, enabling tools to adapt dynamically to the continuum of cognitive impairments.

Summary: Digital Compensatory Strategy Devices

In summary, digital compensatory tools offer advantages over traditional paper-and-pencil methods, including features such as integrated prompts, auto-fill and search functions, greater storage capacity, and advanced capabilities like adaptive algorithms, activity recognition, and real-time data collection. Artificial intelligence has the potential to optimize functionality and reduce logistical barriers in digital compensatory tools. These tools can enhance independence for individuals with cognitive impairments by simplifying tasks, providing reminders, and reducing caregiver reliance. They also support caregivers by reducing stress, cognitive offloading, enabling remote care, and fostering stronger care relationships (Weakley & Farias, 2023), while clinicians benefit from continuous data collection that informs decision-making and early interventions.

Challenges

The advantages presented by new technologies for cognitive training, prompting, and compensation are clear. New personal digital devices have strong computing power, are small enough to carry, and are becoming increasingly affordable. Although technological innovations hold great promise for cognitive rehabilitation, there are numerous challenges that must be addressed as these digital tools continue to evolve. In fact, challenges are so concerning that much of the available technology research focuses on usability rather than effectiveness. Major challenges include technology adoption and efficient and effective training, which is particularly relevant for older adults and individuals with lower digital literacy. Like all analog interventions, adherence is also a challenge for digital interventions, but there are several advantages to digital tools that may be leveraged to increase adherence. Finally, numerous methodological barriers, like battery charging and costs, must be considered and addressed for successful implementation of digital tools. These barriers and technology-based suggestions to overcome them are reviewed below in detail; addressing these barriers through future research will unlock the full potential of digital tools to improve quality of life, reduce burden, and support long-term independence and aging in place.

Encouraging Technology Acceptance and Use

Studies show that older adults are naturally adopting personal digital technologies, like smartphone calendars and reminders, as cognitive prosthetics to aid memory and organization (Beech et al., 2024; Farias et al., 2020; Stojanovic et al., 2023). However, barriers to adoption of digital rehabilitation tools remain and are relevant to participants, care partners, and clinicians. For example, participants may lack familiarity with technology, resist and fear change, and experience accessibility concerns. Often, devices and apps are not developed using co-design or person-centered approaches (Conway et al., 2023; see Table 14.1), leading to digital tools that are not intuitive or desired by older adults. Caregivers also face challenges with accessibility (e.g., costs), integration, complexity, and reliability (Mikula et al., 2024), while clinicians encounter limitations in lack of awareness of available technologies, evidence-based guidance, and scalability (Boyle et al., 2022; Kiselica et al., 2024). Finally, researchers also face practical barriers associated with the rapid pace of technological advancements, making large-scale trials impractical and underscoring the need for improved methodologies to evaluate the efficacy of these interventions more efficiently and adaptively (Øksnebjerg et al. 2020).

Technology adoption will require deliberation and care in selecting the most appropriate digital tools for an individual considering their context and personal goals and needs. Technology selection involves a multistep process that integrates both client-centered planning and theoretical guidance from established technology adoption frameworks. Once a clear goal is established with the client, clinicians must determine whether to incorporate digital tools in the first place. If so, then consideration of the specific tools to use and the best implementation methods is crucial (Schmitter-Edgecombe & Weakly, in press). Frameworks such as the Senior Technology Acceptance and Adoption model for Mobile technology (STAM; Renaud & Biljon, 2008), the Unified Theory of Acceptance and Use of Technology (UTAUT; Venkatesh et al., 2003), and the Matching Person and Technology (MPT; Scherer, 1998; Scherer & Craddock, 2002) model provide valuable insights into factors like perceived usefulness, ease of use, social influence, and the fit between the person, the device, and the environment. These models emphasize the importance of aligning user needs, technological features, and contextual variables to facilitate successful adoption and integration. Clinicians must also proactively identify barriers to tool use, leverage facilitators to enhance training and adoption, and consider the interactions between factors. Drawing upon these and other relevant frameworks (e.g., Dai et al., 2020; Shek et al., 2021; Venkatesh & Davis, 2000), as well as personal experiences, Schmitter-Edgecombe and Weakley (in press) outlined a problem-solving approach for clinicians called TECH. The approach emphasizes the importance of considering potential facilitators and barriers related to Technology, Environment, Coaching/implementation plan and Human/personal characteristics (see Table 14.2) when choosing and training use of technology in rehabilitation.

Table 14.2 TECH Considerations When Selecting and Implementing Technology for Client Use and Training

*T*echnology	*E*nvironment
• Ease of use and learning to use; intuitiveness, use of common language • Perceived reliability and effectiveness of technology • Access to and costs of technology • Privacy and security • Integration and compatibility with existing technology	• Infrastructure available (e.g., fast and reliable Internet) • Social influences • Accessibility of assistance and technical support
***C*oaching/Implementation Plan**	***H*uman/Personal Characteristics**
• Utilizing tailored and culturally relevant training and education • Integrating evidence-based approaches • Creating habit formation and high use frequency • Considering timing and resources required for tool use • Exploration and confirmed usefulness of technology	• Demographics, cognitive, physical ability, personality, and health factors • Digital literacy, self-efficacy, and comfort with technology • Beliefs and attitudes about technology and perceived benefits of technology • Motivation, resistance, and willingness to use technology • Nature of cognitive impairment (e.g., progressive decline)

Fostering Technology Training

Even the simplest digital tools reviewed in this chapter require some level of training to optimize their use and effectiveness. Clinician selection of training methods depends on multiple factors (Ramirez-Herandez et al., 2023), and assessing facilitators and barriers is important (see Table 14.2). Age has been associated with training time in studies introducing new smartphone (Hackett et al., 2025) and smartwatch (Holmqvist et al., 2025) technologies, suggesting that older adults will need more time to learn and practice use of digital interventions. Age-related changes, including cognitive (e.g., working memory), visual (e.g., color vision decline), auditory (e.g., high-frequency hearing loss), and motor changes (e.g., dexterity), must be considered. Effective learning strategies, such as procedural learning, multimodal presentation (e.g., captioning), step-by-step instructions, schema acquisition, and rule automation can be used to improve encoding and retention (Joubert et al., 2024). Further, to foster habitual tool use and tailor the device to the individual's needs, prompting, goal-setting, and problem-solving exercises can be utilized. Based on these design principles, an empirically oriented, clinician-led training for memory notebook use (Chudoba et al., 2020; Sohlberg & Mateer, 1989) was recently converted into an adaptive web-based intervention for training use of the EMMA app (Li et al., 2026; see Figure 14.3).

Adaptive training, the same strategy used for cognitive training mentioned earlier, also may be leveraged for training to use digital rehabilitation tools. Adaptive instruction designed to promote mastery has been found to significantly improve learning

Figure 14.3 Example adaptive web-based training screens: animated instructor (top left); animated characters (top right); skill quiz (bottom left); and clinician (bottom right).

outcomes (Aleven et al., 2017). Automated training via video and web-based platforms also enable opportunities for unlimited repetitions, personalizing learning to align with the user's cognitive abilities. Research suggests that tailoring treatment to individual needs maximizes its effectiveness (Kwok et al., 2020). Advances in technology that allow tracking of user learning metrics during web-based training, combined with machine-learning methods, make personalized training possible while improving learning efficiency. In work developing algorithms to adaptively guide users through the web-based EMMA app training (Li et al., 2026), clinicians first observed older adults with varying cognitive abilities as they completed the web-based lessons. Based on their observations, clinicians decided whether quizzes needed repetition or modules required a second review. These data, along with participant performance on knowledge questions and quiz accuracy, informed the adaptive training algorithms. Overall, web-based training offers advantages for training over traditional methods, including scalability, remote monitoring of progress, and adaptive instruction tailored to individual needs, positioning it as an innovative approach for promoting effective learning of digital compensatory tools. Further, drawing from principles used in app-based development (Tong et al., 2022), user-inclusive participatory design and iterative development can help optimize the web-based delivery of interventions.

Supporting Technology Adherence and Adoption

Despite the many technological innovations in digital rehabilitation, challenges in adherence and adoption persist. For instance, a study on individuals with severe mental illness found that of 11 motivated participants, only five successfully integrated mobile devices (e.g., iPod Touch, iPhone, iPad) into their rehabilitation, with barriers including lack of support and unfavorable environmental factors (Briand et al., 2018). Moreover, a study of children and adolescents with acquired brain injuries revealed that the strongest predictor of reported smartphone use was the professionals' positive attitudes toward the technology (Plackett et al., 2017). Recently, a web-based selection tool and errorless learning training program, FindMyApps, was introduced to help people with mild dementia or MCI and their caregivers identify user-friendly apps (Beentjes et al., 2023).

Several studies report strong adherence to digital interventions in the short term (i.e., several weeks; Hackett et al., 2025; Scullin et al., 2022), though longer-term studies of computerized cognitive training show markedly lower rates of adherence (Turunen et al., 2019). There are many factors that influence adherence, and digital technologies offer powerful tools for understanding and promoting adherence. For example, real-time digital biomarkers (e.g., type, frequency, regularity index, speech, sleep) obtained in real-world environments may provide valuable insights into adherence and introduces innovative methods to support the adoption of digital tools, such as automated booster sessions (Schmitter-Edgecombe et al., 2023). Additionally, real-time feedback through digital metrics allows clinicians to monitor participant progress, assess mastery, and evaluate intervention responses, which also could be used to give feedback to clients as incentives and modify the intervention for greater effectiveness. For example, digital markers from the ReHaGoal App allowed therapists to intervene early and adjust therapy elements by providing actionable information about patient task completion between sessions (Ertas-Spantgar et al., 2024). Access to these real-time digital markers can facilitate more timely and tailored interventions, fostering improved outcomes.

Both learning efficiency (De Wit et al., 2021) and adherence to behavioral interventions (Sr et al., 2020) have been shown to improve outcomes in cognitively impaired older adults. The ability to continuously track digital markers provides significant advantages over traditional adherence measures, such as meeting attendance, daily or retrospective self-reports of completed intervention activities, and staff reviews of completed intervention tasks on selected days (e.g., calendar, workbook). For instance, tracking daily device use and use of its varying components (e.g., minutes used, number unique activities) allows for a deeper understanding of user engagement and uptake of the intervention. A study by Robert and colleagues (2020), which used a web app, called MeMo, to provide training in memory and mental flexibility/attention, demonstrated that the cognitive and behavioral efficacies of MeMo were only observed with consistent, regular use. This underscores how digital markers from such applications can provide critical insights into adherence and the dosage required for effective intervention outcomes.

Technology adoption is essential for sustained long-term use of digital tools. Continuous data collection can provide valuable insights into the characteristics of adopters, offering opportunities to identify individuals likely to benefit from specific interventions and inform the design of better training programs for broader adoption. For example, clinical data and digital markers from the EMMA app were used to compare individuals with MCI who became "adopters" (users at 3 months) to "non-adopters" (Luna et al., 2023). Adopters had higher cognitive language and delayed memory test scores at baseline and engaged with the app more frequently by week two of the 4-week training period. These findings suggest that forming habits of early and consistent use during training can boost adoption rates. Although the data are mixed (e.g., Aramaki et al., 2011; Borella et al., 2023), it has been suggested that booster sessions can reactivate the use of strategies previously learned promoting continued engagement with interventions (Nguyen et al., 2019). Behavioral markers captured by digital tools, combined with machine learning methods, have the potential to enable automated booster sessions at optimal times (Schmitter-Edgecombe et al., 2023). For instance, detecting declining performance in app use could signal a trainable moment, triggering automated, real-time "booster" training. Digital aids can also support routine self-tracking of health and goals, which prior work has shown to be effective in driving health behavior change (Figueiredo et al., 2018). Additionally, machine learning can dynamically adjust motivational support to sustain engagement (Monroe et al., 2023). As adopting new technology requires behavior change, researchers have advocated for including behavioral change interventions, persuasive system design, and motivational frameworks into digital rehabilitation to enhance adoption and sustained use (Bell et al., 2022; Zhu et al., 2024).

Promoting Proactive and Just-in-Time Adaptive Interventions

Continuous and real-time digital markers captured by digital technologies (e.g., daily routine) also have the potential to provide opportunities for both early and real-time interventions (Teh et al., 2022). These behavioral markers can be captured by a variety of platforms (e.g., smart home, app), including wearable sensors (e.g., smart watch, fitness tracker) and cognitive prosthetics (e.g., digital notebooks). One smart home study detected changes in in-home walking speed prior to individuals being aware of the changes and 6 months prior to the clinical diagnosis of MCI, highlighting an opportune time for early intervention (Khan & Jacobs, 2021). Machine learning methods have also been used to map derived digital markers to predictions of functional health scores (Sprint et al., 2022), the quality of everyday activity completion (Dawadi et al., 2013), and abnormal behaviors associated with dementia (Arifoglu et al., 2019). This work highlights how digital technologies and machine learning can be used to detect subtle behavioral changes within the real-world environment, enabling proactive and real-time interventions.

Technology-based strategies can also be used to promote adherence by enabling in-the-moment interventions. Just-in-time adaptive interventions (JITAIs) are designed to adapt to an individual's changing internal and contextual states, delivering the right support at the right time in everyday environments (Nahum-Shani et al., 2018). JITAIs have been applied in addiction research, reducing sedentary behaviors, and managing conditions like blood glucose control (Park et al., 2023; Wang & Miller, 2020). Advanced health technologies combined with machine learning could further extend JITAIs to promote use of cognitive training programs, digital prosthetics, and other positive behaviors, such as exercise, when individuals are most receptive. Furthermore, studies have found that partnering technologies can enhance adherence and treatment efficacy (Schmitter-Edgecombe et al., 2022; Vandelanotte et al., 2018). For example, a pilot trial showed that adjunctive use of a consumer wearable device improved both treatment outcomes and engagement in digital behavioral therapy for insomnia (Aji et al., 2022). Gaming features, in the form of rewards or points, also may be useful for increasing adherence. These findings underscore the potential of leveraging digital tools and machine learning to create timely, adaptive, and impactful cognitive interventions.

Methodological Concerns

Unlike traditional compensatory aids, such as notebooks and sticky notes, digital technologies present a range of logistical concerns that must be addressed for successful adoption, use, and efficacy. The most fundamental requirement of all digital tools is that they require a power source. Although seemingly straightforward, remembering to charge one's smartphone, tablet, or smartwatch is cognitively demanding. Charging behaviors should be reviewed during training and considered when deploying digital tools. Some smartphone apps are associated with increased power resources and may require more frequent charging. Where, when, and how the device will be charged should be reviewed with the participant. If possible, care partners could be asked to assist the client to remember to charge their devices, portable batteries may be used for intervention studies, and digital prompts to remember to charge devices could be incorporated into the treatment plan or study procedures.

Interventions requiring the use of personal digital devices such as tablets or smartphones also should consider the advantages and disadvantages of using personal devices or a designated study/treatment device. Designated devices have the advantage of affording the researcher/clinician access to the continuous data metrics being collected by the device as well as total control over the device and operating system, which is a major advantage when using apps or other software that are impacted by hardware changes and updates to operating systems. An unanticipated update in a user's operating system could lead to dysfunction of an intervention app or cognitive training program. In fact, the rapid innovations in technology make it very difficult to develop and sustain digital tools without a highly competent computer engineering team working to fix problems that arise due to hardware and software updates.

Additional practical barriers include the cost of new technologies, concerns regarding privacy, and the computing storage and skills to process large, continuous datasets. Decreasing costs of digital devices are offset by the development of new and more costly devices with more computing power and capabilities. Maintaining hardware, such as smartphones, laptops, and tablets, that are up-to-date and able to run current versions of software and operating systems can be costly. The cost and availability of Wi-Fi also may preclude access to many new web-based digital tools that are described above. The costs of digital tools and Wi-Fi services partly explain why they have been studied in homogenous samples of highly educated older adults with high socioeconomic status. Storing data also is costly for researchers and clinicians. Cognitive prosthetics and prompting apps that record continuous data from device sensors require the use of secure computer servers to receive and store continuous data collected over days, weeks, and months. Transmission of data to servers also raises important privacy and ethical concerns that need to be fully explained to clients and their care partners (Nebeker, 2024). Large amounts of clinical data also require knowledge of multilevel and longitudinal modeling techniques for analysis and interpretation of results.

Future Directions and Opportunities

There is incredible need for research on the development, adoption, adherence, and effectiveness of digital interventions for cognitive impairments in older adults. Major gaps in our knowledge of this area include head-to-head comparisons of digital tools versus standard cognitive rehabilitation tools (e.g., paper-and-pencil calendars, notes, etc.). Such comparisons would clearly elucidate the advantages and potential trade-offs of new technologies for cognitive intervention. However, these studies may become less relevant as technologies further integrate into everyday life. Studies also are needed to identify the personal characteristics, tasks, and contexts that are ideal for digital tools. For example, some prompting apps may be best for some individuals over others and for specific tasks, and some combinations of digital and analog tools may be ideal for certain situations. This information would facilitate person-centered interventions and increase efficacy. More research is crucial for developing best practices for technology training, particularly for older adults and individuals with cognitive impairment. Finally, framing interventions using neuropsychological theories and principles is crucial to ensure that we do not lose progress as devices and software evolve and become obsolete.

In clinical settings, clinicians should educate themselves about the wide range of technologies that may benefit their patients and prioritize patient goals. Familiarity with assistive technologies increases the likelihood that a clinician will recommend them, especially when they feel confident in their ability to use and explain the technology (Weakley et al., 2019). When considering a device, it is essential to ensure that its features align with the client's rehabilitation goals. Technology may not always be the best intervention option. Considering both potential barriers and facilitators to the client's successful adoption of the technology is important. Models such as the TECH framework can aid in this process by helping evaluate the fit between the user and both their environment and the technology itself.

Clinicians should encourage patients to use their personal devices to manage everyday challenges, ideally by sticking to basic, familiar phone features that can be personalized to the user's needs. Cognitive load and operational complexity should be weighed against potential benefits to ensure the technology provides a net positive outcome. For clients with progressive conditions, technology use may need to be periodically reassessed. The importance of training cannot be overstated. Training should be comprehensive and allow for practice with feedback. Implementation also should include support—whether from caregivers or others—who can assist in learning and using the technology effectively.

In conclusion, technology offers transformative opportunities for advancing digital rehabilitation. By increasing scalability, digital tools can mitigate inequities in access, making interventions available to individuals in rural areas or unable to travel (Kwasnicka et al., 2022). These tools also allow patients to engage in intensive, long-term cognitive training from the comfort of their homes (Repetto et al., 2021). Continuous monitoring of learning performance enables clinicians to identify barriers early, thereby facilitating timely interventions and personalized adjustments to support technology adoption (Ertas-Spantgar et al., 2024). Web-based training programs that utilize adaptive algorithms can align training with the users' cognitive abilities, improving engagement and learning outcomes. Real-time behavioral markers collected in real-world environments may improve the efficacy of digital rehabilitation by enhancing adherence and promoting sustained engagement through timely boosters. Tracking data on intervention components could reveal the impact of dosage, identify the most effective treatment elements, and determine which intervention aspects work best for specific users—advancing precision rehabilitation. Additionally, digital behavior markers can provide opportunities for more proactive health care by offering insights into cognitive and functional status, and by recognizing and predicting changes in health. These capabilities position technology as a powerful tool for improving accessibility, effectiveness, and long-term success in digital rehabilitation.

Acknowledgments

We would like to thank Marina Kaplan for her assistance in gathering notes and references for this chapter. This work was supported by funding from the National Institute on Aging [R35 AG071451 and R01AG062503] and the Office of the Assistant Secretary of Defense for Health Affairs, through the Peer Reviewed Alzheimer's Research Program under Award Number W81XWH-20-1-0654.

References

Adamczyk, P. D., & Bailey, B. P. (2024). If not now when? The effects of interruptions at different moments within task execution. *Proceedings of the SIGCHI Conference on Human Factors in Computing Systems* (pp. 271–278). Associations for Computing Machinery. https://doi.org/10.1145/985692.985727

Aji, M., Glozier, N., Bartlett, D. J., Grunstein, R. R., Calvo, R. A., Marshall, N. S., White, D. P., & Gordon, C. (2022). The effectiveness of digital insomnia treatment with adjunctive wearable technology: A pilot randomized controlled trial. *Behavioral Sleep Medicine*, *20*(5), 570–583. https://doi.org/10.1080/15402002.2021.1967157

Aleven, V., McLaughlin, E. A., Glenn, R. A., & Koedinger, K. R. (2017). Instruction based on adaptive learning technologies. In R. E. Mayer & P. Alexander (Eds.), *Handbook of research on learning and instruction* (2nd ed., pp. 522–560). Routledge.

Allé, M. C., Manning, L., Potheegadoo, J., Coutelle, R., Danion, J. M., & Berna, F. (2017). Wearable cameras are useful tools to investigate and remediate autobiographical memory impairment: A systematic PRISMA review. *Neuropsychology Review*, *27*, 81–99.

Aminikhanghahi, S., Schmitter-Edgecombe, M., & Cook, D. J. (2020). Context-aware delivery of ecological momentary assessment. *IEEE Journal of Biomedical and Health Informatics, 24*(4), 1206–1214. https://doi.org/10.1109/JBHI.2019.2937116

Annese, J., Klaming, R., Haase Alasantro, L., & Feinstein, J. S. (2023). A case of severe anterograde amnesia in the era of smartphone technology. *Journal of Clinical and Experimental Neuropsychology, 45*(5), 498–512. https://doi.org/10.1080/13803395.2023.2254911

Aramaki F. O., & Yassuda, M. S. (2011). Cognitive training based on metamemory and mental images: Follow-up evaluation and booster training effects. *Dementia and Neuropsychology, 5*, 48–53. doi: 10.1590/S1980-57642011DN05010009

Arifoglu, D., & Bouchachia, A. (2019). Detection of abnormal behaviour for dementia sufferers using convolutional neural networks. *Artificial Intelligence in Medicine, 94*, 88–95. https://doi.org/10.1016/j.artmed.2019.01.005

Arntz, A., Weber, F., Handgraaf, M., Lällä, K., Korniloff, K., Murtonen, K. P., Chichaeva, J., Kidritsch, A., Heller, M., Sakellari, E., Athanasopoulou, C., Lagiou, A., Tzonichaki, I., Salinas-Bueno, I., Martínez-Bueso, P., Velasco-Roldán, O., Schulz, R. J., & Grüneberg, C. (2023). Technologies in home-based digital rehabilitation: Scoping review. *JMIR Rehabilitation and Assistive Technologies, 10*, e43615. https://doi.org/10.2196/43615

Avila, R., Bottino, C. M. C., Carvalho, I. A. M., Santos, C. B., Seral, C., & Miotto, E. C. (2004). Neuropsychological rehabilitation of memory deficits and activities of daily living in patients with Alzheimer's disease: A pilot study. *Brazilian Journal of Medical and Biological Research, 37*, 1721–1729.

Ball, K., Berch, D. B., Helmers, K. F., Jobe, J. B., Leveck, M. D., Marsiske, M., . . . Advanced Cognitive Training for Independent and Vital Elderly Study Group. (2002). Effects of cognitive training interventions with older adults: A randomized controlled trial. *JAMA, 288*(18), 2271–2281. https://doi.org/10.1001/jama.288.18.2271

Barnard, P. J., Murphy, F. C., Carthery-Goulart, M. T., Ramponi, C., & Clare, L. (2011). Exploring the basis and boundary conditions of SenseCam-facilitated recollection. *Memory (Hove, England), 19*(7), 758–767. https://doi.org/10.1080/09658211.2010.533180

Beech, B. F., Almeria, A. T., & Schmitter-Edgecombe, M. (2024). Efficacy of digital and non-digital compensatory strategies in supporting prospective memory task completion among community-dwelling mid-life and older adults. *Archives of Clinical Neuropsychology, 39*(7), 849–859. https://doi.org/10.1093/arclin/acae030

Beentjes, K. M., Neal, D. P., Kerkhof, Y. J. F., Broeder, C., Moeridjan, Z. D. J., Ettema, T. P., Pelkmans, W., Muller, M. M., Graff, M. J. L., & Dröes, R. M. (2023). Impact of the FindMyApps program on people with mild cognitive impairment or dementia and their caregivers: An exploratory pilot randomised controlled trial. *Disability and Rehabilitation. Assistive Technology, 18*(3), 253–265. https://doi.org/10.1080/17483107.2020.1842918

Benge, J. F., & Scullin, M. K. (2020). Implications for technological reserve development in advancing age, cognitive impairment, and dementia. *The Behavioral and Brain Sciences, 43*, e157. https://doi.org/10.1017/S0140525X20000126

Bell, I., Pot-Kolder, R. M. C. A., Wood, S. J., Nelson, B., Acevedo, N., Stainton, A., Nicol, K., Kean, J., Bryce, S., Bartholomeusz, C. F., Watson, A., Schwartz, O., Daglas-Georgiou, R., Walton, C. C., Martin, D., Simmons, M., Zbukvic, I., Thompson, A., Nicholas, J., Alvarez-Jimenez, M., ... Allott, K. (2022). Digital technology for addressing cognitive impairment in recent-onset psychosis: A perspective. *Schizophrenia Research. Cognition, 28*, 100247. https://doi.org/10.1016/j.scog.2022.100247

Berry, E., Kapur, N., Williams, L., Hodges, S., Watson, P., Smyth, G.,... Wood, K. (2007). The use of a wearable camera, SenseCam, as a pictorial diary to improve autobiographical memory in a patient with limbic encephalitis: A preliminary report. *Neuropsychological Rehabilitation, 17*(4–5), 582–601. https://doi.org/10.1080/09602010601029780

Bier, N., Paquette, G., & Macoir, J. (2018). Smartphone for smart living: Using new technologies to cope with everyday limitations in semantic dementia. *Neuropsychological Rehabilitation, 28*(5), 734–754. https://doi.org/10.1080/09602011.2015.1094395

Björkstedt, E., Voutilainen, A., Auvinen, K., Hyttinen, V., Jyrkkä, J., Mäntyselkä, P., & Lönnroos, E. (2023). The role of functioning in predicting nursing home placement or death among older home care patients. *Scandinavian Journal of Primary Health Care, 41*(4), 478–485.

Block, C., Santos, O. A., Flores-Medina, Y., Rivera Camacho, D. F., & Arango-Lasprilla, J. C. (2017). Neuropsychology and rehabilitation services in the United States: Brief report from a survey of clinical neuropsychologists. *Archives of Clinical Neuropsychology, 32*(3), 369–374. https://doi.org/10.1093/arclin/acx002

Borella, E., Sella, E., Simonetto, A., Bellorio, N., Lenti, G., Taconnat, L., & Carbone, E. (2023). Effects of strategy-based memory training for older adults: Do booster sessions prompt long-term benefits? *Brain Sciences, 13*(9), 1301. https://doi.org/10.3390/brainsci13091301

Boyle, L. D., Husebo, B. S., & Vislapuu, M. (2022). Promotors and barriers to the implementation and adoption of assistive technology and telecare for people with dementia and their caregivers: A systematic review of the literature. *BMC Health Services Research, 22*(1), 1573. https://doi.org/10.1186/s12913-022-08968-2

Braley, R., Fritz, R., Van Son, C. R., & Schmitter-Edgecombe, M. (2019). Prompting technology and persons with dementia: The significance of context and communication. *The Gerontologist, 59*(1), 101–111. https://doi.org/10.1093/geront/gny071

Briand, C., Sablier, J., Therrien, J. A., Charbonneau, K., Pelletier, J. F., & Weiss-Lambrou, R. (2018). Use of a mobile device in mental health rehabilitation: A clinical and comprehensive analysis of 11 cases. *Neuropsychological Rehabilitation, 28*(5), 832–863. https://doi.org/10.1080/09602011.2015.1106954

Cagiltay, K., Baek, E., Boling, E., & Frick, T. (2008). User-centered design and development. In M. Spector, M. D. Merrill, J. van Merriënboer, & M. P. Driscoll (Eds.),

Handbook of Research on Educational Communications and Technology (pp. 660–668). Routledge. https://doi.org/10.4324/9780203880869

Cannings, M., Brookman, R., Parker, S., Hoon, L., Ono, A., Kawata, H., Matsukawa, H., & Harris, C. B. (2024). Optimizing technology-based prompts for supporting people living with dementia in completing activities of daily living at home: Experimental approach to prompt modality, task breakdown, and attentional support. *JMIR Aging, 7*, e56055. https://doi.org/10.2196/56055

Chang, C., Hinze, A., Bowen, J., Gilbert, L., & Starkey, N. (2018). Mymemory: A mobile memory assistant for people with traumatic brain injury. *International Journal of Human-Computer Studies, 117*, 4–19. https://doi.org/10.1016/j.ijhcs.2018.02.006

Chudoba, L. A., Church, A. S., Dahmen, J. B., Brown, K. D., & Schmitter-Edgecombe, M. (2020). The development of a manual-based digital memory notebook intervention with case study illustrations. *Neuropsychological Rehabilitation, 30*(9), 1829–1851. https://doi.org/10.1080/09602011.2019.1611606

Clay, I., Cormack, F., Fedor, S., Foschini, L., Gentile, G., van Hoof, C., Kumar, P., Lipsmeier, F., Sano, A., Smarr, B., Vandendriessche, B., & De Luca, V. (2022). Measuring health-related quality of life with multimodal data: Viewpoint. *Journal of Medical Internet Research, 24*(5), e35951. https://doi.org/10.2196/35951

Conway, A., Ryan, A., Harkin, D., Mc Cauley, C., & Goode, D. (2023). A review of the factors influencing adoption of digital health applications for people living with dementia. *Digital Health, 9*, 1–20. https://doi.org/10.1177/20552076231162985

Critten, V., & Kucirkova, N. (2019). "It brings it all back, all those good times; it makes me go close to tears": Creating digital personalised stories with people who have dementia. *Dementia, 18*(3), 864–881. https://doi.org/10.1177/1471301217691162

Cuberos-Urbano, G., Caracuel, A., Valls-Serrano, C., García-Mochón, L., Gracey, F., & Verdejo-García, A. (2018). A pilot investigation of the potential for incorporating lifelog technology into executive function rehabilitation for enhanced transfer of self-regulation skills to everyday life. *Neuropsychological Rehabilitation, 28*(4), 589–601.

Czarnuch, S., Cohen, S., Parameswaran, V., & Mihailidis, A. (2013). A real-world deployment of the COACH prompting system. *Journal of Ambient Intelligence and Smart Environments, 5*(4), 463–478. https://doi.org/10.3233/AIS-130221

Dai, B., Larnyo, E., Tetteh, E. A., Aboagye, A. K., & Musah, A. A. (2020). Factors affecting caregivers' acceptance of the use of wearable devices by patients with dementia: An extension of the unified theory of acceptance and use of technology model. *American Journal of Alzheimer's Disease and Other Dementias, 35*, 1533317519883493. https://doi.org/10.1177/1533317519883493

Dawadi, P. N., Cook, D. J., Schmitter-Edgecombe, M., & Parsey, C. (2013). Automated assessment of cognitive health using smart home technologies. *Technology and Health Care: Official Journal of the European Society for Engineering and Medicine, 21*(4), 323–343. https://doi.org/10.3233/THC-130734

Derbring, S., Barbos Nordström, M., Svenningsson, J-A, & Laakso, K. (2023). Effects of a digital reminiscing intervention on people with dementia and their care-givers and relatives. *Ageing and Society, 43*(9), 1983–2000. doi:10.1017/S0144686X21001446

Divers, R., Tassoni, M. B., Hackett, K., McKniff, M., Yamaguchi, T., Ham, L., Matchanova, A., Calamia, M., & Giovannetti, T. (2025). A pilot study of the effect of repeated practice in virtual reality on everyday action performance in real life. *Archives of clinical neuropsychology : the official journal of the National Academy of Neuropsychologists, 40*(8), 1602–1613. https://doi.org/10.1093/arclin/acaf067

Dubourg, L., Silva, A. R., Fitamen, C., Moulin, C. J., & Souchay, C. (2016). SenseCam: A new tool for memory rehabilitation? *Revue Neurologique, 172*(12), 735–747. https://doi.org/10.1016/j.neurol.2016.03.009

El Haj, M., Gallouj, K., & Antoine, P. (2017). Google Calendar enhances prospective memory in Alzheimer's disease: A case report. *Journal of Alzheimer's Disease, 57*(1), 285–291. https://doi.org/10.3233/JAD-161283

Ertas-Spantgar, F., Korabova, S., Gabel, A., Schiering, I., & Müller, S. V. (2024). Guiding patients with traumatic brain injury through the instrumental activities of daily living with the RehaGoal App: A feasibility study. *Disability and Rehabilitation: Assistive Technology, 19*(2), 254–265. https://doi.org/10.1080/17483107.2022.2080290

Evald, L. (2015). Prospective memory rehabilitation using smartphones in patients with TBI: What do participants report? *Neuropsychological Rehabilitation, 25*(2), 283–297. https://doi.org/10.1080/09602011.2014.970557

Fang, C. M., Samaradivakara, Y., Maes, P., & Nanayakkara, S. (2025). Mirai: A wearable proactive AI "inner-voice" for contextual nudging. *ArXiv, abs/2502.02370.*

Farias, S. T., Giovannetti, T., Payne, B. R., Marsiske, M., Rebok, G. W., Schaie, K. W., & Gross, A. L. (2018). Self-perceived difficulties in everyday function precede cognitive decline among older adults in the ACTIVE study. *Journal of the International Neuropsychological Society, 24*(1), 104–112.

Farias, S. T., Gravano, J., Weakley, A., Schmitter-Edgecombe, M., Harvey, D., Mungas, D., Giovannetti, T. (2020). The Everyday Compensation (EComp) Questionnaire: Construct validity and associations with diagnosis and longitudinal change in cognition and everyday function in older adults. *Journal of the International Neuropsychological Society, 26*(3), 303–313. https://doi.org/10.1017/S135561771900119X

Farina, E., Fioravanti, R., Chiavari, L., Imbornone, E., Alberoni, M., Pomati, S., & Mariani, C. (2002). Comparing two programs of cognitive training in Alzheimer's disease: A pilot study. *Acta Neurologica Scandinavica, 105*(5), 365–371.

Figueiredo, M., Caldeira, C., Chen, Y., & Zheng, K. (2018). Routine self-tracking of health: Reasons, facilitating factors, and the potential impact on health management practices. In *AMIA Annual Symposium proceedings, AMIA Symposium, 2017* (pp. 706–714).

Foloppe, D. A., Richard, P., Yamaguchi, T., Etcharry-Bouyx, F., & Allain, P. (2018). The potential of virtual reality-based training to enhance the functional autonomy of

Alzheimer's disease patients in cooking activities: A single case study. *Neuropsychological Rehabilitation, 28*(5), 709–733.

Ge, S., Zhu, Z., Wu, B., & McConnell, E. S. (2018). Technology-based cognitive training and rehabilitation interventions for individuals with mild cognitive impairment: A systematic review. *BMC Geriatrics, 18*, 1–19.

Gómez, C. S., & Rodríguez, E. J. F. (2021). The effectiveness of a training programme in everyday cognition in healthy older adults: a randomised controlled trial. *BMC Geriatrics, 21*, 1–13.

Greber, C., Ziviani, J., & Rodger, S. (2007). The four quadrant model of facilitated learning: A clinically based action research project. *Australian Occupational Therapy Journal, 54*, 149–152. https://doi.org/10.1111/j.1440-1630.2006.00558.x

Hackett, K., Lehman, S., Divers, R., Ambrogi, M., Gomes, L., Tan, C. C., & Giovannetti, T. (2022). Remind me to remember: A pilot study of a novel smartphone reminder application for older adults with dementia and mild cognitive impairment. *Neuropsychological Rehabilitation, 32*(1), 22–50. https://doi.org/10.1080/09602011.2020.1794909

Hackett, K., McKniff, M., Lehman, S., Pinsky, E., Tan, C. C., Kaplan, M., Vallecorsa, G., Serruya, M. D., & Giovannetti, T. (2026). A counterbalanced crossover pilot study of a personalized smartphone reminder application for older adults with cognitive impairment. *Neuropsychological Rehabilitation, 36*(1), 1–35. https://doi.org/10.1080/09602011.2025.2489125.

Hammink, J. H. W. C., Moor, J. A. N., & Mohammadi, M. M. (2023). Influencing health behaviour using smart building interventions for people with dementia and mild cognitive impairment: Expert interviews and a systematic literature review. *Disability and Rehabilitation: Assistive Technology, 18*(7), 1175–1191. https://doi.org/10.1080/17483107.2021.1994032

Hoel, V., Feunou, C. M., & Wolf-Ostermann, K. (2021). Technology-driven solutions to prompt conversation, aid communication and support interaction for people with dementia and their caregivers: A systematic literature review. *BMC Geriatrics, 21*(1), 157. https://doi.org/10.1186/s12877-021-02105-0

Holmqvist, S., Kaplan, M., Chaturvedi, R., Shou, H., & Giovannetti, T. (2025). Longitudinal and combined smartwatch and ecological momentary assessment in racially diverse older adults: feasibility, adherence, and acceptability study. *JMIR human factors, 12*, e69952. https://doi.org/10.2196/69952

Howard, R., Gathercole, R., Bradley, R., Harper, E., Davis, L., Pank, L., Lam, N., Talbot, E., Hooper, E., Winson, R., Scutt, B., Ordonez Montano, V., Nunn, S., Lavelle, G., Bateman, A., Bentham, P., Burns, A., Dunk, B., Forsyth, K., Fox, C., … Gray, R. (2021). The effectiveness and cost-effectiveness of assistive technology and telecare for independent living in dementia: A randomised controlled trial. *Age and Ageing, 50*(3), 882–890. https://doi.org/10.1093/ageing/afaa284

Imbeault, H., Langlois, F., Bocti, C., Gagnon, L., & Bier, N. (2018). Can people with Alzheimer's disease improve their day-to-day functioning with a tablet computer? *Neuropsychological Rehabilitation, 28*(5), 779–796. https://doi.org/10.1080/09602011.2015.1133431

Jamieson, M., Cullen, B., McGee-Lennon, M., Brewster, S., & Evans, J. J. (2014). The efficacy of cognitive prosthetic technology for people with memory impairments: A systematic review and meta-analysis. *Neuropsychological Rehabilitation, 24*(3–4), 419–444. https://doi.org/10.1080/09602011.2013.825632

Jamieson, M., McClelland, H., Goudie, N., McFarlane, J., Cullen, B., Lennon, M., Brewster, S., Stanley, B., McConnachie, A., & Evans, J. (2024). AppReminders—A pilot feasibility randomized controlled trial of a memory aid app for people with acquired brain injury. *Neuropsychological Rehabilitation, 34*(4), 535–571. https://doi.org/10.1080/09602011.2023.2220969

Jamieson, M., Monastra, M., Gillies, G., Manolov, R., Cullen, B., McGee-Lennon, M., Brewster, S., & Evans, J. (2019). The use of a smartwatch as a prompting device for people with acquired brain injury: A single case experimental design study. *Neuropsychological Rehabilitation, 29*(4), 513–533. https://doi.org/10.1080/09602011.2017.1310658

Jamieson, M., O'Neill, B., Cullen, B., Lennon, M., Brewster, S., & Evans, J. (2017, May). ForgetMeNot: Active reminder entry support for adults with acquired brain injury. In *Conference on Human Factors in Computing Systems – Proceedings* (pp. 6012–6023). Association for Computing Machinery. https://doi.org/10.1145/3025453.3025888 [1, 2].

Josephsson, S., Bäckman, L., Borell, L., Nygård, L., & Bernspång, B. (1995). Effectiveness of an intervention to improve occupational performance in dementia. *The Occupational Therapy Journal of Research, 15*(1), 36–49.

Joubert, S., Maquestiaux, F., Enriquez-Rosas, A., Villalpando, J. M., Brodeur, C., & Bier, N. (2024). Smartphone use as an efficient tool to improve anomia in primary progressive aphasia. *Neuropsychological Rehabilitation, 34*(3), 362–387. https://doi.org/10.1080/09602011.2023.2181824

Kaplan, M., McKniff, M., Tassoni, M. B., Holmqvist, S., Halberstadter, K., Chaturvedi, R., Callahan, A., Rosahl, M., Simone, S. M., Manganti, J., & Giovannetti, T. (2026). Virtual reality improves performance of real everyday tasks for older adults with cognitive decline by strengthening task goals. Department of Psychology & Neuroscience, Temple University.

Khan, T., & Jacobs, P. G. (2021). Prediction of mild cognitive impairment using movement complexity. *IEEE Journal of Biomedical and Health Informatics, 25*(1), 227–236. https://doi.org/10.1109/JBHI.2020.2985907

Kim, J., Hwang, M., & Hwang, Y. (2024). An integrative review of the feasibility and effects of the use of location-tracking devices by persons living with cognitive impairment.

American Journal of Alzheimer's Disease and Other Dementias, 39, 15333175241264767. https://doi.org/10.1177/15333175241264767

Kiselica, A. M., Hermann, G. E., Scullin, M. K., & Benge, J. F. (2024). Technology that CARES: Enhancing dementia care through everyday technologies. *Alzheimer's & Dementia, 20*(12), 8969–8978. https://doi.org/10.1002/alz.14192

Kringle, E. A., Setiawan, I. M. A., Golias, K., Parmanto, B., & Skidmore, E. R. (2020). Feasibility of an iterative rehabilitation intervention for stroke delivered remotely using mobile health technology. *Disability and Rehabilitation: Assistive Technology, 15*(8), 908–916. https://doi.org/10.1080/17483107.2019.1629113

Ksibi, A., Alluhaidan, A. S. D., Salhi, A., & El-Rahman, S. A. (2021). Overview of lifelogging: Current challenges and advances. *IEEE Access*, 9, 62630–62641. DOI: 10.1109/ACCESS.2021.3073469

Kueider, A. M., Parisi, J. M., Gross, A. L., & Rebok, G. W. (2012). Computerized cognitive training with older adults: a systematic review. *PloS One, 7*(7), e40588.

Kwan, R. Y. C., Cheung, D. S. K., & Kor, P. P. (2020). The use of smartphones for wayfinding by people with mild dementia. *Dementia (London, England), 19*(3), 721–735. https://doi.org/10.1177/1471301218785461

Kwasnicka, D., Keller, J., Perski, O., Potthoff, S., Ten Hoor, G. A., Ainsworth, B., Crutzen, R., Dohle, S., van Dongen, A., Heino, M., Henrich, J. F., Knox, L., König, L. M., Maltinsky, W., McCallum, C., Nalukwago, J., Neter, E., Nurmi, J., Spitschan, M., Van Beurden, S. B., ... Sanderman, R. (2022). White paper: Open digital health—Accelerating transparent and scalable health promotion and treatment. *Health Psychology Review, 16*(4), 475–491. https://doi.org/10.1080/17437199.2022.2046482

Kwok, E. Y. L., Moodie, S. T. F., Cunningham, B. J., & Oram Cardy, J. E. (2020). Selecting and tailoring implementation interventions: a concept mapping approach. *BMC health services research, 20*(1), 385. https://doi.org/10.1186/s12913-020-05270-x

Lancioni, G., Desideri, L., Singh, N., O'Reilly, M., & Sigafoos, J. (2021). Technology options to help people with dementia or acquired cognitive impairment perform multistep daily tasks: A scoping review. *Journal of Enabling Technologies, 15*(3), 208–223. https://doi.org/10.1108/JET-11-2020-0048

Lazar, R. M., & Mohr, J. P. (2011). Revisiting the contributions of Paul Broca to the study of aphasia. *Neuropsychology Review, 21*, 236–239.

Li, X., Beech, B. F., Hales, T., Van Son, C., Chilton, R., Lujan, C., Duell, B., DeSmet, C., Cook, D., Johnson, R. K., & Schmitter-Edgecombe, M. (2026). Evaluating an adaptive, web-based training program for teaching older adults experiencing cognitive difficulties to use an electronic memory and management aid. *Archives of clinical neuropsychology : the official journal of the National Academy of Neuropsychologists, 41*(1), acaf102. https://doi.org/10.1093/arclin/acaf102

Lintern, G., & Boot, W. R. (2021). Cognitive training: Transfer beyond the laboratory? *Human Factors, 63*(3), 531–547.

Luna, C., Cook, D. J., & Schmitter-Edgecombe, M. (2023). But will they use it? Predictors of adoption of an electronic memory aid in individuals with amnestic mild cognitive impairment. *Neuropsychology, 37*(8), 955–965. https://doi.org/10.1037/neu0000898

McDonald, A., Haslam, C., Yates, P., Gurr, B., Leeder, G., & Sayers, A. (2011). Google calendar: A new memory aid to compensate for prospective memory deficits following acquired brain injury. *Neuropsychological Rehabilitation, 21*(6), 784–807. https://doi.org/10.1080/09602011.2011.598405

Mikula, C. M., Perry, C., Boone, A. E., Benge, J. F., Scullin, M. K., & Kiselica, A. M. (2024). Dementia caregiver insights on use of assistive technologies. *Work, Aging and Retirement, 10*(1), 14–24. https://doi.org/10.1093/workar/waac027

Mihailidis, A., Boger, J. N., Craig, T., & Hoey, J. (2008). The COACH prompting system to assist older adults with dementia through handwashing: an efficacy study. *BMC Geriatrics, 8*, 28. https://doi.org/10.1186/1471-2318-8-28

Monroe, C. M., Cai, B., Edney, S., Jake-Schoffman, D. E., Brazendale, K., Bucko, A., Armstrong, B., Yang, C. H., & Turner-Mcgrievy, G. (2023). Harnessing technology and gamification to increase adult physical activity: A cluster randomized controlled trial of the Columbia Moves pilot. *The International Journal of Behavioral Nutrition and Physical Activity, 20*(1), 129. https://doi.org/10.1186/s12966-023-01530-1

Morrison, L. G., Hargood, C., Pejovic, V., Geraghty, A. W., Lloyd, S., Goodman, N., Michaelides, D. T., Weston, A., Musolesi, M., Weal, M. J., & Yardley, L. (2017). The effect of timing and frequency of push notifications on usage of a smartphone-based stress management intervention: An exploratory trial. *PLoS One, 12*(1), 1, e0169162. https://doi.org/10.1371/journal.pone.0169162.

Nagarkar, A., & Kulkarni, S. (2022). Association between daily activities and fall in older adults: An analysis of longitudinal ageing study in India (2017–18). *BMC Geriatrics, 22*, 203. https://doi.org/10.1186/s12877-022-02879-x

Nahum-Shani, I., Smith, S. N., Spring, B. J., Collins, L. M., Witkiewitz, K., Tewari, A., & Murphy, S. A. (2018). Just-in-Time Adaptive Interventions (JITAIs) in mobile health: Key components and design principles for ongoing health behavior support. *Annals of Behavioral Medicine, 52*(6), 446–462. https://doi.org/10.1007/s12160-016-9830-8

Nebeker, C. (2024). Navigating the ethical maze in digital health research. *The American Journal of Bioethics, 24*(2), 99–102.

Nguyen, L., Murphy, K., & Andrews, G. (2019). Immediate and long-term efficacy of executive functions cognitive training in older adults: A systematic review and meta-analysis. *Psychology Bulletin, 145*, 698–733. DOI: 10.1037/bul0000196

Okoshi, T., Ramos, J., Nozaki, H., Nakazawa, J., Dey, A. K., & Tokuda, H. (2015). Attelia: Reducing user's cognitive load due to interruptive notifications on smart phones. In *IEEE International Conference on Pervasive Computing and Communications (PerCom)*, St. Louis, MO (pp. 96–104). DOI: 10.1109/PERCOM.2015.7146515

Øksnebjerg, L., Janbek, J., Woods, B., & Waldemar, G. (2020). Assistive technology designed to support self-management of people with dementia: user involvement, dissemination, and adoption: A scoping review. *International Psychogeriatrics, 32*(8), 937–953. https://doi.org/10.1017/S1041610219001704

Olsson, A., Persson, A. C., Bartfai, A., & Boman, I. L. (2018). Sensor technology more than a support. *Scandinavian Journal of Occupational Therapy, 25*(2), 79–87. https://doi.org/10.1080/11038128.2017.1293155

Osborne, C. L, Juengst, S. B, & Smith, E. E. (2021). Identifying user-centered content, design, and features for mobile health apps to support long-term assessment, behavioral intervention, and transitions of care in neurological rehabilitation: An exploratory study. *The British Journal of Occupational Therapy, 84*(2), 101–110. https://doi.org/10.1177/0308022620954115

Ownsworth, T., Mitchell, J., Griffin, J., Bell, R., Gibson, E., & Shirota, C. (2023). Electronic assistive technology to support memory function after traumatic brain injury: A systematic review of efficacy and user perspectives. *Journal of Neurotrauma, 40*(15–16), 1533–1556. https://doi.org/10.1089/neu.2022.0434

Park, J., Kim, M., El Mistiri, M., Kha, R., Banerjee, S., Gotzian, L., Chevance, G., Rivera, D. E., Klasnja, P., & Hekler, E. (2023). Advancing understanding of just-in-time states for supporting physical activity (Project JustWalk JITAI): Protocol for a system ID study of just-in-time adaptive interventions. *JMIR Research Protocols, 12*, e52161. https://doi.org/10.2196/52161

Pike, K., Moller, C. I., Bryant, C., Farrow, M., Dao, D. P., & Ellis, K. A. (2023). Examination of the feasibility, acceptability, and efficacy of the online personalised training in memory strategies for everyday program for older adults: Single-arm pre-post trial. *Journal of Medical Internet Research, 25*, e41712. https://doi.org/10.2196/41712

Plackett, R., Thomas, S., & Thomas, S. (2017). Professionals' views on the use of smartphone technology to support children and adolescents with memory impairment due to acquired brain injury. *Disability and Rehabilitation: Assistive Technology, 12*(3), 236–243. https://doi.org/10.3109/17483107.2015.1127436

Ramirez-Hernandez, D., Wong, D., Ownsworth, T., & Stolwyk, R. J. (2023). Which training methods are effective for learning new smartphone memory apps after acquired brain injury? A pilot randomized controlled trial comparing trial and error, systematic instruction and error-based learning. *Neuropsychological Rehabilitation, 33*(1), 139–172. https://doi.org/10.1080/09602011.2021.1993273

Rebok, G. W., Ball, K., Guey, L. T., Jones, R. N., Kim, H. Y., King, J. W., & ACTIVE Study Group. (2014). Ten-year effects of the advanced cognitive training for independent and vital elderly cognitive training trial on cognition and everyday functioning in older adults. *Journal of the American Geriatrics Society, 62*(1), 16–24. https://doi.org/10.1111/jgs.12607.

Renaud, K.V., & Biljon, J.A. (2008). Predicting technology acceptance and adoption by the elderly: A qualitative study. In *Annual Research Conference of the South African Institute of Computer Scientists and Information Technologists*, Wilderness, South Africa, October 6–8, 2008 (pp. 210–219). https://doi.org/10.1145/1456659.1456684.

Repetto, C., Paolillo, M. P., Tuena, C., Bellinzona, F., & Riva, G. (2021). Innovative technology-based interventions in aphasia rehabilitation: A systematic review. *Aphasiology, 35*(12), 1623–1646. https://doi.org/10.1080/02687038.2020.1819957

Richmond, L. L., Morrison, A. B., Chein, J. M., & Olson, I. R. (2011). Working memory training and transfer in older adults. *Psychology and Aging, 26*(4), 813–822. https://doi.org/10.1037/a0023631

Robert, P., Manera, V., Derreumaux, A., Ferrandez, Y., Montesino, M., Leone, E., Fabre, R., & Bourgeois, J. (2020). Efficacy of a web app for cognitive training (MeMo) regarding cognitive and behavioral performance in people with neurocognitive disorders: Randomized controlled trial. *Journal of Medical Internet Research, 22*(3), e17167. https://doi.org/10.2196/17167

Robertson, K., Rosasco, C., Feuz, K., Schmitter-Edgecombe, M., & Cook, D. (2015). Prompting technologies: A comparison of time-based and context-aware transition-based prompting. *Technology and Health Care, 23*(6), 745–756. https://doi.org/10.3233/THC-151033

Sanz Simon, S., Ben-Eliezer, D., Pondikos, M., Stern, Y., & Gopher, D. (2023). Feasibility and acceptability of a new web-based cognitive training platform for cognitively healthy older adults: The breakfast task. *Pilot and Feasibility Studies, 9*(1), 136. https://doi.org/10.1186/s40814-023-01359-2

Sawik, B., Tobis, S., Baum, E., Suwalska, A., Kropińska, S., Stachnik, K., Pérez-Bernabeu, E., Cildoz, M., Agustin, A., & Wieczorowska-Tobis, K. (2023). Robots for elderly care: Review, multi-criteria optimization model and qualitative case study. *Healthcare (Basel, Switzerland), 11*(9), 1286. https://doi.org/10.3390/healthcare11091286

Scherer, M. (Ed.). (1998). *Matching Person & Technology: A series of assessments for evaluating predispositions to and outcomes of technology use in rehabilitation, education, the workplace & other settings.* The Institute for Matching Person & Technology.

Scherer, M. J., & Craddock, G. (2002). Matching Person & Technology (MPT) assessment process. *Technology and Disability, 14*(3), 125–131. https://doi.org/10.3233/TAD-2002-14308

Schmitter-Edgecombe, M., Brown, K., Luna, C., Chilton, R., Sumida, C. A., Holder, L., & Cook, D. (2022). Partnering a compensatory application with activity-aware prompting to improve use in individuals with amnestic mild cognitive impairment: A randomized controlled pilot clinical trial. *Journal of Alzheimer's Disease, 85*(1), 73–90. https://doi.org/10.3233/JAD-215022

Schmitter-Edgecombe, M., Luna, C., Farias, S., & Cook, D. (2023). *Development of an algorithm for real-time delivery of automated intervention boosters to support long-term use of an electronic memory aid.* Poster presented at the Alzheimer's Association International Conference, Amsterdam, Netherlands.

Schmitter-Edgecombe, M., Pavawalla, S., Howard, J. T., Howell, L., & Rueda, A. (2009). Dyadic interventions for persons with early-stage dementia: A cognitive rehabilitative focus. In R. R. Bougham (Ed.), *New Directions in Aging Research: Health and Cognition* (pp. 39-56). Nova Science.

Schmitter-Edgecombe, M., & Weakley, A. (in press). Digital technology in rehabilitation. In Wolfe, T. J., & G. Giles (Eds). *Functional cognition text* (2nd ed.). AOTA Press.

Scullin, M. K., Jones, W. E., Phenis, R., Beevers, S., Rosen, S., Dinh, K., Kiselica, A., Keefe, F. J., & Benge, J. F. (2022). Using smartphone technology to improve prospective memory functioning: A randomized controlled trial. *Journal of the American Geriatrics Society, 70*(2), 459–469. https://doi.org/10.1111/jgs.17551

Seelye, A. M., Schmitter-Edgecombe, M., Cook, D. J., & Crandall, A. (2013). Naturalistic assessment of everyday activities and prompting technologies in mild cognitive impairment. *Journal of the International Neuropsychological Society, 19*(4), 442–452. https://doi.org/10.1017/S135561771200149X

Seelye, A. M., Schmitter-Edgecombe, M., Das, B., & Cook, D. J. (2012). Application of cognitive rehabilitation theory to the development of smart prompting technologies. *IEEE Reviews in Biomedical Engineering, 5*, 29–44. https://doi.org/10.1109/RBME.2012.2196691

Shek, A. C., Biondi, A., Ballard, D., Wykes, T., & Simblett, S. K. (2021). Technology-based interventions for mental health support after stroke: A systematic review of their acceptability and feasibility. *Neuropsychological Rehabilitation, 31*(3), 432–452. https://doi.org/10.1080/09602011.2019.1701501

Sohlberg, M. M., & Mateer, C. A. (1989). Training use of compensatory memory books: A three-stage behavioral approach. *Journal of Clinical and Experimental Neuropsychology, 11*(6), 871–891. https://doi.org/10.1080/01688638908400941

Sprint, G., Cook, D. J., Schmitter-Edgecombe, M., Holder, L. B. (2022). Multimodal fusion of smart home and text-based behavior markers for clinical assessment prediction. *ACM Transactions on Computing for Health Care, 3*(4), 41. https://doi.org/10.1145/3531231

Sr, P. A. A., DeFeis, B., De Wit, L., O'Shea, D., Mejia, A., Chandler, M., Locke, D. E. C., Fields, J., Phatak, V., Dean, P. M., Crook, J., & Smith, G. (2020). Functional ability is associated with higher adherence to behavioral interventions in mild cognitive impairment. *The Clinical neuropsychologist, 34*(5), 937–955. https://doi.org/10.1080/13854046.2019.1672792

Stojanovic, M., Waters, A. B., Kiselica, A. M., & Benge, J. F. (2023). The impact of technology-based compensatory behaviors on subjective cognitive decline in older adults with a family history of dementia. *Applied Neuropsychology: Adult, 32*(4), 1–9. https://doi.org/10.1080/23279095.2023.2247109

Teh, S. K., Rawtaer, I., & Tan, H. P. (2022). Predictive accuracy of digital biomarker technologies for detection of mild cognitive impairment and pre-frailty amongst older adults: A systematic review and meta-analysis. *IEEE Journal of Biomedical and Health Informatics, 26*(8), 3638–3648. https://doi.org/10.1109/JBHI.2022.3185798

Tomaszewski Farias, S., Giovannetti, T., Payne, B. R., Marsiske, M., Rebok, G. W., Schaie, K. W., Thomas, K. R., Willis, S. L., Dzierzewski, J. M., Unverzagt, F., & Gross, A. L. (2018). Self-perceived Difficulties in Everyday Function Precede Cognitive Decline among Older Adults in the ACTIVE Study. *Journal of the International Neuropsychological Society : JINS*, *24*(1), 104–112. https://doi.org/10.1017/S1355617717000546

Tomaszewski Farias, S., Gravano, J., Weakley, A., Schmitter-Edgecombe, M., Harvey, D., Mungas, D., Chan, M., & Giovannetti, T. (2020). The Everyday Compensation (EComp) Questionnaire: Construct Validity and Associations with Diagnosis and Longitudinal Change in Cognition and Everyday Function in Older Adults. *Journal of the International Neuropsychological Society : JINS*, *26*(3), 303–313. https://doi.org/10.1017/S135561771900119X

Tong, C., Kernoghan, A., Lemmon, K., Fernandes, P., Elliott, J., Sacco, V., Bodemer, S., & Stolee, P. (2022). Lessons and reflections from an extended co-design process developing an mHealth app with and for older adults: Multiphase, mixed methods study. *JMIR Aging*, *5*(4), e39189. https://doi.org/10.2196/39189

Turunen, M., Hokkanen, L., Bäckman, L., Stigsdotter-Neely, A., Hänninen, T., Paajanen, T., & Ngandu, T. (2019). Computer-based cognitive training for older adults: Determinants of adherence. *PloS One*, *14*(7), e0219541. https://doi.org/10.1371/journal.pone.0219541.

van Teijlingen, T., Oudman, E., & Postma, A. (2021). Lifelogging as a rehabilitation tool in patients with amnesia: A narrative literature review on the effect of lifelogging on memory loss. *Neuropsychological Rehabilitation*, 17,1–27. https://doi.org/10.1080/09602011.2021.1974891

Vandelanotte, C., Duncan, M. J., Maher, C. A., Schoeppe, S., Rebar, A. L., Power, D. A., Short, C. E., Doran, C. M., Hayman, M. J., & Alley, S. J. (2018). The effectiveness of a web-based computer-tailored physical activity intervention using Fitbit activity trackers: Randomized trial. *Journal of Medical Internet Research*, *20*(12), e11321. https://doi.org/10.2196/11321

Van Etten, E. J., Weakley, A., Schmitter-Edgecombe, M., & Cook, D. (2016). Subjective cognitive complaints and objective memory performance influence prompt preference for instrumental activities of daily living. *Gerontechnology*, *14*(3), 169–176. https://doi.org/10.4017/gt.2016.14.3.011.00

Venkatesh, V., & Davis, F. D. (2000). A theoretical extension of the technology acceptance model: Four longitudinal field studies. *Management Science*, *46 (2)*, 186–204. https://doi.org/10.1287/mnsc.46.2.186.11926

Venkatesh, V., Morris, M. G., Davis, G. B., & Davis, F. D. (2003). User acceptance of information technology: Toward a unified view. *MIS Quarterly*, *27*(3), 425–478. https://doi.org/10.2307/30036540

Wang, L., & Miller, L. C. (2020). Just-in-the-Moment Adaptive Interventions (JITAI): A meta-analytical review. *Health Communication*, *35*(12), 1531–1544. https://doi.org/10.1080/10410236.2019.1652388

Weakley, A., Tam, J. W., Van Son, C., & Schmitter-Edgecombe, M. (2019). Effectiveness of a video-based aging services technology education program for health care professionals. *Gerontology & geriatrics education, 40*(3), 339–356. https://doi.org/10.1080/02701960.2017.1281805

Weakley, A., Liu, X., Duvvur, S., Kaushal, H., Mussi, N., Namboodiri, S., Choi, Y., Farias, S. T. (2021). Interactive care: A web-based platform for remote caregiving and functional independence in older adults with cognitive impairment. *Supplement: Dementia Care Practice (Descriptive), 17*(S8), e055322. https://doi.org/10.1002/alz.055322

Weakley, A., & Tomaszewski Farias, S. (2023). Rehabilitation of neuropsychological deficits: Compensatory approaches. In G. G. Brown, B. Crosson, K. Y. Haaland, & T. Z. King (Eds.), *APA handbook of neuropsychology: Neuroscience and neuromethods* (pp. 357–374). American Psychological Association. https://doi.org/10.1037/0000308-017

Wilson, B. A., Evans, J. J., Emslie, H., & Malinek, V. (1997). Evaluation of NeuroPage: A new memory aid. *Journal of Neurology, Neurosurgery, and Psychiatry, 63*(1), 113–115. https://doi.org/10.1136/jnnp.63.1.113

Wolff, J. L., Benge, J. F., Cassel, C. K., Monin, J. K., & Reuben, D. B. (2021). Emerging topics in dementia care and services. *Journal of the American Geriatrics Society, 69*(7), 1763–1773. https://doi.org/10.1111/jgs.17341

Woods, S. P., Weinborn, M., Li, Y. R., Hodgson, E., Ng, A. R., & Bucks, R. S. (2015). Does prospective memory influence quality of life in community-dwelling older adults? *Aging, Neuropsychology, and Cognition, 22*(6), 679–692.

Woods, S. P., Morgan, E. E., Loft, S., Matchanova, A., Verduzco, M., & Cushman, C. (2020). Supporting strategic processes can improve time-based prospective memory in the laboratory among older adults with HIV disease. *Neuropsychology, 34*, 249—263. https://doi.org/10.1037/neu0000602

Yaddaden, A., Couture, M., Gagnon-Roy, M., Belchior, P., Lussier, M., Bottari, C., Giroux, S., Pigot, H., & Bier, N. (2020). Using a cognitive orthosis to support older adults during meal preparation: Clinicians' perspective on COOK technology. *Journal of Rehabilitation and Assistive Technologies Engineering, 7*, 2055668320909074. https://doi.org/10.1177/2055668320909074

Zanetti, O., Zanieri, G., Giovanni, G. D., De Vreese, L. P., Pezzini, A., Metitieri, T., & Trabucchi, M. (2001). Effectiveness of procedural memory stimulation in mild Alzheimer's disease patients: A controlled study. *Neuropsychological Rehabilitation, 11*(3–4), 263–272.

Zhu, D., Al Mahmud, A., & Liu, W. (2024). Examining behaviour change techniques (BCTs) in technology-based interventions for enhancing social participation in people with mild cognitive impairment (MCI) or dementia: A scoping review protocol. *BMJ Open, 14*(2), e078188. https://doi.org/10.1136/bmjopen-2023-078188

Zhu, Y., Long, Y., Wang, H., Lee, K. P., Zhang, L., & Wang, S. J. (2024). Digital behavior change intervention designs for habit formation: Systematic review. *Journal of medical Internet research, 26*, e54375. https://doi.org/10.2196/54375

15

Technology-Based Interventions for Children with Neurological Conditions

Evidence, Trends, and Future Directions

Shari L. Wade, Anna-Lynne Ruth Adlam, Nicole Viola, Flora Hemming, Kelly M. Jones, Claudia Corti, and Tricia S. Williams

Note

The most up-to-date term for telepsychological interventions is often "telehealth" or "telebehavioral health," which broadly encompasses the delivery of psychological and behavioral health services using digital and remote technologies. In recent literature, "digital mental health interventions" and "online behavioral health interventions" are also increasingly used to denote a wide range of technology-enabled psychological services, including assessment, therapy, and neurorehabilitation delivered through video conferencing, web platforms, or mobile applications. These terms reflect the expansion and integration of technology into psychological care beyond traditional telemedicine models. Throughout this chapter, we will use the term "technology-based intervention."

Early Online Treatments for Pediatric Neurological Conditions: Rationale and Appreciation of the Neurological Context

Previous chapters have focused on leveraging innovative technologies to optimize the precision of neuropsychological assessments. In this chapter, we focus on how technology-based interventions have been developed, expanded, and scaled to address long-standing neurorehabilitative needs of pediatric neuropsychology populations. We also provide practical, clinician-focused suggestions for integrating technology-based approaches into neuropsychological services, based on our experiences of the Teen Online Problem-Solving program (TOPS) and Internet based

Shari L. Wade et al., *Technology-Based Interventions for Children with Neurological Conditions*.
In: *Technology and Neuropsychology*. Edited by: Jared F. Benge et al., Oxford University Press.
 DOI: 10.1093/9780197814116.003.0015

Interacting Together Every day, Recovery After Childhood Traumatic brain injury (I-InTERACT) and InTERACT-North.

Pediatric neurological conditions, including traumatic brain injuries (TBIs), constitute a natural target for technology-based interventions due to their chronic course and lack of neurorehabilitation specialists outside of urban centers. Consequently, some of the earliest technology-based interventions for children focused on pediatric TBIs (Wade et al., 2004). These initial interventions were developed in response to a growing literature underscoring the central role of the family in the child's cognitive and behavioral recovery following a TBI (Gerring & Wade, 2012). Initial technology-based interventions aimed to mitigate common challenges associated with behavioral health care for pediatric neurological conditions, such as geographic isolation/distance from experienced providers, socioeconomic disparities, and stigma around accessing behavioral health services (Fisher et al., 2021; Narad et al., 2019; Vyas et al., 2021). This chapter explores the history, evidence, and status of online neurorehabilitation interventions, including their availability for clinical care.

Beginning in the early 2000s, two contrasting approaches emerged for online neurorehabilitation with pediatric populations: online attention and memory training (e.g., CogMed, CWMT; Klingberg et al., 2002) and online family-centered problem-solving and positive parenting approaches (e.g., Online Family Problem Solving, TOPS, Counselor Assisted Problem-Solving, I-InTERACT/InTERACT-North; Ford et al., 2023; Narad et al., 2017; Wade et al., 2014, 2006b). Although both approaches leveraged the advantages of computerized delivery, drilled-based approaches such as CWMT, aiming to restore cognitive capabilities through repetitive practice, tended to focus on gaming approaches to train specific attention and memory skills. In contrast, family-centered approaches prioritized the provision of didactic information, video scenarios, collaborative family exercises, and targeted problem-solving, behavior regulation, and cognitive communication skills. The following section presents and compares an example of a computerized drill-based training program with an online family-centered approach.

Cogmed Working Memory Training (CWMT)

Cogmed was developed in the early 2000s by neuroscientist Torkel Klingberg and colleagues at the Karolinska Institute. Cogmed is an adaptive, computerized training program aimed at improving working memory and other cognitive challenges, especially in children with attention-deficit/hyperactivity disorder (ADHD). The first published paper appeared in 2002 and included children aged 7 to 12 years (Klingberg et al., 2002). Cogmed modules are tailored for different age groups and typically involve 20–25 online sessions over 5–7 weeks. Individuals work with a certified CWMT coach (often a psychologist, psychometrist, or trained educational professional) who oversees the program remotely. For children and youth, parents or caregivers (herein referred to as caregivers) support the training by facilitating a consistent, distraction-free environment and motivating the child to complete daily sessions. Caregivers communicate progress or challenges to the coach, but they do not assist with the child or young person's actual tasks. Evidence shows medium-sized improvements in verbal and visuospatial working memory, with some transfer effects to executive functions. However, far-transfer effects to academic achievement or behavior are inconsistent, and critiques highlight methodological concerns and limited generalization (Bharadwaj et al., 2022; Etherton et al., 2019; Sala et al., 2019). There is also some evidence to suggest that combining CWMT with metacognitive strategies supports sustained effects more than CWMT alone (Jones et al., 2020). There has been some application to medical populations but with similar null efficacy/transfer findings and related concerns (Calderon et al., 2019; Eve et al., 2016). More recently, caution has been advised in clinical implementation as further research is required to fully examine the effectiveness of CWMT in improving working memory and decision-making in a pediatric acquired brain injury (ABI) population (e.g., brain tumor; Hardy et al., 2013; Phillips et al., 2016).

Online Family Problem-Solving

TOPS is a family-centered, technology-based intervention designed to improve communication, problem-solving, and behavioral regulation in children and adolescents. Unique from CWMT, TOPS was specifically designed to support youth with neurological conditions, such as TBIs, and their families. TOPS includes core and supplementary modules, delivered via structured sessions with families. Content emphasizes collaborative goal-setting, outlining steps of problem-solving and strategies for managing everyday challenges, including behavioral and emotional regulation, and includes videos and exercises to support personalized application to goals (Wade et al., 2006c, 2018) Evidence from five randomized controlled trials (RCTs) and an individual participant data meta-analysis supports improvements in behavioral outcomes, family functioning, and emotional regulation in adolescents with TBIs (Wade et al., 2006a, 2015, 2018, 2019a, 2019b). More recently, the TOPS has been employed transdiagnostically with a range of neurological conditions (Wade et al., 2022) and in studies with epilepsy (Modi et al., 2019) and pediatric brain tumor survivors (Wade et al., 2020).

Comparison of Cogmed and TOPS

CWMT focuses on cognitive training for the child alone, using gamified tasks, while TOPS involves the whole family in therapist-guided sessions. CWMT has consistently been linked to improvements on working memory tasks but demonstrated limited generalizability, whereas TOPS has shown improvements in behavioral and family outcomes. TOPS is closely tied to the child's environment and contextual supports, whereas CWMT is more decontextualized and task-based. Given the empirically established centrality of family/caregiver functioning in promoting behavioral health and the lack of research on integrating these models, the remainder of this chapter is devoted to TOPS and the early-age, family-centered, technology-based interventions, I-InTERACT and Interact-North.

Evolution of Online Family Problem-Solving/TOPS

Online family problem-solving (Wade et al., 2006a, 2006b) grew out of an initial trial of face-to-face family problem-solving therapy to reduce behavior problems and family distress (Wade et al., 2006c). Findings from the initial trial supported the potential efficacy of the program in reducing child internalizing behaviors and caregiver distress, while underscoring difficulties returning to the hospital for in-person treatment. Informed by this trial, Wade and colleagues developed an eight-session online problem-solving program that integrated online learning modules with synchronous videoconferences with a trained therapist (Wade et al., 2004). Session content focused on staying positive/cognitive reframing, problem-solving, cognitive changes, behavioral changes, family communication, crisis management, and planning for the future. Each online learning module included didactic information about brain injury, videos modeling skills, and interactive exercises to reinforce understanding and skill acquisition. Beginning in the third session, families used the five-step problem-solving process (ABCDE: Aim, Brainstorm, Choose, Do It, Evaluate) to develop plans to address goals identified by the young person and their family. Sessions involved the entire family when possible, including siblings and emphasized collaborative goal-setting and problem-solving. Families could also complete up to four supplemental online sessions addressing both individual (e.g., managing pain) and family-level concerns (e.g., marital communication, effects on siblings).

The initial RCT, with 39 children aged 5–16, found improvements in self-management, compliance, and behavior problems, particularly among older children (aged >13 years) and those of lower socioeconomic status (Wade et al., 2006a), as well as significant reductions in caregiver depression and distress (Wade et al., 2006b). These findings underscored the feasibility and potential utility of online family problem-solving while suggesting that the problem-solving approach might be better suited to older children and adolescents.

Four subsequent RCTs with children aged 12–18 provided further support for the efficacy of online family problem-solving in reducing child behavior problems, executive dysfunction, and caregiver distress (Kurowski et al., 2014; Petranovich et al., 2015; Wade et al., 2012, 2014, 2015). An individual participant meta-analysis of 359 participants aged 5–18 years who participated in prior trials confirmed the superiority of TOPS in reducing child behavior and caregiver distress, particularly for adolescents as well as those with greater social disadvantage (Wade et al., 2018, 2019b; Zhang et al., 2019).

Although originally developed and tested with children with TBIs, TOPS content has been adapted for use with adolescent and young adult brain tumor survivors (Survivor's Journey; Moscato et al., 2019; Wade et al., 2020) and adolescents with epilepsy-related executive function deficits (Epilepsy Journey; Modi et al., 2019, 2021). These adaptations integrated the core elements of TOPS with diagnosis-specific content focusing on challenges unique to those populations (e.g., fatigue for brain tumor survivors and medication adherence for youth with epilepsy). Medical providers, TOPS clinicians, caregivers, and young people with neurological conditions provided input that fueled a transdiagnostic adaptation of TOPS (TOPS4ALL). This adaptation supports adolescents and emerging adults across a range of neurological conditions that may impact neurobehavioral functioning, including brain tumors, epilepsy, stroke, spina bifida, cerebral palsy, infectious and anoxic insults, and multiple sclerosis, among others. Taken together, these findings support the utility of TOPS as an effective and accessible tool for improving outcomes following TBIs and other conditions with complex neurobehavioral consequences.

Figures 15.1 and 15.2 depict the current TOPS core and supplemental sessions, respectively. Within the transdiagnostic TOPS4ALL site, the original session on anger management has been broadened to encompass regulating a range of difficult emotions, including fear, worries about recurrence, and sadness. The supplemental sessions have been expanded to focus on "visible and invisible conditions," "managing your medications," and "self-advocacy," and video examples include adolescents and young adults with a range of neurological conditions.

The case study below involves an Italian adolescent who received I-TOPS (Italian TOPS, described in greater detail later; Corti et al., 2025) after a severe TBI. Tommaso's case highlights how the problem-solving framework and heuristics of self-monitoring and emotion regulation can be used to improve executive and emotional functioning.

Tommaso's Journey with I-TOPS

Tommaso, 15 years old, sustained a severe TBI with significant cognitive and emotional challenges, including low processing speed and difficulty regulating anger.

Key Concerns: Dependence on his mother for schoolwork, anger management and emotional self-regulation, social disengagement, and excessive phone use.

I-TOPS Strategies Applied

ABCDE Aim: Structured homework sessions to build independence

STARRS (Stop Think Accept Relax, Reframe, Solve): Calming and reframing techniques for emotional regulation

SMART: Monitoring and adjusting social behavior, reducing phone use

Mother's Role: Actively involved in therapy, she supported strategy use at home and helped Tommaso reflect on challenges and strengths.

Outcome: Tommaso showed improved task organization, emotional regulation, and problem-solving. His mother noted that focusing on both challenges and strengths helped him approach difficulties more constructively.

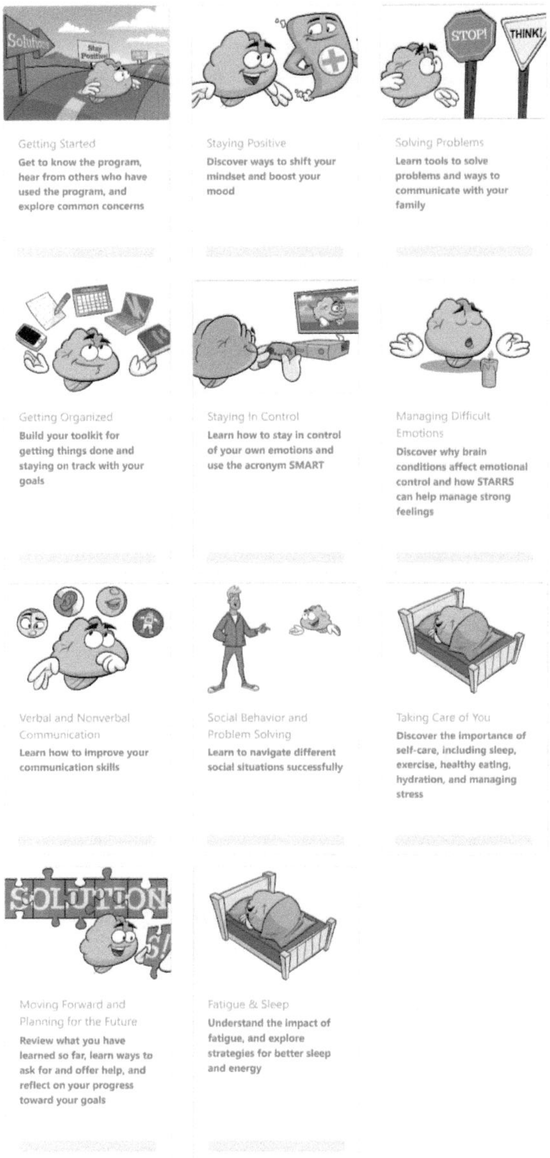

Figure 15.1 Ten core sessions of TOPS USA

Figure 15.2 TOPS USA supplemental sessions

The text box below outlines some of the tips identified by TOPS practitioners to consider when delivering the program. With tailoring and thoughtful adaptation, TOPS, and similar digital health programs, can be used successfully even among families with limited technological resources or experience. Given unique issues with privacy and therapeutic boundaries when delivering treatment into family's homes, initial clarification, ground rules, and troubleshooting can promote engagement and mitigate distractions.

TOPS Clinical Implementation Tips

Support task completion using memory and organizational strategies to help participants engage with web modules and track progress.

Boost family engagement with scaffolding and praise, model website use, solve tech issues, and gradually shift responsibility.

Adapt sessions when content isn't reviewed beforehand by focusing on core concepts and tailoring discussions to family goals.

Use mobile tools by having youth screenshot strategies (e.g., relaxation, self-talk) for quick access.

Adjust session format for cognitive needs by splitting sessions into two smaller sessions focusing one on didactic instruction and one on skill practice.

Clinically, TOPS can be integrated into the recommendations in a comprehensive neuropsychological report. As noted by Kelly McNally, PhD, training director at Nationwide Children's Hospital, "So often we complete our detailed evaluations and identify problems with executive functions, but in many cases, we are really limited in resources available for helping these families, beyond our one-time feedback session. TOPS has given us a great option for that next-step after neuropsychological feedback. We can directly link the content of the TOPS modules to the specific problems identified during our evaluations and that has really helped with caregiver buy-in."

I-InTERACT and Interact-North

Findings from early TOPS trials highlighted its benefit for older youth and the need for an alternative approach to support the needs of younger children and families following brain injury (Wade et al., 2018). Subsequently, I-InTERACT (Internet-based Interacting Together Every day, Recovery After Childhood Traumatic brain injury), a technology-based parenting intervention, was designed to support families of younger children aged 3–9 recovering from TBIs (Aguilar et al., 2019; Antonini et al., 2014; Narad et al., 2017; Wade et al., 2017). The program was informed by well-known behavior caregiver training programs, including Parent Child Interact Therapy, Incredible Years Parenting Program, and Triple P (Eyberg, 1988; Kaminski et al., 2008; Kirkbride et al., 2024; Nowak & Heinrichs, 2008; Schuhmann et al., 1998; Webster-Stratton et al., 2011), but it uniquely provided neuropsychologically informed psychoeducation regarding effects of TBI on emotion and behavior regulation. The original multisite RCT comparing I-Interact (10 core and 4 supplemental sessions), an abbreviated version (i.e., I-Interact-Express; 7 core sessions), and an Internet resource group indicated the efficacy of the intervention. In the full and abbreviated versions, the program led to improvement in parenting skills and reductions in child emotional and behavioral concerns (Aguilar et al., 2019; Wade et al., 2017).

In 2020, I-InTERACT was adapted for a Canadian context at the Hospital for Sick Children (Toronto, Ontario), named InTERACT-North. Leveraging participatory design, the program transitioned to a fully transdiagnostic model, designed to support children aged 3–9 with a wide range of neonatal and early onset neurological and neurodevelopmental conditions, including neonatal stroke, hypoxic-ischemic encephalopathy (HIE), epilepsy, congenital heart disease, and preterm birth, as well as autism spectrum disorder (ASD), ADHD, and genetic syndromes associated with intellectual disabilities (Ford et al., 2023). To expand the program's reach and relevance, all references to injury-related behavioral changes were removed and Interact-North incorporated new content addressing caregiver uncertainty, psychological trauma during the neonatal/congenital period, and early developmental concerns. The program retained key elements of positive parenting skills training, such as warm, responsive parenting and consistent discipline, while incorporating psychoeducation relevant to a wider clinical population. Findings indicated that the transdiagnostic version was both feasible and acceptable, with caregivers reporting that the content was applicable to their child's medical history and experience (Burek et al., 2021; Deotto et al., 2023; Williams et al., 2022).

Interact-North Stepped Care was introduced in 2021, beginning with low-intensity guided self-help in a podcast format, and progressing to more intensive therapist-supported coaching as needed. This version tailors the intervention to the severity of behavioral concerns and needs of the child, as well as the caregivers' capacity (Deotto et al., 2023). Interact-North Stepped Care has now transitioned into clinical implementation initiatives within Canadian institutions (SickKids, Alberta Children's Hospital). Both versions also continue to have condition-specific randomized trials including children born very/extremely preterm (Fisher et al., 2024; Glazer et al., 2025) and children with congenital heart disease (Taylor et al., 2024).

The respective programs combine virtual self-guided psychoeducational modules (approximately 20 minutes long) including video content to help caregivers further develop their parenting skills such as specific praise, use of behavioral contingencies, and caregiver stress management strategies, alongside psychoeducation about common challenges associated with brain injury and medical conditions for both children and their families (see Table 15.1). Information is presented with engaging, interactive features (e.g., video clips of caregivers who are modeling skills, quizzes). After completing each online module, caregivers meet with their therapist virtually (~60 minutes) to review the content using secure, videoconference technology that is compliant with the Health Insurance Portability and Accountability Act (HIPAA) and Personal Health Information Protection. During sessions, module content is reviewed and applied to the child and family's specific circumstances, and parenting skills are individualized and practiced with live coaching while the caregiver and child play together. These coaching sessions reinforce use of positive parenting skills

Table 15.1 I-InTERACT/InTERACT-North Program Session Content

Session	I-InTERACT (TBI)/ I-InTERACT Express (Wade et al., 2017)	InTERACT-North (Congenital/Neonatal) (Burek et al., 2020)	Stepped-Care InTERACT-North (COVID-19) (Deotto et al., 2023)		Interact-North Clinical Implementation (Williams et al., 2025)	
Self-Guided/ Pre-Treatment			Step 1	Podcast: guided self-help, review of parenting strategies during stress and in COVID-19 context	Step 1	Single session consultation to evaluate fit and formulate case conceptualization and session completion
1	Introduction to program, positive parenting skills, special play time	Introduction to I-InTERACT-North, review baseline info, set goals, introduce labeled praise and positive opposites	Step 2	Positive parenting & Special Play Time; Coaching session 1 Introduction to “lead your child”; Coaching session 2	Step 2	Introduction to Special Play time, labeled praises, positive opposites Introduction to “Follow your Child,” PRIDE skills Coaching session 1
2	Positive parenting skills, special play time	Positive parenting skills, PRIDE skills (Praise, Repeat, Imitate, Describe, Enjoy), ignoring problem behavior		Behavior management strategies; Coaching session 3		Introduction to “Lead your Child,” good commands, broken record Coaching session 2
3	Lead your child, compliance/noncompliance, good commands, broken record	Lead your child, compliance/noncompliance, good commands, broken record	Step 3	Consequences, time-outs, rewards; Coaching session 4	Step 3	Consequences and rewards, brain–behavior connection, setting up for success Coaching session 3
4	Behavior management, increasing good behavior	Behavior management, review of outcomes post-brain injury, strategies to increase good behavior				

5	Introduction to consequences for not following directions, time-out technique	Introduction to consequences, effective time-outs, rewards, review time-out scenarios	House rules, consistency; Coaching session 5	Limit setting and options for consequences (time-out, two-choices approach, sticker charts) Coaching session 4
6	Using positive parenting in real life, house rules	Consistency outside home, implementation of house rules	Module 6—Review and consolidation; Coaching session 6	Home rules and family values Coaching session 5
7	Closing thoughts, review key concepts	Closing thoughts, program review	Advanced strategies, future planning; Coaching	Review and consolidation Coaching session 6
8–10	Cognitive problems, anger management, stress management, communication, supplemental sessions (e.g., siblings, school)			
Booster	Booster session 8–12 weeks after core		Booster sessions suggested for skill maintenance	Booster session suggested for 6–12 weeks for maintenance

(e.g., specific praise, giving a good command with follow through) while fostering caregiver responsiveness and positive caregiver–child interactions.

Families and clinicians consistently applaud the virtual approach of this program to increase accessibility by addressing commonly reported barriers to receiving services (Wade et al., 2009, 2020; Williams et al., 2025). In fact, clinicians and family participants have commented how online service delivery to the family's home may offer advantages over in-person sessions, such as increased generalization of caregivers' new skills to their natural environment, as well as clinician access to more holistic and accurate information about family climate, challenges, and distractions, which may lead to more effective troubleshooting and skill application (Antonini et al., 2012; Burek et al., 2021; Deotto et al., 2023; Williams et al., 2025). The benefits of leveraging technology to deliver services directly into family homes, such as improved generalization of skills and richer contextual understanding, highlight a shift in how neuropsychological clinical care is conceptualized and delivered. This shift has important implications for pediatric neuropsychology training, which has traditionally emphasized assessment over intervention.

Over the past 3 years, Interact-North has been offered clinically through a clinical implementation initiative at the Hospital for Sick Children. Through biweekly group supervision sessions, Interact-North therapists have developed a robust set

Table 15.2 Practical Tips/Strategies for Common Virtual Issues Experienced in Interact-North

Interact-North Virtual Delivery Issue	Interact-North Therapist Strategies
Limited/unreliable access to Internet/device	Use local community resources for sessions, divide content by family availability, allow phone use for videoconferencing, shorten sessions, send materials in advance, provide alternative formats (Word docs, phone calls).
Coaching adaptations for virtual delivery	Position camera on caregiver only, allow child to wear mask/costume, conduct coaching with audio only, accept observation via listening, and take qualitative notes even in other languages.
Distractions during virtual sessions	Schedule sessions when siblings are away, give siblings alternate activities, divide session by child, occasionally allow siblings on camera, and provide targeted caregiver praise.
Coaching and communication in virtual real time	Caregivers wear headphones for live coaching, provide feedback after sessions if needed, use chat function for written coaching if child is uncomfortable.
Language and interpreter use	Use interpreters for teaching program portions, provide written module content in Word format for translation, maintain interpreter continuity, leverage online translation tools for website content.

Interact-North Virtual Delivery Issue	Interact-North Therapist Strategies
Confidentiality and documentation	Use secure email templates, avoid personal health information in emails, set boundaries for email topics, document adaptations and safety in secure records, review confidentiality risks and troubleshooting at program outset, ensure therapists have private space and devices.
Optimizing engagement and participation	Discuss importance of consistency at outset, create schedule "contracts," book sessions in advance, send calendar invites, set clear guidelines for no-shows and follow-ups.

of virtual delivery strategies (see Table 15.2) to address the unique challenges and recommendations of delivering behavioral caregiver training via technology-based intervention. These include technological adaptations, flexible scheduling, creative approaches to special playtime observation and coaching, and a strong emphasis on family-centered flexibility. Specific examples are elaborated next incorporating clinical case examples.

Limited or Unreliable Access to Internet and Issues with Device Access

Several families in remote settings have had unreliable Internet access and limited access to devices. Over the years, therapists have suggested using a local medical center or community resource to access sessions and recommended dividing sessions so that some content could be completed when the children were at school and others when they were home. Therapists were flexible about session timing and encouraged the use of a phone for videoconferencing if a computer was not available. When other families had limited device access, therapists shortened sessions, allowed families to use phones for videoconferencing, and sent session materials in advance via email. They also provided alternative ways to access content, such as sending Word documents or using phone calls for check-ins.

Coaching Adaptations for Virtual Delivery

For children who were uncomfortable being on camera, therapists recommended positioning the camera only on the caregiver, allowing the child to wear a fun mask or costume, or conducting coaching with audio only. In one case, the therapist accepted that caregiver–child interactions could be observed by listening rather than watching and taking qualitative notes even when the session was conducted in a language the therapist did not speak.

Distractions During Virtual Sessions

In families with multiple children or distractions at home, therapists suggested scheduling virtual sessions when siblings were at school, giving siblings an activity to do during coaching sessions or dividing the session to focus on one child at a time. This helped ensure that the target child received focused attention, even in a busy home environment. Other strategies included allowing the sibling to be on camera, such as, for example, engaging in the same activity and providing the caregiver focused praise for their ability to provide positive-parenting skills to both children.

Coaching and Communication in Virtual Real Time

Therapists often recommend that caregivers wear headphones during coaching to minimize the child overhearing. However, if the child was uncomfortable with this setup, therapists discussed alternatives, such as providing feedback after the session or using the chat function to provide written coaching.

Language and Virtual Interpreter Use

For families whose primary language was not English, therapists in Interact-North have used interpreters for the didactic/teaching portions of sessions and provided written module content in Word format for easier translation. In one case, the therapist coordinated to have the same interpreter attend each session for continuity and provided Word copies of module content to both caregiver and the interpreter prior to session. Newer strategies have included leveraging online tools to make I-North content accessible in multiple languages for families (e.g., guiding families to use Google Chrome's built-in translation feature to view website text in their preferred language). Plans are also underway to integrate Zoom translated captions, enabling participants (therapists and caregivers) in a session to have their speech automatically translated into real-time captions in another language.

Confidentiality and Documentation

Therapists emphasized using secure email templates, avoiding using personal health information (PHI) in emails, and setting clear boundaries for what could be discussed over email versus in session with families. They also documented adaptations and safety concerns in electronic patient records or other secure systems, especially when delivering the program virtually. In sessions, confidentiality is reviewed at program outset, detailing additional risks (privacy, etc.) with families and troubleshooting accordingly. For therapists, during training and supervision, access to their own personal private space and devices to provide sessions were also emphasized.

Optimizing Engagement and Participation

Therapists also described potential missed appointments, given the flexibility of offering a virtual program. Recommended strategies included discussing the importance of consistency and attendance at the outset, creating a schedule "contract" with families, including booking multiple virtual sessions in advance and sending regular calendar invites and reminders. Also having clear guidelines regarding the number of no-shows and follows-ups offered has been helpful for the team.

The Value of Embedding in Neuropsychology Training Programs

In recent years, there has been growing attention to the role neuropsychologists can play in delivering neuropsychologically informed pediatric and adult interventions (Williams et al., 2025; Wong et al., 2024). Traditionally, the focus of pediatric neuropsychology training has been exclusively on the assessment of cognitive and behavioral outcomes, with recommendations provided for home and school support. While neuropsychological assessment offers critical understanding of the child's needs and rehabilitation goals, it is only one component of neuropsychological practice. This has long been recognized in training guidelines and expectations for neuropsychological competencies and increasingly prioritized as we consider future training and practice (Rey-Casserly et al., 2012; Stringer et al., 2025). Yet clinical training and practices of neuropsychologists continue to be predominantly assessment focused (Sweet et al., 2015, 2021). As clinical neuropsychology evolves, integrating competency models and updated guidelines into training ensures that professionals are prepared to provide high-quality assessments and interventions within virtual environments. The Minnesota Conference guidelines specifically emphasize the necessity of adapting educational frameworks to incorporate skills required for technology-based interventions, reflecting a broader trend in professional practice toward remote care delivery (Stringer et al., 2025).

While many neuropsychology training centers and programs offer didactic assessment training, there is a need for training that equips neuropsychologists with the necessary skills to implement evidence-based, transdiagnostic, neuropsychologically informed interventions. Incorporating and assessing training in these neurorehabilitation strategies into pediatric neuropsychology practices can significantly enhance the well-rounded care that neuropsychologists are able to provide to children with brain injuries and neurological conditions. By emphasizing both assessment and intervention, neuropsychologists can become better equipped to address the multifaceted challenges these children face and use their unique skillset in providing psychoeducation on the brain–behavior relationship, as well as targeted neuropsychologically informed care as part of a multidisciplinary team.

Training the next generation of neuropsychologists to deliver evidence-based virtual care has become increasingly pertinent and vital for sustaining the relevance and accessibility of pediatric neuropsychological practice in the modern era. Recent reflections from trainees in Interact-North have underscored the novelty, value, and importance of embedding virtual care delivery skills into training from the outset (Green et al., 2026). Similarly, neuropsychology trainees who delivered the TOPS program in the United States and Canada reported that it was a valuable part of their training and helped them build competencies in delivering evidence-based online interventions for neurological disorders (Bonnano et al., 2026). Given the growing reliance on digital health services, and cognizant of ever-increasing demands on healthcare services and resources, it is crucial to equip neuropsychologists with the competencies needed to equitably deliver effective, evidence-based care in virtual settings.

Transdiagnostic Versus Diagnosis-Specific Approaches

The transdiagnostic approach to intervention reflects a growing recognition in the field (Cross & Hickie, 2017; Dalgleish et al., 2020; Kennedy et al., 2021; Marchette & Weisz, 2017; Wong et al., 2024), and in pediatric neuropsychology particularly (Burek et al., 2021; Goodman et al., 2024; Mrakotsky et al., 2022; Vyas et al., 2021) of overlapping symptom profiles across conditions and the dearth (or absence) of evidence-based programs for rare conditions. Notably, many neurological and neurodevelopmental conditions share common pathways of risk for emotional and behavioral difficulties, family stress, and challenges in day-to-day functioning as well as factors that contribute to resilience (Licari et al., 2019; Wade et al., 2006; Williams et al., 2019). Thus, as illustrated by TOPS and I-InTERACT/InTERACT-North, transdiagnostic adaptations may offer a responsive and cost-effective approach to address shared mechanisms such as behavioral dysregulation, reduced caregiver competence and confidence, and expectation misalignments. Importantly, transdiagnostic interventions may be especially valuable from a training perspective, allowing students to learn evidence-based intervention strategies that can address the broad spectrum of presenting conditions, recognizing the high degree of comorbidity that characterizes many pediatric neurodevelopmental conditions (Licari et al., 2019).

International adaptations of TOPS further illustrate the transdiagnostic potential of the program. In Italy, the I-TOPS (Italian TOPS) program was expanded beyond TBI to include not only other forms of ABI but also children with genetic syndromes (e.g., Sotos syndrome, Malan syndrome, and Joubert syndrome) or congenital malformations (e.g., cerebellar dysplasia), all of which are associated with significant impairments in problem-solving, social functioning, and affective functioning. This broadened scope was driven by the limited availability of outpatient neuropsychological services and the need for scalable interventions that could address a wider range of clinical presentations. The Italian team adapted the content to reflect cultural communication styles, emphasizing nonverbal cues and emotional expressiveness. Similarly, in the United Kingdom, TOPS was adapted to include adolescents with acquired brain injuries, including brain tumors and central nervous system infections, and modifying the content to reflect the varied etiologies and recovery trajectories of different neurological conditions. Building on these adaptations, the UK team has engaged in an intensive stakeholder engagement process with autistic young people and young people who had been adopted, alongside their caregivers, to shape TOPS into a more purposefully transdiagnostic intervention beyond ABI. This work refined the program's language, delivery pacing, sensory considerations, and relational framing, ensuring TOPS could address both neurodevelopmental differences and how executive function challenges can interact with the early life trauma that young people who have been adopted might have experienced. These adaptations preserved the core components of collaborative problem-solving and metacognitive skill-building while enhancing accessibility and relevance. In New Zealand, although TOPS has not yet been formally trialed, its principles emphasizing relational healing and collective family involvement—further supporting the program's flexibility across diagnostic and cultural boundaries.

Notably, despite the many advantages of transdiagnostic approaches, there is systemic pressure, particularly from funding agencies and some advocacy groups, to create diagnosis-specific versions. TOPS, I-InTERACT, and InTERACT-North have been used successfully to treat behavioral challenges associated with a range of conditions. At the same time, there are current trials testing condition-specific versions. Epilepsy Journey, for example, designed for adolescents with epilepsy and comorbid executing functioning challenges, includes 10 modules aligned with the Behavioral Rating Inventory of Executive Function (BRIEF) domains, paired with therapist-guided, problem-solving sessions. Epilepsy Journey is currently being tested in a multicenter trial comparing online modules plus therapist to online modules alone, therapist alone, and treatment as usual. Similarly, Survivor's Journey was tailored for adolescent and young adult survivors of pediatric brain tumors, addressing survivorship concerns such as fatigue, fear of recurrence, and social reintegration. These adaptations maintained the foundational problem-solving framework, and much of the original TOPS content, while embedding content specific to the lived experiences of each diagnostic group. Evaluations of these programs showed high levels of satisfaction and sustained improvements in quality of life and emotional well-being, although most were assessed through single-arm pilot studies without control groups (Modi et al., 2019; Moscato et al., 2019; Wade et al., 2020). Similarly, as described previously, current trials in Canada and America are evaluating the efficacy of Interact-North and I-InTERACT with families of children with congenital heart disease and prematurity, respectively.

While diagnosis-specific adaptations offer targeted psychoeducation and may enhance relevance for families managing specific conditions, they require separate development and validation, which can limit scalability. Moreover, given the challenges of translating programs developed in a research context into clinical care, diagnosis-specific interventions may be substantially less likely to be adopted over time. Additionally, many conditions are extremely rare, making diagnosis-specific interventions unfeasible and cost prohibitive. However, diagnosis-specific versions may be warranted when condition-specific concerns—such as seizure management or cancer survivorship—are central to family functioning and adolescent well-being. In contrast, transdiagnostic models offer broader applicability and cost-effectiveness, particularly in systems with limited resources or diverse clinical populations. By focusing on shared challenges such as executive dysfunction, emotional distress, and family stress, transdiagnostic programs can reach a wider audience without sacrificing therapeutic depth. Importantly, the success of both models is enhanced when delivered in a contextualized format that embeds skill development within everyday family routines and environments. Contextualized approaches promote generalization of skills and long-term impact by helping families apply strategies to real-life situations, rather than relying solely on abstract training.

Ultimately, both diagnosis-specific and transdiagnostic adaptations of these telerehabilitation programs have demonstrated feasibility, acceptability, and preliminary efficacy. The choice between models may depend on clinical priorities, available resources, and the characteristics of the target population. As these programs continue to evolve, future research should explore how hybrid models—combining core transdiagnostic content with optional diagnosis-specific modules—might offer the best of both worlds, supporting personalization while maintaining scalability. The use of advanced computing including artificial intelligence (AI) to individualize and tailor evidence-based intervention content may offer opportunities to increase tailoring for specific profiles of challenges, potentially promoting both engagement and efficacy.

Cross-Cultural/Cross-National Adaptations and Translations

The TOPS program has demonstrated notable adaptability across international contexts, offering insights into how evidence-based technology-based interventions can be tailored to diverse health care systems, family structures, and cultural values. Grounded in a therapeutic framework emphasizing problem-solving, cognitive reframing, self-regulation, and communication, TOPS has been implemented in Canada, the United Kingdom, and Italy.

In the United Kingdom, TOPS was integrated into the National Health Service (NHS), a publicly funded system with regional variability in access to neuropsychological rehabilitation. The UK adaptation retained the original structure, while reducing the number of core sessions to six, with four optional modules, delivered via videoconferencing. Core UK sessions are presented in Figure 15.3. Families appreciated the flexibility to tailor content to their needs, with high satisfaction reported for modules focused on goal-setting, timetabling, and positive thinking. Adolescents and caregivers described strong therapeutic alliances with their psychotherapists, and the intervention was particularly valued during the post-acute phase of recovery.

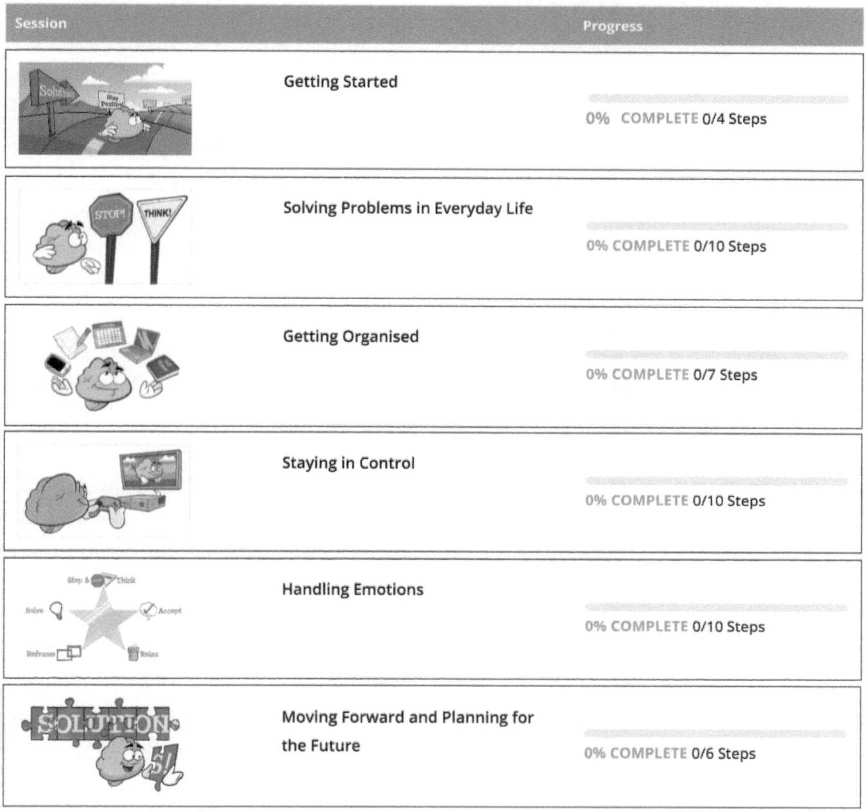

Figure 15.3 Seven core sessions of TOPS UK

Culturally, the UK adaptation reflected Western European norms of individual autonomy and structured educational milestones. In the United Kingdom, adolescents typically face earlier academic specialization compared to the United States, influencing the framing of school-related scenarios. The legal age for driving and alcohol consumption differs from the United States, requiring adjustments to examples used in the modules.

Family involvement in the United Kingdom was centered on the immediate family members—typically one or both caregivers supporting the adolescent. Sessions were dyadic, with a focus on helping caregivers scaffold their child's problem-solving and emotional regulation. Extended family involvement was minimal, reflecting societal norms of independence and privacy.

In Italy, the adaptation of TOPS was accelerated by the COVID-19 pandemic, which necessitated a rapid shift to remote service delivery. The program was implemented to maintain rehabilitation continuity and reach children who had previously lacked access to psychological support in the chronic phase after an ABI. After that, the Italian version expanded the program's scope to include children with genetic conditions in addition to those with ABI. Italian cultural norms emphasize expressive communication, prompting adaptations to video content that highlighted gestures, facial expressions, and emotional nuance.

In New Zealand, particularly within Māori (the Indigenous population of New Zealand) communities, family involvement is conceptualized through the lens of *whānau*—extended family networks that include immediate relatives, elders, and community members. The adaptation of TOPS principles was guided by the Te Waka Oranga model (Elder, 2013), which frames rehabilitation as a shared journey between clinicians and *whānau*, symbolized by paddling a canoe together toward recovery. This approach emphasizes *whānau*, health professionals as equal partners, and collective decision-making, and it takes a holistic approach to well-being. Māori cultural advisors recommended incorporating Te Reo Māori (the Indigenous language of New Zealand), traditional settings such as *marae* (communal sacred place), and practices like *karakia* (prayer). Therapeutic engagement was designed to be inclusive and responsive to Indigenous knowledge systems. Unlike the United Kingdom and Italy, where sessions were typically dyadic, the New Zealand model encouraged broader participation from *whānau* members, recognizing the importance of collective support and cultural identity in the healing process. Although TOPS was not formally trialed, its principles informed culturally tailored rehabilitation efforts.

In Canada, the Interact-North program development and its clinical implementation have involved two iterations of co-design workshops (2021, 2023). Across both, cultural representation and language barriers were reflected in prominent themes and recommendations for tailoring to representing all races and family types in program videos and examples to "ensure that video examples capture differences" in family experience. Families wanted a more accessible learning platform that could be accessed on portable devices, contained more relevant language, and reflected the diversity of the Canadian population that was not reflected in the original I-InTERACT program. This was considered pertinent, given that caregivers new to Canada must learn about "Canadian culture and school systems," which may impact their ability to relate to program content. This also applied to neurodevelopmental diversity representation. Caregivers wanted to ensure that families were not dismissed because of language barriers, and clinical partners recommended that administrators "invest in translation materials upfront into a variety of languages." The program was also responsively designed that enabled phone access, with future iterations considering technology to leverage virtual translation options on both the website and within the Zoom platform.

These international experiences with cross-cultural adaptation and implementation suggests that online neurorehabilitation is broadly acceptable and programs such as TOPS and Interact-North can be tailored to fit varied contexts. Cross-cultural comparisons show that while the therapeutic core can remain constant, the broader contextualization and delivery must be adapted to acknowledge and align with cultural expectations. Effective adaptation and implementation must extend beyond linguistic translation to ensure that approaches to delivery and program content reflect critical cultural nuances across settings, such as how families define role and responsibilities, and view neurological conditions, healing, and well-being. These cross-cultural experiences underscore the importance of designing interventions that are not only evidence-based but also culturally attuned. As we look to future adaptations, these lessons suggest that effective implementation requires co-creation with local stakeholders, responsiveness to cultural norms, and a commitment to equity in access. The experiences in the United Kingdom, Italy, Canada, and New Zealand provide a roadmap for expanding digital neurorehabilitation programs globally and highlight the potential of technology-based intervention to transform neurorehabilitation for children and adolescents with brain injuries across diverse contexts. The next case study involves a Canadian child with history of neonatal stroke who participated in Interact-North with her parents and grandparent. Kai's case highlights how positive parenting, behavioral strategies, and being embedded in a practice of cultural humility within the program improved not only child behavior but also parent confidence and family stress.

A Family in Harmony: Kai's Story with InTERACT-North

Kai, 5, has a history of neonatal arterial ischemic stroke and neonatal seizures.

Key Concerns: Aggression, tantrums, challenges with following instructions, parental stress

Interact-North Strategies Applied

Special Play Time

Consistent Consequences: Two choice technique and sticker chart rewards

Home Rules: "No hurting," "No throwing," immediate time-out for rule-breaking

Consistency Across Settings: Same expectations applied at home by all caregivers and in public

Family's Role: Parents and grandparent collaboratively established and enforced rules, integrating Chinese values of harmony and respect

Outcome: Kai had marked reductions in aggression and tantrums, and improved communication and compliance. Parents shared lower caregiver stress and greater confidence and consistency in their caregiving strategies. The family noted that integrating Chinese cultural values, especially harmony, respect, and family unity, made strategies more meaningful and easier to sustain.

Future Directions

As pediatric neurorehabilitation continues to evolve, the integration of emerging technologies presents both exciting opportunities and complex challenges. Building on two decades of translational research and international adaptation of programs such as (TOPS) and I-InTERACT/InTERACT-North, future directions in digital intervention delivery are increasingly shaped by innovations in mobile applications, AI, predictive modeling, and real-time translation tools. These developments offer the potential to enhance personalization, accessibility, and scalability of interventions for children with ABI and other neurological conditions. However, their implementation must be carefully balanced against considerations of data privacy, neurodevelopmental needs, and technological equity.

One promising avenue involves the development of dedicated mobile applications that integrate seamlessly with existing web-based platforms. These apps could support real-time goal tracking, interactive problem-solving exercises, and gamified modules designed to engage adolescents with executive function challenges. AI offers further potential to transform technology-based intervention approaches. AI-driven "problem-solving wizards" could guide families through therapeutic modules, suggest strategies tailored to their unique challenges, and provide real-time feedback. Adaptive content delivery systems may adjust session pacing and complexity based on user engagement and performance, thereby enhancing therapeutic alliance and reducing clinician burden. In addition, AI-powered therapist dashboards could synthesize session data to inform clinical decision-making and highlight areas requiring additional support. To date, however, limited integration of AI into the TOPS problem-solving wizard underscores the current limitations of this approach, with AI suggestions often mirroring the initial solution, in different more complex language or with details that may be irrelevant for the individual. Moreover, ongoing issues with AI fabrications and hallucinations highlight the need for caution and close scrutiny in its use.

Virtual reality (VR) is being increasingly used in the rehabilitation of motor skills and to a lesser extent memory and executive function challenges. While VR offers the possibility of contextualization, it remains expensive, individual- rather than family-centered, and challenging to integrate into clinical care. Nonetheless, technological advances may support broader integration of VR into some facets of digital pediatric neurorehabilitation.

Machine learning models may also be employed to predict which version of an intervention—that is, therapist-guided, self-directed, or hybrid—is most likely to benefit a given family. By analyzing clinical, demographic, and psychosocial data, these models could support precision matching of intervention modalities, optimizing resource allocation and improving treatment efficacy. Such predictive tools could be integrated into intake assessments or electronic health records to support automated decision-making and reduce dropout rates.

To support international implementation and culturally diverse populations, future iterations of telerehabilitation programs should incorporate real-time translation tools. Headphone-based audio translation during videoconferencing sessions could reduce language barriers and enhance accessibility. Multilingual interfaces and culturally adapted content, as demonstrated in the Italian, UK, and New Zealand adaptations of TOPS, will be essential for global scalability. These features must be designed with sensitivity to nonverbal communication styles and cultural practices, such as the inclusion of Māori customs in New Zealand or the emphasis on gesture-based communication in Italy.

Despite these technological advances, several challenges must be addressed to ensure safe, effective, and equitable implementation. Data protection and privacy regulations vary significantly across regions. In the United States, HIPAA mandates strict controls over personal health information, while the European Union's General Data Protection Regulation (GDPR) requires transparency, data minimization, and the right to erasure. International collaborations and cloud-based platforms must reconcile these frameworks to ensure compliance and protect user privacy. Clear policies, secure infrastructure, and ongoing legal consultation are essential for responsible data stewardship.

Children with neurological conditions may also face unique challenges in engaging with digital platforms. Sensory sensitivities, attention deficits, and executive dysfunction can impact usability and engagement. Interface design must accommodate cognitive load through simplified layouts, visual supports, and adjustable pacing. Session structure should be modular and flexible to reduce fatigue, and therapists must be equipped to provide real-time scaffolding and adaptive strategies to support skill acquisition and generalization.

Finally, technological access remains a significant barrier for many families. Socioeconomic disparities and geographic isolation can limit access to devices, reliable Internet, and private spaces for therapy. Implementation strategies must include the provision of loaner devices, development of low-bandwidth alternatives, and technical support for families with limited digital literacy. Without addressing these systemic barriers, the benefits of technological innovation may remain inaccessible to those most in need.

In sum, the future of pediatric technology-based interventions lies in the thoughtful integration of technology that enhances personalization, accessibility, and cultural responsiveness. These innovations must be pursued with careful attention to ethical, developmental, and contextual considerations. As the field continues to adapt to changing health care landscapes and technological capabilities, ongoing research and collaboration will be essential to ensure that digital interventions remain inclusive, effective, and sustainable.

Conclusions

Increasingly, pediatric neuropsychologists can draw upon a range of technology-based interventions such as TOPS, I-InTERACT, and Interact-North to provide structured follow-up after neuropsychological assessments, thereby extending their clinical reach and impact. Evidence supports the value of technology-based interventions for neuropsychologists and neuropsychology trainees as both an additional tool in their clinical toolbox and a resource to share with other professionals treating these children and families. Embedding training in digital health program delivery in graduate training, internship, and fellowship programs may further build capacity and reduce barriers to care. However, challenges to implementing technology-based interventions into standard pediatric rehabilitation remain, particularly in a time of stretched resources. Yet, by embracing innovation and collaborative learning, we have the opportunity to transform pediatric technology-based interventions and mental health care, making cutting-edge digital care accessible, effective, and an essential part of every child's recovery journey.

References

Aguilar, J. M., Cassedy, A. E., Shultz, E. L., Kirkwood, M. W., Stancin, T., Yeates, K. O., Taylor, H. G., & Wade, S. L. (2019). A comparison of 2 online parent skills training interventions for early childhood brain injury: Improvements in internalizing and executive function behaviors. *Journal of Head Trauma Rehabilitation, 34*(2), 65–76. https://doi.org/10.1097/HTR.0000000000000443

Antonini, T. N., Raj, S. P., Oberjohn, K. S., Cassedy, A., Makoroff, K. L., Fouladi, M., & Wade, S. L. (2014). A pilot randomized trial of an online parenting skills program for pediatric traumatic brain injury: Improvements in parenting and child behavior. *Behavior Therapy, 45*(4), 455–468. https://doi.org/10.1016/j.beth.2014.02.003

Antonini, T. N., Raj, S. P., Oberjohn, K. S., & Wade, S. L. (2012). An online positive parenting skills programme for paediatric traumatic brain injury: Feasibility and parental satisfaction. *Journal of Telemedicine and Telecare, 18*(6), 333–338. https://doi.org/10.1258/jtt.2012.120404

Bharadwaj, S. V., Yeatts, P., & Headley, J. (2022). Efficacy of Cogmed Working Memory Training program in improving working memory in school-age children with and without neurological insults or disorders: A meta-analysis. *Applied Neuropsychology: Child, 11*(4), 891–903. https://doi.org/10.1080/21622965.2021.1920943

Bonanno, K., Bothwell, S. J., Glazer, S., Patronick, J., McNally, K., Scratch, S., Cirincione, L., & Wade, S. L. (2026). Enhancing competencies in neurorehabilitation by integrating Evidence-based intervention delivery into psychology training: A clinical example. *Applied Neuropsychology: Child, 0*(0), 1–9. https://doi.org/10.1080/21622965.2026.2644531

Burek, B., Ford, M. K., Hooper, M., Green, R., Kohut, S. A., Andrade, B. F., Ravi, M., Sananes, R., Desrocher, M., Miller, S. P., Wade, S. L., & Williams, T. S. (2020). Transdiagnostic feasibility trial of internet-based parenting intervention to reduce child behavioural difficulties associated with congenital and neonatal neurodevelopmental risk: Introducing I-InTERACT-North. *The Clinical Neuropsychologist*, *35*(5), 1030–1052. https://doi.org/10.1080/13854046.2020.1829071

Calderon, J., Bellinger, D. C., Hartigan, C., Lord, A., Stopp, C., Wypij, D., & Newburger, J. W. (2019). Improving neurodevelopmental outcomes in children with congenital heart disease: Protocol for a randomised controlled trial of working memory training. *BMJ Open*, *9*(2), e023304. https://doi.org/10.1136/bmjopen-2018-023304

Corti, C., Papini, M., Strazzer, S., Borgatti, R., Romaniello, R., Poggi, G., Storm, F. A., Urgesi, C., Jansari, A., Wade, S. L., & Bardoni, A. (2025). Examining the implementation of the italian version of the teen online problem-solving program coupled with remote psychological support: Protocol for a randomized controlled trial. *JMIR Research Protocols*, *14*(1), e64178. https://doi.org/10.2196/64178

Cross, S. P., & Hickie, I. (2017). Transdiagnostic stepped care in mental health. *Public Health Research & Practice*, *27*(2), 2721712. https://doi.org/10.17061/phrp2721712

Dalgleish, T., Black, M., Johnston, D., & Bevan, A. (2020). Transdiagnostic approaches to mental health problems: Current status and future directions. *Journal of Consulting and Clinical Psychology*, *88*(3), 179–195. https://doi.org/10.1037/ccp0000482

Deotto, A., Fabiano, G. F., Chung, B. Y. T., Wade, S. L., Anagnostou, E., Crosbie, J., Kelley, E., Nicolson, R., Andrade, B. F., Miller, S. P., & Williams, T. S. (2023). Stepping up to COVID-19: A clinical trial of a telepsychology positive parenting program targeting behavior problems in children with neurological risk. *Journal of Pediatric Psychology*, *48*(6), 523–536. https://doi.org/10.1093/jpepsy/jsad032

Elder, H. (2013). Te Waka Oranga: An Indigenous intervention for working with Māori children and adolescents with traumatic brain injury. *Brain Impairment*, *14*(3), 415–424. https://doi.org/10.1017/BrImp.2013.29

Etherton, J. L., Oberle, C. D., Rhoton, J., & Ney, A. (2019). Effects of Cogmed working memory training on cognitive performance. *Psychological Research*, *83*(7), 1506–1518. https://doi.org/10.1007/s00426-018-1012-9

Eve, M., O'Keeffe, F., Jhuty, S., Ganesan, V., Brown, G., & Murphy, T. (2016). Computerized working-memory training for children following arterial ischemic stroke: A pilot study with long-term follow-up. *Applied Neuropsychology. Child*, *5*(4), 273–282. https://doi.org/10.1080/21622965.2015.1055563

Eyberg, S. (1988). Parent-child interaction therapy: Integration of traditional and behavioral concerns. *Child & Family Behavior Therapy*, *10*(1), 33–46. https://doi.org/10.1300/J019v10n01_04

Fisher, A. P., Aguilar, J. M., Zhang, N., Yeates, K. O., Taylor, H. G., Kurowski, B. G., Narad, M. E., & Wade, S. L. (2021). Caregiver and child behavioral health service utilization following pediatric traumatic brain injury. *Research on Child and Adolescent Psychopathology*, *49*(4), 491–501. https://doi.org/10.1007/s10802-020-00737-1

Fisher, A. P., Miley, A. E., Glazer, S., Gies, L. M., Parikh, N. A., Lam, L., & Wade, S. L. (2024). Feasibility and acceptability of an online parenting intervention to address behaviour problems in moderately to extremely preterm pre-school and school-age children. *Child: Care, Health and Development, 50*(1), e13209. https://doi.org/10.1111/cch.13209

Ford, M. K., Roberts, S. D., Andrade, B. F., Desrocher, M., Wade, S. L., Kohut, S. A., & Williams, T. S. (2023). Building I-INTERACT-North: Participatory action research design of an online transdiagnostic parent–child interaction therapy program to optimize congenital and neurodevelopmental risk. *Journal of Clinical Psychology in Medical Settings, 30*(1), 204–215. https://doi.org/10.1007/s10880-022-09875-8

Gerring, J. P., & Wade, S. (2012). The essential role of psychosocial risk and protective factors in pediatric traumatic brain injury research. *Journal of Neurotrauma, 29*(4), 621–628. https://doi.org/10.1089/neu.2011.2234

Glazer, S., McCullough, K., Parikh, N. A., Barnes-Davis, M., Yuan, W., Dudley, J., Williams, T., & Wade, S. L. (2025). Preliminary efficacy of a novel online parenting skills program for caregivers of preterm children with behavioral challenges. *Child Neuropsychology, 32*(4), 1–19. https://doi.org/10.1080/09297049.2025.2579217

Green, R. R., Taylor, M. M., Bondi, B., Désiré, N., Wade, S. L., & Williams, T. S. (2026). Training outcomes in a transdiagnostic, neuropsychologically-informed parenting intervention for children with early brain injury. *Journal of Clinical and Experimental Neuropsychology*, 1-15, Special Issue: Breaking Down Barriers: Transdiagnostic Approaches in Neuropsychology.

Goodman, C. V., Green, R., Taylor, M. M., Wade, S. L., & Williams, T. S. (2024). One-year follow-up of a transdiagnostic telepsychology parenting program for children at neurological risk: Who benefits the most? *Translational Issues in Psychological Science, 10*(2), 135–149. https://doi.org/10.1037/tps0000412

Hardy, K. K., Willard, V. W., Allen, T. M., & Bonner, M. J. (2013). Working memory training in survivors of pediatric cancer: A randomized pilot study. *Psycho-Oncology, 22*(8), 1856–1865. https://doi.org/10.1002/pon.3222

Jones, J. S., Milton, F., Mostazir, M., & Adlam, A. R. (2020). The academic outcomes of working memory and metacognitive strategy training in children: A double-blind randomized controlled trial. *Developmental Science, 23*(4), e12870. https://doi.org/10.1111/desc.12870

Kaminski, J. W., Valle, L. A., Filene, J. H., & Boyle, C. L. (2008). A meta-analytic review of components associated with parent training program effectiveness. *Journal of Abnormal Child Psychology, 36*(4), 567–589. https://doi.org/10.1007/s10802-007-9201-9

Kennedy, S. M., Lanier, H., Salloum, A., Ehrenreich-May, J., & Storch, E. A. (2021). Development and implementation of a transdiagnostic, stepped-care approach to treating emotional disorders in children via telehealth. *Cognitive and Behavioral Practice, 28*(3), 350–363. https://doi.org/10.1016/j.cbpra.2020.06.001

Kirkbride, J. B., Anglin, D. M., Colman, I., Dykxhoorn, J., Jones, P. B., Patalay, P., Pitman, A., Soneson, E., Steare, T., Wright, T., & Griffiths, S. L. (2024). The social determinants of mental health and disorder: Evidence, prevention and recommendations. *World Psychiatry, 23*(1), 58–90. https://doi.org/10.1002/wps.21160

Klingberg, T., Forssberg, H., & Westerberg, H. (2002). Training of working memory in children with ADHD. *Journal of Clinical and Experimental Neuropsychology, 24*(6), 781–791. https://doi.org/10.1076/jcen.24.6.781.8395

Kurowski, B. G., Wade, S. L., Kirkwood, M. W., Brown, T. M., Stancin, T., & Taylor, H. G. (2014). Long-term benefits of an early online problem-solving intervention for executive dysfunction after traumatic brain injury in children: A randomized clinical trial. *JAMA Pediatrics, 168*(6), 523–531. https://doi.org/10.1001/jamapediatrics.2013.5070

Licari, M. K., Finlay-Jones, A., Reynolds, J. E., Alvares, G. A., Spittle, A. J., Downs, J., Whitehouse, A. J. O., Leonard, H., Evans, K. L., & Varcin, K. (2019). The brain basis of comorbidity in neurodevelopmental disorders. *Current Developmental Disorders Reports, 6*(1), 9–18. https://doi.org/10.1007/s40474-019-0156-7

Marchette, L. K., & Weisz, J. R. (2017). Practitioner review: Empirical evolution of youth psychotherapy toward transdiagnostic approaches. *Journal of Child Psychology and Psychiatry, and Allied Disciplines, 58*(9), 970–984. https://doi.org/10.1111/jcpp.12747

Modi, A. C., Mara, C. A., Schmidt, M., Smith, A. W., Turnier, L., Glaser, N., & Wade, S. L. (2019). Epilepsy journey: A proof of concept trial of a web-based executive functioning intervention for adolescents with epilepsy. *Epilepsia, 60*(9), 1895–1907. https://doi.org/10.1111/epi.16317

Modi, A. C., Mara, C. A., Schmidt, M., Smith, A. W., Turnier, L., & Wade, S. L. (2021). Pilot executive functioning intervention in epilepsy: Behavioral and quality of life outcomes. *Journal of Pediatric Psychology, 46*(4), 363–374. https://doi.org/10.1093/jpepsy/jsaa119

Moscato, E. L., Miley, A. E., LeBlond, E. I., King, J. A., Raj, S. P., Narad, M. E., Platt, A., Thompson, A. N., Baum, K. T., Salloum, R., & Wade, S. L. (2019). Feasibility and acceptability of an online problem-solving therapy intervention for adolescent and young adult brain tumor survivors. *Clinical Practice in Pediatric Psychology, 7*(1), 68–78. https://doi.org/10.1037/cpp0000265

Mrakotsky, C., Williams, T. S., Shapiro, K. A., & Westmacott, R. (2022). Rehabilitation in pediatric stroke: Cognition and behavior. *Seminars in Pediatric Neurology, 44*, 100998. https://doi.org/10.1016/j.spen.2022.100998

Narad, M. E., Shultz, E., Yeates, K. O., Taylor, H. G., Stancin, T., & Wade, S. L. (2019). Behavioral health service utilization and unmet need after traumatic brain injury in childhood. *Journal of Developmental and Behavioral Pediatrics, 40*(6), 451–457. https://doi.org/10.1097/DBP.0000000000000681

Narad, M. E., Taylor, H. G., Yeates, K. O., Stancin, T., Kirkwood, M. W., & Wade, S. L. (2017). Internet-based interacting together everyday, recovery after childhood TBI (I-InTERACT): Protocol for a multi-site randomized controlled trial of an internet-based parenting intervention. *DIGITAL HEALTH*, *3*, 2055207617719423. https://doi.org/10.1177/2055207617719423

Nowak, C., & Heinrichs, N. (2008). A comprehensive meta-analysis of triple p-positive parenting program using hierarchical linear modeling: Effectiveness and moderating variables. *Clinical Child and Family Psychology Review*, *11*(3), 114–144. https://doi.org/10.1007/s10567-008-0033-0

Petranovich, C. L., Wade, S. L., Taylor, H. G., Cassedy, A., Stancin, T., Kirkwood, M. W., & Maines Brown, T. (2015). Long-term caregiver mental health outcomes following a predominately online intervention for adolescents with complicated mild to severe traumatic brain injury. *Journal of Pediatric Psychology*, *40*(7), 680–688. https://doi.org/10.1093/jpepsy/jsv001

Phillips, N. L., Mandalis, A., Benson, S., Parry, L., Epps, A., Morrow, A., & Lah, S. (2016). Computerized working memory training for children with moderate to severe traumatic brain injury: A double-blind, randomized, placebo-controlled trial. *Journal of Neurotrauma*, *33*(23), 2097–2104. https://doi.org/10.1089/neu.2015.4358

Rey-Casserly, C., Roper, B., & Bauer, R. (2012). Application of a competency model to clinical neuropsychology. *Professional Psychology: Research and Practice*, *43*, 422–431. https://doi.org/10.1037/a0028721

Sala, G., Aksayli, N. D., Tatlidil, K. S., Tatsumi, T., Gondo, Y., & Gobet, F. (2019). Near and far transfer in cognitive training: A second-order meta-analysis. *Collabra: Psychology*, *5*(1), 1-22. https://doi.org/10.1525/collabra.203

Schuhmann, E. M., Foote, R. C., Eyberg, S. M., Boggs, S. R., & Algina, J. (1998). Efficacy of parent-child interaction therapy: Interim report of a randomized trial with short-term maintenance. *Journal of Clinical Child Psychology*, *27*(1), 34–45. https://doi.org/10.1207/s15374424jccp2701_4

Stringer, A. Y., Fuchs, K., Bordes Edgar, V., Bristow, T., Correia, S., Penna, S., Reyes, A., Whiteside, D. M., Block, C., Bodin, D., Butt, S., Calamia, M., Didehbani, N., Dodzik, P., Dotson, V. M., Fernandes, M., Freece, K., Fuller, R., Getz, G., ... Schmitter-Edgecombe, M. (2025). The Minnesota Conference proposed guidelines for education and training in clinical neuropsychology. *The Clinical Neuropsychologist*, *40*, 1–42. https://doi.org/10.1080/13854046.2025.2520957

Sweet, J. J., Benson, L. M., Nelson, N. W., & Moberg, P. J. (2015). The American Academy of Clinical Neuropsychology, National Academy of Neuropsychology, and Society for Clinical Neuropsychology (APA division 40) 2015 TCN professional practice and "salary survey": Professional practices, beliefs, and incomes of U.S. Neuropsychologists. *The Clinical Neuropsychologist*, *29*(8), 1069–1162.

Sweet, J. J., Klipfel, K. M., Nelson, N. W., & Moberg, P. J. (2021). Professional practices, beliefs, and incomes of U.S. neuropsychologists: The AACN, NAN, SCN 2020 practice and "salary survey." *The Clinical Neuropsychologist*, *35*(1), 7–80. https://doi.org/10.1080/13854046.2020.1849803

Taylor, M., Bondi, B. C., Andrade, B. F., Au-Young, S. H., Chau, V., Danguecan, A., Désiré, N., Guo, T., Ostojic-Aitkens, D., Wade, S., Miller, S., & Williams, T. S. (2024). Stepped-care web-based parent support following congenital heart disease: Protocol for a randomized controlled trial. *JMIR Research Protocols, 13*, e64216. https://doi.org/10.2196/64216

Vyas, S. S., Ford, M. K., Tam, E. W. Y., Westmacott, R., Sananes, R., Beck, R., & Williams, T. S. (2021). Intervention experiences among children with congenital and neonatal conditions impacting brain development: Patterns of service utilization, barriers and future directions. *The Clinical Neuropsychologist, 35*(5), 1009–1029. https://doi.org/10.1080/13854046.2020.1871516

Wade, S. L., Carey, J., & Wolfe, C. R. (2006a). The efficacy of an online cognitive-behavioral family intervention in improving child behavior and social competence following pediatric brain injury. *Rehabilitation Psychology, 51*(3), 179–189. https://doi.org/10.1037/0090-5550.51.3.179

Wade, S. L., Carey, J., & Wolfe, C. R. (2006b). An online family intervention to reduce parental distress following pediatric brain injury. *Journal of Consulting and Clinical Psychology, 74*(3), 445–454. https://doi.org/10.1037/0022-006X.74.3.445

Wade, S. L., Cassedy, A. E., McNally, K. A., Kurowski, B. G., Kirkwood, M. W., Stancin, T., & Taylor, H. G. (2019a). A randomized comparative effectiveness trial of family-problem-solving treatment for adolescent brain injury: Parent outcomes from the coping with head injury through problem solving (CHIPS) study. *The Journal of Head Trauma Rehabilitation, 34*(6), E1–E9. https://doi.org/10.1097/HTR.0000000000000487

Wade, S. L., Cassedy, A. E., Shultz, E. L., Zang, H., Zhang, N., Kirkwood, M. W., Stancin, T., Yeates, K. O., & Taylor, H. G. (2017). Randomized clinical trial of online parent training for behavior problems after early brain injury. *Journal of the American Academy of Child & Adolescent Psychiatry, 56*(11), 930–939. https://doi.org/10.1016/j.jaac.2017.09.413

Wade, S. L., Fisher, A. P., Kaizar, E. E., Yeates, K. O., Taylor, H. G., & Zhang, N. (2019b). Recovery trajectories of child and family outcomes following online family problem-solving therapy for children and adolescents after traumatic brain injury. *Journal of the International Neuropsychological Society, 25*(9), 941–949. https://doi.org/10.1017/S1355617719000778

Wade, S. L., Gerry Taylor, H., Yeates, K. O., Drotar, D., Stancin, T., Minich, N. M., & Schluchter, M. (2006). Long-term parental and family adaptation following pediatric brain injury. *Journal of Pediatric Psychology, 31*(10), 1072–1083. https://doi.org/10.1093/jpepsy/jsj077

Wade, S. L., Gies, L. M., Fisher, A. P., Moscato, E. L., Adlam, A. R., Bardoni, A., Corti, C., Limond, J., Modi, A. C., & Williams, T. (2020). Telepsychotherapy with children and families: Lessons Gleaned from Two Decades of Translational Research. *Journal of Psychotherapy Integration, 30*(2), 332–347. https://doi.org/10.1037/int0000215

Wade, S. L., Kaizar, E. E., Narad, M., Zang, H., Kurowski, B. G., Yeates, K. O., Taylor, H. G., & Zhang, N. (2018). Online family problem-solving treatment for pediatric traumatic brain injury. *Pediatrics, 142*(6), e20180422. https://doi.org/10.1542/peds.2018-0422

Wade, S. L., Kurowski, B. G., Kirkwood, M. W., Zhang, N., Cassedy, A., Brown, T. M., Nielsen, B., Stancin, T., & Taylor, H. G. (2015). Online problem-solving therapy after traumatic brain injury: A randomized controlled trial. *Pediatrics, 135*(2), e487–495. https://doi.org/10.1542/peds.2014-1386

Wade, S. L., Michaud, L., & Brown, T. M. (2006c). Putting the pieces together: Preliminary efficacy of a family problem-solving intervention for children with traumatic brain injury. *Journal of Head Trauma Rehabilitation, 21*(1), 57–67. https://doi.org/10.1097/00001199-200601000-00006

Wade, S. L., Narad, M. E., Moscato, E. L., LeBlond, E. I., King, J. A., Raj, S. P., Platt, A., Thompson, A. N., Baum, K. T., & Salloum, R. (2020). A survivor's journey: Preliminary efficacy of an online problem-solving therapy for survivors of pediatric brain tumor. *Pediatric Blood & Cancer, 67*(2), e28043. https://doi.org/10.1002/pbc.28043

Wade, S. L., Oberjohn, K., Burkhardt, A., & Greenberg, I. (2009). Feasibility and preliminary efficacy of a web-based parenting skills program for young children with traumatic brain injury. *Journal of Head Trauma Rehabilitation, 24*(4), 239–247. https://doi.org/10.1097/HTR.0b013e3181ad6680

Wade, S. L., Stancin, T., Kirkwood, M., Brown, T. M., McMullen, K. M., & Taylor, H. G. (2014). Counselor-assisted problem solving (CAPS) improves behavioral outcomes in older adolescents with complicated mild to severe TBI. *Journal of Head Trauma Rehabilitation, 29*(3), 198–207. https://doi.org/10.1097/HTR.0b013e31828f9fe8

Wade, S. L., Walsh, K., Slomine, B. S., Davis, K. C., Heard, C., Maggard, B., Sutcliffe, M., Van Tubbergen, M., McNally, K., Deidrick, K., Kirkwood, M. W., Lantagne, A., Ashman, S., Scratch, S., Chesley, G., Johnson-Kerner, B., Johnson, A., Cirincione, L., & Austin, C. (2022). Widespread clinical implementation of the teen online problem-solving program: Progress, barriers, and lessons learned. *Frontiers in Rehabilitation Sciences, 3*, 1089079. https://doi.org/10.3389/fresc.2022.1089079

Wade, S. L., Walz, N. C., Carey, J., McMullen, K. M., Cass, J., Mark, E., & Yeates, K. O. (2012). A randomized trial of teen online problem solving: Efficacy in improving caregiver outcomes after brain injury. *Health Psychology: Official Journal of the Division of Health Psychology, American Psychological Association, 31*(6), 767–776. https://doi.org/10.1037/a0028440

Wade, S. L., Wolfe, C. R., & Pestian, J. P. (2004). A web-based family problem-solving intervention for families of children with traumatic brain injury. *Behavior Research Methods, Instruments, & Computers, 36*(2), 261–269. https://doi.org/10.3758/bf03195572

Webster-Stratton, C., Reinke, W. M., Herman, K. C., & Newcomer, L. L. (2011). The incredible years teacher classroom management training: The methods and principles that support fidelity of training delivery. *School Psychology Review, 40*(4), 509–529. https://doi.org/10.1080/02796015.2011.12087527

Williams, T. S., Burek, B., Deotto, A., Ford, M. K., Green, R., & Wade, S. L. (2022). Pandemic perils and promise: Implementation of a virtual parenting intervention during COVID-19 among children with early neurological conditions. *Developmental Neurorehabilitation, 25*(8), 505–517. https://doi.org/10.1080/17518423.2022.2099996

Williams, T. S., Deotto, A., Greenblatt, A., Fabiano, G. F., Green, R., Linga-Easwaran, J., Anagnostou, E., Crosbie, J., Kelley, E., Miller, S. P., Nicolson, R., Rosart, J., Wade, S. L., & Barwick, M. (2025). Scaling up: Facilitators, barriers, and EDI considerations for clinical implementation of a stepped-care early mental health parenting program (I-InTERACT-North). *Implementation Research and Practice, 6*, 1-14. https://doi.org/10.1177/26334895251346816

Williams, T. S., McDonald, K. P., Roberts, S. D., Westmacott, R., Dlamini, N., & Tam, E. W. Y. (2019). Understanding early childhood resilience following neonatal brain injury from parents' perspectives using a mixed-method design. *Journal of the International Neuropsychological Society, 25*(4), 390–402. https://doi.org/10.1017/S1355617719000079

Wong, D., Pike, K., Stolwyk, R., Allott, K., Ponsford, J., McKay, A., Longley, W., Bosboom, P., Hodge, A., Kinsella, G., & Mowszowski, L. (2024). Delivery of neuropsychological interventions for adult and older adult clinical populations: An Australian expert working group clinical guidance paper. *Neuropsychology Review, 34*(4), 985–1047. https://doi.org/10.1007/s11065-023-09624-0

Zhang, N., Kaizar, E. E., Narad, M. E., Kurowski, B. G., Yeates, K. O., Taylor, H. G., & Wade, S. L. (2019). Examination of injury, host, and social-environmental moderators of online family problem solving treatment efficacy for pediatric traumatic brain injury using an individual participant data meta-analytic approach. *Journal of Neurotrauma, 36*(7), 1147–1155. https://doi.org/10.1089/neu.2018.5885

16

How Can Neuropsychologists Shape the Future of Neurotechnology?

Jared F. Benge, Sophie I. Leib, Brittany Wolff, Travis Marchman, and Dean C. Delis

Like all works, this one is a product of its time. The idea for this volume emerged as our field was adapting to a new normal in the aftermath of the global pandemic, an era marked by the accelerated use of technology in nearly every aspect of our professional and personal lives, a reckoning with new socioeconomic, political, and demographic realities, and the mourning of our colleague and pioneer in neurotechnology, Robert Bilder. As editors of a volume on technological innovation, we are acutely aware that what we regard as pragmatic calls to action today may not withstand the test of time, societal evolution, and the next crisis humanity faces. We intentionally invited coeditors who are early in their careers of neuropsychology, hoping to offer a warm handoff of our perspectives on innovations to those who will soon carry the baton forward. Aware that our recommendations may soon be outdated, we nonetheless present the following calls to actions for neuropsychologists committed to shaping the future of neurotechnology.

Neuropsychologists Must Lean into Team-Based Collaborations

As discussed throughout this volume, it has become abundantly clear that no idea, technology, or device exists in isolation. To develop a computerized neurocognitive test, for example, requires building upon decades of technological discovery and innovation ranging from basic hardware engineering, computer software development, front- and back-end design, human factors research, corporate partnerships, usage agreements, Internet infrastructure, cloud storage, and Health Insurance Portability and Accountability Act (HIPAA)–complaint safeguards, just to name a few. This is before even considering the rapidly expanding foundational neuroscience that informs our knowledge on brain–behavior relationships, as well as advances in psychometrics and normative-data collection procedures, all of which remain central to understanding neuropsychological assessment. In short, the future of

Jared F. Benge et al., *How Can Neuropsychologists Shape the Future of Neurotechnology?* In: *Technology and Neuropsychology*. Edited by: Jared F. Benge et al., Oxford University Press. © Oxford University Press (2026).
DOI: 10.1093/9780197814116.003.0016

neurotechnology depends heavily on neuropsychologists' willingness and ability to collaborate closely with experts across these interconnected domains of research and development.

What this looks like will, of course, vary from clinic to clinic and lab to lab. Too often, however, neuropsychologists function in separate divisions or groups. Places where patients are referred or where cognitive problems are addressed in isolation from the broader context of healthcare, science, and society. This siloed approach is antithetical to our vision of the future of neurotechnology.

How do we begin to dismantle these silos? We encourage labs and clinics to regularly host (real or virtual) open houses to allow academic, clinical, and industrial partners to see what it's like to work with individuals with cognitive disorders and to highlight the kinds of resources and collaborations your work requires. In addition, make it a priority to attend workshops, meetings, and conferences in the technology space as a part of your routine outreach and networking. Even if you do not work in academia, your local institutions likely host public colloquia, innovation accelerators, or new product ideas related to technology—search the web, attend, and learn.

Also, in your collaborations, avoid letting the perfect become the enemy of the good. It is, at least in our opinion, better to equip someone with a tech interested in developing tools in the cognitive space with understanding of how a validated cognitive screener (along with appropriate training on administration), a sound activities-of-daily-living questionnaire, modern diagnostic and staging criteria and a clear understanding of the limitations of this approach in evaluating participants than to insist that every participant undergo a 4-hour, in-person evaluation before anything meaningful can be said about cognition. Work with the resources you have and help identify limitations but also help guide paths forward with appropriate nuance, collaborate with people you know, and move forward iteratively rather than remaining isolated.

Change Starts with the Next Patient and Research Project

As we noted in Chapter 1, we are often struck by the remarkable stability of the cognitive batteries used by clinicians and researchers over time. While this in part reflects the maturity and validity of our science and its instruments, it also represents a departure from an earlier era when neuropsychology was characterized by astute clinical observations, creative adaptation of tests for different purposes, and broad, evolving theories about brain–behavior relationships based on those observations.

Has neuropsychology become more change-averse even as technology has transformed the neurosciences? In neuropsychology, we now understand far more about the importance of assessing different domains of cognition, including hot and cold executive functions, the rich interplay between brain health, exercise, and sleep, and how cognitive models built on findings in one culture may not generalize to others we serve. As this volume illustrates, modern advances in assessment, psychometric principles, report writing, and interventions have progressed at breakneck speed. Yet these advances, by and large, have not been translated into routine clinical practice, research batteries, or training programs.

Our capacity to embrace change requires, we believe, intentionality. Can you commit to trying one new test this year in your clinical or research batteries? Will you follow at least one new technology-focused journal and read its abstracts regularly? Could you invite a guest lecturer to your didactic series from the fields of electrical and computer engineering? Can you keep a running journal of how others are incorporating technology into their practice or business, and what you might learn from that? The time has come to make change our professional identity: Let innovation become a defining feature of your practice.

We Need to "See" the Digital Lives of Those We Serve

Neuropsychologists fundamentally try to understand, assess, and improve brain–behavior relationships. But let's conduct a quick thought experiment: How much of your own daily behavior is digital? Chances are, there are few domains of your day-to-day life untouched by technology. Relationships are mediated through texts and social media posts, our commerce is conducted online, our exercise is tracked by our phone, and an open browser tab often guides our thinking about a case we are assessing or a paper we are writing. Digital behaviors increasingly dominate and define many facets of modern life.

We are not philosophers, and we are not here to argue that these changes are good, bad, or irreversible: They simply are. But if our own behaviors are intrinsically shaped by technology, so, too, are the behaviors of those we serve. This means we must look more deeply at how digital behaviors can inform our assessments: How are people functioning in digital contexts? Can technological adaptations enhance their daily functioning? What maladaptive technology behaviors might warrant intervention? And do our test stimuli and questions still seem relevant and capture the skills needed for everyday digital tasks? Staying relevant requires that we truly see what is in front of us, and that is digital behavior.

We Have to Integrate Technology into Training Programs

Psychology training is not a monolith, and the pathways to becoming a neuropsychologist will (and we argue should) remain diverse. Yet just as our theories and practices evolve with science, the core pillars of our training must weave technology into the fabric of what we do. To be clear, the editors of this volume do not believe this requires every training program to add a new course or clinical practicum focused on integrating technology into assessment and treatment (though we suspect some will). Instead, we encourage those teaching foundational graduate courses in neuropsychology to consider how technology is reshaping our field and to incorporate readings and discussion topics on neurotechnology, including chapters from this volume! For practicum supervisors: Do you ask your students about technology behaviors? Do you discuss clinical cases impacted by adaptive or maladaptive uses of technology? Do you model the process of updating your own assessment battery with new tools and digital platforms? And for internship and fellowship directors: When was the last time you reviewed your didactic schedule? Could you find a time slot to invite a guest from another department, campus, or publishing company to discuss innovations, such as new web-based, digital assessment platforms? These small steps can reshape the next phase of digital neuropsychology training and ensure that the next generation of clinicians benefit from the role that these innovations will play in understanding and measuring the human mind.

We Have to Be Vigilant About Security and Safety in the Digital World

As neuropsychology increasingly embraces digital tools, we must remain vigilant about data security and patient safety. Neuropsychological data are often deeply personal, making it both highly valuable and vulnerable in the digital environment. Any breach of security can compromise patient privacy, erode trust in our profession, and expose individuals to harm. This concern grows more urgent as technology evolves, introducing new and often unforeseen risks in how data are stored, transmitted, and accessed.

To mitigate these risks, we must foster a culture of vigilance. This means not only understanding and adhering to existing privacy regulations, but also proactively engaging with our technology partners to ensure they uphold the highest standards of data protection. Neuropsychologists should be encouraged to ask critical questions about how data are encrypted, stored, and accessed. We must also recognize that digital tools can introduce new forms of bias or harm, such as algorithmically driven clinical interpretations that might produce inaccurate or unfair outcomes, or through overreliance on technology that can fail and place a patient or research participant at risk. By prioritizing security and safety from the outset, we can build a digital infrastructure that is both robust and ethical, safeguarding our patients and preserving the integrity of our field.

We Have to Be Vigilant About Equitable Utilization of Neurotechnology

While neurotechnology holds great promise for improving lives, we must ensure its integration does not widen existing disparities in health care. A future in which advanced neuropsychology technologies are accessible only to those with substantial financial resources or where digital assessments are normed on selective homogenous populations is counterproductive. The high costs of developing and maintaining digital tools can create economic barriers that deepen inequalities. Additionally, the very digital behaviors we study may not be representative across all socioeconomic and cultural groups. To prevent this, we must proactively embed principles of equity and accessibility into every stage of development by advocating for public health–focused funding, including diverse samples in our studies, and designing technologies that are useful for everyone.

We Have to Be Realistic About What It Takes to Innovate and Work Within Economic Realities

The calls to action outlined here are ambitious. We must also be pragmatic about the immense effort, time, and resources required for true innovation. A common misconception in our field is that a novel test or technology can be developed quickly with minimal investment, a notion that is quickly dispelled when one examines the realities of the publishing and technology industries. As our colleagues at Pearson have noted in this volume, the development, maintenance, and security requirements of digital assessments, even with growing efficiencies, can require "multiple millions of dollars" in upfront and ongoing costs. This is especially true, given the growing regulatory landscape around data privacy, security, and accessibility. The development timeline can also be extensive; for example, the D-KEFS Advanced required 16 years of sustained collaboration to bring to fruition.

The takeaway here is not to discourage innovation, but to ground it in reality. Groundbreaking neurotechnology is rarely created in isolation or on a shoestring budget; it emerges from long-term, interdisciplinary collaboration. By acknowledging and educating ourselves about the financial and logistical complexities involved, we position ourselves as credible and valued partners in the developmental process, rather than being seen as isolated consultants with unrealistic expectations. Our contribution to the future of neuropsychology and technology depends not only on our ability to generate bold ideas but also on our willingness to understand and navigate the real-world challenges of bringing those ideas to fruition.

While these goals are ambitious, leveraging technology to enhance our assessment tools and treatment services is essential—ultimately allowing us to deepen our understanding of brain–behavior relationships and improve the lives of children and adults affected by neurocognitive disorders.

Glossary

"Agreeableness Effect" (AI Sycophancy) The tendency for large language models, which are optimized to be cooperative, to affirm a user's premise or framing without challenge. This can reinforce a clinician's confirmation bias or lend unwarranted authority to a premature conclusion.

AI as Augmentation A guiding principle emphasizing that artificial intelligence should be used as a tool to support, extend, and enhance a clinician's expertise, rather than as an automated system that supplants or outsources professional reasoning and human judgment.

AI Hallucinations A phenomenon where artificial intelligence models, such as large language models, generate content that is inaccurate, fabricated, or nonsensical, posing a significant risk to quality control and accuracy in automated clinical services.

AI Scribe/Ambient Listening Technology A type of software designed to passively record and transcribe clinician–patient interactions, such as a clinical interview. It uses natural language processing to automatically extract, organize, and categorize relevant historical details and other data into structured report sections, reducing the clinician's documentation burden.

Algorithmic Bias The risk that machine learning models and other artificial intelligence systems will produce inaccurate, unfair, or discriminatory outcomes. This often occurs when the algorithm is trained on data that reflects real-world inequities or lacks diversity, leading to inaccuracies for marginalized groups.

Algorithmic Detection The use of artificial intelligence to analyze "vast swaths of small samples of behavior" (e.g., from passive digital monitoring) to identify patterns, categorize individuals, or detect risk for cognitive decline or self-neglect, often without active user input.

Algorithmic Opacity A significant ethical challenge where the complex, multilayered, or proprietary nature of an AI model makes it difficult or impossible for a neuropsychologist to understand how it arrived at a conclusion. This interferes with the clinician's ability to take responsibility for the evaluation's outcomes.

Anticholinergic Burden The cumulative negative cognitive effect on a patient resulting from the combined use of all medications with anticholinergic properties. Technology, such as AI tools, can be used to calculate this burden from a medication list to help identify potential iatrogenic causes of cognitive impairment.

Artificial Intelligence (AI) Computer systems designed to perform tasks that traditionally require human cognitive capabilities, such as problem-solving or recognizing subtle patterns. In neuropsychology, these tools can assist in data-heavy tasks like record summarization, data organization, and report drafting.

Automated Feedback A feature of digital assessment platforms where the device itself delivers immediate, automated corrections for errors (e.g., visual cues, sounds). This shifts the responsibility of error correction from the examiner to the device, which can reduce examiner burden, minimize measurement error, and help preserve rapport with the examinee.

Automated Summarization Tools Software that uses AI to automatically create a concise and coherent summary of a larger text document.

Biological Definition (of a Disorder) A technological and diagnostic shift, such as in Alzheimer's disease, where the "ground-level truth" of the condition is defined by its biomarkers (e.g., amyloid and tau), rather than by its clinical or neurobehavioral symptoms alone. This change requires neuropsychologists to adapt how they interpret and communicate findings.

Body Doubling A technique, often facilitated by streaming platforms, in which an individual works or studies in real time alongside another person (either virtually or in person) who is also performing a task. This method is used to create a sense of shared focus and accountability, which can be particularly beneficial for neurodivergent individuals in maintaining attention and productivity.

Boston Process Approach (BPA) (Digital) A clinical assessment framework, largely credited to Edith Kaplan, that emphasizes the qualitative analysis of how an individual solves a problem, not just the final score. Digital technologies enhance this approach by capturing and quantifying "en route" behaviors—such as errors, response latencies, and drawing kinematics—in real time, providing insights into cognitive strategies and subtle impairments not observable with paper-and-pencil tests.

Branching Logic A feature in digital forms (e.g., Microsoft Forms) that dynamically alters the subsequent questions a user is shown based on their answers to a previous question. This allows an intake form to be tailored, for example, by presenting detailed follow-up questions only if a patient answers "yes" to having a specific medical history.

CARES A framework for understanding how technology impacts cognitive health in older adults, based on five key areas: Connection, Adaptation, Rehabilitation, Executive Function, and Spatial Navigation.

Classical Test Theory (CTT) The traditional method for scoring tests, which typically involves summing responses across items to get a total score. This method assumes that all items contribute equally to measurement and that a single standard error of measurement (precision) applies to all individuals at all trait levels.

Clinical Nuance Subtle, complex, and context-dependent details observed in a patient's behavior, history, or symptom presentation that are crucial for accurate interpretation. A major concern with automated report-writing systems is their potential inability to capture this clinical nuance, which often requires human expertise and critical thinking.

Co-design (or Participatory Design) An approach to technology development that actively involves community members and diverse end-users in the early design phases. This method is used to improve the cultural relevance, appropriateness, and trustworthiness of m-health tools for the populations they are intended to serve.

"Cognition in the Wild" A term describing the measurement of cognitive and functional abilities as they naturally occur within a person's everyday environment, rather than in the controlled, artificial setting of a clinic.

Cognitive Ecological Momentary Assessment (Cognitive EMA) An assessment method that integrates objective, performance-based cognitive testing into a broader EMA framework. It typically uses smartphones to collect real-time data on a person's cognitive functioning repeatedly and within their natural environment.

Cognitive Offloading The process of using external tools, such as smartphones and GPS, to assist with or take over tasks traditionally performed by our brains, like remembering appointments or navigating.

Cognitive Prosthetic A digital tool or application, such as a smartphone calendar, reminder app, or note-taking tool, that functions as an external aid to support or compensate for cognitive tasks. These tools can be essential for managing organization, time, and memory adherence.

Cognitive Scaffold A conceptual metaphor for the appropriate role of AI, positioning it not as an interpretive authority but as an assistive instrument. It helps structure and support the clinician's own cognitive processes and reasoning, much like a scaffold supports a builder.

Cognitive Training A restorative technique involving the repeated practice of specific cognitive tasks to improve skills like processing speed, reasoning, or memory.

"Cold" Executive Function A component of executive functioning that is primarily cognitive and less influenced by emotion. It encompasses skills such as abstract reasoning, problem-solving, and using feedback to determine a long-term strategy.

Common Data Elements (CDEs) A set of standardized, predefined variables used to ensure that the same essential information (e.g., medical history, psychosocial context) is collected consistently and comparably across all neuropsychological evaluations, improving reliability and reproducibility.

Compensatory Strategies/Cognitive Prosthetics Tools and technologies used to support or substitute for lost cognitive abilities, helping individuals to function more independently. These can include digital memory notebooks, smart pens, or lifelogging devices that aid in recalling past events and managing daily tasks.

Component-Level Information Fine-grained performance data captured by digital tests, such as a digital Trail Making Test (dTMT), that deconstruct a task into its core processes. Instead of only a total completion time, this includes metrics like pause duration, time spent inside each circle, and time between circles, which help isolate the specific cognitive abilities (e.g., inhibitory control vs. processing speed) driving performance.

Computerized Adaptive Testing (CAT) An assessment method where a digital platform dynamically adjusts the difficulty of test items in real time based on the examinee's ongoing performance. This approach can boost efficiency by shortening test batteries and, as seen in tools like the Stricker Learning Span, can offer additional exposures to items an individual struggles to recall.

Convergent Thinking The cognitive process of evaluating, refining, and selecting among multiple ideas to arrive at a single, optimal solution to a well-defined problem. It is closely linked to the brain's executive control network (ECN).

Creativity (Neuropsychological Theory) A skill, viewed as coachable and essential to innovation, that arises from the dynamic interplay between divergent and convergent thinking. It represents a "fluid dance" between the brain's generative (default mode network) and evaluative (executive control network) neural networks.

Cultural Mistrust Skepticism or reluctance among minoritized populations to adopt digital health tools, often stemming from historical and ongoing experiences of discrimination within health care systems. This mistrust is rooted in perceptions that new technologies may perpetuate marginalization, bias, or be co-opted for surveillance.

Culturally Responsive Implementation A framework for deploying digital health tools that intentionally integrates cultural considerations to ensure accessibility and relevance. This involves tailoring content and delivery formats to a community's norms and providing culturally appropriate support services to increase user engagement.

De-identification An essential data security safeguard where all protected health information (PHI) is removed from clinical records. This process, or the use of local, offline models, is necessary before using artificial intelligence tools that are not HIPAA-compliant.

Default Mode Network (DMN) The neural network associated with spontaneous thought, imagination, and daydreaming. It is considered the primary network supporting divergent thinking by allowing for the free-flowing association of ideas.

Differential Item Functioning (DIF) A term describing the failure of measurement invariance. DIF occurs when the probability of responding to an item depends on more than just the person's trait level, such as their demographic group (e.g., sex, age, or race). When DIF is present, scores are not comparable across groups because the construct is not being assessed in the same way.

Digital Behaviors The objective, ecologically valid data generated as individuals use digital tools, such as smartphones, in their daily lives. These data provide "robust and continuous slices of daily activity" that can be passively mined by artificial intelligence to inform diagnostic decisions.

Digital Biomarkers Objective, quantifiable data passively collected from digital devices, such as smartphone keystroke dynamics, general usage patterns, or performance on embedded games. These data hold promise for identifying subtle cognitive changes and distinguishing between neurocognitive diagnostic groups.

Digital Clock Drawing Test (DCTclock) A digital, process-oriented version of the clock drawing task that captures detailed metrics beyond the final drawing's accuracy. It records kinematic data such as "initiation speed" (time to start drawing) and "percent thinking time" (time the pen is off the page), which have been associated with genetic risk (e.g., APOE ε4) and biomarkers for Alzheimer's disease.

Digital Competence A proposed core training competency for neuropsychologists that goes beyond basic technological literacy. It includes understanding the principles of large data, knowing what questions to ask about a new tool, fostering a flexible mindset, and developing the foundational skills to collaborate with interdisciplinary teams of engineering, coding, and statistical professionals.

Digital Divide The disparity between populations regarding their access to and proficiency with digital technology, such as reliable Internet, computers, and mobile devices. This gap disproportionately affects older adults, individuals from lower socioeconomic backgrounds, and certain racial and ethnic minorities, threatening to exacerbate preexisting health care disparities.

Digital Inclusion A framework and goal aimed at reducing the structural inequities that contribute to the digital divide. It involves strategies like educational outreach and collaborative policymaking to ensure underserved communities can equitably access and benefit from digital health technologies.

Digital Natives A term for the generation of individuals who have grown up with ubiquitous digital technology, contrasting with "digital pioneers." Neuropsychologists are currently transitioning from primarily serving the latter to the former, requiring an adaptation of clinical tools and assumptions.

Digital Neuropsychology A future-facing concept of assessment that moves beyond merely computerizing traditional tests. It aims to integrate rich, ecologically relevant data from sources like passive smartphone data, wearable devices, and smart home sensors to capture a person's cognitive and functional health in their everyday environment.

Digital Phenotyping A specific type of passive sensing defined as the "moment-by-moment quantification of the individual-level human phenotype in situ" by collecting data from personal digital devices, such as smartphones or wearables.

Digital Pioneers The term used to describe the current generation of older adults who are the first to have grown up with and extensively used computers and other digital technologies, making them a unique group for studying the long-term effects of technology on the aging brain.

Digital Rehabilitation The process of integrating digital technologies into clinical treatment to help individuals, particularly older adults, maintain or improve cognitive and functional abilities. This can include using technology for training, prompting, and compensation strategies.

Discrimination Parameter (a) An item parameter in IRT models (like the 2PL) that describes an item's ability to discriminate between persons of different trait levels. It is proportional to the slope of the item characteristic curve (ICC) and dictates the height of the item information curve (IIC), with higher slopes providing more information (precision).

Displacement Hypothesis The theory that time spent using digital technology replaces time that could be spent on more beneficial activities, like social interaction or physical activity.

Divergent Thinking The ability to generate multiple, unique ideas or solutions to an open-ended problem. It involves cognitive flexibility and fluency and is considered a cornerstone of creative thought, often associated with the default mode network (DMN).

Ecological Validity The extent to which assessment stimuli and tasks resemble real-world situations to measure how an individual might perform in daily life. Examples include using photos of people with emotional expressions or introducing distracting stimuli during a task.

Equivalence (of Assessment) The research-supported finding that neuropsychological test scores obtained through teleneuropsychology are, on average, comparable and not meaningfully different from scores obtained during traditional, in-person administration.

Equivalence Testing A specialized statistical method, distinct from traditional difference testing, designed to determine if an effect (e.g., the score difference between teleNP and in-person) is not meaningfully large. It tests whether the difference is small enough to be considered practically or clinically irrelevant.

Everyday Function The ability to perform daily living tasks essential for maintaining independence, such as shopping, meal preparation, or managing finances.

Executive Control Network (ECN) The neural network responsible for goal-directed behavior, working memory, and inhibitory control. It supports the evaluative, convergent thinking functions of creativity, such as assessing the novelty and appropriateness of ideas.

Flatland Fallacy A conceptual critique of traditional assessment, suggesting that by relying on "low-dimensional" tools (like static paper-and-pencil tests) and linear interpretations, clinicians risk misinterpreting the true "multidimensional nature" of complex cognitive deficits.

Flow A state of deep immersion and energized focus in an activity, described by Mihaly Csikszentmihalyi, where one's skills are perfectly matched to the challenges at hand. This state is thought to facilitate creativity by allowing the default mode network and executive control network to work in concert without self-critical interference.

"Glitz" Lesson A lesson in test development cautioning that "flashy" or technologically impressive digital features (e.g., generic, real-world distracting sounds) do not always translate to better clinical utility or sensitivity. Effective digital design must be rooted in neuropsychological principles, not just technological novelty.

Health Equity by Design A principle for mitigating bias in clinical algorithms that involves proactively embedding fairness and equity into the technology's development process from the beginning, rather than attempting to correct discriminatory outcomes after deployment.

High-Dimensional Data The rich, high-frequency, and fine-grained data (e.g., precise response times, movement patterns) yielded by digital approaches. These data offer greater precision and sensitivity to subtle deficits compared to the "low-dimensional" (e.g., single summary scores) data from traditional paper-and-pencil tests.

High-Verisimilitude Tasks A type of performance-based functional assessment designed to appear highly realistic and similar to a real-world activity. Examples include simulated tasks for navigating an online pharmacy, managing a web-based bank account, or using a telephone portal.

HIPAA-Compliant Platform A secure, cloud-based artificial intelligence system that meets rigorous data protection standards, including encryption, access controls, and a business associate agreement (BAA). Clinicians are ethically and legally required to use such platforms when handling any protected health information (PHI).

Home-to-Home A teleneuropsychology delivery approach where both the neuropsychologist and the patient participate in the appointment from their respective homes, a model that became common during the COVID-19 pandemic.

"Hot" Executive Function A component of executive functioning that involves cognitive skills that are influenced by emotional factors. It is particularly relevant in decision-making tasks involving risk, rewards, and losses, and includes skills like emotional inhibition and risk aversion.

Human Oversight (or Supervision) The non-negotiable ethical principle that a qualified clinician must maintain vigilant supervision over all AI-assisted work. The human expert bears full and final responsibility for verifying all data, guiding all clinical reasoning, and ensuring the accuracy of all conclusions.

Hybrid teleNP Approach A flexible practice model where some clinical services (like interviews or feedback sessions) are provided remotely via telehealth, while other services (such as complex, hands-on testing) are conducted in-person.

ImPACT (Immediate Post-Concussion Assessment and Cognitive Testing) A computerized neurocognitive assessment tool used to measure cognitive function (e.g., memory, reaction time) following a concussion. It is commonly used in sports for baseline testing (assessing athletes before a season) to help inform return-to-play decisions after an injury.

Insight Learning ("A-ha!" Moment) A phenomenon, first demonstrated by Wolfgang Köhler, where the solution to a problem appears suddenly and completely. Neuropsychologically, it is linked to a rapid neural reorganization that brings a nonobvious solution into conscious awareness.

Instrumental Activities of Daily Living (IADLs) Complex tasks that are necessary for an individual to live independently within a community, such as managing finances, shopping, taking medications, and using transportation. The ability to perform these tasks is increasingly shaped and mediated by technology.

International Classification of Functioning, Disability, and Health (ICF) A framework from the World Health Organization (WHO) that conceptualizes functioning from a biopsychosocial perspective. It considers the interaction between body structures (e.g., brain health), activity limitations (e.g., difficulty learning software), participation restrictions (e.g., inability to work), and environmental factors, such as technology, that can either impede or facilitate performance.

Intra-individual Cognitive Variability A metric, uniquely captured by high-frequency Cognitive EMA, that measures the fluctuations in a single person's cognitive performance over time. It is increasingly recognized as a sensitive early marker for brain dysfunction.

Item Characteristic Curve (ICC) A visualization in item response theory, typically a sigmoidal function (S-shaped curve), that plots the mathematical relation between a person's level on the latent trait (e.g., depression, on the X-axis) and their probability of endorsing a specific item (on the Y-axis).

Item Response Theory (IRT) A framework of psychometric models that describe the relationship between observed item responses (whether dichotomous or multicategorical) and the hypothesized underlying latent trait (e.g., depression) that is believed to be responsible for the shared variance in those responses. Unlike classical test theory, IRT estimates the relation for each item, provides standard errors that vary by ability level, and allows for valid comparisons across different test forms.

Iterative Refinement (or Dialogue) The process of interacting with an artificial intelligence as a dialogue rather than a single command. It involves reviewing the artificial intelligence's initial output, correcting errors or omissions, and then reasking refined questions to gradually shape the most accurate and usable results.

Keystroke Dynamics A passive sensing metric derived from monitoring a person's natural typing patterns on a smartphone touchscreen keyboard. These dynamics, such as typing speed or error rates, can be used as digital biomarkers for processing speed and executive function.

Large Language Models (LLMs) A type of artificial intelligence model trained on a massive amount of text data to recognize, summarize, translate, predict, and generate content.

Location Parameter (b) An item parameter in IRT models that represents an item's difficulty. It is the point along the latent trait continuum where an individual has a 50% probability of endorsing the item (in 1PL and 2PL models). Items with high positive locations are more "difficult" because they require a higher level of the trait for endorsement.

Longitudinal Measurement Burst Designs An intensive assessment schedule in which short periods of very frequent data collection (e.g., multiple times per day) are embedded within a longer study period. This method is used in Cognitive EMA to improve reliability and sensitivity to cognitive changes.

Mail Merge A software function (e.g., in Microsoft Word) that automates the creation of documents by pulling data from a structured source, like a spreadsheet, and inserting it into designated fields within a template. In report writing, this allows a clinician to automatically populate a report template with a patient's specific scores and history from a master spreadsheet.

Master Spreadsheet In a custom-built reporting system, this is a central spreadsheet (e.g., Microsoft Excel) that consolidates all patient information from multiple sources—such as digital history forms, electronic medical record exports, and test score data—into one organized location to be used as the data source for the final report.

Measurement Invariance A psychometric property, currently understudied in teleneuropsychology, that assesses whether a test or battery of tests is measuring the same underlying cognitive construct in the same way across different administration modalities (e.g., in-person versus remote).

Media Multitasking The act of simultaneously engaging with multiple forms of media, such as watching TV while texting or browsing the web.

Micro-Response Data Capture A capability of all-digital assessments to capture fine-grained performance data at a millisecond level. This allows for the development of new and numerous process scores, such as the standard deviation of response times, which are not possible to capture with traditional print-and-pencil tests.

Minnesota Conference (MNC) Guidelines Updated guidelines for neuropsychological training that, for the first time, propose incorporating innovation and technology as a core competency for neuropsychologists, to be embedded across the curriculum.

Mobile Health (m-Health) The use of mobile devices—including smartphones, wearable activity trackers, wireless sensors, and other portable technologies—to support health care services, remote patient monitoring, and public health interventions.

Modular Calculators Purpose-built software tools, often web-based or downloadable, designed to perform a single, specific set of functions, such as converting raw scores or calculating reliable change indices. These tools may be "test-agnostic" or prepopulated with norms for specific measures.

Natural Language Processing (NLP) A branch of artificial intelligence that enables computers to understand, interpret, and generate human language.

NIH Toolbox A comprehensive suite of standardized, computerized tests designed to assess cognitive function, motor skills, sensory perception, and emotional health across the lifespan (ages 3–85+). It is used in both research and clinical settings and has shown utility in identifying subtle cognitive changes in conditions like prodromal Alzheimer's disease.

Passive Sensing (or Passive Activity Detection) An assessment approach that involves the remote, continuous, and completely unobtrusive monitoring of behaviors using sensor technology. Data from in-home sensors or personal devices (e.g., smartphones, wearables) are used to objectively quantify real-world functioning like mobility, sleep, or social activity.

Performance-Based Functional Assessments (PBFAs) A method of assessment that moves beyond questionnaires to quantify an individual's actual performance on a given task. In a technological context, this may involve prompting an individual to complete a task on an actual website or in a highly realistic simulated environment.

Photo-Taking Impairment Effect The phenomenon where a person's memory for a specific object or event is worse if they took a picture of it compared to if they simply observed it.

Prepotent Response An overlearned, automatic, or impulsive response that is immediately triggered by a stimulus (such as reading a word). Many executive function tasks require a person to actively inhibit this initial, prepotent response to generate a more difficult, conflicting, or correct response.

Process Approach A neuropsychological framework, notably championed by Edith Kaplan, that emphasizes a careful analysis of the types and frequency of errors an individual makes. It operates on the principle that errors are not just failures but are "windows into brain function," revealing how an individual is struggling with a task.

Prompt Engineering An emerging professional skill involving the deliberate structuring of clear, context-rich instructions (prompts) to communicate effectively with an AI. Effective prompts often include role framing (perspective), task definition (purpose), format specification (output style), and contextual constraints (scope).

Prompting Technologies Digital tools designed to provide reminders, alerts, or cues to assist individuals with prospective memory failures—that is, remembering to perform a future action.

Prospective Memory The cognitive process of remembering to perform a planned action at a future time. Digital tools like calendar alerts and reminders are often used to assist with this type of memory.

Psychometric Equivalence Evidence demonstrating that a digital version of a test produces scores that are highly consistent with and statistically comparable to the traditional paper-and-pencil format. This supports the construct validity of the digital administration, suggesting that the digital norms and reliability data are applicable (e.g., WAIS-5 on Q-interactive).

Q-interactive A digital assessment platform from Pearson that uses two iPads (one for the examiner, one for the examinee) connected via Bluetooth or Wi-Fi. It allows for the digital administration of comprehensive cognitive assessments like the WAIS-5, featuring real-time scoring and automated reporting.

Regression-Based Norms A sophisticated normative method that uses a statistical formula to derive a standardized score by considering multiple variables at once (e.g., age, education). Automated tools are essential for this process, as manual calculation is complex, time-consuming, and prone to error.

Simulation Sickness (SS) A type of motion sickness with symptoms like nausea, dizziness, and headache that can be induced by exposure to 3D-simulated environments. It is an important consideration when using virtual reality with clinical populations.

"Smartphone Dependent" A term describing individuals who own a smartphone but do not have broadband Internet access at home, relying on their mobile device for all online activities. This status is more prevalent among individuals with lower incomes and lower levels of formal education.

Social Drivers of Health Framework A framework used to consider how various sociodemographic variables—such as educational access and quality, economic status, social and community context, and neighborhood environment—impact health outcomes and an individual's exposure to and ability to use technology

Speed-Accuracy Trade-off The inverse relationship between speed and accuracy when performing complex, timed cognitive tasks. Digital assessment allows for the capture of new measures to analyze this relationship, revealing whether a person's performance reflects a sacrifice of accuracy for speed (impulsivity) or a sacrifice of speed for accuracy (excessive caution).

Stereotype Threat A psychological phenomenon where individuals from minoritized groups may underperform on cognitive tests due to the pressure of potentially confirming a negative stereotype. This can be triggered by discriminatory experiences and may lead to inaccurate assessment conclusions and further health inequities.

Structured History Protocol for Neuropsychology (SHiP-NP) A standardized, structured tool developed by the National Neuropsychology Network (NNN) designed to streamline the comprehensive collection of a patient's biopsychosocial history, including medical, psychological, educational, and familial factors, using common data elements.

Tech Readiness A patient factor related to the "digital divide" that refers not just to a person's access to technology, but also their confidence, familiarity, and ability to use Internet-ready devices and software independently for a telehealth visit.

Technological Audit A proposed framework for ethically evaluating new artificial intelligence models before clinical use. This interdisciplinary audit involves scrutinizing all components of a model, including its Input Data (e.g., was the sample representative?), Model Design (e.g., were choices documented?), and Cultural Context, to assess for fairness and bias

Technological Disclosure A component of informed consent where patients or retaining parties are made aware of when, how, and to what extent artificial intelligence tools are being used in their evaluation, such as assisting in summarizing records or drafting parts of a report

Technological Literacy An individual's familiarity and comfort with using digital tools and platforms. A lack of technological literacy can impact the validity of a digital assessment by impairing test engagement or introducing an unintended cognitive load

Technology and Innovation (as a Core Competency) A training competency proposed by the Minnesota Conference (MNC) wherein neuropsychology trainees are expected to develop technological literacy and the critical thinking skills necessary to evaluate and ethically implement innovative tools and data streams in their practice

Technology-Enabled Services (TES) A framework for integrating digital tools into clinical care. The chapter stresses the need for culturally responsive implementation of TES, which involves tailoring content to be culturally relevant and providing support services to increase engagement and accessibility for all individuals.

Telehealth The delivery of health-related services and information via electronic communication technologies.

Telehealth Triage Consultation Appointment (TTCA) A brief, remote consultation model used to triage referrals. It helps to clarify differential diagnoses, determine if a full neuropsychological evaluation is necessary, and provide psychoeducation, often dramatically reducing clinic waitlist times.

Teleneuropsychology (teleNP) The use of audiovisual technologies, such as videoconferencing, to conduct neuropsychological assessments and consultations remotely with patients.

Test Information Curve (TIC) A plot in item response theory created by summing all the individual item information curves in a test. It describes the amount of measurement precision (information) the entire test provides at different levels of the latent trait. The inverse of this function provides the conditional standard error of measurement, which shows how precise a person's trait score estimate is.

Unsupervised Remote Testing A method of assessment where a patient completes cognitive tests on their own device (e.g., smartphone or computer) in their own environment (e.g., at home) without the direct, real-time supervision of a clinician

Virtual Reality (VR) A simulated, three-dimensional environment that can be explored and interacted with using special electronic equipment, such as a headset.

Voice Biomarkers A digital assessment method where machine learning algorithms are used to analyze acoustic and linguistic features of a person's recorded voice (e.g., from verbal fluency tasks or picture descriptions) to detect patterns associated with cognitive impairment.

Index

For the benefit of digital users, indexed terms that span two pages (e.g., 52–53) may, on occasion, appear on only one of those pages.

Tables, figures, boxes, and labels are indicated by an italic *t*, *f*, *b* and *l* following the page number.

www.ingramcontent.com/pod-product-compliance
Ingram Content Group UK Ltd.
Pitfield, Milton Keynes, MK11 3LW, UK
UKHW040715021026
476226UK00012B/96

9 780197 814086